The Critics Hail the Works of Linda Goodman:

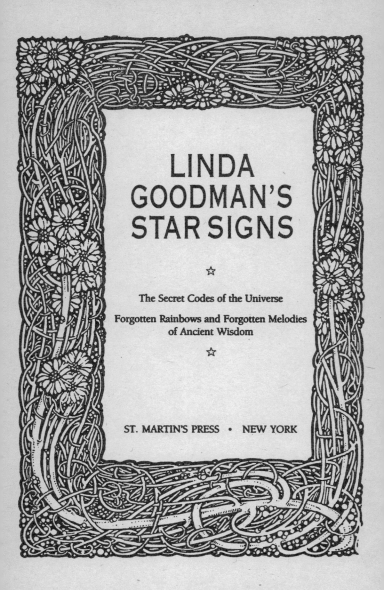

LINDA GOODMAN'S STAR SIGNS

☆

The Secret Codes of the Universe

Forgotten Rainbows and Forgotten Melodies
of Ancient Wisdom

☆

ST. MARTIN'S PRESS · NEW YORK

LINDA GOODMAN'S STAR SIGNS

The Secret Codes of the Universe

Forgotten Rainbows and Forgotten Melodies
of Ancient Wisdom

ST. MARTIN'S PRESS   •   NEW YORK

Mannu

Grateful acknowledgment is made for permission to quote from "On a Clear Day You Can See Forever" by B. Lane & A.J. Lerner. Copyright © 1965 by Burton Lane & Alan Jay Lerner. All Rights Administered by Chappell & Co., Inc. International Copyright Secured. ALL RIGHTS RESERVED. Used by permission.

Author photo on inside back cover by Bill Robbins.

Library of Congress Catalog Card Number: 87-28375

ISBN: 0-312-91263-3   Can. ISBN: 0-312-91264-1

St. Martin's Press hardcover edition published 1987
First St. Martin's Press mass market edition/November 1988

10 9 8 7 6 5 4 3 2

Editorial Consulting
by
Robert A. Brewer
★

with Everlasting Love

I dedicate this

and all my future books

to "my sneaky guru"

Aaron Goldblatt

who has patiently, throughout all incarnations, guided
my creative efforts and spiritual enlightenment with
the infinite gentleness and wisdom of a Master Avatar;
and who has been . . . is now and ever shall be . . .
responsible for all my miracles . . . every single one
of them manifested only through his faith.

*"Be not forgetful to entertain strangers; for
thereby some have entertained angels unawares."*

HEBREWS 13:2

*"My children, errors will be forgiven. In our obsession
with original sin, we do often forget . . . original innocence."*

POPE INNOCENT OF ASSISI
A.D. 15th Century

this book is also for

Nona
with one perfect snowflake
for endless galaxies of reasons

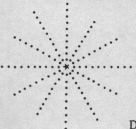

Nahtan
the apple of my "I"

Dr. Charles A. Musès
whose wisdom never fails

Sally . . . Bill . . . Michael . . . and Jill

and in loving memory of
Sam O. Goodman

". . . and God shall wipe away all tears from their eyes; and
there shall be no more death . . ."

REVELATION 21:4

the birth of these star signs was made possible
in various ways, for a number of reasons, by the
following people, to whom I would like to say "thank you"

first and foremost . . . Robert A. Brewer

Toni Lopopolo (the Laurel Lily Lady) . . . Robin Kessler . . . George
and Alice Rostad . . . Patrick, Lenore, Norman, and Corinne Lobo . . .
Ted and Jean Fraites . . . Harold and Kathleen Finstad . . . Don
Matthews . . . Sue and Bill Fox . . . Tom Demeo . . . Dan Delaney . . .
Carol, Star, and Sunshine Rainey . . . Sue Kelly . . . Suzanne Finstad
. . . Allen Matthews . . . Harry Musante, Jr. . . . Carol Pozy . . .
Connie Larsen . . . Olive and Carol Twinem . . . Gladys Cunningham
. . . Sgt. Robert Meza . . . John Forsman . . . Louis Cicalese . . . Mike
Nelson . . . Judy Carr . . . Charles Collie . . . Julie Bogash . . . Dora
Elliott . . . Renier Milan . . . Joshua Rappaport . . . Vicky Sparks . . .
Pat Franklin . . . Charles Hurst, D.D.S. . . . Neal Brawner . . . Harriet
Snare . . . Mary Jo Anne Valko . . . Inga Danville . . . John Eastlack,
Esq. . . . Mercedes Hernandez . . . Jim Gaidula . . . Paul O'Driscoll . . .
Dan Schow . . . Harold and Carol Nay . . . Sahle Adanu . . . Lance
Reed . . . Pat Callison . . . Ruth Cook . . . Bill Slawson, Jane Schaefer,
Rosemary MacIntyre and Fredo Killing, of the Antler's Plaza Hotel in
Colorado Springs . . . Jerome A. Perles, Esq. . . . Garry R. Appel, Esq.
. . . George Rosenthal . . . Howard Hughes, Jr. . . . and last, but
certainly not least . . .

Philip di Franco, the Lion . . . Dame Thelma Dunlap, the Bull

also

Arthur Mitchell Klebanoff

the "wise man," who, for the second time, as with *Love Signs*, parted
the Red Sea, so this book could get out of Egypt !

A grateful acknowledgment
and the reason for it . . .

The completion of this book was delayed by a typical Aries accident:
a blow on my head that caused my shocked spine to pop out its 5th
lumbar vertebra, which then pinched my sciatic nerve, and kept on
pinching it for a very long, painful time. Now I want to express my
gratitude to the man who got me back to the typewriter

John Wm. Perry, M.D.
Hollywood, California

who is everyone's ideal of a perfect physician, because he combines
the nostalgic, comforting bedside manner Norman Rockwell painted
with a brilliant knowledge of modern medical marvels and
techniques — plus the strong healing magnetism of Scorpio. "Dr.
John" is a specialist in internal medicine, diagnosis, and a pioneer in
sports medicine. He's been the official doctor for numerous sports
figures and teams, including the Washington Redskins and the Los
Angeles Rams — and is now the official doctor for this Aries Ram,
who, under his expert care, went from a painful "quarter-back" to a
"half-back" to, finally, a well back.

also

Marianna Clunie, Libra . . . and Aurie Salazar, Gemini

Dr. John's serene staff . . . two angels of mercy. Both of them Air
Signs, of course. What other Sun Sign element would angels be ?

and two final bear hugs for:

Ralph Bergstresser
Scottsdale, Arizona

who additionally (and not for the first time) blessed me with many
magics he brought back from Atlantis, by way of Jupiter.

LINDA GOODMAN'S STAR SIGNS

Both the prose and verse quotations used throughout the text and at the beginning of each chapter have been taken from the author's forthcoming work, *Gooberz*.

CONTENTS

★ ★

3

GURUS, GHOSTS, AND AVATARS

the Rocky Mountain "highs" of magnetic power points and
astral vibratory frequencies, including clairaudience and
clairvoyance at ten thousand feet above sea level

4

DÉJÀ VU

the laws of Karma and reincarnation: how yesterday's vices
and virtues result in today's sorrows and joys . . . how to
balance these for a happier Present and Future

5

WHILE THE SOUL SLUMBERS

the study of numerology, based on the Hebrew Kabala teachings and
the Chaldean Alphabet . . . the one and only true and correct system
of numbers

6

FORGOTTEN RAINBOWS

the power of Color in your life . . . the human aura . . .
permanent weight gain and weight loss through Color . . .
and other magics—including the powers of gems and crystals

7

FORGOTTEN MELODIES

harmonic communications among humans . . . the power of Silence, Sound, and Music . . . the synchronicity and Oneness of the Universe . . . how to use these to manifest magic and miracles

329

8

LEXIGRAMS . . . AND THE WORD DRUIDS

the use of words to penetrate the meanings of ancient codes
. . . the profound mysteries of the English language . . . and
how to lexigram the secrets of words, names, titles, and
phrases

419

9

PHYSICAL IMMORTALITY

a thought transformation, leading to the achievement
of cell regeneration

509

AFTERWORD

remarks from the author to her readers on the subjects of
astrobiology and *Gooberz*

579

FOR THE PILGRIM'S PROGRESS

a recommended reading list of books on metaphysical and
occult studies . . . both fiction and nonfiction

591

Note to my readers: Sometimes, when reading this kind of book containing a variety of information, the reader is tempted to check the Contents and turn directly to a chapter in which there's a particular interest. Please try not to do that with *Star Signs*, because if you do, you'll be missing so much. You really do need to read the chapters consecutively, as they were written, for a full understanding of the material in each. If any chapter is read out of context, the meaning will be confusing, and not having the foundation of previous chapters, it will not be very helpful.

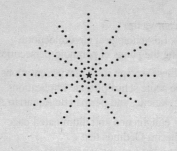

INTRODUCTION

am I the innocent victim
of a new kind of psychological circumlocution
or am I suffering the pangs of paranoid persecution ?

why do I feel these strange solar plexus sensations
as I ponder the acute schizophrenic implications
of this frenetic, kinetic, and peripatetic Aquarian Age ?

where is the enlightened and illuminated page
of Freud's Electra-Oedipus text
that will hint what I might expect next
in this perplexing pattern of non sequitur human behavior ?

what unseen galaxy of stars
holds the true wisdom of the Easter gladness
and the answer to all this other madness
of the Aquarian Age ?

★ ★ ★ ★ ★ ★

"When the Moon was in the seventh house, and Jupiter aligned with Mars," it brought the dawning of the Age of Aquarius, in all of its colorful, bizarre, upside-down, and dizzy glory, frightening the conservatives out of their stiff molds, and delighting the free-spirited nonconformists.

Along with the wild hairdos, gypsy clothing, and shocking lifestyles bearing the unmistakable Uranian stamp of individuality, an important signature of the New Age is the swiftly growing interest in metaphysics and the supernatural, spreading like wildfire all over the world. Seductively, it has beckoned high school and college (even grade school) students, housewives, career women, the so-called "jet set," film stars, government officials, staid businessmen, politicians, and Boards of Directors. Already, representatives of some of America's largest companies, such as IBM, AT&T and General Motors, to name only a few, have met in lengthy seminars to discuss how metaphysics might be able to help their executives compete in the world marketplace.

Chaldean–Hebrew Kabala Numerical Alphabet

A – 1	H – 5	O – 7	V – 6
B – 2	I – 1	P – 8	W – 6
C – 3	J – 1	Q – 1	X – 5
D – 4	K – 2	R – 2	Y – 1
E – 5	L – 3	S – 3	Z – 7
F – 8	M – 4	T – 4	
G – 3	N – 5	U – 6	

These businesspeople believe the esoteric mysteries will show them how to decrease their losses and increase their profits, while new apostles of the occult are equally convinced that, in addition to holding the solutions to their personal problems, these same esoteric mysteries contain an answer to the threat of approaching natural cataclysms and the nuclear holocaust — the final Götterdämmerung. They are right. The ancient wisdoms do possess such solutions and answers, with certain reservations, depending on the interpretation and application of — and obedience to — their truths. Every coin has two sides, and the golden coins of mysticism and metaphysics are no exception.

Astrologers are not surprised at this burgeoning of a newborn belief in the occult. It has been foretold for centuries; long anticipated by esoteric Initiates. And be assured that it will continue to advance like a tidal wave throughout the coming decades of the next two thousand years of the New Age, as the Aquarian "children," spanning all generation gaps, dance a little crazily down the Yellow Brick Road toward the Uranus-ruled, Emerald City of Oz. But beware, Dorothy, lovable Lion, Tin Man, Scarecrow, and innocent Toto ! The land of Oz is not the true Emerald City of enlightenment. There may be a few good faeries with genuine magic wands hovering here and there, but Oz is awash in a surplus of glittering pseudo Wizards, hiding behind every Lollipop Bush and Gingerbread Tree.

Essentially, of course, it is good that humans are, at long last, beginning to realize who they really are — to recognize their own marvelous magical abilities. Behind the explosion of the current mass quest for illumination are the forgotten rainbows and forgotten melodies of remembered miracles. Earthlings are finally becoming dimly aware that they are, in truth, *spirits,* imprisoned in flesh Body Temples, and afflicted with an eons-old amnesia of each individual's true identity and birthright of divinity.

It's a good thing, this dawning of awareness, yes, but there are dangers: the false prophets who can sink the human spirit into an even deeper darkness rather than cause it to rise into the light of true understanding of each individual's mission on this weary Earth, this waning planet . . . at history's twilight hour.

You must remember that, under Universal Law, Light shining from a mountaintop will inevitably attract the darkness.

The dark forces on Earth cannot halt the Aquarian Age earthquake of illumination, nor banish the new hunger for supernatural knowledge and ancient wisdom, but they can use the growing tide of enlightenment for their own nefarious purposes by twisting its message and distorting its clarion call of truth.

As an example of such abuse, an article by Robert Lindsey of *The New York Times* News Service points out that in the early 1980s, recruiting slogans at the Army War College in Carlisle, Pennsylvania, read: "Be All That You Can Be." Lindsey notes that researchers into the growing phenomena of esoteric *group* (that's the Key Word) programs cite this as clear evidence of a significant influence on the Armed Services by credos such as est, Lifespring, and other "New Age" programs and seminars spreading into certain quarters of the military.

These researchers discovered that a number of officers at the Army War College in Carlisle in the early 1980s were graduates of such programs as est, and were dedicated to creating a "New Age Army." According to participants in the study, these officers envisioned the training of soldiers in transcendental meditation (in groups), extrasensory perception, magic, and certain hypnotic techniques. The researchers further contend that est, Lifespring, and other group instruction seminars continue to this day to influence all branches of the Armed Services.

Such a warning to the wise should be sufficient, but it seems not to be. This has to be the non sequitur supreme. Think about it. The use of alleged "spiritual" enlightenment to teach soldiers how to kill more efficiently is surely the ultimate contradiction.

A certain "psychic-medium," currently being promoted and near worshipped by a growing number of major film stars, as well as "ordinary" truth seekers, has been raised to the stature of a saint by followers who congregate in group meetings to become "illuminated" and receive "past life readings" from the "psychic-medium" who, while in trance, becomes "an ancient seer," with voice changes and all the other trappings of medium seances.

Each apostle of this "holy one" has paid from $400 to $1,500 to become enlightened by listening for several hours to "the voice from thousands of years ago." That adds up to a handsome sum when you multiply it by the twenty to fifty or so people attending each group seance. Devoted followers of this "seer" frequently tell others, with incredible naïveté, that "the occult information must be valid because the seminars are so very expensive. You get what you pay for, and why not pay for the best ?" What a pathetically wrong yardstick this is to measure the sincerity of one who claims to be a "Master," even though a small portion of the teachings of "the ancient one" are esoterically sound. The false prophets often surround falsehood with a soft blanket of truth, to disguise the lie. In this instance, the expensive California seer sought by major film stars, housewives, and business executives teaches those who come to be enlightened that "you are Divine, and the divinity in you can do no harm. Therefore, you are incapable of wrongdoing." "Even murder ?" her apostles ask. "Yes," answers the "sage," leaving the seekers really out on a limb, "if you have a good reason for the murder, you may kill without sin." Good grief, Charlie Brown and Lucy. Whatever do you think of that ?

Still, the outrageousness of such teaching is somewhat diluted, I suppose, in the minds of the "seer's" students, by consideration of the "religious wars" — the Crusades. "Go forth, sons of Assisi," shouted the Catholic Bishop. "War is beautiful !" — and further consideration of the 15th and 16th centuries, during which the Catholic Church brutally mutilated and murdered more than five hundred thousand innocent women accused of being witches.

The California trance medium is apparently following the lead of psychiatrists who tell their patients, "If it feels good, do it." — the hypocrisy of the Mormon Church that forbids followers to smoke or drink, while the Church owns some of the largest liquor and tobacco companies in the world — and the precepts of other religious leaders who teach that "holy wars" justify murder. Not all Mormon and Catholic leaders are guilty of such philosophies, of course, only a certain few among the Hierarchies, but . . .

Add the Hebrew religion to this strange religious philosophy. The Chosen Ones Moses led out of the wilderness today shoulder their guns and drop their bombs from the sacred womb of Israel with the same fanatical fervor as America's "proud" Green Berets. It would appear that man can always invent an idealistic reason for murder when it suits him to do so. Considering modern female world leaders, so will woman, when given the opportunity of authority over others, who follow the leader like bleating sheep in the holy name of patriotism.

The beloved mystic, Edgar Cayce, who led a life of near poverty, did not charge hundreds of dollars for the very real help he gave to thousands of people. For a brief time those representing him accepted a small voluntary donation, but most of the time those who sought and received his counsel could not afford even this. While Jesus imparted wisdom during the Sermon on the Mount, or frequently while walking barefoot along the shores of Galilee, Peter and the other disciples are not on record as collecting money from the seeking — or banning those who were poor from receiving the knowledge of the Master. Nor did the Nazarene sail around the world on expensive yachts between his lessons to the multitudes and to individuals, as have those persuasive spiritual salesmen who founded most of the major "group seminar sessions."

Beware of those glittering pseudo-Wizards of Oz who promote enlightenment like used car salesmen in group seminars costing a small fortune, especially when the leaders of these programs are wealthy men who remain aloof from the individual seeker, their wealth earned from the gullibility of their students, taught by high-pressure junior salesmen.

The problem of money and spirituality is not new. There is nothing wrong with earning large sums of money. What matters is *how* you earn it and what you do with it after you've received it. You need not apologize for earning your daily bread (even large bushels of it) for any sort of labor you do which contributes something to the world, on any level. To receive cash compensation, you must put back into the world something of value, whether it be paintings, specialized services, clothings, automobiles, refrigerators, music, or entertainment. As long as you cheerfully and willingly give away half of what you have to those less fortunate, you needn't be ashamed to be a millionaire — or even a billionaire — because you have let go of *half,* thereby allowing this "green energy" to circulate. (Also because you earned it by honest work.) Money is not evil. Only the use of it and the means of gaining it can cause it to be.

However, there is a singular rule and metaphysical precept concerning the relationship between money and spiritual counsel. The rule is clear, and repeated in every holy work of every religion. *Money must not change hands between esoteric teacher and student.* This is why all churches, Catholic, Protestant, or Synagogue, do not permit their priests, ministers, or rabbis to accept money from the parishioners. These "teachers" are supported, their needs supplied by the church, which is, itself, supported by voluntary and anonymous donations from the general public.

It's unfortunate, for example, that there are no "churches" to support astrologers. They must "earn their daily bread" in some other manner, and perform their astrological counseling during their precious free time. It's unfortunate, yes, but not as much so as when astrologers charge for their readings, since the ancient teachings say that the one who heeds not the warning forbidding the exchange of money between teacher and student will soon "lose the gift of perception," and consequently will no longer be sought by the "students."

To write about esoteric subjects or personal paths of enlightenment in books is not against this law. Books by everyone from actress Shirley MacLaine to Ruth Montgomery and dozens of astrological and metaphysical writers spread enlightenment in the spiritually approved way. The money received by the authors is for their labors at the typewriter, the talent of stringing words together, earned over years of practice and hard work. To earn your bread by writing is the same as to earn your bread by being a craftsman in any endeavor. (But they'd still be best advised to share half of it with others in need !)

The money rule, is not the only roadmap you'll need on your journey down the Yellow Brick Road of metaphysics to the enchanting Oz of enlightenment. You need to also be forewarned, therefore forearmed, against the loss of your own individuality by trusting those who seek to control your mind and your personal intuition (teaching from within) through a form of mass hypnosis.

Dr. Edwin Morse, a former member of the University of Wisconsin's psychology faculty, following a study of self-help groups such as est, Lifespring, Forum Insight, and Actualizations states that "the graduates of such group programs, former cult members, are often psychologically scarred." He further contends that these groups are subjected to well-known and effective "hypnotic procedures — and are not being told about it."

You do have a choice, whether you realize it yet or not. You can choose the dangerous turn in the Yellow Brick Road to enlightenment by following the deceptive Detour Sign to "group illumination," and risk becoming lost, while you pay, not only a high toll charge in dollars, but the higher price of stilling the always wise voice of your own personal Higher Self — your own intuition . . . being taught from within.

Or you can choose an intimate Personal Odyssey, learning to *listen* to the voice of the Angel of your Higher Self. This is the road which will lead you directly to the Emerald City of enlightenment, not the Oz of pseudo wizards. And you need not walk the road alone. The words of an old song contain a true promise . . . *"I believe for everyone who's gone astray . . . someone will come, to show the way."*

Yes. You are entitled to your own Guru. Your own personal Adept or Avatar, who will not only emanate the wisdoms of all past Messiahs, but who will lead you into understanding that you, too, are a Messiah. You needn't look in the Yellow Pages of the telephone directory to locate this special one who will walk along the path with you until you're able to walk alone. Then, how do you find the "Guru" you decide to seek alone, without turning your precious mind over to others in expensive, dangerous group seminars ? It's really quite simple. Desire. Genuine desire. Desire, when it stems from the heart and the spirit, when it is pure and intense, possesses awesome electromagnetic energy. Released into the ethers each night as the mind falls into the sleep state . . . and each morning as it returns to the conscious state . . . it will surely and certainly manifest that which has been imaged. You can rely upon this ageless promise as surely as you can rely upon the eternally unbroken promise of sunrise . . . and spring.

Often, the initial manifestation of your quest is a series of strange "coincidences," which are not coincidental at all . . . leading you to certain books written about a variety of metaphysical subjects. You can be led to such esoteric works in several ways. Sometimes through a chance remark from friends . . . often through your own seemingly aimless but subconsciously purposeful browsing. You'll soon learn to judge yourself whether a book's contents are misleading or wise by listening to the voice of your own Higher Self, whispering into your inner ear. You'll learn to *feel* the messages in a short while. Some books you may reject, and others you will inwardly know are teaching a facet of universal truth you can accept.

This is not always but usually the first step you must take alone before the manifestation of your own personal Guru, who will then impart ancient wisdom on a warm and precious one-to-one basis. To aid you with this initial step, I've included at the end of this book a section from *Love Signs* called "For the Pilgrim's Progress," with some additions. It's not intended to be a complete list of all worthy occult and metaphysical works — just some of those to which I was blessedly led on my own star quest for truth, and which I've personally found to be deeply insightful. I believe they will be of equal help to you, but you must, nevertheless, judge for yourself.

Reading about metaphysical subjects is normally necessary as a preparation for personal counseling from your own Avatar. Aries Thomas Jefferson said, "I cannot live without books." One can, of course, and some have risen to illumination without them, but they are undeniably a swift shortcut to enlightenment.

After you've demonstrated your sincerity of desire by reading the books to which you've trusted your own Higher Self to lead you, by Universal Law, you'll be ready for your personal teacher, who will instruct you in the Socratic method: by helping you remember what you already know but have forgotten. Basically, the Socratic method consists of the teacher asking the students questions, not telling them something. When, instead of a statement being made, a question is asked, the computer brain scans its stored memory bank (of this and other lifetimes) and usually comes up with an answer you didn't even realize you knew. But you do know — everything there is to know, written indelibly upon the ethers, in what has been called the Akashic Records. You can read them, as did mystics like Edgar Cayce. You have only forgotten how.

Every action ever taken, every word ever spoken — remains — on a higher frequency vibration — and may be magnetized back into conscious awareness under certain conditions. To claim that you are unable to do so is like owning a radio, possessing AM and FM, an On switch — and numerous frequencies or stations — and saying that there is no way you can tune in to WABC or whatever "spot on the dial" you choose. An infant, of course, sitting before a radio switched to Off, could not tune in to the various frequencies. And humans are infants, relative to their present state of enlightenment. But all infants eventually mature, as will all humans eventually reach spiritual maturity. Remaining with this analogy, it's possible that, by some accident, the radio before which the infant is sitting may be switched on and music is heard. The infant didn't deliberately tune in to that "station," and has no idea where it's coming from . . . but listens happily, and is soothed by it. This is similar to an adult human who accidentally experiences a flash of déjà vu, clairaudience, or clairvoyance.

How will you and your teacher-Guru find each other ? One of the oldest metaphysical adages, existing even before the recorded history of the Tibetan Priesthood, is: *"When the student is ready — the teacher will appear."* As strange as such a prophecy may seem to you as a beginning pilgrim, it is totally true. I know of many who have experienced it, and I can attest to its truth and reliability myself, as I have . . . through intense desire . . . found, over the years, three such personal Gurus, Avatars, or Adepts . . . not by seeking them, but simply by *desiring* their manifestation, by preparing, and being willing to wait until they appeared, wholly without my calling them. I've told of only one such unannounced, startling manifestation I have personally experienced in the Preface to this book — and there are other references in Chapter 3, *Gurus, Ghosts, and Avatars.*

I assure you that you will discover more fathoms of peace, wisdom, and contentment by taking the necessary steps toward manifesting an Avatar who will be considering nothing but your own personal illumination than by attending a hundred expensive seminars or group workshops. And no money will change hands. All true enlightenment and every final mystical initiation must occur, not in groups, but in a close relationship between teacher and student. *When the student is ready.*

No, these will not be "spirit guides" from another world, but quite tangible flesh-and-blood people (some even possessing a minor flaw or two to "keep their molecules together while present on an Earth vibrating with such negative energy forces as currently"). Yes, they will appear disguised as "ordinary" humans, albeit the awesome magics they will demonstrate to you . . . sometimes in a startling way . . . at other times simply through an unguessed wise manner of setting examples you will slowly but finally comprehend. And so . . . the safest and purest way to learn the esoteric mysteries is to properly prepare yourself in the manner I've described for the manifestation and certain appearance of a very personal teacher, who will lead you into a comprehension of what you think of as magic, but which is only a higher level of what you think of as reality. Remember that "meta" is a Greek word meaning "beyond," therefore, metaphysics is simply "beyond physics." Beyond the fiction of fact lies truth ?

Neither should you blindly accept, on your quest for truth, the validity of the star sign codes of the Universe I offer in this book — until you have practiced and carefully tested each one, so that you can decide for yourself rather than take my word for it.

Mystical knowledge is power, and power will always tend to corrupt. Spiritual wisdom is the priceless key of those who earnestly desire to help others, as well as to attain personal joy and happiness — and is equally the dangerous master of those who wish to control others, who seek only personal benefit. When used with unselfish motive, there is no end to the wonders such knowledge can materialize. But if used for selfish purpose, it will inevitably boomerang back upon the user all manner of tragedies and disasters. This is one of the great laws of the Universe, which cannot be broken. It is inflexible, unswerving, and eternally undefeated.

Esoteric mysteries must be approached cautiously, with reverence and compassion, with a genuine desire to use their magics to end the world's suffering . . . to relieve the pain of individuals . . . and to bring happiness to friends and strangers alike. Yes, and also to enemies. Even especially to these. Then it will follow that joy and happiness will likewise descend upon its user in abundance. Endless miracles will manifest when love and peace rule in the heart of the one who has mastered the arts and sciences of ancient wisdom with goodwill and loving intent.

There is no more effective resolve to follow in these — and in all other matters — than the affirmation of Francesco Bernadone of Assisi, spoken aloud and sincerely meant each new morning of each day.

> Lord, make me an instrument of your Peace
> where there is hatred, let me show love
> where there is injury, let me give pardon
> where there is doubt, let me have faith . . .
> where there is darkness, let me spread Light
> where there is sadness, help me find Joy !
>
> Grant that I may not so much seek . . . to be understood
> as to understand
> to be loved . . . as to love
>
> Then . . . miracle shall follow miracle
> and wonders shall never cease

★ ★ ★ ★ ★ ★

The intention of this book is to reveal, among several other metaphysical codes, a key to wisdom previously comprehended by only a few initiated Masters, a secret hidden for centuries "in plain sight" (the safest place to hide the sacred) and unsuspected by the mundane intellect, long blinded to the *simplicity* of truth. I've christened this enlightenment Lexigrams, a method of acquiring astonishing insights into a person or "a thing" by using the letters of the name, title, or phrase in a certain way. Combining Lexigrams with Numerology (the *correct* Chaldean-Kabala system) — which is also demonstrated in the book — brings a new kind of awareness that causes the thoughts to spiral into a penetration of the deeper enigmas of existence . . . accomplishing the same benefits obtained from transcendental meditation, but more surely and more swiftly. More swiftly because the comprehension gained through Lexigrams and Numerology (as well as the other codes in the book) is spontaneous, and creates a sort of spiritual chain reaction in the mind. More surely because these universal codes do not require the difficult achievement of a total submission of the personal ego and consciousness.

When prejudiced blindfolds are removed, answers to all conceivable questions can be seen, even the proof of their validity, through a multiplicity of codes and signs beyond — yet inseparable from — astrology. As unrelated to planetary influences as these prisms of knowledge may first appear, they nevertheless all initiate from the Luminaries (Sun and Moon) and the stars or planets. They are the Star Signs of wisdom, awaiting your discovery.

As with *Love Signs*, *Star Signs* contains a number of controversial concepts of a moral, philosophical, and intellectual nature, in the areas of science and religion.

To some of you, these concepts will be inspiring — to others they will appear strange and startling — to still others they could be deeply disturbing. They are presented here as truth, and will be recognized as such by many of you — just as they may be viewed as otherwise by some.

I've shared my personal discoveries of truth with you because I believe that any kind of search implies an obligation to exchange with others what has been found, in the interest of hastening the sunrise of harmony on Earth, the ultimate Peace.

However, I do not ask — nor do I even expect — any of you to regard my concepts as *your* truth, unless they should happen to agree with your own personal enlightenment and private convictions.

Partial truth — the seeds of wisdom — can be found in many places. In primal instinct may partial truth be found . . . in earthly law, social custom, scientific research, philosophy, and religious doctrine. The seeds of wisdom are contained in all scriptures ever written . . . especially in art, music, and poetry . . . and, above all, in Nature.

But *real* Truth can be found in one place only — in every man's and woman's communion with an eternal Source of hidden Knowledge within — which each individual must seek and find for himself or herself.

We may point out the path to others, but each must walk along that path alone — until every single "lost one" has made the whole journey — and all of us have finally reached the Light of full-born Wisdom at the end of the Way . . . where we began, a long-forgotten Time ago.

— Linda Goodman

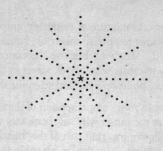

PREFACE

It is with an odd mixture of misgiving, inspiration, and excitement that I've decided to publish this book, based on a diary I kept in Colorado in 1970. Misgiving because the concepts presented in it raise issues likely to create some shock waves in the already churning oceans of religious, philosophical, and scientific thought.

It's necessary to your comprehension of these "shock waves" that you understand at the outset why this book was written. The explanation will also allow me to shift part of the "blame" or the "credit" — whichever word applies — for the far-out subjects of the text, since, in reality, I had little control over the channeling of the material.

I've always written my books in such a way as to share many of my personal feelings and experiences with you, my readers, because I trust you — and I'm still following that pattern of taking you into my confidence. It makes me feel closer to you, as it makes you feel closer to me, which so many of you have told me in your letters.

And so, this is how it all came about.

Once upon a lonely time, when I was in California on a promotional tour for my first book, *Sun Signs,* staying in the haunted suite 1217* of the Hollywood Roosevelt Hotel, *a stranger knocked on my door*. The year was 1970. The month, January. New Year's Day.

Several years earlier, while I was talking with Lucille and David Kahn in New York (my home at the time), we had drifted into a discussion about Masters, Avatars, Space People, Gurus, and Adepti. David Kahn, since deceased, was the mentor of the well-known and beloved mystic, Edgar Cayce — who encouraged Cayce's work and provided his living expenses during the early years. For the longest time I'd been mesmerized by the ancient Tibetan adage of, *"When the student is ready, the teacher will appear,"* and so I asked David a question.

"What precisely," I wanted to know, "does that mean ? How

---

* Now renumbered by the hotel's new owners as 1221.

does such a teacher appear ? Does he just knock on the door some unexpected day or night, and when you answer — there he is ?"

David and Lucille glanced at each other with a mysterious smile, then David turned to me and replied quietly, "Well, yes . . . something like that."

Now we can return to "once upon a time," a few years later, in suite 1217, at the Hollywood Roosevelt Hotel, on January 1, 1970.

When I answered the stranger's knock, I saw standing there in the open doorway a plump man, shaped rather like a Buddha, wearing the incongruous combination of a proper business suit, suede loafers — and a snow-white turban fastened in the center with a pearl stickpin. He had an irresistible, almost childlike smile and an impeccably gracious manner. I soon learned he was an "initiated" Hatha Yoga *and* a Zen Buddhist who had spent thirty years in a monastery in India, under a vow of silence. I'd never heard of anyone being both a Hatha Yoga and Buddhist, but then, I was still very much a novice in such matters. His complexion was creamy olive; his eyes, not brown, but black and piercing.

He apologized for the intrusion, saying that he had read my first book, *Sun Signs,* and some of the passages in it caused him to perceive that I was already aware of many mystical secrets, but was still questing for more "star signs" of truth — and he felt that perhaps he might be able, in some small way, to guide me along the path of light. His voice had musical intonations, with a pronounced British accent. Later, he told me he'd been educated at Oxford, and had lived for some time in London.

He offered no explanation of how he had managed to locate me, and I didn't ask, feeling that such a direct question was forbidden by some esoteric rule of conduct. I didn't *know* this, but I *sensed* it.

Of course I invited him to come in, curious, yet not alarmed. For the next several hours we chatted like old friends . . . although . . .

there seemed to be a strange pattern to our talking. I had the impression that our speech was, in an inexplicable way, speeded up, because our words were exchanged so swiftly, almost without pause, sentences tumbling over one another . . . and at times I could have sworn we were speaking simultaneously, like a double track on a tape.

I had a thousand and one questions for him, and each was answered no less than profoundly. Excited and exhilarated as I was to be learning so much in such a brief time, I felt a surge of regret when he told me he would soon have to leave, because he was late for an appointment at the Griffith Park Observatory.

"But before we part," he added, "I have a message to relay to you from the Masters of Karma, channeled through me by the Higher Forces."

Oddly, such an unusual statement neither alarmed nor surprised me. But it certainly fascinated me. "Message ? What kind of message ?" I asked.

"About your future. There are some events ahead in time even an astrologer as experienced as yourself cannot fully penetrate, because they lie above and beyond the natal and progressed planetary configurations."

"And what, then, is ahead in time for me ?" Involuntarily, my pulse quickened, and I felt a sudden chill. He spoke slowly and very deliberately.

"Soon you will be going to the mountains."

"The mountains ? Do you mean Tibet ? The Alps . . . Switzerland maybe ? I've always wanted to go there."

He smiled enigmatically, and his reply was noncommittal. "To a higher altitude. For the purpose of raising your vibratory frequency, and receiving several gifts of illumination from teachers, who will appear without your seeking them."

"Without my seeking ?"

"Is that not how I came to you this day ?"

"Yes, of course. Is it related, then, to the ancient Tibetan adage I've heard that, *when the student is ready, the teacher will appear* ?"

"*Quite.*" (I was later to learn that was his favorite word of approval.)

"Well, it all sounds rather spooky." I smiled, to show him I was joking, but I was only half-joking. There was an unreal sensation about this conversation. His next words were completely unexpected . . . and shocking.

"After your retreat in the mountains, you will travel back here to California, where you will meet your Twin Self."

"Twin Self ? Don't you mean Twin Soul ?"

"No. There is an important difference in the definition of the two terms, as you will soon learn for the purpose of teaching others."

"Are you saying that I'll learn this difference while I'm in the mountains, from the teacher I'll meet there without my seeking ?"

"Partially. But you will be *fully* enlightened to this only after you have met the man who is the other half of yourself. Following your meeting, you will write a book about everything you will teach one another. However, you must not make it available to your readers until after you have written and published a book you will also write, about your experiences of enlightenment in the mountains, which will occur, in Earth Time, *before* you meet this man." He waited, but I made no comment. Then he continued.

"After you've met, it will become clear to both of you that your mutual mission, as written in the Akashic Records, is manifold. You are to make others aware that such phenomena as magical cognition, the seeing of auras, the power to ordain happiness and erase misery, the ability to attain spontaneous remission of illness, and the achievement of immortality — do not belong exclusively only to a few Masters, but are possessed by all Earthlings, and may be developed to as high a degree as they desire."

Again he waited, and again I remained silent, not wanting to express my reaction to these words aloud, as I thought to myself that there was no way I could ever be capable of meeting such a challenge as he presented, with or without the "other half of myself." He might as well have told me that the following day I would be able to manifest a spacecraft out of the ethers, hop in, press a button, and zoom off for a weekend on Mars or Saturn. The manifold mutual mission he described was so unattainable as to be amusing if it hadn't been so overwhelming.

My silence didn't seem to disturb him. His enigmatic smile remained, and his eyes continued to burn into mine like a laser beam. After a moment or so, when it became obvious that I was not going to respond, he simply went on with his incredible statements.

"An important part of the illuminations the two of you will seed into the sleeping awareness of humans is the importance of *love* to men and women, the various paths they may take toward a reunion with the Twin Self . . ." He paused, and his voice took on a sterner tone, making his next words sound like a warning. ". . . . and the danger, once the other half has been found, of both becoming what have been called 'fallen angels,' destroying their sacred, for-eons-awaited Oneness through the grave sins of false pride, selfishness . . . and unforgiveness. It is further written in the Akashic Records that this, too, is part of the mission you and another assigned yourselves long ago, to be accomplished in this present incarnation. The task will be extremely difficult, but you must not allow yourselves to be discouraged. You must also be aware that, if you should fail in your mutual mission, there are others — not only others who will be simultaneously teaching the same truths — but others who will replace you, should you give up. For the teaching itself is the priority, and it shall not be allowed to fail. Earth Time is growing short — so short that the approaching moment of human choice between enlightenment and extinction must now be measured by the year instead of by the century.

Another pause from him. Another silence from me.

"Your task will require much courage, because you will face disbelief and ridicule. You will also face the challenge of many false teachings, contradictory to your own, which are even now swiftly spreading throughout the world. For these are the days of the false prophets predicted by John in *Revelations* in your Christian scriptures."

My mind contained, superimposed, two thoughts. The first was a surge of thankfulness that, at some time during our conversation, I had asked him if he minded my turning on my small tape recorder, so that I could later recall at least a portion of what he was telling me, because I knew I was likely to forget much of it, or believe I had dreamed the entire incident, and he had agreed. But, as I glanced down, I saw that the tape had run out — I had no idea when. Then, glancing at the clock on the table, I saw that barely a minute or so had passed since I'd turned on the ninety-minute tape, and I knew positively that the things he had been saying, which were naturally still clear in my memory, could not possibly have taken such a brief time as a minute or so. It puzzled me, but more, it frightened me — in the sense that all things not completely understood are frightening when they occur.

The second superimposed thought was that his words had made such a profound impression on me, I didn't trust myself to comment — especially his statement that Earth Time is growing so short that "the approaching moment of human choice between enlightenment and extinction must now be measured by the year instead of by the century." Consequently, until I had a chance to assess all of this within, I knew I had to change the subject in self-defense. So I did.

Clearing my throat nervously, I finally spoke. "Forgive me, but I've always believed," I pointed out rather smugly for a novice, "that the Akashic Records refer only to past events and actions — to former incarnations or lifetimes — and not to either the present or the future."

He smiled again. "But what Earthlings call the Past, Present, and Future are all one, you see — taking place simultaneously. By the way, the word *simultaneously* contains within it the letters of the words *no time* and *time is a lie* — which is what the word 'simultaneously' really means. Think deeply about this."

I did. *Very* deeply. And it was at this instant that my enlightenment to Lexigrams was born (Chapter 8).

He went on, his expression making it clear that he knew the seeds he had just planted with that word had taken root, and would soon flower. In fact, he seemed to be positively elated. His face fairly beamed.

"I know it seems incomprehensible to you now, but after a while you will understand, and when you do, you will have mastered how to exist, for temporary periods, whenever you should wish, in what is called the Eternal Now, a Higher Dimension of Time. There are many such dimensions. Earthlings now exist in the Third Dimension, and are ready to graduate into the Fourth Dimension."

His words chimed a carol somewhere in the back of my mind.

"For some reason," I told him, "what you just said about an Eternal Now reminded me of the lyric to a song about . . . 'on a clear day, you can see Forever,' my favorite tape cassette. I play it all the time. It's the recorded score from the stage musical and later film, starring Barbra Streisand, written by Alan Jay Lerner and Burton Lane, called *On a Clear Day*. For some strange reason, I always seem to miss seeing the film when it's playing in a theatre near me, but I love the title song, especially the verse to it, before the chorus."

"Will you sing it for me ? I would very much like to hear it."

Shyly, softly, and unsure, I sang to him the words and melody as well as I could recall them.

Spoken: "Why, Daisy ! You're a bloody miracle ! Could anyone among us have an inkling or a clue . . . what magic feats of wizardry and voodoo you can do ?"

Sung: ". . . and who would ever guess . . . the powers you possess . . . and who would not be stunned to see you prove . . . there's more to us than surgeons can remove ! So much more than we ever knew . . . so much more were we born to do ! Should you draw back the curtain, of this I am certain . . . you'll be impressed with *you* ! On a clear day, rise and look around you . . . and you'll see who you are ! On a clear day, how it will astound you . . . when the glow of your being outshines every star !

"You'll feel part of . . . every mountain, sea and shore. You will hear, from far and near . . . a world you've never heard before. And on a clear day . . . on that clear day . . . you can see Forever . . . and ever . . . and evermore . . ." I finished, slightly off key.

He clapped his hands like a small boy. "That was beautiful ! It describes so perfectly the powers possessed by all Earthlings, each man and woman . . . yet they remain unaware of it."

He closed his eyes for a heartbeat, then . . . . .

"You have missed seeing the motion picture, *On a Clear Day,* for a reason you do not as yet suspect. I believe that you and your Twin Self will see it together . . . and that the seeing of this film together, the 'simultaneous' sharing of its seedings about Time and reincarnation, will be the first experience to open your Third Eyes. For it will contain certain subliminal messages for both of you.

"Yes, it is a clear day when one finally comprehends the mystery of making miracles. Thank you again for singing those words to me."

I blushed. "I'm sure I didn't sound like Barbra Streisand," I murmured, feeling a wave of embarrassment at having spontaneously burst into song before a stranger. But his next words erased those feelings.

"And why should you sound like her ? Your Earthling composer and musician, Paul Winter, who plays to whales and dolphins in the ocean, and who has played duets with wolves and eagles in the woods, in the key of Earth, D flat, causing them to respond and 'sing' with him in perfect harmony, made a wise observation. *It would be a sad and quiet, lonely forest if no bird sang except the nightingale.* And so, once again, I thank you for singing to me."

"Thank *you* for your message," I replied. "It's such a lovely event to anticipate, like a song in itself . . . some familiar but forgotten melody I'm sure I'll hear in the back of my mind until the meeting with my Twin Self really happens. Yes, lovely . . . oh ! I just realized that *lovely* and *lonely* are very similar words, but with such very different meanings !" The Lexigram seeds he had planted were already beginning to flower in my consciousness. As I spoke, I was thinking of my own loneliness, an affliction I'd begun to fear was to be permanent in my life.

"Yes, similar words, true," he agreed, "with, as you say, quite different meanings. What makes them different is a third word, hiding in one of them, that answers all questions, solves all problems, heals all pain."

"What word is that ?" The Lexigram blossoms were unfolding, and fascinating me.

He smiled. "The word *love*. Notice that the word *lovely* contains the word *love* within it. The word *lonely* does not."

He paused. "Love is all."

"I see," I told him. And for the moment, I did.

For a timeless Time, then, we both remained silent. There was a humming stillness in the room that seemed to vibrate like some sort of energy force, the kind of stillness so tangible you can almost *feel* it, you know? I know this sounds contradictory, but the stillness grew louder, until I became aware of a growing sense of uneasiness and apprehension.

I looked at the clock. It was exactly twenty minutes past one P.M. Twenty after. I remembered something my Irish elf mother (grandmother) told me when I was a child. Something . . . I'll share with you in Chapter 3 of this book . . . and more of it in Chapter 8.

In the humming quiet between us, I was aware of the stranger still staring at me, unblinking, his eyes like burning coals. I finally found my voice, and asked him hesitantly, "Just exactly when — in present time — am I supposed to be destined to meet this man who is . . . my Twin Self?"

"It is written that your reunion shall take place near Christmas, in December of 1970. As Time is calculated here on Earth . . . at the end of this year."

"Reunion?" I was confused. "Since we'll be meeting each other, I assume, for the first time, why do you call it a reunion?"

"You will not be meeting for the first time. You have lived countless lives together in former incarnations — even in this present one."

This was too much for me to untangle. "But," I persisted, "if we have not yet met in this incarnation, which I am absolutely certain we have not . . . then why do you say, 'in this *present* one'? It doesn't make sense. It isn't logical. Is it some kind of a riddle?"

"Yes, a riddle. One you may solve yourself, with his help, for you will teach each other many things. And now I really must leave you." He rose from his chair, causing me to feel a sharp stab of disappointment, because I knew that, this time, he would really leave.

Suddenly, the stab of disappointment was replaced by a surge of inexpressible happiness, enveloping me like a fine mist, and I felt so grateful to this kind stranger who had promised me such a perfectly marvelous Christmas gift as meeting my own Twin Self. Who hasn't secretly longed for just such a miracle?

He walked toward the door, and I followed; then he stopped in front of a table at the entrance to the small hallway of the suite. On it was my miniature altar, consisting of an alabaster statue of St. Francis of Assisi . . . Francesco di Bernadone . . . with his beloved birds and animals . . . a bowl of fresh daisies . . . and several votive candles burning in ruby-red glass holders, like the ones in St. Patrick's Cathedral on Fifth Avenue in New York City. I carry my small altar with me when I travel, using it to evoke minor magic and ordain baby miracles — for myself and others. It's rather like a portable cathedral. Of course, one doesn't really need such accoutrement to manifest magic or miracles. All one needs is a direct line of communication to one's Higher Self — or, if you prefer, to one's own God, Whoever He, She, or They may be — on the desert, in the woods, on a mountaintop, on the shore, or even walking along a crowded city street. But, speaking for myself, I feel the presence of angels with more certainty, and am able to spiral my thoughts more purely, when my senses are thus sweetly incited by subtle ritual.

My uninvited but most welcome visitor stood there before the flickering candles, very still; then in a low voice asked me to close my eyes while he offered a prayer.

I did as he requested, bowing my head, and as I stood beside him in the scented dark, the musty, mystical fragrance of my Morning Star "church incense" seemed richer than usual, and my thoughts drifted, until I became aware that he had placed his hand gently on the top of my head, like a blessing . . . and then began to chant in a strangely familiar, musical language, similar to the Latin of the Mass, yet which was, I could tell, *not* Latin. The melodious sound of his chanting, blended with the sweet scent of the incense in the black velvet behind my closed eyes, after a while transported me back into a magical childhood Christmas Eve, when I had slipped through the huge carved wooden doors of St. Raphael's Convent to hear the nuns singing "Silent Night, Holy Night" in their soft voices, a capella . . . I could smell oranges and cinnamon in the air.

Suddenly, his chanting stopped, the light pressure of his hand on my head lifted, and I reluctantly returned from the past to the present, opening my eyes slowly, as if awakening from a dream. When I turned to say good-bye to my new friend, he was gone. Simply disappeared.

True, I had come out of my trancelike state and opened my eyes slowly enough for him to have had time to slip through the door — I mean to have slipped *out* the door. Or would *through* it be more appropriate ?

But I had heard no sound of the door opening or closing. Shivering, I took the blue-flowered comforter folded across the bottom of the bed, sank down into the plump sofa chair by the window that looked out on the small white cross, planted on the far hill behind Graumann's Chinese Theatre across Hollywood Boulevard . . . tucked my feet under, and wrapped the comforter around me.

It was a disturbing experience, but as I sat in the chair, snugly enfolded in the soft clouds of the comforter, an errant thought swam through the floods of my fear, from childhood's vast ocean of memories . . . my Baptist Sunday School teacher mother's voice, quoting from the New Testament . . . "Be not afraid, for thy Comforter shall come." I smiled, then, to myself, at the incongruity of the play on words. Cosmic acuity aside, I was on the verge of believing it had all been a dream from the beginning. But there was the tape. And then I noticed, on the glass-topped table beside the chair, the small white card the stranger had handed me only seconds after I'd invited him to come into the room. I hadn't really looked at it before, assuming it was a business card. Now I saw that it was blank, except that printed in the center in small violet letters were the words: EXPECT A MIRACLE.

There was something else on the table beside the small white card I'd been given. An unopened box of Goober's peanuts, the kind sold in the lobby of every film theatre in America. This, the stranger had definitely *not* given me, and I knew I had not placed the box of chocolate-covered peanuts there myself. Where could they have come from, I wondered, unless the turbaned one had left them there when I wasn't looking ? That must have been what happened, I told myself. There was no other explanation. But . . . *why* would he have done so ?

The Goober's peanuts troubled me more than a little, because they were, in a complex way, associated with a traumatic relationship in my past. Back then, I had studied only the rudiments of basic numerology (I was later to be initiated into this art and science in more depth, during my predicted retreat in the mountains) . . . so I quickly scribbled down the numerical value of the letters in "Goober," and realized that the singular of the word must be spelled with three o's — as Gooober. The plural had to be spelled with only two o's and a "z" instead of an "s" — as in Gooberz. The proper numerological vibrations of words make worlds of difference. Again, I reminded myself of my promise to the me-of-me, that I would learn more, when I had time, about this deeply mystical and powerful code of the Universe, taken from the Hebrew Kabala, and steeped in the traditional wisdom of the ancient Chaldeans.

For a long time I sat in the chair by the window, trying to memorize everything that had occurred during the stranger's visit, so I wouldn't later forget anything important, even the slightest nuance of his words. Somewhere in my metaphysical studies in the past I had heard of or read about those Rosicrucian Adepti (called by many other names as well) who were able to disappear then reappear before one's physical vision by changing their vibratory frequency of angstrom units per second . . . speeding up the rate to become invisible to the naked eye, and slowing down the rate to become physically visible.

I had heard — and read — of such magic, but that never prepares one for the actual witnessing of it. I had not hallucinated. There was, you see, the box of Goober's peanuts — and the small white card.

If the stranger had not been real, but merely an etheral vision I had invoked, then they could have appeared on the table only through what is called "telaportation," and it was easier to accept that I had met an Adept — after all, they most assuredly do exist — than to believe that I had "apported" the chocolate-covered peanuts and the card.

★ ★ ★ ★ ★ ★

Now I know my mind was programmed by the stranger on that mystical, prismed New Year's Day to magnetize me toward the geographical location destined as the place for my next step in what he had called illumination. Back then, however, once I'd recovered from the initial shock of the arcane incident, I never imagined such a thing, for I believed that I control my own mind, as we all do . . . do we not ?

A few weeks after my return from California to New York, on a snowy February day, I had lunch with a friend who had just returned from a vacation in Colorado. She was full of her trip, as enthusiastic as a travel agent about this colorful western state, the scene of the "Pikes-Peak-or-Bust" gold rush of the 1890s — and disappointed that she'd had to leave there so soon to get back to her job in Manhattan before she'd had time to make a side trip to Cripple Creek.

"What is so special about Cripple Creek ?" I asked her.

"It's a tiny former gold-mining town, high in the mountains, ten thousand feet above sea level. I believe the population is only a few hundred people, waiting around, I guess, for the price of gold to go high enough to mine it from the ground again. Cripple Creek is nestled in a valley, with woods all around, protected by the Sangre de Cristo mountain range — the Continental Divide. My brother and his wife were there last year, and they say it's absolutely breathtaking . . . so beautiful . . . no humidity at all in the summer . . . pure air . . . and snow-capped peaks, just like Switzerland . . . or Tibet . . . and . . . ."

The rest of her words faded in and out, because I'd been transfixed the moment she had spoken the words, *"high in the mountains."*

"What does Sangre de Cristo mean ?" I asked her.

"The blood of Christ, I think. Anyway, my brother says most people in the area believe that Cripple Creek is haunted. He told me he had the odd feeling himself that he'd been there before . . . a kind of . . . what do they call it . . . a déjà vu ? So did Elaine. She told me that she knew exactly where the Old Homestead was before anyone told her. That's the oldest red-light house in the West, so we teased her about why she knew . . . told her she probably worked there as "one of the girls" in her last life. But she also knew where the Abraham Lincoln gold mine was before it was pointed out to her. She said Tenderfoot Mountain and Mount Pisgah were places she felt she had seen before . . . and some of the deserted log cabins on the edge of town had a familiarity about them that made her feel . . . well, strange."

I said nothing to my friend about my inner thoughts, but by the time we'd finished lunch and parted — she, to return to the ad agency on Madison Avenue where she works, and me, to walk slowly home to West End Avenue through a flurry of snowflakes — I had made a decision, remembering what I had been told about "the teacher appearing when the student was ready — high in the mountains." I would go to this haunted little gold-mining town and retreat for several months, to test the stranger's prediction.

While I was there, I told myself, I would complete my next book, *Love Signs* — and assuming that I somehow, while there, learned the metaphysical secrets he had promised, I would also keep a diary as the basis for a future book about my experiences.

So I flew to Colorado in April of 1970, and everything the turbaned one had prognosticated came true . . . some of it unexpectedly. I learned many secrets from several teachers who appeared without my seeking them. I also endured several personal tragedies in Colorado while I was learning, but these you will not be reading about in this particular book. Only the magic.

★★★

CRIPPLE CREEK, COLORADO

> *for gold miner and poet, Julian Davis*
> *who loved each rock and tree*
> *and who lingers still . . . for me*
> *on Bennett Avenue*
> *walking through the ghosts of living strangers*
> *not one of them so real as he*

★★★★★★

ten thousand feet above the level of the sea
high-hidden on the sunrise side
of the wandering Continental Divide

is a magical kingdom

where a clean wind blows
and the white star of Bethlehem glows through the clouds
of winter's snow-veiled skies

a microcosm Tibet

where the lonely and searching still travel

to mine the fool's gold of wealth
or Nature's truer treasures . . . rooted there
as surely as the sturdy Bristlecone pines

those ancient mysteries few have thought to seek
   beyond the protective purple shadows
of the Sangre de Cristo guardian range
    where lies the town called Cripple Creek

sleeping in a sweetly scented valley
surrounded by the scarred hills of man's greed
and the greener woods of meditative solitude

  a Heaven-sent, sometimes hell-bent
community of fallen angels . . . and occasional saints
fighters and writers, cowboys and painters
the self-sufficient and the proud . . . the tortured and the damned
yet even these infused with the alchemy
    of transmutation into blessed

    a singing Shangri-la

wearing the mask
of a tough, hard-hearted town
spilling over with yesterday's memories
  and eight months pregnant
with tomorrow's not yet shattered dreams

    where horses, cows, and velvet-eyed burros
      wander the dusty roads and by paths
    and "mountain canaries" sing the restless to sleep

    where midnight is silent . . . and passions run deep
    where raw courage is absorbed
    from the mountains' mute strength . . . pure white
    snows
    and the brilliant turquoise sky

Teller County's glittering "Bowl of Gold"
    of the new Aquarian Age
discovered by a trembling few, after passing through
                       the Tunnel of Time

        then hearing echoes of coded whispers
        in the twilight zone of neighboring Victor
        Goldfield's haunted Bull Mountain
        and Phantom Canyon's chanting Narrows

    those reflections of Stonehenge

        where the watchful Third Eye
        can see the faint, still-flickering lights
        of the druids' enchanted Twelfth Night rites

        and the weary spirit learns to wait
        for the eternally certain, however late
                      return

        of spring's reincarnated promise
           to the heart

                            Linda Goodman

1

LABORS OF LOVE
AND
THE MONEY MYSTIQUE

astrological career guide . . . and the
achievement of simultaneous financial
security and financial freedom

he wanted to be a composer, a writer, a doctor . . . maybe an
artist
to heal, he said, people's bodies, minds and spirits
it didn't matter which, just one of the three
and the healing of the other two
                    would surely follow, he believed

but he had become an engineer, and secretly despised it
the Highways of the State employed him
                    as the Pharaohs employed the slaves in Egypt
to lift and measure stones to build their silent tombs

dusty roads . . . are so unlike sterile medical laboratories
nor do ditches much resemble a vaulted concert hall
or the polished ceilings of an art museum

              he did manage to save enough cash
                    to buy a typewriter
              one-two-three dreams, you're out !
                    and who is the Umpire — Fate ?

                    ★ ★ ★ ★ ★ ★

OW MANY engineers dream of being physicians, and
how many doctors dream of being engineers ? How
many scientists long to be musicians, and how many
musicians long to be scientists ? There are millions
upon millions of men and women who are discon-
tented, depressed, and unhappy square pegs in round holes (or round
pegs in square holes), whose talents, abilities, and "daydreams" (in
reality, the wise urgings of the Higher Self) are sadly mismatched with
the way they earn their daily bread. It's not only a deplorable waste of
manpower and womanpower, it's a tragic waste of human happiness
and joy, which are the birthright of every individual on Earth.

    And so, before pondering and perusing the star-sign codes of
ancient wisdoms, you'll find it both sensible and practical to first fol-

low the metaphysical paths to contentment and happiness in your work, since it involves more than a third of your time — to learn how to improve your financial affairs, since a certain amount of financial security is necessary to free the mind to fly into the higher realms — and to consider your health, because, of course, your physical well-being takes priority over everything.

This is why I've decided to first present this chapter about *Labors of Love the Money Mystique* and then the *Apple a Day* chapter, your astrological and numerological health guide. Without these three basic needs of the body and the mind, the spirit is not in the mood to contemplate the deeper waters of esoteric mysteries. When you truly love your work, when you can pay the rent or mortgage on time and feel physically fantastic, then you can start skipping up the mountain to Gurism. Note to Webster: I just invented that word.

When I first moved to Cripple Creek, Colorado, where I'd been directed by the turbaned Guru, in the manner I related in the Preface, I felt like a spiritual pilgrim who had located Tibet or Shangri-la. Somehow, I sensed that many secrets and mysteries were hidden among the bristlecone pines dotting the hillsides — and that "Guru" had been right. I learned much during my retreat to the mountains (which was later to become my permanent residence) — and wrote it all down in the diary that was to become this book.

My first morning there I awoke happily sniffing the cool, clear, pure mountain air, and immediately decided to take a walk through town, consisting of five blocks of a paved street called Bennett Avenue. All the other streets in this little Christmas-card town are dirt roads, but with their own kind of magic. Every time it rains there, which is nearly every day (meaning there's a rainbow every day over my funny little crooked, slipping-off-the-time-track 1890 house) . . . people walk around, both tourists and the 600 or so permanent residents, staring at the ground in this very strange way. They're looking for spots of sky blue — in the dirt, not above. At the turn of century, when this area was the thriving gold camp of the West (Pikes Peak or bust !) folks also mined turquoise. As the turquoise was carried in carts, by burrows, much of it fell off and became imbedded in the dirt — so that today, when the rains wash the dirt roads, pieces of turquoise appear suddenly, here and there, like a sudden spring surprise. All Indian tribes claim that turquoise carries powerful good luck vibrations.

During my walk in a misty rain that early morning, searching for a lucky chunk of blue stone, I bumped into the least likely Cripple Creeker to become my first acquaintance in what was to be my new adopted hometown: the Chief of the C.C. Police Department. His name was — and is — Dale Simpson. He's a Pisces, with a soft voice, a gentle smile, a typical Neptunian love of talking — and a talent for also being a very good listener.

We introduced ourselves, then stopped at the Palace Hotel dining room with its player piano tinkling away, for a chat and a cup of coffee. (Imagine the Chief of Police in New York taking time out for coffee and flapjacks to the tune of "Let Me Call You Sweetheart" !)

As soon as I discovered that he was a Pisces, I shook my head doubtfully. "A round peg in a square hole, or vice versa." I told him chidingly. "I don't mean to be rude, or to offend you, but I can't imagine why a Piscean like yourself would choose a job or a career as a police chief."

Like most people ruled by the planet Neptune, he wasn't in the least offended by my candid remark. He was curious.

"I don't know much about astrology," he admitted with a friendly grin, "except that my sign is Pisces. Why are you so surprised at my occupation ?"

"Well, because it's the last job that any astrologer, which I am, would ever counsel a Pisces to pursue. You see, I happen to believe that people should 'labor with love,' that the employment or career should harmonize with each person's character, personality, and inner goals — or dreams — since that's the only way to be truly happy. And . . . " — I smiled at him — "I can't see a Neptune-ruled Fish being happy performing the duties of a police chief — although there are other Sun Sign people who would find such an occupation challenging and stimulating."

"That's interesting, and I'd like to tell you why it is. But first, will you explain how you know all that ?"

"As I said, I'm an astrologer, and I've made a study of it. I'm continually amazed that people don't take it more seriously, when it's such a reliable guide to career success — and to every other area of life. There would be lots more contented and successful people if, for example, those who were born to be associated with the theatre as actors, directors, producers, and so forth, didn't settle for, say, the medical profession — or those who were born to be lawyers weren't, instead, pursuing a profession in landscaping . . . and so on. They become more frustrated with their lives every year, and it never occurs to them why they are unfulfilled. They don't realize that they're round pegs in square holes, or vice versa. Being completely happy with and challenged by your work is one of the surest ways to make your dreams come true. Now, you promised to tell me why you thought what I said was interesting."

"Maybe one of the reasons so many pegs and holes don't match," Chief Simpson mused with natural Neptunian insight, "is because the parents don't try to help their children find out what they really want to become in life, but instead, intimidate them into preparing for a profession Mother and Father think is right, and the child has no choice until it's too late."

I wondered if this had been the case with Dale Simpson and his own parents. But if so, it had probably started long before the job as Police Chief, and I didn't feel it would be polite to ask.

"I'm sure not going to make that mistake with my children," he continued, staring out through the screen door at the entrance to the dining room as if he were lost in thought. "They're on their own when it comes to their future."

"That's a very Piscean attitude," I told him, "a hands-off policy. With children, friends, relatives. Like Aquarius, Pisces believes in the motto of live and let live. It's a rare Fish who tries to interfere in anyone else's life, except to now and then make a suggestion — and even then usually only when asked. But . . . why did you say it was all interesting ?" I persisted.

"Because," he answered slowly, and more than a little sadly, "you're absolutely right about what you said. I can't say that this job fulfills me in any way. Mostly, it frustrates me and drains me of energy."

"That's because crime and punishment, or disciplinary action of any kind, are not pursuits natural to your disposition. You're too sympathetic to apprehend 'bad guys.' An association with guns and violence — shooting and arrests — all that goes against your very essence. It's a wonder you haven't become ill from it. However, you'd make a good Sherlock Holmes–type detective, without the violence and arrests. You're naturally equipped to solve mysteries. As a Pisces, your personal mission is to help other people solve their emotional and psychological problems — sometimes simply by being an understanding, compassionate listener. You need to be involved in something that allows your imagination full scope, in an artistic or any other kind of career — where you can dream yourself into discovering startling answers to things. Albert Einstein was a Piscean, and he certainly brought imagination to mathematics, with his abstract math and theories of Relativity."

"You're right about the possibility of becoming ill too," he nodded. "I've already had one mild heart attack, and I've had a half-dozen other minor health complaints the past few years I never had before. I've always had a strong constitution . . . until recently. I've been thinking about retiring and finding something else to do. What you've said may help me make the decision. By the way, everything you just mentioned about Pisces people . . . the sympathetic understanding . . . and helping people in all those ways . . . sure fits a Pisces woman I know here in town. Her name is Ruth Cook, and she teaches grade school. Everybody around here says she's the best teacher in the County." He chuckled. "Maybe in the whole State. And like you say, she loves every minute of her work. She's doing what comes naturally for her, no doubt about that. And the kids in her classes really learn. She makes them *want* to. They're all crazy about her, because they know she cares."

"What is your wife's Sun Sign ?" I asked.

"Junie is a Scorpio. She works at the Post Office, and she enjoys it there. I think she must be a round peg in a round hole." He laughed. "Is that a good job for Scorpio ?"

"Great. Scorpio is a Fixed Sign, and Fixed Signs are born Organizers. They're good at what's called 'watching the store,' experts at pulling the strings together to make everything go smoothly. I'm glad to hear your Scorpio wife handles the mail. Makes me feel a lot more secure about today's Pony Express."

"The Postmaster, Bud Sanders — he's a Scorpio too."

"Terrific. I've been losing so much confidence in the postal system these days, I've almost felt like sending birthday cards Federal Express. With *two* Scorpios in charge here, I can stop worrying. Senator Muskie was quoted in *The New York Times* last month as saying that the Government ought to turn over the problem of inflation to the United States Postal Service. He said "they might not be able to solve it, but they could sure slow it down." We both laughed.

"Junie replaced another friend of ours, LaVerne King, who was with the Post Office for years before she retired. LaVerne is a Virgo."

"Fantastic ! Virgos have an innate ability to bring order out of chaos. I'll bet all the zip codes were correct when she was there. I'd almost think somebody around here uses astrology for hiring your postal people."

Before Chief Simpson climbed back into his police car after his coffee break with me, he said he'd like to know more about astrology and professions, if I had time to tell him someday, so I promised to type it out for him.

Here's an expanded version of the astrological career guide I prepared for Chief Simpson, including all twelve of the Sun Signs.

But first, consider the truest words ever expressed on the subject of working, written by the poet from Lebanon, Kahlil Gibran, who warned that work must be performed with genuine love, or it's a waste of time and energy; that if you cannot work with love, it's better that you do nothing until you do find such work, meanwhile accepting charity from those who do labor with love. For, as Gibran expressed so beautifully, *"bread baked without love is a bitter bread, that feeds but half man's hunger."*

There are thousands of parallels to that wisdom. If you're a singer who hates your audiences, your performance feeds but half their hunger for music. If you're a writer who would secretly prefer to be an attorney or a doctor, your written words will feed but half the hunger of your readers, and your books won't sell. If you're a teacher who would rather be an actress, your instruction will satisfy but half the thirst for knowledge in your students. And so on. The examples are endless.

The personal unhappiness and failure to achieve resulting from round pegs in square holes (and the opposite) is not a new discovery by any means. But sometimes a truth is repeated so often it loses its meaning, the edge of its brilliance becomes dull, and it needs the razor sharpening of a new image, or a rediscovery.

Remember that you were born to excel in some kind of occupation, profession, or career. There is something you can do better than anyone else in the world, by bringing to it your personal touch of magic, based upon the individual character, personality, inner motives, and dreams of your Sun Sign — (also based on certain other aspects in your rectified horoscope, but the Sun Sign is an excellent place to begin).

The Sun "leaves" one sign and "enters" the next at a different time on each cusp day, depending on the year. Therefore, if you were born on a cusp day (i.e.: April 20th or May 21st or August 23rd, etc.), you must know the hour and minute of your first breath on that cusp day to know which is your Sun Sign. Any astrologer can give you this information quickly.

When you have determined your Sun Sign, use the following career guide to begin the path toward your personal Labor of Love.

CARDINAL SIGNS are: Aries   Cancer   Libra   Capricorn

If your Sun Sign is Cardinal, you were born to earn your daily bread as a LEADER of thought and action. You'll never be truly content in a subordinate position, carrying out the concepts of others, unless you're using it merely as a stepladder to the top. To labor with love, you must either be the Big Boss — or be *your own* boss. You must either be at the head of things, the one in charge — or be self-employed as the captain of your own ship, so to speak. Working in an occupation that prevents you from conceiving and exploiting your own ideas could result in physical fatigue, mental tension, and emotional depression, which can eventually lead to chronic illness.

All four Cardinal signs were born to lead or to be self-employed. However, the *kind* of work most harmonious with the spirit is *individual* with each of the four Cardinal Sun Signs, depending on the Element of the sign, i.e.: whether you're a Cardinal FIRE sign Leader (Aries) — a Cardinal WATER sign Leader (Cancer) — a Cardinal AIR sign Leader (Libra) — or a Cardinal EARTH sign Leader (Capricorn).

Aries: You'll be successful in a profession that harmonizes with your Cardinal FIRE nature. Fire translates into anything exciting and capa-

THE KARMIC WHEEL OF LIFE

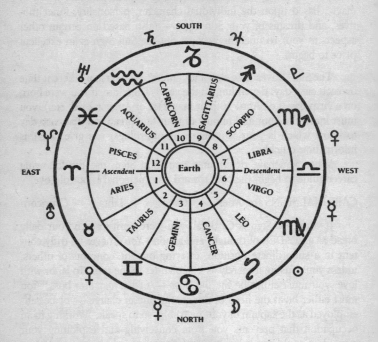

THE SYMBOLS

Aries ♈	Libra ♎	Mars ♂	Pluto ♇
Taurus ♉	Scorpio ♏	Venus ♀	Jupiter ♃
Gemini ♊	Sagittarius ♐	Mercury ☿	Saturn ♄
Cancer ♋	Capricorn ♑	Moon ☽	Uranus ♅
Leo ♌	Aquarius ♒	Sun ☉	Neptune ♆
Virgo ♍	Pisces ♓		

SUN SIGN BIRTH PERIODS

ARIES:	Part of March 20th into April 20th
TAURUS:	Part of April 20th into May 21st
GEMINI:	Part of May 21st into June 21st
CANCER:	Part of June 21st into July 22nd
LEO:	Part of July 22nd into August 23rd
VIRGO:	Part of August 23rd into September 23rd
LIBRA:	Part of September 23rd into October 23rd
SCORPIO:	Part of October 23rd into November 22nd
SAGITTARIUS:	Part of November 22nd into December 21st
CAPRICORN:	Part of December 21st into January 20th
AQUARIUS:	Part of January 20th into February 19th
PISCES:	Part of February 19th into March 20th

ble of arousing instant enthusiasm in yourself and others. You need to "lead the parade on a white horse," trailing red ribbons and pink balloons — and to have the opportunity to display your talent for penetrating straight to the heart of any issue. You belong in any endeavor that allows you to attract attention and be recognized, preferably where there's someone to lovingly protect you from your often misplaced trust, naïveté, generosity, and rashness — but not fence you in, because you cease to function when you're not totally free to give of yourself and impulsively pioneer all kinds of new beginnings. You'll cheerfully and successfully initiate just about anything. You're a great, even a flawless "opener." But leave the closing of deals and the tying up of loose ends to others, *please*. Thank you.

Cancer: You'll be content and inspired in a profession that harmonizes with your Cardinal WATER nature. Water translates into anything absorbing, deep, constantly moving, with an aura of mystery to stir the imagination. In your occupation or career, whether in education or one of the Arts, you need considerable privacy while you work — to be able to hide within your crab shell while you move first sideways, then backward, until you're good and ready to lunge forward, straight ahead. Your profession must leave lots of room for your vivid imagination to expand and provide plenty of time for travel, with frequent changes of scenery, but you'll always need a home base. You'll remain deliciously contented when your occupation is one requiring you to take customers or clients to breakfast, lunch, or dinner *very* frequently. Working in any field associated with *food* or *money* in any way whatsoever is your idea of "heaven." You're also superbly suited to "mothering," "fathering," or taking care of others. Cancer cares. You belong in an endeavor where you can keep most of your dreams and plans secret until you sense it's time to implement them — one that will bring you a certain amount of public attention (though you'll deny this !) — and which allows you to live near your mother.

Libra: You'll labor with love in a profession that harmonizes with your Cardinal AIR nature. Air translates into anything that lets you keep moving mentally and involves the intellect. You're an excellent arbitrator and judge of crime and punishment (but not violence). You need some sort of outlet for your innate sense of fairness — to be able to balance the pros and cons of everything and everyone around you. You'll be more fulfilled and successful when you work in partnership with a compatible and harmonious person (but not another Cardinal Sign, please — unless you mutually decide at the outset which one is to be the leader. If it's another Libra, the two of you will *never* decide !). You'll be a blessing in any career that allows you to settle disputes among others, pour oil over the troubled waters, and hold periodic discussions and debates, whether you manufacture, sell, or demonstrate cosmetics (Libra is the sign of beauty !) — or shovel manure on the farm.

Capricorn: You'll labor with love in a profession that harmonizes with your Cardinal EARTH nature. Earth translates into anything that's solid, stable, and practical, with a firm foundation and a strong growth potential. You're happier leading behind the scenes, in most cases, but there's always the exception that proves the rule. You were born for an occupation or a career where you can guide and counsel others (if you're not self-employed) — where you can use your vast storehouse of past experience to enhance your unsuspected perception of the future. Job security (or career or professional security — same thing) is what will always magnetize you toward any occupation. No pie-in-the-sky gambles for you. You're happy only when you're involved in a gold-embossed sure thing, with the potential of taking you up to the very top of the career mountain, where you've been headed since you were twelve years old. There's never been any doubt about it.

FIXED SIGNS are: Taurus   Leo   Scorpio   Aquarius

If your Sun Sign is Fixed, you were born to earn your daily bread as an ORGANIZER of thought and action. You'll never be happy or succeed in reaching your true goals when the organizational structure is left to others. To work with love, to achieve fulfillment in your career or profession, and all that goes with it, you must be the one who's unquestionably responsible for the success of any company or venture you're part of, whether it's your own or someone else's — and surprisingly often, you'll be equally fortunate when it's someone else's rather than your own. You're completely contented only when you're type-cast, so to speak, in the role you play so well: that of "keeper" to others in the astrological zoo who need one, and goodness knows there are lots of *those* ! You must be the one who "makes it all happen," who properly delegates authority and pulls all the loose ends together everyone else leaves flapping in the wind, causing things to run smoothly and efficiently. Let the Cardinal Signs lead the parade, let the Mutable Signs communicate back and forth, you need to feel — indeed, to *be* — the rock everyone leans on, the one who holds the center together. Becoming permanently involved with any occupation that gives you no responsibility for what goes on around you could result in physical fatigue, mental tension, and emotional depression, which can lead to chronic illness.

All four Fixed Signs were born to organize and be responsible for the outcome of whatever they're involved with. However, the *kind* of work most harmonious with the spirit is *individual* with each of the four Fixed Signs, depending upon the Element of the sign, i.e.: whether you're a Fixed EARTH Sign organizer (Taurus) — a Fixed FIRE Sign organizer (Leo) — a Fixed WATER Sign organizer (Scorpio) — or a Fixed AIR Sign organizer (Aquarius).

Taurus: You'll labor with love in a profession that harmonizes with your Fixed EARTH nature. Earth translates into anything solid, stable, and practical, with a firm foundation and a powerful potential for growth. You need to gather all the facts, then sit on them quietly (and often stubbornly !) until you believe it's time to act on them, always after careful consideration. You'll labor with love in any field that allows you to checkmate the impulsive behavior of others, while building a sound future for yourself. Structuring huge empires and large corporate operations for yourself — or others — is what magnetizes you and makes it possible for you to sit behind a desk and burn the midnight oil. You will be deeply depressed unless you're involved in a career or a profession that gets bigger and better every year, whether you're into banking, farming, real estate — or the production of teddy bears.

Leo: You'll labor with love in a profession that harmonizes with your Fixed FIRE nature. Fire translates into anything exciting, original, daring, and capable of constantly inspiring you. Working in a situation that doesn't permit you to take charge and organize everything in sight will bring on your Lion's roar of angry frustration. You need to express yourself openly, creatively, and artistically in some way — and you must be respected and appreciated, or you won't be worth a nickel — to yourself or anyone else. You know best how matters should be handled, and you must never become involved in a position where you're expected to follow orders based on how others believe things should be done. You're right nine times out of ten, you really are — and to be curbed in your efforts to implement your always original, always expansive concepts will make you a most unhappy person indeed. Running the show is an absolute necessity for you, and when you finally settle into an occupation or a career where your superior talents are recognized and respected, the resulting self-esteem will guarantee huge success. Any occupation that permits you to bring about dramatic results is the answer to your huge need to be free — just to be yourself — and prove what you can do to people who don't suspect how wise you truly are.

Scorpio: You'll labor with love in a profession that harmonizes with your Fixed WATER nature. Water translates into anything absorbing, deep, silently progressing, with an aura of mystery capable of stirring the floods of imagination. In whatever career you choose, you need to be permitted to penetrate its heights and its depths, to experience intensely — and to gather knowledge about all facets of your occupation or profession, so that you can retain it for future use. You have an inner conviction (whether you realize it consciously yet or not) that "knowledge is power" — and power leads to success. When your superb ability to "watch the store" is exercised, you *really* watch the store ! Nothing escapes your Eagle eye. What you don't actually see, you *sense*, with your highly developed insight and intuition. You belong in any field that will allow you to investigate its assets and its liabilities, and permits you to work alone as much as possible, so you can put into practice your inflexible standards of excellence. You'll apply your keen investigative talents to anything you touch, because you can't rest until the mystery, the problem, or the troubled situation is cleared up or solved. You prefer to be left to your own devices, and you strongly resent your methods being questioned, even by superiors, whether you're in acting, politics, or plumbing.

You're not the type to burn bridges behind you prematurely, because your strong will and churning emotions are usually checkmated by your realization of the value of caution and practicality. (I said *usually* !) Consequently, you may not express your displeasure for a long time. You'll keep your feelings within, and appear to go along. But when you sense that the time is right, and you've reached a position of self-sufficiency, you'll make it quite clear that it's to be done your way — or you'll leave. Case closed. By the way, if Piscean Police Chief Dale Simpson had been born under either Capricorn or Scorpio, he wouldn't have been a round peg in a square hole. Detective and police work aren't the only harmonious pursuits for these latter two Sun Signs, of course, but they are certainly among them. A Capricorn police chief, however, probably wouldn't be satisfied until he rose to Police Commissioner — and a Scorpio police chief would be strongly inclined to perhaps use the job as a springboard into politics. But neither of these two Sun Signs would be troubled by exposure to the necessary scenes of violence connected with such professions as Pisces would be. Also, Capricorn and Scorpio would find it easier to administer appropriate punishment to criminals, in fact, to punish the rest of us, too, when we goof !

Aquarius: You'll labor with love in a profession that harmonizes with your Fixed AIR nature. Air translates into anything which is — in your case — unpredictable, unorthodox, unexpected, changing — and involves the intellect. You need to be permitted to concentrate while standing on your head, should the mood strike you, so you can come up with those astounding lightning flashes of insight and genius. You'll never be either happy or successful in an occupation that requires you to conform to a strict schedule. Yes, you're a peachy-dandy organizer, but you have to do it *your way.* Your curiosity will cause you to invent new methods of doing just about anything, and you'll be impatient with work done the same old way as always. You'll add your own pretzel twist to the way things are done. Since your gregarious nature attracts friends easily, and you like people (if you're a typical Water Bearer), you'll likely become pals with your co-workers and your boss. You'll find it hard to see the difference between them, with your broad and normally tolerant brotherhood and sisterhood charisma. You'll be more contented in a job or career that allows you to answer mainly to yourself, since your flashing streak of originality needs plenty of space and freedom to turn old methods into innovative new ones. As a Fixed Sign, you won't "suffer fools gladly," and when you're pushed to follow orders you believe are outdated and inefficient, you can become more than a little stubborn, which is why you should seek freedom of expression in your line of work above financial compensation, in the beginning at least. You belong in any position or career that allows you to sort out the jigsaw pieces of problems, then abracadabra them into brilliant solutions — and permits you to play marbles with jelly beans on your lunch break.

MUTABLE SIGNS are: Gemini   Virgo   Sagittarius   Pisces

If your Sun Sign is Mutable, you were born to earn your daily bread by being a COMMUNICATOR of thought and action. You'll never be happy when you're forced to be responsible for the chaos around you, when you're expected to sit behind a desk, or remain in any one place and take charge. You'd be miserable "leading the parade" like the Cardinal Signs or "watching the store" like the Fixed Signs. You need to constantly circulate, travel, move around, and communicate ideas (and ideals) between the Cardinal Leaders and the Fixed Organizers. You'd be equally happy being self-employed, assuming that your self-employment allowed you to communicate to the public some new and different viewpoint of standard ideas, preferably either abstract or inspiring. To work with love you must have complete freedom, a variety of activity, periodic change, lots of coffee breaks, long lunch hours, and interesting assignments. Working at a job that ties you down in any way, forces you to take complete charge and be responsible for the actions of others could result in physical fatigue, mental stress, and emotional depression, which could lead to chronic illness.

All four Mutable signs were born to communicate. However, the *kind* of work most harmonious with the spirit is *individual* with each of the four Mutable Sun Signs, depending on the Element of the sign, i.e.: whether you're a Mutable AIR sign Communicator (Gemini) — a Mutable EARTH sign Communicator (Virgo) — a Mutable FIRE sign Communicator (Sagittarius) — or a Mutable WATER sign Communicator (Pisces).

Gemini: You'll labor with love in a profession that harmonizes with your Mutable AIR nature. Air translates into anything that's unpredictable, keeps you floating around, and challenges your sharp intellect. Although you're so versatile, you could be successful in just about any sphere of endeavor imaginable; you'd really have it made if you published a new dictionary or spent your time making up new crossword puzzles. Choosing professional bridge or chess as a career would bring you certain fulfillment, but never mind, you'll play mental chess with your co-workers in any occupation lucky enough to pin you down long enough to say you work there ! You need a career that will allow you to bring to it your great capacity for variety — one that will permit you and your Twin (your own alter ego) to sweep out the dusty corners both symbolically and literally and open up the windows to let in the fresh air of new thoughts and ideas. You belong where you can use your considerable charm and vivid imagination — where your quick intelligence and verbal glibness is given free rein. *Never* allow yourself to get stuck in a position where you're expected to punch a time clock, or you'll be miserable. I know a Gemini man who counsels students, nine to five, at a college. The counseling part is fine, but he's most unhappy with the lack of *change* in his job. Yet, he's determined to remain a few more years until he gets his retirement benefits. (It's his Cancer Ascendent and Cancer Moon Sign.) As unhappy as he is, he won't do anything to lose the security of retirement. He should leave his ever-present Twin sitting behind the desk, and let the other Twin start looking around for something new and exciting to do with his life.

Virgo: You'll labor with love in a profession that harmonizes with your Mutable EARTH nature. Earth translates into anything practical, stable, well-planned, and capable of paying you what you're worth. (You'll insist on the last.) But that needn't be synonymous with stuffy or boring. You need a chance to purify the disorder around you, with your clear thinking and exquisite sense of discrimination. You belong in any endeavor that can benefit from your cool head and mild manner, for you very much *need* to be *needed* — but which also gives you gobs of time to be alone, far from the noisy zoos of chattering people. Your ability to see mistakes, your talent for spotting the flaws everyone else misses make you indispensable wherever you settle down to do your thing. If you work for yourself, say as a doctor or a lawyer, you'll make fewer errors in judgment than others in these professions — and in the latter case, you'll be a genius at discovering the faux pas of the opposing attorney's briefs. In the former, no one would need a "second medical opinion" after your diagnosis, since you'll have considered every detail of every symptom and every test several times before giving a verdict. You'll never find personal fulfillment or success being a leader. You're ideally equipped to let others lead while you help them keep a tight ship. You need a career where your ability to find error is an indisputable asset, not a liability, as when Virgo President Lyndon Johnson (who was a square peg in a round hole) cheerfully announced that he was helping to solve the energy problem by turning out all the electric lights in the White House himself each night. Presidents should be Cardinal or Fixed, never Mutable. John Kennedy was one of those "exceptions that prove the rule." Still, he led as a Mutable *Communicator,* undeniably.

Sagittarius: You'll labor with love in a profession that harmonizes with your Mutable FIRE nature. Fire translates into anything exciting, original, slightly dangerous, or challenging in either a physical or a mental sense. You need an occupation where you can express yourself enthusiastically, where your idealism is appreciated. You simply cannot stay in one place. You need a change of scenery at the very minimum of once a year, and you may even have thought of joining a circus as a way to escape humdrum monotony. There's a saying among astrologers that Sagittarian Archers retire before they get their first job, an exaggeration meant to convey your restlessness and need for change. Some Archers leave home as early as twelve or fourteen to chase "the impossible dream." Let's hope you never realize quite all your impossible dreams, because life would then begin to lack luster for you. You'll bring a touch of magic (and an Emmet Kelly, clownlike humor) to any profession with a degree of risk to it, from the stock market to mountain climbing. You belong in a field that dares you to take chances, to gamble on tomorrow's sure win — where you can contribute your triple whammy of winging optimism, inspiration, and idealism, including, but not limited to, sports, religion (which has always intrigued you) or space travel — wherever you can zing those arrows of truth. The atmosphere of the place where you hang your Dorfman hat for temporary periods between vacations must be cheerful and outgoing, open and completely candid, packed with congenial people. You can't stand "sneaks," but if you should get yourself fired for calling your boss one, don't worry, you'll get a new job right away. Who wouldn't want a merry, lovable Centaur-racehorse around? You're honest to a fault, and now I hear you complaining that honesty is not a fault. It depends on how brutally truthful you are. People's feelings are sensitive, you know. An employer (or even a co-worker) just doesn't like being told, "Gee! You're a really good-looking guy in spite of that big bump in the middle of your nose. And I don't think people should call you camel-nose." Take it easy, okay?

Pisces: You'll labor with love in a profession that harmonizes with your Mutable WATER nature. Water translates into anything that definitely moves around, as water must do, is many layered or multi-leveled, somewhat mysterious — and flexible. You'd be a great trouble shooter for *The New York Times* or a department store — an equally terrific Priest in the Confessional, psychiatrist, psychologist, or marriage counselor.

People are going to be dumping their problems on you anyway, so you might as well get paid for listening to them, and that's not a materialistic view, just sensible — because the people who come to you will never fail to be greatly benefited, and your fee will normally not be more than they can afford, so it's money well spent. With your nature, however, you'd probably forget or neglect to send a bill for your services, so you'd need a good accountant or business manager. All things considered, you're probably better off to just give your listening ear free of charge, so it doesn't trouble your conscience, and earn your bread in some field that urgently needs your sensitive perception and uncanny ability to solve mysteries. Even a field like science. Einstein was a Piscean, you know. He brought the Neptune vision and far-out concepts to mathematics, resulting in the creation of a whole new and thrilling dimension of time and space. Pisceans enjoy swimming in artistic and creative waters, where they are undeniably contentedly at home, yet more Fish should dive into the ocean of science, where the Neptunian sixth sense, open Third Eye, and innate intuition are qualities desperately needed to bring about a long-awaited Utopian marriage between science and mysticism. If these reluctant mates don't marry soon, so that technology and esoteric wisdom become One, it may be too late for the wedding — and there won't be any place to go on the honeymoon, if you comprehend what I mean, which, if you're a psychic Piscean, you will.

You have little desire to lead any parade, unless you're one of those rare, more aggressive "shark-type" Fish, and you're happiest when you're helping others find the way to self-discovery. Your gentle manner and subtle humor are an asset to any kind of business. You'll find more opportunities to succeed when you choose a profession where you can develop your uncanny ability to dream and make your dreams come true. Any occupation that allows you to demonstrate your rare capacity for listening sympathetically and nurtures your imagination will bring you self-fulfillment. Both children and adults sense immediately that you truly care about them, and your very presence has a healing effect, whether you labor with love in a hospital or in a greenhouse. Plants know you love them too !

There's no use making a list of specific professions, careers, and occupations for each Sun Sign, because that doesn't matter in itself. It can be any kind of career or employment you can think of, as long as the *kind* of work done *within* that profession is harmonious with one's nature. It doesn't make any difference whether a Cardinal sign (Aries, Cancer, Libra, Capricorn) is involved in fire fighting or an advertising agency, as long as he or she is Fire *Chief* or the President of the advertising firm (or at least, at the head of its major accounts). It doesn't matter whether a Fixed Sign (Taurus, Leo, Scorpio, Aquarius) is associated with a florist or a dairy, as long as he or she is responsible for organizing the productivity involved, and is in charge of the activity. It makes no difference whether a Mutable Sign (Gemini, Virgo, Sagittarius, Pisces) has chosen the profession of writing, the law, or Big Government, as long as he or she can spend the working hours *communicating* with everyone, and not leading or being responsible for what's happening. The same Virgo, for example, who would make a superb writer, needing very little editing, should never try to run a publishing house. The Virgo who would make a meticulous and successful lawyer would be miserable as head of the Bar Association. Virgo President Lyndon Johnson, for example, received as much high praise for his well-performed job as Senate Majority Leader (communicating with other Senators and government officials) as he received criticism for his attempt to lead the country. Follow the natural path of your Sun Sign. If you're a Leo, it's okay to be a farmer, but make sure it's your own farm, and a very *large* one !

★ ★ ★ ★ ★ ★

Like everyone else, you have experienced from time to time in your life, even when you were in grade school or high school, flashing images in your mind of vivid scenes. Scenes of yourself as a Senator, an actor or actress, a scientist, a Chef in a French restaurant, a newspaper columnist, an attorney, a Judge, a teacher or professor, a telephone operator, a secretary, a designer, an architect, a baker or a candlestick maker. You have called these flashing images "daydreams" or "wishes." Wishes are the dreams you dream when you're awake.

Your so-called "daydreams" are urgings from your own Supraconscious, not merely "wishes" to be briefly enjoyed, then wistfully forgotten. These images originate from the wise Angel of your Higher Self, who repeatedly urges you, by seeding into your mind a picture of what you were born to do, to take your destined place in the jigsaw puzzle of Life.

Some of you who are reading this are saying to yourselves, "But I'm too *young* to pursue such lofty ambitions" — or "I'm too *old* for anything like that to happen to me." Nonsense. As you'll learn in the chapter on Physical Immortality in this book, chronological age is a complete illusion, only made to *appear* real by the false programming of the mass collective subconscious for centuries. *What* you do has absolutely no relationship to *when* you do it.

George Bernard Shaw was 94 when one of his plays was produced. Mozart was seven years old when his first composition was published. When he was 20, Mickey Mantle hit 23 home runs in his first full year in the major leagues. Golda Meir was 71 when she became Prime Minister of Israel — and she was a *woman* yet ! William Pitt II was only 24 when he became Prime Minister of Great Britain. Ted Williams, at 42, slammed a home run in his last official time at bat. Benjamin Franklin became a newspaper columnist at the age of 16 — and a framer of the United States Constitution when he was 81. A woman I know named Rachel planned to be a concert pianist, changed her goal suddenly because she loved to cook, and baked brownies for friends. Her business now grosses seven million dollars a year. She didn't think she was too young or too old. She simply followed her own daydreams with persistence.

You say you *have* tried to pursue your daydream images but they must have been a false lead to your destiny because you have failed to materialize them over and over again ? You call that the reason you haven't yet manifested your personal miracle ? It's not the reason, it's just an excuse.

Once upon a time there was a young man who was born to poverty-stricken parents. He wasn't able to go to school, so he taught himself. He dreamed of being a lawyer, but no one would hire him.

When he completed military service, he decided to use his self-administered study of the law to enter politics, so he ran for a seat in the Senate. He was defeated by a large majority.

So he temporarily retired from the law and politics and became a storekeeper. His store went bankrupt, and he spent the next seventeen years of his life paying off his debts, picking up whatever odd jobs he could. But his daydreams continued to urge him on.

He fell in love, married, struggled to support his family, and then again entered politics — as a candidate for Congress. He was elected by a very narrow margin, but when he ran for re-election, he was humiliatingly defeated.

Next, he tried to get a position with the United States Land Office, but they refused to hire him. It seemed that everywhere he went, he was ridiculed because of his poor background, his lack of education and social graces. He held up his head, ignored his hurt pride, and decided to run for the United States Senate. Both his friends and enemies, even his family, laughed at him behind his back. Once again, he was defeated.

Eventually, he was nominated for Vice-President at the political convention of a major party. On the final ballot, he lost again — to a political unknown. Running again for the Senate, he waged a campaign which captured the imagination of a nation, but which resulted in only another defeat.

Still, he never stopped following his "daydreams." He didn't dwell on his failures. He continued to intensely and fiercely pursue the ideals and principles in which he believed. And finally, at the age of fifty, wounded by heartache and scarred by repeated defeats, but still clinging fast to his destined life path, Abraham Lincoln became President of these United States.

More recently, in the late 1970s and early 1980s, a student at Harvard named William Gates made a courageous decision to drop out of college and pursue his personal vision. His dream was to give computer microchips more power, a chip telling them what to do and how to do it. After relinquishing the certain future his Harvard degree would have guaranteed, he got together with a couple of bright genius-type young men and formed a company called Microsoft. IBM leased his innovation for their own computers, and in 1986, about three years after he took his big gamble, his company was generating several million dollars annually, and his own shares were worth 540 million dollars. He followed his dream. He believed in his vision. His daydreams were real to him. William Gates heeded the flashing messages from his Higher Self, the true prophecy of his future. Have you listened to yours ?

Don't discard your daydreams as impotent wishful thinking. *Listen* to them with your inner ear. *See* them with your Third Eye of wisdom. "Let those who have ears, hear; let those who have eyes, see." Follow your "daydreams" energetically, intensely, fiercely — courageously, even when it means *temporarily* sacrificing financial security. Your "daydreams" are your blueprint for success and happiness. Believe in them. Believe in yourself. Then follow "the second star from the right . . . and straight on till morning !"

★ ★ ★ ★ ★ ★

There's a mystique to money most people never realize. It's more than just paper and coin. As a medium of exchange among people all over the world, it possesses an unguessed power of its own, and when the secret of that power is recognized and put into use, money will multiply in several amazing ways. Learning the secret of money is one thing. Using your knowledge of its secret is another — and often difficult to grasp for many reasons we're now going to analyze, for the purpose of erasing them — which is the only way you'll ever achieve true financial security and financial freedom simultaneously. Here's a verse expressing the secret of money poetically. Then we'll discover the practical side of it.

★ ★ ★ ★ ★ ★

. . . and tonight I'm remembering

those bubbly moments of bittersweet
when a tapped-out stranger stops us on the street
to ask you for a dime or a quarter
a fellow Earthling, who's lost his or her way for a while

you always smile, then give the lost one five dollars
or ten . . . or twenty
even when you're broke yourself
and it's your very last five . . . or ten . . . or twenty

then, when the Taker looks shocked, as they always do
you call back, over your shoulder

"Listen, if you want any more
just give half of that away
don't save it for a rainy day !
rain rhymes with pain
. . . give rhymes with live !"

★ ★ ★ ★ ★ ★

Using the astrological career guide to lead you to your own "labor of love" is helpful knowledge, but there's no avoiding the fact that it's all linked to success, which to most people means money or financial security — an association difficult to escape in our present society. One can't be much help to one's self or to others in this day and age by walking barefoot down dirt roads, or preaching and teaching along the seashore. Even a sleeping bag and a bowl of soup for the homeless requires money. In addition to your personal necessities and helping the homeless, there are also those organizations dedicated to saving the planet on which we all live from annihilation. Achieving that miracle likewise requires money.

There's little chance for the survival of either individuals or the planet unless and until we all get it together swiftly enough to halt the approaching manmade and natural cataclysms. As it once was in Atlantis, it is again history's eleventh hour for a multitude of reasons, from acid rain to the insanity of the nuclear arms race. The possible Götterdämmerung is now being measured by the year instead of by the century. Therefore, because Time itself has become the Great Dictator, we need the green energy of money to make a difference in *time* . . . *this* time. There's enough of it to go around, if it were handled differently, and not hoarded. There is nothing negative in having money, only in how it's spent or used by those who possess it. Greenpeace, for example, needs the green energy of money to continue its efforts to save the whales, dolphins, and seals from cruel slaughter and mindless extinction. We urgently need organizations like Greenpeace, the Sierra Club, and all other such dedicated groups — and *they* need *money*. A brief but powerful verse, written by this book's consulting editor, Robert A. Brewer, a marine biologist, expresses with consummate clarity what I'm trying to communicate.

> where were you
> when the great whales were crying out for mercy
> and the fish were disappearing
>   from our poisoned rivers and streams ?
>
> did you write one letter ?
> did you sing one song ?
>   or did you just sit there
> telling yourself
>   that your letter would not be read
> your song would not be heard ?
>
> where were you
> when the Earth began to die ?

★★★★★★

Actually, there are only three reasons why anyone works.

(1) The most common reason for working is to earn your daily bread to pay for your basic necessities, which you need in order to survive and be able to go to work, so you can get enough money for your basic necessities, which you need so you can continue to work to earn the money to pay for your . . . and so on. It's called the treadmill existence, and aptly named.

(2) To become immensely wealthy — or famous. Whether the goal is the former or the latter or both, these people fall into the same category.

(3) To keep one's self from fading into a nonperson, which you would surely become if you couldn't do the work you're doing, because it's an obsession, a dream that consumes you — and you don't do it to earn your daily bread — you do it for the reason that it provides "hyacinths for the soul." You would do it even if you were paid no money at all, because you can't *help* doing it. Quite simply, you love it. Your work is a labor of love. Therefore, you're guaranteed to achieve inner fulfillment, outward success — and if you're genuinely devoted to the dream — also bushels of money, under Universal Law.

(4) These are the rare ones who inherit their money, and who don't actually work at anything but hiring people to make sure their inheritance doesn't disappear, and that their wealth increases through investment. They're hardly worth considering, since there are so few of them. The sons of wealthy empire builders seldom inherit, along with the money, the father's driving ambition (or dream obsession). Occasionally, a grandson does, but . . .

Obviously, what is needed is some sort of gigantic miracle that could transmute or convert all the bored, weary, and frustrated people in Group 1 — and all the tense and hyper people in Group 2 — happily into Group 3. Don't you agree ? Of course, it won't be easy, since Groups 1 and 2 share the same blindness to the reality of the Money Mystique.

You would think, wouldn't you, that everyone would make an intense effort to become part of Group 3 ? It's logical. But it doesn't always happen that way. You see, the people in Group 2 think they don't need to join Group 3, because they believe they already have the formula for success, although they're gravely mistaken. The equally misguided people in Group 1 aren't sure just *what* it is they want, and even when they are, the necessity of survival takes priority because the ideal labor of love for them individually doesn't always beckon from the Classified Ads during the same week the rent is due. Thus begins the endless treadmill of existence. And since humans are, unfortunately, creatures of habit, well . . .

Universal Law regarding money is mysteriously contradictory. Never mind all those self-help books that purport to tell you how to do it. No matter which formula they counsel is used, *working hard to make money is not how you make money*.

The immense fortunes in America (and the same rule applies to other countries) always have been and always shall be built upon the deceptively fragile foundation of a dream by men who labored with love and were obsessed by an idea. When they added the letter "L," for love, to the idea, it became an *ideal* that eventually, inevitably, and miraculously brought benefit to the world, while simultaneously producing a never-ending flow of money. *Women* obsessed by an idea-ideal that resulted in changing the world and accumulating a fortune ? None have been permitted such achievement yet, but their time is swift approaching, for "women's dreams are made of sterner stuff, and they will manifest soon enough." (I guess it's all right to plagiarize a line from one of my own poems ?)

Consider the great wealth accumulated by Group 3 people like Frank W. Woolworth, Andrew Carnegie, George Westinghouse, the *original* Henry Ford and John D. Rockefeller — and Howard Hughes.

(I refer to Hughes, Junior, *not* Senior. The latter belonged to Group 2 — and never mind the negative things you've been told about the former. Ninety percent of it is made up of deliberately planted lies and distortions, which will soon be exposed in particular forthcoming books.)

These incalculable fortunes were built by men who didn't give a ginger snap about making money. They were single-mindedly consumed only with the dream, the idea transmuted into an ideal, by adding the "l" for love of their work. Then the money materialized in awesome and ever-increasing amounts, under what the science of metaphysics calls the Universal Law of Magnetic Attraction — and the first rule of that law is to work with love — to pursue your daydreams until they lead you into a labor of love.

There have been only a rare few in Group 2 who set out to accumulate wealth, with money being the sole motive, who have succeeded in permanently achieving that goal. Most fail dismally, without ever coming close to their images of King Midas and his gold. The large majority of the remaining, who temporarily *appear* to have succeeded, aren't able to retain their wealth. Because it doesn't bring them a trace of genuine happiness, inevitably their inner depression causes them to make some miscalculated move that eventually results in the loss of their wealth in various ways.

Those rare few who don't fail to accumulate, and who don't experience the misfortune of losing their wealth, end up as pathetic creatures, full of abject misery, looking and behaving (as only one example) like "poor" J. Paul Getty, who, regardless of his enormous fortune, refused to pay the ransom for his grandson's life until the kidnappers sliced off the boy's ear and mailed it to him. To end up like these rare few who manage to hang on to it (but can't take it with them when they go) could hardly be the desire of any sane person who perceived the certain future of such avarice. Charles Dickens's Scrooge was more than a fictional character to be considered during the Christmas season. He is a prototype of particular Group 2 people in every society, perhaps somewhat exaggerated to get the point across, but very real.

When the Money Mystique is ignored, whether through greed or through ignorance of the Law, the money gained either gradually dwindles away — or is accumulated to the level of stagnation within the spirit of the one who hoards it, bringing all of the accompanying miseries of *the fear of loss*.

"Oh, ye of little faith ! Why are you so concerned with your riches ?" shouted Francis of Assisi in the Vatican to the jewel-encrusted Bishops and Cardinals, who blushed with shame and flushed with rage that this ragged, barefoot monk should dare to criticize his "religious superiors."

As for Francis of Assisi, remember that there are some who engage in a labor of love, yet do not accumulate bushels of money. But this is not a denial of the Laws of the Money Mystique. It occurs through personal choice because these few unintentionally discover, along the way, something of equal importance to them individually: that a modest financial security permits them to periodically retreat from the madness of society and commune with Nature, while this same modest financial security also allows them to devote much of their time to relieving the suffering of those still existing in the darkness of ignorance, i.e.: voluntary monks, social workers, and teachers who love to teach. (Teachers today are so grossly underpaid, they *have* to fall into this category, or leave the profession.)

The Universal Law concerning money is simple, as all great truths are simple — i.e.: the Nazarene's Golden Rule and Lincoln's Gettysburg Address. Unfortunately, however, *simplicity* is the very quality that causes ancient wisdom to be so difficult for humans to master. Adult humans, that is. Children grasp it quickly and naturally, until the power of their innocence is gradually diluted and finally destroyed by the growing process, through the constant conditioning and programming of their minds with falsehoods by adults (who were once children themselves). A vicious circle.

In fact, the Money Mystique is so very simple, you'll have to struggle hard to obey it and practice its rules, experiencing a great deal of both mental and emotional pain in the attempt — until you finally escape the withering clutch of *the fear of loss* and conquer it. Becoming a joyful member of the brotherhood and sisterhood of the Money Mystique requires, like everything else, that you pay your dues.

The first rule is to find what kind of work will allow you to labor with love, thereby entering Group 3. The second rule is giving. Once you've followed the first rule, you'll soon be earning money far and above your basic needs. After you've paid your debts and taken care of all of your essential needs of living (which include, in addition to necessities, also vacations, rest, travel, and "hyacinths for the soul") — then give away *half* of every remaining surplus dollar you earn through working with love. Let go. Repeat: *let go.*

HALF ? ! I can feel your shocked response. I hear it in the voices and see it in the faces of each of you reading this . . . as I sense it in your minds. Yes, *half.* The word is not a misprint or a typo. Just . . . *give* it away ? Yes, just give it away. After you have also spent it freely to gain your reasonable personal requirements for happiness, which may include a cottage in Wales, for all I know. As long as you don't concentrate on accumulating it and investing it, so that "money earns money," (which is against Universal Law) it doesn't matter whether you give it or spend it, relative to its continuing to increase. The giving part — as opposed to letting go through freely spending — is an additional booster to the continuation of the flow and required by the Law of Karma for personal happiness, the reward of spiritual enlightenment.

As I've already warned you, the law is so absolutely *simple*, you will have extreme difficulty in (1) comprehending it (2) believing it and (3) practicing it.

After you've openly and freely (not cautiously and fearfully) tried it only *once,* you'll need no further convincing, because this amazing

Law will then go into effect. Within a shockingly brief period of time (which will vary, depending on several factors) the money you "crazily" — "naïvely" — and "extravagantly" gave away will not only return to you, it will return in an increased amount, often threefold or fourfold . . . in a completely unexpected manner, from a likewise completely unexpected source.

Don't ever *loan* money. *Give* it. It will return, and always multiplied, but (and this is important) not necessarily or always from the same source where it was given — rarely from the one to whom you gave. It will return from the Universe itself, which is synchronized to the harmonics of the Law of Giving.

The Money Mystique may bring a few shudders to stockbrokers, bankers, and insurance companies, but it needn't. When the initial shock wears off, stockbrokers will realize that investments in new companies and corporations may not meet the spiritual requirements met by giving, but does meet the Money Mystique requirement of *circulating* green energy into the Universe. What they do with their personal funds can then follow the circulation law, plus the booster law of giving. As for insurance companies and salesmen, they can ease their trembles by knowing that reasonable insurance for families and people who are too ill to work is certainly acceptable. It's the large fortunes in insurance that break the laws of the Money Mystique, causing relatives to wish for the insured one's death, to fight shamefully among themselves . . . and too often even lead to murder.

Bankers ? They needn't be overly concerned. What they will lose in interest on unnecessarily large Savings Accounts they'll more than make up for through the increased flow of the new checking accounts resulting from spending and giving. Bankers have all their bets covered ! What do I mean by the harmonics of the Law of Giving ? All of Nature gives freely, or there would be no grass, no flowers, no fruit. No trees. To tune in to this all-embracing Giving, which returns a thousandfold, is to become one with Nature Herself. The apple tree doesn't say, "I'll give only to the deserving." Nor does the gentle, brown-eyed cow, with her milk. For, without giving freely, the apple tree would die; the cow's milk (like hoarded money) would dry up and cause her to be ill. The Sun, also a Giver — of warmth and light — shines upon the godly and ungodly alike, with the same life-giving energy. All of existence depends upon giving . . . to exist.

The secret of the Money Mystique is that the green energy of money travels in a magnetic circle. Let go of it, and it follows that invisible circle of pure and powerful energy, infallibly returning to you multiplied, flowing through you and outward in its circular path (like the boomerang mystery) — and back again. Over and over, continuously, without end. You will have become, then, the center for this energy, the catalyst for its flow — and it will never stop returning to you, each time increased. Bread cast upon the waters does return, as the carpenter taught, including the daily bread you earn from working with love. It will cease only when you cease to give. Then the magic circle is short-circuited. The Law operates, remember, on the principle of electromagnetic energy, much like Nikola Tesla's alternating current. Don't allow a temporary small sum of money cause you to cease to give. If you have only twenty dollars, spend or give away — circulate — ten dollars. The key word is that your small sum is *temporary*.

To suddenly let go, and discover the miracle of how to thereby literally obtain wealth, is hard. You've been conditioned and programmed since childhood to be "frugal, cautious and economical — to be practical and hang on to your money." Consequently, it's natural for you to believe that what I'm writing here is utter nonsense. But I hope you don't. You may think that the counsel of "letting go" — giving — or even spending (as I pointed out, the Universe doesn't care which, as long as you toss it in some manner back into the world at large) is a ridiculous way of obtaining money. If you were told, when you only possess, say, four hundred dollars, and therefore can't afford to buy or even rent the house of your dreams, to spend two hundred dollars of the four hundred to buy a special lamp or quilt or chair for the house to *guarantee* you'll soon be living in it, you'd probably ask:

"How can I *get* money by giving away or spending what little I have ? It's not logical. It's extravagant."

Think whatever you like. As I said, I'm sure you will soon become convinced of the truth of the Money Mystique the first time you decide to try it. All I can tell you from my own experience is that following the law of the Money Mystique has never failed me. But I can speak only for myself. If you're still suffering from the grip of the fear of loss, why don't *you* do that ? Speak for the elf of your own s-elf. You'll be surprised at what happens to the you-of-you.

I wish I could make everyone understand how exciting it is to synchronize yourself with the harmony of the Universe pulsing around you, and tune in to giving. There's such a wild sense of euphoria that comes when you realize you're free of the chains that bound you to the green paper called money — when you finally comprehend that the swiftest and surest way to *get* it is to *give* it. It's FREEDOM ! An overwhelming and sudden awareness — a *knowing* — that you're no longer tied to the desperate need to fear and worship money. You'll be pleasantly shocked to realize, at last, that it's only paper ! And dirty, wrinkled paper at that. Like a discarded chewing gum wrapper. There is no possible way to express such a feeling in words. You must risk the initial sharp pain of letting go, and experience it yourself. Follow the law of the Money Mystique, and watch what happens within a "self" — your own s-elf — you only thought you knew.

Wealthy people like the Rockefellers, the Fords, the Kennedys, and so on, have always given, and their accumulation of money never stops. Granted, the motive has, for the most part, been one concerned with corporate tax write offs. But that's one of the strangest things about the Money Mystique. Its laws aren't concerned with motive once the magnetic energy circle has been spun into motion — only with the circulation of green energy back into the Universe from where it came. The motive for giving does matter, of course, to the advancement of the heart and spirit, but the motive doesn't affect the boomerang action of money's circular route and multiplied return. Perhaps . . . the Law isn't affected by motive because the very act of letting go itself creates so much intense energy it neutralizes all motives into good. Whether or not you use it to penetrate the mystery of money is up to you. Free Will is a precious gift.

The astrological alchemy for making the big leap into Group 3 I've already given. When you've found your personal labor of love, you'll soon begin to accumulate enough green energy to start your own magic circle of giving. But neither I nor anyone else can force you into illumination. The time for growing-knowing is individual, dictated by your own Higher Self. That's always the best way. To judge for yourself. It fattens the intuition and makes it grow.

A Mantra for the Money Mystique

I've been broke, but I've never been poor. Being broke is temporary. Being poor is a state of mind.

— Mike Todd

★ ★ ★ ★ ★

2

AN APPLE A DAY

an astrological and numerological health guide
including vegetarianism —
and other current problems
and their esoteric, holistic solutions

AN APPLE A DAY

. . . keeps the doctor away

. . . the most persistent memory fragment
of the time when I started to talk
is the recollection . . . after I'd learned to walk
of everyone fearing I would catch pneumonia
from running out into the rain

before that, I crawled out into it, in pure bliss

they were forever warning . . .
"you are sure and certain to catch pneumonia"

only they said it pronouncing the "p" and a double "e"
to make me laugh
and for years I called it that . . . pee-nee-monia

"you'll catch pee-nee-monia for sure and certain"
I would shake my finger and tell my dolls

★ ★ ★ ★ ★ ★

 HAT LITTLE girl and her dolls were the victims of a highly contagious epidemic of medical fear. Astrology teaches with absolute verity that (for one example), if at birth there was no affliction related to the Ascendent and/or the sixth house of health in Pisces or Gemini — and no planet afflicted by a malefic in Pisces or Gemini (Gemini ruling the lungs, and Pisces associated through the mutable cross of sympathetic parts of the body) — there is no way that you are ever going to succumb to pee-nee-monia, or even pneumonia. Never mind how much the foregoing sentence sounds like Greek to the astrological layman, you can depend on it being true, with no exceptions.

With none of these Pisces-Gemini afflictions in the birth chart, you could sleep in the rain overnight or be caught in a snowstorm and not contract pneumonia. Likewise, with none of these Pisces-Gemini afflictions in your birth chart (and this will drive the American Cancer Society into a frenzy of fury) — *whatever* your birth aspects, someone smoking a cigarette near you, or several people smoking across the room will not cause you to develop lung cancer (the latest dire warning from the white-coated gods of the ACS). The only way that what is called "passive smoking" can affect you is if you find the smell of tobacco unpleasant. Some do, some don't. I find the odor of alcohol personally offensive, but it's certainly not going to cause me to develop the disease of alcoholism. The exposure of your lungs to the carbon monoxide emissions of cars and buses, compounded by industrial smog, is deadly to all of us, but that person lighting a cigarette at a nearby table will *not* give you lung cancer. That so many actually believe such a ridiculous and unfounded claim is an example of how easy it is to hypnotize or program the human brain with repetitious lies of any kind.

Granted, smoking will certainly not benefit your lungs or any other organs which may be the weak links in your body chain — and not smoking or smoking low-tar cigarettes in moderation, and not inhaling, is the best choice for your general health — but lung cancer you will not get, assuming the aforementioned birth chart. Even without the latter you will not be in any way affected by a smoker in the room, any more or less than you're affected (or offended) by the reek of alcohol fumes or, if you are a vegetarian, by the stench of butchered animal flesh cooking nearby.

Every profession has its flaws — and its black sheep. The medical profession is no exception, although its image makers would like us to believe otherwise. Like Caesar's wife, modern medicine has been "above reproach" for the past half century or longer.

It was not always thus. The pendulum swings. During the time of the Civil War and through the turn of the century, the credibility of the medical professions was questionable, to say the least. Physicians bought large ads in newspapers and tacked up flamboyant posters (which you've probably seen reproduced on wallpaper in the rest rooms of certain restaurants) offering medical panaceas they claimed would simultaneously cure your sore toe and chronic backaches, stop nosebleeds, cause luxuriant hair to grow on your bald head, relieve constipation, banish hives and boils, bad breath and snoring — *and* resolve your marital problems. It must be admitted that, if one elixir did all that, it would surely make anyone's marriage substantially happier !

Patients were "bled" by Dracula-like leeches attached to their skin to remove impurities from their bodies — and when a lone and dedicated physician, Dr. Ignaz Semmelweis, dared to suggest (and proved it) that fewer women would die from the puerperal infection called "childbed fever" if the attending doctors and midwives would simply wash their hands in a chlorinated lime solution before delivering the laboring mothers of their infants, he immediately became a pariah in the medical community. His death in an insane asylum was the reward bestowed upon him by his professional peers for his stunning contribution to life.

Then the AMA was conceived and born (I trust by those who first washed their hands) — the powerful American Medical Association — whose members soon aligned in spirit with the FDA, the Federal Drug Administration, in a mutual mission to clean up shabby medical and drug practices, with the goal of changing the carnival sideshow image of both the healers and the pharmaceutical alchemists who compounded the chemicals the former prescribed. Medical schools with strict academic requirements were established, high standards of ethics were imposed . . . and abracadabra ! The tackiness disappeared, replaced by hygenic medical practices and dogma, further glamorized by the sterile chrome laboratories and operating rooms of the newly emerging and exciting field of medical research. Slowly, but very surely, medicine grew into the status of almost a religion, supported by congregations of patients in awe of its white-coated high priests, who would not tolerate the slightest criticism of themselves or their profession, and, in fact, demanded a kind of respect that nearly amounted to worship. Who would dare to contradict anyone who began a conversation with, "Well, my *doctor* told me that . . . ." ? Very few.

Now the pendulum is swinging in a new and different direction. There are still those sincere medical men and women who are genuinely devoted to their healing work. But as malpractice suits steadily rise, and are duly reported in the media, the general public is gradually becoming aware that the warmly remembered family doctor of Norman Rockwell's paintings has gone the way of the dinosaur. We're living in an age of specialists.

Medical people who set broken bones, replace limbs amputated in accidents, repair scarred and disfigured faces, treat severe burns, remove bullets and dangerously diseased or ruptured organs and start hearts beating again after they have stopped, deserve our respect and support, even our affection.

Such professional and compassionate ones who perform miracles of healing do still exist, here and there, like Dr. James Huperich and Dr. Raymond Wong, of Hollywood Presbyterian Medical Center, a healing haven with caring ones like Carmen Sosa, under the enlightened guidance of hospital personnel such as Sy Schneider. I mention only those medical people I've personally experienced, although there are, naturally, a number of others. My son Michael's life was literally saved by these people and this particular medical center. Nevertheless, it's growing undeniably more difficult every year to locate a sincerely dedicated physician.

We've been made only too knowledgeable of the many deaths and deformities caused by both the medical and the pharmaceutical professions to feel comfortable in continuing to genuflect to the high priests of medicine with the same degree of awe they expected of us in the past.

As a result, a growing number of people are turning to homeopathy and holistic medicine, a revolution seeded by the popularity of books about the "sleeping prophet," Edgar Cayce, and further fruited by the flower children and the back-to-Nature movement of the Sixties, which hasn't faded into oblivion, but is gathering more apostles every year.

We don't want to lose our good doctors, and we don't want the historic swinging pendulum to swing us all the way back to the elixirs and leeches of the nineteenth century. We'd like a happy medium, if possible — a change in the direction of medicine able to give us what medicine has always promised and never delivered: permanent good health, by giving priority to the practice of prevention over diagnosis and treatment, as does homeopathy and medical astrology. (We wouldn't even have the medical profession's current semi-approval of acupuncture if former President Richard Nixon hadn't been ailing when he visited China, and became convinced of its effectiveness.)

No, we don't want to swing back to the nineteenth century's medical practices, but swinging back to even before then, to ancient China, might not be so bad.

There were three types of doctors in ancient China. The first kind merely cured your disease, and was the least of the three. The second was an expert in diagnosing an illness, not only after it appeared, but earlier, shortly *before* it appeared. He was higher on the medical ladder. The most skilled, most venerable, and most respected physician was the one who kept his patients so healthy that they never manifested any form of sickness in the first place, a Taoist ideal. This medical "caste system" was nothing if not logical.

And it went further. A doctor in ancient China (oh, turn back the clock !) was paid only when his patients got well, when he had healed them — and in some districts the doctor was under strict obligation to make economic amends or restitution should a patient become worse or continue to be ill under his care, because it was considered that, if he had not kept his patients healthy, then their diseases were fully his responsibility.

Every time a patient died, a lantern of a certain shape was hung outside the attending doctor's office, and a doctor with too many of these lanterns swinging at the front door could be assured of a slow business. Physicians who complain today about the high insurance caused by malpractice suits should be glad they weren't practicing in ancient China, when the doctors were blamed for everything (unjustly) and the patients given no responsibility for their own mental attitudes causing their illnesses to linger. Why must everything be one extreme or the other ? A little of each would be nice, with physicians and patients taking *equal responsibility* for good health.

If I may be permitted a respectful suggestion to the medical profession, physicians and surgeons would benefit by paying more attention to the founding father of their profession — Hippocrates, who based his knowledge on astrology. Every doctor, upon being presented with his or her medical degree in whatever specialty, before taking over the authoritative role of dictating to us about our own bodies (surely a precious and privately owned possession) takes the "Hippocratic Oath." Therefore, is it too much to ask that the wisdom of this founding father's counsel be respected and followed in the practice of medicine ?

Consider some of that wisdom from Hippocrates. He wrote in his diaries that "He who practices medicine without the benefit of the movement of the stars and planets is a fool." No pussyfooting around with innuendos or Greek double-talk there. (Much like the well-known legal adage that "he who represents himself in a court of law has a fool for a lawyer.") Hippocrates further stated firmly this warning: "Touch not with iron that part of the body ruled by the sign the Moon is transitting."

His counsel may need some interpretation for the medical people who have ignored the astrological wisdom of their founding father for so long they haven't a clue as to how to translate his words.

It means this: One does not perform a surgical procedure with a knife (iron) upon a part of the patient's body which is ruled by (associated with) the astrological sign through which the Moon is moving at the time. The Moon remains in one sign approximately two and a half days, and this information can be easily obtained from an Ephemeris, calculated by astronomers — or a Farmer's Almanac.

According to Hippocrates, and proven repeatedly in surgery, disobeying this law will inevitably result in one of three failures of any surgery performed at the wrong time: (1) complications, including infection — (2) unusually slow and painful healing and recuperation — and (3) fatality. The last of the three possible results of disobedience of the law is behind the too frequent and well-known medical explanation that: "The operation was a success, but the patient died." In the case of (3), death can result from any number of causes, including the anesthetic administered. The results of (1) and (2) are by far more frequent, and result (3) is rare. Nevertheless, observing the warning of Hippocrates is clearly the wisest course.

Some examples: When the Moon is in Taurus, ruling the neck and throat, one should not perform a tonsillectomy. When the Moon is passing through Scorpio, ruler of the reproductive organs, a prostate operation or a hysterectomy (removal of the tubes, ovaries, or uterus) should not be performed. When the Moon is in Capricorn or Aries, the former ruling the teeth and bones, the latter ruling the head in general, no dental surgery or other surgery related to the bones or any part of the head should be performed. And so on. Later in this chapter is a list of the various parts of the body ruled by each of the twelve signs.

Personally, I never accept anything counseled by anyone without first investigating its validity, and that includes the astrological advice of Hippocrates. But, unlike the medical profession's attitude toward the stars and planets, neither do I disbelieve it until I've checked into it to a satisfactory degree. I investigated the counsel of Hippocrates concerning this particular law, and found it to be valid each time. I'll give only a few examples here, among the many instances I've checked.

Jeff Chandler, a film star of the Fifties, entered the hospital to undergo spinal surgery for a slipped disc. It was a common and comparatively simple surgical procedure, requiring only a few days of hospitalization. He died on the operating table from "unknown causes." That day the Moon was transitting the sign of Leo, ruler of the heart, the back, and the spinal column.

Bertha Todd, first wife of the producer of *Around the World in 80 Days*, Michael Todd, who was later married to Elizabeth Taylor, cut her finger on a broken glass. The next day she decided to go to the emergency room of a Los Angeles hospital and have the cut closed with a few stitches by the intern on duty, a minor bit of surgical attention. On the way to the hospital, Bertha and her attorney stopped for coffee at a Beverly Hills drugstore. When they arrived at the emergency room, Bertha was afraid the stitching might be painful, so she requested an anesthetic. She was given two, but they weren't effective. The third one took Bertha out of the realm of all pain. She died within minutes. That day the Moon was transitting the sign of Gemini, ruler of the shoulders, arms, hands, and fingers. With Bertha Todd and Jeff Chandler, "the operations were a success, but the patient died."

A close friend of mine in Pittsburgh sent both of her children to the hospital at her doctor's suggestion that they have simultaneous tonsillectomies. One was suffering from a severe tonsil inflammation, the other less severe. It was during the time, not so long ago, when physicians advised wholesale surgery of this kind (which they've only recently counseled against). If you had four children, might as well stuff them all into green nightshirts and yank out their tonsils at one time. Those who didn't need it then "were sure to need it eventually." Only later did the medical people decide that tonsils have a job to perform in the body and should never be removed except for excellent cause. Back then, the wholesale removal was recommended. It was more efficient and practical. And there was also the advantage of a cut rate of the surgeon's fee for multiple removal, as opposed to the expense of a single tonsillectomy.

The day the two children entered the hospital the Moon was transitting the sign of Taurus, which is, as I've already mentioned, ruler of the neck and throat. One child developed a severe infection as a complication of surgery, which was touch and go for a while, but he eventually responded to treatment with antibiotics. The other child, a girl, endured a long recuperation — five weeks in the hospital — during which time it was discovered that a piece of tonsil remained and had to be removed in a second surgical procedure later.

The medical community openly confesses that at least five percent of all deaths in hospitals are "unexplainable." Could the astrological counsel of Hippocrates explain them ? They will never know until they make an attempt to find out. Doctors needn't suddenly leap into practicing the wisdom of Hippocrates by becoming astrologers. That's expecting too much. But the very least of the obligations implied by their Hippocratic Oath would be a carefully controlled observation of past patient case histories and current surgical operations, to check the results. All they need is an Ephemeris or an Almanac — and a few brief words of instruction from any competent astrologer.

Since the Moon, as I've said, remains in any particular sign for only about two and a half days, a *necessary* (many of them are not) operation need not be postponed for a great length of time by those who respect Hippocrates. If the medical profession won't protect its patients, they can perhaps protect themselves by scheduling their own operations, giving the doctor some plausible excuse, such as: "If I don't take my vacation this week, I won't be able to take it at all this year. It postpones the surgery for only three days, doctor" — or "It's more convenient for me — and for my family — to have my surgery next Friday instead of next Tuesday." All any patient needs to beat the system is an imaginative excuse, an Ephemeris or Almanac — plus a healthy respect for his or her own body, a realization that it doesn't belong to the medical trust to do with as they please, but to one's own self. It wouldn't be wise to request a rescheduling of surgery by saying, "You see, doctor, my astrologer says . . ." The medical community isn't quite that enlightened yet, on the whole. Maybe soon.

Assuming you get lucky and find a doctor who will be at least partially sympathetic to your views about the no-no dates for surgery, he or she may ask you why this should be. Here is the foundation behind the counsel of Hippocrates concerning "Touch not with iron that part of the body ruled by the astrological sign the Moon is transitting."

Even the stuffiest scientists now recognize and realize that the Moon controls the ocean's tides as well as the timing of the opening and closing of oysters. Any police chief can tell you that the department dreads the nights of the Full Moon, because it brings on a great "tide" of criminal activity, filling up the police blotters with double or triple the number of crimes compared to other times. The Moon also controls the monthly menstrual cycles of women.

Now, since it's a recognized fact that the Moon has the power to move around all the great bodies of water in the oceans on Earth, and since it's an equally recognized fact that more than eighty-five percent of the human body consists of water, the Moon controls your body and emotions to a degree most people don't suspect.

Surgery interrupts the as yet undiscovered *tidal flows* in the body by the unnatural process of opening up the body and allowing air to enter. Consequently, those parts of the body which are ruled by whatever astrological sign the Moon is transitting at the time are especially sensitive and vulnerable. That should explain the counsel of Hippocrates sufficiently to even the most closed medical minds, let alone to an open-minded physician or surgeon.

Medicine has always treated the disease the patient has. Medical astrology and homeopathy treat the patient who has the disease — and there's a vast and vital difference. Your individual birth chart (nativity or horoscope) indicated at the moment of your first breath of life on this Earth the weak links in your body's chain reactions. That's why medical astrology is more concerned with the *diagnosis* and *prevention* of disease than with treatment. If it's known at birth that a baby's nativity indicates a strong predisposition to diabetes, for example, the parents can control the diet of this small human early enough to prevent the adult the child will become from ever developing diabetes. "An ounce of prevention is worth a pound of cure" is a true adage.

Remember that the stars incline, they do not compel. Translated, that means that your nativity or horoscope shows which diseases and accidents to which parts of your personal body you are *inclined* to suffer. If you take the proper preventive measures, these astrological birth warnings will have accomplished their purpose, and you need *not* become ill in the manner indicated in the horoscope as the body's *inclination*. But if you do *not* take such preventive measures (for the reason that you're ignorant of your own nativity's warnings), then your body will be inclined to respond to the electromagnetic "pulls," and what were originally only possibilities will then become realities.

There is nothing fatalistic about astrology. The behavior of humans is where the responsibility for predictive tragedy lies — their refusal to heed the warnings of the birth chart or to take the astrological advice that would prevent the occurrence of *all* negative events foreshadowed in the horoscope, not just those concerning health.

Medical astrology provides the medical profession (if they would only accept and recognize it) with the true original cause of the breakdown of certain organs in each individual's body. Every physical illness, without a single exception, is the result of the initial cause of certain mental and emotional attitudes. As just two of these, for example, the emotional seeding that causes arthritis is resentment, bitterness, and frustration held inside, controlled — and not allowed to express itself outwardly. Be honest, say what you feel — or get a punching bag.

Heart disease and heart attacks are caused by (a) the lonely longing resulting from not being loved (b) the inability to give or return love — or (c) the inability to love one's self. The emotion of love and the human organ of the heart are inseparable.

Anger is deadly and swift in its effect. When you become really violently angry with someone — or about something — I mean a raging fury, whether or not it's justified, and whether or not it's held in or allowed to spill out — it nevertheless creates bile, and the bile buildup triggered by the anger seldom takes more than a few months, sometimes only weeks. The result ? An excruciatingly painful gall-bladder attack and the manifestation of gallstones. It's a dreadful and painful price to pay for anger. Forgiveness is as practical as it is spiritual, since it not only strengthens the soul, it keeps the body healthy. If you've ever suffered a gallbladder attack, if you've ever had gall-stones, ask yourself with whom or with what you were furiously angry a few weeks or a few months prior to the attack. It shouldn't be hard to remember. The memory of anger or rage strong enough to create bile (whether suppressed or expressed) stays with you awhile. Think hard about it. It will surprise you, and also teach you an important lesson about uncontrollable rage. It also affects the spleen. Why do you think "bile" and "spleen" are used to describe violent emotions ?

Your birth chart infallibly reveals not just your susceptibility to particular diseases and accidents, not just the organs composing the weak links in your body's chain reactions, but also the mental and emotional attitudes responsible for causing specified parts of your body to attract accident or infection. Beyond this, the birth chart contains the knowledge of the *timing* of illness and possible accident, indicating *when* you'll be the most vulnerable to one or the other, so that they can be prevented or circumvented through an advance change in your individual mental and/or emotional behavior indicated to be the initiatory cause.

If accident or disease has already occurred, the nativity will indicate which mental or emotional attitudes must be changed to reverse the progress of the illness or promote swifter healing of the body parts which have undergone accident. Sometimes your own instincts can cause such a reversal, producing what doctors call "spontaneous remission," the medical term used when no apparent cause for recovery can be found. Astrology accurately analyzes character, personality, physical strengths and weaknesses, and much more — but is equally helpful as a timing device.

★★★★★★

Never forget that what you *eat* and what you *think* is what you *are*. The food taken into your body is what gradually . . . slowly but surely . . . forms your thought patterns. And your thoughts, both conscious and subconscious, are in absolute control of your body's health or lack of it.

An apple a day, as the old adage goes, may well keep the doctor away, because fruit is the food most beneficial to your body's well-being. It's good to become a vegetarian, but the ultimate goal is to become a fruitarian . . . and eventually a *part-time* breathtarian, gaining all your body needs from the very air you breathe (assuming one can find any smog-free air these days — except in places like Cripple Creek, Colorado, ten thousand feet above sea level, with pure, clean air). The person striving for perfect and permanent good health finally graduates into becoming a full-time fruitarian and part-time breathtarian, no longer needing to kill life in order to sustain life. The so-called food chain (destroying life to maintain life) is not as holy and Nature-endorsed a pattern as you've been programmed to believe — nor as necessary as you've been taught.

Reaching that ultimate in well-being cannot be accomplished overnight. It takes at least fifteen years — and a change of attitude or thought patterns. Deciding to become an instant vegetarian, for example, after eating meat for many years, can shock the body into severe illness, as happens only too often, causing people to mistakenly believe that vegetarianism is "bad for you."

Before beginning the course of becoming a vegetarian, it's first necessary to desire to do so for the correct reasons. The first reason is genuine compassion for our animal brothers. It will save a lot of time if I quote here from an interview in *The New York Times* with an unenlightened rancher, feeling perhaps the beginning sensations of compassion but not yet illuminated to the truth of the cruelty of butchery and ranching.

In the interview, the rancher was discussing his cows with the reporter. He talked about how small calves are raised in terms of expenses, profit and loss; how much you need to get for their dead bodies and the dead bodies of cows and steers (calves liver, hamburger, steak, and roast beef) in order to earn a living for yourself as a rancher. Everything he said in the interview applies also to mother and baby sheep and pigs (lamb chops, pork chops, ham, and bacon).

"You know," the rancher said to the reporter, "you can almost get sentimental about these little fellers. Do you know," he continued, "that the mother cows can tell their own calves in a herd of a thousand or more ? And didja know that when we separate them calves into the shipping corrals, the mothers stand there outside by the fence just shrieking and bellowing in sounds you ain't never heard no cow make. As if they know what's happening. Sometimes they'll just stand there for a week or more after the calves are gone, without eatin' nothin' at all. Some of them, their throats get raw from all that bellowing, and they can't swallow. Time comes you have to drive those mother cows away from there or they'll starve themselves to death." (More loss, no profit — can't allow *that*.)

You've been taught that your body must have protein (meat) to be healthy. You've been taught a myth. In plain language, a lie — on a par with the nineteenth-century leeches.

No matter what you've been raised to believe, chopping off the head of a turkey or a chicken also brings pain and suffering.

Fish die more slowly, after their tender mouths are torn by the sharp point of the tackle, or, if caught in a net, thrashing around in agony, gasping for "air" — water to them. Fish are an important part of Nature's ecology; they perform vital functions swimming in rivers, streams, lakes, and oceans during their brief lifespan. And by the way, Jesus was not a fisherman. Instead, he magnetized certain of his apostles away from killing sea life by promising to make them "fishers of men." There's no record of his eating flesh of any kind himself.

As for the fish, not all of them are carnivorous cannibals, eating other fish. Many are vegetarians, existing on algae, seaweed, and other kinds of plant growth in the ocean. Whales eat tons of plankton, which also provides more than seventy percent of the oxygen humans breathe, and which is rapidly disappearing from our man-poisoned waters.

It's worth noting that the percentage of carnivorous opposed to vegetarian fish closely matches the current percentage of carnivorous opposed to vegetarian humans. There are other meaningful reflections between animal and human habits, and the former imitate the latter, not the other way around. I don't have the time, space, or inclination to fully debate the evolutionists here, but that's the way it is.

Gorillas, for instance, are vegetarians and very gentle creatures, as primate expert Diane Fossey discovered by observing them closely for many years. So are chimps, yet, when one chimpanzee, in a perverse mood spontaneously and unnaturally happens to kill a flesh animal, and toys around with eating it (though his surprised stomach may make him quickly ill), he is immediately glorified by the other chimps (even though they remain basically vegetarians), feared, respected, and made the dominant male of the group — until another male chimp takes a whim to do the same. Then the new killer becomes the dominant male. A clear mirror reflection of human behavior.

There are many examples in the fish and animal world proving that the carnivorous aspect of the "food chain," so holy to biologists, is *not a necessity for healthy survival.* Jungle animals who eat the flesh of other animals ? Regardless of what you learned in school about Darwin's theory, men taught animals to be carnivorous. There was no blood shed in Eden, when this Earth was an "Eden Heaven," many millions of years before the Atlantean, Lemurian, and paleolithic periods, about which more in Chapter 9. If cows and calves, sheep and lambs, mama and papa and baby monkeys and gorillas, giraffes and hippos can survive in good health as vegetarians, there's no reason why lions, tigers, leopards, and others can't do the same, given enough time to restore their digestive organs back to their original state.

Have you ever wondered why the Catholic Church counsels its followers to celebrate Lent by forgoing red meat, as a holy thing to do ? Ask a Jesuit priest the reason behind this edict of Rome, and you will, at the very least, hear some absolutely fascinating double-talk.

Since I've given the Catholic Church a few slaps of criticism in this book, it deserves a pat on its ancient back when it's right. The 1987 stand taken by the Roman Church against artificial insemination, surrogate mothers, and test-tube babies demonstrates that regarding these moral questions, the Church is vibrating in harmony with Universal Law. Creating new life without the positive-negative, electromagnetic energy force exchanged in a male-female union constitutes definite disobedience to Nature's Law, which happens to *also* be the Law of our Creators, and could have unsuspected and serious repercussions. This is not the place to go into great detail about why — such a discussion belongs in future books — but meanwhile, one might ordain swift enlightenment so that these spiritually dangerous practices may halt.

The Roman Church is likewise right in its stand against the genetic engineering our "mad scientists" are now performing on flora and fauna, certain to disrupt Nature's balances, as it causes great suffering to helpless animals.

Sometimes the healing treatments of particular medical people cause one to wonder if we aren't living in what will someday be called the "dark ages of medicine." A friend of mine from Colorado fell ill several years ago with a persistent virus she had picked up in the Orient. She grew progressively weaker, and pain consumed her entire body. For a time she considered the homeopathic treatment recommended by a holistic medical person I told her about, but she finally decided instead to seek help in a series of expensive clinics. The physician at the last clinic placed her on a thirty-day diet consisting of nothing but *raw meat*. I felt a combination of deep sorrow and intense outrage when she died a few months later. It was some time before I could pass a hospital without feeling a flame of anger within myself.

Fresh air, fruit and vegetables, and lots of sleep are the requirements for the body to heal itself of illness. So what happens when you're in the hospital for the purpose of becoming well ? The windows are locked tightly with a key, permitting not a single breath of fresh air, as the patient lies there, breathing in the very unhealthy carbon monoxide from his or her own breath.

Your hospital diet, with very few exceptions, consists of red meat, undercooked and bloody, and often cold. White sugar is used liberally, even in the tuna fish salad in many hospitals. It makes one wonder if the dieticians graduated from a speed course at a fast-food chain. Sleep ? It's difficult, if not impossible, to sleep so your body can begin its healing process when you're periodically awakened by temperature-taking (the schedule designed to fit the hospital's convenience, not yours) and the loudspeakers in each room for calling nurses and doctors jerk you awake, causing the astral to plunge back into the body with a spasm.

★★★★★★

When your feeling for our fish, fowl, and animal brothers and sisters dawns within your heart and soul, and your mind begins to realize the intense harm done to your body through eating traumatized flesh of all kinds, you can't suddenly become a vegetarian. As I mentioned before, this can be dangerous to your already poisoned system. As I also mentioned earlier, it takes fifteen years to complete the cycle. Here is the path recommended by one of my personal

Avatars, a Hatha Yoga. (The number of years is important, related to numerology and related spiritual matters as well as to the physical body's needs.)

The ideal way to cleanse your body temple of the impurity of years of eating animal flesh is to begin by eliminating all "red meat" — beef, steak, hamburger, pork, ham, and bacon — for a *five-year period*. During this five-year period, eat both fish and fowl — vegetables and fruit — breads, cereals, and all dairy foods (eggs, milk, cheese). For one day each week of these first five years, take nothing into your body but fruits and/or natural fruit juices. This allows your body to become gradually accustomed to fruit, avoiding the negative result of your surprised bowels responding with diarrhea.

During the *second* five-year period, eliminate fish and fowl and eggs (unfertilized chicken embryos, of course) — but continue to eat all kinds of vegetables and fruit — breads, cereals, and the dairy foods of milk and cheese. Again, choose one day a week to take into your body only fruits and/or fruit juices during this second five-year period.

During the *third* five-year period, you will be ready to eliminate all vegetables which grow *under* the ground — along with red meat, fish, fowl, and eggs. Your diet now consists of only vegetables which grow *above* the ground, fruit, breads, cereals, milk, and cheese. As with each of the three five-year periods, again choose one day a week to take into your body only fruits and fruit juices.

You have now spent fifteen years preparing your physical system to sustain itself on fruit alone, now eliminating *all* vegetables, *all* dairy foods — and eating breads and cereals only when you feel the need for them. You have become a fruitarian. Remember that a fruitarian diet must include plenty of tomatoes and nuts of all kinds, along with other fruits. Some people have claimed that fruit is the food placed on this Earth from the beginning, and the only "food" the body needs. But, you see, fruit is not simply a food. It's not part of the "food chain" in its usual definition. Essentially, fruit is a *cleanser* — a purifier of the body. Your body can take care of its own needs involving blood, tissue, and so forth. But it needs the cleansing that fruit supplies. I've known a number of people (mostly Gurus) who are pure fruitarians, and they are all amazingly strong and healthy individuals. (I'm not quite there myself; I'm only in the second five-year period.)

When you've become a fruitarian slowly and safely, the stools and urine have no odor, the skin is clear, the eyes sparkle, and the mind is more alert. The important thing to remember is that vegetarianism and becoming a fruitarian can be harmful to your health unless achieved gradually and gently over a safe fifteen-year period of purification. Then you can become a breathtarian, gaining all that your body needs from the proper breathing of fresh air and Prana (the Life Force energy) — and occasionally or periodically eating fruit to cleanse your body of impurities, such as one week each month.

You may believe it's impossible to survive on the air you breathe, but it can be done, under the proper conditions. A woman named Therese Neuman, of Bavaria, who was carefully observed by several respected physicians, lived for 20 years without food — drinking only pure water and eating one thin communion wafer per day. Her death was accident-related, not from disease. Francesco Bernadone, of Assisi, is known to have frequently fasted (been a breathtarian) for 30 to 90 days at a time with no negative health results. It was after these long fasting or breathtarian periods that he was seen levitating by his monks. Unfortunately, pure water and pure air are both in short supply on our planet these days, so becoming a complete breathtarian may have to wait until a miracle of reversal in the Aquarian Age. Meanwhile, becoming a fruitarian is a giant step forward for body, mind, and soul.

All of these paths to permanent good health, please remember, must be approached with caution and common sense. There are some health addicts who become so obsessed with the concept of vegetarianism, they want to turn their newborn infants into vegetarians, beginning with their first food. This is extremely dangerous. The infant has inherited "the sins of the flesh" from the parents and ancestors, and can no more endure a sudden vegetarian diet than an adult. The same *three stage* course is safe, except that, according to my Hatha Yoga Avatar, with infants and children, it should take the form of: two *six*-year periods and a final *seven*-year period, with the same food regimen as given in the three five-year periods for adults, totaling nineteen years of preparation, from whatever age the child is when the program is initiated. Should the purification program begin at birth, then the infant should be fed all dairy products, all vegetables, fruit, bread and cereals, *plus* fish and fowl — eliminating only red meat during the first six years . . . and so on . . . with the *second* six-year period following the food intake of the second *five*-year adult period, and the final *seven*-year period matching the final adult *five*-year period.

Meat-eating races have always been warlike and aggressive, all through history, whereas non-meat-eating races have been passive and peaceful. As for hunting, I rarely enter into discussions with hunters, being an Aries. Too many Mars fireworks might explode. The excuse many hunters give to justify murdering wildlife is that they are "clearing out the excess population — otherwise there wouldn't be enough food, and the animals die anyway" makes me feel that their thought patterns are only a fraction removed from finding murder a likewise "practical and humane" way to "clear out" overpopulated areas of China and India and America's slums. In a worldwide sense, mankind (and here the chauvinistic term is appropriate) has always found war to be an "ideal" solution to "clear out" population. Nature herself is fully capable of solving her own problems, without man's "helpfulness," comprised of murder and killing. My Cherokee Chief has a bumper sticker that reads: JOIN THE ARMY. SEE THE WORLD. VISIT EXOTIC PLACES AND MEET INTERESTING PEOPLE — THEN KILL THEM.

I personally know several hunters who are otherwise kind, gentle, generous, and truly good people, possessing only this one blindness. Nevertheless, as much as I deeply and dearly love Colorado and my hometown of Cripple Creek, I manage to go to California or New York during hunting season there.

My favorite Cherokee Indian legend, which is really a true story passed down through many generations, is about the vegetarian Indian called Snow Foot, who would kill no living creature. When the deer in the forest near his tent grew older and sensed their death was near, they came to Snow Foot, knelt down before him, gazed at him for a long, still moment with their gentle brown eyes . . . then died. It was their way of offering him their dead bodies for use in making clothes to protect him against the cold, and moccasins for his feet . . . in gratitude for not participating in hunting them down and allowing them and their families to live out their life spans in the wilderness in peace.

★ ★ ★ ★ ★ ★

The Aquarian Age will bring new miracles to the field of medicine, Nature's unsuspected secrets of well-being and healing. There are hundreds of these, but I'll mention only one of them here: the magic of carrots. In 1985 John and Margaret Blamford, she approaching the chronological illusionary "number age" of 40, and he approaching the chronological illusionary "number age" of 50, had despaired of ever being able to have the baby they longed for. They had been told by the medical people that Margaret was "too old" to bear a child without risk, and John's sperm count was too low to ever allow him to become a father.

Margaret, with her woman's intuition and inexplicable feminine instinct, thought about rabbits and their amazing reproductive patterns. She knew that all domesticated rabbits eat carrots, so she put her husband on a carrot diet for several months. Every single day the hungry man gobbled carrots in every form — grated in salads, diced and cooked in casseroles, and raw in between meals. A strict carrots-only diet.

Magic ! The rabbit recipe worked like a charm, as carrot-crunching John and his esoterically inclined wife, Margaret, of Trent, England, became the proud parents of a beautiful, healthy baby girl. Margaret wasn't "pixilated" — she had simply tuned in to her Higher Self, and one of Mother Nature's secrets dawned in her conscious mind. Dr. Andrew Stanway, in his book, *Why Us?* (a commonsense guide for childless couples) explains that carrots contain an abundant supply of zinc, which is known to pep up and increase the sperm count in males. Nondomesticated rabbits and hares, who run freely in the woods, eat few, if any, carrots — and they don't reproduce anywhere near as frequently as the domesticated carrot-nibblers.

The Blamfords, after being told there was no hope for them, finally realized their dream by imitating the bunnies, but astrobiology could create the same miracle for couples who are childless for reasons different from low sperm count, though not excluding the latter. Astrobiology (see Afterword) is equally as reliable and helpful for couples who want to conceive as it is for those who use it for dependable, safe birth control. There are "many roads to Rome," as the old adage goes.

★ ★ ★ ★ ★ ★

Hair may not be closely related to health, but I can't resist giving you this helpful astrological hint. If your hair is cut short (male or female) and you'd like to keep it that way without so many trips to the barber or beautician, have it cut each time at the apex or the day of the *Full* Moon any month. It will grow noticeably more slowly, and therefore need less frequent cutting. Cappies, Bulls, and Virgos, think of the money you'll save !

If you're a woman who has cut her hair and regretted it, and are impatient to have long tresses again, trim the ends of your hair yourself *ever so slightly,* just a smidgin, at the apex of the *New* Moon, and it will grow visibly much faster. You're going to need that Ephemeris or Farmer's Almanac for lots of reasons ! If one of your local bookstores can't help you, you can order either or both from the Bodhi Tree Bookstore in Los Angeles, California — or the Samuel Weiser bookstore in New York City. All Farmer's Almanacs are the same, but regarding the Ephemeris, you need only the ten-year Ephemeris, not the thousand-year edition. The former is less expensive.

★ ★ ★ ★ ★ ★

Now, here are some very helpful astrological and numerological guides for your general health. First, the astrological guide.

When you read the following, remember that your individually calculated and rectified (the exact hour and minute of your first breath) nativity contains your *complete personal* health picture, all the strong and weak links in your body's chain reactions. These Sun Sign indications are only general. Nevertheless, in approximately eighty percent or more cases, the problem areas will center in the parts of the body ruled by your Sun Sign. Not always, but usually. Just don't believe it's the whole story. For a complete health analysis you'll need a carefully rectified horoscope and a competent person trained in medical astrology to interpret it for you.

Wouldn't it be a blessing if that competent person could be a professional physician who has also studied astrology ? Wouldn't that be simply ideal ? There's small chance of your locating such a medicine man because only a few exist, as rare as the dodo bird, but we can dream, can't we ? And dreams, don't ever forget, are the first step in manifesting wishes into reality.

★ ★ ★ ★ ★ ★

SUN SIGN RULERSHIPS OF THE BODY

♈	*ARIES:*	head, face (except nose), the cerebral hemispheres of the brain
♉	*TAURUS:*	neck, throat, larynx, tonsils, carotid arteries, and jugular vein
♊	*GEMINI:*	shoulders, arms, fingers, lungs, thymus, and upper ribs
♋	*CANCER:*	stomach, diaphragm, breasts and thoracic duct, lymph system
♌	*LEO:*	heart, aorta, the back, and the spinal cord
♍	*VIRGO:*	large and small intestines and the pancreas
♎	*LIBRA:*	kidneys, equilibrium and balance — sometimes skin by association
♏	*SCORPIO:*	nose, genitals, descending colon, rectum, the blood, urethra, sometimes the back, by association
♐	*SAGITTARIUS:*	hips, thighs, liver, veins, femur bone, and sacral region
♑	*CAPRICORN:*	teeth, bones — the kneecaps and the skin
♒	*AQUARIUS:*	lower legs and ankles, varicose veins, and circulatory system
♓	*PISCES:*	the feet and toes, *sometimes* the lungs and intestines by association — and, in reality, the entire body system related to "leaks" and the draining of fluids

What medicine calls "the sympathetic parts of the body" came directly from the astrological computations of Hippocrates. The sympathetic parts of the body mean that when particular symptoms occur in one part of the body, your doctor will look to one of the other three "sympathetic" parts to see where the trouble may have initiated. You can comprehend this easily by studying the drawings of the three astrological "crosses" on page 63.

Notice that two of each of the four signs in each Cross are *opposite* each other (180 degrees apart in the horoscope circle) — and all four signs in each Cross are *square* to each other (90 degrees apart in the horoscopic circle). See the astrological wheel drawn on Page 10. It defines the sympathetic parts of the body.

Now go back to page 61 and study the body rulerships of each Sun Sign. Here are only a few examples of how it works. First, the Cardinal Cross. Look at it again. Then study the parts of the body ruled by these particular four Cardinal Signs.

Aries rules the head, Libra rules the kidneys and bladder. The symptoms of Libra kidney or bladder problems often begin with severe *headaches* (Aries). Cancer rules the stomach. Capricorn rules the skin (among other things). When you take into your stomach food which disagrees with you or to which you're allergic (Cancer) — your *skin* breaks out in a rash (Capricorn). A *toothache* (Capricorn rules the teeth) gives you pain in the head and face (Aries). Aries and Capricorn are *square* to each other, just as Aries and Libra are *opposed* to (opposite) each other.

Now the Fixed Cross. Look at it again. Then study the parts of the body ruled by these particular four Fixed Signs.

Aquarius rules the lower legs. Leo rules the heart (among other things). One of the first symptoms of heart trouble is pain in the lower legs. Leo and Aquarius are *opposed* to (opposite) each other. Taurus

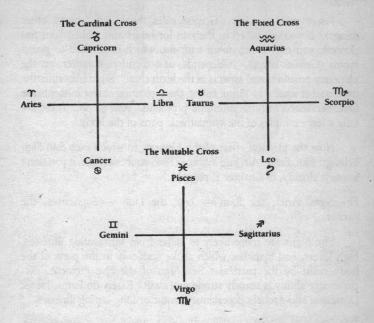

The Cardinal Cross
♑
Capricorn

The Fixed Cross
♒
Aquarius

♈   ♎   ♉   ♏
Aries   Libra   Taurus   Scorpio

The Mutable Cross

Cancer
♋

♓
Pisces

Leo
♌

Ⅱ   ♐
Gemini   Sagittarius

Virgo
♍

rules the throat, neck, and vocal cords. Scorpio rules the sex organs (among other things). When a boy goes through puberty (a Scorpio sexual change), his vocal cords (Taurus) also undergo a change, and his voice deepens. Taurus and Scorpio are *opposed* to (opposite) each other. Leo also rules the spine. One of the first signs of *spinal* meningitis is a sore *throat* (Taurus). Taurus and Leo are *square* to each other. Likewise, Leo and Scorpio are *square* to each other in the Fixed Cross. Scorpio rules the colon (among other things). Leo rules the back and spine. The symptoms of severe colitis or infection of the colon are often felt first as pains in the lower back area.

Now the Mutable Cross. Look at it again. Then study the parts of the body ruled by these particular four Mutable Signs.

Pisces rules the feet. Gemini rules the Lungs (among other things). If you've walked in the rain for hours and soaked your *feet* (Pisces), you may come down with flu, which could lead to pneumonia (Gemini-lungs). It depends, as I mentioned earlier, on the planetary positions and aspects in the birth chart. Sagittarius rules the liver, and is *square* to Virgo, ruling the intestines. Liver ailments are first manifested through intestinal problems. And so on. These are only a few examples of the sympathetic parts of the body.

Now the physical effect of the *Elements* to which each Sun Sign belongs: Fire, Earth, Air, and Water. (Find your Sun Sign, if you don't know it already, in Chapter 1, page 11.)

Fire Signs: Aries, the Ram — Leo, the Lion — Sagittarius, the Archer

Fire Signs are more likely to suffer from fulminating illnesses, high fevers, and maladies which strike suddenly in the parts of the body ruled by the particular Sun Sign of the Fire Element. Recuperative ability is usually strong and swift. Rarely do Rams, Lions, Lionesses, and Archers experience chronic or long-lasting illnesses.

Earth Signs: Taurus, the Bull — Virgo, the Virgin — Capricorn, the Goat

Earth Signs are more likely to suffer from deep-rooted physical ailments, taking years to develop, and often becoming chronic for periods of time. Also emotional depression. The recuperative abilities of Bulls, Virgins, and Goats are powerful, but often slow.

Air Signs: Gemini, the Twins — Libra, the Scales — Aquarius, the Water Bearer

Air Signs tend to suffer from mental stress and psychological disturbances, nervous breakdowns, breathing difficulties, and circulatory problems. Recuperative powers are unpredictable.

Water Signs: Cancer, the Crab — Scorpio, the Eagle — Pisces, the Fish

Water Signs are prone to peculiar illnesses, difficult to diagnose and lingering in nature. Also severe melancholia. The recuperative abilities are completely self-controlled, whether or not this is realized on a conscious level.

Remember that your individually calculated and rectified (the exact moment of the first breath) nativity contains your *complete* health analysis, *all* of the strong and weak links in your body's chain reactions. The foregoing Sun Sign and Element indications are only general, although more than seventy-five percent of the time, the most recurrent problem areas and types of illnesses will occur in the parts of the body ruled by the Sun Sign, and be of the nature of the Element of the Sun Sign. Just be sure you realize that it's not the whole story. Meanwhile, *combining* these Sun Sign and Element indications with the numerological health analysis of the single number of your day of birth in the following interpretations will be most helpful, a surprisingly reliable guide, as you will see.

★★★★★★

The true system of numerology is defined and explained in Chapter 5, and this is only a small preview of the magic of numbers, as they relate to your health only, involving your *day* of birth, rather than Chapter 5's full explanation of the numbers of your date of birth and the numerological revelations of your name.

You are a Number 1 if you were born on the 1st, 10th, 19th, or 28th day of any month.

You are a Number 2 if you were born on the 2nd, 11th, 20th, or 29th day of any month.

You are a Number 3 if you were born on the 3rd, 12th, 21st, or 30th day of any month.

You are a Number 4 if you were born on the 4th, 13th, 22nd, or 31st day of any month.

You are a Number 5 if you were born on the 5th, 14th, or 23rd day of any month.

You are a Number 6 if you were born on the 6th, 15th, or 24th day of any month.

You are a Number 7 if you were born on the 7th, 16th, or 25th day of any month.

You are a Number 8 if you were born on the 8th, 17th, or 26th day of any month.

You are a Number 9 if you were born on the 9th, 18th, or 27th day of any month.

The Number 1

The colors that harmonize with the Number 1 vibration are: all shades of sunny or golden yellow, bright orange, and royal purple.

Number 1 people will notice a subtle beneficial change in their general well-being and can increase their positive essence by wearing topaz or amber next to the skin.

The 1 vibration brings a tendency to suffer from heart problems in some form, such as palpitation and irregular circulation — lower back pain, accidents to the spine, sometimes high blood pressure and astigmatism, and should have their eyes tested frequently. Their physical weaknesses will be intensified by negative emotions — and diluted or even negated by positive emotions, forgiveness, and a cheerful attitude. Sometimes sexual disorders may surface, such as frigidity in women and impotency in men. But these problems are temporary and can be reversed by the right mental control. 1 people can bring on illness through their exaggerated sense of pride and ego.

When they learn to become more tolerant, more flexible, they'll see a marked improvement in the general health.

October, November, and December of *every year* are the months when most ill-health symptoms — mental or physical — sickness or accident — will strike the Number 1 person, brought on by negative emotional attitudes, depression, stress, or overwork. 1 people should practice remaining serene each year as these months approach. After a while, practice makes perfect, and they'll be able to greatly dilute or even negate the tendency toward illness or accident at these times. The practice of serenity should begin at least a month before each month just given.

The foods which should be eaten frequently by a 1 person are: raisins, barley bread, barley, oranges, lemons, and dates. The principal herbs which will go a very long way toward the eventual achievement of permanent good health for a Number 1 person are: saffron, camomile, eye bright, St. John's wort, cloves, nutmeg, sorrel, borage, gentian root, lavender, bay leaves, thyme, musk vervain, and myrrh.

When these herbs are taken in a liquid form by a person born on the 1st, 10th, 19th, or 28th day of any month, any year, they act as Nature's tranquilizer and tonic. A remarkable and swift change will be noticed when three or four teaspoons are taken to relieve anxiety, tension, depression, anger, or other mental or emotional disturbances. The liquid should be taken (one tablespoon) twice a week on a regular basis, and more when necessary under stress.

How can you obtain your herbs in liquid form ? My friends at the Herb Products Company in California, who have been in the homeopathic business for more than a quarter of a century, will make up the herbal liquid for you. They have a list of all the herbs for each number, from 1 through 9, so all you need do is call them and give them your number (in this case Number 1) and they'll blend the magic for you. They'll tell you over the phone the cost (minimal) of the size bottle you want. Then you send a check in that amount, and they'll mail your herbal tonic.

The telephone numbers are (213) 877-3104 or (818) 984-3141. The address is:

> John W. DuVall, Jr.
> Herb Products Co.
> 11012 Magnolia Blvd.
> North Hollywood, California 91601

The Number 2

The colors that harmonize with the Number 2 vibration are: Light green, pale yellow, silver, violet, and lavender.

Number 2 people will observe a subtle beneficial change in their general well-being and can increase their positive essence by wearing emeralds, pearls, or moonstones next to the skin.

The 2 vibration brings a tendency to suffer from stomach problems and digestive disorders. They're susceptible to ptomaine poisoning, and should be careful of the foods they eat and the water they drink in a foreign country. Gastric troubles and internal growths (usually benign) are possibilities. The breasts and chest area are vulnerable to problems. Most complaints of 2 people are lingering and chronic, caused by their refusal to let go of anxiety, and when they learn to do this, recuperation will be much swifter.

January, February, and July of *every year* are the months when most ill health symptoms — mental or physical — sickness or accident — will strike the Number 2 person, brought on by negative emotional attitudes, depression, tension, anxiety, or overwork. 2 people should practice remaining serene each year as these months approach. After a while, practice makes perfect, and they'll be able to greatly dilute or even negate the tendency toward illness or accident at these times. The practice of serenity should begin at least a month before each month just given.

The foods which should be eaten frequently by a 2 person are:

lettuce, cabbages, turnips, cucumber, melon. The principal herbs which will go a very long way toward the eventual achievement of permanent good health for a Number 2 person are: chicory, endive, rapeseed, colewort, moonwort, linseed, water plantain, and ash of willow.

When these herbs are taken in liquid form by a person born on the 2nd, 11th, 20th, or 29th day of any month, any year, they act as Nature's tranquilizer and tonic. A remarkable and swift change is noticed when three or four teaspoons are taken to relieve anxiety, stress, depression, anger, or other mental or emotional disturbances. The liquid should be taken (one tablespoon) twice a week on a regular basis — and more if necessary under tension. The way to obtain the herbal liquid for Number 2 people is explained at the end of the Number 1 analysis.

The Number 3

The colors that harmonize with the Number 3 vibration are: all autumn colors, such as yellow and burnt orange, rust . . . also, turquoise and sky blue. 3 people often share a love of purple with the 1 people.

Number 3 people will notice a subtle beneficial change in their general well-being and can increase their positive essence by wearing turquoise next to the skin.

The 3 vibration brings a tendency to suffer from overstrain of the nervous system, usually brought on by overwork and lack of sleep. They're inclined to have severe attacks of sciatica and neuritis, various forms of skin troubles — and are vulnerable to accidents to the hips. There may be complaints concerned with the liver and aches in the thigh or hip area.

December, February, June, and September of *every year* are the months when most ill health symptoms — mental or physical — sickness or accident — will strike the Number 3 person, brought on by negative emotional attitudes, depression, stress, or overwork. 3 people should practice remaining serene each year as these months approach. After a while, practice makes perfect, and they'll be able to greatly dilute or even negate the tendency toward illness or accident at these times. The practice of serenity should begin at least a month before each month just given.

The foods which should be eaten frequently by a 3 person are: beets, bilberries, asparagus, cherries, barberries, strawberries, apples, mulberries, peaches, olives, rhubarb, gooseberries, pomegranates, endive, pineapples, grapes, almonds, figs, hazelnuts, and wheat and all-wheat products. The herbs which will go a very long way toward the achievement of permanent good health for a Number 3 person are: borage, dandelion, ewerwort, lungwort, sage, mint, saffron, nutmeg, cloves, sweet Marjoram, and St. John's wort.

When these herbs are taken in liquid form by a person born on the 3rd, 12th, 21st, or 30th of any month, any year, they act as Nature's tranquilizer and tonic. A remarkable and swift change is noticed when three or four teaspoons are taken to relieve anxiety, tension, depression, anger, or other mental or emotional disturbances. The liquid should be taken (one tablespoon) twice a week on a regular basis and more if necessary under stress. The way to obtain the herbal liquid for Number 3 people is given at the end of the Number 1 analysis.

The Number 4

The colors that harmonize with the 4 vibration are: electric blue and cobalt blue — silver-gray and ocean green.

Number 4 people will notice a subtle beneficial change in their general well-being and can increase their positive essence by wearing sapphire, quartz, or a stone containing a blend of azurite and malachite next to the skin.

The 4 vibration brings a tendency to suffer from mysterious ailments difficult to diagnose, mental disorders, melancholy, anemia, poor circulation, pains in the head and back, accidents from electricity or lightning, and injuries to the lower legs. 4 people can derive great benefits from electrical treatment of all kinds, hypnosis, and mental suggestion. They are strongly warned to avoid taking or being given drugs — and although everyone would be healthier being a vegetarian, Number 4 people in particular will become chronically ill unless they avoid highly seasoned foods and all forms of red meat. Their physical weaknesses will be intensified by negative emotions — and diluted or even negated by positive emotions, a calm spirit, and patience. There is a possibility of problems with the reproductive organs, occasional impotence in men and frigidity in women, but the latter can be banished with mental concentration and the realization that the complaint is psychological, not physical.

January, February, July, August, and September of *every year* are the months when most ill health symptoms — mental or physical — sickness or accident — will strike the Number 4 person, brought on by negative emotional attitudes, depression, stress, or overwork. 4 People should practice remaining serene each year as these months approach. After a while, practice makes perfect, and they'll be able to greatly dilute or even negate the tendency toward illness or accident at these times. The practice of serenity should begin at least a month before each month just given.

The foods which should be eaten frequently by a 4 person is spinach. The principal herbs which will go a very long way toward the eventual achievement of permanent good health for a 4 person are: sage, pilewort, wintergreen, medlars, Iceland-moss, and Solomon's Seal.

When these herbs are taken in liquid form by a person born on the 4th, 13th, 22nd, or 31st day of any month, any year, they act as Nature's tranquilizer and tonic. A remarkable and swift change is noticed when three or four teaspoons are taken to relieve anxiety, stress, depression, anger, or other mental or emotional disturbances.

The liquid should be taken (one tablespoon) twice a week on a regular basis — and more if necessary under tension. The way to obtain the herbal liquid is explained at the end of the Number 1 analysis.

The Number 5

Just as 5 people can usually harmonize with people born under all kinds of numbers, they can normally wear all colors, but those which harmonize best with the 5 aura are: pearl gray, light green, and silver. *They should not wear dark colors*, even when they are given as the colors of their Sun Signs.

Number 5 people will notice a subtle beneficial change in their general well-being and can increase their positive essence by wearing aquamarine gems, platinum, or silver next to the skin.

The 5 vibration brings a tendency to attempt too much mentally; to deplete the energies, which can lead to nervous breakdowns. 5 people live too much on their nerves, and may suffer from insomnia, twitching in the face or eyes, and "phantom pains" in the shoulders, arms, and hands. Even under minor mental tension they can become irritable and nervous. They're advised to practice grace under pressure, to try to remain calm and patient when events around them are stressful. Sleep and rest and quiet surroundings will have a noticeable healing effect.

June, September, and December of *every year* are the months when most ill health symptoms — mental or physical — sickness or accident — will strike the number 5 person, brought on by negative emotional attitudes, depression, stress, or overwork. 5 people should practice remaining serene each year as these months approach. After a while, in this way they'll be able to greatly dilute or even negate the tendency toward illness or accident at these times. The practice of serenity should begin at least a month before each month given.

The foods which should be eaten frequently by a 5 person are: carrots, parsnips, sea kale, oatmeal, oatmeal breads, parsley, and nuts of all kinds, especially hazelnuts and walnuts. The principal herbs which will go a very long way toward the eventual achievement of permanent good health for a Number 5 person are: sweet marjoram, champignons, caraway seeds, and thyme.

When these herbs are taken in liquid form by a person born on the 5th, 14th, or 23rd day of any month, any year, they act as Nature's tranquilizer and tonic. A remarkable and swift change is noticed when three or four teaspoons are taken to relieve anxiety, stress, depression, anger, or other mental or emotional disturbances. The liquid should be taken (one tablespoon) twice a week on a regular basis — and more if necessary under tension. The way to obtain the herbal liquid for Number 5 people is explained at the end of the Number 1 analysis.

The Number 6

The colors that harmonize with the Number 6 vibration are: the pastel shades of every color, especially pink and blue — sometimes earth tones, such as chocolate brown and deep green, but these are secondary to the pastels.

Number 6 people will observe a subtle beneficial change in their general well-being and can increase their positive essence by wearing opals next to the skin . . . and sometimes, copper.

The 6 vibration brings a tendency to suffer from infections of the throat, nose, and upper part of the lungs — also the chest and breast area. Women influenced by the 6 are prone to breast problems and sometimes "milk fever" in childbirth. There are often mild heart complaints, which lead to irregular circulation of the blood. The bladder and kidneys are vulnerable, and 6 people should avoid foods with sugar. As a general rule, 6 people have a strong, robust constitution when they either live in the country — or visit frequently a place where they can have plenty of fresh air and exercise. If they live in the city, they should make a serious effort to spend frequent weekends and vacations in the country.

May, October, and November of *every year* are the months when most ill health symptoms — mental or physical — sickness or accident — will strike the Number 6 person, brought on by negative emotional attitudes, depression, tension, anxiety, or overwork. 6 people should practice remaining serene each year as these months approach. After a while, practice makes perfect, and they'll be able to greatly dilute or even negate the tendency toward illness or accident at these times. The practice of serenity should begin at least a month before each month just given.

The foods which should be eaten frequently by a 6 person are: all kinds of beans, parsnips, spinach, melons, apples, peaches, apricots, figs, walnuts and almonds — especially almonds. The principal herbs which will go a very long way toward the eventual achievement of permanent good health for a Number 6 person are: mint, marrows, motherwort, pomegranates, juice of maidenhair, fern, daffodils, wild thyme, musk, violets, vervain, and rose leaves. Isn't that a lovely combination ? Lucky 6 people !

When these herbs are taken in liquid form by a person born on the 6th, 15th, or 24th day of any month, any year, they act as Nature's tranquilizer and tonic. A remarkable and swift change is noticed when three or four teaspoons are taken to relieve anxiety, stress, depression, anger, or other mental or emotional disturbances. The liquid should be taken (one tablespoon) twice a week on a regular basis — and more if necessary under stress or tension. The way to obtain the herbal liquid for Number 6 people is explained at the end of the Number 1 analysis.

The Number 7

The colors that harmonize with the Number 7 vibration are: sea green, light yellow, aqua, pink, and white. 7 people should avoid wearing black *or dark colors*, even when these are indicated by the Sun Sign.

Number 7 people will observe a subtle beneficial change in their general well-being and can increase their positive essence by wearing an amethyst or emerald next to the skin. Water lilies and lotus blossoms will curiously lift their spirits when the heart is sad, lonely, or longing.

The Number 7 brings a tendency to suffer from anxiety. These people are more easily affected by worry, annoyance, and frustration than others. As long as their personal and business affairs are running smoothly, they're capable of producing amazing amounts of work, at home or in the office. But when they become worried by circumstances around them or the behavior of other people, they're inclined to imagine that things are worse than they are, and fall into melancholy, which results in extreme physical fatigue. Unusually susceptible to their surroundings, they soak up negative situations and attitudes like a sponge.

When they feel they're genuinely needed — and appreciated, 7 people will cheerfully take on any responsibility, and are unusually conscientious in carrying out their work. It's difficult for them to realize that they're not as strong physically as they are mentally; often the body is frail, and the 7 person attempts too much for his or her own strength, a major cause of all their health problems. They're inclined to have extremely delicate skin, sensitive to the sun and friction, perhaps some peculiarity regarding perspiration — and eating things that disagree with the digestive system frequently results in boils, pimples, and rashes.

January, February, July, and August of *every year* are the months when most ill health symptoms — mental or physical — sickness or accident — will strike the Number 7 person, brought on by negative emotional attitudes, depression, tension, anxiety, or overwork. 7 people should practice remaining serene each year as these months approach. After a while, practice makes perfect, and they'll be able to greatly dilute or even negate the tendency toward illness or accident at these times. The practice of serenity should begin at least a month before each month given.

The foods which should be eaten frequently by a 7 person are:

lettuce, cabbage, endive, cucumbers, mushrooms, apples, cranberries, and the juices of all fruits. The principal herbs which will go a very long way toward the eventual achievement of permanent good health for a 7 person are: chicory, colewort, linseed, ceps, and sorrel.

When these herbs are taken in liquid form by a person born on the 7th, 16th, or 25th day of any month, in any year, they act as Nature's tranquilizer and tonic. A remarkable and swift change is noticed when three or four teaspoons are taken to relieve anxiety, stress, depression, anger, or other mental or emotional disturbances. The liquid should be taken (one tablespoon) twice a week on a regular basis — and more if necessary under tension and stress. The way to obtain the herbal liquid for Number 7 people is explained at the end of the number 1 analysis.

The Number 8

The colors that harmonize with the Number 8 vibration are: indigo, all shades of brown, dark green, and navy blue.

Number 8 people will observe a subtle and beneficial change in their general well-being and can increase their positive essence by wearing a diamond or onyx next to the skin.

8 people are more liable than others to suffer from troubles with the liver, bile, intestines, and excretory part of the system. They have a tendency to develop migraine headaches, diseases of the blood, rheumatism and autopoisoning. They are advised to avoid meat of all kinds, since they are especially allergic to animal food.

January, February, July, and December of *every year* are the months when most ill health symptoms — mental or physical — sickness or accident — will strike the Number 8 person, brought on by negative emotional attitudes, depression, tension, anxiety, or overwork. (Spells of deep depression are more common with 8 people than with those influenced by any other number.) 8 people should practice remaining serene each year as these months approach. After a while, practice makes perfect, and they'll be able to greatly dilute or even negate the tendency toward illness or accident at these times.

The foods which should be eaten frequently by an 8 person are: spinach, carrots and wild carrots, broccoli, and celery. The principal herbs which will go a very long way toward the eventual achievement of permanent good health for a Number 8 person are: wintergreen, angelica, sage, plantain, pileworth, ragwort, shepherd's purse, Solomon's seal, vervain, elder flowers, gravel root, and mandrake root.

When these herbs are taken in liquid form by a person born on the 8th, 17th, or 26th day of any month, any year, they act as Nature's tranquilizer and tonic. A remarkable and swift change is noticed when three or four teaspoons are taken to relieve anxiety, stress, depression, anger, or other mental or emotional disturbances. The liquid should be taken (one tablespoon) twice a week on a regular basis — and more if necessary under tension or stress. The way to obtain the herbal liquid for Number 8 people is explained at the end of the Number 1 analysis.

The Number 9

The colors that harmonize with the Number 9 vibration are: crimson or ruby red (with no orange tones), true blue, and pure white.

Number 9 people will observe a subtle beneficial change in their general well-being, and can increase their positive essence by wearing a ruby next to the skin.

The 9 vibration brings a strong tendency to suffer from headaches, extremely high fevers, illnesses that strike suddenly, are fulminating, and usually disappear as quickly as they appeared. It's very rare for a 9 person to develop an illness that lingers or is chronic, and should this occur, it's most important to have such sickness correctly diagnosed, since it's opposed to the very nature of the 9 essence. The recuperative powers are vital and swift. 9 people seldom avoid chicken pox, smallpox, scarlet fever, or scarletina and such. 9

people should be careful not to take chances during sports or other such activities, since they're prone to accidents to the head, cuts, and burns. There may be more than the average tooth problems and frequent trips to the dentist (which they hate). 9 people are especially warned to avoid rich foods, alcoholic drinks, and wines of all kinds.

February, April, May, October, and November of *every year* are the months when most ill health symptoms — mental or physical — sickness or accident — will strike the Number 9 person, brought on by negative emotional attitudes, depression, tension, anxiety, or overwork. 9 people should practice remaining serene each year as these months approach. After a while, practice makes perfect, and they'll be able to greatly dilute or even negate the tendency toward illness or accident at these times.

The foods which should be eaten frequently by a 9 person are: onions, garlic, rhubarb, horseradish and tomatoes (unless there's an allergy to these initiating from some planetary aspect in the horoscope). The principal herbs which will go a very long way toward the eventual achievement of permanent good health for a Number 9 person are: mustard seed, wormwood, betony, spearwort, white hellebore, ginger, pepper, broom, rape, madder, hops, danewort, and juice of nettles.

When these herbs are taken in liquid form by a person born on the 9th, 18th, or 27th day of any month, any year, they act as Nature's tranquilizer and tonic. A remarkable and swift change is noticed when three or four teaspoons are taken to relieve anxiety, stress, depression, anger, or other mental and emotional disturbances. One tablespoon of the liquid should be taken twice a week on a regular basis, and more if necessary under tension or stress. The way to obtain the herbal liquid for Number 9 people is explained at the end of the Number 1 analysis.

★★★★★★

You'll notice that particular colors and gems were given at the beginning of each Single Number in the foregoing health analysis. The colors constitute a portion of your aura when it's harmoniously balanced, as related to the *day* you were born.

Another portion of your aura when it's harmoniously balanced is composed of the colors of your Sun Sign — another portion is composed of the colors of the Ascendent or Rising Sign of your Nativity or Birth Chart (Horoscope). Completing your personal rainbow (your aura) are the colors representing all of your planetary positions at birth: the astrological signs in which the planets and Luminaries (Sun and Moon) were located when you drew your first breath.

However, the *predominating* auric colors having an effect upon your tranquility and well-being are those colors representing the *day* you were born — your Sun Sign — and the Ascendent or Rising Sign of your Horoscope. Here are the colors — and gems — of each of the 12 Sun Signs. Study them, and then we'll discuss how to use them.

ARIES:	(Mars)	9	ruby or crimson red, true blue, and white
TAURUS:	(Venus) Pan-Horus	6	rose pink, all shades of blue, brown, and deep-green
GEMINI:	(Mercury)	5	pearl gray, light green, and silver
CANCER:	(Moon)	2	light green, pale yellow, silver, violet, and lavender
LEO:	(Sun)	1	sunny yellow, orange, sometimes purple
VIRGO:	(Mercury) Vulcan	5	pearl gray and silver (as in Gemini 5) — but also forest green and white

LIBRA:	(Venus)	6	rose pink (as in Taurus 6) — but also pastel shades of every color, especially light blue
SCORPIO:	(Pluto)	0	black, blood red, burgundy, wine, and maroon
SAGITTARIUS:	(Jupiter)	3	autumn colors, such as yellow, bright orange and rust — also turquoise. Sagittarius sometimes shares the love of purple with Leo
CAPRICORN:	(Saturn)	8	indigo, navy blue, all shades of brown, and dark green
AQUARIUS:	(Uranus)	4	electric blue and cobalt blue, silver gray, and ocean green
PISCES:	(Neptune)	7	emerald green, light yellow, pink, and white

★★★★★★

ARIES:	ruby	*SCORPIO:*	bloodstone
TAURUS:	sapphire	*SAGITTARIUS:*	turquoise
GEMINI:	aquamarine	*CAPRICORN:*	diamond (and onyx)
CANCER:	moonstone and pearls		
LEO:	topaz	*AQUARIUS:*	mixed azurite/ malachite
VIRGO:	green or white jade		
LIBRA:	opal	*PISCES:*	emerald and amethyst

A later chapter, *Forgotten Rainbows,* will define your aura in more detail. Here we're concerned only with the colors and gems you can use to benefit your health and general well-being because of their influence over your emotions.

How to Use Your Personal Colors and Gems

For the moment, ignore the *numbers* just given for each of the 12 Sun Signs.

Now read again the first two paragraphs of your individual Single Number health analysis, which tell you how to use the colors and gems that vibrate to the *day* of your birth.

Memorize the *colors* and *gems* of the astrological sign which is your individual Sun Sign. (See Page 11 for the Sun Signs periods of birth if you don't know your own Sun Sign.)

If you know the Ascendent or Rising Sign of your Nativity or Horoscope, memorize also the colors and gems of that particular astrological sign — but make sure that your birth chart has been correctly rectified, so you can be certain of it. If you're not sure, it's safer to forget your Ascendent and use *only* the colors and gems of your *day* of birth (given under each Single Number health analysis) — and the colors and gems of your *Sun Sign.*

The combination or blending of the colors and gems of your day of birth — your Sun Sign — and your Ascendent Sign (only if you're absolutely sure of it) — will be surprisingly helpful in helping you to achieve the emotional tranquility necessary as a foundation for good health.

Some Examples

If you're a Leo, born on August 13th, the single number 4 is your birth number. (See page 66.) Use the colors and gems given in the Single Number 4 health analysis — and combine them with the colors and gems given for the astrological sign of Leo, which is your *Sun Sign* (see pages 79, 80) — then add the colors and gems of the astrological sign of your Horoscope's Ascendent, assuming you are certain of it. (*If not*, as I said, *disregard it*.) Wear the gems next to your skin and use the colors in your clothing and in your surroundings as much as possible.

If you're an Aries, born on March 27th, the single number 9 is your birth number (the day of your birth). Use the colors and gems given in the Single Number 9 health analysis — and combine them with the colors and gems that vibrate to the astrological sign of your Horoscope's Ascendent, assuming you are certain of it. (If not, disregard it.) Notice that the number of your *Sun Sign* is 9, the same as the single number 9 of the day of your birth (March 27th: 2 plus 7 = 9). Therefore, you're under a *double* 9 influence, and everything stated in the Single Number 9 health analysis relating to your day of birth is intensified.

IMPORTANT

Remember that you must not use the *number* of your *Sun Sign* to read any particular Single Number health analysis, as it *will not apply — unless it happens to be the same as the single number of your day of birth*. The *numbers* for each Sun Sign are given *only* to guide you should you happen to have the *double influence* of a single number, such as the Aries example in the foregoing paragraph.

Some Additional Examples

If you're a Taurus Sun Sign, born on May 7th, 16th or April 25th, the single number of the *day* of your birth is 7. The number of the Sun Sign of Taurus is given as 6. *Do not read the Single Number 6 health analysis* given in this chapter — because *it will not apply to you*. If you're a Taurus Sun Sign, born on any of the above days equaling the single number 7, read *only* the Single Number 7 health analysis — but combine the *colors* and *gems* given in the Single Number 7 health analysis with those given for the Taurus *Sun Sign* — and those given for the astrological sign of your Horoscope's Ascendent, if you are certain of it. Otherwise, disregard the Ascendent and use only the colors and gems of the single number of your birth *day,* combined with the colors and gems of your *Sun Sign.* Wear the gems next to your skin, and use the colors in your clothing and in your surroundings as much as possible.

A Reminder

In all cases, study the *type* of illness related to your Element (Fire, Air, Earth or Water) — the parts of the body ruled by your Sun Sign — then study the Single Number health analysis for the *day* of your birth — and finally, the colors and gems given for your *day* of birth, your Sun Sign and your Ascendent (if you know what it is) and combine these.

★★★★★★

Before leaving the subject of your health, let's consider the disease or the physical, mental, and emotional disharmony called cancer.

In 1984, a Los Angeles hospital tried an experiment with a dozen or so children doomed to die from "terminal illness," mostly cancer. None were over the age of twelve, I've been told, and this is important, as we'll see shortly. The dying youngsters were told to close their eyes tightly, then imagine (image or visualize) a brilliant white light. One of the children, a small boy, was photographed for a television news show while he was imaging. "I see it, I see it, I see it !" he cried ecstatically as his eyes were squeezed shut. It moved me — and I'm sure other viewers also — to tears.

The boy recovered. Nearly all of the children involved in the white light experiment displayed spontaneous remission of their allegedly "terminal" illnesses.

The important ingredient in this particular group of miracles was the chronological age of the patients. None over twelve. The pineal gland is the Third Eye of mystical teaching. It's been medically discovered that in children under the age of twelve, the pineal gland is soft and malleable, like clay. In humans past the age of twelve (adults) the pineal gland is as hard as a rock, proving what young people secretly believe, that most adults "have rocks in their heads." The pineal gland is the seat of spiritual wisdom. Children have imaginary playmates, who are actually very real — they see and talk with small fairies and nature spirits — they tell their parents that "Uncle Charlie (dead for several years) sat on my bed last night and told me stories." They do these things until they are so repeatedly chastized by adults: "You simply must stop *lying*. Uncle Charlie could not possibly have visited you. He's dead — and there are no such things as druids and faeries and imaginary playmates. Your friend 'Peggy' does not exist, so you must stop talking to her aloud as you do. People will think you are crazy" — that their Third Eyes become hard and impotent, blind to real truth. Sometimes spankings accompany the scoldings.

I always wondered, once I decided to dive into the deep waters of astrology (and later explore the caverns and caves of numerology), after I'd started to meditate on the astrological symbols of the twelve signs, from Aries through Pisces, why people couldn't imitate the marine crab, which is the symbol of the sign Cancer, the Crab. When the marine crab loses a claw in some manner, it will swiftly grow a new one. Why not humans ? Are lizards and crabs more evolved than we ? A lizard can grow a new tail if the original one is cut off or lost in some manner.

So now we know that a human body can lose a finger and grow a new finger. Do you believe, then, that one could also grow a new arm or leg after having lost either ? Or perhaps even a new kidney ? If your answer is "yes," congratulations ! You're already an honorary "druid" (Nature Spirit), and well on your way to the enchanted world of enlightenment. If your answer is "no," I have a second question for you.

Why *not?*

★★★★★

One "terminal" two-year-old boy with cancer kept drawing butterflies with a black crayon in St. Raphael's Hospital. A clear picture, his doctor, Bernie Siegal, tried to tell the boy's parents, of the despair all around him (from concerned and negative-thinking parents and relatives). The butterflies were the small child's attempt to believe in tomorrow; the black crayons he always chose revealed that the fearful thoughts of others were overpowering what could have been the kind of miracle so easily manifested by the faith, innocence, and profound wisdom of childhood, a situation which should also be familiar to the readers of this chapter by now. The sad part of it is that the boy's relatives, like most relatives of allegedly "terminally ill" children, are not aware that their genuine concern and nondeliberate negativism is so damaging to the natural healing process.

In Dr. Siegal's book, *Love, Medicine and Miracles,* published in 1986 by Harper and Row, he tells of his attempt to teach patients how to master meditation and imagery, how to picture their bodies successfully fighting cancer. One of his true stories is about a small boy with a brain tumor. Several of his doctors had given up, and had stopped treating him; his family was waiting for him to die. But this boy opened his Third Eye, as adults seldom do. He began to regularly image his cancer cells being bombarded by video-game rocket ships. In a short time, the brain tumor and the cancer disappeared.

Now Dr. Siegal is one of my medical heroes, along with my own Dr. John Perry, of Hollywood, California.

Dr. Perry doesn't realize how wonderfully he practices the holistic healing methods. It just comes naturally to him. As he's said to me often, "I always treat my patients as complete individuals. *They* are the priority, not the disease or infection they have — because the very same disease or infection will act in a totally different way with each person." When his patients have a good day, he invariably exclaims with genuine pleasure, "Isn't that just *wonderful* ! You're in the home stretch now !" I can personally attest to the rare and unique charisma he possesses in somehow making each patient feel that whatever *might* be the problem, it isn't all that serious, and even if it is, it is most certainly curable and reversible. It's an attitude (real, not feigned) that makes a whole universe of difference. Dr. Perry expertly and professionally employs all modern methods of diagnosis and treatment, all the benefits medicine has to offer, then mixes these with genuine caring and an optimistic sort of *knowing* that a healing *will* take place, as long as the patient *believes* it will. This is a doctor whose compassion is part of his very nature. In 1968, he became one of the ten founders of the Western Special Olympics for physically handicapped youngsters (covering seven states) which, in 1972, became the California Special Olympics. A large slice of his free time is cheerfully given to this project which has brought such happiness to these children, and has made impressively positive changes in their mental conditions.

He loves to play golf (most doctors do, because golf is one of the most relaxing of pastimes), but he seldom has time to play. He adores traveling, but very rarely has an opportunity to do so. There is always a patient or two who needs him, and he continually cancels his few and far between social engagements to make an urgent house call. (Yes, a house call. Some doctors still make them.) It's easy to see why this intense Scorpio healer is able to almost *will* his patients to recover. To him; all illness, including cancer, is an unnatural condition, his personal enemy — and good health a normal and natural state of being — not the other way around, as many medical people see it. Too many physicians become so hypnotized by being around sickness so much, they subconsciously begin to think of it as normal and expected. It's easy to drift into such an attitude, but Dr. John Perry is in no danger of that ! His powerful drive and energy is highly contagious. No one can avoid "catching it" from him. It infects everyone around him.

★★★★★★

A book that will have a strong influence on your thinking, make the deepest impression on you, and perhaps be responsible for changing your attitude toward cancer, is by Dr. Max Gerson, called *A Cancer Therapy — 50 Cases*. It's still available at most health food stores, or if not, most of them can order it, because it's still in print.

His research was logical, and made sense, emphasizing the metaphysical rule that you can't go wrong in anything you do if you follow the *natural patterns* of Nature.

Dr. Gerson's methods were simple and basic, as was his theory, and when he put them into practice, they proved themselves time and time again.

He was convinced that cancer could not spread, and would quickly reverse itself if the body's immune system could be restored. And the way to do this, he believed (and repeatedly proved), was to eliminate from the cancer patient's diet all liquids and foods except those heavy in *fiber content*: certain cereals, and fresh raw fruits and vegetables, eating these exclusively, along with a substantial intake of several vitamins, chiefly C and E (D-alpha tocopherol E, not mixed tocopherols) for periods ranging from ninety days to six months or so.

Most of his patients were cured within the 90-day period. The "terminal" ones, instead of *eating* fresh raw fruits and vegetables, drank the *juices* of fresh raw fruits and vegetables, took the prescribed amount of vitamins, and ate or drank nothing else. It took somewhat longer for them to restore their bodies' immune system, but the result of reversal of the disease was the same as with the swifter healings. Those in the first group also drank the juices of the fresh fruits and vegetables as well as eating them raw for their *fiber content*. Both groups received lots of sunlight, lots of rest and sleep, lots of fresh pure water — and large doses of confidence and optimism from relatives who believed in Dr. Gerson's treatments. Confidence is highly contagious, and was also a major factor in the visible and rapid improvement in the condition of the patients under Dr. Gerson's care.

Although the medical profession at the time shrugged its collective shoulders regarding Dr. Gerson's discoveries, today, finally, these same physicians are recommending the eating of high fiber-content foods for the "prevention" of cancer.

Max Gerson was no "health fad nut," which some of his enemies called him behind his back (and some still do). Rather, he was a professional, careful, and accredited physician, who permanently cured Dr. Albert Schweitzer's wife of tuberculosis after several other doctors had failed to do so. Dr. Gerson possessed the vision and inspired determination of a pioneer in any field, as did vitamin C's proponent, Dr. Linus Pauling, and one of vitamin E's proponents, Dr. Shute of Canada.

★★★★★★

Everything I have said about cancer applies to aids. (I refuse to give it capital letters.) Aids need not kill through paralyzing the body's immune system. Now that *does* deserve capital letters. Aids NEED NOT KILL.

★★★★★★

When I began to write this chapter, I happened to see a television special about aids.

Near the close of the program, a man who was diagnosed as suffering from "advanced aids" was interviewed. His doctors told him on camera it was a certainty that he would be dead within a year. He didn't believe them. He truly did not. You could see it in his eyes as he stated firmly that he expected to heal himself — and live. I don't know if he was gay or heterosexual or bisexual, and I don't care. I wept for him. Not tears of sorrow and compassion. Tears of joy ! And I couldn't resist saying aloud to his bright, brave, and confident face on the television screen, "Right on ! And . . . expect a miracle !"

★★★★★★

3

GURUS, GHOSTS,
AND
AVATARS

the Rocky Mountain "highs" of magnetic power points
and astral vibratory frequencies,
including clairaudience and clairvoyance
at ten thousand feet above sea level

was it a mystical chill I felt that night ?
it was odd to shake so uncontrollably in a public dining place
to feel such an icy shiver
when I was sitting within three feet
                              of a roaring fireplace

  I saw him look at you
and you . . . look back at him

and . . . what did he say then . . . that strange man ?

  "when an astral entity," he said, "from any level of awareness
  whether it be the astral of one who has died
  a space traveler . . . or merely the astral of someone
                                        somewhere, asleep
  when such an entity, out of body
          in whatever form, from whatever dimension
  approaches . . . comes near one's vicinity
  that entity is vibrating at such a higher rate
          of angstrom units per second
  than the vibratory frequency of most humans
          that it causes a marked drop in temperature
  as the air currents are suddenly cooled . . .
          and the change is so sharp and unexpected
  that one might . . . shall we say . . . feel a draft ?"

everyone laughed

            then you whispered
                  "Darling, did you see a ghost ?"
            and offered me your sweater

                    ★ ★ ★ ★ ★ ★

F YOU'VE read my Preface to this book, which I assume you have, you know that the star sign codes I'll be writing about were revealed to me in the Rocky Mountains, where the Guru told me I would be going on a sort of retreat, to be instructed. As I also mentioned in my Introduction, I kept a diary while I was there, planning to later use my notes to write a book about my experiences. Since *Star Signs* is, therefore, based on my diary notes, it seems appropriate to share with you the haunted setting of the place where I was told, "when the student is ready, the teacher will appear."

Actually, more than one "teacher" appeared during my mountain retreat in Cripple Creek, Colorado, which I later decided to make my permanent residence. I experienced several arcane meetings there, some of which will form the basis for future books. Legend claims that those who possess a knowledge of the deeper mysteries of the macrocosm of Heaven and the microcosm of Nature often nestle themselves in the quiet forests of the Earth's highest altitudes, and as I've mentioned, Cripple Creek is 10,000 feet above sea level. I'd like to tell you what these Avatars or Gurus taught me about magnetic power points and ghosts which, I must confess, I never believed in until my arrival in this former gold-mining town in the Rockies.

A magnetic power point is a place where intense emotions have repeatedly occurred, making the surrounding area sensitive to all manner of vibrations. You can, as people have often said, "feel it in the air." Stories about haunted houses abound all over the world, usually in places where several murders or other evil events occurred. No one can walk near the concentration camps in Germany without sensing the heavy clouds of depression and tragedy. That's on the negative side. On the positive side, other magnetic power points also exist, like churches centuries of years old, or shrines, where millions of candles have flickered over hundreds of years, and millions of prayers have been spoken, leaving their unmistakable impressions upon the ethers. One feels calm and peaceful and tranquil in these places, just as one feels vaguely disturbed and sad in other places heavily charged with the electromagnetic intense emotions of past events.

Cripple Creek is thus highly charged and fairly quivering with intense vibrations — of a mixed sort. During the gold rush of the late 1880s and 1890s, emotions ran high in this mountain town . . . and dreams multiplied themselves. There were major fires, murders, fervent religious teachings and preachings, houses of prostitution, greed, lust, and all the shimmering fantasies gold has always stirred in human hearts. Definitely a magnetic power point.

Cripple Creek was called the Bowl of Gold by gold-mining king Winfield Scott Stratton. Is it mere coincidence, or a deeper synchronicity of blood tie harmonics that my maternal elf-mother's (grandmother's) maiden name was Stratton — and Stratton is also my father's middle name ?

The area is known as The District, which includes Cripple Creek, the neighboring town of Victor, about five miles or so south . . . and several now deserted but once booming little towns with names like Independence and Goldfield. One of the deserted gold mines between Cripple Creek and Victor is called The Abraham Lincoln. Then there's the still-open-for-tourists gold mine called The Mollie Kathleen, on Tenderfoot Mountain, looking down on the town . . . The Stratton mine, and many others. In Victor is a long-shuttered silent film theatre called the *Isis*.

The District was the scene of the "Pikes-Peak-or-Bust" gold rush at the turn of the century. Stratton claimed that Cripple Creek, situated in a valley, is the center of a "bowl of gold" created by the long ago eruption of a volcano — and that only a fraction of the gold there was taken, even during all the frenzied mining activity of the 1890s. It could all happen again, they say, if the Old-Timers' persistent predictions that the price of gold will rise to an all-time high by the late 1980s or early 1990s, making the mining of it economically feasible once again — is more than just wishful thinking. I have a hunch that it's more.

Miners are unexpectedly psychic. Miners *know* things. They don't understand how they know, they just know. After all, they're the ones who discovered and recognized the elusive Tommyknockers, those wee folk who play mischievous tricks yet who also sometimes miraculously protect the men who labor deep within the bowels of the Earth.

If The District should become, during the approaching 1990s, the stage for an encore of the gold mystique drama, there will be a regrettable difference. The lead players won't be riding out on horseback to stake their claims, followed by their stubborn but patient burros, back-packed with bundles of colorful dreams. They'll be riding to their conglomerate-controlled domains in jeeps and pickup trucks.

Meanwhile, both Cripple Creek and neighboring Victor (where Lowell Thomas was born, raised, and ran the local newspaper, and where Jack Dempsey trained for his fights) are currently inhabited by more ghosts than people — more potbellied stoves than pots of gold at the end of the rainbow. The population of Victor is said to be around two or three hundred, give or take a few restless roamers — and Cripple Creek's population is between seven and nine hundred, depending on whether you believe the census takers or the Old-Timers, who count more accurately, they insist, because they include the lively ghosts overlooked by uninitiated outsiders. I don't overlook the ghosts there. I only wish I *could* overlook them !

It's a considerable drop from New York's ten million or so bodies and souls, if you count the suburbs and the subway car and sidewalk sleepers. Manhattan doesn't have many ghosts. Since ghosts are composed of a finer etheric substance than flesh, they would probably melt away in the polluted air. Los Angeles is different. Hollywood attracts a hardier breed of phantoms, able to breathe the smog and still do a respectable night's work haunting.

Most occult tomes tell you that ghosts, phantoms, and such, belong to the astral world of dreams, and are not at home on the material plane in the third dimensional level. It doesn't seem to matter anymore whether that's true or not, because I'm about to conclude that there's no difference between them — dreams and reality. Or is it just that these two concepts are mirror-reversed, and what people believe is one — is, in actuality, the other ?

When you fall asleep at night, leaving behind the so-called world of "reality" for the world of dreams, have you noticed that — no matter *how hard you try,* as you're drifting off to slumberland, to hold on to the "reality" of the sounds of the television, traffic, or the dog snoring — they fade away into oblivion ?

Conversely, when you awake in the morning, leaving behind the so-called "dream world" for the world of reality, have you likewise noticed that — no matter *how hard you try,* as you're waking up, to hold on to the sights and sounds of the "dream" you just had — they fade away into oblivion in exactly the same manner as the sights and sounds of "reality" fade when you're falling asleep ?

Polarized points of view, interchangeable — indisputably. And so, which is the "dream," and which is the "reality" ? Who is to say ? How do you really know that this very waking moment is not the dream, and last night's dream the true reality ? The ancient wise ones taught that "dreams are the true reality." Aristotle wrote: "Life is an imitation of art . . . and art is an imitation of reality; therefore, life is but an imitation of reality." The reality of dreams. The Tibetan monks in bygone centuries, when they prayed, chanted repeatedly, "This is the world of illusion . . . this is the world of illusion."

I suppose the Bible Fundamentalists, who still image God as a kindly man with a snow-white beard, would view such an interchange as sacrilegious. Speaking of Divinity, one of the first things I noticed when I arrived in Colorado's glorious Rockies was a sign proclaiming the state as "God's Country." It was the hint of exclusivity that bothered me a little, since it insinuates that He isn't concerned with crowded cities anymore, and that's obviously where He's most needed just now.

Maybe She is watching over the cities for Him. I mean my Mother Who art in Heaven, right alongside my Father Who art there. As you can see, I'm not a follower of the patriarch concept. It takes a positive-negative energy force . . . male-female . . . to create anything at all, whether flesh infants or solar systems. Any other concept is a direct denial of the laws of both physics and metaphysics.

When you begin the drive up to Cripple Creek, just before you come to the twisting, serpentine, winding road named Ute Pass after the Ute Indians who once lived in the area, you pass a town called Manitou — Manitou meaning "Great Spirit" or God, which should be spelled properly "Mannitou," according to numerology. (You'll understand why the Great Spirit's name should contain two n's instead of one when you've studied Chapter 5, *Numerology*.)

As you drive by Mannitou (let's don't misspell the Great Spirit's name), on your right is something the Utes dreamed into reality, called the Garden of the Gods. It's a stirring and awesome sight of mute power and grandeur, even from a distance.

The Utes allowed no members of any Indian tribe at war with any other tribe to enter there, and walk along its sacred ground. Only those red men (and women) who were at peace with their brothers (and sisters) were permitted to participate in the mystic rites of esoteric initiation within that haunted, hushed sanctuary of sunrise-dyed, strangely shaped red rock formations . . . as reddish in hue as Scarlett O'Hara's "red clay of Tara." Nowhere else in the vicinity is the earth red colored . . . except for a place a few miles beyond Cripple Creek, called, appropriately, Phantom Canyon. There are several theories among geologists concerning the cause of the red rock and red clay, but no one really knows for certain.

The violent thunderstorms — or electrical storms — occurring frequently in the mountains have never made me gloomy. They exhilarate me, and stir me profoundly. Thunder and lightning seem to evoke some deep and long-buried sense of power in me, as though I could stop it or start it if I chose. As though . . . everyone else could do it, too, if they remembered how to project such power. Like an invisible energy force everyone long ago possessed, then lost. The only thing is, I'm not sure whether I feel good or bad about it — whether it's a positive or a negative memory bell I hear chiming in the back of my mind.

★★★★★★

Until I learned about vibratory frequencies, I could find no rational reason to believe in ghosts, although I was certainly not a complete sceptic, since the entire spectrum of mystical and metaphysical subjects had won me to the side of the "invisible" long before I first went to Colorado. Still, ghosts were . . . well, something else again. I was aware that they were usually seen — or more frequently reported — in "haunted" magnetic power point areas of both high spiritual vibrations (churches, shrines, and so forth) and the lower vibrations of crime and evil (mass murders, satanic rites, and so forth).

And so it was that I didn't even "believe" in the ghosts seen and heard in my own "haunted" house there on Carr Avenue — whether they were seen and heard by myself or others — until one of the Gurus I mentioned explained it to me. Before then, I laughed it off, but uneasily, because I couldn't explain away what kept happening.

First, there was the "party." Nearly every night after I first arrived (and less frequently during later weeks, months, and years) I actually had to stuff cotton in my ears to be able to sleep through the noise. The house was filled with the sounds of a gala party, including the tinkling of glasses, muffled conversation and laughter (loud enough to hear clearly, but too indistinct to make out the words) — and the music of a piano, accompanied by a man and a woman singing a duet at intervals (again, clearly heard, but too indistinct to make out the lyrics).

The first night I slept there it happened. My initial response was that the man from whom I rented the house I later bought had left a radio on somewhere. So I rose from the couch in the den (where I slept the first few nights, being still too apprehensive to sleep in one of the upstairs bedrooms) — and walked into the kitchen, which seemed to be the room from where the party sounds were coming. As soon as I entered the kitchen, the party seemed to be coming from the basement. Gingerly, I opened the basement door, and cautiously peeked down into the darkness. Then the sounds seemed to be coming from the front porch.

Annoyed, I thought that perhaps my neighbors, whom I hadn't yet met, were having a party, and were being quite inconsiderate to allow the noise to be so loud when other people were trying to sleep. So I opened the front door and walked out on the porch. The houses on either side of me were dark and silent, as were all the houses visible across the street. Then the party noise stopped as suddenly as it began, proving it couldn't have come from a radio accidentally left on by the landlord somewhere in the house.

Standing on the porch at that moment, looking up at the midnight blue sky, sparkling with every single star in the heavens (a sight I had never seen through the smog in New York) I heard a new noise. It sounded like a rushing brook or stream, punctuated by a faint but distinct drumbeat. I must confess that for a few seconds I was thoroughly frightened. After a moment's reflection, I realized, with a sudden shock, that I was hearing the sound of my own pulse and heartbeat, the flowing rhythms of my own blood in my veins — in my inner ear. The sounds of silence. Utter silence. Since I had never stood in the night at any time in my life surrounded by total silence, it was a curious and fascinating experience. "Silence is *noisy* until you become accustomed to it !" I thought, as I listened to the roars and pulsing rhythms of my own body. Then . . . the bray of a burro (they call them mountain canaries) split the air for a second. Afterward, silence again.

I must have remained on the front porch for nearly a half hour, pondering "the sounds of silence." Finally, I walked back inside the house, closed the door, climbed back on the couch, pulled the grandma quilt up under my chin, and fell asleep. For a very short time. It couldn't have been more than a few minutes until I was awakened again by the "wild party," the tinkling glasses, conversation, laughter, piano playing, and singing. It rose in pitch louder and louder as I tossed and turned, as unable to sleep as if a television set had been turned on full volume next to the couch. Realizing now that it was no use to search for the source of the party sounds, I turned on my side, covered my exposed ear with a pillow . . . and eventually fell back to sleep.

When I related the incident (which occurred periodically over a period of time . . . and still does on infrequent occasions, fifteen years later), I was told that "everyone who's ever lived in that house has heard the same wild party." Neighbors and others informed me that my house had once, for a couple of years, been used as a sort of annex to The Old Homestead (still standing) — called the "oldest red-light house in the West." It was evident that they all believed the party noises were made by the ghosts (or astrals) of the "ladies of the evening" of long ago, and their male customers. I smiled politely, and although I had no more logical an explanation for what I *knew* I was hearing every few nights, I somehow still couldn't fully accept ghosts as the cause.

Nor was I overly impressed to hear that all the former residents of the house had shared my experience. After all, there was no real proof of this, since none of them were around to attest to the truth of it, so it could have been merely rumors, spread by the gullible.

However, it wasn't long until I began to have guests visit me, from time to time, in my red brick "haunted" house — friends and relatives from out of town. I was always careful never to mention the "Old Homestead Party Ghosts." Yet, nearly all of my guests, with very few exceptions, were wide-eyed at breakfast, following their first night in the house, and could hardly wait to tell me about the "loud party" my neighbors must have been having the night before. Their descriptions matched what I had been hearing to the smallest detail. A couple of them were even able to identify one of the duets (which I'd never been able to do) as "I'll Take You Home Again, Kathleen." All of my guests believed firmly in the "ghost theory," once they'd been told. I was the only holdout, but I was gradually weakening.

I have never, to this day, heard a baby cry in my house. But four separate guests who spent a week or more with me over the years could barely sleep at night because of being awakened every couple of hours by the sound of a baby crying and sobbing loudly, sometimes from the foot of the stairs, occasionally in the old-fashioned bathroom.

As I pondered all this, I remembered what I'd been taught about sound. A sound, spoken or musical or otherwise, once sent into the ethers, never ceases to exist. It just keeps rising on higher frequencies (like the dog whistle humans cannot hear, but dogs can) — until the *average* human ear can no longer detect the sounds. But they are still out there . . . somewhere. A book called *Breakthrough,* published by Richard Taplinger of Taplinger Publishing in New York, now out of print, unfortunately (but possibly available through the used bookstore circuit), details experiments conducted by major universities, using blank tapes and specific, complex methods, to "pull out of the ethers" such long-ago-spoken words. They were successful, as the book reports, in picking up many voices and considerable conversations, mostly in foreign languages, but could not, of course, pinpoint the source or the time the words were originally spoken. The book concludes by quoting these scientists as saying that "we now know that we can record from the ethers the higher frequency sounds, music, and words initiated long ago, but it will likely be many years until we can do this *selectively*." Meaning that it will take much more experimentation to be able to successfully retrieve the spoken words of Abraham Lincoln's Gettysburg Address, even though they are indisputably still vibrating, as clear as ever, somewhere out there in the ethers. Nevertheless, such magic is not only possible, it's probable under the influence of the curious, questing, unpredictable Uranus (ruler of Aquarius).

I feel strongly that such a breakthrough is certain to occur during the Golden Age of Aquarius, but remember that the Aquarian Age will be around for about 2,000 years. Until such a miracle occurs, we'll have to rely on those who possess an unusual degree of what is called "clairaudience" (sensitivity of the inner ear) to pull long-ago sounds from their hiding places. After pondering all this, I was finally convinced of the reality of the sounds and voices. It all made sense. But I attributed them to the "higher frequencies" — not to actual ghosts. I still had much to learn.

The wild party and the crying baby were not the only "ghost hauntings" in my Carr Avenue, slipping-off-the-time-track house. One night, the first year I lived there, I held a party at my house for the cast of the famous melodrama staged every summer at the charming old Imperial Hotel in Cripple Creek. At the height of the party, while the guests were wandering all over the house (it's rather like a museum, slightly musty smelling, filled with antiques of yesteryear) . . . drinking punch and carrying on dozens of separate conversations, as people do at such gatherings, a loud gasp and a stifled scream were heard from the young couple seated on the old fainting couch in the parlor.

Both of them were visibly frightened nearly out of their wits; their eyes were opened wide, and they were staring at the corner of the room beyond the old Ben Franklin wood stove. They sat there stiffly, unmoving, staring hypnotically at the spot, not blinking, for several minutes, while everyone was asking insistently, "What is it ? What's wrong ? What do you see ?" — since none of the rest of us could see anything unusual in the corner.

The girl spoke first. "It's . . . it's a man, with straight black hair and a black mustache, wearing a black, formal frock coat. He . . . looks so sad." Then she spoke louder, clearly agitated, "Can't you see him ? He's standing right there. Just look !" She was trembling, and obviously disturbed.

"Do you see it too, Paul ?" someone asked her husband. He didn't answer, just gulped hard a few times, and nodded his head up and down. Eventually, he found his voice. "The guy is there. He's standing there. Can't any of you see him ?" he asked, agitated, glancing from one person to another. Again, everyone answered that they could see nothing. Then someone suggested that Paul walk over to the corner and touch the man . . . see what he felt like. At this point, his wife stood up abruptly from the couch, grabbed her husband's arm, and said, "Paul, let's get out of here. *Now*. Please take me home." She was so upset that there were tears in her eyes. Her husband nodded, and they both walked out the door, ran down the steps, got into their car and drove off, without even saying "Good-bye" or "Good night" to the rest of the startled guests — or to me.

Ever since that incident — not always, but nearly always — when I or anyone else happens to go to that corner of the parlor, perhaps to take a book from the antique bookcase there, it is icy cold. Even when the rest of the room is toasty warm, and a wood fire is blazing in the old Ben Franklin stove. When I say icy cold, that's not an exaggeration. It's cold enough to cause involuntary shivers, from both the unexpectedly chilly air and the admittedly apprehensive and uneasy feeling of knowing that this is where a "ghost" was seen. For the longest time I didn't understand the coldness in that corner, not until I later learned about "higher vibratory frequencies" causing a change in the air currents and a sudden drop in temperature . . . when an astral entity of any kind is near.

I could explain the phenomenon of the sounds heard through clairaudience, but the *sight* of a human, whether transparent or solid, still troubled and mystified me. I wasn't to comprehend such phenomena until several other "ghost sightings," as well as sounds, came to my attention. Personally, I've never "seen" any*thing* — or any*one*. My only personal experience in Cripple Creek has been the equally trembling one of clairaudience — hearing sounds through the "inner ear" from a higher frequency than the physical human ear can hear. As for other "ghost" hauntings. . . .

There was Maggie. Or rather, there is Maggie, the live-in, mischievous and lovable ghost (or astral) of the Sarsaparilla Ice Cream Parlor on Bennett Avenue. Maggie has gained quite a bit of fame over the years, among the town's residents, reporters from Colorado's major newspapers — and thousands of tourists.

Because ghost sightings are growing more commonplace — nearly everyone has some sort of experience with some type of ghost or astral — and because the explanation for such sightings is part of basic metaphysical laws — also because Maggie has been seen and heard by so many people of unquestionable credibility and integrity, it's important for you to learn about her in some detail. I know the story of Maggie, of course, but I can't always recall the finer points of her eccentric manifestations over the years.

And so, while writing this book, I called Ken and Katherine Hartz, the owners of the building that houses the Sarsaparilla Ice Cream Parlor, and asked them to write down as much about Maggie as they could . . . so I could help my readers comprehend her amazing manifestations. Ken and Kathy obliged, by telling the story on a tape cassette and sending it to me. I think it's best if I simply quote Kathy, in her own words, rather than try to tell the story myself. Afterward we'll see what my Gurus offered by way of explanation.

Please keep in mind that Kathy (a Virgo) is extremely critical of the slightest distortion of the facts, the kind of person called "the soul of honesty," and although she is more sensitive and intuitive than the average person, she is still a Virgo, inclined to subject people and things to her microscopic scrutiny, to suspect and question, not blindly accept. In fact, Katherine Hartz is the very last person anyone would expect might "see ghosts" — or even hear them. She is by nature Practical with a capital "P."

From Katherine (Kathy) Hartz — Cripple Creek, Colorado

As you know, Linda, the old Farley Lampton building we now own in Cripple Creek, on the corner of Bennett Avenue and Third Street, had been vacant for many years when we bought it and turned the huge first floor into the Sarsaparilla Ice Cream Parlor and Gift Shop. It was the first structure built after the big fire in 1895 that burned down nearly the whole town. The land had already been cleared, and the building materials were all piled in sidecars up on Tenderfoot Mountain, so they began building the next morning. Cripple Creekers recover from their tragedies pretty quickly. Instead of sitting around crying and complaining about the fire that destroyed everything, they just began to rebuild the town as fast as they could. That's why all the brick buildings on Bennett Avenue have 1895 carved in them — the year of the fire — and the year of the rebuilding of Cripple Creek.

Of course, our building is also the largest in Teller County. Ken and I could never understand why nobody seemed to want it all those years. But I'm glad they didn't, because otherwise we wouldn't have been able to buy it, and I loved it from the first moment I saw it. It was the most beautiful, beautiful building ! And so steeped in the past. I remember that when you first moved here, and wanted to walk down to the post office, you kept walking straight toward the Sarsaparilla, then came inside, confused, and said, "I don't know why I'm here. I keep thinking it's the post office, but I know it isn't." You must have lived here, Linda, back in the gold rush days, in another incarnation, because the building actually was a post office for several years between 1895 and 1910. Lots of newcomers here make the same mistake, so maybe they lived here before too.

When we bought the building, a woman had a rock shop in it, and she told us there were strange "energies" in the building. She said everyone noticed it. But it didn't frighten me because she said these "energies" were always heard or felt upstairs on the third floor, and since I planned to live on the first floor while we were building the gift shop and the Sarsaparilla Ice Cream Parlor, there seemed no reason to be concerned about "ghosts" on the third floor. Anyway, I found it to be more intriguing than frightening.

Before we moved in, Charlie Frizzell, a well-known local artist, and a group of his friends lived in the building. They told me that one night they all decided to have a sort of seance on the third floor, in the ballroom, and it simply scared them to pieces. They were really frightened — I never did get the details of what happened — but they said none of the girls would stay inside the building after that; they slept in cars parked on the street. Charlie then asked me, "Aren't you afraid to stay here alone when Ken is in Denver, Kathy?" The energies in this building are real. Too many people have experienced them, including myself, for them to be imaginary.

(*Kathy is a very precise Virgo.*) "Of course I'm not frightened," I told Charlie. "No way. Why should I be? Nothing is going to harm me. My Guardian Angel (*she meant her Higher Self*) is with me all the time, and wouldn't allow anything bad to happen to me."

After a few days, Charlie and all his friends moved out, and I was alone, living in the back of the first floor, while Ken was in Denver taking care of our business and our home there, planning to come to Cripple Creek on weekends to help supervise our remodeling. Nothing happened for several days, and I decided that the woman who had the rock shop there had an active imagination, that's all, and Charlie and his friends were just trying to tease me — although he seemed so sincere, and everyone knew him as a serious and earnest young artist.

The last day I was there alone — I was going to join Ken in Denver the next day — I thought I would go up and check the second and third floors, make sure all the windows were closed and everything was as it should be before I left for Denver. So I climbed up to the second floor, and walked down the huge, long hallway.

I checked all the doors and windows, and when I got more than halfway down the hallway, I heard the distinct sound of high-heeled shoes walking directly above me. At first I thought that maybe one of the girls who had been staying in one of the rooms hadn't left yet, and was upstairs on the third floor packing up her clothes. I knew I had to check to make sure before I left and locked the building. So I went to the stairway that leads up to the third floor, and was surprised to see that there were two doors leading up to the third floor, each with glass in them, and Charlie and his friends had wired the first door together with coat hangers. No one could have gone through the first door, then the second door to the third floor and left the first door so tightly wired. The footsteps suddenly became louder, and sounded nearer . . . but still above me, still coming from the third floor.

I suppose my pulse raced a little faster, but I wasn't really frightened, just a little uneasy perhaps — and determined to go up to the third floor ballroom and take a look around. As I was trying to untwist the wire coat hangers to gain entrance, the footsteps stopped abruptly. I glanced up, through the glass in the two doors, and saw a woman standing there, as clear as could be, at the top of the stairs, beyond the second door. This was the first time in my life I'd ever had such an experience as "seeing a ghost," yet I wasn't afraid. I can't explain why. I wasn't disbelieving either. I saw what I saw, as clear as anything — the same as seeing a flesh-and-blood person — yet I knew she was a ghost, not a real person. Don't ask me how I knew. I just knew. (*Kathy herself, as I've learned over the years, vibrates to a very high frequency.*)

She was just beautiful, Linda. Really beautiful ! She appeared to be in her early twenties. Her hair was in Gibson girl–style, and she had large, piercing brown eyes. She was slender, and was wearing a white blouse with tiny tucks in the front and a sort of mandarin collar, open at the neck . . . a brown cotton skirt, embroidered with small rosebuds, that came just above her ankles . . . and she had on high-heeled boots. These were evidently the high heels I had heard walking on the third floor.

I stood there staring at her, and she at me, for a few seconds, and then we shared a . . . well, I guess you would call it a mental telepathy conversation. I could hear her voice, and yet, somehow, I knew I was hearing it with my . . . inner ear . . . is that what you call it ? Well, she said "hello" . . . and a few other words I can't seem to remember, and without thinking about it, I called her Maggie when I spoke to her. It never occurred to me to call her anything else, and over the years she's always answered to Maggie. It's interesting that each person who has had contact with her, either through sight or sound, without any knowledge of my calling her Maggie, has always instinctively thought of her and spoken of her as "Meg" or "Margaret" — all names related to Maggie. So . . . she was Maggie to me immediately.

I told her that she was welcome to stay in the building, that I was happy to have her, but that she would have to observe certain rules.

I said aloud to her, "You may take care of the building and watch over it if you wish, Maggie, and take care of us too — that would be nice — but none of your spooky friends, no bad energies, none of that can ever be here. Otherwise, you will just have to leave." Then I told her that she was more than welcome to stay, and that if she had time, she could even come and visit Ken and me in our home in Denver. That was just about all the conversation — or communication — there was. And as I said, it was more like a mental telepathy thing. When I stopped speaking, after a few seconds, Maggie just sort of faded away . . . gradually, not abruptly. I stood there for a while, thinking about the strangeness of it, then finally went downstairs, fixed myself a cup of coffee . . . and thought about it some more.

The next day I went home to Denver. When Ken and I returned the following spring, everything in the building was just as we left it. No signs of any mischief or destruction or anything. But then . . . after a few weeks, things began to happen to let us know that Maggie was around. Like the fragrance. When she's near, you can actually smell a very soft scent, like a cologne . . . or white roses. Nothing heavy or overpowering . . . just a soft fragrance.

Over the years, Maggie has materialized for a couple of people, but never again for me. One of her manifestations was experienced by a boy who worked for us in the ice cream parlor, and lived in the building, as many of our young people do in the summer.

One night, we had a big party in the ballroom, with a band. Everyone was dressed in long, old-fashioned ball gowns, and we danced until quite late, because we were all enjoying ourselves so much. Early the next morning, this kid went in to one of the upstairs bathrooms to brush his teeth and wash his face before he came downstairs to the ice cream parlor to begin work. While he was scrubbing his face, he sensed that someone was standing behind him. He thought it was one of the other kids who worked and lived there, so he turned, expecting to see one of the boys, and instead, he saw Maggie. She was just kind of leaning over, trying to see what he was doing. It frightened him so badly he didn't even stay for breakfast. He left that morning, after telling us the story nervously, and never returned. He seemed to be dreadfully upset by the experience. He told us that Maggie's hair was done up in the same style I had seen her wearing, but her clothes were different. She was wearing, he said, a long dress made of cream-colored satin, with lace trimming . . . as though (we thought) she had attended our party in the ballroom the night before.

Maggie is a benevolent ghost. You know, Linda, that she's never really tried to frighten anyone — and you know that our building has the most wonderful feeling about it. No one has ever felt any danger or been unable to sleep or anything like that. There's always a very warm, soft feeling when Maggie's around. It's as if she's part of the family now. She loves us, and we love her. Lots of people have come here and wanted to see her so they could take her picture. Some reporters from the major papers have even brought their cameras and slept up in the ballroom all night, hoping to see her and take a photo of her for the papers. But no one has ever been able to take a photograph of her. Maybe someday . . . but not so far.

Someone asked us once if we wanted to get rid of Maggie, and said they could bring a person who could exorcize her. I told them,

"Don't be silly. This is her home. Why would we want to get rid of her? She's lovely and very nice. She can stay here as long as she wants to stay." We've already told Maggie that if she wants to go on to whatever dimension she may belong in, it's fine with us. We've even told her how to look up into the sky, and see the light — and that, if she wishes it, there will be someone to take her hand and lead her to where she can be with others like herself, maybe even people she knew. But she doesn't seem to want to do that. She seems contented to stay right where she is.

Sometimes we think she has gone, after several months go by with no one sensing any sign of her, you know? Then, when we're least expecting it, there will be a cool breeze and the white roses fragrance again . . . softly . . . or some other indication that she's still in the building.

There was the time when we hired a new girl, who was going to live in the building with us for the summer, while she worked in the Sarsaparilla. The room she chose was on the second floor, near the stairway up to the third floor (or ballroom). While the girl was hanging her clothes in the closet, she heard a voice say, very clearly, "Oh, how nice! You're going to stay with us! Welcome!" To say she was startled or surprised would be stating it mildly.

The girl came downstairs, and said to the other waitresses, "I don't think that's funny at all, what you did. You all know I'm afraid of Maggie, and I just don't think tricks like that are amusing."

And the girls all told her that they had not done such a thing. They had all been working, and they were a little annoyed that she would think they were lying. They told her again, "We didn't say a word. It was not us," and the girl finally said, "Well, all right, but I don't really believe in Maggie. I think the whole thing is silly, but it still scares me."

A day or so later, this girl was making coffee in the Sarsaparilla, and telling the other waitresses how she didn't believe in Maggie, and she still believed they were trying to frighen her, and all that. That day we had about eight tables of tourists and Cripple Creekers, having lunch — and there were about nine kids working in the kitchen. Did I tell you the girl's name was Laura ? Well, anyway, Laura was talking about how all this business about Maggie was just a bunch of stuff, and "I don't believe in her" and so on . . . and suddenly all the glasses on the bar came floating through the air, and one hit Laura on the back. The glasses all fell to the floor, but none of them broke. Everyone in the ice cream parlor saw it happen — and Laura just stood there, with her hands up in the air, saying, "I believe, I believe in you, Maggie !" The customers were in a state of shock.

Needless to say, Laura moved out that evening, and also stopped working for us. She used to drop in once in a while to have a hot fudge sundae, but she never stayed long, and she always sat near the front door. She wouldn't sit at any of the tables in the back, near the ice cream bar. Lots of people in town witnessed that particular little show of Maggie's. The tourists witnessed it, too, and some of them come back now and then, in the summer, and remind us of it.

Another thing Maggie does a lot is call out your name when you're not expecting it. She did that to you once, Linda, remember ? Now, this is very audible, as you know. A person will hear his or her name being called loudly, and turn around, and there's no one calling. Then all of a sudden, they say, "Oh, it's only Maggie again," and go on about their business. When it happens to me, I just say aloud, "Maggie, be quiet. I'm working, and I don't have time for games right now." Then she stops calling.

Another thing, Maggie sings. Her voice is lovely, a delicate soprano. She sings Irish arias and ditties and funny little songs, and several people, including Ken and myself, have heard her singing and dancing with her high-heeled boots in the ballroom, doing the polka.

Maggie also used to play the concertina. I didn't know what a concertina was at first, but I soon found out. Other people in the building heard it too. The first four or five years after we moved in, she really played that little instrument, quite loudly sometimes — and gently at other times. But no one has heard her playing in recent years.

The main thing is that Maggie's presence is a comforting thing. Everyone says there's something so warm and nice about just sitting in the Sarsaparilla . . . just sitting there makes them feel good and happy somehow. You've said that many times yourself, Linda. I know what they mean, because Ken and I feel it too. Sometimes, when I'm feeling down in the dumps and blue or depressed . . . sometimes just worn out from all the work that needs to be done, especially during the busy season . . . or when I'm really worried about something . . . Maggie will come near . . . I'll smell that soft, soft cologne or white roses fragrance, and a warm feeling comes over me. I can telepathically hear her saying to me, "It's all right, Katherine. I'll give you strength. I'm here, and you don't have to worry. I'll take care of you." It gives me a distinct warm and soft and comfortable feeling when I'm alone.

Somehow, you just know that whoever or whatever Maggie is, she was never a bad person. She had to be — or has to be ? — one of the nicest people who ever lived — or haunted — in Cripple Creek. At first, we did some investigation, but we never learned anything helpful. We asked Fergie Ferguson, who used to have a business in the building years ago, and he told us that he'd never heard of a murder or a tragedy or anything like that connected with a young woman. We did find out that there was a funeral parlor there at one time, called the Farley Lampton Funeral Home. But that's all we were ever able to discover, and none of it seemed to explain Maggie's presence.

I'll close by reminding you that lots of people who have spent the night in our building have heard a baby crying loudly — like the one people hear at your house, Linda. I've never heard it myself, but other people have, and it disturbs them, because it's such a sad and pitiful kind of crying. We still wonder if maybe the baby belongs — or belonged — to Maggie, but, of course, we don't know . . . and I guess we never will. Every summer we wonder what Maggie will do this year at the Sarsaparilla. Now a new summer is coming up, and we hope she'll be back. We miss her so much when she goes away for a while. So does everyone else.

And that's the story of Maggie, told by her loyal friend, Katherine Hartz. By the way, Kathy's husband, Kenneth, is a businessman who also teaches astrology courses. His Sun Sign is Libra, and I believe he's still trying to make up his mind about Maggie ! He knows perfectly well that she does exist, in some form, but he still hasn't balanced his Libra Scales regarding exactly where she came from . . . and why she's there.

★ ★ ★ ★ ★ ★

As I've pointed out, it wasn't until I later learned about vibratory frequencies (angstrom units per second) from one of my mountain retreat Gurus that I finally comprehended that ghosts are indeed real, not imaginary.

First, it may help to ponder the definition of angstrom units. An angstrom unit is one hundred-millionth of a centimeter, a unit used in measuring the length of light waves.

Each person vibrates to a completely individual electromagnetic frequency of angstrom units (light waves) per second. When that frequency is raised or increased, the physical body is not visible to another person's physical vision. When the frequency is lowered or decreased, the physical body again becomes visible to the physical eye.

The way I was able to comprehend it was through the analogy of an electric fan. When the electricity is off, and you look at the fan, what do you see ? You see a circle. Portions of the circle (the blades of the fan) are opaque (solid) and you cannot see through them. Other portions of the circle (the spaces between the blades) you can see straight through to the other side — or to whatever is behind the fan.

So . . . part of the circle is visible, part is invisible. The blades are dense matter — the spaces in between the blades are — just air.

Now, when you turn on the fan at the Low Speed, it begins to spin at a certain frequency, and for a time, the circle *appears* to be dense and solid. You can't see through it at any point. Then, when you press the High Speed, the frequency increases and the circle changes from an *apparently* solid mass to a full circle of air, with no dense matter obstruction, and you can see straight through the *entire circle*. It may seem to be an optical illusion, but it's not. It's reality. What is the difference between the solid circle of the fan you *cannot* see through — and the empty circle you *can* see through at all points ? *The rate of speed at which the blades are spinning.* Therefore, to the vision of the physical eye, the difference between the visible and the invisible is — the speed at which the object seen — or unseen — is vibrating.

I trust that makes it easier for you to understand the visible and invisible worlds (objects and people). It did for me.

A person in astral form, whether recently or long dead — or simply sleeping, and temporarily out of body — is "spinning" so fast, vibrating at such an increased rate of light waves or angstrom units per second, the average person in the physical world cannot see him or her with physical vision; therefore, the astral one is invisible.

Sometimes, a man or woman who is ultrasensitive, unconsciously raises his or her rate of frequency for a few moments, and can then see with physical vision forms that remain invisible to others who are not so finely tuned. Consequently, some people can — on occasion, for brief periods, usually only seconds — "see a ghost." The astral form thus seen is not always that of a "dead person," but is nearly always believed to be. In the case of Maggie, the astral is undoubtedly that of a woman who died long ago, but in other cases of "seeing ghosts," the astral could just as well be that of someone — from anywhere — who happens to be asleep at the time, and whose astral body is wandering around — an extraterrestrial being (a space person) or a Master, a Guru, or an Avatar. With the sleeping person, the incident is usually purely accidental, caused by the sensitivity of the viewer, not by the sleeper's astral.

However, regarding the latter Avatars, they are all capable of consciously and deliberately either raising (increasing) or lowering (decreasing) the frequency vibration of their bodies whenever they choose, to become invisible — or visible — to those who are less enlightened, and who are therefore vibrating at a lower rate of angstrom units per second. This vibratory ability was demonstrated to me by one of the "teachers" who came to instruct me in Colorado, and evidently also by Nahtan on that spooky New Year's Day at the Hollywood Roosevelt Hotel in Suite 1217 — now renumbered to Suite 1221. (See Preface). The initial shock of seeing such a demonstration with your own eyes, sans any kind of "hallucinatory drugs," with a perfectly clear mind, is frightening, awesome, mind-boggling, and bizarre beyond description. But after more than one demonstration of it, the whole thing becomes rather natural, like watching an electric fan. I'm aware that some of you may not believe what I've related in this paragraph, but I can't allow myself to be concerned about that. I have a pretty heavy and deep-rooted "thing" about honesty, and I don't make up stories. Whether you accept it or reject it, I wanted to tell you that such appearances and disappearances are quite real, and they do happen. Those who have observed such "phenomena" feel much the same way Abraham Lincoln might have felt if someone had handed him an odd-shaped piece of hard plastic, told him to hold it to his ear, and he heard Mary Todd speaking to him from Virginia — or showed him a square box, then told him to press a button and he could actually see General Lee addressing his troops in the South. Everything strange and mysterious is relative.

As we are now aware, hearing sounds on a higher frequency, such as the wild party in my "haunted" Cripple Creek house, is called clairaudience. *Seeing* an astral which is vibrating at a higher frequency is called clairvoyance. Some people possess clairaudience, some possess clairvoyance, and some possess both gifts. Then there are those "appearances or disappearances" which occur because they are deliberately willed by a Master, Avatar, or Guru who can control his or her own vibratory frequency to become visible or invisible even to those who do not possess the gift of clairvoyance — or to utter words or sounds which can be heard even by those who do not possess clairaudience.

Therefore, both "hearing" and "seeing" a ghost is possible, sometimes separately, sometimes simultaneously, through a combination of clairaudience and clairvoyance.

Can such entities move objects, manipulate matter ? Yes, they can. Astral entities of any of the several kind I've already described are not simply floating etheric "impressions" or images. They are controlled by the astral's Overself (Spirit or Higher Self) and the *still existing and functioning* mind and soul, none of the three of which die or cease to exist or operate after the death of the flesh body, upon which, in life, the astral is superimposed, matching the physical body in appearance exactly. And the mind, soul, and Overself are definitely capable of manipulating matter, as they are equally capable of raising and lowering the vibratory frequency of the astral of the dead or sleeping flesh body.

If the ventriloquist's dummy is broken or discarded, can the ventriloquist still manipulate matter, speak, move a cup or whatever "he" (it — they) could do while controlling the discarded puppet's "strings" ? Of course. Because it was *never the puppet who accomplished the speaking or any other action*. It was the ventriloquist (or puppeteer) who was responsible all the time — and the ventriloquist or puppeteer (choose your analogy) was not discarded when the puppet (body) was discarded. Until the puppeteer or ventriloquist chooses a new puppet to control and guide, he or she has a certain amount of free time, so to speak. However, relatively few puppeteers choose haunting as an occupation between incarnations. There are more productive and enlightening, not to mention interesting, things to do in other dimensions. One of the situations causing some, though not all, hauntings is that the still existing mind and soul are magnetized to a location where intense emotion was experienced while the flesh body was existing. And the Overself (Spirit or Higher Self) must go along, even though often reluctantly. Why ? Free Will.

Does this sound strange to you — much like the mailroom person telling the President of General Motors what to do, with the latter meekly following along, just to be there if needed ? Well, here's a surprise. That's exactly the way it is.

Your Overself (or Spirit — or the Angel of your Higher Self) is always there . . . never separated from your mind and soul (which are, by the way, outside the body) . . . either in life or in death. Always there, lovingly ready to guide and help you over the rocks when things get rough, but unable (because of the gift of Free Will) to force wisdom or power upon you. This "Guardian Angel" — the real you . . . the you-of-you . . . possesses all wisdom, all truth, all innocence, and all power. But He or She cannot initiate effective communication. You must do so (and here the term "you" means your own mind [operating through the computer brain] and your own soul [operating through the Third Eye]). You must initiate and establish communication. You must, with your Free Will, choose and decide to tune in to your Higher Self and receive, thereby, all the power which has always been your birthright, since your first incarnation into a flesh body . . . and all through your subsequent incarnations, including, of course, the present one. One might say it's eternally true that "it's your move" in the spiritual game of chess.

All of this may be difficult for you to comprehend, but it may become more clear and understandable through drawings illustrating this "holy trinity" of the you-of-you. On the next page is just one quick sketch to help your imaging.

Notice the double pyramid formed by the connection between the holy trinity. This is a most important point, as you will learn in

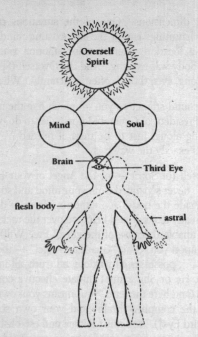

Chapter 7, *Forgotten Melodies*. Notice also that the two pyramids thus formed are base to base, not top to top.

A word here, before we go on, relating to the mind and the soul. Let's use capitals to make it more clear. The Mind — of both men and women — is Masculine. It operates through the Masculine Brain — in both men and women.

The Soul — of both men and women — is Feminine. It operates through the Feminine Third Eye — in both men and women. This is why; as I've mentioned elsewhere in other chapters, there is a little man in every woman and a little woman in every man; also why it's perfectly natural and desirable for a man to show compassion, to weep, to enjoy poetry, and possess other sensitive qualities, and he shouldn't be considered "effeminate" because of this feminine side of his nature. Jesus wept.

Yet, small boys in our society are continually told that "men don't cry. Men don't embrace. Be a little man . . ." and so forth.

Conversely, it's perfectly natural and desirable for a woman to show courage and independence, to seek a career or a profession where her talents and abilities may be used, and she shouldn't be considered "tough, unfeminine, or pushy" because of this masculine side of her nature.

Yet, small girls in our society are continually commanded to "be a Lady. Keep your opinions to yourself. Don't be a tomboy" . . . and so on.

The core of all the problems on this Earth today is that the Masculine Mind, operating through the Masculine Brain, has allowed technology to surpass spiritual wisdom at the price of threatened annihilation.

The appearance of women's liberation is a healthy sign that our Creators are attempting to seed into the minds of all Earthlings that it's time the Feminine Soul (in both men and women) — operating through the Feminine Third Eye — is equally recognized. The Queen, in other words, must sit on her throne beside the King if there is ever to be Peace in the Kingdom. Kingdom. Named after him, notice. Or if the will of our Creators is to "be done, on Earth, as it is in Heaven."

The tragic thing is that some women, who yearn (justifiably) to be free, believe that the way to freedom is to become a man, defeating the whole holy purpose, and planting the seeds for a matriarch society, which, I assure you, would be equally as detrimental to human happiness as the patriarch society we've suffered under for so long. The key is a wrong interpretation of the word "equal." It must be realized that men and women are not equal. They are, they must be, and they always shall be — *different*. The ideal is not that they become a Unisex, but that they remain separate, with equal rights and equal powers.

That's the flaw in the thinking of the feminine gender today. The flaw in the thinking of the male gender can be described by an illustration given in, I believe, the Aries-Leo section of *Love Signs*. The Leo (King) says to the Aries (Queen) in angry frustration: "How can I make you my *equal* until you first recognize that I'm your *superior* ?" That macho statement needs no interpretation. It speaks for itself, and it symbolizes the angry frustration of the male in today's society.

What does all this have to do with the subject matter of this chapter ? Everything. The title is *Gurus, Ghosts, and Avatars,* and each Guru or Avatar who appeared during my mountain retreat in Colorado to teach lessons "when the student was ready" took great pains to explain that the masculine-feminine principal, contained in the Yin and Yang of art, electricity, science, and human union is the prismed crystal through which the reflected rainbow spectrum of all truths is seen.

★ ★ ★ ★ ★ ★

The analogy of the President of General Motors reminds me of what I've been instructed — and you may find interesting — concerning one's personal Guru "when the student is ready." You'll remember that in the Introduction to this book, I counseled you to seek your own personal Guru when you are ready, who will then teach you how to finally communicate with the most reliable Guru of all — your own Higher Self.

After a while, when perhaps more than one "teacher" has manifested, then disappeared and left you alone to try your new "wings," when you are ready to become an Initiate and be completely illuminated, you are given two Gurus. Not always simultaneously, but never very far apart in time sequence. One of these is kind, patient, gentle, mild, and nonintrusive — peaceful and quiet, almost to the point of timidity. His responsibility, for whatever period of time he's required to spend with you, is to demonstrate only by example. He may not tell you anything or demand anything. He is only to quietly and continually demonstrate by his own behavior what you should imitate. He may not correct you, "scold" you, or point out your weaknesses. When he is gone, your heart will nearly break with your belated understanding of his mission — but you will have learned much, and you'll begin to walk in his footsteps.

The other one will anger you, frustrate you, and annoy you, but he will demand — and receive — your awed respect. Respect for his intellect, his seemingly endless esoteric knowledge, and his powers. He is like the trainer who must prepare the dog (not a derogatory example) for "best of show." His responsibility is to severely discipline, test your faith in him — and in yourself — in a number of ways. You will rebel until you submit. When he leaves, you will have learned the lesson of humility, the most necessary requirement for final initiation. Then he will appear again, when you least expect it, to lead you the rest of the way into enlightenment, no longer stern and deceptive (deception was only a test of your faith) — with twinkling eyes and a demeanor that demonstrates the equality beween you.

Finally, your "kind Guru" will manifest again, and you will be so inexpressibly happy to see him, to at last understand the mission of both of them, that "your cup will runneth over."

The divine plan is for each person to reach the point of evolvement needed for his or her own personal Avatars to appear. And their mission, as I've already explained, is to teach you to reach at-onement with the ultimate "Guru" — your own Higher Self.

This is why the spread of what is called both trans-channeling and trance-channeling (channeling through another person, who is in trance) can be misleading, and should be approached with much caution. I wish I could recall who said it, because it's so very appropriate, but someone observed that receiving spiritual counsel in this way is like dialing a series of numbers at random on an astral telephone, and having no way to verify who's going to answer the call. Seeking knowledge through a medium can, on rare occasions, be valid and helpful, as so many learned through Edgar Cayce. But Cayce and Jesus of Nazareth both faced the frustration of those they tried to help and teach by insisting upon relying on the teacher for everything, ignoring the most important lesson being taught, expressed in the Nazarene's words: "All things which I have done, you can do also. Go, thou, and do likewise — and more." You can expect to read those words several times in this book. They deserve much repeating.

"Spirit Guides" from other levels of awareness are — not always, but too often — misleading, and sometimes even diabolical, leading you in the opposite direction from the top of the mountain you're longing to reach.

The best known member of The Great Brotherhood of Elders, to which all Gurus and Avatars belong, is the Adept called the Comte de St. Germain. (The "St." doesn't stand for the Catholic term of "saint," but is part of a French surname.) William Shakespeare, according to all of the world's most respected metaphysicians, was one of the several identities of St. Germain, who was also, it is said, Sir Isaac Newton and Sir Francis Bacon.* The latter names periodically appear in literary studies of Shakespeare's works by scholars, who theorize that one or the other of them was the actual author of the Bard's plays. The Count of St. Germain was also a friend of General Lafayette's, who, when our founding fathers were quarreling and disputing certain points of our Declaration of Independence, stood up in the back of the room and made such an impassioned speech about Freedom that when he was finished, they all grabbed their quill pens and signed. St. Germain is also rumored to have been the subject of Rembrandt's mysterious painting, called the "Polish Rider." Further, he was the

---

*The puzzle of how one Avatar could assume several identities during the same time period is explained in Chapter 9.

one, as history records, who warned Marie Antoinette of the coming French Revolution, but she didn't heed his warning, and thus lost her head to the guillotine. As did, also, of course, her husband, Louis XIV, and a number of other members of the royal family. Their small son, "the lost Dauphin," was smuggled out of the palace in a laundry basket, and the several books written about what is alleged to have happened to him fascinated me in high school history class.

Historians of the day have recorded that St. Germain was also the mysterious alchemist who taught cell regeneration to several ladies of the French court, causing young men of nineteen and twenty to fight duels for their romantic favors when these noblewomen were chronologically eighty to ninety years old. I trust they were all spiritually enlightened, or they could not have mastered these lessons of regeneration from "the Master."

Of all the St. Germain identities, the one I'm fondest of is Isaac Newton, because, when he was debating the validity of astrology with Edmund Halley of Halley's comet fame, and Halley was ridiculing this art and science, Newton won the argument by stating simply — and firmly: "Sir, I have studied the matter. You have not." And with that, he clicked his heels, bowed sharply — and left.

It's said that St. Germain is still among us today, using a new identity . . . and I have reason not to doubt it. . . . .

★ ★ ★ ★ ★ ★

There are Avatars . . . and there are Avatars. Some possess their own flesh bodies (a number of these many centuries old, by Earth Time, as will be explained in Chapter 9) . . . others take over the body of an Earthling, whose mind and soul make a perfect channel, and with the consent of that body's Overself (Spirit or Higher Self) uses this person as a channel for enlightenment of the world, at certain times in Earth's history when some vital discovery or invention is needed for the continued evolvement of the world. This is called "overshadowing."

All the great composers were thus "overshadowed" in channeling the Music of the Masters, as they themselves believed . . . chorded fragments of the "Music of the Spheres" . . . to the degree that Earthlings were ready to receive these harmonic frequencies. Humans today would be in even worse shape than they are had it not been for the great symphonies which have touched the souls and moved the hearts of millions.

One of these Avatars indisputably used as a channel was Yugoslavian Nikola Tesla. Many people even quite seriously believe that Tesla was an extraterrestrial. He's part of the haunted setting of Cripple Creek, where I was, myself, channeled with the star signs in this book. And so, this is yet another experience in the mountains I should share with you. This one began before I even walked into my haunted house for the first time . . . on my first trip up the winding road from Colorado Springs to the miniature Tibet or Shangri-la called Cripple Creek.

As with Kathy Hartz and Maggie, I believe the story would best be told in the words of a real estate agent, Finbar O'Malley, who drove me up into the mountains upon my arrival because Leland Feitz, the owner-landlord of the house I had rented, was out of town at the time. Here is our conversation on that star-crossed day, as best I can recall it. It was my first knowledge of Nikola Tesla. . . and includes another strange and mysterious incident many of you have experienced yourself.

★★★★★★

I'll close my eyes for a moment and imagine myself in the car with Finbar, then write out our conversation for you, from memory. We passed Woodland Park, after leaving Colorado Springs, then when we reached a tiny place called Divide, we turned, and headed down a long stretch of road lined with spruce and aspen. Well, not exactly "down" the road . . . we were gradually but very surely driving in the direction of another 5,000 feet or so higher than the altitude of the Springs. Can you picture us in the car ?

"Cripple Creek," Finbar informed me, "is almost two miles high, straight up toward the sky. On some days there, the clouds hang down so low you can actually reach up and touch them — if you jump a little. Where you're going to be staying is ten thousand feet above sea level."

"Just the right altitude for miracles," I replied spontaneously, then wished I hadn't, because I could see my remark had aroused the curiosity of this man I hardly knew, and had no desire to know better. No reflection on Finbar O'Malley as he is an agreeable and likeable sort of chap. But it was, after all, the me-of-me I had traveled to "God's Country" to become better acquainted with, not more strangers. There are enough of those in New York.

"What kind of miracle were you expecting to happen up here?" he asked, curious, yet rather guardedly, I thought.

"Oh, just any old kind I might find buried somewhere near a Bristlecone pine tree, unnoticed for centuries or longer. I'm not fussy about miracles." I needed a subject-changer. The weather.

"Someone told me the sky bursts open frequently in the mountains with violent electrical storms. Is that true?" It worked.

"Oh, maybe once a month or so, sometimes more often, especially in the summer. It depends on the atmospheric conditions. This is only the second week of April, so you'll probably see quite a few of them before fall. Now and then there's an electrical storm in the middle of winter up here. While it's snowing. Damnedest thing. Gives you an eerie feeling. Folks don't ordinarily associate the thunder and lightning of an electrical storm with snow. But it happens up here in the mountains. They say that's why Nikola Tesla came up here to conduct his experiments. Because of the electrical storms at ten thousand feet . . . and higher. Pike's Peak, where they say he pulled off some of his light shows, is closer to fourteen thousand feet."

Nikola Tesla. I'd noticed the name on some kind of commemorative plaque in the park near the Colorado Springs airport as we drove by and stopped for a minute or so for a stalled car ahead of us.

Curious, I turned to Finbar, and asked, "Who was he ?"

"Some kind of a scientist or inventor. Folks claim he was a genius. I even heard somebody say once that he believed Tesla was a Space Man, like Spock and those characters on TV in *Star Trek*." Finbar chuckled at the very idea of anything so far out, then continued.

"He sure had a lot of peculiar habits. Real eccentric, he was. Somethin' funny about his inner ear, they say — whatever that is. Thing is, his ears were so sensitive, he could even hear a fly light on a table, and it sounded to him like an explosion. They say he could hear a clock ticking two or three rooms away. He was in pain a lot of the time because of the sensitive ears, you know ? Then there were the visions."

"Visions ?" I asked, my curiosity growing.

"Yep. He invented all kinds of electrical devices. Drew complicated blueprints for electric- and solar-powered cars and planes, stuff like that no one had ever even thought about. But he didn't draw the blueprints for his electric cars and spacecraft and planes and so on the way most of those guys do. He claimed that he had visions — that each time he had one of these visions, the whole thing just popped up in his mind like it was a screen or something. And his 'mental pictures,' as he called 'em, were complete right down to the smallest detail. Weird." Finbar shook his head.

"He was a psychic or a mystic or whatever it's called, they claim. He could sort of see things before they happened. Like the time lots of folks heard him tell a friend not to take a certain train. The friend listened to Tesla, and didn't get on. A few hours later the train ran off the track and killed everybody on board."

Again, Finbar shook his head in a gesture of half disbelief and half wonderment. Then he went on with his oddly familiar dissertation. Why familiar to me? Maybe I already knew it on a higher level? Has that ever happened to you? I mean, when you hear something for the first time, something you've never heard before, yet you sense that you already know it before the person finishes telling you?

"Tesla's the one who discovered AC — or alternating current, not long after Tom Edison discovered DC — direct current, you know. Edison didn't like it much, I guess. Took out big ads in the New York newspapers warning everybody that their houses might catch fire and burn down if they used Tesla's alternating current. Old Tom claimed it was unsafe and a dangerous hazard, whether it was used outdoors or indoors. Tesla was working for Edison for a while, but that caused a split between them. Finally, George Westinghouse and J. P. Morgan backed Tesla's crazy ideas, and Tesla came out here to Colorado Springs to build a laboratory for his experiments. Later, he proved his AC current was safe. That's all they use in homes today, of course."

I waited for Finbar to continue, fascinated . . . yet troubled by the sense of "this has happened before" . . . a kind of déjà vu flash.

"They say Tesla was all upset when they split the atom. He said it would bring on nuclear power, which could end the world. He kept trying to convince J. P. Morgan and his money backers that the world would run out of energy in the near future, and that nuclear energy would destroy it — but that his method was safe and pure. He said it would give everybody all the energy they needed without polluting the air, which he predicted in the early 1900s would be a big problem before the end of the century. He was right. Too bad nobody listened. Sure is a big problem. Especially in Denver now. Just like Los Angeles and New York, maybe worse."

Finbar was quiet for a moment, then went on. "Tesla was a strange one, for a fact. Looked a lot like Howard Hughes. Acted a lot like him too. Kinda brooding and moody. He wouldn't shake hands with anybody. Something about mixing up auras, but I'm not real sure what an aura is.* They say Tesla climbed Pikes Peak alone more than once. That's it, over there to the left, the one with all the snow on it. I guess he wanted to try some of his crazy experiments with lightning. Climbed right up to the top, he did, in the middle of the worst storms you can imagine, according to what they tell around here. He used to pull in lightning with the tower he built, with J. P. Morgan's money, down in the Springs. Then, after a storm, he'd run out with his helpers and screw light bulbs right into the ground. They'd light up, just as if they'd been screwed into a lamp that was plugged in an electric outlet. Just screwing them into the dirt. Isn't that wild ?" Finbar once more shook his head in a gesture of combined respect and disbelief. "Tesla said it had something to do with the Earth's magnetic field."

. . . then it happened

Suddenly, without warning, we were enveloped in a velvetlike cloud of heavy silence, that grew . . . and grew . . . seeming to wrap itself around the car like a smothering blanket. Even the hum of the car's engine sounded muffled . . . somehow distant, far away.

For a measureless time the silence remained, until it became uncomfortable. Finbar said nothing, his eyes fixed, staring ahead, unblinking. I tried to think of something to say to break the silence between us, and found I could not.

Ripping into the silence, a yellow streak of lightning snaked across the sky, accompanied by a crash of thunder that seemed to split open a mass of clouds overhead. The sun turned dark for one frightening instant, then shone forth again, as bright as before. No rain.

---

*See Chapter 6, *Forgotten Rainbows*.

Just a warning flash, the kind I'd heard sometimes comes as a sign that a storm is approaching in this high altitude. Still there was silence. I wanted to ask Finbar about the sudden thunderclap and bolt of lightning that seemed so disconnected with reality, appearing and disappearing as swiftly as they did. But I simply could not speak. Nor could he.

After a while . . . at last I found my voice. "Is it twenty minutes *until* the hour — or twenty minutes *after* ?" I asked.

The car swerved slightly as Finbar quickly glanced at the watch on his left wrist, then swallowed hard before he replied.

"It's twenty minutes till three." He looked at his watch again. "*Exactly* twenty minutes till three," he repeated in a low voice. "*Right on the second.* How . . . did you . . . ?"

Then I did that dumb thing I do sometimes, even though I'm not an Aquarian. I forgot Finbar's name. That kind of instant amnesia everyone gets occasionally with people they've only just met (except for Aquarians, who do it all the time !). I'm sure it's happened to you too. And you're embarrassed to ask, so you take a chance that you're right. When you're wrong, it's . . . well, you wish the ground would open up and swallow you, right ? I thought I remembered his name. I was wrong.

I laughed. "I'm surprised to hear an Irishman ask how I knew the exact time, *Michael*," I said. "I thought all Gaelic people knew about the 'sudden silence' superstition. In fact, my own Irish grandmother, whose parents were born in County Cork, is the first one who told me about it."

Still the man beside me did not relax. If anything, he was even more tense, and his voice remained very low.

"Told you . . . about what ?"

"About the strange thing that sometimes happens when two or

more people are talking together. All of a sudden there's a dead silence, and no one seems able to break it for the longest time, no matter how hard they try. It's as though everyone's lips were sealed, or everyone had somehow been mesmerized into a trance. After the silence gets to be downright embarrassing, someone finally manages to speak, and break it. And usually, no one even comments on it aloud. Everyone just goes right on talking about whatever it was they were talking about before it . . . happened."

Finbar said nothing, but his sunburned, freckled hand tightened on the steering wheel. I felt a flush rise to my cheeks. Had he decided I was pixilated, the Gaelic term for not having it all together ? I finished my story nervously.

"My grandmother (I called her my elf-mother) told me that when the sudden-silence thing occurs, it's almost always — at least about ninety-five percent of the time — either twenty minutes till — or twenty minutes after the hour. Any hour. I've tested it most of my life, since I was about fourteen years old, every time an unbreakable silence falls when I'm talking with another person . . . or a group of people. And she was right. Almost every time, that's where the clock hands point. Twenty till . . . or twenty after . . . whatever hour.

"There have been only a few times over the years, maybe three, that it hasn't worked. Day or night. When you ask the person or people you're with when it happens if it's twenty till or twenty after, and you're not wearing a watch yourself, and there's no clock visible anywhere, they're always shocked," I finished lamely. "Like you are right now."

Finbar remained silent, although he nodded, with a faint, polite smile.

"I've always wondered why it happened," I went on, trying to fill what was now a different and definitely uneasy kind of silence in the car. "I mean, I've tried the experiment so many times, and observed how amazingly it works, I'm sure there must be a reason for it. Maybe involved in the laws of physics. Or metaphysics. It obviously has something to do with the fourth dimension of time. I'm very much interested in numerology, but I've never found a solution to it in any numerology books I've read. I'm going to study it more up here this summer, maybe the Kabala too. I know I'm going to figure out the answer someday. Maybe in the mountains I'll dream the answer. Little mysteries like that intrigue me, and I can't rest until I've solved them."

Finbar cleared his throat, then spoke as if he hadn't paid any attention to a word I'd been saying.

"My name," he said, "is Michael." He paused. "Michael Finbar O'Malley. You had no way of knowing that. And . . . you knew the exact time, too, although you're not wearing a . . . . uh . . . I guess you've more or less explained how you knew . . . but . . . are you what they call psychic ?"

Once more the conversation had taken a wrong turn. I desperately reached for another subject-changer. As Finbar shifted gears, I shifted subjects, perhaps not too smoothly.

"No, I'm not psychic. That is, no more than everyone could be by just opening up the mind and allowing things to channel through. It's simply a matter of tuning in to a higher level of awareness. Anyway, the name was probably just a coincidence. I didn't realize I called you Michael till you brought it up."

A double lie. I *had* realized it. And nothing on this planet is a coincidence. Or on any other planet. Or in any Solar System or Universe. However major or microscopic, every event is linked to an unguessed, invisible, interlocked cosmic pattern. But this was neither the time nor the place to engage in the untangling of such complexities. I tried to sound cheerful and reassuring as I fumbled into an abrupt change of subject.

"Michael is a common name. Lots of people are named Michael." Then the briefest pause. "Where did Nikola Tesla live ?"

"Mostly in Colorado Springs. Now and then, though, he stayed in Cripple Creek, when he was doing some things on Mount Pisgah or Tenderfoot . . . and Pikes Peak. But nobody seems to know for certain exactly where. Probably because he came and went for only a few days at a time, I suppose, when the storms were brewing."

Finbar's apprehension seemed to have returned momentarily, as he murmured, "It's funny you should ask."

"Why is it funny ?"

"Well, maybe not funny. I guess the word is . . . strange."

"All right, then, why strange ?"

"Because you anticipated something I was about to tell you . . . and because of the fact that . . ." He hesitated. I remained silent, waiting. It seemed the wisest thing to do.

"Well, there's a strong rumor that he sometimes stayed in a two-story red brick house across from the school and gymnasium, between Third and Fourth Streets. The house was built in the late 1880s by a jeweler from New York named Goldsmith or Goldblatt or something. Later, it was used as a kind of annex to the Old Homestead, when they had an overflow of customers on a weekend. After that, it was a boardinghouse that rented out single rooms."

"The Old Homestead ?" Brief questions were decidedly safer. I remembered my friend mentioning the Old Homestead back in New York. Was it my imagination that Finbar was speaking faster than usual ? As though he were trying to cover up words he wasn't saying ?

"Yes. It's one of the oldest red-light houses in the West. If you like, I'll drive you past there when we get to Cripple Creek. It's a museum now. You might like to go in and have a look around. They have guides there who give real interesting talks about the Madam, Pearl DeVere, and all the swingin' that went on there during the gold rush, like the bells over the beds the girls used to ring when they looked out the window and saw the cops comin' up the front walk. Pearl's story has a sad ending, but I won't tell you now or I'll spoil it for you."

He picked up speed, his words tumbling out faster and faster. "Most of the furnishings inside are authentic, back from when the place was doing business as usual. If you like antiques, you'll enjoy going through the Old Homestead, and also the main museum at the train depot. Victor has a museum too. And there's the Melodrama at the Imperial Hotel in Cripple Creek, just down the hill from . . . the house you'll be . . . living in."

Was I imagining it, or did he hesitate ?

"Just walking into the lobby of the Imperial makes you feel like you fell asleep and woke up in the nineteenth century. And the plays there are . . ."

"Maybe some other time, Finbar," I interrupted. "I'd like to drive around with you and see all those places, or walk to them myself later, but I want to get settled in the house before dark." Why had he called my question about Tesla strange ?

"Can't say that I blame you. Night isn't the best time to unpack in a house you've never . . . been in or lived in before. Especially when you're alone. Then there's that warning of a storm maybe bein' on the way. If one of those wild ones blows up, it won't be a very cheerful greeting for your first time in the mountains. It could make things kinda gloomy. Too bad."

"Finbar . . ." I looked directly at him, and spoke deliberately. "Why did you say it was strange when I asked you about where Nikola Tesla stayed when he was in Cripple Creek ?"

He didn't answer. Except for clearing his throat again several times loudly, he remained silent, as if he hadn't heard me. But I persisted.

"What's the name of the street where the rooming house you said he might have stayed in is located ? The one across from the high school and the gymnasium ?"

A long pause. Then . . .

"Carr Avenue. Three fifteen Carr Avenue. Named after Governor Carr."

Quickly, I reached in the pocket of my cherry-red poplin Windbreaker with the attached elf hood (my favorite for a number of years, patched and repatched), and pulled out a folded sheet of notepaper. I stared at it.

"Three fifteen Carr Avenue ? Why, that's . . . the address of the house I'm renting from you." I trembled slightly, for no particular reason.

"Yes, well . . . yes," he mumbled, his face turning a rosy pink. "That's true, it is. That's why some folks say the house is haunted, I guess. But there's no real proof Tesla ever stayed there, you understand. It's only a rumor." He grinned at me reassuringly.

"Well, I hope the rumor is true," I answered, smiling what I tried to make a bright smile, my voice projecting a cheerfulness I didn't feel. "Then I'll have something exciting to write about to everyone back in New York."

Finbar then threw me one of his widest Irish grins, to show me he had now recovered from his fear of being a captive companion in a car with a witch. I had evidently convinced him, with my feigned casual reaction to the shock of the thought that Tesla had lived in the house where I was going to be staying alone — that I wasn't going to turn him into a toad, or cast any spells he couldn't handle. I grinned back at him, trying to appear nice and normal, although inwardly, I felt anything but normal.

Suddenly, I turned to Finbar as we drove down the winding road to Cripple Creek, and asked, "He's not still alive is he ? I mean Tesla."

"Oh, no. He's been dead for years. Died in New York, after the government — or somebody — set fire to his laboratory and burned it to the ground, with all his papers and research notes. It just about broke his heart, they say. He went back to New York after old J. P. Morgan pulled back his financial backing, and they tore down his lightning tower, or whatever it was — in the Springs. Seems that Morgan got scared when he found out that one of Tesla's inventions was a thing where, if folks just had an antenna in their backyards, they could pull in all the electrical energy they'd ever need for anything — to run their homes or farms — right out of the air, without it costing them a penny. Guess Morgan thought that would be milking the cow for free, so to speak. And by then, Edison and the government were gettin' together, all cozy, so nobody approved of Tesla figurin' out a way to give away electricity to folks for nothing.

"Some say Tesla died of heartbreak. He was a broken man all right. Heartbroken and financially broken. Others say he died of injuries from when he was struck by a car when he was crossing the street near the New Yorker Hotel, where he was staying. I read in some book that there were those who didn't believe the car running him down was an accident. Some folks claim it was the Nazis, because he was working on something that would have won any war for our side. He had a lot of supporters. Mark Twain thought he was brilliant, and they were good friends."

Finbar was silent for a few seconds. "There are also those who say that aside from the accident injuries, Tesla might have lived forever . . . or still be living. But that's a far-out theory if there ever was one. No intelligent person would believe it."

In view of Finbar's last statement, I decided not to say aloud what I was thinking, which was: "I believe it."

Finbar continued his tale as we turned down Bennett Avenue, past the Cripple Creek District Museum and the train station. "Tesla got to play one last joke on everybody, though. His funeral was held in the Cathedral of St. John the Divine, in New York. Hundreds of scientists and famous people attended the services. And there were reporters and photographers from just about every big newspaper and magazine in the world. Well, they were all using Eastman Kodak film in their cameras, and they took a lot of pictures of Tesla in his open casket, up on the altar.

"Then they stepped back. It was kind of a dramatic moment, because, just after they took the last picture, a ray of sunlight hit Tesla's head from one of the stained glass windows, and folks heard a loud clap of thunder, but it wasn't raining. The weird thing was, all those pictures they took . . . I read where it was more than fifty — every single one of the negatives was blurred. Couldn't see a thing. Eastman Kodak couldn't figure it out. So Tesla got the last word, in a way."

I was silent, thinking, as Finbar finished his story. "It's too bad this country has suppressed Tesla's work. Kids in school never hear about him. All the textbooks say is that Edison discovered electricity. But we wouldn't have electricity in the form we have it today without Tesla's alternating current — AC. Poor fella. They say Marconi stole Tesla's invention of short wave energy, or radio, after Tesla let Marconi come into his lab and see what he was doin' with all those experiments."

"For shame, America, for shame." I murmured softly, but Finbar didn't hear me. He wound up his Tesla tale with a startling piece of information.

"Tesla was a shy man, they say. Like I said, from the one picture I ever saw of him, he looked a whole lot like that Howard Hughes fella. Black hair. Black mustache. Dark eyes. He didn't like to have his picture taken, so he must have maybe zapped the cameras in the church somehow . . . maybe with one of those electromagnetic light waves he was always experimenting with in his laboratories. Anyway, they've never been able to figure out what happened.

"And then there's this invention he was workin' on before he was hit by the car. Called a Tesla coil, I think. They use it in some process today they call Kirlian photography . . . taking pictures of the human aura, whatever that is. I've heard tell his Tesla coil is some kind of static electricity he claimed would repair bone marrow, make broken bones knit faster, heal arthritis and just about everything else. It's supposed to stop any kind of pain with just one or two treatments. Gives you a positive mental attitude too — even removes the desire for drink and drugs. It's supposed to tune in to . . . what did I read ? . . . to the vibratory frequency of each cell or something. I figured the plans for it were burned when his New York laboratory caught fire, but there's a rumor he taught somebody who worked in his lab how to build one . . . some fella who's living out west. . . ."

Finbar's voice trailed off as we drove up in front of my new home. I didn't comment on his last words. There seemed to be nothing to say. But there was a lot to think about.

★★★★★★

After the ghost sighting in my house I've related to you, I pondered the Tesla story a great deal. Could the ghost in the corner have been the astral of Tesla, haunting the house he had once lived in ? Finbar's description of him matched what the frightened couple had seen that night. Then, too, I later read a number of books about Tesla, and learned that he was fond of wearing evening clothes. He was a formal man. A lonely man too. A Cancerian, deeply attached to his mother. She invented a number of things herself, yet she couldn't read. After I thought about the "corner ghost" haunting my little slipping-off-the-time-track house, I felt more comfortable about it. If it was Tesla, I thought, I wish he would communicate. Actually . . . finally . . . he did. But that story I'll have to save for still another future book.

One night during an electrical storm in Cripple Creek, I sat on the front porch, watching the yellow-white serpents of lightning streaking across the sky . . . and meditating about . . . a legend. A legend concerning a Priest . . . or a Priestess ? . . . of the lost continent of Atlantis . . . who is supposed to have buried, beneath the Earth, just before that once fair land was inundated . . . *magnetic fields* . . . to attract, during the Aquarian Age, those souls who would shine the beams of Love and Light into the darkness. More "New Age" thinkers every year have taken up residence in Cripple Creek, Victor, and the surrounding areas.

In alchemy, gold is called magnetic. And . . . there was Winfield Scott Stratton, the gold-mining king, calling Cripple Creek the "bowl of gold" . . . formed from the eruption of a volcano that simultaneously carved out the valley where the town lies . . . . . . and saying that the gold rush of the late 1890s only scratched the surface . . . and what about the possible approaching gold rush the Old-Timers predict for the early 1990s ? . . . (Why did such a thought as that fly through my mind ?) . . . the haunted Garden of the Gods . . . where only those with peace in their hearts were allowed by the Ute Indians to come and pray. . . . to chant . . . musical mantras.

Gold. Magnetic. Magnetism. Alchemy. Nikola Tesla. The Utes. Magnetic power points. Clairaudience. Clairvoyance. Ghosts. Voices. Sounds from yesterday. Maggie. Vibrations measured by angstrom units of light waves per second.

. . . . *magnetic fields buried beneath the Earth* . . . .

Yes, Cripple Creek is a strangely haunted place. Hiding many secrets, veiling many mysteries. Why am I here ? I wondered.

When I'd first arrived . . . that first morning of awakening there . . .

when I saw the deep green woods everywhere, all around . . . and the snow-capped mountain peaks in the background . . . I sensed there was something magical about the place.

This is the forest primeval, I thought . . . with murmuring pine and hemlock. Longfellow. Well, not hemlock. And no oak or maple either. But enough murmuring pine, spruce, and aspen to fill a hundred Grimm's fairy tales . . . with the fragrance of some dark green, echoed promise . . . wafting on the cool, crisp breeze in the pure, clean mountain air that fairly sparkles with electricity. A proper place, indeed, for any kind of star quest.

I solved the mystery of "twenty till and twenty after" while I was there. To my own satisfaction, at least. I'll tell you about it in Chapter Eight. Don't peek ahead — just wait. That's a rhyme ! So you must obey it. Obeying anything said in rhyme is an old Irish superstition I just made up !

★★★★★★

For many years I wasn't certain of the meaning of the word serendipity. I thought it meant something like peace or serenity. After all, the word 'serenity' is contained within it. Then one of my Colorado Avatars signed a note she left on my porch with "Serendipity," so one day I asked her (yes, this particular Guru was female) the real meaning of the word. I remember how fascinated and delighted I was with her answer. She told me that the meaning and its origin was much more exciting than 'serenity.'

The word 'serendipity' was coined in 1784 by Horace Walpole, after a Persian faerie tale called *The Three Princes of Serendip,* in which the three princes make miraculous and unexpected, fortunate discoveries ! And so, the word means: *an aptitude for making fortunate and magical discoveries . . . . unexpectedly.*

My retreat to the Rockies was most certainly serendipitous. And

I trust that my sharing of the haunted setting where these star signs were born will bring you serendipity too.

In closing this chapter about Gurus, Ghosts, and Avatars, magnetic power points and vibratory frequencies, I'd like to leave with you a few coded words in a very brief verse, written by one of my Avatars under one of his several current Earth identities of Kyril Demys . . . although he has written many brilliant and inspired works of much greater length — both in the Present . . . and several hundred years ago.

> *the ageless melody, unheard, heals*
> *the healing vision, unseen, leads*
> *the true leaders, unknown, rescue*
> *the rescuers, immortal, know . . .*

4
DÉJÀ VU

the laws of Karma and reincarnation:
how yesterday's vices and virtues result
in today's sorrows and joys . . .
how to balance these
for a happier Present and Future

there is much I have learned
yet, much I still seek to fathom

in some silent depths I feel mysteriously drawn to
probe
for lost Essenic pearls of truth
which first appear, then disappear
in swirls of deep, green water

wisps of love . . . hazes of
fear
sometimes distorted . . .
sometimes clear

and always the question
why ?

what is this insistent pull on my mind ?
what is it urging me to find ?

is it simply a need to pursue, with
Aries persistence
the reason for humanity's continued
existence ?

no, I fear it is something more . . . long lost on a
forgotten shore
calling me on and on . . . to explore . . . the
ancient laws
of Karma

★ ★ ★ ★ ★ ★

VER SINCE high school, like everyone else, I suppose, I've been somewhat intimidated by dictionaries, slightly in awe of the erudite folk who compile them. It takes courage to contradict Webster, nearly as much as it takes to contradict the Bible — although in the latter case, I must point out that the word "Bible" does contain the word "lie," thereby hiding a great mystery, one we'll try to partially penetrate in the first page of Chapter 7, when we ponder some of the secrets of the book of Genesis.

Recent editions of Webster's have finally sanctioned the inclusion of the word "Karma." That's good. It proves that Karma has joined the parade of "new words in common usage." You hear it spoken just about everywhere these days, yet few of those who use the word fully comprehend the concept behind it. Even when they believe they do, more often than not they're mistaken. Like Webster. Regretfully, I must tell you that the dictionary's definition of Karma is . . . well . . . wrong.

Karma: "*. . . the force generated by a person's actions, held in Hinduism and Buddhism to perpetrate transmigration, and to determine his destiny in his next existence.*"

Most assuredly, that definition contains serious flaws to anyone other than a Buddhist or one of the Hindu faith, and after all, there are other philosophies than these which are founded on Karma, such as astrology, numerology, metaphysics — and in the beginning, before it was suppressed, and removed from the Holy Works, also Christianity.

Maybe it's Merriam, not Webster, who's guilty. The cover reads: *New Merriam-Webster Dictionary.* I have such warm, walking-through-red - and - gold - autumn - leaves - smelling - crisp - football - weather - and-the-smoke-of-bonfires schoolday memories associated with good old Webster, I'd prefer to blame Merriam.

So Mr. Merriam does not get an "A" for accuracy on his dictionary report card. Maybe a B plus, though, because I do rather like his opening phrase: *"the force generated by a person's actions."* Those words evoke a powerful image of how the whole thing works. Because the law of Karma is, indeed, a force — a force composed of electromagnetic energy — and it is most certainly generated by a person's actions. But that's only half true, and half is not whole.

As for the first flaw in Merriam's definition, if he felt obliged to present the misleading doctrine of transmigration in his dictionary (albeit correctly based on certain Hindu and Buddhist beliefs), he should be fair enough to give equal space to the other side of Karma and reincarnation, which is definitely antitransmigration. I promise him, if dictionary compilers are concerned with such matters, the logic of the truth of Karma shall prevail, and he will not be born again as an anteater or a water buffalo. As a matter of fact, one need not die at all, but that's a deep subject we'll share in a later chapter called *Physical Immortality*. The main thing to remember for the time being is that in no way will you be born again into the body of an insect or an animal, fish or fowl.

To begin with, you can choose to govern and ordain your personal destiny — to be the master of your own fate. Don't ever forget that, because it's as important to your happiness as the end of the nuclear arms race and the nuclear-waste-caused acid rain is to the survival of the planet.

Whether you consciously realize it yet or not, you've enrolled yourself *by choice* (on the level of your Higher Self) in a spiritual classroom. And the school of Karma (macrocosm to microcosm) is just like any Earth school in most respects. In Earth schools, when you graduate the fifth grade, you move on to the sixth grade (the next level) — and if you've learned particularly well, you may even skip a grade or so. But should you *fail* the fifth grade, what happens ? You remain right there where you are until your teachers feel you've learned enough to be advanced to the next grade (or level). You don't get plunked back into the fourth or second grade or kindergarten, just because you failed your fifth grade exams. And that should end the confusion about transmigration. Likewise, you don't get plunked back into the body of a grasshopper or a kangaroo when you've failed a certain grade (level) of human existence. You remain in the same general type environment, life after life (incarnation after incarnation), until you're ready to pass your tests and advance into the next grade — or level of enlightenment — equipped with a body temple made of finer substance (cell regeneration), a more evolved mind and illuminated spirit with which to meet the challenges of the higher grades, all the way up to the spiritual "college courses." Eventually you receive your "Master's" degree.

If you're wondering whether or not the spirit, in the long-forgotten past, ever chose to incarnate into mineral, insect, or animal form . . . reflected in the poet's musing . . . "when I was a tadpole, and you were a fish" . . . . and should you also be wondering why half the astrological signs are represented by animals . . . why animals are on Earth, and what manifested them here, eons upon eons ago, know that there is an answer to such puzzlings. They are all matters relating to a personal enlightenment and esoteric instruction I've experienced . . . part of the true story of Genesis. It still needs more support from the teachings of one far more illuminated than myself, and I feel that such full verification is several years away. When I'm sufficiently instructed and prepared, and when I'm told the time is right, I will write about all these "twelfth night secrets." But it's a delicate and complex subject, and considering the controversy it could create among both the sincere Bible Fundamentalists and the Darwin disciples, it might have to be presented as science fiction. For the present, it's sufficient for you to realize that there is an explanation for the animal enigma, and that it does not necessarily contradict or oppose either the creation theory or the evolution theory, but rather enriches and expands both, bringing them together in harmony.

As long as we're discussing animals related to the falsehood of transmigration, I'd like to give you my answer (since it relates to both

Karma and Lexigrams) to the question I've heard literally hundreds of times: "Why should it be that God (or god) spelled backward is dog ?" It's not just a coincidence. Unless they're severely beaten, starved, or fall victim to rabies, dogs demonstrate the closest thing to "god-love" humans can experience. No matter how much a dog is ignored or neglected — or sharply spoken to — no matter how often you forget to feed or water him or her when there are other things on your mind, your dog is still there, gazing at you adoringly, eyes brimming over with pure love. No matter how badly a dog is treated, he or she is still ready to protect you, defend you, and love you. The wells of understanding and compassion are fathoms deep. A dog forgives and forgives and forgives . . . endlessly. Nothing you do, short of violent and repeated beatings, will kill a dog's undying love for and loyalty to both master or mistress.

A dog is not only your best friend, but also the best example you'll ever have of what love is all about. It's taught (falsely and incorrectly) by some transmigration doctrines that the next step *up* in reincarnation from dog form is human form. Wrong as such doctrine is, I wonder why those who believe in it consider from dog to human one level *up*. Dogs are more patient, faithful, loyal and loving, forgiving and compassionate than most humans — except for those poor, tortured dogs bred and trained by *people* to attack and kill, such as pit bulls and Dobermans (include cock fights, bullfights, and most scientific testing laboratories). I use the term "people" rather than humans here because I don't consider such people to *be* human. They're several levels below human and many levels below animals. Those who abuse the smaller and more helpless (animals) or the innocent (children) have heavy-heavy Karma ahead, and they richly deserve it.

As I said earlier, the dictionary's definition of Karma is only partially correct. Further, the part in Merriam's definition about Karma "determining a person's destiny" is misleading.

One portion of it which is incorrect, and, I might add, glaringly obvious, is Merriam's choice of pronouns, i.e.: ". . . to determine *his* destiny in *his* next existence." Well, *really*. Are we to accept the insinuation that only men are given the chance in a future life to atone for goofs and faux pas in the past and present ones ? With all due respect, I suggest that the dictionary compilers take more frequent coffee breaks during their work, so they have time to read an occasional newspaper or magazine to inform them of the revolution. That is, the dawning of the golden Aquarian Age, as they seem not to have noticed, has been gradually seeding the masculine brain with this far out and curious idea that women are entitled to all of the same positive-negative aspects of Life as men — and are, therefore, surely also entitled to their own personal slice of Karma.

Now, it's true that Karma does, indeed, "control destiny," but that's only part of the picture, and when you give only a partial glimpse of truth, you leave truth seekers with false impressions. In this instance, they're led into believing that their personal fate or destiny is governed *entirely* by this mysterious force called Karma. Since it's represented to be totally in charge, without equivocation, just forget it. Why try at all, when nothing you do — or don't do — is going to change a single turn of the karmic wheel you set in motion yourself, so long ago you can't even remember giving it that initial spin ?

I'd like to fatten the dictionary definition of Karma.

Is the irresistible force of Karma, as the dictionary definition indicates, the *sole determining factor* in your personal destiny ? Yes and No. It depends.

Karma is the determining factor in your destiny *only when you allow it to be,* by ignoring its inflexible laws. In this respect, it's very like your astrological birth chart, which is logical, since your horoscope is simply a picture, using coded symbols, of all the major and still viable vibrations you've set up around yourself in this life, through your now forgotten actions in a series of past incarnations — and with which you must deal in the current one.

The less you believe in astrology, the more your chart fits you like a tight glove (because you haven't yet learned how to graduate from a pawn in the chess game to a King or Queen). It's always interesting to "read" the birth chart of a sceptic and watch the shock when the smallest detail in that person's life is exposed, which spooks him or her into wanting to know more about this "silly parlor game," with the dawning awareness that the art and science of astrology is neither silly nor a game. (Except for those newspaper and magazine astrological predictive columns, which have no more relationship to true astrology than the game of Monopoly has to actual real estate transactions.)

You see, while you're still uninitiated, the planetary movements keep you "in line," prevent you from drifting too far afield of your karmic obligations. Only when you believe in — then investigate — and finally comprehend astrology (and numerology) are you released from the restrictions placed on you by your birth chart. There's an ancient wisdom that teaches "the chart of a saint is impossible to read." Why ? Because the "saint" (and note that the word contains "sin" for an excellent reason we'll go into later in the lexigram chapter) has risen *above* the natal chart, and is free of it.

Enlightenment causes your personal aura to vibrate at a vastly increased rate of angstrom units per second. This vibratory frequency makes you immune to the electromagnetic vibrations bombarding you from the cosmos in a pattern commensurate with the positions of the planets when you drew your first breath, at which instant the more than forty billion electric cells in your brain were programmed, like a computer — which is precisely what the brain is (and manmade computers are but a pale imitation of it, as we've discussed earlier).

You might say that en*light*enment is a form of deprogramming, granting immunity from the control of your destiny by planetary movement. The same is true of the force of Karma, which is what planetary movement is all about. Ignore Karma's rules, and it keeps a tight and relentless rein on your life. But when you grow to *care* enough about Yesterday, Today, and Tomorrow — when you begin to see these as an Eternal Now, and not separate slices of Time, then you'll know how to take over the reins of your personal destiny — in fact, to *ordain* exactly how it shall be. *"Seek the truth, and the truth shall set you free."* Free of the karmic yoke. It's a never-ending puzzlement to me how people can continue to confuse the words of the humble carpenter from Nazareth into webs of complexities, when he exerted such effort to make them simple and clear.

One final example of the astrological chart and its relation to your karmic destiny, and then we'll go on to a more detailed definition of the word Karma itself. Image your horoscope as a karmic playpen, where you are confined for your own good (to work out your *necessary* Karma). In the microcosm example of the baby, when it grows stronger and wiser, it's lifted out of the playpen, and has the freedom to wander about, more or less as it chooses. The same with you when you've grown spiritually strong enough and mentally wise enough to wander by yourself and make your own mistakes (new Karma) if you choose, which I hope you don't. This is called being under the law of *Instant* Karma, (with Karma from all past lives erased and paid in full) which is a heavy soul test in itself, as we'll soon see. But first, exactly what is Karma ?

The law of Karma is based solidly upon the rock of Newton's law of cause and effect: for every action, there is a reaction. John hurts Mary, and Mary (in a future existence) meets John in a new body, with a different name (sometimes a different sex) — and hurts John back, through a dim awareness (on a subconscious, not a conscious level) that he formerly hurt *her*. Then comes a new lifetime for both, and now it's John's turn to hurt Mary again — then Mary's to hurt John — with each becoming the channel for the other's boomerang Karma in a chain of dreary, seemingly endless lives (incarnations).

Such a chain of Karma can be broken in only two ways.

1. The one most recently hurt (in a previous existence) is John. He is enlightened to the truth of karmic law, and refuses to be the continuing channel for Mary's Karma. He realizes that his inex-

plicable urge to hurt her is somehow "coming to her" (he senses this subconsciously) — but he makes a *conscious* decision to refuse to become a channel for her karmic retribution (what she has coming, under karmic law). In effect, Mary is *forgiven* by John, and the chain of Karma breaks. (Mary is fortunate.) A broken karmic chain brings freedom to *both* people who have been linked to it.

2. John is not yet sufficiently enlightened to behave as described in the previous paragraph, but Mary is enlightened to the truth of karmic law, and responds to the hurt inflicted on her by John by saying to herself (and *meaning it*), "What must I have done to this person to cause him to hurt me so ? I've done nothing to cause such hurt in this life, but I must have hurt him in a former life or I wouldn't be in this position. I can experience no luck, good or bad, that I didn't bring on myself by initiating a like action in a former incarnation. Therefore, I not only deserve this, but perhaps more." Mary, in other words, is willing to pay her karmic debt gracefully and willingly, without bitterness or resentment. Once Mary has accepted the hurt as *her own responsibility*, and holds no resentment to plant itself in the seed atom of the heart, and therefore be retained in subconscious memory in the next life, she has *broken the chain of Karma* through a different kind of forgiveness — through an understanding that will be carried over to the next existence when she meets John again.

That's how it works. The karmic chain can be broken by *either one* of the two people bound by it (and, of course, you have karmic ties with many people . . . not just one). It can be broken either by the potential *giver* of the Karma — or by the potential *receiver* of the Karma.

Remember, you have no luck — either good or bad — that you don't deserve because of your actions, whether in this life or in an earlier one. Every action set in motion will remain in motion until it is negated by a balancing of the laws of cause and effect — a leveling of the karmic debt. It's inescapable. In a moment, I'll give you another example of how to balance your Karma. What causes all the confusion is forgetfulness. Karmic amnesia is a tragic thing. To learn from past experience requires some remembered knowledge of the lessons of that past experience. The word "memory" contains the two words "more" and "me." If you could only remember more, you would have more of yourself. It's been said that just the *belief* in reincarnation will gradually bring the memory of past lives as a gift to an illuminated spirit.

However, you must become *illuminated* to receive the gift of karmic memory, capable of tuning in and out of memory *selectively* — just as you might tune in or out of a radio station or a television channel. Otherwise, chaos would result in the mind and brain, leading to insanity. Imagine how it would be if you could *not* tune in a radio station or television channel *selectively*, and all stations or channels were bombarding you simultaneously. You would hear and see nothing but senseless and frightening chaotic confusion. That's why, at your current level of evolvement, you're protected from such certain insanity of simultaneous karmic memory by a form of spiritual amnesia, until you begin to vibrate on a high enough frequency to be able to be *selective* in karmic recall.

The pattern of Karma is not difficult to grasp. What is the mysterious force set into motion by your actions ? Karma. How is this force controlled and directed ? By the Higher Angel of Yourself, the teacher in your spiritual classroom. How do you break the chain of Karma ? By getting in touch with your own Higher Self, via tuning in, as to a radio station or television channel, on the right frequency. How do you accomplish this ? Through electromagnetic energy — magnetic attraction. Where do you obtain this energy ? From *desire*. Through intense wanting — needing — seeking — desiring. Intense desire creates an energy wave that joins others on the same frequency level, and varying degrees of enlightenment occur.

Once again, "Seek the truth, and the truth shall set you free." The first steps toward seeking the truth are wanting, wishing, needing, desiring. Reading all the books on the subject of Karma and reincarnation you can find. If your desire to *know* is sincere and intense, not just idle curiosity, you'll begin to experience flashes of déjà vu that can lead you into the realms of self-discovery you need in order to selectively remember long ago and far away. You will have *ordained* such memory, karmic recall — and you will get it. "Ask and you shall receive." It's that simple.

It may seem like a non sequitur, but it is, in fact, *so* simple that it's often difficult to grasp, unless you "become as a little child" — the requirement given by the Galilean to "enter the Kingdom" (of your Higher Self).

It won't happen immediately, but it will happen, and it will be an exciting surprise when it does. You'll see. The time is swiftly approaching in this Aquarian Age for all karmic circles to complete themselves, for all Twin Selves, separated so many eons ago, to find each other and unite again in perfect Oneness, bringing about the ultimate Harmony of the Universe. The time will soon come when clear and total recall, vivid images of déjà vu will replace current karmic amnesia . . . and memories of paths once walked together will be brought into sharp focus by choice, so that everyone might visit long-forgotten, precious events of past lives. The Time Machine envisioned by H. G. Wells is not a scientific instrument, not an invention accomplished through the laws of physics, but a method of travel *within yourself*, built upon the laws of metaphysics, (*beyond* physics). As Wells himself wrote, ". . . the day will come when we shall walk again in vanished scenes . . . stretch painted limbs we thought were dust . . . and feel the sunshine of a million years ago."

Meanwhile . . .

. . . until you train yourself to receive flashes of former lives, and are successful in achieving this from time to time, there's an effective alternate way to balance your Karma. First, when something severely negative happens to you, *realize* that you inflicted the same kind of suffering on someone (most likely that same person) in a previous existence, or *you would not be receiving it now.* Accept *full responsibility* for the negative situation, even though it appears *on the surface* that you're innocent of causing it. Remove from your mind and heart *all* bitterness and resentment toward the giver of the hurt, and *know* that he or she (not comprehending the first method of breaking the karmic chain I described a few pages back), is merely the channel for this particular Karma, which you set into motion yourself in a former life, never mind that you can't now remember doing so.

Such total and sincere acceptance (it must be genuine and deeply felt, not just an act) will, of itself alone, considerably lighten the burden of the particular Karma you're experiencing, and you'll sense it right away. Often, the person will seem confused or vaguely ashamed, and stop the negative action, either immediately, or gradually.

Next step: meditate on the *polarity* of the negative action — the thing which is now happening to you, but which you did to another in a former incarnation — and perform that polarity action (or several) of the opposite quality toward one or several people, including the person who is causing your suffering. Quite often, this will balance the scales of Karma so that the cause of your suffering is permanently removed, and matters turn rightside up again swiftly (usually shockingly). You may need a couple of brief examples.

This is a true story. A friend of mine in Charleston, West Virginia, was shaken when his doctors told him he had contracted a rare disease for which medical science has no cure, and which would gradually, over the period of less than a year, completely paralyze him. He first accepted responsibility for this Karma. He realized that he had caused someone (or several people) to be paralyzed in a former life, and having set the situation into motion, the *reaction* of his initial action was now attempting to balance the scales, under karmic law.

(Karmic law is quite impersonal.) He could have initiated such action by being a hit-and-run driver, running from the scene of an accident, leaving his victim paralyzed — he could have inflicted paralysis on another in the "wonderful sport" of football or boxing — he could even have been one of those in Rome in charge of throwing the Christians to the Lions in the Coliseum. Next, he meditated upon several forms of *polarity action,* and made a decision.

He resigned from his job, and at a substantial financial loss, while suffering increasing pain, he offered his services to a crippled children's hospital in a nearby city for a modest salary, barely enough to allow him to rent a small furnished room near the hospital grounds. He read aloud to the children, assisted with their physical therapy, and performed several unpleasant but necessary menial janitorial tasks. During the first week, he was so moved by the cheerful smiles and noncomplaining attitudes of the children, many of whom had been diagnosed as terminal, he forgot about his own illness, except at night, when the pain seemed to take over more severely in his limbs, making it difficult to sleep. Three months after he began working with the crippled children, he noticed his pain had substantially subsided, and a couple of weeks later, he had no sensation of discomfort at all. Returning to Charleston for a scheduled series of medical tests and treatments, his amazed doctor told him that all signs of the fatal disease had disappeared. "Spontaneous remission" is what his doctor called his complete recovery (the medical term for a miracle). Karmic law, as I said, is impersonal. It's not concerned with *how* the scales are balanced, *only that they are balanced.*

Here's another example of lifting Karma. When a woman is told that she is barren, that she can't conceive a child for whatever medical reason (except an upside-down uterus), there's a karmic cause for this tragedy of unfulfilled longing. She has either repeatedly refused to bear children for selfish reasons in several past lifetimes, or has abused them in some manner. So she decides to adopt a child. (I'm not leaving out the husband, I'm just concentrating on the woman's individual Karma in this example.) What happens after the adoption ? A physician friend of mine in New York, and another in California, told me that the statistics are as high as seventy-five to eighty-five percent. Of what ? Seventy-five to eighty-five percent of women diagnosed as barren (including those whose husbands have a low sperm count) who then adopt a child, discover soon afterward, to their delight, that they've become pregnant.

The barren woman has been made so by her Karma, the teacher of her lessons in the spiritual classroom, so she'll comprehend what it's like to be alone and childless, and consequently carry over this subconscious memory into the next existence, during which she will neither refuse to bear children nor abuse them. However, when she indicates that she's *already learned* this karmic lesson of atonement by taking in a motherless child to give it love, the karmic burden is lifted. Naturally, the husband's Karma is also lifted, since it's entwined with hers.

In those cases where adoption takes place and the woman does not later become pregnant, then the action against children in a former life has been extremely negative (perhaps even murder), leaving a Karma which requires more than one act of atonement in more than one incarnation to balance it out. Still, by taking in a baby needing love and care, and treating it as her own, she is gradually erasing past karmic debts, and is on her way to a complete absolution of them. At least she's going forward instead of going backward . . . or standing still.

There are as many examples of Karma as there are people on this Earth, each with thousands of minor and major facets of karmic cause and effect entangling the events in their lives. The one wide-sweeping and instant way to break each karmic chain is to forgive everyone who hurts you, even *before* they ask — even when they *never* ask. Not only will forgiveness break your karmic chain, but also theirs — unless and until they go running out to make new Karma for themselves — and unless and until you do the same.

If someone steals from you, you can be sure that you've stolen from someone, most likely that same person, by whatever name and in whatever body (the temple of the soul) he or she resided in during a relationship in a former existence. When you receive kindness and compassion, financial aid — or any kind of *apparently* undeserved favor — from someone in this life, it's not undeserved at all. You can be sure that you performed the same service for that person in a previous incarnation, and he or she is magnetized by karmic law to return it now. It works both ways, you see. The John-hurts-Mary, Mary-hurts-John pattern can also be John-*helps*-Mary, Mary-*helps*-John karmic chain . . . and that's the "golden chain that binds."

Again, the words of the Nazarene were simple and clear. "Do good unto all those who hate you and say all manner of evil against you . . . if a man strikes you on the right cheek, turn and let him strike you on the left cheek . . . and if any man will sue thee at the law, and take away thy coat, let him have thy cloak also. . . . Resist ye *not* evil." In other words, pay your karmic debts gracefully, without complaining, without bitterness or resentment, and the karmic yoke will be miraculously lifted from you — assuming your "grace-ful" acceptance is balanced with a positive act that will balance the former negative action in the karmic scales. First, accept. Then, forgive. And finally, atone. Become at-one with yourself.

I might add, in reference to certain modern religious movements, that just speaking the words, "I accept Jesus as my Saviour and God as my King" does not constitute a magical mantra to remove karmic responsibility. Such spiritual laziness will accomplish no miracles. You never hear these people quoting Jesus concerning the major flaw in their philosophy, do you ? "Judge not that ye be judged." The "Jesus saves" mantra often sounds less like a blessing than an unspoken threat. Believe as I believe, or you'll burn in hell . . . . and all you need do to achieve happiness is to repeat a few words . . . presto ! I'm afraid that's not quite all there is to it. And what of those who believe in the teachings of Avatars other than the Nazarene ? Those who follow the equally wise precepts of Mohammed and Buddha — (profoundly wise, that is, excluding the false doctrine of transmigration, which may have been a distortion of the original teaching).

The frequently misunderstood and misinterpreted Old Testament's *"an eye for an eye, and a tooth for a tooth"* is *not* meant to counsel retribution and retaliation. It refers to the law of Karma, the law of cause and effect. For every action there is equal *re*action. Take away someone's sight, and you will lose yours (unless you learn how to atone and cancel the Karma). Take even so much as a tooth with malicious intent, and someday, somewhere, somehow that person will take a tooth from you . . . and so on . . . whatever the injury, whatever the theft, whatever the hurt done to another might be.

You might ask, "What difference will it make if I have to pay later for what I do now if I can't remember it in a future life ?" Does it make any difference to anyone that you've seen suffering severe affliction in this present life ? Obviously, it makes a great difference. And so will it to you — *then*. The suffering person you see at present would give anything to be able to change the past that caused it — too late. People forget that they are preparing for their *then* — right *now*.

Reincarnation and the law of Karma so clearly and totally explain the reason for the differences between the sighted and the blind — the healthy and the crippled — the poor and the wealthy — the fulfilled and the lonely. Yet the leaders of all organized religions and creeds today, when they're asked to explain such apparently unfair and cruel judgment (assuming only *one* life or existence) from a supremely benign Diety, respond only with: "no comment" or "we are not to question these things." My response to the latter is: We are not to question ? Not so ! The Nazarene specifically counseled that we are to "seek the truth."

Perhaps these religious leaders are pleading a sort of spiritual Fifth Amendment, based on "whatever they say might incriminate them" — or might expose the lack of a foundation beneath their moral teachings ? That solid, that beautifully just and logical foundation is Karma — its road maps being astrology and numerology, concepts held by the Essenes, who were among those from whom Jesus learned during his eighteen "lost years," the accounts of which were also removed by the ones who committed their spiritual surgery upon the words of the Galilean as written in the "new testaments" of his disciples.

The important truth one must always remember about Karma is that every man and woman began the long journey together — and each will *positively* reach the same destination — at an individual time, through an individually chosen method of travel, on an individually selected path, using a likewise individually selected roadmap (religious belief). As the poet Kahlil Gibran succinctly expressed it: "You cannot rise higher than the highest which is in each of you — nor can you sink lower than the lowest which is in each of you." Everyone is headed toward the same destination, the eventual arrival equally assured for each, regardless of the chosen mode of travel. Incidentally, when one adds the "y" for *you,* the word "destination" contains the word *destiny*.

The concept of Karma and reincarnation, astrology and numerology, were removed from the Christian Bible (remember that the word Bible contains the word 'lie' in Lexigram code) through the sacrilegious surgery of the early church "fathers" (the patriarch system has never allowed church mothers) at various times in the past, including the Council of Trent in A.D. 300, and the Council of Constantinople in A.D. 553, aided by Emperor Justinian and Empress Theodora, who insisted that all references to these concepts be removed from the Holy Works, and the Pope acquiesced. Fortunately, these sacrilegious surgeons missed a few in their haste, such as the verses of Ecclesiastes, which describe astrology and the planetary movements related to human behavior . . . and several brief discourses between Jesus and his disciples referring to multiple reincarnations . . . to name only two examples.

★ ★ ★ ★ ★ ★

The song "People," from the stage musical and motion picture, *Funny Girl*, observes that "lovers are very lucky people . . . they're the luckiest people in the world." Oh, yes, they are. So very true are those words.

Lovers are very lucky people in a karmic sense, the most fortunate of all those who are making the long, weary journey back home. Lovers may suffer more from the negative chains of their mutual Karma than others, but they also rejoice in higher levels of ecstasy from Karma's positive rewards than others do. They're blessed with a more intense desire (energy, remember ?) to draw back the curtains veiling former relationships shared in previous incarnations. Instinctively, they're more aware of how to tune into the Angels of their Higher Selves.

All lovers are linked by the silver cords (and musical chords) of déjà vu, the shared memories of past reciprocal tenderness and passion — yes, and also past reciprocal hurt and pain — realized fleetingly but intensely during those enchanted moments of staring deeply into each other's eyes, because the eyes are the windows of the soul . . . and spirit.

Few modern authors have written about Karma (except for those recommended in the *Pilgrim's Progress* section at the end of this book) but many poets have used it as a basis for their works. Elizabeth Barrett and Robert Browning were Twin Selves, and Elizabeth's familiar sonnet, *How Do I Love Thee?* has a karmic theme . . . as does this portion of a Rossetti poem . . .

> I have been here before. . .
> I know the grass beyond the door
>   the sweet, keen smell
> the sighing sound, the lights around the shore

you have been mine before
'though how or when I cannot tell
yet, just when at that swallow's soar
　　　　your neck turned so . . .
I knew it all of yore

'though age, faith or creed
may keep us now apart . . .
one travels the hill, the other, the lake
I claim you still for my own love's sake
delayed 'though it may be for more lives yet
much is to learn, much to forget
e're the time be come for taking you
but the time will come . . . oh, yes !
　　　　　　　　　　　　the time will come

★ ★ ★ ★ ★ ★

As for the fourteenth line in these Rossetti verses, such reunion need *not* be "delayed . . . for more lives yet." When lovers understand how to employ the law of Karma, the waiting may not be necessary; fulfillment is attainable in the present incarnation for both. . . when they listen to the whispers of the Higher Angels of themselves . . . and forgive one another.

If you ever happen to be debating the truth of reincarnation or Karma with someone who denies its existence, ask that person to explain or to account for *déjà vu*, those inexplicable, yet very vivid and very real — and often very provable flashes of another time . . . another place . . . striking one unexpectedly. Such déjà vu recall has been experienced by millions of both private and public people, from Ralph Waldo Emerson to Henry Ford, General Patton and many others. You can read about what happened to convince them of the truth of Karma in the books listed in the *Pilgrim's Progress* section following Chapter 9, among them, *Reincarnation in World Thought*, edited by

Cranston and Head — or their second book, *The Phoenix Fire Mystery*, especially the first one, my personal favorite, although the second one is equally enlightening. They may be out of print now, but any good used bookstore should be able to locate them for you through its "grapevine."

A postscript: While writing this chapter, I found another dictionary in my den, and I was right about blaming Merriam instead of Webster for the definition of Karma I gave you earlier ! This dictionary is called *Webster's New World Dictionary* — no mention of Merriam. The Webster definition, while still a touch chauvinistic, omits transmigration, and it gives a clear and correct meaning of the word.

KARMA: *the totality of a person's actions in any one of the successive states of his existence, thought of as determining his fate in the next*

"Quite"

★ ★ ★ ★ ★ ★

5

WHILE
THE SOUL
SLUMBERS

the study of numerology,
based on the Hebrew Kabala teachings
and the Chaldean Alphabet . . .
the one and only true and correct system of numbers

Mystical
Meanings
and
Practical
Applications
of
Numbers

. . . for, did not the Egyptian Adepti teach
        "put the mysteries of wisdom into
practice
        and all evil will flee from you" ?

numerological contains the two words
    magic and logical
yes, the science of numbers is wise
as "Abstract Al" Einstein knew
in the Wonderland of higher mathematics

    everything in Heaven and on Earth
    is arranged according to numerical discipline
    . . . and the laws of metaphysics
    are as inflexible and reliable
    as those governing the ordinary physics
                        of matter

numbers are not dead — no, ciphers live !
and they give to the mind that seeks a knowing
in the dawning light of the spirit's growing
answers.

        ". . . while the soul slumbers
        God speaks to us in numbers"

★ ★ ★ ★ ★ ★

O COMMENCE, it's necessary to point out certain facts about the little understood and much maligned art and science of numerology, for those of you who might have been led astray in the past.

There are several numerical alphabets and numerological systems of calculation, and goodness knows how many books written about them. This is a pity because *only one* numerical alphabet, that which has been handed down by the ancient Chaldeans and the Hebrew Kabala, is valid. Likewise, there is only one system of numerological calculation which is true and reliable — the Chaldean and Kabala system, also used by the Essenes, who taught Jesus of Nazareth during his eighteen "lost years."

Most people in today's society have an attitude toward numerology ranging from amused scepticism to downright disbelief and ridicule. I don't blame them. There's plenty to be amused by — and sceptical or disbelieving of — in the majority of books on the subject. Most of them are no more reliable than a numerical alphabet and system you made up yourself would be.

Consequently, numerology has come to be considered only a sort of parlor game, using "hot numbers" for betting on lotteries and horse races ("hot numbers" based on false alphabets and systems). To most people, numerology is a joke, not far removed from fortune-telling — more or less "a fun thing." Rather than allow the reputation of numerology to grow worse, I believe it's time to try to explain the only true numerology, and trust that the knowledge of it will remove some of the existing stigma against a remarkably helpful art and science, as people learn to use the correct alphabet and system, and observe how infallibly it works.

There are several ways the misguided pied pipers of numbers distort the truth of numerology, but it's sufficient to know this: a reliable guide to the *wrong* books written about numerology is the numerical alphabet they contain. If you read anything on the subject of numerology, and it's based on the numerical values of each letter of the alphabet *other than the following one,* the system taught in such a book will *not* work, is not reliable, and your study of such a numerological system will be a waste of time. Using any numerical alphabet other than the following one, and expecting your numerological calculations to be correct and helpful, is tantamount to applying astrology in your life from an astrology book that describes Aries as timid — Leo as introverted — Gemini as stable and stuffy — and Capricorn as impulsive and extravagant, for example. The wrong numerical alpha-

bets give numerology as bad a name as the daily newspaper astrological predictions give to astrology — although *monthly* predictions,
in a general sense, based on the Sun Sign alone, do have a limited
validity.

The correct Chaldean-Hebrew Kabala numerical alphabet has already been shown in the Introduction on page xxvii. But I want to
present it again here, so it's handier while you're learning the system of
calculating numbers given in this chapter.

Chaldean–Hebrew Kabala Numerical Alphabet

A – 1	H – 5	O – 7	V – 6
B – 2	I – 1	P – 8	W – 6
C – 3	J – 1	Q – 1	X – 5
D – 4	K – 2	R – 2	Y – 1
E – 5	L – 3	S – 3	Z – 7
F – 8	M – 4	T – 4	
G – 3	N – 5	U – 6	

Before you place your faith in even this correct system of numerology, you should try its calculations for yourself. Then you'll be able
to discover *how* it works — but most important, *if* it works. You
shouldn't accept that from me or anyone else — only from your own
experience. Speaking for my own self, I've never been a real sceptic
about numerology; nevertheless I always need to know the *why* of
every esoteric science, and then I have to test it repeatedly to be certain it's valid. Many well-known historical figures have had complete
faith in the power of numbers (including the founders of America, as
we'll learn more about in Chapter 7, *Forgotten Melodies*), but I've al-

ways needed to experience everything for myself before I totally trust it. I had the same attitude about astrology, when it first beckoned me. After I had taken the time to really study it, and cast charts for people I knew, I could see there was no use doubting it. It simply works.

As I said in the Introduction to this book, but it bears repeating, there are a multiplicity of star signs and universal codes which are beyond — yet inseparable from — astrology. Each astrological sign has its ruling planet, and each planet vibrates to its own *number*. As unrelated to planetary influence as numerology, sound, music, and color may seem, they all, nevertheless, *initiate* from the Luminaries (Sun and Moon) and the planets — and are the star signs of wisdom.

King Solomon asked God to give him wisdom as "the greatest gift he could receive," and was granted this gift simply because he asked for it. *"Ask and you shall receive." "Knock, and it shall be opened unto you." "Seek the truth, and the truth shall set you free."*

In the Book of Solomon included in the Apocrypha, King Solomon, "the Wise," expresses his gratitude for this gift of "unerring knowledge of all things that are" . . . "all things that are secret or manifest" . . . in these words:

I thank Thee, O Great Creator of the Universe that Thou hast taught me the secrets of the Planets that I mayest know the Times and Seasons of things, the secrets of men's hearts, their thoughts and the nature of their being. Thou gavest me this knowledge, which is the foundation of all my Wisdom.

Astrology is inseparable from numerology, and Solomon was a wise king indeed, aided in his thoughts and deeds by both of these arts and sciences. Yet, alas ! He was also a chauvinist ("the secrets of *men's* hearts"), raised in the bosom of a patriarch society. Our Mother Who art in Heaven has forgiven Solomon and all of Her sons who

have turned away from Her unknowingly, and so I shall forgive him
— and them — also.

As for King Solomon's unintentional chauvinism, a quick but
pertinent digression. Are you aware that *all Mother Goose rhymes are
riddles to be solved* ? Some of them are easy to decode, others more
difficult. I'd like to share with you this particular verse of hers, which
hides more than one mystery. First, you must realize that Humpty
Dumpty is a symbol for our Earth. Then read "between the lines."
I've given you a clue for decoding the first layer of its message in my
self-composed second verse.

> Humpty Dumpty sat on a wall
> Humpty Dumpty had a great *fall*
>
> All the King's horses, and all the King's men
> couldn't put Humpty together again.
>
> No, all the King's horses, and all the King's men
> couldn't put Humpty together again
> until all the Queen's women forgave all the King's men
> Then the miracle of love healed all Humpty's hurts
> and made him whole and complete once again.

★ ★ ★ ★ ★ ★

The origin of numbers is unknown, although it's certain that
Hermes Thoth knew a great deal about them, eons ago, before Atlantis. The ancient Chaldeans, Egyptians, Hindus, Essenes, and the wise
ones of the Arabic world were masters of the hidden meanings of
numbers. Certain of these enlightened ones discovered what today is
known as the Precession of the Equinoxes, calculating that such an
occurrence takes place every 25,850 years. How they arrived at such
a calculation is a mystery. By observation ? That answer requires that
they had to be around in the same flesh bodies for longer than the
approximately twenty-six thousand years of the precession. Could

they possibly have calculated to such a fine degree without instruments ? Our modern science, after laboring for hundreds of years, has been able to do nothing but prove and acknowledge the accuracy of the calculations of these ancient ones.

Some things must simply be accepted, with the certainty that the answers will reveal themselves . . . at the allotted time. Because everything, as poetically and astrologically observed in the Book of Ecclesiastes of our Holy Works, has an allotted time. "To everything there is a season, and a time for every purpose under the heaven . . ."

The study and practical application of numerology is not contrary to anyone's religious beliefs. It's merely one of the many facets of the harmonics of the Universe and synchronization to Nature's laws. Earthlings bring suffering upon themselves by not complying with these simple and logical laws. If they would learn how to harmonize with them, then happiness, health, and success would be attainable, instead of an ever-beckoning, seemingly impossible dream. People call Nature and "Fate" unjust, cruel, and unfair, *yet they remain unwilling to take the time and trouble of learning in which direction these irresistible forces are moving.*

Most of those who pray "Thy will be done on Earth, as it is in Heaven" have no intention of attempting to discover just what that "will" is which is obeyed in "Heaven," and broken by Earthlings nearly every hour of their lives. Organized religion, all Churches, are, in essence, monuments to the unknown and mysterious, *yet the already known lives within each man and each woman.* "Seek ye first the Kingdom within, and all these things shall be added unto you." Earthlings have tried every spiritual creed, and they've all failed to bring the comfort needed. The keys or "star signs" to the mysteries of the Universe were once entrusted to priests, rabbis, and prelates, who long ago lost the truth in their cloisters and monasteries — or buried it in their secret ceremonies and shrouded rituals.

Astrology and numerology are eternally interlocked and interconnected. The true solar year begins when the Sun enters into the Spring Equinox between the 21st and 23rd day of March each year, then appears to pass through each astrological sign of the zodiac of 30 degrees each, one after the other, Aries through Pisces, which takes slightly less than 365½ days, making our calendar year popularly (albeit a tad incorrectly) accepted as 365 days . . .

Each 24 hours, as the Earth revolves once upon its own axis, the twelve signs in their turn pass once over each portion of the Earth. Simultaneously, the Moon revolves around the Earth in a lunar month of 28 days — exactly like the hour hand, minute hand, and second hand of a clock.

Each astrological sign has its own planetary ruler. And each planet vibrates to a certain *number*.

9 is the number of the planet Mars, ruler of Aries.

6 is the number of the planet Venus, ruler of Taurus and Libra (until the true ruler of Taurus, Pan-Horus, is discovered).

5 is the number of the planet Mercury, ruler of Gemini and Virgo (until the true ruler of Virgo, Vulcan, is discovered).

7 is the number of the planet Neptune, ruler of Pisces.

8 is the number of the planet Saturn, ruler of Capricorn.

4 is the number of the planet Uranus, ruler of Aquarius.

3 is the number of the planet Jupiter, ruler of Sagittarius.

2 is the number of the Moon, ruler of Cancer.

1 is the number of the Sun, ruler of Leo.

0 (zero) is the powerful number of Pluto, ruler of Scorpio.

Remember I told you that all the star sign codes begin with the planets. The vibratory frequency then continues in an unchanging magnetic direction or pattern.

★ ★ ★ ★ ★ ★

It's very important for you to keep clearly in your mind, as you read the following few pages referencing the "3-legged stool man," that I am not referring to "evolutionary man" in the sense that the Darwinists and proponents of evolution interpret his origin and existence. The Darwin theory is partly correct and partly incorrect. Its major flaw lies in the omission of a vital fact, which is the true "missing link" in the chain they've tried to forge of the genesis of a puzzle they've only dimly comprehended and tried to piece together from the findings of geology and archeology, only the "bare bones of a skeleton of truth," so to speak.

They are correct in their assumptions of the various stages of man's evolutionary process (but absolutely incorrect regarding animals) — while omitting the most important piece of the puzzle: how prehistoric man got that way. They seem to imply that the "cave man" evolved from animals, leaving dangling the questions of where the animals came from, and why they are still here. Can you handle an amazing statement ? You haven't found the answers in anything written in books by evolutionists, geologists, or archeologists, but you don't need to because *you know every detail of all the answers yourself.* You've only forgotten. The mission of this book and the two books that will follow it is to *teach you how to remember those answers.*

The answers you already know but have forgotten (just as the cave man forgot how to count) which will be given in future books — will not contradict the Darwin theory, only enrich it and give it the foundation it's always needed.

Meanwhile, allow me to remind you again that the 3-legged stool man referred to within the next few pages refers to man *after the fall* from innocence and wisdom. (If you possess the former, you automatically possess the latter.)

Such a fall from grace has occurred, not once, but many times on this planet — and each time initiates an earth-cataclysm of such gigantic and destructive proportions that only a few humans survive it, scattered all over the world, separated, lonely, lost, and unable to communicate with one another. In their desperate struggle for bare survival (those who possess the survival instinct; others give up quickly), and suffering also from mutation caused by cataclysm, they develop a gradual amnesia of all former knowledge, and must slowly and painfully regain it. These fallen angels, these lost souls constitute the so-called "cave man" of the paleolithic period.

For instance, each of the planets and constellations must be rediscovered for the wisdom of astrology and astronomy to be recaptured. Likewise with the wisdom of numbers. The numerical system of both numerology and third-dimensional mathematics must each time be rediscovered and relearned (as with the 3-legged stool man illustration below.)

Then the process of what is called evolution begins, described by the evolution proponents with much accuracy. Along with it comes the process of relearning and remembering LOVE, a word that seems to arouse contempt in historians, geologists, and archaeologists, who ignore as meaningless the fact that the word LOVE is contained within the word EVOLUTION. They won't even discuss the matter, believing it to be a mere coincidence, therefore remaining blind to its urgent message. (See Chapter 8.) Love does not hide within evolution coincidently, but wisely and truly so — as an eternal star sign code.

Evolution progresses at different speeds in different ways in various parts of the planet geographically. One clue: the word "Incan," related to the ancient Incans, means "the lost ones." Another clue: the "creature" known as Sasquatch, or Bigfoot, is far more than what most people define as a creature. And by the way, the word CREATURE contains the word CREATE. Why don't you spend some time wondering why ? A prediction and a promise for tomorrow: Very soon now, a Lion will uncover many of the secrets of Bigfoot, an event foretold by the decoding of the mystery of the Egyptian Sphinx, the man-lion guarding the Great Pyramid of Giza. And now, let's meet our "3-legged stool man."

1-2-3 are the first numbers "man" comprehended. He placed a stick on the ground, representing himself — or the number 1. Then he placed another stick on the ground, representing his mate. Now he had the number 2 — or 2 sticks. He placed the tip of the 2 sticks representing himself and his mate so that they touched at the top, and were separated at the bottom, in a tentlike shape. After this, he placed a third stick on the ground, horizontally across the bottom, representing the child, the total of the 3 sticks then forming a triangle, the oldest known spiritual symbol: father — mother — and logos child. Soon our slowly comprehending man drew a circle around the 3 sticks, to protect himself, his mate, and his child from outsiders or evil. Then he stood the 3 sticks on end, contemplated the circle — and the concept of the first 3-legged stool was born.

For ages, the number 7 has been regarded as the number of mystery, representing the *spiritual* side of things — whereas the number 9, the end, or the finality of the series upon which all our materialistic calculations are built, has for an equal number of ages been regarded as the number of electrical energy and all life upon this planet in a *material* sense. The number 0 represents power (which is why it's the number of the planet, Pluto, ruler of Scorpio, since Pluto is the most powerful of all the planets). Add 0 to any number, and the more zeros you add, the more "powerful" the number becomes. From 1 to 10 to 100 to 1,000 to 100,000 to 1,000,000, and so on. The number 0 is considered to be the number of Eternity (the Eternal Now ?) — the serpent, eating its own tail. Positive energy feeding into negative energy, resulting in a third energy, which is both, yet neither, and all-powerful.

It's most significant that Friedrich Kekule, who made the monumental discovery of the benzine ring structure, which paved the way for the theoretical aspect of organic chemistry, said that he dreamed repeatedly of "a snake eating its own tail," shortly before the concept occurred to him. His Higher Self was sending him a Morse Code message.

The number 1 is the first number comprehended by our 3-legged stool man. It represents, according to the ancients, the First Cause, the Creator, or God, call it what you like.

When you take the number 1 and add the symbol of Eternity — 0 — in a figure representing 1,000,000 or more, then divide it by the mystical number 7 (representing the spiritual side of things) — you get the number 142857, which has been called, from the beginning of time, the "sacred number." For example:

$$7 \overline{\smash{\big)}\,1,000,000}$$
$$142857$$

Add as many zeros as you like, and keep dividing by 7 through all of eternity, and you will always get repetitions of the same sacred number. Why is this a "sacred number"? Because these numbers, when added together, equal the double number 27, and when you add the 2 and the 7 of 27, you end up with 9 — the number of electrical energy and all material life on this planet. This is also what is referred to in the Bible (never mind those satanic implications in horror films that try to scare you) in the statement the "666 is the number of man and the number of beast." Of course it is. 666 adds to 18 and 18 adds to 9, which is the number of all life on Earth.

$1 + 4 + 2 + 8 + 5 + 7 = 27 = 9$. Sacred Number of Eternity.

Now, just think of that! When you take the number of the First

Cause, or the *Creator* — 1 — then add the zeros — 0 — of *Power,* and divide by 7, the number of mystery and the *Spiritual* side of things — you get the sacred number 142857, which, when added, then produces the number 9 — material *Life.* That's the whole story of existence, *n'est-ce pas* ?

Why is 7 the number of mystery relating to spiritual matters ? First, take the *seven* days of Creation, as symbolically referred to in Genesis — and the Seventh Heaven referred to several times in the Holy Works. The seven churches — the seven thrones — the seven Seals — the seven-day march around the walls of Jericho — and on the 7th day, the walls fell down, when Joshua blew the right note on his Ram's horn. There are 7 generations from the birth of David to the birth of Jesus in Bethlehem ("who shall be born of the House of David").

Ezekiel speaks of "the seven angels of the Lord that go to and fro through the whole Earth," which is believed by metaphysicians to refer to the magnetic power points which radiate through the Earth, and could be the basis for Nikola Tesla's magnetic fields in the Earth, upon which he based his discovery of alternating current. This mysterious power is also spoken of in the Book of Revelation as "the seven spirits of God sent forth into all the Earth." And . . . look at all these additional repeats of the spiritual number 7:

> The seven spirits of the Egyptian religion.
> The seven Angels of the Chaldeans.
> The seven Devas of the Hindu religion.
> The seven Sephiroth of the Hebrew Kabala.
> The seven Amschaspands of the Persian faith.
> The seven Archangels of Revelation . . . and on and on . . .

In every religion, the number 7 symbolizes the mysterious "God Force," or spiritual power. It's inescapable. Remember, the number of the planet Neptune, ruler of Pisces, the Fish, is 7. The Fish was the symbol of Christianity during the time of Jesus, who was born during the Age of Pisces (the previous Age to this Aquarian Age). The miracles performed by the Nazarene were all Neptunian, mysterious and spiritual in essence. (Just a preliminary touch of Lexigrams here — when you take the word "essence," and remove the "c" for Christ, the word you have left is Essene. It was among the Essenes up in the mountains where Jesus spent many of his "lost years," learning numerology and astrology, among other studies.)

It was probably the Essenes who first discovered what the Chaldeans and Hindus also knew: that the number 7 is the *only number capable of dividing the number of Eternity* — of continuing itself as long as the number representing Eternity lasts, and yet, at every addition of itself, produces the number 9, the basis of all material calculations, and the entire edifice upon which human life depends and human thought finds expression. Even stranger, astronomers are puzzled by the seven-day week, first conceived in the Book of Genesis, because the period of 7 days doesn't fit precisely into either months or seasons of the year. It is said to be "a number man would not naturally adopt."

The *material* number 9 fascinates me personally even more than the magical facets of the spiritual number 7, mostly, I guess, because it's the number of my favorite planet, Mars — ruler of my Aries sun sign. The number 9 can do even more "magic tricks" than the number 7 in proving itself to be the number of electrical energy, the Alpha and the Omega (beginning and end of everything) — and of all human life on Earth, on the material plane of existence. Let's put 9 through its tricks.

To begin with, when you add together all the numbers in our numerical system . . . 1 + 2 + 3 + 4 + 5 + 6 + 7 + 8 + 9 . . . you get the number 45, which, when you add the 4 and 5, becomes *nine*. There's no escaping or denying it. In this Third Dimension we live within on our present level of evolvement, 9 is the Big Boss.

The number 9 cannot be destroyed, no matter how many times you multiply it or add it to its own multiple, and *this is true of no other number*. 2 times 9 equals 18, which adds to 9. 3 times 9 is 27, which adds to 9. 4 times 9 is 36, which adds to (or reduces to) the single number 9 — and so on, into infinity. To repeat, *9 cannot be destroyed — and neither can the human life it represents be destroyed.*

We have the 9-day prayers of the Novenas in the Catholic Church. In Freemasonry (based on astrology) there is the Order of the 9 Elected Knights, and in the working of this order 9 roses — 9 lights and 9 knocks must be used.

A Great Sidereal Year is 25,920 years. When added, these figures become 18, which reduces to the single number 9. The Sidereal Year is closely related to the Precession of the Equinoxes: the length of time it takes for all the planets to return to their original positions and relationships to each other. It takes 72 years to complete one degree of this equinoctical precession. 7 + 2 equal 9. *Any* number of degrees of equinoctical precession equate to 9. Two degrees, for instance, take 144 years — three degrees take 216 years — five degrees take 360 years — ten degrees take 720 years — and so on. All of which add to or reduce to 9. This is no accident or coincidence. It's part of the synchronized harmony of the Universe.

John Nelson, former head of RCA Laboratories in New York, used astrology to calculate weather conditions for RCA. He told me he had discovered that when two planets are "square" to each other in a particular latitude/longitude, a thunderstorm occurs. In astrology, in a human horoscope, a square is an aspect of "tension" — and planets "square" each other when they are exactly 90 degrees apart. 9 again. (Remember that this isn't necessarily negative, because thunderstorms "clear the air" in a most refreshing way.)

Government cycle researchers and experts have observed that important changes, with sweeping worldwide implications, occur every 180 years on Earth. 1 + 8 + 0 equal 9. The 360 degrees of the astrological circle (or any circle of life) add to 9. It takes 9 months of gestation to produce the birth of a child. There are 86,400 seconds in a day, adding to 18 and reducing to 9. There are 24 hours in a day, and when the 2 and 4 are added, you get 6, which is an upside down 9, a vital point, as we shall soon see.

The human mean normal respiration rate is 18 times a minute, and 1 + 8 equal 9.

The mean normal heartbeat or pulse rate is 72 times a minute. 7 + 2 equal 9.

The average number of heartbeats per hour is 4,320 — 9 again.

The average number of respirations per hour is 1,080 — 9 again.

In 24 hours, your heart beats an average of 103,680 times — equaling 9.

In the same 24-hour period, respiration occurs an average of 25,920 times — *exactly the same number of times as there are years to a Great Sidereal Year* !

Is it any wonder that the Scriptures tell us 666 (9) is the number of man and beast ?

In astrology, the *harmonious* aspects or angles formed between the planets are 30 degrees — 60 degrees — and 120 degrees. These add (or reduce) to the single number of either the *harmonious* 6 or 3. Whereas, the *disharmonious* or tense aspects or angles formed between the planets are 45 degrees — 90 degrees — and 180 degrees — all of which equal 9. This indicates the importance and desirability of attempting to rise *above* the Third Dimensional Awareness of Time and its stresses (9) into a happier, more harmonious state of being. (6). As I said, more soon about the urgent connection between the numbers 9, 6 and 3.

Mystics claim (and there's convincing scientific evidence) that *all measurements* (inside and out) of the mysterious and enigmatic Great Pyramid of Giza (built by Osiris, not Cheops, and millions of years earlier than now believed) — before Cheops and Time itself changed the measurements — each added to a multiple number which, when added, then reduced, equaled the single number 9. 9 is called the Red Dragon in alchemy.

The Novendiale (9) was a Fast held in the early Roman Catholic Church to avert or prevent catastrophes and calamities (Earth cataclysms) of all kinds, and from this ceremony came the modern day Catholic practice of Novenas, the prayer services lasting for 9 nights as I mentioned earlier.

On the 9th day, the Romans buried their dead. Both the First and the Second Temple of the Jews were destroyed on the 9th day of the month the Jewish people call Ab. (Remember that the number 9, from antiquity, has symbolized the Alpha and the Omega, the Beginning and the End.) Today, the Jews who follow the ancient orthodox Hebrew religion may not wear the Talith and Phylacteries until the Sun has set on the 9th day of Ab. The earliest Hebrew writings say that "God" descended to the Earth, walked among humans and talked with them — 9 times.

All these examples of the vibrations of the number 9 should give you plenty of food for thought, a veritable numerological banquet for an esoteric gourmet. But to truly understand, to fully comprehend the number 9, you must first penetrate the meaning of the numbers 6 and 3, their relationship to one another — and to the number 9.

9 is the number of Mars — aggression — penetration — *Man*. 6 is the number of Venus — love — compassionate passivity — *Woman*. (6 also rules money and other things, as 9 rules other things, too, but now we're concerned only with the *Male-Female* vibrations of the 6 and 9.) And so . . .

The number 6 symbolizes Venus — Love — Woman.

The number 9 symbolizes Mars — Conflict — Man.

When the number 6 is added to the number 9, Conflict is destroyed, and Love is victorious. Together, the 6 and 9 equal 15 — and when the 1 and the 5 are added together — they equal 6 again. Venus. Love. *Love is all.* In any confrontation between Venus and Mars, Venus wins in the *final outcome*. It cannot be otherwise under Universal Law.

This is surely a most reassuring cosmic code message from our Creators.

Here are a few more mysteries hidden within the numbers 6 and 9. We just saw what happens when these two numbers are added together. 6 is victorious. Now let's place them together, side by side, noting that each number is the other, turned upside down, and mirror reversed.

69

When 6 and 9 are side by side, they form the astrological symbol for the sign of Cancer, representing parenthood.

Cancer: **69**

The two circles of the symbol of Cancer, **6** and **9**, represent the mother's breasts. The total form of each of these two numbers reflects the form and general shape of spermatozoa. ❀ Quite logical, when you think that the numbers reflecting the female breasts and the male spermatozoa, both intimately connected with childbirth, are the numbers representing the two creators of new life: the woman and the man. Equally logical is that the *number* of Cancer is 2.

The astrological sign of Cancer is ruled by the Moon. Our first Moon landing took place in July, the month of Cancer. The year was 1969, which contains, of course, in the last two digits, the 6 and the 9. Such serendipitous synchronicity !

So, as we now see, 9 is 6 re-*versed*, and 6 is 9 re-*versed*. Translated, this means that 9 is a new *verse* of 6, and 6 is a new *verse* of 9. A "new verse" (new poem or new musical sound) is always created when anything at all is re-*versed*. There's a little woman in every man, and a little man in every woman. Therefore, it's not wrong, but perfectly natural, for a man to be sensitive — and for a woman to be courageous.

The Compound number 15, which is reached by adding together the 9 (man) and the 6 (woman), is called by the ancients "the number of magic and mystery." And indeed it is.

Magic and mystery . . . yes. When man and woman unite in love that's magic ! When their mutual love leads into a sexual union between them, mental, spiritual, and physical ecstasy is achieved, new life is conceived . . . and that's mystery !

The number 6 and its "half number," 3 (representing Jupiter, the planet of religion and ruler of Sagittarius), are an integral mathematical part of the *Nine Mystery* — the third-dimensional concept — with 9 equaled by 3 times 3 — 6 equaled by 3 plus 3 — and 9 equaled by 3 plus 6.

Jesus was found in the Synagogue discussing deep esoteric matters with the High Priests and Rabbis when he was 12 years old. 12 reduces to the number 3. He began his ministry and teaching at the age of 30 — another 3. He was crucified at the age of 33, reducing to 6, which is the reversed 9. He suffered on the cross for 3 hours. At the 9th hour he was pronounced dead. On the 3rd day he arose.

Only when Earthlings learn to re-*verse* (employ a new musical sound) the *material* number 9, by transforming it into its harmonious polarity number of 6, will there truly be Peace on Earth. For, it bears frequent repeating that 6 is the number of Venus and Love . . . and *Love is All.*

I've already shown you the magic tricks number 9 can do, and the number 6, the re-*versed* 9, is capable of equally magical behavior. But before I prove it to you, let's consider the total *Nine Mystery.*

The *Nine Mystery,* composed of only three numbers, 3 - 6 - 9, is the deepest of all mysteries demonstrated by mathematics (the calculation) and proven by numerology (the interpretation).

Remember our 3-legged stool man who discovered the numbers 1 - 2 - 3 . . . then the 0 (zero) ? What he didn't suspect was that those numbers alone: 1 - 2 - 3 and 0 summarize our entire Three Dimensional World. (The Fourth Dimensional World of the Eternal Now is another matter.)

Now, imagine our 3-legged stool man from the beginning, when he first placed a single stick on the ground to represent himself, conceiving the number 1 (Original Cause or Creator) . . . then added a second stick to represent his mate, conceiving the number 2. . . . then added a third stick horizontally, to represent the child, conceiving the number 3, the 3 sticks then forming a triangle, the oldest known symbol of all religions . . . and finally conceptualized the number 0, by drawing a circle around the 3 sticks on the ground, to protect himself, his mate, and his child from harm. Now meditate on this drawing for a moment . . .

Code: 1 - 2 - 3 - 0

I meditated on it one night during my Cripple Creek retreat as I fell asleep. When I awoke the next morning, I scribbled some notes on the pad beside my bed . . . and a few days later, I began to draw the numbers and the letters of the alphabet, and made what was, to me at least, a profound discovery. Doubtless all mathematicians are aware of it, and most certainly "Abstract Al" Einstein was — but it was news to *me*, and so illuminating, I felt like Christopher Columbus proving the world was round ! Here's my enlightenment: Each number, 0 through 9 — and each letter of the Anglo-Saxon alphabet, from A through Z — was born from — or may be transmuted into — the triangle or the circle. In fact, everything in our Third Dimensional awareness, when reduced to its primary base, including the rectangle, octagon, pentagon, hexagram, and so on — can be *coded* as the Universal key of 1 - 2 - 3 - 0 or:

Isn't that exciting ? It spirals my thoughts upward into all kinds of mysteries of existence. I'll just draw 3 numbers for you, as examples — and 3 letters of the alphabet. You can do the rest yourself, like a puzzle. It's fun !

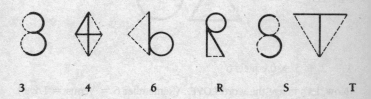

3   4   6   R   S   T

It makes you wonder what symbols would be like in the *Fourth* Dimensional awareness. I used to meditate a lot on the fact that we are three dimensional objects, and when the Light (the Sun) shines "through" us, we cast a *two dimensional* shadow. Therefore, could there not be a *fourth dimensional* Self, with an even brighter Light than our Sun causing it to cast the "shadows" of a *third dimensional* you and me ? And . . . perhaps also *fifth dimensional* beings, casting the "shadows" of our *Fourth Dimensional Selves* . . . and so on, up the line . . . and even beyond . . . in higher levels, since we can count only to 9 in this Third Dimensional awareness.

What does the number *above* 9 look like ? The zero — 0 — the circle. There is no such thing as a straight line. Eventually, every

Alpha (the beginning) meets its Omega (the end) — and joins it, forming a circle. So, if you were high enough to "look down" on an allegedly straight line, you would see that there was no beginning and no end to it after all: The Nazarene said, "*I am the Alpha and the Omega.*" The Beginning and the End are the same. Full serpent circle.

All of this relates to the Eternal Now, the Einsteinic discovery that Past, Present, and Future are not separate slices of Time, but are all One — and simultaneous. More about this in later chapters. For now, let's return to the Universal Code.

Universal Code: 1-2-3-0   Add the numbers, and you get 6 — Love.

$1 + 2 + 3 + 0$ equals 6

Now, let's image the word **LOVE**. (Remember 6 = Venus = Love.)

Here's one of the magic tricks I told you number 6 can do — but it's still part of the sacred *Nine Mystery*, as you will see.

The formula for our Third Dimensional Awareness is 1-2-3-0 . . . and this formula equals 6. Love. So, we'll take the Universal Code for Love and combine its numbers or digits, then add them in columns.

0-1-2-3 = Love   Below are all numerical variations of Love.

0123	1032	2310	3210
0132	1023	2301	3201
0231	1320	2103	3102
0213	1302	2130	3120
0321	1203	2013	3012
0312	1230	2031	3021
1332 = 9	7110 = 9	12888 = 27 = 9	18666 = 27 = 9

Now, if you were adding columns of money, there would be a vast difference between $1,332 and $18,666. But to the Universe, it's all *nine*. Note that there are 6 combinations in each column, and 24 multiple combinations (2 + 4 = 6) — and 96 digits in all columns (9 + 6 = 15 = 6). There's no way to separate the strange connection of the 3 - 6 and 9.

Multiplication of 3	Multiplication of 6	Multiplication of 9
2 × 3 = 6 – 6	2 × 6 = 12 – 3	2 × 9 = 18 – 9
3 × 3 = 9 – 9	3 × 6 = 18 – 9	3 × 9 = 27 – 9
4 × 3 = 12 – 3	4 × 6 = 24 – 6	4 × 9 = 36 – 9
5 × 3 = 15 – 6	5 × 6 = 30 – 3	5 × 9 = 45 – 9
6 × 3 = 18 – 9	6 × 6 = 36 – 9	6 × 9 = 54 – 9
7 × 3 = 21 – 3	7 × 6 = 42 – 6	7 × 9 = 63 – 9
8 × 3 = 24 – 6	8 × 6 = 48 – 3	8 × 9 = 72 – 9
9 × 3 = 27 – 9	9 × 6 = 54 – 9	9 × 9 = 81 – 9
Total 51 = 6	Total 48 = 12 = 3	Total 72 = 9

Notice that the number 3 repeats the vertical pattern of 6-9-3 . . . 6-9-3 (from top to bottom) and so on, no matter how many times it's multiplied. And the number 6 repeats the pattern of 3-9-6 . . . 3-9-6 . . . and so on, no matter how many times it's multiplied. This is all part of the *Nine Mystery, and 3 and 6 are an integral part of it.* As for the 9 column, the pattern is another indestructible 9-9-9-9 vertically.

I'm going to repeat myself now, for clarity.

The number 6 symbolizes: Venus Love Woman ♀
The number 9 symbolizes: Mars Conflict Man ♂

As I've already demonstrated, these numbers of sexuality are equally as much each other as they are themselves, because 9 turned upside down is 6 — and 6 turned upside down is 9. So, 9 is a 6 re-*versed* (a new verse) and 6 is a 9, re-*versed*.

Look again at the multiplication tables for the numbers 3 — 6 — and 9, and their sequence patterns. Once again, the 3 sequence pattern is 693-693-693, repeatedly. The 6 sequence pattern is 396-396-396. And, as we've already seen, with 9, it's always and eternally 9. (I refer to the sequence pattern of numbers reading vertically in the last column of each table.) Now, try it yourself, the same multiplication test, with any 3 of the other numbers of your choice besides these three. You'll find no numerical sequence pattern. Just an unrelated group of numbers.

No other number, not even the spiritual 7, can perform such multiplication magic as can be demonstrated with the 3 — 6 — and 9 of the Third Dimensional Nine Mystery. By the way, 3 plus 3 equal 6. 6 plus 6 equal 12 (which reduces to 3). . . likewise 3 plus 9. And 3 plus 6 equal 9. The 3, 6, and 9 cannot be divorced or separated in any mathematical manner. And there are *three* of these mystery numbers. Remember the 1-2-3-0 of the Universal Code, which is also *three* numbers, plus the 0 of increased power.

We're now agreed, I should think, that 9 is the King of the Numbers. Should you need further proof of the number nine's right to rule all life and electrical energy on this planet, ponder this: 9 is the only number capable of *giving life to every other number*, because, when 9 *adds itself* to each number, that number *is not lost*. 9 gives it back its identity and its "life."

9 plus 1 = 10 = 1 again   9 plus 2 = 11 = 2 again   9 plus 3 = 12 = 3 again

9 plus 4 = 13 = 4 again   9 plus 5 = 14 = 5 again   9 plus 6 = 15 = 6 again

9 plus 7 = 16 = 7 again   9 plus 8 = 17 = 8 again

No other number added to other numbers has this power.

★ ★ ★ ★ ★ ★

One more number magic . . . another cosmic message for tomorrow. Let's ponder again the demonstration that the number 9 (war, conflict, and aggression) can never win a victory over the number 6 (love and peace) because, when you add the 6 and 9, you get 15 — which, when adding the 1 and the 5 equals 6 again.

Next, let's add the conquering 6 to the spiritual number seven. 6 plus 7 adds to 13 — and the 1 plus the 3 of the 13 adds to the single number 4. The number 4 is the number given to Uranus, the ruling planet of Aquarius. Isn't that happy news about the future of this "unpredictable" (except through numerology) Aquarian Age ? Love (6) and spiritual enlightenment (7) will, during the Uranus-ruled (4) Aquarian Age, in the final inning, defeat war, conflict, aggression, and technology, no matter how they may *appear* to be losing the battle during the times of testing. The Earth will *not* be destroyed by nuclear insanity, nor by the Nature cataclysms it may be karmically destined to endure. There may be extensive damage and tragedy, yes, if Earthlings don't halt their negative behavior in time — but in the final analysis, love and peace will triumph !

It can be no other way, having been ordained by the inflexible mathematical order of the Universe . . . and its harmonics. Therefore, the cosmic numerical code to the future of the Aquarian Age unlocks the key to a happy tomorrow, regardless of the fears of today. Pollyanna would love it ! So would Abstract Al Einstein. I'll bet he knew it years ago. Meditating the marvels of numbers can cause your thoughts to soar as if they had wings and could fly to the place where all mysteries are born ! So . . . sleep in peace tonight, and dream of sixes and sevens.

★ ★ ★ ★ ★ ★

All right, are you ready ? Our class in applied and practical numerology is now in session, so you can learn how to use the unguessed power of numbers in your personal life when you need a little extra magic. First, there are certain rules you must know before we get into the actual instructions for the calculating process itself.

Read that last sentence again slowly, will you please ? Thank you !

I hope the lessons are fun. All lessons should be, but most of them are boring because teachers forget the Socratic wisdom of learning, and the students sense it. That is, no one can teach you anything. All an instructor can do is *help you remember what you already know.* And so . . . learning is remembering.

I'm sure you'll recall what we learned a few pages back — that the word "memory" contains the two words "more" and "me." Memory equals "more me." More you. More everyone.

An echo of this wise Socratic method of instruction comes to us down through the centuries from Diogenes, the eccentric Greek who wandered around carrying a lantern, looking for a completely honest man. (Do you suppose he might have had more luck if he had been looking among the feminine sex ? Sorry. I couldn't resist that female chauvinist piglet bite !) Anyway, one morning while Diogenes was walking down a dusty road on his weary quest, he met up with a very bored Alexander the Great, who had already conquered most of the known world by the time he was in his late teens — and the two of them had a sort of rap session. Finally, Alexander, much impressed with his new friend's intense and determined devotion to his goal, asked Diogenes if there was anything he could do to help him.

"Only stand out of my light," replied Diogenes.

That's what all teachers should try to do — stand out of their students' "light," and allow them to slowly but surely regain the knowledge buried in subconscious memory. That's why, with numerology as our subject, I'm going to first give you the basic rules — next give you the methods of calculating, plus some examples of how it's done — and finally stand back and let you "remember" the fine tuning of interpreting the definitions of the numbers, beginning on Page 226.

To begin with, you'll soon notice, when we've finished with the rules and progressed to the how-to-do-it portion, that I'll be using the word "entity" a lot. Let me explain what I mean by that term. Just as in astrology, a Broadway play or musical, a corporation, a book — or an event of any kind (wedding, purchase of a house, etc.), which is "born" or consummated at a certain *time,* has a birth chart (horoscope) as valid as the birth chart of a human baby (or animal) — likewise in numerology do these foregoing "entities" possess, relative to their *name* and the *day* they were "born," representative Key Numbers, the same as a person.

For example, consider the musical, *My Fair Lady,* Margaret Mitchell's *Gone with the Wind,* the stock brokerage firm of Paine Webber and other entities, such as your wedding day, the day you met a particular person, etc. All these are "entities," with a representative *birth number* (the *day* of incorporation — or of the event) and/or a *name number*.

Before I demonstrate how to find your birth number and your name number (both Single and Compound numbers), you must memorize the following basic rules of numerology.

The double or Compound numbers 11 and 22 are called Master Numbers. This means that *when being added to another number, they may not be reduced* — i.e.: the number 11 may not be added together or reduced to the number 2, and the number 22 may not be added together or reduced to the number 4. These two Master Numbers must always be added to other numbers in the numerology process as 11 and 22. Only when the *total* of the numerical value of the *name* is 11 or 22 may these numbers be added to produce the single 2 or 4 as the Key Number of the name, and only when a person was *born* on the 11th or 22nd may these numbers be reduced to 2 or 4 to equal the single Key Number of birth. (I'll give you some examples of this later.)

It's important to read the last two paragraphs regarding the Master Numbers 11 and 22 more than once to be sure you completely comprehend and don't ever forget this vital rule of numerology when you begin to work out your own calculations.

A final reminder regarding the "things" represented by the word "entity." When you're reading the single number and compound number definitions representing an *entity*, you must read them with a slightly different sense of interpretation than you would read them when they represent a *person*. You'll begin to acquire a feeling for it with practice. Certain statements in the definitions of the single and compound numbers given later in this chapter are clearly describing a person, not a "thing," but they also contain particular basic statements made which apply to an *entity*. To master the art and science of numerology yourself, you must learn to be adept in the technique of *intuitive interpretation*, and gradually become facile in *adapting* the seeds or the foundation of a definition or an analysis of a number to fit the goals, motives, and *general character or personality* of the "entity" you are trying to understand.

The Single numbers from 1 through 9 are called the root numbers, and they denote what the person or entity appears to be in the eyes of others or the world. The double or Compound numbers indicate the hidden karmic influences behind the scenes, so to speak, and foreshadow the destiny of the individual or entity. However, when that destiny is a negative one, I've given, in the compound number definitions, the way in which these karmic currents can be controlled and turned in a new and more fortunate direction. Always remember that you are, in the final analysis, in charge of your own fate, the captain of your soul and destiny. When you apply certain disciplines, you need not submit blindly to negative Karma, but will learn how to dilute its effect through your actions — by understanding how to balance the scales. (See Chapter 4.)

Once more, keep in mind the following:

Single numbers represent what a person or an entity *appears to be* in the eyes of others. They are the numbers of individuality and personality.

Compound or double numbers reveal or indicate the karmic influences, and foreshadow the destiny of the person or the entity, which can be controlled and eventually neutralized by heeding the advice given in the definitions of these numbers. You'll find the definitions of both the Single and the Compound numbers near the end of this chapter. You won't need to read them until you've first learned how to calculate your own numbers.

Another way of expressing the difference between the Single and Compound numbers is that the Single numbers from 1 through 9 belong to the physical or material side of people and entities, while the Compound numbers (double numbers) belong more to the spiritual side of life, such as Karma. One might say that the astrological planets and signs — and the numbers comprising numerology — are symbols for the language of our Creators. As written at the beginning of this chapter, "While the soul slumbers, God speaks to us in numbers."

When you've learned how to use numerology by obeying the following instructions of calculation, you'll find it surprisingly practical. Not only will you discover more about yourself and others, including the equally important "entities" in your life (book titles and pub dates if you're a writer — film or play titles and opening dates if you're a producer, and so forth) — but you'll be able to observe karmic patterns — and be able to choose *fortunate days* for all important meetings or events — the signing of documents — the initiation of trips and the like — and the favorable days for incorporating businesses, commencing new projects, etc. The fortunate numerological dates should be particularly helpful and beneficial regarding legal matters, courtroom dates, and the like, for attorneys — *and* their clients, when the selection of such dates is possible. Of course, there are times when a choice is not possible, but when it is, it would be wise to be guided by numerology in the manner you're about to learn — or remember — and you'll discover that such knowledge is of inestimable value. (Fortunate numerological dates generally coincide with the harmonious transits and progressed aspects of the horoscope.)

Now we're ready to learn (to remember) how to discover your own Single and Compound Key Numbers, and those of other people and entities.

Once again, here is the alphabet printed earlier in this chapter, repeated for your convenience. Study it as you practice your own calculations.

Alphabet

A = 1	N = 5
B = 2	O = 7
C = 3	P = 8
D = 4	Q = 1
E = 5	R = 2
F = 8	S = 3
G = 3	T = 4
H = 5	U = 6
I = 1	V = 6

$$J = 1 \qquad W = 6$$
$$K = 2 \qquad X = 5$$
$$L = 3 \qquad Y = 1$$
$$M = 4 \qquad Z = 7$$

You've probably noticed that there is no letter equaling the number 9. The accepted explanation for this, passed down orally through the centuries, is that, in the most secret esoteric orders, it has been said that the number 9 is synonymous with the "mystery name" of the Supreme Power over life, which has 9 letters; therefore, it may not have a single letter of the alphabet representing it. I accept this reason, since I don't possess the knowledge to refute it, and because the system works without the 9 being used as a value for a single letter of the alphabet.

However, if the *single* number of the *name* of the person or the entity being analyzed is 9 — or if the single *birth number* of the person or entity is computed to be a 9, by being born on the 9th, 18th, or 27th day of the month, then the meaning for the Single number 9 given in the Single number definitions on Page 244 should be used.

Examples

Let's begin with two interesting and well-known people: Abraham Lincoln and Jesus of Nazareth.

Study these examples carefully. Notice that below each letter in the name is the numerical value of that letter. These numbers are then added across, horizontally, to reach a Compound number, which is totaled below, then reduced to a Single number. (See Abraham.) Do the same with each separate name (or word, with an entity). Finally, add the *Single numbers* of each name (or word) to reach the final *Key Numbers*. Note how this is done in the following example.

After you have calculated the Compound Key Number of the

name (or title or phrase or whatever) — add the two numbers of the Compound Key Number to arrive at the *Single* Key Number. If you'll carefully study the Abraham Lincoln example, it should be clear.

A B R A H A M   L I N C O L N   Born February 12th
                                       $1 + 2 = 3$

Compound Key Number of *birth* is 12
Single Key Number of *birth* is 3

A B R A H A M   L I N C O L N
1 2 2 1 5 1 4   3 1 5 3 7 3 5 $7 + 9 = 16$

Total: 16 = 7   Total: 27 = 9 $1 + 6 = 7$

Compound Key Number of *name* is 16
Single Key Number of *name* is 7

Therefore, Abraham Lincoln's Key Numbers are 12 and 3 (birth numbers) — and 16 and 7 (name numbers). 12 - 16 - 3 - 7.

Don't move on past the Abraham Lincoln example until you are quite sure that you understand how the final four Key Numbers were calculated, whether it takes five minutes to completely comprehend these steps — or two hours. Don't read further until each step is clear to you.

Do you see how each of Lincoln's four Key Numbers was reached ? Are you *sure* ? All right, then we can move on to a *partial* definition of these numbers representing Abraham Lincoln.

Let's take the Key Numbers of the *name* first — the Single 7 and the Compound 16.

When you read the definition of the Single Number 7 in the definition pages near the end of this chapter, you'll see that it fits the *personality and character* of our Civil War President perfectly — how he *appeared to others.*

The 7 definition (given near the end of this chapter) tells you that Lincoln "had remarkable dreams." That he possessed "a calming and quieting magnetism which had a great influence over others" — that he "disliked following the beaten path and had peculiar ideas about religion and unique, unorthodox political views." It tells you that Lincoln "cared little about material possessions" — and that he blessed others with his "sympathetic understanding of pain and suffering." Also that others often "unburdened their troubles and problems" to him. The Single Number 7 analysis tells you that Lincoln was "not judgmental or prejudiced," that he was "tolerant of the views of others." This sums up the man's personality with accuracy, does it not ?

Abraham Lincoln's *Compound* Key Number of his name is 16. Among other revelations, this karmic number is symbolized as the Shattered Citadel — a "Tower struck by Lightning, from which a man is falling, with a Crown on his head. A strange fatality awaits one — the defeat of one's plans is threatened." All this clearly fits President Lincoln. The complete analysis of the Compound Number 16 near the end of this chapter also contains the method by which Lincoln could have avoided the negative karmic destiny of the 16, or greatly diluted it — but he did not. The 16 analysis explains in what manner he chose *not* to avoid or neutralize his Karma. (For one thing, he did not heed his warning dreams.)

Also contained in the definition of Lincoln's *Single* Key Number 7 (of his name) is the warning *not* to wear black or dark colors, and, of course, this is the only color ever worn by Lincoln — his black frock coats, black trousers, and black stovepipe hat (which was the custom of the day) although others relieved the black occasionally with other colors in their personal lives, at home, and such. Lincoln did not.

Moving from the Key *name numbers* (single and compound) of Abraham Lincoln, let's study his *birth numbers*. People born on a day of the month consisting of a Single number do not have a Compound birth number, only a Single birth number. But those born on a day of the month consisting of a double number, have *both* a Single and a Compound *birth number*. Lincoln is one of the latter.

Lincoln's *day* of birth is February 12th. Therefore, the *Compound Key Number* of his *birth* is 12 — and the *Single Key Number* of his *birth* is 3, adding the 1 and the 2 of the 12.

When you read the meaning of the Single Number 3 and the Compound Number 12 in the Single and Compound Number definitions, beginning on Page 230 and Page 251, you'll get an even clearer picture of the man. Read the entire analysis of the 3 and the 12 for a full picture. *In part,* the meaning of 3 is a person who bases every action upon a "great ideal" — and who is "shockingly blunt of speech." 3 people are challenged by "tests of physical strength." Lincoln entered into several such tests of strength in his youth — and then, too, we have Lincoln, the rail splitter, who beat all comers in contests of log chopping — and Indian arm wrestling. The 3 analysis describes a person who is an odd blend of "the wise philosopher and the happy-go-lucky clown." An apt description of Lincoln. The 3 definition also reveals that these people are "crushed when denied the higher halls of learning." Think of Lincoln, who had practically no formal schooling, and was crushed by this lack. But he didn't allow it to defeat him. He set about to study law on his own, under great hardship, and became the most brilliant lawyer of his time — an excellent example for anyone who shares Lincoln's Single Key Number 3. (3 people are intensely determined to obtain higher education, and therefore, usually *do,* but are more deeply disappointed than others when it's denied.)

Abraham Lincoln was an Aquarian. You will see in the enclosed analysis of the Single Number 3 that this number is *harmonious* with his Aquarian Sun Sign.

As for his Compound *birth number* of 12, study the definition of the Number 12, and you'll learn much more about Lincoln. A *partial* glimpse of its meaning is: "The Sacrifice or the Victim — one who is sacrificed for the plans and intrigues of others." Anyone who has studied American history, and is familiar with the vast amount of political intrigue and deception surrounding his Presidency will quickly see how appropriate this is.

Study this brief sample analysis of Abraham Lincoln's *birth* numbers and *name* numbers carefully until you completely comprehend them, because it's the very best way to learn all the nuances of calculating the Key Numbers of the person or entity you're personally interested in analyzing, especially yourself.

Jesus Christ . . . Jesus of Nazareth

This name is one of the most revealing I've ever calculated, and the strangest. We've already seen the mysterious link between the numbers 3, 6, and 9. Further, this mystical relationship of the numbers 3, 6, and 9 assumes great importance in its association with the Single and Compound Key Numbers of the Nazarene's name.

The child Jesus was found in the Temple discussing profound spiritual matters with the Rabbis at the age of 12, which adds to 3. He began his mission of wandering ministry at the age of 30. Another 3. He was crucified at the age of 33, adding to 6, which is the reversed 9. He suffered on the cross for 3 hours. At the 9th hour he was pronounced dead. On the 3rd day he arose. Bringing in the 9 vibration again, there were 18 "lost years," during which time the activities of

Jesus are unrecorded in the "modern" Scriptures, and 18 adds up to 9. His life was repeatedly locked into the mystery of the three numbers 3 - 6 and 9 I wrote about before. And, as I've already pointed out, adding the 3, 6, and 9 equals 18, which adds or reduces to 9 once again. 9 is the number of Beginnings and Endings. "I am the Alpha and the Omega." Now let's calculate the Key Numbers of his name, and you'll discover even more mystery.

J	E	S	U	S		C	H	R	I	S	T	
1	5	3	6	3		3	5	2	1	3	4	9 plus 9 equals 18

Total: 18 = 9   Total: 18 = 9   18 = 9

It's odd that the name Jesus equals the compound number 18 and the single number 9 — and the name Christ has *exactly the same value*. But even stranger, let's evaluate the numerical value of the three words so frequently used to identify him: Jesus of Nazareth.

J	E	S	U	S		O	F		N	A	Z	A	R	E	T	H
1	5	3	6	3		7	8		5	1	7	1	2	5	4	5

Total: 18 = 9   Total: 15 = 6   Total: 30 = 3

9 plus 6 plus 3 equal 18   Compound Key Number: 18

18 = 9   Single Key Number: 9

An amazing synchronicity of vibratory influence ! These three words, so often used to describe the man born in Bethlehem, equal, respectively, the mysteriously linked numbers 9, 6, and 3. When added, they equal 18 again, which reduces once more to 9, making the Key Numbers for this three-word description the single 9 and the compound 18, *exactly the same numerical value* as the word JESUS — the word CHRIST — and the *two-word* name JESUS CHRIST.

It was clearly impossible for him to avoid the *Compound* number

18 as his destiny, nor did he make any attempt to escape it, as an ordinary man with equal esoteric knowledge would be inclined to do. Neither could he escape (with so many repetitions) the *Single* number 9 — the Alpha and the Omega. The entire life destiny of Jesus is contained in the influence of the 3, 6, and 9 — and the compound 18.

When you read the full meaning of the Number 18 in the Compound number definitions that begin on Page 249, you'll see a strange symbolism which, when you use your esoteric imagination, closely describes (in code) the scene on Calvary with the Roman Centurions casting dice at the feet of the crucified Messiah, for the prize of his robe. Essentially, the Compound Number 18 indicates "materialism striving to destroy the spiritual side of the nature." It represents a person who is "associated with uprisings and revolutions" — plus "deception from both friends and enemies." Rather an accurate capsule summary of the drama of his mission, and the purpose behind it, wouldn't you say ?

★ ★ ★ ★ ★ ★

Now let's use an American film star, Robert Redford, and calculate the Key Numbers of his name, to demonstrate the importance of the rule of *not* reducing the Master Numbers 11 and 22, when adding them to other numbers.

R O B E R T	R E D F O R D	
2 7 2 5 2 4	2 5 4 8 7 2 4	22 plus 5 equals 27
Total: 22 = 22	Total: 32 = 5	27 = 9

You should have learned enough now to see that the Single Key Number for the name of Robert Redford is 9 — and the Compound Key Number is 27. The definition, in part, of the Number 27 is that "the creative faculties have sown good seeds, which will reap a fine harvest." The rest of this definition equally fits Robert Redford — but if you had *reduced* the 22 of Robert to a 4, then added it to the Redford number 5, you would still get the correct Single Key Number of 9 — but you would have *missed* the most *important* influence in his life, that of the Compound Number 27.

Remember that you may reduce the Master Numbers 11 and 22 *only* when they are *Key Numbers*, and must be added or reduced to obtain the *final Single Key Number* of the name or the day of birth. In other words, to repeat what I wrote earlier, if the Compound Key Number of the name is 11 or 22 (after having added the single numbers of the several names), the 11 or 22 may then be reduced to the 2 or 4 to create the *Single Key Number*. Likewise, if a person is born on the 11th or 22nd day of the month, then the 11 or 22 is the Compound *Key Number of the birth* — and to obtain the Single Key Number of the birth, you may add the 11 to obtain the single 2 or the 22 to obtain the single 4. The only time you *may not* reduce these two Master Numbers is when they are being added as separate parts of a several word name or entity, such as in the Robert Redford example I just demonstrated. Study it again. Study it until you fully comprehend the rule about 11 and 22.

Now, I've been "standing in your light" enough, so I'm going to help you by demonstrating a few more examples of people and entities — that is, demonstrating the system of calculating the Key Numbers, as I did with Robert Redford, Abraham Lincoln, and Jesus (not necessarily in that order !) — but I'm not going to give you any hints as to the *interpretations* of the Key Numbers. You should be able to handle that yourself by this time, when you study the Single and Compound number definitions beginning on Page 225 and Page 249.

Remember that when you're trying to analyze a *person*, the enclosed definitions are self-explanatory — but when you're analyzing an *entity*, you have to intuitively "pick up" what is given in the definitions that applies more specifically to an *entity* rather than to a person. You're going to learn (remember) how to "read between the lines" in a metaphysical sense, and condense the "person" definitions so that they more briefly and clearly describe a "thing" — an event or an entity.

First, we'll try a few more people. Then the entities. By the time you're through studying these calculations — and then the definitions of the Key Numbers of these further examples, you'll be ready to begin penetrating the mysteries of your own name, the names of friends and relatives — and your own special entities (corporate structures, books, plays, special dates and events, and so on).

E L I Z A B E T H   T A Y L O R   Born: February 27th

2 plus 7 equals 9

Single Key Number of *birth*: 9
Compound Key Number of *birth*: 27

Now, let's calculate the Single and Compound Key Numbers of Elizabeth's *name*.

E L I Z A B E T H   T A Y L O R
5 3 1 7 1 2 5 4 5   4 1 1 3 7 2

Total: 33 = 6   Total: 18 = 9   6 plus 9 equals 15

1 plus 5 equals 6

Single Key Number of *name*: 6
Compound Key Number of *name*: 15

And so, Elizabeth's four Key Numbers (for birth and name) are: the single 9 and the single 6 — the compound 27 and the compound 15. Remember that the *Single* numbers of both the birth and the name describe the personality and character of the person or entity, as they appear to others — and the *Compound* numbers of both the birth and the name represent the karmic path of destiny, what is hidden or buried.

Therefore, Elizabeth's four Key Numbers are 9, 27, 6, and 15. The 9 and the 6 describe her personality and outward behavior. The 15 and the 27 represent her hidden karmic destiny. I can't resist making one comment, although I've promised not to help from now on with the definitions. Elizabeth, being a Pisces, I've always wondered about her occasional flashes or outbursts of impulsive action. 9 being her Single birth number answers that puzzlement once and for all. (You'll notice, when reading the enclosed Single Number definitions, that they give you a way to compare the person's Sun Sign with his or her single number — or numbers.)

Let's try two more well-known names. This reminds me of the old vaudeville joke you've probably heard about the out-of-towner who was lost in New York, and asked an Italian pushcart peddler how to get to Carnegie Hall. The man threw his hands in the air and cried out, "*Practice, practice, practice !*" There's a moral in that joke. I'm giving you all these examples so you can practice, practice, practice — which is the only way, not only to eventually be good enough to play a concert in Carnegie Hall, but to master the ancient art and science of numerology. Another American film star.

J A N E   F O N D A   Born: December 21st

                             2 plus 1 equals 3

Single Key Number of *birth*: 3
Compound Key Number of *birth*: 21

J A N E   F O N D A
1 1 5 5   8 7 5 4 1   3 plus 7 equals 10

Total: 12 = 3   Total: 25 = 7   10 equals 1

Single Key Number of *name*: 1
Compound Key Number of *name*: 10

Jane Fonda's four Key Numbers are 1, 3, 10, and 21. (Look up the meanings.) The Single Key Numbers of 1 and 3 describe the personality and character of Jane as she appears to be to others — and the compound Key Numbers of 10 and 21 represent her karmic destiny path, what is hidden or buried.

S A M U E L   C L E M E N S   Born: November 30

3 plus 0 equals 3

Single Key Number of *birth*: 3
Compound Key Number of *birth*: 30

S A M U E L   C L E M E N S
3 1 4 6 5 3   3 3 5 4 5 5 3   22 plus 1 equals 23

Total: 22 = 22   Total: 28 = 10 = 1   2 plus 3 equals 5
Single Key Number of *name*: 5
Compound Key Number of *name*: 23

And so, the Key Numbers of Samuel Clemens are 3, 5, 23, and 30. (Look up the meanings which apply.)

However, author Samuel Clemens *changed his name* to Mark Twain. In so doing, he didn't much improve his vibrations — the 23 is a fine number for success — although he may have become, through the change, somewhat more gregarious, and less a "hermit" than the Number 30 allowed. Still, the change to Mark Twain brought one distinct advantage — the acquisition of the Compound Number 17, which (as you'll see in the enclosed definitions) *guaranteed that his name would live after him.*

M A R K   T W A I N
4 1 2 2   4 6 1 1 5   9 plus 8 equals 17

Total: 9   Total: 17 = 8   1 plus 7 equals 8

Single Key Number of *name*: 8
Compound Key Number of *name*: 17

You'll also notice, when you look up the definitions of these numbers, that Samuel Clemens also gave himself a goodly helping of self-discipline when his new name, Mark Twain, influenced him with the Single Number 8, but also added, unfortunately, the sadness and depression of the 8, along with its wealth vibrations.

Jane Fonda is a Sagittarian. So was Samuel Clemens aka Mark Twain. Both of these Archers are influenced by the Single Number 3. In their cases, the 3 has a *double influence,* since 3 is the number of the planet Jupiter, and Jupiter is the ruler of Sagittarius.

Next, let's try some "entities." We've had enough examples of people.

G O N E	W I T H	T H E	W I N D
3 7 5 5	6 1 4 5	4 5 5	6 1 5 4
Total: 20 = 2	Total: 16 = 7	Total: 14 = 5	Total: 16 = 7

2 plus 7 plus 5 plus 7 equals 21

Compound Key Number of Title: 21   Single Key Number of Title: 3

Look up the Key Numbers for this American classic novel and motion picture about the Old South, and see how perfectly they fit. In particular, the first paragraph of the meaning of 21.

Now an immensely popular and successful Broadway musical and motion picture.

M Y	F A I R	L A D Y	
4 1	8 1 1 2	3 1 4 1	5 plus 3 plus 9 equals 17
Total: 5	Total 12 = 3	Total: 9	

Compound Key Number of Title: 17   Single Key Number of Title: 8

You'll notice as you become adept in numerology that in interpreting an entity, such as *Gone with the Wind* and *My Fair Lady,* the Compound Key Number is often more descriptive and revealing than the Single Key Number. The Single numbers of the birth and/or name of entities are also valid, but sometimes it takes a little intuitive work to apply them, since entities possess multiple facets not known to the general public The Compound Key Numbers, however, will reveal the path of destiny of the entity.

Another entity example is the stock brokerage house of . . .

P A I N E   W E B B E R

8 1 1 5 5   6 5 2 2 5 2   2 plus 22 equals 24

Total: 20 = 2   Total: 22 = 22 (22 cannot be reduced here)

Look up the meaning of the compound number 24, and you'll see why Paine Webber is such a successful company.

Let's try one more "person" example, since it teaches us such an important lesson of courage. Helen Keller was a Cancerian, and her Sun Sign helped her fight to overcome the disability of being blind, deaf, and speechless. Cancer's essence is ultrasensitive, which Helen had to be to receive the messages patiently sent to her by her teacher, Annie Sullivan — and Cancer is tenacious. Without these Lunar qualities of sensitivity . . . imagination . . . and tenacity, Helen might never have found her way out of her dark and silent world. But she also had the help of her numbers, and their influence likewise blessed her.

H E L E N   K E L L E R   Born: June 27th
                                       27 equals 9

Single Key Number of *birth*: 9
Compound Key Number of *birth*: 27

H E L E N   K E L L E R
5 5 3 5 5   2 5 3 3 5 2   5 plus 2 equals 7

Total: 23 = 5   Total: 20 = 2

Single Key Number of *name*: 7
Compound Key Number of *name*

Supporting the beneficial influences of her sensitive, intuitive, and tenacious Cancerian Sun Sign were Helen Keller's birth and name Single and Compound Key Numbers. (Read the definitions of them in the section beginning on Pages 225 and 249.) The 7, which is the number of Neptune-ruled Pisces, gave her the spiritual strength she needed. The 9, which is the number of Mars-ruled Aries, gave her the physical stamina and drive she equally needed, and the fiery determination necessary to keep on fighting against "the impossible."

Finally, her Compound Key Number of birth — the 27 — foreshadowed her eventual victory over her afflictions — her glorious triumph of the spirit as she held audiences spellbound all over the world by demonstrating how she had overcome "insurmountable" obstacles to find happiness. Helen Keller made everyone who saw her believe in miracles.

The Single numbers of each name in a person's whole name — or of each word in a title or a phrase — mean absolutely nothing. Ignore them. The Compound "Total" numbers of each name and each work — i.e.: the 23 of Helen and the 20 of Keller — or say, the 33 of Elizabeth and the 18 of Taylor — carry only a mild and secondary influence, but the effect is not very strong, and is usually diminished by the more powerful strength and vibratory influence reached by adding them to a Single number, then adding the Single numbers to create a Compound *Key Number*. Always, the most important influences to be considered are the Single and Compound *Key Numbers* of *both* birth and name.

The reason the former numbers deserve small attention, and are less personal and individual than the Key Numbers is that, after all, every Elizabeth is a 33, and every person with the surname of Taylor is an 18, for example. Still, 33 is a mighty fine number, subliminal or not, and I wouldn't mind possessing it myself, however mild or neutralized by the stronger Key Numbers of birth and name.

★ ★ ★ ★ ★ ★

When numerology is used to select the name of a corporation, company, or business, a book or play title — to change a name, or the spelling of a name — don't forget this basic rule. The way numerology "works" is through magnetic vibration. Before I explain that, let me give some illustrations.

I had lunch a couple of years ago in New York with the manager of the Bonwit Teller department store and one of the buyers from Bloomingdale's. We were discussing something store people everywhere (including furniture and appliance store managers) call "the nine mystery." Let's say an item is priced at ten dollars, and isn't selling. After many years of experimenting, store people discovered a startling fact they proved over and over again — that they can actually *raise* the price of the item to eleven or twelve dollars — as long as the price tag reads $10.99 or $11.99. Almost immediately it will start to sell briskly, after moving at the pace of a snail for weeks, or even months.

Over the years, experienced buyers and department managers of anything from shoe stores to boutiques know that all they need to do to start a previously unpopular item moving is to either lower the price by one cent — or *raise* it to a reasonable figure — add 99 to it — i.e.: $7.99 — $21.99 — $149.99 — and so on, and it will attract buying customers. The two men admitted that, although everyone in the business knows this to be a fact, they don't understand *why*. ($12.96 or $12.94 won't do.) Nothing they've ever learned about customer psychology explains why a person would be more willing to pay a higher price than a lower price if the price ends with .99. I told them why, and I'm not sure they believe me, but they found it fascinating.

You already know that 9 is the number of Mars — action. Since numbers speak directly to the subconscious, when the customer sees the number 9, especially when it's repeated twice or more, an action message is instantly flashed through the brain's telepathic network that says: "Buy now — move now — act now" — and the conscious mind tends to obey this subliminal conditioning or programming, causing the customer to impulsively make the purchase, not every time, of course, but quite often, as reflected in the store's sales receipts.

This has a great deal to do with how numerology works, through the vibrational frequency of the *constant repetition* of a number — the repeated impression of its vibration upon the ethers (and subconscious minds everywhere) required for it to be fully effective. In other words, the more often you send out a particular single or double number's vibration, via the spoken, written, or printed word, the more powerful it is in its influence. So it doesn't do much good to select a name for a business or whatever — or to change the numerical vibration of your own name — if you're the only one who knows about it.

Samuel Clemens would not have received the added benefit of the 17 of Mark Twain (promising that his name would live after him) if he had kept the name change a secret. Instead, "Mark Twain" was printed over and over on hundreds of thousands of books (eventually, millions) — and in various other ways over the years, including his spoken introductions at countless social affairs as "Mark Twain."

Therefore, when you already have Key Numbers you consider to be fortunate and harmonious with your inner goals — and *especially* when you've adopted a new vibration by choosing a new name for an entity, adding a name or initial to your own name, or changing the spelling of a name, don't expect to see much difference unless you make a special effort to "send out the new vibration" to impress itself upon the ethers and reach as many subconscious minds as possible, à la Mark Twain. Sign your new name (or the title of an entity) as frequently as possible, print the new name on business cards, handing out as many as possible, be sure you're introduced by the new name at business meetings and social functions — have your bank checks printed with the new name — and *increase its power every chance you get — in every way possible.*

When you're considering adopting a new vibrational influence by changing the Key Numbers of your name, there are several ways to do this. Naturally, few people would want to completely change the surname. But some surnames are adaptable to having a letter added or subtracted to achieve a new and more favorable single and/or compound Key Number.

Most people would prefer to achieve the new vibration by either *subtracting* one of *two* "given" or "first" names — or adding a new first name. It's also possible to simply add an initial between the first and last names to obtain the desired numerical influence. When any of these steps are taken, as I've already explained, you can increase the power of the new name by having it printed on checks, letterheads, stationery, and business cards. However, adding a new first name — or adding an *initial* (single letter) between the first and last names — has less chance of a power increase because you lose the added magnetic energy of your name used in introductions to others — and of others *thinking* of you that way.

It's rare for people to use *two* first names in an introduction, and even more rare for them to use a middle initial. If you change John Mendenhall to John L. Mendenhall to achieve the magical compound Key Number of 15 instead of the 12 of just plain John Mendenhall, your friends and associates aren't likely to introduce you as "John L. Mendenhall" — they'll probably still *call* you John Mendenhall, and continue to *think* of you that way. Even though you have the new name with the added initial L. printed on checks and such, you lose some of the power that comes from repeated vibrations.

The "exception that proves the rule" is when the two first names are hyphenated, or consist of the more commonly thought of and more commonly pronounced double names, such as Mary Ellen, Mary Kathleen, and so forth. Use your own logical judgment in the case of double names.

It's true that you can add an initial and just through its *printed* repetitions still observe remarkable changes in your life, but the changes with more possibilities of a power increase are: (a) to *remove* one of your first names, assuming you have two of them, and assuming that gives the desired new numerical value — (b) *add* a new first name (preferably with a hyphen, i.e.: Mary-Jane or joined as Mary-jane) assuming you already have only one, and insist that others refer to you in that way — or (c) change the *spelling* of either the first or the last name (surname).

You may have two "given" or first names plus a surname, and discover that using only the *initial* of the second name causes all three names to achieve the single and/or compound number you want — or *conversely,* you may discover, if you've already been using only the initial of your second name, and this gives you an undesirable Key Number, that *spelling out your second name in full,* and insisting that people refer to you in this manner (plus all the other power increase suggestions I've described) will obtain the result you want.

But the easiest and the most effective way to make a change is to either adopt a different or similar first name — or change the *spelling* of either the first name or the surname. When either of these two methods are not possible or desirable, you may use the other methods I've illustrated.

The main thing to remember is to do all you can to increase the number of times the magnetic energy of the new name is impressed upon the ethers — and upon the minds of others. Let's hope you enjoy the challenge of the name you have now, and don't choose to change, but to make the very best of its influence. Obviously, that's much less trouble, and you should remain with your own name if you feel you can handle it — *except for the rules which apply* to the strange numbers 4 and 8. I've written about them on Page 269 following the definitions of the single and compound Key Numbers, so be sure to read about them if your name (or birth *day*) produces the Single number 4 or 8.

The reason that the Key Numbers of your day of birth exert a stronger influence over your life than the Key Numbers of your name is, obviously, that while you can choose to gradually change the vibratory influence of your name by changing the spelling in some way, you cannot change the day of your birth.

You may be wondering, "Are all the first names to be added to the last name (or surname) to produce the Key Numbers ?" The answer is that when you are determining the numerical influences of the Single and Compound numbers in your life, whether you are satisfied with them, or wish to change them, it is the *most used first name or names* which should be added to the surname or last name to produce the Key Numbers representing you.

Also, those people with titles must consider the title before their names as *an additional* number. For example, you've already studied the illustration of Abraham Lincoln's birth and name Key Numbers, and their meanings. But he was also referred to frequently as "President Lincoln."

```
P  R  E  S  I  D  E  N  T        L  I  N  C  O  L  N
8  2  5  3  1  4  5  5  4        3  1  5  3  7  3  5
```

Total: 37 = 10 = 1   Total: 27 = 9   1 plus 9 equals 10

1 plus 0 equals 1

Single Key Number: 1
Compound Key Number: 10

When you read the definition of the Single Number 1 and that of the Compound Number 10, you'll quickly see how this title and name, "President Lincoln," and the Key Numbers it produced as an *added* influence over his life path, were most fortunate for him, helped him overcome some of the negative influences of his birth and name Key Numbers, and gave him the strength to carry out his mission. However, he was *simultaneously influenced* by the compound birth Number 12 and the compound name Number 16, as illustrated by the events I referred to before, including his assassination — and also the several severe and painful political defeats he endured before being nominated for the Presidency.

Because of this, a person who has calculated the Single and Compound Key Numbers of birth and name, should also calculate his or her title and surname together to discover the *added influence* of these additional Key Numbers, since a person's title is so frequently used — or impressed upon the ethers. Such as President Lincoln, Senator Kennedy, Congresswoman Luce, and so on.

Another example of the foregoing is physicians. If a doctor's name is, for instance, John Perry, the Single and Compound Key Numbers of that name will certainly influence his life. However, he is called and known as "Dr. Perry" as often as John Perry. Perhaps even more often. Therefore, the calculation of the Key Numbers for "Dr. Perry" is important as a secondary influence. The Single and Compound Key Numbers of both names should be taken into consideration, since both names exert power over the life. The same is true of professors. A man may be called James Dorchester by many people, but if he is equally as often called Professor Dorchester, he must consider the Key Numbers of both names. Returning to the title of "doctor," should you calculate Doctor Perry or Dr. Perry ? The latter, because the abbreviation is nearly always used in writing the name, and when people *say* it, they seldom think of it in their minds as having six letters, but rather mentally image it as "Dr."

In the case of someone in the military, the same rule applies. Douglas MacArthur, for instance, was equally as often called General

MacArthur, so both names would influence his life. Whether the title is General, Lieutenant, Sergeant, Ensign, or whatever, normally both the given first and last name should be used, as well as the title, i.e., Henry Miller and Lieutenant Miller.

If a woman's name is Penelope Mason, and nearly everyone she knows refers to her by the nickname "Penny" — or Penny Mason — then the latter is *the most used* name (with the most frequently repeated vibrations into the ethers to increase the power of the numbers representing it) — and is, consequently, the name which should be used in numerical calculations.

Another question some people may ask is: how do you calculate the Key Numbers of a name containing two words in the surname ? The clearest way to answer this is by the following example, using the name of a friend of mine, Philip di Franco. It's the "di Franco" that creates the problem. Should he treat "di Franco" as one word — or two ? The answer is: *as two words*.

```
P H I L I P        D I      F R A N C O
8 5 1 3 1 8        4 1      8 2 1 5 3 7
```

Total: 26   5   Total: 26

2 plus 6 = 8
2 plus 6 = 8
8 plus 5 plus 8 = 21
2 plus 1 = 3

Single Key Number of name: 3
Compound Key Number of name: 21

Let's try it by calculating "di Franco" as a *one-word* surname.

```
P H I L I P        D I F R A N C O
8 5 1 3 1 8        4 1 8 2 1 5 3 7
```

Total: 26   Total: 31   2 plus 6 = 8
                                                      3 plus 1 = 4
                                                      8 plus 4 = 12
                                                      1 plus 2 = 3

Single Key Number of name: 3
Compound Key Number of name: 12

Notice the difference made in Philip's Key Numbers based on whether his surname is treated as one word or two words, as it's spelled. The Single Number 3 describes him perfectly, and is the Key Number in both calculations. But . . . read the meaning of the Compound Number 21 and the Compound Number 12. Who would exchange the 21 for the *reversed* 12 ? Besides, the 21 fits his karmic pattern, judging by his life to date, far more than the 12.

In summary, those who have a two-word surname should treat it as two words — not as one word — when they're calculating the Single and Compound Key Numbers of their names.

This next advice is probably the most vital part of numerology for you to comprehend. It concerns what happens when you alter the Compound and Single Key Numbers representing you, by changing, in one way or another, the numerical value of your name.

Let's say an actress or singer adds the letter "E" to her first name or surname, and makes every effort to *increase the power* of the new numbers this name change creates. First, she should remember that it *takes time,* usually from a few months to a year or so, for the new vibration to noticeably begin to affect her and her life pattern. And when this change does occur, she should *not expect her life to suddenly and permanently become a solid "bed of roses."*

As an example, let's say that she begins to experience a number of events and opportunities which lead to career successes, her financial situation changes from negative to substantially positive, she makes fewer enemies than before, and more good friends. Then, unexpectedly, her marriage ends in divorce *for any number of reasons* related to her husband's or her own attitude and behavior (observed in her astrological birth chart) — and she has no astrologer to counsel her. She may then begin to blame the name change for the divorce, because she fancied that adding an "E" to her name to produce new and more favorable Key Numbers would guarantee that nothing whatsoever of a negative nature could ever again occur in her life. She is wrong. Nothing under the Sun can give that kind of a solid insurance against every single disappointment caused by her Karma.

Numerology does not have the power to completely erase Karma.

What numerology does have the power to accomplish in your life is to remove many *unnecessary* obstacles from your path, to cause your business and personal affairs to run more smoothly — and *to allow you to take full advantage of your potential,* as revealed in your horoscope, by removing frustrating restrictions which are preventing you from realizing your goals and, most important, from performing your individual mission on this Earth. This mistake of misunderstanding was made by a beautiful and talented singer whose name was a 12, and adding the "E" made it 17; an obviously beneficial change, but she misunderstood as described in the previous two paragraphs and deleted the "E" later. She should not have done so.

When you change your Key Numbers, you will absolutely see a great difference, a marked improvement in all your affairs. But every time you stub your toe, or someone steals your billfold walking home from the theatre, don't blame it on numerology. A word to the wise should be sufficient. Only the unenlightened would expect one hundred percent "heaven on Earth" simply by increasing the positive power of numbers in the life — and they *are* very much a positive power when they are properly employed and properly understood. But they cannot — and should not — replace your own personal and individual *responsibility* to do all the things needed to achieve happiness, contentment, and success. If numerology removed your free will choice to such an extent, it would not be positive, but a negative force in the Universe, resulting only in postponing the inevitable karmic responsibilities until a future incarnation — and this is contrary to its purpose for existing as a valuable guide for men and women on their path to truth and self-awareness.

★ ★ ★ ★ ★ ★

When you're calculating the Key Numbers of the name of a person or an "entity," and you get a Single Key Number, but no Compound Key Number, what do you do ? Must you accept that the person or entity has only a Single number influence — and if a person, remain frustrated in discovering what the karmic mystery contained in the Compound number definitions might be ? No.

In such cases, here is what you do. I'll explain by giving you the example of my own name — and my first two books as "entity" examples.

L I N D A   G O O D M A N
3 1 5 4 1   3 7 7 4 4 1 5   5 plus 4 equals 9

Total: 14 = 5   Total: 31 = 4

Single Key Number: 9
Compound Key Number: none

Using the name Linda Goodman as our example, here is what to do if the name you are calculating gives you only a Single Key Number, and does not give you a Compound Key Number. You may do something that has no validity, *except in this particular instance*. Take the Total Compound numbers of both names, and *add them* together to produce a Compound *Key Number*.

Example: Linda is a 14. Goodman is a 31.

$$\begin{array}{r} 14 \\ + 31 \\ \hline 45 \end{array}$$

And so, 45 becomes the Compound Key Number of Linda Goodman. When you look up this number in the definitions given of the Compound numbers, beginning on Page 249, you'll see that 45 has the same value (or vibration) as the number 27. Therefore, the Compound Key Number of my *name* is 27.

L I N D A   G O O D M A N'S   S U N   S I G N S
3 15 4 1   3 7 7 4 4 1 5 3   3 6 5   3 1 3 5 3

Total: 14 = 5   Total: 34 = 7   Total: 14 = 5   Total: 15 = 6

5 plus 7 plus 5 plus 6 equals 23

The compound Key Number of this book's title is 23, with which I am very pleased. The reason my publisher and I decided to use the possessive, and call it "Linda Goodman's Sun Signs" instead of "Sun Signs" by Linda Goodman, is because the former title is a 23 — and the latter title (Sun Signs alone) is an 11. I wasn't too happy with the 11, and so the official title included all four words. This meant that the vibration of the number 23 received a great power increase with each book printed (and read) — and had to be listed as that four-name title on the best seller lists, etc.

However, there were a number of newspaper releases, interviews, and various write-ups about the book in which it was referred to as simply *Sun Signs*, and readers referred to the book between themselves as the two-word title — "Have you read *Sun Signs*" — or "May I borrow your copy of *Sun Signs* ?" Every time the magnetic vibration of 11 was sent out in this way, its influence over the book increased.

When you read the definition, you'll see why that wasn't very fortunate, and certain aspects of my relationship with my publishers

— later — reflected the negative side of the Compound number 11, although the Compound Key Number of the four-word title, the fortunate 23, balanced things to some extent.

I do try to learn through experience, so when I decided on a title for my next book I wanted to make sure that the vibration was equally fortunate and harmonious with — or without — my name as part of the title — since my publishers insisted that the "Linda Goodman's" possessive be part of it. Nevertheless, I knew that some people would still refer to it *without* the use of the possessive form of "Linda Goodman's" — which is why I finally chose Linda Goodman's Love Signs, because the vibration of "Love Signs" alone, even though that wasn't to be the official title, is equally favorable. Illustration:

```
L I N D A      G O O D M A N'S      L O V E      S I G N S
3 15 4 1       3 7 7 4 4 1 5 3      3 7 6 5      3 1 3 5 3
Total: 14 = 5   Total: 34 = 7    Total: 14 = 5   Total: 15 = 6
```

5 plus 7 plus 3 plus 6 equals 21

The Compound Key Number of this four-word title is 21, a most fortunate number. Should people begin to refer to it with the "unofficial" title of Love Signs alone, I knew it would be influenced by the strong Single Number 9 (the 3 of "Love" and the 6 of "Signs" equals 9).

But remember the rule to follow when you have a Single Key Number, but *not* a Compound Key Number. You add the Compound numbers of the names (in this case, the two words "Love" and "Signs") — and the resulting number is the Compound Key Number.

So . . . since the Compound number of *Love* is 21 — and the Compound number of *Signs* is 15 . . .

$$\begin{array}{r} 21 \\ + 15 \\ \hline 36 \end{array}$$

As you'll see in the Compound number definitions, the number

36, like the Compound number of my name, 45 — is equal to 27, a most fortunate number.

Too many people associate numerology with "lucky numbers." There is no such thing in numerology as a guaranteed-always-lucky number. However, the Single Key Number of the day of your birth does vibrate harmoniously with you in most situations. Therefore, not always, but frequently, when you keep important appointments on a day of the month that harmonizes with your day of birth, things will usually turn out to be more fortunate than not.

For example, if you were born on the 1st, 10th, or 19th day of any month, you're influenced by the Single number 1, and you should try to arrange important meetings on one of those days. If you were born on the 2nd, 11th, 20th, or 29th, you're influenced by the Single number 2, and should try to arrange important meetings on one of these days — and so on with all the numbers. (Except for the karmic numbers 4 and 8, for reasons explained beginning on Page 269.) Let's call the rule described in this paragraph Rule Zebra. The reason it needs a name is because I'm going to refer back to it shortly.

The priority Single and Compound Key Numbers of your birth are derived from the *day* of your birth.

However, if you wish, you may calculate your *entire* birth date to find a *secondary* Single Key Number (personality and character) and a *secondary* Compound Key Number (karma and destiny). Sometimes this secondary method of using the entire birth date gives you only a milder subliminal influence. Sometimes it will amazingly intensify the influences of the priority Key Numbers of the *day* of birth, as in the following example of a person I know, using Rule Zebra.

This person is a Leo, born on August 13, 1945. The Single Key Number of the *day* of his birth is 4 — the Compound Key Number of the *day* of his birth is 13. These are his priority birth numbers.

Now, let's use his entire birth date to arrive at his secondary Single and Compound Key Numbers. August 13, 1945.

First, August is the 8th month. The number 8 has a relationship with the Single Key Number 4 of his birth *day,* as you will note when you read the section about the strange numbers 4 and 8, beginning on Page 269. The people influenced by 4 and 8 find these two numbers mysteriously appearing and repeating themselves.

The year, 1945 adds (or reduces) to 19, which reduces to 10, which reduces to the Single number 1. (The Chaldean system does not use the numerical value of the *letters* of the month, but its numerical sequence: January is the 1st month — a 1 — etc.) Here is how we calculate the Lion's entire birth date.

8	August is the 8th month
4	Single number of the *day* of birth
_1_	reduced Single number of 1945

Total: 13 = 4

Therefore, this particular Leo's priority and secondary Single and Compound Key Numbers are:

DAY OF BIRTH (Priority Key Numbers)   *ENTIRE BIRTH DATE* (Secondary)

Single Key Number: 4   Single Key Number: 4

Compound Key Number: 13   Compound Key Number: 13

Rather astonishing. This Lion's *name* (not given here for reasons of privacy) also creates the Single numbers 4 and 8. The names and birth dates of most of his close relatives are also 4's and 8's. Likewise, his telephone numbers and addresses over the past years produce 4's and 8's. You'll discover, when reading the section about the numbers 4 and 8, that this is a perfect example of the influence of these "numbers of fate" (not necessarily negative).

Back to Rule Zebra. When you're applying Rule Zebra, use the

Single Key Number of the *day* of birth, and also use the Single Key Number of the entire birth date.

However, *never* use the entire birth date to calculate your Single number for the purpose of your *health* analysis. (See Chapter 2: *An Apple a Day,* which contains a chart to aid you in determining your Single number for a health analysis.)

When you use all these numerological star sign codes of wisdom, and add your Sun Sign description from my book, *Sun Signs* (or any other good astrology book), you'll have a more complete picture of your complex and many-faceted self. The Lexigram codes in Chapter 8 will reveal even more.

"You are endless galaxies, and you have seen but one star."
— from *Sun Signs*

All these calculations may seem like a lot of work, but assuming you follow the several rules of increasing the power of your numbers, it will be well worth the effort, many times over.

When you've mastered the numerical calculations (much easier than they seem at first glance), you'll be able to see in which direction those "powerful, invisible forces" described at the beginning of this chapter are flowing, so you can flow along with them, and get in tune with the harmony of the Universe. You'll find that you are able, to a large extent, to control events instead of allowing them to control you, simply by understanding how to change a major part of your "fate" by changing your numbers. You'll also learn more about the people you love. And finally, you'll be able to decode certain numerological secrets about your Karma, each of these Compound numbers containing its own mystery of how to benefit from the number's positive aspects — and eventually erase the negative aspects.

★ ★ ★ ★ ★ ★

A warning: Some numerology books place great emphasis on

your "compatible" numbers, claiming to tell you which number person you'll get along with best, based on your birth or name Single number.

Numerological compatibility does not work with any reliable degree of dependability, and it would be unwise to base your relationships on this weak branch of the numerology tree.

Numerical compatibility is based on what seems to be logic, which is why you might be deceived. For example, these books tell you that, for instance, a Number 1 person is compatible with a Number 9 person. They say this because 1 is the number of the Sun (ruler of Leo) — and 9 is the number of Mars (ruler of Aries) — which is like saying that Leo and Aries are compatible, which they definitely are.

But suppose that the Number 1 person is a Cancerian, and the Number 9 person is a Libra. The Sun Signs of Cancer and Libra are *not* generally harmonious or compatible, and the power of this Sun Sign influence will take priority over the alleged numerical compatibility (or lack of it).

Your Sun Sign character and personality will also dominate the personality analysis of your birth and name Single Numbers — although the latter will be most helpful in helping you understand an *additional facet* of your total personality. This relationship between the Sun Sign and the Single Key Numbers of name and birth is explained in the analysis of each Single Key Number, beginning on Page 225, telling you how your Single Key Number clashes or blends with your normal Sun Sign personality.

★★★★★★

The definitions of the Single numbers and double, or Compound, numbers are based on the Tarot and ancient writings, and like the numerical value of the letters of the alphabet, do not "belong to" any individual numerologist. Each individual astrologer or numerologist adds his or her own style of expression to these definitions, but the basic foundation of them is as old as thought itself. As an individual seeking truth and guidance from the planets and numbers, you may (and should) develop your own form of esoteric interpretation, reading "between the lines" when you're trying to apply the definitions to a specific person, event, or situation. In other words, you have a personal obligation and responsibility to add *your own effort* to the process, to sharpen your own intuition through the study, and use of these star sign codes to wisdom.

The origin of the Chaldean and Hebrew kabalistic alphabet is lost in antiquity. It's believed that the system was originated by the Chaldeans, who were adept in numerous magical arts and sciences, then passed down to the Hebrews, and the knowledge became part of the Hebrew Kabala, but no one claims to be certain who initiated it in the beginning. The word "Kabala" is spelled in various ways in its translation from Hebrew to English, but I prefer this spelling because it equals the compound number 10 — and you'll see how logical that is when you read the definition of this number.

And now, the definitions of the Single numbers.

Definitions
of
Single
Numbers

The Number 1

The Number 1 vibrates to the Sun. It represents creativity, protection, and benevolence. 1 is the number of original action, the initiating basis of all other numbers.

A person or entity is influenced by the Number 1 if born on the 1st, 10th, 19th, or 28th day of any month in any year. People or entities born on the 1st are stamped with the distinctive imprint of the Number 1. So are those born on the 10th, 19th, or 28th day of the month, but these will, *in addition,* be challenged to unlock the karmic mystery of the *Compound* number — 10, 19, or 28, as the case may be — in their lives. The same is true of the Single and Compound number of the *name* of the person or entity being analyzed.

The Number 1 attitudes and characteristics will be periodically exhibited by the 1 person or entity, and will *interact* with that person's or entity's personality in different ways, depending on the individual Sun Sign.

When the Sun Sign is:

LEO: The 1 vibration *intensifies* the Sun Sign personality traits.

AQUARIUS: The 1 vibration sometimes *opposes* the Sun Sign motives, but, with effort, can be used to *balance* the Sun Sign nature.

ARIES, SAGITTARIUS, GEMINI, LIBRA: The 1 vibration *harmonizes well* with the Sun Sign character, motives, and personality patterns.

SCORPIO, TAURUS, VIRGO, CANCER, PISCES, CAPRICORN: The 1 vibration is in *sharp contrast* with the basic Sun Sign instincts. When it surfaces on occasion in the personality, the behavior is so unusual, relative to the person's or entity's normal or natural Sun Sign attitudes, it startles others, and often surprises the Number 1 person as well.

The Meaning of the 1 Vibration

The following definition of Number 1 applies to both people and entities. 1 people possess a strong sense of self-worth, and a marked dislike for criticism. A 1 person demands — and usually gets — respect; will insist on organizing and controlling everything and everyone around. The underlying desire is to be inventive, creative, and strongly original. These people are quite definite in their views, and can be stubborn when thwarted. They dislike restraint, and must feel free. They'll almost always rise to some position of authority in whatever they undertake. Otherwise, they'll pout in the corner, nursing a bruised ego and frustrated ambitions. They insist on being looked up to by the mate, friends, relatives, co-workers — and even by the boss !

They'll protect the weak, defend the helpless, and take on the burdens of others as long as "the others" will do exactly as the Number 1 person dictates. They know everything better than anyone else, and consider their opinions to be superior, if not flawless. The great majority of the time they are right, which understandably annoys the people they lecture. They're strong on lectures. But 1 people are also unbelievably susceptible to compliments (sincere, not phony, and they can detect the difference). Genuine appreciation will get them to bend over backward to please. Pride is their weakest point. When the pride is wounded, 1 people lose all their virtues and become most unpleasant. When they're appreciated and respected, no one can be more generous and benevolent. But they can be dangerous when ignored. Being in love and being loved is as vital a necessity to them as the very air they breathe.

Although the disposition is easily wounded, enemies are quickly forgiven after they bow down and apologize. The only way to win a confrontation with a 1 person is to be humble, say you're truly sorry, and you'll be graciously excused. The Number 1 person resents familiarity from strangers, but is extremely warm and affectionate with those who are loved and trusted. There's a fondness for children and young people, but often some sadness connected with a child. The 1 person enjoys fine clothes and jewels, impressive cars. Even a cloistered monk with a 1 vibration will keep his robe mended, and the cord around the waist will not be torn or tattered. All Number 1 people are blessed with a visible inbred sense of dignity.

The Number 2

The Number 2 vibrates to the Moon. It represents imagination, parenthood, and sensitivity. 2 is the number of conception, childbirth, and dreams.

A person or entity is influenced by the Number 2 if born on the 2nd, 11th, 20th, or 29th day of any month, in any year. People or entities born on the 2nd are stamped with the distinct imprint of the Number 2. So are those born on the 11th, 20th, or 29th day of the month, but these will, in addition, be challenged to unlock the karmic mystery of the Compound number — 11 — 20 or 29, as the case may be — in their lives. The same is true of the Single and Compound number of the *name* of the person or entity being analyzed.

The Number 2 attitudes and characteristics will be periodically exhibited by the 2 person or entity, and will *interact* with that person's or entity's personality in different ways, depending on the individual Sun Sign.

When the Sun Sign is:

CANCER: The 2 vibration *intensifies* the Sun Sign personality traits.

CAPRICORN: The 2 vibration sometimes *opposes* the Sun Sign motives, but, with effort, can be used to *balance* the Sun Sign nature.

SCORPIO, PISCES, VIRGO, TAURUS: The 2 vibration *harmonizes well* with the Sun Sign character, motives, and personality patterns.

ARIES, LIBRA, GEMINI, SAGITTARIUS, AQUARIUS, LEO: The 2 vibration is in sharp contrast with the basic Sun Signs instincts. When it surfaces on occasion in the personality, the behavior is so unusual, relative to the person's or entity's normal or natural Sun Sign attitudes, it startles others, and often surprises the Number 2 person as well.

The Meaning of the 2 Vibration

The following definition of Number 2 applies to both people and entities. 2 people are dreamers, with a tendency to fear the unknown or the unfamiliar. They are extremely imaginative and inventive, but not always as forceful as could be in carrying out their plans and ideas. Not all, but most 2 people are seldom as strong as those born under the single birth numbers of 1, 9, 3, or 6.

These people possess a very romantic nature, and are secretly what is called "psychic." The intuition is highly developed. One of the traits for 2 people to guard against is "fearing shadows of fears." A 2 person fears every conceivable kind of loss: loss of love, property, money, friendship, employment — loss of loved ones through death or any other kind of separation. These people need a home base, and although they adore to travel the globe as frequently as finances permit, they must have a home to return to. In no way can a 2 person be a "soldier of fortune," to whom home is where you hang your hat. They are fanatically devoted to or involved with (in either a negative or positive sense) the parents, especially the Mother. They make ideal parents themselves, but they must be careful not to smother their children with possessive love.

This is the "chicken soup" vibration, since all 2 people are ultra concerned with the well-being of friend and relatives. They hover over everyone, making sure they don't catch cold, throw money away foolishly, and so forth. "Have some hot chicken soup and wear your boots or you'll catch your death of pneumonia." 2 people are extremely cautious, and dislike gambling or taking chances. They love money, but like to accumulate it in a safe, stable way, then invest it securely, so it can increase through dividends and interest. The 2 vibration is secretive, and never lets anyone know what the next move might be. They're experts at wheedling secrets from others, but they won't allow you to invade their own privacy. They'll veer from right to left and backward, then lunge forward in a surprisingly aggressive manner toward their goals. Money seems to stick to them like glue, so you'll almost never find a 2 person (or an 8 person) on public welfare or food stamps. These people are charitable (especially with family), and are prone to heading charity drives, but it chills them to even think about accepting charity themselves. It insinuates a failure to protect their assets, which is a cardinal sin to the 2 vibration. When 2 people learn to overcome fear, possessiveness, and unnecessary caution, their imagination, adaptability, and intuition can carry them to the fulfillment of all their many dreams.

The Number 3

The Number 3 vibrates to the planet Jupiter. It represents idealism, higher education, foreign travel, and religion. 3 is the number of optimism, movement, expansion — and the Holy Trinity of the body, mind, and spirit.

A person or entity is influenced by the Number 3 if born on the 3rd, 12th, 21st, or 30th day of any month in any year. People or entities born on the 3rd are stamped with the distinctive imprint of the Number 3. So are those born on the 12th, 21st, and 30th day of the month, but these will, in addition, be challenged to unlock the karmic mystery of the Compound number — 12, 21, or 30, as the case may be — in their lives. The same is true of the Single and Compound number of the *name* of the person or entity being analyzed.

The Number 3 attitudes and characteristics will be periodically exhibited by the 3 person or entity, and will *interact* with that person's or entity's personality in different ways, depending on the individual Sun Sign.

When the Sun Sign is:

SAGITTARIUS: The 3 vibration *intensifies* the Sun Sign personality traits.

GEMINI: The 3 vibration sometimes *opposes* the Sun Sign motives, but, with effort, can be used to *balance* the Sun Sign nature.

ARIES, LEO, AQUARIUS, LIBRA: The 3 vibration *harmonizes well* with the Sun Sign character, motives, and personality patterns.

PISCES, VIRGO, CAPRICORN, SCORPIO, TAURUS, CANCER: The 3 vibration is in *sharp contrast* with the basic Sun Sign instincts. When it surfaces on occasion in the personality, the behavior is so unusual, relative to the person's or entity's normal or natural Sun Sign attitudes, it startles others, and often surprises the 3 person as well.

The Meaning of the 3 Vibration

The following definition of Number 3 applies to both people and entities. 3 people base every action (even when they are misguided and the action is a negative one) upon the foundation of a great ideal. They aim high for truth, and nothing less than truth will satisfy them, whether they seek the truth of a love affair, a friendship, a career, politics, or religion. They are not easily put off by evasive answers or deception, and they can spot a lie, a distortion, or dishonesty a mile away. Some of them achieve the goal of truth, others are misled into believing their own illusions, but they never stop searching. The 3 vibration is fiercely independent, seeks total freedom of speech and movement, and cannot be tied down. Travel is an absolute necessity, mingling with others and seeing the world, learning everything there is to know about every country and its people, every intellectual concept, every philosophy.

They tend to look at the bright side of everything, and their optimism is contagious. Even Capricorns with 3 as the birth number will shock themselves with these occasional bursts of sheer Pollyanna optimism.

Because of the shining quest for truth, the 3 person is either an agnostic, an atheist, or intensely devoted to a religious principle, i.e.: nuns, ministers, monks, rabbis, and priests. Religion is an important part of the life of a 3 person or entity, whether religion is fervently, fanatically accepted or bitterly rejected. The attitude is never neutral.

Physical challenge inspires the 3 people or entities; therefore sports play a major role. The 3 vibration is shockingly blunt of speech, candid to a fault, and outraged at duplicity of any kind. There's a genuine love for animals and a strong tendency to defend the underdog human with the same loyalty they show to their dogs, horses, and other pets. There's a marked indifference to family ties, and marriage works only when freedom is total. The 3 vibration is associated with tests of physical strength, gambling, and taking a chance, whether at the casinos or on the floor of the stock market. The 3 person or entity will take a chance or bet on just about anything. Their bubbling optimism is delightfully contagious.

3 people or entities often display an odd blend of the wise philosopher and the happy-go-lucky clown, and a sense of responsibility is sometimes lacking. Some of the goals, dreams, and ambitions are serious; others are silly and frivolous. Pursuing an education matters a great deal to 3 people, and they are crushed when they're denied the halls of higher learning for whatever reason. They make excellent "armchair lawyers" or professional attorneys, since the Planet Jupiter, represented by 3, rules the law.

The Number 4

The Number 4 vibrates to the planet Uranus. It represents individualism, originality, inventiveness, and tolerance. 4 is the number of unconventional behavior and sudden, unexpected events — also of genius.

A person or entity is influenced by the Number 4 if born on the 4th, 13th, 22nd, or 31st day of any month, in any year. People or entities born on the 4th are stamped with the distinctive imprint of the Number 4. So are those born on the 13th, 22nd, or 31st day of the month, but these will, in addition, be challenged to unlock the karmic mystery of the Compound number — 13 — 22, or 31, as the case may be — in their lives. The same is true of the Single and Compound number of the *name* of the person or entity being analyzed.

The Number 4 attitudes and characteristics will be periodically exhibited by the 4 person or entity, and will *interact* with that person's or entity's personality in different ways, depending on the individual Sun Sign.

When the Sun Sign is:

AQUARIUS: The 4 vibration *intensifies* the Sun personality traits.

LEO: The 4 vibration sometimes *opposes* the Sun Sign motives, but, with effort, can be used to *balance* the Sun Sign nature.

GEMINI, LIBRA, ARIES, SAGITTARIUS: The 4 vibration *harmonizes well* with the Sun Sign character, motives, and personality patterns.

SCORPIO, TAURUS, CANCER, VIRGO, CAPRICORN, PISCES: The 4 vibration is in *sharp contrast* with the basic Sun Sign instincts. When it surfaces on occasion in the personality, the behavior is so unusual, relative to the person's or entity's normal or natural Sun Sign attitudes, it startles others, and often surprises the Number 4 person as well.

The Meaning of the 4 Vibration

The following definition of Number 4 applies to both people and entities. 4 people are seldom understood by their friends and family. They're an enigma to everyone they know. They make their own rules, and these rules don't always match those of society. Marked individuality colors every thought and action. If there's a different way to do anything, the 4 person will find it. Their speech and actions frequently shock others, and it often seems the attempt to shock is deliberate. It is. 4 people live in the future, caring little about the present. They're light years ahead of others in their ideas and ideals. Going along with this trait is an innate talent for prophecy, for knowing what will happen tomorrow long before tomorrow arrives. Their life-style ranges from unconventional to the bizarre, yet their "crazy" ideas are successful more often than not.

Anything far out or off the beaten path appeals strongly to the 4 person's questing, curious nature. For example, a 4 person with a well-aspected Jupiter in the natal horoscope has an excellent chance to be the first person to tame and make friends with Sasquatch or Bigfoot — or locate and swim along with Nessie, the Loch Ness monster. If the 4 person also has a Scorpio Sun or Moon, the discovery, if attempted, is almost certain to be successful. That's because such incredible, unproven, and so-called unscientific theories never deter, but instead excite the 4 person, who is deeply convinced of the reality of whatever can be conceived in the mind. To be told that a thing is impossible only intensifies and spurs the 4 person's resolve to prove it is possible. The phrase "mission impossible" rings the great bells of mental challenge in the very soul of a 4 person.

Although the 4 vibration advocates change in every area of life, from politics to art, these people are strangely reluctant to accept change in their personal habits, which remain rather fixed. They can be quite stubborn when people try to dictate to them or try to mold them into a more acceptable social pattern. Because prophets are often unrecognized in their own time, and because 4 people live far into the future, their grandest and truest visions are often ridiculed or ignored. They're fascinated by U.F.O.s, and their secret wish is to be contacted and taken aboard, hopefully not to return to the chaos of Earth. Reform movements like Women's Liberation and Equal Rights for Minorities attract the 4 people, who are genuinely dedicated to tolerance and brotherhood (and sisterhood). Friendship is vital to the 4 vibration, and these people — not always, but usually — have bushels of friends from all walks of life. Money means little to them; they're as likely to mix with Kings as with paupers — they care nothing about class distinction, have no desire to impress anyone, and would just as soon live in a van, a tent, or a sleeping bag as in a mansion. It's not that they're prejudiced against comfort or wealth, it's because they simply don't *notice* their surroundings. They live in their imaginations. One of their finest virtues is the tendency to "live and let live." The 4 person doesn't give a ginger snap what you do or say, however outrageous or against his or her own principles — and expects you to return the same consideration.

The Number 5

The number 5 vibrates to the planet Mercury. It represents communication, movement, and versatility. It's the number of the intellect and both written and oral expression.

A person or entity is influenced by the number 5 if born on the 5th, 14th, or 23rd day of any month in any year. People born on the 5th are stamped with the distinctive imprint of the number 5. So are those born on the 14th or 23rd day of the month, but these will, in addition, be challenged to unlock the karmic mystery of the Compound number of 14 or 23, as the case may be, in their lives. The same is true of the Single and Compound number of the *name* of the person or entity being analyzed.

The number 5 attitudes and characteristics will periodically be exhibited by the 5 person or entity, and will *interact* with that person's personality in different ways, depending on the individual Sun Sign.

When the Sun Sign is:

GEMINI, VIRGO: The 5 vibration *intensifies* the Sun Sign personality traits, and gives the ability to create magical changes in the appearance and behavior.

SAGITTARIUS, PISCES: The 5 vibration sometimes *opposes* the Sun Sign motives, but, with effort, can be used to *balance* the Sun Sign nature.

ARIES, TAURUS, CANCER, LEO, LIBRA, SCORPIO, CAPRICORN, AQUARIUS: The 5 vibration, due to its peculiar mingling power, either *harmonizes* with or *sharply contrasts* with the 5 person's Sun Sign characteristics, depending on the mood of the moment. The nature of the 5 is endlessly changeable and adaptable, bringing a curious tendency to be in harmony with one's self when one wishes, and at odds with one's self at other times. It's never easy to know a 5 person. The dreams change like quicksilver. When 5 is the single number of either the birth or the name of a Virgo or Gemini, the mercurial qualities are even more pronounced.

The Meaning of the 5 Vibration

The following definition of Number 5 applies to both people and entities. 5 people possess a great deal of natural charm, and, as a general rule, are innately courteous. They're quick to spot mistakes and flaws, and will not hesitate to point them out when they see them. The 5 vibration is super-critical and incapable of ignoring mistakes (their own, as well as those of others) and it's associated with a love for movement and travel. Change is a never-ending necessity for 5 people. Change of scene, change in relationships, residence, spiritual and political beliefs, and so on. There's a strong tendency to overanalyze people and situations. It's difficult for a 5 person to submit to the feelings and the intuition; the intellect is determined to find logical answers. This obsession with analysis can ruin personal relationships for those who allow themselves to be ruled by the 5 vibration. Even love can wear out under such continual (and usually unnecessary) scrutiny. Love is made of instinct and feelings, not logic. 5 people tend to "talk love to death" instead of just letting it be, allowing it to become part of them, without questioning its whys and wherefores. Love has nothing to do with logic. Most people enjoy being in the company of a 5 person, since the outward persona is unusually pleasant and soothing. Because 5 is the vibration of intellect, those under its influence are extremely bright, of higher than average intelligence, and mentally alert. Nothing escapes their notice. They seem to be fine-tuned to the smallest detail. When financial or other circumstances don't permit the frequent travel all 5 people need, they'll travel in their minds, and since their minds are so acute, their "daydreams" are vivid enough to satisfy the restless urges within them for a time, at least.

According to the ancients, the number 5 has an association with what is called "earth-magic." Curiously, the number 5 brings a longing to believe in magic, elves, faeries, and mysteries of Nature, along with a need to pin everything down and view it under a mental microscope, two qualities which are in direct polarity to one another, causing those under the influence of 5 to find it difficult to understand themselves. 5 people are sometimes high strung; they live on their nerves, and crave excitement. They're quick in thought and decision, often impulsive in their actions. They have a keen sense of new ideas and inventions, are willing to take risks, and are born speculators. Writing, advertising, public relations, and publishing are fortunate 5 occupations. 5 people possess an admirable elasticity of viewpoint, and the ability to rebound swiftly from blows of fate, which seem to leave no long-lasting impression on them.

The Number 6

The Number 6 vibrates to the planet Venus. It represents the feminine essence, compassion, and (until Venus gives up her rulership of Taurus when the planet Pan-Horus is discovered) also money. 6 is the number of love and romance.

A person or an entity is influenced by the Number 6 if born on the 6th, 15th, or 24th day of any month, in any year. People or entities born on the 6th are stamped with the distinct imprint of the Number 6. So are those born on the 15th and 24th day of the month, but these will, in addition, be challenged to unlock the karmic mystery of the Compound number — 15 or 24 — as the case may be — in their lives. The same is true of the Single and Compound number of the *name* of the person or entity being analyzed.

The Number 6 attitudes and characteristics will be periodically exhibited by the 6 person or entity, and will *interact* with that person's or entity's personality in different ways, depending on the individual Sun Sign.

When the Sun Sign is:

AQUARIUS, TAURUS, LIBRA: The 6 vibration *intensifies* the Sun Sign personality traits.

SCORPIO, ARIES: The 6 vibration sometimes *opposes* the Sun Sign motives, but, with effort, can be used to *balance* the Sun Sign nature.

ANY OTHER SIGN: The 6 vibration will, at times, *harmonize* with the Sun Sign character and personality patterns, and at other times, *contrast sharply* with them. At the latter times, the behavior is so unusual, relative to the normal behavior, it startles others, and often surprises the Number 6 person as well.

The Meaning of the 6 Vibration

The following definition of Number 6 applies to both people and entities. 6 people seem to magnetically attract others to them. They're genuinely loved by their friends and associates — and when they become attached themselves, they're devoted to the loved one. There's more idealism and affection than sensualism in the love nature. These people are born romantics with a strong sentimental streak, no matter how they deny it or try to hide it. The 6 vibration brings a love of art and a deep affinity for music. These people love nice homes and tasteful furnishings, pastel colors, and harmony in their surroundings.

They love to entertain their friends and to make people happy, and they simply cannot abide discord, arguments, unpleasantness, or jealousy — although they can display intense jealousy themselves if they're threatened with the possible loss of someone (or something) they love. The 6 vibration makes friends easily, and they tend to enjoy settling disputes between their friends, business associates, and relatives, at which times they appear to be as peaceful and as docile as lambs — until their stubborn side surfaces; then they don't seem quite so sweet !

Money often comes to them without effort, sometimes through their own talents and abilities, sometimes through inheritance or through wealthy friends or relatives. But they're warned to watch for a tendency toward the extremes of extravagance and stinginess. There's seldom a neutral attitude toward finances. It's either one or the other, taking turns in the nature. The love of beauty of all kinds in every area of life is pronounced. Most 6 people are deeply attached to Nature in some way, and love spending time in the country, near the silent woods and singing streams, which has a tranquilizing effect on their emotions. A fondness for luxury marks the 6 vibration. Ugliness is extremely offensive to them. They admire the tasteful and shrink from loudness and vulgarity. Their manners are, as a general rule, impeccable, and in their associations with others they are usually polite. However, when they feel strongly about anything, they won't hesitate to make their opinions known. They're fond of discussing and debating politics and other matters, and they usually win, because of their logic . . . and their irresistible smiles.

The Number 7

The Number 7 vibrates to the planet Neptune. It represents spirituality, sensitivity, sympathy, and mystery. 7 is the number of illusion and delusion, sometimes deception — but also the number of healing and miracles, faith — and dreams that come true.

A person or entity is influenced by the number 7 if born on the 7th, 16th, or 25th day of any month, in any year. People or entities born on the 7th are stamped with the distinctive imprint of the Number 7. So are those born on the 16th or 25th day of the month, but these will, in addition, be challenged to unlock the karmic mystery of the Compound number — 16 or 25, as the case may be — in their lives. The same is true of the Single and Compound number of the *name* of the person or entity being analyzed.

The Number 7 attitudes and characteristics will be periodically exhibited by the 7 person or entity, and will *interact* with that person's or entity's personality in different ways, depending on the individual Sun Sign.

When the Sun Sign is:

PISCES: The 7 vibration *intensifies* the Sun Sign personality traits.

VIRGO: The 7 vibration sometimes *opposes* the Sun Sign motives, but, with effort can be used to *balance* the Sun Sign nature.

SCORPIO, CANCER, CAPRICORN, TAURUS: The 7 vibration *harmonizes well* with the Sun Sign character, motives, and personality patterns.

GEMINI, SAGITTARIUS, AQUARIUS, ARIES, LIBRA, LEO: The 7 vibration is in *sharp contrast* with the basic Sun Sign instincts. When it surfaces on occasion in the personality, the behavior is so unusual, relative to the person's or entity's normal or natural Sun Sign attitudes, it startles others, and often surprises the Number 7 person as well.

The Meaning of the 7 Vibration

The following definition of Number 7 applies to both people and entities. 7 people tend to have remarkable dreams. Sometimes they talk about them — and sometimes they keep them to themselves. But they do dream more than most. Secretly, they have an intense interest in esoteric mysteries, mythology, spacecraft or U.F.O.s . . . and the entire forest of the unknown. They often possess the gifts of intuition and clairvoyance and a certain quieting, calming magnetism which has a great influence over others. Often, their mere presence has a soothing effect on a troubled person. The 7 vibration is associated with peculiar ideas about religion, a dislike of following the beaten path, and a tendency to adopt political beliefs which are unique and somewhat nonorthodox. It's not unusual for a 7 person to discover, found, or believe in a new religious concept.

The 7 person will either travel extensively at some time in the life or else read avidly books about foreign people and faraway lands. Many people influenced by the 7 vibration are strongly attracted to the sea and at some time are associated with sailing, water sports, or the Navy. There's a tendency to be anxious about the future, which is why 7 people need to know they have a rock of financial security somewhere in the background, lest the waters of fate sweep them away.

Yet, they care little about material possessions or accumulating great wealth. 7 people can earn large sums of money through their original ideas, but they're likely to make substantial contributions to charities or institutions. When they gravitate toward the arts, they make fine dancers, singers, poets, writers, actors, or actresses.

In their own quiet, laid-back way, people influenced by the Number 7 have ambitions they don't discuss with others, and these are always tinged with a philosophical outlook. They bless others with the grace of their sympathetic understanding of pain and suffering, which is why friends, relatives, and business associates unburden their troubles to the 7 person. There's a strong leaning toward privacy in the 7 vibration, and these people prefer to keep their own problems to themselves. They shrink from prying questions, and have a horror of "big brother" or anything they consider to be an invasion of their privacy.

Refined manners, an artistic temperament, and a sensitive nature make up the 7 essence, and don't let these people fool you with their sometimes taciturn nature . . . you'd be surprised if you knew all the strange thoughts that swim through their minds when they're communing with themselves. If you can coax them to talk about what they're thinking, you'll not only be surprised, you'll be fascinated when you learn the secrets of their Neptunian world. But the 7 person must find you trustworthy before he or she shares these inner streams of contemplation . . . and you'll have to earn that trust by proving you're not judgmental or prejudiced. 7 people are rarely either.

The Number 8

The Number 8 vibrates to the planet Saturn. It represents wisdom, learning through experience, stability, patience, and responsibility. 8 is also the number of financial security, caution, restriction, self-discipline and self-control.

A person or entity is influenced by the Number 8 if born on the 8th, 17th, or 26th day of any month, in any year. People or entities born on the 8th are stamped with the distinct imprint of the Number 8. So are those born on the 17th or 26th day of the month, but these will, in addition, be challenged to unlock the karmic mystery of the Compound number 17 or 26, as the case may be, in their lives. The same is true of the Single and Compound number of the *name* of the person or entity being analyzed.

The Number 8 characteristics and attitudes will be periodically exhibited by the 8 person or entity, and will *interact* with that person's or entity's personality in different ways, depending on the individual Sun Sign.

When the Sun Sign is:

CAPRICORN: The 8 vibration *intensifies* the Sun Sign personality traits.

CANCER: The 8 vibration sometimes *opposes* the Sun Sign motives, but with effort, can be used to *balance* the Sun Sign nature.

PISCES, SCORPIO, VIRGO, TAURUS: The 8 vibration *harmonizes well* with the Sun Sign character, motives and personality patterns.

ARIES, LIBRA GEMINI, LEO, SAGITTARIUS, AQUARIUS: The 8 vibration is in *sharp contrast* with the basic Sun Sign instincts. When it surfaces on occasion in the personality, the behavior is so unusual, relative to the person's normal Sun Sign attitudes, it startles others, and often surprises the Number 8 person as well.

The Meaning of the 8 Vibration

The following definition of the Number 8 applies to both people and entities. 8 people are normally quiet, reserved, and shy. They don't obviously push ahead, but slowly and surely they will get where they want to go, and nothing will stop them from achieving their ambitions. The shyness and reticence is a cover for an intense drive to reach the top of the profession or career. They make excellent teachers and counselors, *most* of them could be successful in the tough game of politics (although now and then there's a sour apple in the barrel) — and they excel at anything that requires patience and intelligent deduction.

Those influenced by the 8 vibration may have poor health in childhood, but they grow more robust when they reach maturity, and longevity is common with 8 men and women. These people are willing to wait for their plans to bear fruit, and they use the waiting time wisely. It's rare to find an 8 person procrastinating or "goofing off." They have an inborn sense of duty and responsibility that won't allow them to take a careless attitude toward what is expected of them.

Most of those born under the 8 influence are as reliable as a grandfather clock, and as cozy to be around as a grandma quilt or comforter. They have a rich sense of humor, but one has to watch for it; it's subtle and never obvious. These people behave as if they don't care a peanut what people think of them, and they appear to be turned off by compliments, yet inwardly they care very much what people think of them, and if the compliments are sincere, they secretly enjoy them, although they'll hide their pleasure, for fear they might be considered weak. To be considered weak is the very last thing they want to happen.

Although the 8 vibration, like all the single number birth vibrations, interacts always with the person's Sun Sign, and the traits aren't always present — they only surface on occasion — most 8 people have very deep and intense natures and great inner strength. They often play an important role in life's drama, and many times are the instrument of Fate for others. There's a tendency toward fanaticism in religion, and they'll stick by what they believe relentlessly, in the face of all opposition. They make loving friends, but bitter enemies.

Although 8 people appear to be cold and undemonstrative with those they love and trust, they can be shyly affectionate and warmly devoted. They're often lonely, needing desperately to be loved, and they're capable of great sacrifices for an ideal, an ambition, or for those who depend on them. They grow younger in appearance and behavior as they grow older — they look and act younger at fifty than they did when they were twenty. They're as demanding of themselves as they are of others, but for all the outward attitudes of wisdom and maturity, self-control, and discipline, the 8 person's heart is lonely and longing, and they need to learn that the pursuit of happiness is not a sin.

The Number 9

The Number 9 vibrates to the planet Mars. It represents aggressive action, penetration, courage, and conflict. 9 is the number of originality and initiative . . . also the contradictory traits of vulnerability and naïveté.

A person or entity is influenced by the Number 9 if born on the 9th, 18th, or 27th day of any month, in any year. People or entities born on the 9th are stamped with the distinct imprint of the Number 9. So are those born on the 18th and 27th day of the month, but these will, in addition, be challenged to unlock the karmic mystery of the Compound number 18 or 27, as the case may be, in their lives. The same is true of the Single and Compound number of the *name* of the person or entity being analyzed.

The Number 9 characteristics and attitudes will be periodically exhibited by the 9 person or entity, and will *interact* with that person's or entity's personality in different ways, depending on the individual Sun Sign.

When the Sun Sign is:

ARIES: The 9 vibration *intensifies* the Sun Sign personality traits.

LIBRA: The 9 vibration sometimes *opposes* the Sun Sign motives, but, with effort, can be used to *balance* the Sun Sign nature.

LEO, GEMINI, SAGITTARIUS, AQUARIUS: The 9 vibration *harmonizes well* with the Sun Sign character, motives, and personality patterns.

CAPRICORN, CANCER, TAURUS, VIRGO, SCORPIO, PISCES: The 9 vibration is in *sharp contrast* with the basic Sun Sign instincts. When it surfaces on occasion in the personality, the behavior is so unusual, relative to the person's normal Sun Sign attitudes, it startles others, and often surprises the Number 9 person as well.

The Meaning of the 9 Vibration

The following definition of Number 9 applies to both people and entities. 9 people are not stubborn, but they are determined to get what they want, and there is a difference. Stubbornness reacts and determination initiates. 9 brings a tendency to be impulsive and make snap decisions, later regretted. Although the temper will flare rather frequently, these people are quick to both forgive and forget an injury. They're vulnerable to their enemies because their first instinct is to trust everyone. Since they're so direct themselves, they expect others to be the same — and others often are not. Deviousness and manipulation always come as a shock to 9 people. As a general rule, they're incapable of such behavior and motives themselves, and dishonesty catches them off guard nearly every time, until they learn to be more cautious.

One of the most beneficial virtues of the 9 vibration is the ability to penetrate straight to the heart or the core of a situation instead of indulging in circumlocution and the slow process of analysis. The Mars rulership of 9 allows these people to get directly to the point swiftly, and this makes them extremely impatient of slower thinkers, which doesn't help them win popularity contests. In fact, impatience with the mistakes of others and with errors of thinking they see instantly is one of the traits 9 people find the most difficult to control.

The familiar catch phrase "what you see is what you get" perfectly describes the 9 personality (when it surfaces to interact with the Sun Sign nature) because of the complete lack of guile. It's against the very essence of the 9 vibration to plan complex strategies or to play games to get what they want from other people. It's so much easier to simply demand what they want ! Since such straightforwardness is unexpected by the other person, 9 people usually get what they want by catching the opposition by surprise. Many people are touched by the visible vulnerability and childlike quality of the 9 person, and feel protective toward him or her; others see these qualities as foolish, one of the reasons that 9 people are seldom truly respected by friends and business associates — until that Mars temper and courageous spirit comes forth, like a battle cry, and those who underestimated the 9 vibration's pure energy will take a sudden, shocked step backward.

There's a strong tendency toward vanity. At least that's what it appears to be on the surface. But 9 people are not vain, even though they are admittedly almost constantly concerned with their appearance. The true root of this attitude is fear of rejection, because, beneath all their bravado, 9 people inwardly tremble with a lack of confidence. As self-assertive as they may seem, they need continual reassurance that they are liked — respected — admired — and loved. For all the pushiness and independent airs of 9 people, they're secretly very unsure of themselves. Generous to a fault and normally extravagant (unless the Sun Sign cancels this trait most of the time . . . although it will still be evident on rare occasions in anyone born as Number 9) — 9 people need no lessons in giving. The first instinct is to give, to let go, and let tomorrow take care of itself.

Definitions
of
Compound
Numbers

10
The Wheel of Fortune

10 is symbolized by Isis and Osiris. A number of rise and fall, according to personal desire. The name will be known for good or evil, depending on the action chosen. 10 is capable of arousing the extreme responses of love or hate — respect or fear. There is no middle ground between honor or dishonor. Every event is *self*-determined. 10 is the symbol of LOve and LIght, which create all that can be imagined, and also contains the code: Image 10 Ordain. Image it, and it shall be. Ordain it, and it will materialize. The power for manifesting creative concepts into reality is inherent, but must be used with wisdom, since the power for absolute creation contains the polarity power for absolute destruction. Self-discipline and infinite compassion must accompany the gift of the former to avoid the tragedy of the latter. *Discipline must precede Dominion.* Unfortunately, some 10 people fail to realize their power potential, and consequently harbor deep-seated feelings of frustration, causing them to feel unfulfilled, and to occasionally behave in a somewhat proud and arrogant manner to cover such unnecessary feelings of inferiority.

11
A Lion Muzzled — A Clenched Fist

This is a number of hidden trials and treachery from others. It represents two members of the same or the opposite sex — or two opposed situations. In either case, compatibility of interest is lacking, and interference from a third force must be conquered. The difficulties may also arise from *the illusion* of separation. It's necessary to unite divided goals to avoid a sense of frustrated incompletion. The third, interfering force can be a person or an idea; and it can take the form of a refusal to see the other side as an obstacle to harmony. The origin of the separating force must be identified, an attempt made to seek compromise. Occasionally, conflicting desires within one's own self are seen as in a reflecting mirror. Two forces or two desires stand apart and must ultimately unite for happiness. Yet, each must remain individual, even after being joined, for each possesses its own worth.

12
The Sacrifice — The Victim

One will periodically be sacrificed for the plans or intrigues of others. The number 12 warns of the necessity to be alert to every situation, to beware of false flattery from those who use it to gain their own ends. Be suspicious of those who offer a high position, and carefully analyze the motive. Although duplicity is not always present, forewarned is forearmed. There is a degree of mental anxiety, caused by the need to sacrifice personal goals to the ambition of others. A secondary meaning of this number should be considered. The figure 1 is the teacher (whether it be a person or Life itself). The figure 2 is the kneeling, submissive student. Sometimes, the result of severe emotional stress and mental anguish creates amnesia, forgetfulness of lessons previously learned. 12 represents the educational process on all levels, the submission of the will required and the sacrifices necessary to achieve knowledge and wisdom, on both the spiritual and the intellectual levels. When the intellect is sacrificed to the feelings, the mind will be illuminated with the answers it seeks. Look within for the solution. Attention paid to the requirements of education will end suffering and bring success.

13
Regeneration — Change

13 is not an unlucky number, as many people believe. The ancients claimed that "he who understands how to use the number 13 will be given power and dominion." The symbol of 13 is a skeleton, or death, with a scythe, reaping down men in a field of new-grown grass, where young faces and heads appear to be thrusting through the ground and emerging on all sides. 13 is a number of upheaval, so that

new ground may be broken. It's associated with power, which, if used for selfish purpose, will bring destruction upon itself. There is a warning of the unknown and the unexpected. Adapting to change gracefully will bring out the strength of the 13 vibration, and decrease any potential for negative. 13 is associated with genius — also with explorers, breaking the orthodox and new discoveries of all kinds. If you were born on the 13th day of any month — or should the Compound Key Number of your name be 13 — you'll need to read carefully the section of this chapter related to the numbers 4 and 8, beginning on Page 269.

14
Movement . . . Challenge

Magnetic communication with the public through writing, publishing, and all media-related matters is associated with the 14. Periodic changes in business and partnerships of all kinds are usually beneficial. Dealing with speculative matters brings luck; likewise, movement and travel associated with combinations of people and nations can be fortunate. However, both gains and losses are sometimes temporary, due to the strong currents of change, which are ever-present. 14 warns of danger from accidents related to natural elements, i.e.: fire, flood, earthquakes, tornados, hurricanes, tempests, and so forth. (This is not an absolute, merely a warning to be cautious.) There is risk involved in depending on the word of those who misrepresent a situation. It's a mistake to rely on others. Rely on the intuition, the self, the voice within. The "luck" of 14 includes money dealings and speculative projects, or "betting," but there's always a danger of loss due to wrong advice from others, or overconfidence.

15
The Magician

15 is a number of deep esoteric significance, the alchemy vibration through which all magic is manifested. It's extremely lucky and carries the essence of enchantment with it. 15 is associated with

"good talkers," eloquence of speech, and the gifts of music, art, and the drama. It bestows upon the person or entity represented by it a dramatic temperament and strong personal magnetism; a curiously compelling charisma. The 15 vibration is especially fortunate for obtaining money, gifts, and favors from others, because of its powerful appeal to the altruistic nature of people. However, there are no roses without thorns, and the ancients warn that 15 rules the lower levels of occultism when it is associated with the single numbers 4 or 8. Such people will use every art of magic — even black magic, hypnosis, and mental suggestion — to carry out their purpose. Or the contrary is true. The 4 or 8 person will become the victim of others using the same methods. Consequently, if the 15th is the birth date, and the *name* number is 4, 13, 22, or 31, the spelling of the name should be changed to equal a Compound number that reduces to the Single number 1, such as 10 or 19. If the *birth* date is the 15th, and the *name* number is 8, 17, or 26, the spelling should be changed to equal the number 6 or 24. If the *name* number is 15, and the person was born on the 4th, 13th, 22nd, or 31st day of the month, the spelling of the name should be changed to equal 6 or 24. If the *name* number is 15, and the person was born on the 8th, 17th, or 26th, the name number should be changed to equal 6 or 24.

It's important to read the section beginning on Page 269 about the numbers 4 and 8 for a fuller understanding of the reason behind this advice.

Other than this warning, the Compound number 15 is extremely fortunate. If you were born on the 15th day of any month, and the Compound number of your name is also a 15, you're blessed with the ability to bring great happiness to others and to shine much light into the darkness, *assuming you don't use this magical and fortunate vibration for selfish purposes.*

16

The Shattered Citadel

16 is pictured by the ancient Chaldeans as "a Tower struck by Lightning, from which a man is falling, with a Crown on his head." It warns of a strange fatality, also danger of accidents and the defeat of one's plans. If the name equals the Compound number 16, it would obviously be wise to change the spelling of the name to avoid this vibration. If the birth date is the 16th day of any month, the challenge of the 16 must be carefully met, so that its effect may be diluted to a milder vibration. To avoid the fatalistic tendency of the 16 as a birth number, one must endeavor to make all plans in advance, making certain that any possibility of failure is anticipated and circumvented by careful attention to detail. The 16 brings with it the Single number 7's obligation and responsibility to *listen to the voice within,* which will always warn of danger through dreams or the intuition *in time to avoid it.* The inner voice must not be ignored. As I partially explained earlier regarding the fact that the name "Abraham Lincoln" is a 16, Lincoln was warned repeatedly of his *potential* assassination by his dreams . . . and also by several "sensitives" or "mediums" who were brought to the White House by Mary Todd Lincoln. He did not heed these many clear warnings, and refused to take the necessary precautions, therefore, was unable to avoid his fate. But it could have been avoided, and this is important for the person whose birth number is 16 to remember. To find happiness in ways other than leadership at the top (the Tower and the Crown) — to renounce fame and celebrity — is another way of decreasing the negative aspect of the 16. Lincoln did not choose to do so, feeling it was more important to attempt to keep the nation united than to enjoy the fulfillment of a private life, although he accepted the Presidency with much reluctance and a profound sadness.

17
The Star of the Magi

This is a highly spiritual number, and was expressed in symbolism by the ancient Chaldeans as the 8-pointed Star of Venus. The Star of the Magi is the image of Love and Peace, and promises that the person or entity it represents will rise superior in spirit to the trials and difficulties of earlier life, with the ability to conquer former failure in personal relationships and the career. 17 is "the number of Immortality," and indicates that the person's (or entity's) name will live after him — (should one decide to die, that is, which is a choice, as you'll learn in the *Physical Immortality* chapter). This is an extremely fortunate Compound number, with one warning. It reduces to the Single number 8, so it's important for anyone with 17 as a Compound Key Number to carefully read the section about the numbers 4 and 8 at the end of this chapter.

18
Spiritual-Material Conflict

Of all Compound numbers, 18 has the most difficult symbolism to translate. (Read again on an earlier page of this chapter the relationship of 18 to Jesus.) The ancients describe the Compound number 18 with the following image: "A rayed moon, from which drops of blood are falling. A wolf and a hungry dog are seen below, catching the falling drops of blood in their opened mouths, while still lower, a crab is seen hastening to join them." 18 symbolizes materialism striving to destroy the spiritual side of the nature. It often associates the person or entity represented by it with bitter quarrels within the family circle — with wars, social upheaval, and revolution. In some cases it indicates making money or achieving position through divisive tactics, through war or other conflict. It warns of treachery and deception from both "friends" and enemies; also danger from the elements, such as fire, flood, earthquakes, tempests and explosions, electrical shock or lightning. If the Compound number of the name is an 18, the vibration should be negated immediately by changing the spelling of the name to equal a more fortunate Compound number. If the birth number is an 18, extreme caution and care must be taken to meet the challenges and dangers of this Compound number. The only way to dilute or diminish its effect on the life is by spiritual means, by unfailingly and repeatedly meeting deception and hatred from others with generosity, love, and forgiveness, by "turning the other cheek," and returning good for evil, kindness for cruelty, honesty for dishonesty, honor for dishonor. In this way, the vibration 18 may be used for great success in illumination and enlightenment. Those born on the 18th day of any month have chosen themselves (on the level of the Higher Self), between incarnations, this channel of birth (as did Jesus) as the greatest of all testings of the soul for worthiness. Another way to dilute the negative aspect of the 18 is to change the number of the name (whatever number it may be) to any favorable Compound number which adds or reduces to the single 6, by changing the spelling of the name. In addition to the attitude just counseled, this will also help to turn the tragedy of the 18 into triumph. Remember what we've learned about the 6 (Love) always and without exception conquering the 9 of conflict ? (1 plus 8 is 9.) Adding the 6 vibration (with its related number 3) was also chosen when the life pattern of Jesus of Nazareth was planned, as I've already explained. People born on the 18th day of any month would be wise to plan everything of importance on the 3rd or 6th day of any month, or on a day adding to the 3 or 6, especially the 6 — and to add the 6 vibration to the life in every way possible, i.e.: addresses, telephone numbers, and any other way they can think of (there are many) to emphasize and increase the power of the number 6 in the personal life and career. In this way may one be victorious, in both the spiritual and material worlds, over the restrictions of the 18.

19
The Prince of Heaven

19 is one of the most fortunate and favorable of all Compound numbers. It is symbolized as the Sun, and is called the Prince of Heaven because it indicates victory over all temporal failure and disappointment. It blesses the person or entity represented by it with all of the power of the Compound number 10, without the danger of abuse inherent in the 10. This number promises happiness and fulfillment — success in all ventures as well as in the personal life. Of course, if 19 is the same number, it must be considered along with the birth number, which might not be as fortunate. So nothing is perfect, but regardless of the influences of another, possibly negative number, the 19 will smooth the path and greatly dilute any negative vibrations one must deal with in the full numerological analysis.

20
The Awakening

In addition to being called "The Awakening," this Compound number is also pictured by the ancient Chaldeans as "The Judgment." It has a peculiar interpretation, and is symbolized as "a winged angel, sounding a trumpet, while from below, a man, woman, and child are seen arising from a tomb, with their hands clasped in prayer." At some time in the experience of the person or entity represented by the number 20, there is a powerful awakening, bringing a new purpose, new plans, new ambitions — the call to action for some great cause or ideal. There may be occasional delays and obstacles to one's plans, but these may be conquered through developing patience (the challenge of the number 20) and by continually cultivating faith in one's own powers to transform. 20 brings the blessing of vivid precognitive dreams, plus the ability to manifest the happy ones and cancel the negative ones. It is not a material number, therefore is doubtful regarding financial success. If large sums of money are necessary for practical support of the new cause or ideal, then one may choose a more positive materialistic number by changing the spelling of the name, assuming the 20 is the *birth* number. If the 20 is the *name* number, then, hopefully, the birth number will bestow a more fortunate financial vibration. However, those who are comfortable with their 20 vibration seldom care about matters of finance. Money is not important to them — and the 20 will, as a general rule, provide enough for the basic necessities.

21
The Crown of the Magi

21 is pictured as "The Universe," and is also called "The Crown of the Magi." It promises general success, and guarantees advancement, honors, awards, and general elevation in the life and career. It indicates victory after a long struggle, for the "Crown of the Magi" is gained only after long initiation, much soul testing and various other tests of determination. However, the person or entity blessed with the number 21 may be certain of final victory over all odds and all opposition. It's a most fortunate vibration — a number of karmic reward.

22
Submission — and Caution

22 is symbolized by the ancients as "a Good Man, blinded by the folly of others, with a knapsack on his back, full of errors." In the image he seems to offer no defense against a ferocious tiger which is about to attack him. It's a warning number of illusion and delusion. It indicates a good person (or entity) who lives in a fool's paradise; a dreamer of dreams who awakens only when surrounded by danger, when it's often too late. It warns of mistakes in judgment, of placing faith in those who are not trustworthy. If 22 is the birth number, the person it represents should exercise caution and watchfulness (since the birth number cannot be altered) in both career and personal matters. The karmic obligation here is to be more alert, to curb "spiritual laziness," and develop more spiritual aggressiveness — to realize your own power to change things, to prevent failure by simply ordaining

success. When this personal responsibility is recognized, practiced, and finally mastered, the 22 person can be in control of events, no longer blinded by the folly of others, and will see ideas achieved and dreams realized. Anyone born on the 22nd day of any month needs to carefully read the section about the numbers 4 and 8, beginning on Page 269.

23
The Royal Star of the Lion

This is a karmic reward number. 23 bestows, not only a promise of success in personal and career endeavors, it guarantees help from superiors and protection from those in high places. It's a most fortunate number, and greatly blesses with abundant grace the person or entity represented by it. As always, the 23 must be considered along with other Single and Compound Key Numbers making up the full numerological analysis, which may not be quite so fortunate. But other numbers don't have much of a chance to bring about serious trouble when the Royal Star of the Lion is present during difficult times. No number can challenge the Lion's strength and win.

24
Love — Money — Creativity

This number is also most fortunate, another Compound number of karmic reward, justly earned in past incarnations, particularly when it's the birth number. It promises the assistance of those with power, and it indicates a close association with people of high rank and position. It greatly increases financial success, and the ability to achieve happiness in love. It denotes gain through romance, the law, or the arts, and a magnetism which is extremely attractive to the opposite sex. The only warning related to the 24 is self-indulgence and a certain arrogance in love, financial, and career matters, because everything comes so effortlessly. It's wise to remember that if the 24 is abused in the present life, it could revert to an 18 or some other extremely difficult birth number in the next. So one is warned not to fail to appreciate the benefits of the 23 and the 24 Compound numbers, and not allow such good fortune to cause selfishness or a careless attitude toward spiritual values. The temptation to indulge in promiscuity must be avoided; likewise a tendency to overindulgence of all kinds.

25
Discrimination and Analysis

25 bestows spiritual wisdom gained through careful observation of people and things, and worldly success by learning through experience. Its strength comes from overcoming disappointments in the early life and possessing the rare quality of learning from past mistakes. The judgment is excellent, but it's not a material number; therefore, financial benefits of a substantial nature must be gained through other Compound numbers in the full birth and name numerological analysis.

26
Partnerships

This Compound number vibrates, in a strange way, to a unique kind of power, based on compassion and unselfishness, with the ability to help others, but not always the Self. 26 is full of contradictions. It warns of dangers, disappointments, and failure, especially regarding the ambitions, brought about through bad advice, association with others, and unhappy partnerships of all kinds. If 26 is the Compound Key Number of the name, it might be best to change the name to achieve a more fortunate influence. If 26 is the birth number, and therefore cannot be altered, the person is counseled to avoid partnerships and pursue the career alone, not heeding even the well-intentioned advice of others, but follow only the personal hunches and intuition — although these should be carefully examined for flaws before acting on them. 26 people should begin at once to stabilize the income, to save money, and not behave in an extravagant manner or invest in other people's ideas. Invest in your own future, be generous with others, especially those in need, but also build a solid foundation for the future for yourself. If your *name* is a 26, or if you were born on the 26th day of the month, you should read carefully the section about the numbers 4 and 8 at the end of this chaper. (2 plus 6 equals 8, so 26 = 8.) It's most important advice for you — or for anyone you know whose name number is 4 or 8, or who was born on the 8th day of the month — or any date that reduces to 4 or 8, such as the 13th, 17th, 22nd, 26th, or 31st.

27
The Sceptre

This is an excellent, harmonious, and fortunate number of courage and power, with a touch of enchantment. It blesses the person or entity it represents with a promise of authority and command. It guarantees that great rewards will come from the productive labors, the intellect, and the imagination, that the creative faculties have sown good seeds which are certain to reap a rich harvest. People (or entities) represented by the Compound number 27 should always carry out their own original ideas and plans, and not be intimidated or influenced by the diverse opinions or opposition of others. 27 is a number of karmic reward, earned in more than one previous incarnation.

28
The Trusting Lamb

28 is a number of puzzling and frustrating contradictions. It symbolizes a person (or entity) of fine promise, even genius, and great possibilities, with the capability of achieving impressive success, and the 28 person frequently does realize such success, only to see everything taken away unless he or she has carefully provided for the future. It indicates loss through misplaced trust in others, powerful opposition from enemies and competitors in business or career, danger of serious losses in courts of law — and the possibility of having to begin the life path over and over again. If 28 is the *name* number, one might wish to change the spelling to achieve a more harmonious and

fortunate number. When 28 is the *birth* number and therefore can't be altered, the karmic lessons of prudence, caution, and well-laid plans must be learned and practiced. When this is done, the negative aspect of the 28 vibration will be substantially diluted. The key is to look before you leap.

29
Grace Under Pressure

The 29 is a number of perhaps the heaviest Karma of all. It tests the person or entity it represents for spiritual strength, through trials and tribulations echoing the Old Testament story of Job. The life is filled with uncertainties, treachery and deception from others, unreliable friends, unexpected dangers — and considerable grief and anxiety caused by members of the opposite sex. It's a number of grave warnings in every area of the personal life and career. When 29 is the Compound Key Number of the name, it's obvious that the spelling of the name should be changed to lift this difficult vibration, unless one is a masochist.

If 29 is the birth number, and thereby unavoidable, conscious effort must be made to dilute and eventually to negate, neutralize, or erase this karmic burden. It can, to a great extent, be eased by choosing a new name (or spelling) with a strongly positive Compound Key Number. Further than this, the person born on the 29th day of any month should do everything advised in Chaper 4 concerning Karma and reincarnation.

In the specific instance of the 29 vibration (bringing with it also the secondary vibration of 11, which should also be read regarding the way to relieve the karmic burden) — remember that the development of absolute faith in goodness and the power of the Self . . . the constant and energetic cultivation of optimism . . . will act as a miraculous medicine for the problems of the number 29.

After all, Job's burdens were finally lifted, when he had learned to accept full responsibility for his troubles, and not to blame others or seek revenge for the hurts he suffered. Not only did his long bad-luck streak end at last, he was given back everything he'd lost, several times over. So, if you were born on the 29th, change the vibration of your name to a powerful number, such as 19, follow Job's example, and soon you'll be as happy as — or happier than — anyone else. Interestingly, the name "Job" equals the powerful Compound number 10 — a difficult vibration to defeat.

30
The Loner — Meditation

This is a number of retrospection, thoughtful deduction, and mental superiority over others. However, it belongs completely to the mental plane, and those represented by it often put all material things to the side, not because they *have* to, but because they *wish* to do so. Consequently the Compound number 30 is neither fortunate nor unfortunate, because it can be either, depending entirely upon the desire of the person (or entity) it represents. The vibration of 30 can be all-powerful, but it is often indifferent, according to the will of the person. Those whose name equals 30, or who were born on the 30th day of any month, generally count few people as their friends. They tend to be taciturn loners, preferring to be alone with their own thoughts. Social functions and public gatherings are not their style. 30 doesn't deny happiness or success, but fulfillment is more often found in retreating from the chaos of the market place, so that one's mental superiority may be used to develop something worthwhile to the world . . . to write ideas which may change the world . . . or to protect and develop one's personal talents, such as art or other gifts. It indicates a lonely, yet frequently rewarding life pattern.

31
The Recluse — the Hermit

Those whose birth or name number is 31 should first read the analysis of the foregoing Compound number 30, because the 31 is very similar to it, except that the person (or entity) represented by this number is even more self-contained, self-sufficient, lonely, and isolated from others. Quite often, genius is present, or at least high intelligence. At some unexpected time in the life, the glittering promises of the world will be suddenly rejected for the peace and quiet of Nature, or, if the response to the 31 is not quite that pronounced, there will nevertheless eventually be a degree of retreat from society in some manner. The 31 person is sometimes opinionated, an advocate of political change, while remaining fixed in personal habits. Even in a crowd, a 31 person will often feel a sense of loneliness and isolation.

32
Communication

This Compound number has the same magical power to sway masses of people as the 14, the same help from those in high positions as the 23. Add all this to the natural ability to charm others with magnetic speech, and it's clear why 32 is sometimes known, by modernizing the symbolism of the ancients as "the politician's vibration." The complexities of advertising, writing, publishing, radio, and television are not always, but usually are an open book to the 32 person, who tends to work well under pressure. But there's a warning note sounded within this seemingly happy melody. 32 is a very fortunate number if the person it represents holds inflexibly to his or her own opinions and judgment in both artistic or intangible matters and material matters. If not, the plans are liable to be wrecked by the stubbornness and stupidity of others.

33

This number has no individual meaning of its own, but carries the same vibration as the 24 — except that the magic of love, the extent of originality and creativity, and the promise of eventual financial success are deepened and increased. Due to the double 3, people whose name equals 33 are more fortunate in every way when involved in a harmonious partnership of some kind with the opposite sex, which applies to the career as well as to romantic and marital relationships. This a number of well-deserved karmic reward. 33 people are advised not to abuse the astounding luck which will descend on them at sometime during the life by allowing it to tempt them into laziness, overconfidence, and a feeling of superiority. When a sense of humor and genuine humility accompany the 33 vibration, it's a wonderfully fortunate number.

34　　Has the same meaning as the number 25.

35　　Has the same meaning as the number 26.

36　　Has the same meaning as the number 27.

37

This number has a distinct potency of its own. It's associated with an extremely sensitive nature — good and fortunate friendships — a strong magnetism with the public, often in the area of the Arts — and productive partnerships of all kinds. It places an emphasis on love and romance, and sometimes too much emphasis on sexuality. Attitudes toward sex may be unconventional (but this aspect may not always be present). There is a pronounced need for harmony in relationships. Happiness and success are more easily attained when in partnerships with another rather than when operating alone as a single individual.

38　　Has the same meaning as the numbers 11 and 29.

39　　Has the same meaning as the number 30.

40　　Has the same meaning as the number 31.

41　　Has the same meaning as the number 32.

42　　Has the same meaning as the number 24.

43

The ancients claim that this is an unfortunate number, and if the name equals a 43, the spelling should be changed to equal a more fortunate Compound number. It is symbolized by the tendency toward revolution, upheaval, strife, conflict, and war. It carries the vibration of repeated disappointment and failure.

44   Has the same meaning as the number 26.

45   Has the same meaning as the number 27.

46   Has the same meaning as the number 37.

47   Has the same meaning as the number 29.

48   Has the same meaning as the number 30.

49   Has the same meaning as the number 31.

50   Has the same meaning as the number 32.

51

This number possesses a strong potency of its own. It's associated with the nature of the warrior, and promises sudden advancement in whatever one undertakes. It is especially favorable for those who need protection in military or naval life, and for the leaders of any "cause" unrelated to war. Yet, it also brings the threat of dangerous enemies and the possibility of attempted assassination; therefore, it is clearly wise, should the name equal 51, to change the spelling to equal a safer Compound number — and forget the glory.

52   Has the same meaning as the number 43.

★★★★★★

Notice that the Compound numbers end with the number 52. This is the reason given by the ancients. It's somewhat obtuse, but I didn't invent numerology, and since I've tested it, discovered that it works, and that it's a helpful and reliable guide, I don't try to penetrate all the veils of mystery around it.

According to the Chaldeans, when you pass the root number 9, you multiply 9 until the Compound number 45 is reached. Then you add the mystical 7 to the 45, producing 52, which represents the 52 weeks in our calendar year. When the 52 is then multiplied by the mystical 7, it produces the number 364, equaling the number of days in a year in ancient times. The Chaldeans used the 365th day of the year as the one great festival holiday (holy day), when no work was allowed to be performed by man, woman, child, or animal.

You may be thinking that you know as little after reading the foregoing as you did when you started. But there it is, for those who are simultaneously mathematically and spiritually inclined. Whether or not you comprehend the reason for the rule, it must be observed. The Compound numbers stop at 52.

All Compound numbers reached through your calculations that are higher than 52 must be added to reach a new Single and/or Compound number. Example: 53 and 63 reduce to the Single numbers 8 and 9 respectively. Another example: 74 and 87 reduce to the Compound numbers 11 and 15 respectively. So when you're dealing with a name that produces a Compound Key Number past 52, you must use the Single or Compound number it equals when you add the two numbers of the Compound number past 52.

You may need some more examples. If the Compound Key Number of your name is *higher* than the number 52, you must find a new number as follows:

53 = the Single Key Number 8.   No Compound Key Number.

54 = the Single Key Number 9.   No Compound Key Number.

55 = the Single Key Number 1.   The Compound Key Number 10.

56 = the Single Key Number 2.   The Compound Key Number 11.

57 = the Single Key Number 3.   The Compound Key Number 12.

58 = the Single Key Number 4.   The Compound Key Number 13.

59 = the Single Key Number 5.   The Compound Key Number 14.

60 = the Single Key Number 6.   No Compound Key Number.

and so on . . .

It's interesting to note that the ancients say: When the Compound Key Number of the name is higher than the number 52 — and *will not be added* to equal a new Compound Key Number (such as in the above examples of 53 — 54 — and 60) it indicates a person who has paid most of his or her karmic debts, and has less Karma to balance out than the average person. Naturally, this will not hold true when you personally decide to change the spelling of your name yourself; it applies only to a name given to you by destiny, i.e.: the name your parents bestowed on you, guided by their own Higher Selves. (Compound Numbers represent one's Karma.)

The Compound Key Number of the day of birth, of course, is not involved in this rule, since the highest compound *birth* number is 31.

Four and Eight . . .
the Numbers of Fate and Destiny

These are known (especially when combined) as the "Numbers of Fate" and the "Numbers of Karma" and hard luck seems to pursue those whose lives are dominated by the 4 and the 8.

When the 4 or the 8 is the Single number of the day of birth, such as the 4th, 8th, 13th, 17th, 22nd, 26th, or 31st, the number has been chosen by the person it represents in the wiser state of grace between incarnations. The Higher Self (soul or spirit), realizing that there are heavy karmic debts to be balanced, which have been delayed or procrastinated for too many lifetimes, chooses the magnetic birth channel of the 4 or the 8 to insure that these long overdue karmic obligations are faced and finally neutralized. On the level of awareness between incarnations, the full import of the karmic chain is comprehended.

It's somewhat analogous to the decision of a student who has continually postponed studying for exams or a test, and as the deadline draws near recognizes that it's time to get serious and make up for the procrastination — no more fun weekends, no more stalling or goofing off. It's "cram time" — time for extra-hard study and attention to scholastic obligations.

Naturally, one can't avoid the 4 or 8 vibration as a *birth number,* nor *should* one be able to, since the 4 or the 8 guarantees that the person influenced by it will be placed involuntarily in specific situations where particular Karma will be balanced in the present existence. Therefore, you might think it unwise to try to remove any further 4 or 8 influence from your life, because its purpose for being there is so spiritually sound. But this is not necessarily true.

The Single number of the name being a 4 or an 8 is an entirely different matter, since one doesn't choose one's own name (except in certain religions). The parents choose the name (guided subconsciously by the powerful influence of the 4 or 8 birth number — or else blindly choose a name with this vibration for no good reason) — and the person bears it, for better or for worse. Therefore, to change the spelling of the name so that it equals a more fortunate Single number is not unduly interfering with Karma. It's a free will choice — and a sensible way, if this be the desire, of making an individual's path in the present existence considerably smoother and less fatalistic.

When 4 or 8 is the *birth* number, care should be taken to avoid the numbers 4 and 8 in all other ways, such as address and phone numbers which add to a Compound number that can be reduced to the single 4 or 8 — and to avoid taking important action or planning significant events on dates equaling either of these two numbers, such as the 4th, 8th, 13th, 17th, 22nd, 26th, or 31st. Most people can handle the 4 or 8 vibration alone. It's the combination of them — the doubling up and increasing the power of the 4 and the 8 that becomes powerfully fatalistic, and causes these unfortunate people to attract far more than their share of bad luck, losses, heartbreak, and disappointments.

Let's consider the two numbers separately, since there's a degree or two of difference between them. We'll begin with the 8.

People whose birth number is 8 seem to be influenced by a more pronounced fatalistic vibration. They are more "children of Fate" than the 4 people. They can be just as strong of character, as noble, devoted, hard-working, and self-sacrificing as others (and frequently even more so) but may feel that they don't receive the rewards they're entitled to or the recognition they deserve. The road to success is a hard one, strewn with obstacles. Although they often manage to rise to a position of high authority, it burdens them with stressful responsibilities, great anxiety, and long hours. 8 people not infrequently manage to accumulate wealth (in fact, the accumulation of wealth at some time in the life is a definite part of the 8 influence — depending on the position of Jupiter in the birth chart) — but the wealth may not bring any real or lasting happiness. In addition, 8 people are often required to pay too high a price for love, which almost invariably brings with it suffering of some kind.

Here's an example: A man born on the 8th, 17th, or 26th day of the month marries a woman born on the 4th, 13th, 22nd, or 31st day of the month (or whose name equals the single number 4). By thus combining the 4 and the 8, the power of these numbers is increased, and the 8 man will experience many blows of fate, mental tension, and emotional sadness in the married state.

Under the law of magnetic attraction, 4 and 8 people seem to be irresistibly drawn together in all kinds of relationships: love, marriage, friendships, and business associations — relatives and relatives by marriage. The combination cannot be called fortunate, at least not in a worldly sense, although it's common for 4 and 8 people to demonstrate a deep devotion to one another (or one does, to an almost fanatical degree, even when the other doesn't). "For better or for worse," especially during times of illness or other misfortune. Some of the greatest examples of self-sacrifice in history are found when 8 and 4 people marry. The most pronounced aspect about this combination in marriage is sacrifice of some kind. Yet, great good can come from such suffering; the couple can create unusually gifted children — or produce the legacy of classical music, poetry, memorable writing of books, plays, and so forth.

The 8 people who observe the numbers 8 and 4 continually influencing the life regarding dates of important events, telephone numbers, addresses, etc., associated with sorrow, disappointment, and bad luck, should avoid these numbers whenever possible, by changing the spelling of the name (if it equals the Single number 4 or 8) — addresses, telephone numbers, and the like, which add to a Compound number that reduces to a 4 or an 8. They should avoid keeping important engagements or planning significant events on the 4th, 8th, 13th, 17th, 22nd, 26th, or 31st day of the month — and alter these to produce the single number 6 (including the name number if necessary). The 8 person should try to carry out all important plans on the 6th or the 24th day of the month, but *not* the 6 reached through the Compound number 15. Read the reason for this in the analysis of 15 under the Compound number definitions.

8 people who follow this advice, who alter the 4's and 8's in their lives to the single number 6, will substantially reduce their "bad luck," and be able to control the curious fate that seems to follow them.

They may not, however, be able to avoid all relationships with other 4 or 8 people, because most of these are karmic obligations which must be dealt with and balanced. Most of the 8 person's *close* friends, business associates, and relatives will usually be a 4 or an 8 by birth, or have names which equal one of these two numbers.

The 4-8 vibration is increased if the 8 person is a Sun Sign Capricorn or Aquarian, since 8 is the number of Saturn (ruler of Capricorn) and 4 is the number of Uranus (ruler of Aquarius).

A most important thing to remember is this: Some 8 people may prefer to carry out *the full force and meaning* of the 8 influence, not fearing the consequences, because they feel that forewarned, they can handle the negative aspect of the 8 — and they wish to increase the power of wealth, stability, responsibility, and so forth that the 8 influence brings. Should an 8 person make such a decision, then they should try to do everything important on the 8th, 17th, and 26th days of the month, and if the *birth number* is 8, they should change the spelling of the name to likewise equal a single 8 (but not in such a way that it equals the Compound 26). In doing this, they'll greatly increase their chances for material success, but they will lead curiously fatalistic lives, seeming to be "stamped by fate" on whatever path of life they choose.

However, those 8 people who choose to increase the power of the 8 in their lives rather than avoid it must take care to avoid the number 4 whenever possible — because it's the combination of these two numbers that brings strong magnetic negative influences to bear upon them.

This is why the 4 people should not, under any circumstances, increase the power of the number 4, since a double 4 equals an 8.

They should avoid, once again, the combination of these two numbers. And because an extra 4 here and there, along with the birth number of 4 (born on the 4th, 13th, 22nd or 31st) will bring, by addition, the 8 influence to bear, creating the very combination the ancients warn to avoid.

According to the Chaldeans, the number 4 as a birth influence is not quite so heavy an influence as the birth number 8. People with 4 as a birth number will find that the 4th, 13th, 22nd, and 31st days of the month are of major significance in both their business and personal affairs — sometimes in a negative sense, yet equally as often in a positive sense. Their own addresses and phone numbers and the like — and the dates of birth of people close to them (especially relatives, since the 4-8 combination greatly influences group family Karma) will be 4's or 8's far more often than can be attributed to coincidence. If your birth number is 4, check into it, and you'll be surprised.

Example: 1003 Main Street (a 4); Phone: 689-2402 (adds to 31, reduces to 4). Either with or without the area code, and sometimes both ways.

A rare few who have chosen the number 4 as the birth channel are illuminated souls who have erased all past Karma by balancing it in previous lives, and have incarnated in the present existence to "rescue" a Twin Self who has become — or in danger of becoming — a fallen angel. In such cases, the 4 vibration is chosen to aid in keeping this person on the path of light; to lessen the temptation to form new, negative Karma, thereby also becoming a fallen angel in the attempt to rescue the fallen other half of the Self.

In this instance, the 4 is an extremely protective influence — and in all other cases (which form the majority of the 4 people) the 4 is not so much to be dreaded as to be recognized as a helpful means to discipline one's self in the present incarnation, which is not a negative situation, but quite positive in a spiritual sense.

★ ★ ★ ★ ★ ★

Numerology and Death Predictions

A famed numerologist who called himself Cheiro, extremely popular in America and abroad during the first part of the twentieth century, was, in my opinion, a brilliant professional in a technical sense, but was a dangerously negative practitioner. His books contain a generous sprinkling of his boasting about how he successfully predicted the exact day of death for numerous clients (mostly royal figures and world celebrities) — either their own deaths, or the deaths of their mates and parents, and so forth. Cheiro possessed the serious flaw of esoteric fatalism, which has caused thousands of people to (justifiably) fear astrology and numerology. (He was also an astrologer.)

Death can no more be prognosticated by numerology than by astrology, and if Cheiro was correct on several well-publicized occasions, it was due to the unfortunate result of the deplorable practice by esoteric professionals of planting a negative seed in the mind of the individual, which has the magnetic power to actually bring about the feared event. It's a form of hypnosis, and has the power to cause things to happen that would never have happened with the proper guidance. Those who make such predictions to the people who trustingly look to them for counsel are the direct cause of the unnecessary deaths they program into the trusting minds they advise. To face the truth of it, such counselors are guilty of unintentional murder.

Never have faith in a numerologist or an astrologer who claims to predict the death of anyone. It's simply not possible. But it *is* possible for such deaths to occur through the fulminating growth of fear. On those occasions when the ethical professional sees a dangerous period coming up for an individual, whether it's an ordinary person, a King, or a President, his or her responsibility is to warn the person of the approaching testing period — and *instruct the person what to do to avoid any serious or fatal experience.* And remember that such "tricky" transits occur in everyone's life periodically, with a fair amount of frequency; therefore, you obviously sidestep them by rechanneling the indicated planetary energy, or you wouldn't still be here.

This "death prediction" situation so intensely concerns me that I feel you may need a specific illustration. I've already told you that I consider Cheiro to have been a brilliant numerologist, but also a most fatalistic one. There are some rules of numerology he recommends that I strongly disagree with, and consequently will not be giving you in this chapter, but these are in the minority. *Most,* even if not all, of his teachings are insightful and reliable. But you have to take the "whole cake" into consideration before taking a large bite, if you see the analogy.

For example, Cheiro (and he's not by *any means* the *only* esoteric professional, astrologer or numerologist, guilty of such behavior) had several sessions with King Edward VII of England. King Edward was born on November 9th. Therefore, the Single Key Number of his birth was 9. His marriage took place in the year 1863, which Cheiro added to get another 9. He was supposed to have been crowned on the 27th of June (which reduces to 9), and was actually crowned on August 9th, making another 9.

Now, there's no doubt that King Edward's Single Key Number of *birth* was the Number 9, and it follows all the rules of numerological harmony that important events would occur in his life on "9 days," such as the 9th, 18th, and 27th. But Cheiro dove into very muddy esoteric waters when he took it further, realizing the strange link I've already told you about concerning the 3, 6, and 9.

He decided, for inexplicable reasons of his own, that since there is a mysterious connection between 6 and 9 (which I've explained) that Edward would *die* when these two root numbers "came together" — that the age of 69 would be a fatal year for the King. He went even further, and decided that since 6 is the number of Taurus, and the month of Taurus is May, that King Edward's death would come on May 6th, in his 69th year.

Cheiro *repeatedly* made this fatal prediction to Edward VII, to the point that the King began referring to Cheiro as "the man who won't permit me to live past 69." Over and over, in various meetings with the King, Cheiro reinforced his death prediction, and even Cheiro himself stated that "the King *never forgot* the fatal prediction."

On May 6th, in his 69th year, King Edward suddenly became ill — and died. Cheiro notes this "successful prediction," among others, in all of his books. What happened is painfully obvious. King Edward was powerfully hypnotized, his subconscious deeply programmed with the negative seed that his death would occur on May 6th, in his 69th year. And so, he obliged. It happened for *absolutely no reason at all except for the programming initiated and constantly reinforced* by his numerologist. I'm sure Cheiro never realized that he was guilty of the King's death, and I'm equally sure that wasn't his intention; however, the truth is the truth — and ignorance is not, to me, an acceptable excuse.

Just think how many people were born on the 9th day of the month, people to whom important events happened on the 9th, 18th, or 27th. According to Cheiro's flawed reasoning, they must *all* die during a month ruled by 6 — on the 6th day of that month — when they reached the age of 69. And I don't need to tell you how ridiculous *that* is. Cheiro based his prediction of death on a misinterpretation of the link between 6 and 9, which has no basis in fact whatsoever, in any esoteric sense. The same kind of weak and false premises are used by astrologers who claim to predict death.

Poor Edward was actually hypnotized into fulfilling this false death prediction. This true story proves again what you should never forget — the awesome power of the mind. What you *believe* will happen — *will* happen. What you fear will inevitably come upon you.

You can change your so-called "destiny" by simply changing your thoughts. Your thoughts create your environment and all the events taking place in it, whether you want to believe that or not. It's not enough to just change your thoughts, however. A great deal of negative can be transmuted into positive that way, but you must also try to balance your Karma in all the ways explained in the *Déjà Vu* chapter. Remember that death is an event which is positively, one hundred percent controlled by your own will. You are the only person who knows when you will die. Not only *when* — but *if*.

The Mysteries
of the
Number Twelve

Before we close this chapter about numerology, we should spend some time together studying the various codes of the Compound Number 12. I don't mean the analysis of 12 in the Compound Number definitions which relates to an individual's Karma, but the number 12 itself.

> On the East, three Gates; on the North, three Gates; on the South, three Gates; on the West, three Gates. And the wall of the city had twelve foundations, and in them the names of the twelve apostles of the Lamb.
>
> Revelations 21: 13

There are 12 astrological signs, from Aries through Pisces. The Earth makes one orbit of the Sun through these 12 signs in the same amount of time the Moon takes to orbit the Earth 12 times. The planet Jupiter is larger than all the other planets in our solar system combined, and Jupiter takes about 12 years to complete one orbit of the Sun.

All great spiritual leaders have had 12 followers. The 12 tribes of Israel were founded by the 12 sons of Jacob. The people of Greece worshipped 12 gods, and there were 12 princes of Ishmael. The great Osiris of Egypt had 12 followers — and the Aztec Quetzalcoatl had 12 disciples. There are 12 gods in the Brahman Zodiac.

King Arthur had 12 Knights of the Round Table. Buddha had 12 disciples. There were 12 altars of St. James and 12 divisions of Solomon's Temple.

A Board of Directors is composed of 12 executives, and there are 12 men and women on a jury. There are 12 basic mineral salts in homeopathic medicine. When gold is weighed, there are 12 ounces to the pound; likewise with the weighing of drugs. There are 12 inches in a foot. Most fascinating of all, the Earth's minerals are also ruled by the number 12. For example, all diamonds have 12 sides and must be cut along these 12 axes.

As we know, Jesus chose 12 disciples (the Single 3 again in his life: See Pages 197–198). As with all spiritual leaders and their followers, Jesus was the 13th — or the Master. Each of the 12 apostles represents one of the 12 Sun Signs. The 13th is the Master, who has learned to combine the positive qualities of each of the 12 Sun Signs, and to conquer the negative traits of each. The Master combines the courage and innocence of Aries with the patience and stability of Taurus, the versatility and mental alertness of Gemini, the sensitivity and protectiveness of Cancer, the nobility, generosity, and love of Leo, the exquisite discrimination of Virgo, the fairness and justice of Libra, the depth of knowledge of Scorpio, the honesty and idealism of Sagittarius, the endurance and wisdom of Capricorn, the prophetic vision and tolerance of Aquarius, and the compassion and enlightenment of Pisces.

He has learned to cast away the rash, impulsive behavior of Aries, the stubbornness of Taurus (which is only Taurus patience turned inside out), the irresponsibility of Gemini, the fears and possessiveness of Cancer, the arrogance of Leo, the critical hair-splitting of Virgo, the indecision of Libra, the revenge and retaliation of Scorpio, the blunt speech of Sagittarius, the coldness and ambition of Capricorn, the unpredictable behavior of Aquarius, and the evasiveness, timidity, and deception of Pisces. Do you see now why the number 13 (the Master) is not really "unlucky," as most people mistakenly believe ?

Legend claims that each apostle (disciple) was the full embodiment (positive and negative blend) of a particular Sun Sign. Legend further claims that Peter, as you might guess, was an impulsive, fiery Aries. (I can't recall which one was a Leo, but since it wasn't Peter, then he surely had a Leo Ascendent or Moon !) The unfortunate Judas (using the negative side of the sign) was a Scorpio. John, the Beloved, was a Pisces — Thomas, the Doubter, a Virgo — and so on.

Paul was a Gemini, and that certainly makes sense. Glib Paul, with such a gift of verbal persuasion that he pulled off the nearly impossible mission of the necessity to teach the Jews that circumcision was "a requirement for salvation" — and the equal necessity to preach to the Gentiles that it was *not* an absolute requirement to be saved. Read Paul's Letters to the Romans — Chapter 2, Verses 25 through 29 — to see how Mercury-sly he was in handling this contradiction. I can't read it myself without laughing aloud at his mental adroitness and typical Gemini "double talk." In a holy cause, of course.

Some extremely intelligent and respected metaphysicians of ancient times have claimed that John the Baptist was a Scorpio prophet, with a fiery Sagittarian Moon or Ascendent, and there's no argument that he was blunt and outspoken. Considering this eccentric "lifestyle," he must have had several planets in Aquarius also.

These same esoteric scholars have alleged that Mary the Mother and Mary Magdalene were both Aries — and there have been several books written by astronomers (I'm trying to locate one a Guru of mine told me about), claiming that Jesus himself (although finally the Master of all 12 Sun Signs) was by birth a Leo, due to errors in various calendars of past and present. The authors point out that in addition to the calendar errors they calculated, the shepherds would not have been "tending their flocks" when the Angel appeared to them — in winter months. They say that late July and August was the most likely period when they would have been camping out with their sheep in the hills and highlands of Jerusalem, Nazareth, and Bethlehem, as only one of several evidences of the credibility of their claim that Jesus was born a Lion.

Their concept substantiates Rudolf Steiner's inspired revelation that Mary the Mother and Mary Magdalene were split pieces of the soul, spirit, or "Higher Self" of Isis, the Twin Self of Osiris, who was murdered and dismembered into 14 pieces by his brother, Set — because it's claimed that each time a "piece" of the spirit or soul of Osiris is incarnated, it has been decreed that such a birth be under the sign of Leo, the Lion, ruled by the Sun — and Jesus of Nazareth is said to be one of the incarnated 14 pieces of Osiris. (Osiris was called the "Sun god.") Likewise with "the two Marys," prophesied to be incarnated each time under the sign of Aries the Ram ruled by Mars. Each incarnation of the "two Marys" is said to be as *both* mother and mate to each incarnation of each of the 14 pieces of Osiris. Two of my Gurus have taught me that this prophecy should be considered to mean *either* a Leo Sun Sign *or* a Leo Ascendent — and *either* an Aries Sun Sign *or* an Aries Ascendent.

There are two Fixed Stars (among others such as Castor, Pollux, Arcturus, etc.) astronomers have named Isis and Osiris. These two Fixed Stars, Isis and Osiris, have been astronomically charted in their movements as having approached near Earth on only two occasions in the historically recorded past: at the time of the birth of the babe in Bethlehem — and at the time of the birth of Francesco Bernadone (St. Francis of Assisi). This is claimed to indicate that both Jesus and Francis of Assisi were incarnations of one of the 14 pieces of Osiris. Metaphysicians say that both King Arthur and Lancelot (Camelot was not myth, but a reality in a never-recorded past) were themselves each a piece of the soul or spirit of Osiris — and that Guinevere and the mother of Arthur were themselves each one of the two split soul pieces of Isis. Isis, her soul split into 2 pieces, is also said to have been incarnated as both Claire Faverone (Francesco's "Lady Poverty") and the Lady Pica, mother of Francesco — again lending support to the continual reincarnation of Isis as "both mother and 'mate,' or 'love,' of each incarnated piece of Osiris." This explains clearly the terrible "pull" on Guinevere in choosing between Arthur and Lancelot, since her own Higher Self recognized them both as reincarnated pieces of Osiris.

Evidently, the Fixed Stars called Isis and Osiris also approached near the Earth in their movements back in uncharted antiquity at the time of the true Camelot. Now astronomers have charted the movement of these two Fixed Stars to approach near the Earth for the third time during the Aquarian Age.

The latter supports the legend that at sometime during the Aquarian Age, the 14 pieces of Osiris will be reincarnated in one man, who shall then be reunited with Isis, her own two split soul pieces reincarnated in one woman. Then, according to prophecy, the two of them shall spread the Light of Love and Pax et Bonum into Earth's darkness, at history's twilight hour, initiating the promised "two thousand years of Peace," to begin during the latter part of the Aquarian Age.

Part of the Isis-Osiris legend is that the concept for many of the world's greatest musical compositions, operas, and literary works (including Shakespeare) were seeded into the minds of these composers and authors by the Masters of Karma, so that particular compositions, operas, and literary works would enlighten in the still sleeping Higher Consciences of Earthlings different facets of the star-crossed love story of the Twin Selves of Isis and Osiris, which I plan to relate in a future work.

Among these are said to be (only a partial list) Madame Butterfly and her Lieutenant Pinkerton . . . Tristan and Isolde (the names "Tristan" and "Isolde" even contain the words "Isis" and "Osiris" within them) . . . Titania and Oberon, of *A Midsummer Night's Dream* . . . Romeo and Juliet . . . Hamlet and Ophelia . . . and a number of others. Notice that the name "Osiris" contains within it the letters of the name "Isis." He shall always protect her spirit within his own — and they may never be permanently Earth-separated.

It is further both prophesied and decreed that the joined spirits of Isis and Osiris, during the early portion of the Aquarian Age, will not be identified or recognized as their true selves, to prevent an encore of the dark sins of "divinity" and "worship" — and may not even themselves be aware of their true identities, but will nevertheless work together in harmony to begin to spread the Light and Love of Pax et Bonum (Peace and Good) into the darkness.

If those legends are true, it certainly is encouraging. Like the old, familiar carol, "Joy to the World" ! Mother Earth can surely use such an approaching benevolence to heal her deep and nearly fatal wounds. It can't be repeated too often that the number 6 (Love) will always be victorious over the number 9 (war and conflict), in both numerology and mathematics. The legends and the message of numbers fit perfectly together, like the completion of a jigsaw puzzle.

6
FORGOTTEN RAINBOWS

the power of Color in your life . . .
the human aura . . .
permanent weight gain and weight loss
through Color . . . and other magics —
including the power
of gems and crystals.

maybe Rembrandt and da Vinci's jeweled colors
            were real . . . not just painted
the way life looks through crystals of tenderness

you smiled at me tonight
at the bottom of the stairs
        with so much love in your eyes

all you said was . . .

        "let's walk in the woods tomorrow, at sunrise
        just you and me . . . alone
                            before the world's awake
        I'll show you
                    how to make a deer come near
        by remaining very, very still
                    projecting kindness"

and all I said was . . .
        "I'll set the alarm for five"

                    but we were stained glass
            ruby red and cobalt blue
    and the choir was singing

                ★ ★ ★ ★ ★ ★

 LL THOSE who deeply love seem to be fine-tuned to
the colors of the spectrum, because they're vibrating
to a higher frequency. Reds are redder, blues are
bluer, and yellows are more brilliant. In fact, all the
senses are thus heightened by love. Fragrances are
more hypnotic, music more inspiring, food tastes better, and the sense
of touch is more intense. Twin Selves vibrate to an even higher frequency than other lovers or mates, and can often see one another's
etheric halos or auras.

One of the forgotten rainbows is the human aura. Extending approximately two to four inches and *outlining* the head and body is what is called the etheric. Depending on conditions in your spiritual self, the etheric is seen as either smoke grey, blue, white, pale yellow or gold, and is more easily perceived by the physical eye than the aura itself. Beyond the etheric is your aura, containing every color of the rainbow spectrum, some brilliant, some muddy, in all shades of each. It measures anywhere from three to five feet in circumference. Your aura is the you-of-you, completely individual, reflecting the condition of your *astral* body, which continually impresses itself upon your physical body.

Plants and animals (even objects) also have auras. Under the right conditions, you can see it with physical vision, usually peripheral — or with the Third Eye, or pineal gland, located in the center of your forehead, between your eyebrows. The Nazarene's statement, "Let those who have eyes, see; let those who have ears, hear," refers to this Third Eye and to the Inner Ear, where is heard the clear, small voice of your Higher Self. Your aura is a large, ovoid or egg-shaped radiance surrounding your entire body, front, back and sides, the colors within it precisely reflecting your mental and emotional state and your physical health, constantly changing. It's your own personal rainbow . . . or dark cloud of depression and illness.

Once upon a time, long ago, many people could see one another's auras, and nearly everyone could perceive at least the etheric. The latter is the origin of the halo, passed down by story and legend, therefore shown around the heads of religious figures by the master painters of the past, who themselves were open channels for Higher Masters to express truth. Earthlings have long since lost the ability to see the aura, or even the etheric, although there are a rare few today who have retained the gift in their present incarnations. The beloved mystic of Virginia Beach, Edgar Cayce, was one of these. He saw the complete aura around everyone when he was a child, and was startled to eventually learn that others couldn't see it. Because he saw each person walking in a rainbow of changing color and light, he assumed that others could also.

Even though you have *temporarily* lost the gift of seeing auras, your aura is, nevertheless, of vital importance to your health, happiness, and spiritual evolvement. Invisible though it may be to you at present, it is there, and esoteric wisdom begins with your acknowledgment and understanding of its very real existence. My personal Gurus and Teachers have counseled me that one should repeat the positive aloud at every opportunity, and never the negative, to prepare one's self for eventually reclaiming this great gift. In other words, never say aloud to anyone, "I can't see auras, not even the etheric halo." Instead, repeat aloud as often as possible when you discuss such matters with others (and even alone) . . . "I can't see the etheric or the human aura *yet* — but I know I will be able to *soon.*" Your subconscious will pick up the message eventually, and your Higher Self will answer it.

Until "soon" arrives, you can still do a number of things to acknowledge your awareness of your aura — and to protect, "polish," and purify your auric egg. Everyone has noticed the odd behavior of humans when they're on an elevator, especially a crowded elevator. Without exception, each person feels strangely introverted and uncomfortable, most of them either staring at their feet or gazing intently at the changing floor numbers above their heads, lighting up with each stop, their features as frozen as if they were watching the countdown for the final nuclear blast-off — until they reach their floor destinations, then they quickly exit, often with a sigh of relief.

The overlapping and mixing of the auric eggs of the passengers on a crowded elevator is what creates the tension and uneasiness in everyone (except for a few fast-talking Geminis, accustomed to blending with the other half of themselves). When someone else's auric egg overlaps or brushes with your own, you feel it instantly, sometimes sharply, sometimes faintly — but the contact will always be felt. This is why, when someone tiptoes up behind you to surprise you, or simply passes by closely behind you, you *sense* that person's presence before you hear or see it. A different auric egg has penetrated the substance of your very personal sheath. Then there are those people who insist on leaning very close when they talk with you, causing you to feel uncomfortable. What causes the uneasiness is that the person has interpenetrated your auric egg with his or her own. Lovers, of course, or parents and children, find this overlapping most pleasurable, but to others it can cause extreme discomfort. When it happens to me I always say, as courteously as possible, with a smile, "You're into my auric egg — do you mind if I move back a bit ?" This response to unexpected or unsolicited closeness is the unguessed reason behind the familiar phrase of the seventies and eighties — "I need my space" . . . or "Give me my space."

The texture of your personal rainbow, your auric egg, is electromagnetic. Consequently, as you mix with other people when you're shopping, working or just walking, your aura will magnetically pick up tiny bits and pieces of the auric texture of others — along with becoming saturated with the magnetic pieces of your own negative emotions throughout the day. Your aura then needs cleansing.

When you take a bath or a shower (preferably a shower) all those magnetic bits you picked from others and from your own negative thoughts and emotions wash right down the drain. This is the effect of the element of water on the auric texture. As the washing off process occurs, the aura slowly draws back *within* the body, so that if you were seen by a mystic, the latter could not see a trace of your aura or etheric. Did you ever notice that, after you take a bath or shower, and step out of the tub, for about thirty to sixty seconds you feel noticeably weak ? It's because your aura has drawn within. Then, after you dry yourself, the sense of slight weakness is replaced by a surge of energy and well-being. This is because the aura has gradually projected itself out again, glowing in its normal state, and cleansed of the clusters of all those negative bits and pieces of electromagnetic energy, which were washed away by the water.

This is the source of the spiritual counsel "Cleanliness is next to Godliness." It's impossible to retain, for some time following a bath or a shower, negative feelings of any real depth — those which bombarded you before you cleansed your aura. When you're feeling exhausted, angry, fearful, grief-stricken, worried — take a bath or a shower. Wash off your aura — cleanse your aura. You'll find it impossible to feel those negative emotions to any substantial degree afterward. You'll be calmer, more peaceful, and better able to deal with the problems that created your tension or stress . . . for several hours at least, until the aura becomes saturated again with negative "bits" from other people and from your own thought processes and emotions. Although they don't comprehend how or why it works, and they certainly have no thought of the human aura, doctors in mental institutions often order severely emotionally disturbed patients to submit to sitting in a tub of running, warm water for periods of time. The technique of hosing angry crowds with water is a deplorable thing for police to do, but the water does have the effect of quieting down the violence and restoring a temporary stability. It's an ugly practice, but once again, it was initiated because the effect of water on the human aura had been observed, even by those who never heard of the term "aura," let alone ever observed one.

The shades of the spectrum rainbow and the Music of the Spheres — color and sound — exert a still unrealized but great power over every area of your life, from physical, mental, and emotional health to your personal relationships. The Forgotten Rainbows and the Forgotten Melodies. (The power of sound will be discussed in a later chapter.)

Consider the color red — ruby red or crimson red. It has an amazing influence over the sleeping awareness, and creates specific vibrations in the mind, certain natural responses. Unfortunately, those in charge of matters like traffic control lacked any knowledge of metaphysics when they decided to use the color red to mean Stop — and the color green to mean Go. To the subconscious, red means

GO ! GO ! CHARGE ! The color green, conversely, speaks to the subconscious with flash messages like: Be cool. STOP. Wait. Rest.

The unenlightened ones who set up the Stop and Go traffic signals chose the color red for Stop because they believed it would be interpreted by the drivers as "Danger !" And so it is — to the *conscious* mind. But to the *subconscious,* remember, the message is *also,* as I just pointed out: GO ! GO ! CHARGE !

I've conducted a fair amount of research on the subject, and I've learned that, for many years after the first Red and Green traffic lights were installed, the offenses of "running a Red Light" were extremely high, and began to lower only very slowly, as drivers gradually reprogrammed their basic, built-in subliminal responses to the colors red and green. Relative to all the "running a Red Light" offenses, most of those who do it usually seem confused, and are unable to explain *why* they did it.

During busy traffic hours in large cities, there are frequent traffic tie-ups associated with the false message of the green, so-called GO Light. The cars blast their horns in repeated, deafening complaint to the car in the front of the line, while the driver frequently just sits there, in a trancelike state, staring at the Green Light that may be saying "GO" to his conscious mind, but contradicts the message with the response from the *sub*conscious of "Cool it. Stop and rest awhile."

A friendly word of advice: Don't run Red Lights — ever. However, if you're ever motioned to pull over by an officer of the law who accuses you of running a Red Light, confess immediately and contritely that you *did* run the light (if you did) — or tell him courteously and add earnestly that you don't believe you're guilty (if you didn't run the light). It wouldn't be wise to explain to him that you can't be held fully responsible for following your subconscious urgings just because the people who created traffic lights were metaphysically color blind, unless you want a swift ticket and perhaps also a sanity hearing or sobriety test (unless the officer is a Pisces). You may be personally enlightened, but that doesn't mean the whole world is equally as illuminated, in particular the Police Department. Cripple Creek's former Police Chief Dale Simpson (see Chapter 1) is one of the few men in blue who would accept such an explanation, and it's not likely you'll be running any Red Lights there. Cripple Creek doesn't even *have* any Red Lights. Everything there is Green . . . and laid back.

Let's return for a moment to the Forgotten Rainbow of your aura — auric sheath or auric egg — with proof that humans at one time, long ago, were fully capable of seeing the aura, as did Edgar Cayce and some others later, and were also capable of decoding its color keys. For example, a certain shade of lime green in the aura indicates jealous, possessive feelings — dark rust red signifies anger — a particular shade of mustard yellow represents fear — dark or indigo blue means depression — purple indicates sexual arousal — black reveals deep melancholy and bitterness, a desire for revenge — and so on.

Our Anglo-Saxon language has inherited this wisdom (more about the English language in a later chapter on Lexigrams) and passed it down to people today who haven't the slightest notion of why they employ descriptive phrases such as: "He's pea green with envy" — "She has a red hot temper" — "He's a yellow coward" — "She has the blues" — "He's in a black mood" — "He felt a purple passion." People never ask themselves why they make such observations. Does a person's face actually turn the color green when he or she is envious or jealous . . . actually turn brick red when angry — turn yellow when afraid — blue when depressed — or black when melancholy and revengeful ? Of course not. When people use such phrases to describe someone's mood or temporary state of mind they are either seeing those colors in the person's aura with unguessed, Third Eye vision — or they're responding to the ancient knowledge and wisdom still inherent in what is called "the mass, collective subconscious," containing the matching of certain colors to certain emotions, as revealed in the forgotten rainbow of the auric sheath or egg.

Color can be used with startling results in every facet of your life. Its power is only recently beginning to be recognized by the medical world, psychiatric institutions, the fashion world, marketing people, and large corporations.

A MAGICAL SECRET

One of the major current concerns in America, indeed, all over the world, is weight loss and weight gain. For reasons I'll soon explain, all diets are impotent in achieving *permanent* weight loss or weight gain, and some are harmful to the general health, as well as frustrating and difficult to follow. Lasting and successful weight gain or weight loss can only be achieved through color, not calories.

It seems as if the world is made up of only two kinds of people: the plumpies who want to lose weight and the skinnies who want to gain weight — plus "10" Bo Derek and Christopher Reeve (Superman) — and even they once belonged to either the former or the latter group.

The most popular topic for books, magazine and newspaper articles, and television these days is diet. Diet, diet, diet — exercise, exercise, exercise. Diet and exercise books and video tapes are sweeping the world marketplace, with the disappointing result that we still have generally the same number of plumpies and skinnies as ever. Those who temporarily lose weight gain it back swiftly — and those who temporarily gain weight lose it again just as quickly.

We've been offered high-protein diets, low-protein diets, and no-protein diets — high-carbohydrate diets, low-carbohydrate diets, and no-carbohydrate diets. There are the bizarre diets, such as the avocado diet, the rice diet, the banana diet, the raw meat diet — and the complicated menu diets one can only observe properly by hiring a full-time chef or dietician to meticulously plan the intricate slices and spoonfuls of this or that for each meal each day of the week. We have diet candies, liquid diets — diets approved by prominent physicians, health food faddists, and traveling Yogis. *None of them work.* Some are successful for brief periods, then everything goes back to Square One, and it all has to start over again. Both the plumpies and the skinnies are also promised weight loss and weight gain (muscles for the machos) through jogging, aerobics, dancing, or strenuous workouts on torturous machines.

Some people swear by the newest diet craze, and some people swear *at* it. Regarding the *quantity* of food intake, some people eat like the proverbial horse, and remain as skinny as a rail. Others eat like elephants and look like them. Some people count their calories as if they were counting the money in their bank balances, and others ignore them, stuffing themselves with all kinds of goodies. The vegetarian is positive that meat causes you to gain weight or lose weight (as the case may be) — and the carnivorous beef and steak eaters sneer at the "rabbit food" and alfalfa sprouts munched by the former.

Millions of people starve themselves with periodic fasting to lose weight, then, in a matter of weeks, all the fat returns. Fasting is marvelous as a cleansing of body, mind and spirit once a month for three days, but it has absolutely nothing to do with permanent weight loss. Other millions trying to *gain* weight devour foods rich in calories, and don't give a tinker's dam about cholesterol, but find they're still wearing size 13 collars in shirts sold only in the boy's department (if men) or Size 1 dresses in pre-teens (if women) — and are still flat-chested (both sexes).

Then enter the physicians. (Genuflect, please.) One doctor tells you that the problem is your thyroid, your liver, or your pituitary gland. Another doctor tells you that you need Vitamins. A different doctor says Vitamins are dangerous, and taking too many may be the real cause of your weight problem. The health food fanatics preach that you need wheat, bran, mega-doses of Vitamins, and no dairy foods, whether you're trying to lose or gain — either one. A few "psychic mediums" are always hiding around the corner to tell you it's your astral body which is afflicted, and you need to repeat your mantras more often.

The entire diet scene is a snake pit of coiling contradictions, a three-ring circus of confusion and misplaced activity — and utterly exhausting to the mind and the spirit, let alone to the poor, battered, punched, massaged, jogged, stretched, aching, starved, or stuffed body. It's all so unnecessarily complicated.

Are you one of the plumpies, overweight, longing to be slim and trim ? Are you one of the skinnies, frail, emaciated, longing to be muscular and sturdy (if you're a man) or rounded and curvaceous (if you're a woman) ? Or are you completely contented with your perfect body ? If your answer is "yes" to the last question, skip this section, but read the rest of the color chapter. If your answer is "yes" to either of the first two questions, keep reading. You're about to receive a magic wand from the days of ancient alchemy, one of the codes of universal wisdom among the many star signs you never dreamed existed.

A page or so back, I stated that successful and lasting weight gain or weight loss can only be attained through color, not calories. A calorie is simply a unit to measure heat, and is not what causes weight gain or loss. One fine day the New Age thinkers in the medical profession will recognize and confess this. However, *and this is most important,* you *can* add weight or lose weight *temporarily* by adding or cutting down on calorie intake because *your brain has been constantly programmed with the erroneous information that calories are the key to gaining or losing pounds.* The programmed brain is an immensely powerful Master of Illusion. Nevertheless, false is false, true is true, and the *truth* is that *calories have nothing to do with weight.*

My Hatha Yoga-Zen Buddhist (see the Preface to this book) told me during our New Year's Day esoteric talk that he had once walked far into the desert to die. (I'm not sure if this was a true story, or just his Guru method of seeding metaphysical concepts into my mind.)

He said that he remained there in the desert for "about four weeks," taking with him three large canteens of water to sip now and then — to "keep him lucid till the end." Most of the fantasies and thoughts and images passing through his mind were of deep green woods and forests and clear, blue-green streams of water. (Note the natural visualization of the colors blue and green.) During his attempted desert "suicide" via starvation, he made friends with a small, curious desert rat, who sat there, he said, and communicated with him silently. At first, he lost weight rapidly, and into the third week he was so thin that his bones seemed about to penetrate through his skin. Then, quite unexpectedly, and nearly as rapidly as he had *lost* weight, he began to *gain* weight. At the end of the following week, still without a bite of food, only sipping water, his normal weight had nearly returned.

At the close of his story (whether true — or make-believe *for the purpose of teaching*), the turbaned one remarked casually, "In this manner, many years ago, did I first begin to comprehend that calories have nothing to do with weight loss and weight gain in the final analysis, depending, of course, upon one's control of one's own falsely programmed brain." He did not add the color secret to his esoteric instruction, evidently knowing that I was to be illuminated to that portion of it soon enough, during the mountain retreat he had predicted, from a teacher who would appear without my seeking him.

We'll discuss the calorie illusion later, but first let's consider the relationship of color to weight. Both overweight and underweight people suffer from the same disease (dis-ease): an imbalance of color in the human aura. They have succumbed to LOCH (pronounced "lock"): Lack of Color Harmony. How does color effect the gaining or losing of weight ?

Food (and never mind the calorie count) is nothing more than Light and Color. The growing plant (fruit or vegetable) absorbs light from the Sun through the process of photosynthesis, then transmutes the light into particular colors. When you take the food into your body and digest it the material breaks down and changes back into light and color. Light and color form the connecting link between idea and form, consciousness and the Supraconscious (your Higher Self), just as there is a direct relationship in the growing plant between light and the emergence of color.

The LOCH condition of underweight in the skinnies, who try and try, yet can't seem to retain their ideal weight, *no matter how many calories they consume,* is the result of an auric color imbalance, due to a lack of the blue-green ray. To restore the color balance of their auras, these people must take into their bodies, for a patterned period of time — in specific ways — the *blue-green* color ray. Yin.

Likewise with the LOCH condition of being overweight in the plumpies, who try and try, yet can't seem to keep the weight off, *no matter how few calories they consume.* It's the result of an auric color imbalance, due to a lack of the *red-gold* color ray in their auras. To restore the color balance of their auras, these people must take into their bodies, for a patterned period of time — in specific ways — the *red-gold* color ray. Yang.

There is a three-step formula for taking into the body afflicted with LOCH the needed blue-green ray (to gain weight) or the red-gold ray (to lose weight). Following the procedures faithfully will allow you to tune in, vibrate to, and absorb the color lacking in your aura in sufficient amounts.

First, the color formula for the plumpies, who want to *lose* weight. Then the color formula for the skinnies, who want to *gain* weight.

If you strictly observe the following instructions, not only will you lose weight safely and surprisingly swiftly, you'll remain at the ideal weight for your individual bone structure and height for a very long time, often permanently — until and unless your aura becomes imbalanced again by absorbing too much Yin, and not enough Yang — or unless and until you abuse the eating process, and thus allow your programmed brain to cause you to once again falsely believe that calories can put on pounds. Then, of course, you must cure your LOCH the same way. However, this rarely happens once you have balanced your personal auric rainbow. I can promise that you'll be astounded at how swiftly and efficiently this "color diet" (a phrase containing the letters of another phrase: "let color do it") will melt away your excess weight. It's so amazingly successful, you'll become nearly fanatic about it, and wonder why you ever tortured yourself with fasting and all those ineffective, sometimes dangerous "diet fads" (a phrase containing the letters of the words "fat" and "die fast").

THE MAGICAL, FORGOTTEN RAINBOW FOR OVERWEIGHT PLUMPIES

You'll need some equipment, but it's well worth the little time and trouble it takes to obtain it. You will need: (a) a metal lamp, the kind used by typists, preferably either brass or metal painted white or red — with a rubber goose neck that can be twisted up or down or sideways — and a firm base, a least two and a half inches in circumference (so it won't topple over on the bed) and (b) a red bulb, *not clear*, but *opaque*, like the bulbs used for EXITS in theatres. It should be 100 watts, but in any case not less than 75 watts. Most light stores carry these bulbs, or can order them for you.

You'll also need: (a) a small cassette player, such as a Walkman, with earphones, unless you have stereo speakers in your bedroom, which will serve as well and (b) one or two or three tape cassettes of music with pronounced drum beats — *red Mars music* (more about this later). The best and most effective is a tape of John Philip Sousa marches — or tapes of loud rock music with heavy rhythm and drum beats, etc. A tape of marching bands in a parade you recorded yourself will serve as well.

The final equipment you'll need is: four 8- to 10-ounce glasses, ruby red (not orange-red) glass. Because ruby red glass is not sold everywhere, they may have to be ordered from a major department store or glassware store. Red plastic glasses are just as effective if they're the right size and the color is ruby red or crimson red, and *not* orange-red. You'll also need an egg timer that can be set to ring.

The three steps to your Forgotten Rainbow miracle.

These three steps must be followed without any interruption in the daily routine, so that a patterned response to the color treatment is established. In the case of the red-gold-yellow treatment to lose weight, the exposure to the needed color rays must be followed for at least forty-five days, fifty-four days if necessary — but need not be followed for longer than sixty-three days. Remember that to cure your LOCH and restore color balance to your aura, you should take your color-music baths *at the same time each day,* which will allow your body to establish the necessary conditioned response. The times of greatest power for thus recharging the colors of the aura with the energizing rays that are lacking are sunrise, high noon, and sunset — or as close to these times as possible. Choose which time is easier to fit into your daily schedule, and stay with it each day.

STEP 1.

Go into your bedroom and darken it by pulling the shades and drawing the drapes. Remove all your clothing and lie down on the bed, with your small tape cassette player. (Unless you have stereo speakers in the room, which will serve as well.) *Make sure there is a clock with a large face on the night table beside the bed,* so the time may be easily seen, with your egg timer next to it. Insert the tape into the cassette player and position the earphones.

Place your small metal desk lamp containing the red bulb between your knees and, holding it firmly between your knees (or thighs), so it won't topple over, use the gooseneck to aim the shade with the red bulb directly toward your solar plexus (between the breastbone and the navel), about two feet from your skin.

Set the timer for fifteen minutes, then turn on the cassette player and the lamp. Relax your nude body, and erase all negative thoughts from your mind. Allow the red-Mars music to enter your "inner ear" through the earphones as loudly as you find to be comfortable, while your solar plexus is being bathed in red light. Keeping your eyes closed is helpful, but not absolutely necessary.

When the fifteen-minute period ends, signaled by the timer, and seen on the clock face, lay the small metal lamp *on its side* at the bottom of the bed, so that the red light from the bulb is aimed one to one and a half feet away from the soles of your feet (while still lying on your back). Set your timer for an additional fifteen minutes, and lie relaxed, erasing all negative thoughts from the screen of your mind, and continuing to listen to the red-Mars music through the earphones, as the red color bath penetrates the soles of your feet (leading to all other parts of your body).

When the second fifteen-minute period of your color bath has ended, as signaled by the timer and seen on the clock face (double insurance for the correct timing), turn off the red lamp and turn off the tape.

That's the end of Step 1, and it has taken only thirty minutes in all, only a half hour out of your busy day. Remember, once a day — at whichever "power time" you've chosen, sunrise, high noon or sunset (or as near these times as possible, just so it's the same time every-day), you must take your color bath — for no less than forty-five days, fifty-four days if necessary, and no more than sixty-three days.

A quick summary of Step 1: fifteen minutes of the red ray ener-gizing your solar plexus — fifteen minutes of the red color bath to the soles of your feet — listening via earphones (or room stereo) to the challenging, exciting red-Mars music during the entire half hour period.

A word of caution: After a few days of the red color bath treat-ment, if you should feel feverish or exhausted, switch to an *orange* bulb for two or three days, then return to the red bulb. You can expect elimination from both bowels and kidneys to increase as the weight lowers rapidly over a period of days, but if your body responds to this energizing with diarrhea for more than one day, again, switch to an *orange* bulb, continue the treatment of Step 1 for two or three days, then *switch back* to the red bulb.

The plumpies who have hypertension or tachycardia (rapid heart beat) should take the entire Step 1 treatment at all times with an orange bulb, instead of a red bulb. The effect will be slightly slower than the red color bath, but perfectly safe. Red will raise the blood pressure temporarily, which is not in the least harmful to the average person, but is not recommended for those with hypertension or high blood pressure. In the latter cases, Step 1 is perfectly safe with an *orange* bulb (although slightly slower) — because the color orange will stimulate the body, allow the aura to absorb the red-gold ray and raise the pulse rate *without* raising the blood pressure. If you do *not* suffer from high blood pressure, hypertension or tachycardia, the *red* bulb color bath is absolutely safe for the *entire period*.

These interstellar light charges irradiate the body's batteries and the aura, and since the body must gradually adapt to these new color patterns in the aura, the *regularity* and *consistency* of these daily "cosmic charges" are vital to the success of your color diet. It's not something you can start, then stop, then start again — or the entire effect will be lost, and there will be no magic. Don't begin it until you're fully committed to complete the forty-five-, fifty-four-, or sixty-three-day cycle, at the same time each day . . . plus the additional steps.

STEP 2.

Still the weight *loss* color diet. Fill two of your four 8- to 10-ounce red glasses with bottled water. Then place them outside, where the Sun's rays fall on them for at least three hours, preferably all day. This will solarize the water with the red-gold ray. It's already been proven scientifically that when sunlight reaches water through a colored glass container the chemical content of the water is measurably altered, each time in a different way, depending on the color through which the light of the Sun reached the water. It's called solarizing. You can protect the water from insects and other particles by sealing the top with Saran Wrap, which won't affect the solarization process.

When your two ruby red glasses of water have been solarized place them somewhere to reach room temperature (the Yang temperature) and set the other two outside to be solarized. In this way, you can drink two delicious glasses of red solarized water a day — morning and evening. While two are reaching the Yang room temperature, the other two are being solarized. You'll notice a refreshing difference in the taste of your red solarized water. Many people say it tastes like fresh spring water or well water. (Do not refrigerate it.)

STEP 3.

You've now taken the red-gold ray into your body, and eventually into your aura through the red lamp color bath — the red-Mars heavy drum beat, pounding, parade march music — and the red solarized water. During this same forty-five-, fifty-four-, or sixty-three-day treatment of the color missing from your auric rainbow, which has caused your condition of LOCH, you must increase your absorption of the red-gold ray through the food you eat. It's quite simple. You eat only those foods which are colored red, gold, yellow, orange — or white. Why add white ? Because white "throws off," and does not "hold in or retain." There are plenty of foods in this color spectrum to choose from. You certainly won't suffer any hunger pangs.

You can eat as little or as much of these foods as you please, without gaining weight, paying no attention whatsoever to either the quantity of the food you eat — or the calorie content. When you've completed the minimum forty-five-, maximum sixty-three-day color cycle, you may then eat any of the foods on the red-gold list — *plus* any of the foods on the blue-green list (given following this red-gold list). In fact, you may eat whatever you want at the end of the cycle.

Here is a partial list of the foods in the red-gold spectrum you can eat sparingly or stuff yourself with, depending on your mood or your perference. You may add any other foods you wish to the list, as long as they are colored red, gold, yellow, orange, or white. Eat *no foods* colored green, blue, blue-green, yellow-green, or brown.

The food list for plumpies

Beets
Red cabbage
Strawberries
Tomatoes
Red onions
Mustard and
    ketchup
Nectarines
Cherries
Radishes
Spaghetti
Chili
Butter — (yes,
    butter)

Red wine — red
    grapes
Red grape juice
Cranberries
Milk — especially
    cream
Pomegranates
Red raspberries
Popcorn
Papayas
Apricots
Bananas
Corn
Carrots

Grapefruit
Lemons —
    lemonade
Oranges
Yellow peppers —
    red peppers
Mangoes
Rutabagas — yams
Rhubarb
Pumpkin
Mayonnaise
Cornmeal muffins
All cheeses,
    including cottage
    cheese

The food list for plumpies continued

Eggs in any form
Honey
Red caviar
Any kind of rice
(except brown
rice)
Watermelon
Yellow melons —
pineapple

Chicken — yellow
noodles and
chicken gravy
Red or white ice
cream if made
with honey
Honey-vanilla ice
cream

All cereals derived
from golden
wheat or oats
Peaches
All potatoes —
except french fries
(but don't eat the
skins of brown-
skinned potatoes)

Let me explain about the skins of foods in relation to what is inside. Watermelon, of course has a green skin, but is red inside. Since no one ever eats the skin of a watermelon, the plumpies may safely eat the red inside of a watermelon. They may also eat the *red skins* of red-skinned potatoes, *plus* the inside of such potatoes — and the *inside* of brown-skinned potatoes, but *not* the brown skins; brown being a part of the blue-green spectrum, corresponding with Nature and all growing green plants, which are blended with brown (such as trees and the like). Plumpies may safely eat *any red- or yellow-skinned fruits and veggies, unless the insides of them are part of the blue-green spectrum.* *Avocados* are out for the plumpies, being brown on the outside, and a combination of green and yellow-green inside. They belong, as you'll see, on the list for skinnies. Plumpies may eat golden chicken gravy — but no brown gravy. They may eat chicken, but no fish. You'll have to wait until your LOCH is cured before returning to your favorite Sushi bar or Japanese restaurant. (Yes, even fish like shrimp belong on the skinnies' list, never mind the orange stripes on the outside.)

Study the list, use your imagination to add other foods, and you'll see that the plumpie color diet won't make you "feel starved." Forget those "reducing salads" and other green things you've always thought would cause you to lose weight. They'll have just the opposite effect, causing you to add weight to your already overweight LOCH. And here are some other color therapy rules.

Products made with white sugar or white flour are no-nos for *both* the plumpies and the skinnies while they're taking the color treatment. White sugar and white flour destroy the color balance of your body and your aura, even though white sugar does not add weight, as you've been falsely led to believe — or as your brain has been falsely programmed. Any sweets made with yellow gold honey are in the proper color spectrum for *losing* weight — and brown sugar or raw sugar products are in the proper color spectrum for *gaining* weight. All sugar *substitutes* are no-nos for both plumpies and skinnies — and even when you've become perfectly balanced, and your LOCH is cured, white sugar, white flour products, and sugar substitutes are best not eaten, purely for health reasons.

You may think that red meat should belong on the plumpie food list in the color treatment, simply because of the red color (from the poor animal's blood, of course). However, all red meats are taboo for the color treatments of both plumpies and skinnies — not because the color is right or wrong, but because the chemical response of your shocked body to this (rotted) *cured* flesh of mammals (our animal brothers and sisters) upsets the entire healing process of any kind of illness or disease, including LOCH — in addition to its being detrimental to your general health. Even if you have no desire to become a vegetarian, don't expect the color treatment to work if you eat red meat during the color cycle time period.

The booster suggestions for the magical color *weight loss* program are:

1. The wearing of red, yellow, gold, orange, or white clothing as often as possible — and the wearing of green, blue, blue-green, greenish-yellow, turquoise, brown, or black clothing as seldom as possible.

2. The mental visualization of the red color bath twice a day. Make sure these two periods are at the same time each day. While standing, breathe deeply and correctly for one minute. Then visualize sparkling ruby red or crimson red light streaming up from the ground below (although you should do this indoors) and mounting in intensity, as the red waves of color envelop your body externally until they reach the top of your head — for one full minute. End the visualization booster by imaging — for one full minute — the same vibrant, red energy beaming downward from the top of your head, and penetrating every cell and organ within your body, as you breathe deeply and correctly for one full minute. The color image visualization takes only two minutes, twice a day, four minutes in all.

3. When outdoors, summer or winter, wear as often as possible red-, rose-, orange-, yellow-, or gold-tinted sunglasses. The color spectrum entering your body through the retina of the eye is a powerful booster.

After a week or so of booster suggestion Number 2, twice a day at a convenient time, at home or the office, you'll be surprised how quickly you will master visualization, until it will seem that you truly see the red rays with physical vision, in the same way that you will someday be able to see auras.

The three steps outlined here plus the boosters which comprise the ancient alchemy color treatment for the LOCH of the plumpies so they may safely, surely, and permanently lose weight are simple and painless. They contain nothing harmful to your health. Let's brief the formula:

1. The daily half hour color baths — and Yang music treatments.

2. Two glasses of red solarized water per day.

3. Eating only the foods in the red-gold-yellow-orange-white spectrum. The three boosters of clothing, color visualization, and sunglasses.

You'll be amazed at how swiftly this color secret causes you to shed pounds, exactly where you need them to melt away, not in the wrong places. It's mysterious and exciting to see it work. The first time you lie down on your bed with your red lamp and marching music, you'll feel somewhat foolish. But here's a hint.

Before you start, try on a pair of jeans you have to pin together at the waist with a safety pin, because they're so small and tight on your overweight body (whether you're overweight by ten pounds or sixty pounds or more). Shower immediately following your color-music bath. (This is assuming you've had your two glasses of red solarized water the day before.) After you shower, dry yourself, then try on the jeans again.

After the first, second, or third treatment (often after the very first one) you'll be surprised to discover that, although the jeans may still be too snug for comfort, you can at least fasten them without the safety pin. A week or so later (or sooner) you can fasten them comfortably — and wear them. A couple of weeks later you'll treat your red bulb and red glasses as if they were chips from the Hope Diamond, with a grateful reverence, as the pounds melt away while you're neither starving yourself nor fasting, and eating as much of the red-gold foods as you desire when you're hungry. Yes . . . definitely magic !

Why the music ? Because color and sound are equally important to human well-being — and every sound or type of music vibrates to a particular color. Therefore, taking into your body, which will eventually and gradually manifest in the personal rainbow of your aura, the needed and temporarily missing spectrum hues, through both color itself and the music or *sound* vibration of that color, speeds up the process. Sound and color are inseparable.

THE MAGICAL, FORGOTTEN RAINBOW TREATMENT
FOR UNDERWEIGHT SKINNIES

This formula will be easy — easy for the author at least ! The color treatment for healing the underweight LOCH is precisely, step-by-step, the same as the treatment for the LOCH of the overweight plumpies, with the following exceptions. Read the three Steps I've just described for the *overweight* LOCH condition, and change only these aspects of the formula:

STEP 1.

Use a *blue* bulb, instead of a red bulb. Make sure that the blue bulb is 75 or 100 watts, and is opaque, rather than clear. The lamp you use for your color baths should be metal, painted brown, tan, or any shade of blue or green.

Instead of the cassette tapes of the red-Mars marching bands — loud, rock and roll or other drum beat music, substitute tape cassettes of soothing ocean sounds or birdsong you can find on a series of tapes called "Environments," carried in most record stores — or other soft, *blue-green Venus music,* with strings, violins, and the like, sometimes called "Music To Make Love By" . . . or orchestral arrangements of pieces like "Clair de Lune" or "Moonlight Sonata," etc.

STEP 2.

Instead of the ruby red glasses, you'll need four 8- to 10-ounce cobalt blue or electric blue glasses (a bright and vibrant, but not dark blue). Other than the color of the glass, the solarized water formula is to be followed exactly as given for the plumpies — with this one exception: In your case, you shouldn't drink the water at room temperature, but should drink it ice cold. Refrigerate your *blue* solarized water while the other two are solarizing.

STEP 3.

Regarding the three booster suggestions given in the overweight color treatment, the skinnies must change the instructions to this: Wear, as frequently as you can, clothing in any shade of blue, green, turquoise, blue-green, greenish-yellow, brown, or black. *Avoid* as much as possible wearing clothing in any shade of red, yellow, gold, orange, or white. It's a strange contradiction that plump people like to wear black, because they believe it makes them look thin. It does. It make them *look* thin — but conversely, black "holds in" and retains, causing weight gain in color therapy. The opposite is true of white — the skinnies should never wear it while on the color therapy "diet" — and the plumpies *should* wear it (never mind that they believe it makes them *look* heavy), because it will help them lose weight.

The booster suggestion of the sunglasses changes for the skinnies, too, naturally. They should wear sunglasses in any shade of blue, green, smoke, or brown (with no rose or yellow tint).

As for the visualization booster, including the breathing and color imaging, follow the same directions given for the plumpies, changing the color visualized from red to forest green, cobalt blue, electric blue, or sky blue. Also, while plumpies should perform the visualization booster standing on the floor, those who desire to *gain* weight should perform it standing barefoot on green grass, whenever possible. The green color ray from the grass entering the soles of the feet, along with the blue-green mental image of blue or green, greatly increases the intake of the blue-green spectrum.

As already stated, the plumpie color treatment must be followed for either forty-five, fifty-four, or sixty-three days — no number of days in between, because these numbers match the red-gold ray. However, the color treatment for underweight skinnies, who wish to *gain,* must be followed for a minimum of forty-two days, fifty-one days if necessary — but no longer than sixty days. And no number of days in between, because these numbers vibrate to the blue-green ray.

In both cases of LOCH, if you miss a day or two, you must begin all over again, because you will have disrupted the necessary continuity of the conditioned response aspect of the color therapy. This is why you shouldn't begin your color treatment until you're prepared to fully commit to the schedule and strictly observe the three Steps of the formula.

The last change for the skinnies that differs from the color requirements for the plumpies is the food list. If you're in the group of skinnies, and wish to *gain* weight, you must eat *only* those foods which are colored blue, green, blue-green, greenish-yellow, or brown, and eat them as frequently and in as much quantity as possible. *Avoid* all foods colored red, orange, gold, yellow, or white. Here is a partial list of foods which will allow the skinnies suffering from LOCH to balance their auras by taking in the missing and needed blue-green-brown color spectrum. You may add any other foods you especially like, since this isn't a complete list, as long as they are colored blue, green, or brown. Including chocolate (made with raw or brown sugar). *No honey.* Remember that white sugar and white flour products will not make you gain weight, as you've been erroneously taught, but they will cause the color harmony you're seeking to go out of kilter.

The food list for skinnies

Blueberries
Blue or green grapes
Plums
Blackberries
Brown gravy — brown rice
Green cabbage
Sashimi (*not* white rice Sushi)
Coffee
Asparagus
Spinach

Broccoli
Kale
Green spinach noodles or green pasta
Powdered carob - chocolate for cold (Yin) drinks — mixed with water, not milk.
Celery

Avocados
Parsnips — parsley
Peas
Green beans
Lima beans
Limes
Kiwi fruit
Green honeydew melons
Artichokes
Green-skinned apples

The food list for skinnies continued

Cucumbers
Mustard greens
Lettuce
Pickles — olives
Fish of any kind —
    except fried
All Japanese food,
    except white
    rice
Artichokes
Skins of brown-
    skinned

potatoes, *not*
    the insides
Green peppers
Green onions
Blue grape juice
Brussel sprouts
All blue-, green-, or
    brown-skinned
    fruits and
    veggies
Margarine

Black caviar
Peanut butter
Brown rice
Pistachio nuts
All other nuts you
    like
Any sweets made
    with raw sugar,
    brown sugar,
    or syrups

So . . . there you'll sit in a restaurant, ordering avocado or spinach salad on a bed of lettuce, while everyone wonders why in the world you're "dieting," when you're so "thin," not realizing that your sparse lunch is causing you to *gain* weight. Magic !

Why is butter nonfattening for the plumpies — and why are you skinnies told you must eat margarine to gain weight ? Because butter fluoresces yellow, and margarine fluoresces blue-green under fluorescent light. It should really create a lot of talk — the plumpies stuffing themselves with baked potatoes, smothered in butter and sour cream (but no chives) — while the skinnies are eating only the brown potatoes *skins,* and munching on all that "diet food," such as lettuce and greens and pickles and olives.

Remember that the color diet won't work if you practice just one phase of it, the solarized water — *or* the foods — *or* the color bath. All three Steps must be part of the entire treatment. As for teas, now that you've become a color expert, I'm sure you can assign all the available teas to the red-gold ray or the blue-green ray, depending on the color of the tea. But remember that the plumpies should drink their teas (and other liquids) hot, because they lack the red-gold Yang ray — and the skinnies should drink their teas (and other liquids) cold, because they lack the blue-green Yin ray.

Remember that the red-gold ray is Yang, and the blue-green ray is Yin. Green is the spectrum color that balances the liver and the spleen by activating the pituitary gland, stimulating its growth potential, and sluggish action of the pituitary is the problem with many severely underweight people. The red-gold ray stimulates the pituitary in the opposite way.

Back to the illusion of calories, which are units to measure heat and nothing more, regardless of the false programming of medical science to date. Do you still believe it's the consumption of an excess of calories that causes you to gain weight, the gobbling down of sweets and so forth — and that cutting down drastically on calories, pasta, milkshakes, and the like is a sure way to lose weight ?

Consider the huge animals on Earth, such as the elephant, the rhino, and the hippo — also the enormous prehistoric dinosaurs. These creatures need tons of weight to frame their huge body skeletons. But did you ever see an elephant eating apple pies and strawberry sundaes — or a hippo munching buttered toast ?

What do elephants and other large creatures (who need to weigh tons in order to survive) eat ? They eat *exclusively* the blue-green-brown color ray. So do cows and bulls. Ponder the pure and simple logic of it. And don't leave out the great whales, who also weigh many tons, and whose diets consist entirely of the blue-green color ray and small fish (which are among the foods to eat for those who want to *gain* weight). You can't argue with wise Mother Nature. You see, the large animals were never programmed with the falsehood that the intake of calories causes weight gain, so they go merrily along, munching blue-green and brown vegetation, nearly zero calories, and grow heavier with each mouthful.

I'm reminded of our small friend, the bumblebee (who probably remains small because he snacks all day on yellow pollen from lots of red, gold, yellow, and orange flowers !). I'm reminded of him in the context of programming. According to all the inflexible rules of aerodynamics and the laws of physics, regarding body weight in relation to wing span, the bumblebee cannot fly. But no one ever told the bumblebee this, so the little fellow flies around anyway, blissfully ignorant of the "fact" that he can't fly.

I wonder if the old truism "ignorance is bliss" could be used to apply to the programming of the human brain with error. Does breaking a mirror really bring seven years of bad luck ? When a black cat crosses your path will you surely soon hear of a death ? If you believe so, yes. Just as calories will make you fat, if you believe they will. The true definition of superstition is: programming of the mind. Is it not ? Think about it. A familiar computer term is GIGO (garbage in — garbage out), meaning that the "facts" popping up on the computer screen are only as reliable as the information that was programmed into it. Likewise with the human brain, of which the electronic computer is but a pale imitation.

So shall we dump the GIGO calorie illusion into the trash bag of medical falsehoods ? Yes, let's do ! When you've completed your color treatment for whichever LOCH you may have you'll finally realize the truth of the calorie myth, and hopefully won't succumb in the future to the false programming you've been subjected to all of your life, so that, after your aura is restored to perfect color harmony, you'll eat anything you please, without subconsciously — and consciously — *expecting* to gain weight . . . therefore, you won't !

One last tip for the plumpies. When your color treatment of the red-gold ray has balanced your auric rainbow and your weight has become ideal for your individual body structure, you may — weeks or months later — suddenly go on a big binge of foods you formerly falsely believed were fattening. If so, and assuming your falsely programmed brain hasn't quite yet realized the lie of calorie intake, you may feel like a toad, about to explode, and your tummy will swell up like a balloon. Programming. Nothing but programming. Yet the swelling looks and feels very *real*. Don't panic. Relax. You can quickly erase the false programming and your body's visible and immediate response to it. And you needn't return to your forty-five-, fifty-four-, or sixty-three-day treatment, with its three Steps plus the boosters to accomplish it.

All you need to do to balance the situation is to lie on your bed, calmly watching television or reading, while taking in the red ray through the soles of your feet (as detailed in Step 1) for a half hour or so. The next morning you'll awaken, go into the bathroom, shower — then come out and view yourself sideways in the mirror. Abracadabra ! Your slightly ballooning tummy of the night before will be nice and flat again. *Definitely* magic ! And so quickly. A humongous binge may take two or three nights of this booster, but never more than that — and usually one will suffice. However, don't let this *partial* red color bath cause you to continue your erroneous calorie GIGO. Your objective, remember, is to be *free* of your brain's GIGO permanently. Also, don't consider this partial color bath a *substitute* for the three Steps and boosters of the color treatment cure for LOCH, since it's only effective *after* you've *completely* followed the forty-five-, fifty-four-, or sixty-three-day schedule.

Note: It occurs to me, relative to the solarized water portion of the color treatment, that you may wonder if you can solarize water in your ruby red — or cobalt blue — glasses on a cloudy day. The answer is yes, you can. The light from the Sun with the power to solarize the water will be just as effective on a cloudy as on a sunny day — and in a somewhat diminished sense, even in the rain. In the instance of the latter, regarding the diminished solarization power, drink three or four glasses of the red or blue solarized water the next day, instead of two glasses.

By the way, in case you've been frightened by scary stories for and against — not only calories — but also the dangers of cholesterol and the necessity of protein — don't fret. Relax. *Green* yourself or *blue* yourself. Metaphysicians and medical astrologers know that the dangers of cholesterol are exaggerated, and the need for protein is the same kind of false programming as the power of calories. (Elephants don't eat "minimal daily requirements of protein," and they do quite nicely, thank you. They also live a looooooooong time.) But even if you still mistakenly believe these illusions, you can comfort yourself with the knowledge that the eggs and cheeses are on the plumpie list of foods and the *apparent* lack of much protein on the list can't hurt you for only forty-five, fifty-four, or sixty-three days.

Another proof of the power of the red ray to lose weight, and of the blue ray to gain weight: the Doppler effect, science has called it. In the late 1800s, Dr. Johann Christian Doppler discovered an important effect concerning light waves, which contain the entire rainbow spectrum, plus infrared and ultraviolet. He observed that, as light approaches a person or an object, the closer it gets, the more *blue* it becomes — and the further away it extends, the more *red* it becomes. Red is the color that *casts out,* and blue is the color that is *absorbed and retained.*

When two people are investigating their psychic ties and telepathic abilities, through experiments with one another at a distance, using esp or mental telepathy — sending and receiving messages — the sender should *send on the red ray* — and the receiver should *receive on the blue ray.*

One last reminder regarding the color treatment. Those of you who do suffer from LOCH should read everything counseled for *both* the plumpies and the skinnies, whichever group you belong to, because (a) you'll learn what *not* to do — and (b) you might miss a pertinent fact relating to the entire condition of both kinds of LOCH.

Now that we've realized how everyone can successfully become a "10" like Bo Derek and Superman Christopher Reeve, we can continue with some other aspects of the relationship between your health, happiness, and well- being — and color. Let's return to the discussion of the medical profession today in the preceding chapter, "An Apple a Day," but this time associated with color.

✶ ✶ ✶ ✶ ✶ ✶

First of all, it's necessary to comprehend that you are a holy trinity, composed of body, mind, and soul. Your Spirit (the Angel of your Higher Self) watches over the three, but is not an integral part of the Earthling You.

This Holy Trinity of You is forever inseparable, and if only allopathic medicine would realize and comprehend that vital truth, we would be nearly all the way home — to permanent good health. However, allopathic medicine (unlike homeopathic and holistic medicine and medical astrology) treats the three parts of the trinity of you as if they were each individual, self-supporting facets of a human, failing to understand that they cannot be separated.

Physicians treat the Body — psychiatrists treat the Mind — and Religion treats the Soul — separately. Such erroneous thought and practice makes the task of the Spirit (your Higher Self or Supraconscious) extremely difficult. The Holy Trinity of You should be treated in a homeopathic sense. As I remarked in Chapter 3, allopathic medicine treats the disease the patient has, while homeopathic medicine treats the whole person who has the dis-ease in his or her aura, reflecting the problems in the other two parts of the Holy Trinity.

When only *one* of the three parts of the Trinity of Body, Mind, and Soul falls ill or stops functioning properly the other two will quickly follow. Remember, they are inseparable. Conversely, when one of the three is correctly and properly healed, the other two will likewise follow. The key words are "correctly and properly" — through thought, color, and music.

You may already be aware that research some time ago developed an instrument called the Aurotone, that makes sound and music *visible* — and makes color *audible*. It reproduces sounds and musical notes in color, transferring each color to a sound equivalent; each sound or musical note to a color equivalent. But you may not be aware that thought itself produces color . . . and responds to color. *Thought is color. Thoughts possess color*.

Consequently, either color or music or thought may be used to successfully restore the balance of harmony in your body and your aura. And when two are used, or all three, the healing power and adjustment of the individual's auric harmony is intensified. You'd best read this paragraph several times until you fully comprehend it.

A brief example of the Aurotone revelations: C major vibrates as red — the note of E vibrates as yellow — the musical note G vibrates as blue — and so on. Each musical note on the Scale also vibrates to a particular planet and astrological sign.

Consequently, it's conceivable and entirely possible for a musician to compose and play your personal Nativity, or birth chart, through its various natal planet positions and aspects, including both the harmonious and discordant chords indicated by your Horoscope (which is actually a symbolic picture of your past incarnations). When you heard this music it would deeply stir your Spirit with both recognition and inspiration. Although setting a Nativity to music is an enormous musical challenge, it can be done, and it would be a wonderful thing to possess your own personal and individual S-elf as music, don't you think ? Composer Robert Ellis, of Seattle, Washington, is currently working on this exciting project, and I'm sure you'll be hearing about it soon.

Color and music (more about music in the following chapter, "Forgotten Melodies") play a vital role in man's and woman's physical evolution and spiritual evolvement, whether or not they're aware of it. The seven notes of the musical scale and the seven visible colors of the rainbow spectrum have a direct effect on what Hindu philosophy calls the seven subtle bodies surrounding and interpenetrating the flesh body — and the electromagnetic frequencies and radiations of these seven subtle bodies are responsible for the color substance of your aura — auric egg — or auric sheath. The great metaphysician, Goethe, taught that all the color frequencies of white light are raised or lowered to meet the needs of the evolution of our planet Earth, as well as all Earths in countless solar systems.

Currently, a kind of role switching is taking place. It seems that many psychologists are attempting to become psychiatrists — and many psychiatrists are trying to become psychologists. They're both at least investigating the inner and outer human. They sincerely want to release the stress and tension from their patients, but they're still unaware of how to teach them to do it themselves. Nonetheless, we owe the dedicated ones (not the sexual perverts who have been raping their patients of late) a debt of gratitude for broadcasting the important message that the emotions of men and women are more contributory to illness than the germs in their body — even though they haven't yet realized that the former constitute the cause, and the latter the effect. The mind materializes the germs, causing them to manifest. The mind also causes germs in the body to be virulent or impotent and harmless. It's all in the state of mind, another term for your "physical" resistance to illness. Many doctors are exposed to the germs of highly contagious diseases constantly, yet don't "catch" the illness. When you're trying to help other people, your own body resistance grows stronger.

Food intake is nothing but the breakdown of color vibrations. Disease treated with initially impressive but temporary success with drugs, chemotherapy, chemicals, and antibiotics in response to germ attacks — must be treated, for *permanent* healing, by changing the color-sound frequencies of the patients, which balances the color harmony of their auras. This is part of the New Age medicine, and when it becomes understood, the nineteenth and twentieth centuries will be looked back upon as "the dark ages of medicine."

In both benign and malignant tumors there is a color disharmony present, creating severe stress and strain which causes cancer cells to multiply. The correct application of color and sound (music) can reverse the progress of the dis-ease and return the cancer cells to normal. It's the nature of, the natural inclination of every cell in your body to return to its normal structure and frequency rate when the color imbalance has been corrected, and there are a number of ways to accomplish this. Unfortunately, there's not enough space here to go into the subject thoroughly. Color therapy, or Chromotherapy as it's called, is an immense, detailed, and specific field of knowledge, requiring a book of it's own — and a very thick one at that.

I don't presently have any plans to write such a book myself in the future, but if I ever do, I can tell you this. Before attempting to counsel the general public concerning such a delicate and complex matter as color therapy or Chromotherapy for *treating diseased organs,* which can be as dangerous to your health as it can be healing and helpful, I would study the subject carefully for several years; then consult with those who have studied for several decades. Only after such preparation would I counsel men and women about how to use color to heal a serious disease in any part of the body by using colored prisms, screens or bulbs, filters — or imaging color directed toward various parts of the body and particular organs of the body.

To attempt to write or lecture about such an intricate and innately medical matter can be a dangerous practice for a layman when what is being taught is specific, but the medical profession isn't concerned about it because they believe the entire subject is harmless and amusing. It is not.

What do you think would happen if someone advised you to take a particular chemical prescription for a certain ailment, and that medication was for a totally different disease ? If you followed such misguided advice, as any good physician will affirm, you could become seriously ill — even die.

What doctors — and the general public — fail to realize is that color therapy has a much greater power (for good or ill) to heal or harm the body than a physician's chemical prescriptions. *Much* greater. Therefore, you can imagine what the *wrong* color counsel regarding healing the physical organs of the body (or the mind, for that matter) can do when taught by someone who has only brushed the surface of the vast study of Chromotherapy, and believes that he or she is ready to teach it to others. There are, alarmingly, several of these men and women who, during the past couple of years — and presently — are treating individuals — lecturing — or holding seminars — without any but a fragmented and cursory or general knowledge of what they believe themselves capable of teaching. There are dozens of books written on the subject, and many of them are in complete disagreement regarding which color can heal or harm which organ of the body. There's no way of knowing which of these books have been read by the amateurs, dazzled by their new discovery of esoteric matters, who feel themselves qualified to instruct you about color healing and imaging.

Most of these unprepared and uneducated instructors mean well, they don't intend to harm their audiences or students, but because of well-intentioned ignorance, that's exactly what can happen.

I don't believe myself to be so qualified (and I may never be) at present, even though I've been partially instructed by Chromotherapists from Europe, who possess medical degrees, and who are also practicing physicians. So think what someone who attends the wrong lecture or has chosen the wrong book to read can do to damage those who listen to misguided color counsel in a group seminar. As for the color diet in this chapter, I'm sure no doctor could complain of the foods given for the plumpies and skinnies for the periods of time suggested. Both lists contain healthy foods. As for the precious "proteins" and such the medical profession swears by, when you're back to your normal weight, you're free to believe or disbelieve in medical faith for or against protein, carbohydrates, cholesterol, and the like.

Relative to everyone's growing sense of the importance of color, hospitals have finally recognized the power of green to soothe and calm, which is why surgeons now wear green masks, caps and gowns, and most hospital walls are painted green. Mental institutions long ago discovered that, with manic depressives, if they placed them in a room where everything was green or blue during their manic or hyper stage, they would almost immediately calm down — and when, in the depressive stage of silent inactivity and despondency, the patients were placed in a room where everything was colored and painted bright red and yellow, they would almost immediately come out of their near catatonic trances and become cheerful and active.

If you're going to an important business meeting or an important social event, think about what image you want or need to project, and what image you *don't* want to project. If you want to present an aggressive image, wear red — and visualize red. If you choose to present an intellectual image, wear blue (but not dark blue) — and visualize blue. If you want to present optimism, wear yellow or orange — and visualize these colors. If you need to present an image of calm, the one who pours soothing oil on troubled waters, wear green (but not lime green) — and visualize green. If you need to be stable, serious, and disciplined, wear black and white. If you want to be loved, and to project love, wear rose pink or light pink — and visualize these shades of the rainbow.

I have a friend in New York, an artist-photographer, who once had the idea of having his entire, large, one-room apartment done all in grey. The walls and ceiling were painted grey, the drapes, carpeting, furniture, pillows, and lamp shades were all grey — varying tones of grey. He intended the solid grey room to form a background, he said, for his visitors, guests, business associates, and friends. The people, he said, would add the color — by the clothing they wore — like brilliant, colored jewels in a soft grey setting. It was undeniably a lovely, artistic concept, but when he was alone in his grey room he became so depressed he couldn't create or work, and after a few months he called in a decorator to change the color scheme.

Speaking of jewels or gems, the Egyptians used these as a booster for the color treatment of illness and disease. Even today, this practice continues in both Egypt and China, and has recently spread to Europe and America, where the "average person" is becoming aware of and fascinated by the various magics possible with the proper use of gems. Gems are concentrated, pure and single colors, not mixed colors, and are therefore, because of being unadulterated, quite potent and powerful in their effect on your body. See the chapter titled "An Apple a Day" and Chapter 5 for the jewels you should wear next to your skin — not to cure illness (because this requires specific colors for specific diseases) — but to harmonize with your individual personality, and bring out the positive qualities you possess, bestowed by the *day* of your birth *and* your Sun Sign together.

When a particular gem is rotated the color rays within are released. Egyptians and other Eastern people are aware that the planets strongly influence human behavior, in a physical, emotional, and spiritual sense — and gems possess the same color ray as the planet to which they vibrate. (Again, refer to Chapters 2 and 5.) Consequently, gems worn against the skin exert the same influence as the planets, except that it's milder, much less forceful. Nevertheless, the effects can be noticed and felt.

Crystals and pure, unalloyed metals possess the highest proportions of etheric substance of anything in inanimate Nature. Alloys do not possess a cohesive wholeness, because they emanate two types of vibrations. This is why the ancient alchemists, Egyptian healers, and seers used only highly refractive crystals and pure, unalloyed metals in their work. Their faith in these cannot be called mere superstition because today's modern electrician has also found that batteries and circuits require pure, unalloyed metals — and the crystal is used as a detector in wireless telegraphy because it is sensitive to the vibrations of the ether.

This is why crystal and pure gems have always been considered the most magical of physical substances — because they are the most measurably etheric. Now do you see why "seers" have, since ancient times, used a ball of pure crystal as a focal point for meditation ? It's clearly not quite so "wacky" as it's made to seem by esoteric sceptics.

Metaphysicians have long known of the communicative quality of quartz crystal, yet only recently have others (who ridicule metaphysics) discovered how to make use of the communicative qualities of quartz crystal in watches and time keeping. They fail to realize that they've only touched the surface of the magic of quartz. During the time of Atlantis, more than 500 hours of spoken data could be recorded on a piece of quartz crystal not much larger than your thumbnail. Those who find this hard to believe should ask themselves (time being relative) if King Henry VIII of England might not have responded the same way to the information that so many hours of spoken data — or music — could be recorded (and played back) on a thin slice of tape that resembled a brown ribbon. The material of the tape itself would have been quite a shock to Henry, let alone hearing the "magic tricks" it could do. Yesterday's "fantasy" becomes tomorrow's science.

There are some tests you can try to prove certain truths about color, and these are only two of them. Color possesses temperature. Red, orange, yellow, and infrared are the "hot" colors, producing heat that creates strong chemical reactions in the flesh body. Red combined with yellow (creating orange) has the highest temperature. Blue, violet, ultraviolet, and to a lesser degree, green, are the "cool" colors. You can measure the temperature of color by placing a thermometer in a glass of red solarized water — or in a glass of cobalt blue solarized water. The thermometer placed in the red solarized water will rise to a higher degree than the one placed in the blue glass of solarized water.

Before placing a thermometer in a glass of red or blue solarized water, be sure the water is at room temperature, not just brought in from the hot sunlight exposure or taken from the refrigerator.

Color and white light also possess force and weight. You can prove this and measure the degree of force or weight of white light (or colored light, using a colored lens) by using a flashlight and a sensitively balanced scale. The scale will tip in the direction of the light, either more or less, depending on the color of the light — or whether it's white light. If you experiment, use a perfectly balanced, sensitive pharmaceutical scale.

Taking a brief trip down the Nile back to Egypt again, in certain temples in Egypt, archaeologists have found convincing evidence that particular rooms were constructed in a design which allowed the rays of the Sun to enter broken up into the seven colors of the spectrum. Since these were healing temples, the healers of the day would diagnose which color or colors the individual person lacked in the aura, then send that person into a room to absorb the color ray or rays he or she needed for the restoration of health — and direct them to take a color bath. This was also one of the many facets of the building of the Great Pyramid of Giza, a mystery too profound to delve into in this book at this time. (And long ago, the Nile was blue . . . so blue !)

Although I believe in only a *part* of the Darwin theory of evolution (the reason will be given in a forthcoming book), anthropologists and Darwinists have correctly claimed that what they call prehistoric man — and what I call Earthlings after the Fall, and after a certain major disaster on the planet — could not see colors. They could discern only black and white. The ability to see color, anthropologists claim, "developed slowly." Not true. The ability to see color was present "in the beginning," then was lost after the Fall . . . and is *returning* slowly. Today, we have two extremes: people who are "color blind," a kind of throwback to the past — and those rare ones, like Edgar Cayce, who can see the human aura because they're gifted with extrasensory perception of color, a kind of glimpse into the future. During the Aquarian Age, men and women are going to need to increase their sense of color and their physical perception of it, if we're all to adjust and respond to the swiftly growing challenges of science — some positive, some negative — spawned by the inherent curiosity of this Uranus-ruled period of history. Color and music . . . our recognition of the power of both, and our proper use of both . . . is what will save us from the Götterdämmerung.

Relative to this need, amazing miracles await those who begin now to study and comprehend color. Life itself is color — and because of this, color can prolong life by curing the improper balance of color in the human aura — or destroy life by creating a color imbalance. Several noted metaphysicians, among them Goethe, Steiner, and F. M. Alexander, have stated that, if one's Primary Color Control in one's individual aura is not disturbed, is kept in balance, then one need not ever either become ill or age. Remember not to confuse the word age with maturing. Here the meaning is not meant to be aging past a healthy maturity.

The seven colors of the spectrum and the invisible color rays must vibrate in each person rhythmically and harmoniously through the aura. When this rhythm and harmony is disturbed an imbalance occurs, causing illness — and when that imbalance becomes too great, death occurs. However, in the musical rhythmic harmony of balanced colors in the aura, death is banished and eternal life may be achieved. Men and women can live in the same physical body eternally. There need be *no aging* when there is no awareness of time. When your aura is color balanced, your thoughts the right color, and you use color wisdom to keep your Holy Trinity of body, mind, and soul, in harmony, you can live forever, providing the nuclear madmen don't blast us involuntarily into another dimension. But . . . good news ! They won't, for the reason given in the analysis of the 6 and 9 in Chapter 5, about numerology.

Physical immortality is explained in the final chapter of this book; how to achieve it, the secrets of those who already have achieved it, why it's possible and attainable when everyone has reached the enlightened state of eternal life in the same physical, improved, and perfected body. But don't rush ahead to that subject now, skipping the chapters in between. You'll need the understanding of the next several chapters if you want to successfully penetrate the mysteries of physical immortality. Right now all you need to realize — and *know* — is that no one need be ill — age — or die.

On that note, we'll program the information about forgotten rainbows into our brain computer, and move on to forgotten melodies and the harmonics or synchronization of the Universe. Mozart, Beethoven, and other musical "masters" will join us astrally as we discover how the Great Pyramid of Giza was constructed, with those very heavy, perfectly joined stones . . . how Joshua caused the walls of Jericho to come tumbling down . . . and many more star signs of magic, mystery, and ancient wisdom.

7

FORGOTTEN MELODIES

harmonic communication among humans . . .
the power of Silence, Sound, and Music . . .
the synchronicity and Oneness of the Universe . . .
how to use these to manifest magic and miracles

Natural Harmonics
and
Off-Key Notes

his eyes were gentle
    but his voice flashed fire, as he said . . .

> "everything in Nature and in human nature
> is composed of Color and Sound . . . these are
> the forgotten rainbows and forgotten melodies
>   of universal harmony

> "the life force emanates
>   from high frequency sound . . . and music
> each 'note' corresponding to each 'tone' of color
> and you must always remember
> that, to create any prismed spectrum
>   there must be a Light
> there are no colors cast at night
>   without the Light"

then I thought of the stained-glass windows
    in the chapel at St. Raphael's
how . . . dark . . . the chapel seemed to me at night
when no Light was shining through them
and how silent and less holy a place it was

    without the chanting of the nuns

★ ★ ★ ★ ★ ★

 OLOR AND Sound. The Rainbow Spectrum and the
Music of the Spheres. We've learned the importance
of color to life itself in the previous chapter, "Forgotten Rainbows." As for the equal importance of
sound, it's been emphasized so simply and so directly, Earthlings have missed its great significance.

In the Beginning was the Word . . .

Our Universe was created by sound. As were all other Universes. Our Creators did not act. They spoke. They said, "Let there

be Light," and there was Light. The formation of all solar systems out of chaos and the void of darkness was brought about by the spoken Word of our Creators — both of them — as the Christian Scriptures still tell us. You would think, wouldn't you, that by now, with all the sacrilegious surgery committed upon the holy works, the plural pronouns would have been removed by the patriarchs? Evidently, certain words of truth are divinely protected, and aren't easy to remove. These have stuck like glue to the pages, down through the Ages. (I rhymed that on purpose, because rhyme is part of the great secret of the English language.) For example, as we've already noted in an earlier chapter, there are contradictory pronouns in the Bible, right from "the beginning."

> And God said, Let *us* make man in *our* image,
> after *our* likeness . . . (was he perhaps talking to himself ?)
> > Genesis: Ch. 1, Verse 26

> In the image of God created *he* him, male and
> female created *he* them . . .
> > Genesis: Ch. 1, Verse 27

I've always wanted to debate this point with a Jesuit Priest, a Rabbi or a Mormon Bishop, but it would only lead back into the circles of convoluted reasoning programmed into these misguided theologians. They casually dismiss the "us" and "our" pronouns in Genesis, just as they gloss over the eighteen lost years of Jesus in the New Testament. Best to "let sleeping dogs (gods backward) lie." Nevertheless, "us" and "our" remain there, twinkling truth, with a stubborn determination, almost as though the words themselves were alive, as they truly are, which you'll discover in the next chapter, "Lexigrams."

Just as there are *tones* of *colors* in the Rainbow Spectrum which can't be seen with physical vision, such as ultraviolet and infrared, there are *colors* of *tones* in the Music of the Spheres which can't be heard with physical hearing. "In the Beginning," certain sounds produced differing sets of vibrational frequencies in the ethers. Some of these were of such low frequency that they formed particles of what we call "matter," or physical substance. There could be no light, as we know it, without minute specks of matter in the ethers to reflect it.

There's an intimate connection between color and sound and all other expressions of life. Sound is on a lower level of the scale, and comes just above the form and substance of matter. Consequently, sound is the intermediary between the higher level of abstract ideas in the Mind — and concrete form. Sound is capable of molding the ethers into shapes, and through these shapes, the corresponding power of the Mind is able to make an impression on physical matter.

Humans have no idea of the power of the sounds they create and send out into the ethers through their spoken words. If they did, they would swiftly realize that anything at all may be caused to materialize through the process of imaging it vividly and intensely in the Mind, then speaking aloud the sounds or words describing it — and, finally, observing its materialization into an actual object or event on the physical level of matter. The "magic wand" is the energy of the Mind and the energy of Sound. As Einstein proved, and modern science now accepts, energy and matter are interchangeable.

The foundation beneath this process, however, must be strong and supportive, or it will all "fall through" with no effect, just as a house will fall down when the foundation crumbles. That foundation is the absolute confidence of *knowing* that "if you have faith as tiny as a mustard seed, *nothing* shall be impossible unto you." Once the foundation has been built, and remains sturdy, the three steps of: Image in the Mind — Ordain through the spoken word — and Manifest into the physical world — allow any man or woman to create his or her own miracles.

However, like everything else, the magic is subject to the First Law of both Physics and Metaphysics — the Law of Polarity — meaning that, when these three steps are used, and what is imaged in the mind and ordained through the spoken word (whether you realize that's what you're doing or not) — is in any way negative, the very thing you do not wish to happen will occur with equal certainty. This immutable law is described (but seldom heeded) in phrases such as "what you fear will come upon you" . . . and President Franklin Roosevelt's warning, during World War II, that "we have nothing to fear but fear itself."

Fear is so powerful an emotion, it actually projects a scent or an odor, a most unpleasant one. Animals scent fear in a human or in another animal instantly. Fear, you may not realize, is also a most powerful faith, capable of literally changing the law of physics. Fear is *faith in the negative,* and strong faith manifests its images as swiftly and surely when projected by negative current as by positive.

So many people I know long desperately for something, such as marriage to a certain person, and because of fear and doubt, use the powerful magic wand of Image-Ordain-Manifest to bring about the opposite, which it will always surely do. Then they wonder why. They blame the failure of happiness to manifest or materialize on some Deity or some force they call "fate" or "destiny," when all the time, they are the ones totally responsible for the outcome. Or they blame it on astrology, not realizing that all astrology can do is to indicate the *timing* of certain strong *opportunities,* making the Image-Ordain-Manifest process much easier, *but the stars incline, they do not compel,* and in the final analysis, Free Will can work against the positive opportunities presented by the cosmic vibrations of the planets (the music of the spheres). The good side is that Free Will can also mitigate any negative astrological indications (the sour notes in the symphony of sound, whether silent or audible). You are the Producer and the Director of the drama of your life. You cast all the characters in it, who mingle and act with you. Astrology wrote the script at your birth, on assignment from you, or from your actions in a former incarnation. But in the present life drama, you can either produce it or throw it away and write a new script (as many microcosm producers in Hollywood do on occasion). Because you're also the star of the show, it's sometimes difficult for you to realize how many "hats you wear" in the production. If you did, you would know that you can change any scene — any time you wish.

The difference between Avatars or Gurus and the average Earthling is that the former have their Third Eyes open. They "listen to the music" and thus are fully aware that they've cast themselves on the stage of life in a play or drama they have the power and authority to alter whenever they desire to do so intensely enough. How? By changing the unheard melody through tuning in to the "Puppeteer," the Higher Self or Spirit, and ordaining a script change, or even replacing one of the players whenever they wish. Not wishing or hoping or praying. Ordering, commanding — ordaining.

Remember in the Introduction to this book the Guru's first seeding of Lexigrams by calling my attention to the fact that the word **SIMULTANEOUS** contains the words **NO TIME**, a hint of the angstrom unit measurements of light waves? For instance, the life force energies demonstrated by Cleve Backster's research (detailed later in this chapter) causing communication between humans, between plants, between plants and humans and between all living entities, used by dolphins also in a telepathic sense, occurs *simultaneously*, or with the speed of light . . . taking **NO TIME**. Imaging and ordaining is likewise accomplished *simultaneously* and manifested later "in time," occasionally also simultaneously.

Regarding the various musical themes in the harmonics of life sounded by astrology, did you know that all British monarchs are crowned at a moment of time calculated by astrologers? They always have been — and still are. When Prince Charles takes the throne, the crown will be placed on his head at a time British astrologers (behind the scenes) have calculated as propitious. Astrology is quite respectable in England, even among the Royals — also in Europe, India, China and the Arab world.

Astrology is defined by nearly all television stations as "fun and games." Psychics are presented in a serious manner on TV's dramatic series, especially detective shows, in which the predictions or visions of a psychic are always proven to be correct — and likewise smiled upon Shirley MacLaine's *Out On a Limb* (as they well should have). However, when it comes to astrology, the television codes undergo a drastic change. An early FCC ruling still observed by individual TV stations and networks states that astrology *cannot be presented on television without a disclaimer printed on the screen warning audiences that astrology is being presented as pure entertainment only, and is not to be taken as a serious science.*

Ronald Reagan has long believed in astrology, and has relied upon it to guide his major decisions for several decades. A large photograph of Reagan hangs on the wall in the office of California astrologer Carroll Righter, along with photos of his other clients — and under Carroll Righter's guidance, Ronald Reagan asked to be sworn in as Governor of California at the extremely odd hour of three minutes past midnight. Likewise, he asked to be sworn in as President of the United States in a *separate* ceremony at *precisely* 11:57 A.M. on the day before the official swearing-in ceremony, and therefore took the oath of office twice.

Belief in astrology in high government places is not new. President Franklin Roosevelt consulted astrologers regularly. So did President Abraham Lincoln. George Washington and our founding fathers were all astrologers themselves. Former Vice-President Walter Mondale has written me to express how helpful he found my books *Sun Signs* and *Love Signs* to be. Former Vice-President Nelson Rockefeller was an astrological client of mine, who wrote to me for astrological counsel on two occasions. The popular New York astrologer, Evangeline Adams, who counseled the likes of J. P. Morgan, who would not make a move on the stock market without her advice, was the granddaughter of President John Quincy Adams and the great-granddaughter of President John Adams.

The power of one's negative mental energies (discordant musical chords) over astrological vibrations often occurs regarding financial transits and progressed aspects observed at a certain time in a person's natal chart. Using such financial vibrations as an example, people never seem to realize that they can't ordain wealth while simultaneously imaging poverty. As producer Mike Todd once said, "I've never yet seen anyone save for a rainy day that the rainy day didn't come, right on schedule." Truer words are seldom spoken. It's not easy to walk the tight rope or thin line between the spiritual insurance of absolute *knowing* — and the worldly insurance of caution, but Perfect Balance takes lots of practice on a "tightrope," as any circus performer can tell you.

The power of spoken (or written) words will be studied in detail in the following chapter about Lexigrams, but for now, consider the following evidences of the power of sound. First, you may be wondering about the power of sound compared to the power of color, but you shouldn't be, because each color corresponds to a certain note or chord, and each note or chord corresponds to a certain color. Therefore, whether you use the power of Red through color, or through its corresponding sound of certain Red words or its individual chord of music in the key of C-major, it's all the same.

A relatively recent discovery has been an instrument called an Eidophone. It consists of a tightly stretched drum surface, covered evenly with a very moldable, pastelike substance. Sounds and words are uttered beneath the drum by human voices (happy, positive words) — and the sounds of such spoken words cause beautiful shapes to form in the flexible paste, exact replicas of trees, ferns and flowers, as they are in Nature.

If sand is spread on the drum surface instead of the pastelike substance, then the sounds of "happy" words spoken beneath the drum cause the sand to produce precise geometrical designs, rather than plant forms. These are called Chladni figures, after their original discoverer, inventor Ernst Chladni, who enlightened the late 1700s and early 1800s to several secrets of our environment.

When ugly, obscene or vulgar words are spoken beneath the drum, creating discordant or disharmonious sounds, both the paste and the sand form chaotic patterns, with no shape or form.

It's been repeatedly observed and carefully recorded that plants will grow faster, healthier and taller when "the music of the masters" is played near them continually, symphonies and the like. When loud and discordant rock music is played near them continually, the plants are sickly, grow very slowly, and their growth is stunted, the full height two to four inches shorter than the plants *who* were lullabyed by the harmonious chords of symphonic music.

More evidence of the power of sound is birdsong. Assuming you don't live full time in the city, have you noticed the chorus of birdsong, like a thousand elfin choirs, all day long in the spring ?

Have you also noticed that the birdsong ceases during the summer months, except at dawn and twilight ? When you're having a picnic in the woods or your back yard on a summer afternoon you'll hear only an occasional, faint chirp from the top of the tallest trees. Have you ever wondered why ?

There's a magical reason for this little-known phenomenon of Nature. The singing of the birds sets up a particular sound vibration that promotes the growth of the young leaves of trees, plants and flowers, so the birdsong is fairly constant all day long in the spring, while the new growth is occurring.

In summer, the birdsong ceases, except at dawn and twilight — and sometimes, if not quite all of the leaves are full, also during the early morning hours of summer. After the leaves are full the chemical activities of the trees, grass, plants and flowers change every day in the summer — at dawn and at twilight. At night, all plant life breathes in carbon dioxide. At dawn and early morning, in the summer, they breathe out pure oxygen. The times of the changeover are heralded by the birds; are actually stimulated by the birdsong, but the sterile rules of biology recognize only the synchronicity of it, typically ignoring the clear evidence of cause and effect, unable to explain any other reason for Nature's precise timing of the seasonal and daily fluctuations of birdsong. In winter months, of course, St. Francis' beloved feathered friends fly south, to where other green miracles need the growth signals of the sound of their singing.

Isn't it lovely to know that the birds tell the grass, plants, trees and flowers when to grow, by setting up the sounds necessary to their chemical activity by singing — all day long in the spring, and at dawn and twilight in the summer ? How can anyone think that birds lead useless, lazy lives ? There's a reason for their singing ! I'm sure that Francesco Bernadone knew all about this truth of Nature.

How superbly logical, then, for the word **NATURE** to contain the word **TUNE**, since **NATURE** herself creates the miracle of the song or the **TUNE** of the birds causing the growth of Her green trees, grass, plants and colorful flowers. I couldn't suppress this mini-Lexigram until the next chapter; it's important that you meditate on it now. Nature does, indeed, consist of many chords of music, many sounds, including the "tunes" sung by the birds. Think about this wonder-ful (full of wonder) proof of the way sound impresses itself on the ethers to manifest the physical "mattering" of the "matter" of all growing things. The birdsong is necessary to Nature outdoors because various unseasonal and unexpected climatic conditions would otherwise frequently halt growth — and greenhouse plants, artificially grown, would thrive more luxuriantly if recorded birdsong were played to them.

Why aren't children taught this natural magic in school ? Because, unfortunately, much truth is not yet taught in schools. They're still teaching youngsters that Thomas Edison was the "inventor of electricity," only a half truth, never telling them that Edison merely used, in his own invention of light bulbs, DC, or Direct Current, while Nikola Tesla discovered AC, the Alternating Current used today almost exclusively.

Our grossly underpaid educators and teachers deserve a large measure of our sympathy for their thankless work, especially today, with the explosion of youthful pregnancies and child drug addicts threatening to destroy the entire educational system.

Our schools are graduating *seven thousand* children a year (as of 1987) who cannot read and are classified as illiterate. Yes, there is a crisis, creating serious discordant notes in the harmonics of the Universe.

Do you suppose that children might want to learn to read and might be concentrating less on sex if they weren't being so bombarded with it on the media and in the classrooms ? Could it be that they wouldn't so desperately be seeking the "other worlds" of drugs if they were being taught about all the other worlds under their very noses, bursting with mysteries and wonders . . . and promises for tomorrow ?

It's possible that they're *bored* out of their socks with sterile learning, causing them to tune into the sexual and drug releases with which their young minds are being unceasingly programmed, and which has led to an additional crisis, growing by leaps and bounds — juvenile stress. Child psychologists are at a loss as to how to deal with it. Maybe both the children's boredom and stress would end if they were to be exposed to the magic and miracles of the Universe, teaching them how to *tune into* their powerful Higher S-elves (they know all about elves) and by so doing, transform the adult-programmed, approaching nuclear Götterdämmerung into a golden Age of "wonders that never cease."

The suicide rate of teenagers, which has doubled during the past decade and is the second highest cause of death between the ages of twelve and nineteen, would fall markedly if the teens were inspired with the exciting future of long-forgotten rainbows and melodies, instead of looking forward to nuclear destruction.

Meanwhile, a teenager somewhere kills himself or herself, commits suicide, every nine minutes. *Every nine minutes.* What were you doing yesterday ? Whatever it was, while you were doing it, seventy-two teenagers were taking their own lives. Today also. And tomorrow, another seventy-two of them. And the next day . . .

If you're reading this book, and you're between the ages of twelve and nineteen, have you been tossing the idea of suicide around in your mind ? While you're tossing it around, figuring that killing yourself might be like kicking the ball to make your point for the final winning score — or at least to even the score (with this screwed-up world and everyone in it) — I have a very personal and intimate story to share with you.

One night, some years ago, but not too many (and not for the first time) I, too, decided to seek oblivion. It seemed to me to be a country mile more intriguing, not to mention more peaceful, than continuing to swim around, trying to stay afloat and avoid the sharks in the chaotic waters of confusion threatening to drown me, in both a personal and general sense, you know ? I kept thinking about what a bitter acquaintance of mine had said: "There are only two kinds of people in the world — bastards and victims." It wasn't hard to figure which group I belonged in.

Since I don't have what it takes to be in the first group, and I was weary of being in the second group, it made sense to go somewhere else where there was another club to join — where neither of the other two existed. I wasn't sure of the directions to wherever it was I would be going after I was dead, but I wasn't sure of the directions here either, where, just when you think you've learned the rules, it's halftime . . . change sides.

Actually the reasons aren't important. God knows there are whole bushel baskets of them to choose from, right ? I was living in New York at the time. (That's one good reason right there !)

I had read an ad in the paper about a telephone number for a suicide prevention group called "Why Kill Yourself ?" (WKY.) So I dialed the number, having decided I was checking out for sure, but curious to see if anyone had a logical argument against my decision. It was a Sunday morning. Gloomy Sunday.

The phone rang several times, then a tape-recorded message was activated, and a pleasant male voice with a southern accent spoke these words: "Good morning ! This is one of your friends you've never met. We're really interested in talking with you about why you want to die. Please call us back Monday through Friday, between ten A.M. and four P.M. Next Thursday is Thanksgiving, so we'll be closed all day. Bye !"

I burst out laughing. I couldn't control myself, it was hilarious. Then I walked over to the mirror, and gazed at my face looking back at me, without realizing it, also staring into my Third Eye, which I later figured is why I seem to get all of my best ideas when I'm staring into the mirror, washing my face, brushing my hair or teeth or applying makeup. Has that happened to you ? (If you're a boy or a man . . . like, when you're shaving or blow-drying your beard ?)

Well, anyway, I spoke aloud to my mirror image. "Look, knuckle-head, now that you know you can't take off on a permanent astral trip (assuming you want to debate the travel plans with someone first) before ten in the morning or after four in the afternoon — and never on weekends or holidays, why don't you hang out a little longer and see if this (expletive deleted) pineapple-upside-down-cake-freaked-out world has any more laughs to offer ? Don't cancel your trip to the cemetery, just postpone it, and who knows ? Maybe the Universe will abracadabra your own Guru in MacArthur Park to tell you why some-one left the cake out in the rain, and help you remember the recipe so you can bake a new one." I did — and it did.

The cake wasn't really ruined, just a little damp. And I found more laughs too. In fact, I discovered there's more to laugh about than to cry about in this lunatic asylum where the wise ones are locked up (people protesting nuclear madness) and the really flaky ones are running around free. Then I was absorbed in the challenge of how to reverse or re-*verse* the situation, and pretty soon it became as exciting as working on a blueprint for breaking out of Alcatraz, like that old Clint Eastwood movie.

There are lots of laughs ahead for you too. Not only laughs, but also a few certified miracles in assorted sizes, colors and sounds that are going to really blow you away — not into a casket — into a workable Time Machine capable of taking you on trips that will make an acid trip seem as mild as drinking the sassafras tea Peter Rabbit's Mum used to brew. I absolutely promise you that, druid honor — and I have this thing about not breaking promises. Trust me, okay ? No. Toss out that question mark and give it a period. *Trust me.*

Anyhow, people forget funerals so quickly today, probably because they have trouble separating the real deaths from the ones in the movies and on TV. They all just kind of blend together, consequently they don't have the same shock effect they used to have. So those callous creeps you want to *really* know how *really* miserable you *really* are won't even get the message. They'll just expect you to pop back up, like Bobby Ewing on *Dallas,* your dramatic farewell gesture and (admit it) bid for some genuine sympathy just a part of somebody else's dream. It's a weird world today, that's for sure. But weirdness can be fascinating if you keep your sense of humor. Besides, look what you're doing to the whales and dolphins. Who else is going to learn how to talk to them if you don't ?

Wander around this Wonderland the way Alice did in the slithy toves, rap with caterpillars puffing on their hookahs, zonk the Red Queen and help the Mad Hatter resolve his Time hang-up by setting his pocket watch for the Eternal Now. Alice had a ball, she did, as everything grew curiouser and curiouser. So can you.

Now, go stare at your Third Eye in the mirror (it's between your eyebrows) and flash some fragments of the future. Read this whole chapter (and the others too), ride your bike, talk to a tree or a plant, paint your room yellow, lexigram your problem (next chapter), check your karmic numbers, get yourself a purple plate (end of this chapter) and use it to mellow out the person who's so hot, but acting so cool; teach your dog some new tricks. Remember, if there's anything in this not-quite-yet-God-forsaken world you don't want to be, it's a statistic. You can think of fifteen million other things that are more satisfying than being a statistic. Statistics never have fun, and lord knows they don't have any laughs. I'll talk to you later. Now I have to go back to talking turkey to the adults who are playing trivial pursuit with your tomorrow, and see if I can beat them at their own game. They're the ones who need help, not you. That is, not you when you're being the real you-of-you, if you know what I mean — and you do.

★★★★★★

The discordant crescendos and clashing chords of sexual and drug abuse are disrupting the harmony of the Universe, because humans are an inseparable part of the symphony.

The war on drugs would be more quickly and efficiently won if our government halted the incoming supply of drugs flooding the country, which it has the ability to do if it chooses — or if it at least removed the astronomical profit from selling and pushing, as was done in England, by setting up clinics where addicts can legally purchase drugs until they can withdraw from them gradually. If people can't make tons of money pushing drugs, then people stop turning on other people, constantly creating new addicts. It's that simple. It takes an awful lot of crime to support a habit you desperately want to lose, but in the meantime forces you to somehow obtain *a thousand dollars a day* — or more. It will soon cost two thousand dollars a day, then three thousand dollars a day. The drug pushers are like the bathtub gin pushers during prohibition; they never get enough. They always want more. This is so logical one feels silly even pointing it out.

The enormous, completely-out-of-control drug Frankenstein afflicting our children today, along with their parents, is the direct responsibility of our government. It owes Americans a huge karmic debt. The dominant characters in the first act of the tragic drama of drugs are intelligence officers, military personnel and an array of scientists, working either directly or indirectly for the United States Government, beginning in the early 1950s. Now that the whole thing has gotten so out of hand that it threatens to destroy America herself, I do believe it's our government's duty to make a giant and genuine effort to accept the blame and repair the damage — and they can never successfully do the latter until they've had the grace to admit the former.

There are some facts so simple and so obvious that even the Mad Hatter at a tea party in the White House rose garden could see the logic. But then, there are those who appear to be a lot madder than Alice's Hatter who have been in charge of things in Washington for the past couple of decades.

It's time the White House made a serious effort, not just one based on political public relations, to help America's helpless, drug-addicted men, women and children, a responsibility that deserves a wide margin of priority over the stockpiling of nuclear eggs, of which we have enough now to blow up ten Universes.

As for the sour notes in the symphony of universal harmony sounded by sexual abuse, again, the word "abuse" applies to adults, not children. The proposed sex education programs are clearly necessary if young girls are going to continue to become pregnant in such droves. But the sex education proponents are missing some points in all the wild frenzy about the subject.

One thing being overlooked is the old familiar adage that "an ounce of prevention is worth a pound of cure" — no matter what is being prevented or cured. No one ever talks about or seems to notice the fact that teenage pregnancies in the 1940s and 1950s, when there was *no* sex education in schools, were nowhere near the alarming epidemic proportions of the 1980s. Those who are shouting both for and against sex education are ignoring the real cause of all this increased sexual activity among children. Sex education is needed, because the fire is out of control, but the lack of sex education in schools is not what started the fire — and not what caused it to burn out of control.

Nothing will change, with or without sex education in schools, until the real reason children are now concentrating on sex to such an obsessive degree is recognized.

They're being saturated by a tidal wave of sexually stimulating material. With these sex images floating around their heads, what are they supposed to be thinking about — daisies and bunny rabbits ? Bemoaning the fact that children are becoming sexually active at ten and twelve is like dumping a white woolly lamb in a pile of manure, then shaming it for being so dirty. Blaming the out-of-control sexual fires burning throughout the schools on a lack of sex education is only a front for the real cause.

Teaching sex in school is one thing. Teaching moral values is another. Even the first grade may be too late for the latter. One of the very real wisdoms of the Catholic Church, scattered among the flaws it shares with other orthodox religions, and to the best of my knowledge, exclusive with the Roman Church, is the truism of *"Give me a child till it's seven."* Meaning that Holy Mother Church (give the patriarchs credit for that correct term) has discovered, through the experience of centuries, that the moral values and religious teachings seeded into a child's mind from birth to the age of seven years will nearly always remain throughout the ensuing years, despite conflicting social and environmental influences.

The Church is astrologically correct. (There's a deep metaphysical mystery behind that age of seven years, revealed in *Gooberz.*)

If revelations of cosmic intelligence were to be taught in schools, using the amazingly effective Socratic method of asking, rather than telling, the children of the Aquarian Age might *remain children* as they mature, retaining the power to turn this new Age into what our Creators meant it to be.

What a lightning flash of Love and Light would illuminate our schools if there were classes in esoteric astrology (not the twisted and distorted form of it currently practiced by charlatans) — in numerology, Lexigrams, natural magic, the wonders of the Oneness of the Universe, the forgotten rainbows and forgotten melodies of color and sound — and holistic health. The children then would be so intensely fascinated, inspired and challenged they wouldn't have any time or interest to give to premature sexual activity or drug experimentation. These would swiftly be ignored in the excitement of making miracles.

Children understand miracles. That is, they do until their Third Eyes are sealed shut by their parents, relatives and teachers. Everyone would make straight A's on their report cards if, instead of cutting up helpless frogs in biology class, they studied why frogs and crickets sing at night, why birds sing at dawn. You think I'm imaging a Utopia or Shangri-La ? Well, yes. But why must Utopia and Shangri-La (Thy Kingdom come on Earth, as it is in Heaven) be given permission to exist only in a dim and undefined Future ? Why not in the Present, since Past, Present and Future are all One — another shining truth not taught to children in our society. What a shame. Children would not only grasp the concept quickly, they would even be able to teach the teachers a thing or two about Einstein's Relativity and the Eternal Now.

There's not a child, not a single boy or girl who wouldn't be fathoms more interested and excited in how Joshua caused the walls of Jericho to crumble (about which more later in this chapter) — or about the fascinating research into the intelligence of plants by India's Sir Bose, Dr. Harold Burr, Cleve Backster and others — than in long and explicit explanations of sexual intercourse between humans. The former two areas we'll be covering shortly — the latter is something children will learn for themselves when they mature and fall in love. Mother Nature is a peerless, unsurpassed teacher in the classroom of love. And love can't really be taught. It happens naturally, as does sex, when children aren't bombarded with it prematurely. First love, then sex. Everything spins upside down when the natural order of these two profound experiences is reversed — and it's not easy to turn it rightside up again.

The singing of the birds is only one of many phenonoma all around us emphasizing the importance of sound, which would be easily comprehended by children, but is apparently too simple and direct for most botanists to grasp its deep significance.

Sound caused the building of the Great Pyramid of Giza. The original Pyramid, subsequently structurally altered by later Pharaohs, was built by Osiris, not Cheops (Khufu), many millions of years earlier than our geologists have wrongly calculated and presently believe. Osiris knew how to use the mighty power of sound, chanted harmonies and intonations. Those huge stones, so perfectly aligned — through a power modern science ignores; therefore, an engineering feat modern science couldn't possibly achieve — were levitated into precise position by certain sounds or mantras, sung or chanted by Osiris and his Twin Self, Isis (her name contained within his), at intricately calculated astrological times, measured by particular alignments of the Sun, Moon and planets.

Some of the most wondrous sounds of the harmony of the Universe are the *sounds of silence,* and one of these is . . . dolphin talk. These beautiful creatures of the sea have been around for perhaps sixty million years (or longer) — enough Earth time to have accumulated a lot of wisdom. Dolphins make certain sounds, but it's their mental telepathy communication . . . the sound of their silence . . . that marine biologists of vision are trying so hard to decode. Dolphins can talk, but you have to converse with them in their own telepathic language. Some humans already have received their messages . . . . also some who were *nearly* human, shortly before they fully became so.

I'll explain what I mean. If you saw the motion picture *Star Trek IV,* you'll remember the scene where Spock swims underwater, in a tank holding a captive dolphin, and "talks to it." The dolphin talks back to Spock, who returns to Captain Kirk and translates for him what he's been told by the dolphin — which of course turns out to be quite true.

That was fiction, or science fiction, which always becomes reality in the future. But here's something that's definitely not fiction.

A friend of mine in California, who is also a friend of the man who makes the purple plates we'll learn about at the end of this chapter, and who has asked that his name not be used here because he's not quite ready to make his findings public, told me an amazing true story of dolphin experiments in Russia — some here in America, but very top secret.

You understand, I trust, that there are "white hats" and "black hats" in every government agency, whether it's our FBI and CIA or Russia's KGB. Whether in government or organized religion, there are the "good guys" and the "bad guys" and the "medium guys" or the "gray hats."

My friend, because of a friendship with a relative of a "white hat" Russian KGB agent, was able to obtain permission to enter that country and observe some of their dolphin experiments and their results. These are research projects in metaphysics and related subjects conducted in the Soviet Union far beyond those described in Sheila Ostrander and Lynn Schroeder's book, *Psychic Discoveries Behind the Iron Curtain.*

Only a small part of the dolphin sound experiment is this: Pregnant women are placed in the water each day of their pregnancy, with a dolphin. A marine biologist is present at all times for safety reasons. The woman remains in the water for fifteen to twenty minutes a day. During these visits, the dolphin communicates with the fetus. To be more exact — (because the fetus, as you will learn in Chapter 8, is not yet human, because the breath of life, its first breath, when the essentially water-breathing creature becomes an air-breathing creature, is when actual life begins) — to be more exact, the dolphin in some way, through that same life force energy connecting all living things Cleve Backster has observed, in some way programs a portion of the more than forty billion electric cells in the physical brain of the fetus during these prenatal visitations.

The infant is then delivered *underwater* (in a sterile tank without a dolphin, of course). All kinds of marvelous things occur when any infant is thus delivered, but this isn't the place to go into all of them. For one thing, it prevents improper breathing in this tiny human, and avoids the terribly damaging trauma of being born in the accepted way. These babies don't cry, and can sleep with their faces in water for minutes at a time for several weeks, gradually adjusting to breathing air. There is no fear and no fright in this kind of gentle birth, and it's recommended — only when an expert is in charge — for every birth.

These Russian infants, with whom a dolphin has communicated prenatally, or rather communicated with the brain cells of the fetus, become "super children." In every imaginable way. My friend attests to seeing with his own eyes one of these dolphin-programmed, born-underwater babies, who, at the age of twelve weeks, was walking and talking with the ease of an average three-year-old child.

Do you find this difficult to believe? A small Earthling is capable of these powers, even *without* dolphin communication — and how much *more* so with help from these wise ocean creatures. The CBS network program *Sixty Minutes* has already interviewed a young American boy of ten who is an amazing genius. When this child was only *seven weeks old*, he was talking, saying "hello" clearly to his father, and repeating other words distinctly a few weeks later. When he was only three and a half years old, instead of scribbling with crayons, he was reading biographies of Albert Einstein and Nikola Tesla.

The world is, indeed, full of wonders, in this dawning of the Age of Aquarius. My friend says that the Russian metaphysicians claim it's theoretically possible for a dolphin-trained child, by the time he is twelve years old, to be able to use his Third Eye as a laser beam and dematerialize or neutralize nuclear missiles in flight. Makes our War Department's Star Wars project seem impotent. It would be much cheaper and much safer to experiment with dolphin babies — in the cause of peace, would it not? There is no evidence that the Russians are experimenting for any cause other than peace. Indeed, the reason their psychic research has been so successful thus far is that the researchers well understand the universal laws governing such matters, and they couldn't have progressed this far with anything but a positive goal. Perhaps this is why it's been predicted that Russia will someday become "the most spiritual country in the world," eventually aligning itself with America in the struggle against negative forces threatening Earth's survival.

★ ★ ★ ★ ★ ★

Dolphins communicate with, as dolphin friend Jim Cummings has written, a rich and varied set of sounds — and "it seems they have also developed (or perhaps never abandoned) the ability to share information telepathically. . . . . . humans are now noticing that, when they quiet the endless verbal chatter echoing through their language-filled brains, there is a quieter, more universal mode of communication and knowing waiting to be tapped."

Some marvelous things are being accomplished regarding dolphins by Joan Ocean and Jean-Luc Bozzoli through their *Dolphin Connection,* in Laguna Beach, California.

Joan receives communications from the dolphins, some of which have been technical in nature, and which are passed on to scientists for interpretation and application. She is not alone. People in Colorado, California, Florida and Australia have reported messages from dolphins concerning social interactions, human history and music.

Joan has been taken for rides by dolphins, and expressed amazement at their incredible power combined with their sensitive and synchronized movements. Jean-Luc felt that the variety of sonar and audible vibrations filling the water was like "being in the middle of a concert."

As those involved with the *Dolphin Connection* have learned, simple people living in magic *can* make a difference. If you would like to contact these people, join their gentle efforts and be part of their dream for harmony on Earth, you may write to them in care of The Dolphin Connection — P.O. Box 4077, Laguna Beach, California 92652 — USA.

★ ★ ★ ★ ★ ★

I thought this a most unusual wish
to be part of a classroom in a school of fish
and decided you must be joking with me

but you said, quite seriously

I'm not joking at all
fish are wiser than most people surmise

is that what your secret assignment is ?
are you going to try to teach dolphins to talk ?

you looked straight into my eyes
when you replied

if I ever became friends with a dolphin
I would never presume to try to teach such a creature

more evolved than most humans could ever be
on the contrary, I would try to learn
all the levels of insight and depths of wisdom
a dolphin might be kind enough
                                    to share with *me*

train dolphins for secret missions ?
I'd prefer to train them how to remain free
that is . . . if I were ever to meet one
and the two of us
should happen to share a cup of tea

            then you smiled
            and changed the subject . . .

                                                    from *Gooberz*

★ ★ ★ ★ ★ ★

Felix Mendelssohn, the great-grandson of the composer, began experimenting with the power of sound because of his interest in the recognized phenomenon of the power of musical notes, when sung in certain keys. He knew, and was fascinated by the fact that, when a singer hits a particular note in a certain musical key, the sound thus sent into the ethers will instantly shatter a glass — each glass possessing its own individual vibratory frequency, which will respond only to the exact corresponding musical sound.

Every material object and each human being vibrates at an individual frequency of angstrom units per second, a measurement of light waves, as we learned in Chapter 3, "Gurus, Ghosts, and Avatars" — and will respond to that particular individual frequency produced by a sound, which is why you sometimes feel a tingle in the back of your neck when you're in a concert hall, listening to a symphony. Somewhere, within the chords and sounds filling the hall, you're hearing your personal frequency, just as a glass shatters in response to its very individual frequency sound.

Before there was Maria Callas, there was Rosa Ponselle. Even Maria herself called her "the greatest singer of all of us." Ponselle (1897–1981) possessed an incomparable voice. In 1954, RCA tried to record her at home in Baltimore, but her voice shattered more than a glass. It shattered all of RCA's equipment !

★★★★★★

Mendelssohn's research, conducted with his Third Eye wide open, led him to realize that the biblical account of Joshua and the crumbling of the walls of Jericho was literal, not symbolic. As he knew, and as everyone who's ever been in the Army knows, when a group of soldiers are marching "in time," rhythmically — left, right, left, right — toward a hastily constructed bridge, the Sergeant will call out a command to "Break step !" before the men actually reach the bridge, especially if it's a fragile one. Why ? Because the *rhythm* of all those feet, pounding the ground "in time" together, sets up a vibration that has the power to damage or destroy the bridge structure.

Mendelssohn then concluded that the armies led by Joshua approached the walls of Jericho "in step" together — thousands of feet pounding the ground in unified tempo — which produced a mighty and particular vibration in the Earth, so that when Joshua (who was metaphysically knowledgeable) then blew a particular note on the Ram's horn, the combination of marching feet in rhythm and the *individual frequency* note or tone of the wall structure sounded clearly on the Ram's horn caused the walls of Jericho to respond, and come "tumbling down," perfectly fulfilling a natural law of harmonics. How pleasingly appropriate that a descendant of a musical composer, a musical "Master," should have uncovered this truth of sound, as related to Joshua.

The same principle applies to the certain rhythmic sound frequency sacredly chanted by Osiris possessing the powerful energy to move even huge stones and rocks, levitating them into precise alignment in forming the Great Pyramid of Giza.

If science today refuses to heed the logic of Mendelssohn's discovery of why the walls of Jericho came tumbling down — or the logic of how the Pyramid was built by levitation caused by musical sounds and incantations — one might deduce that it's because these events happened so long ago, so far back in antiquity. But that doesn't explain why the natural magic of birdsong and the modern Eidophone are likewise ignored by the boys with microscopes, yardsticks, calculators and computers, who still can't grasp or comprehend the definite forms and radiations produced in the ethers by sound — even by (and perhaps especially by) our spoken words. One can only ordain that someone soon rips off the blindfolds and dark glasses of dogma they're wearing, or, at the rate present-day technology is going, we'll be blasted back into the Stone Age on the glorious wings of science before we've had a chance to experience the wonderland of the new, golden Age of Aquarius. There are positive signs that the needed miracle may occur in time Reading more or less between the lines of medical journals and scientific periodicals of the early 1980s, the hints are there that a few sleepy Third Eyes are being gradually awakened.

As I mentioned in an earlier chapter, we still possess the saving grace of the music of the "masters," directed into the minds of the great composers of the past, who were pure channels, born with a natural musical genius.

The reason for those stirring symphonies, operas, works like "The Messiah," the eternally uplifting music of Christmas carols and certain old church hymns being channeled was to guide material-minded humans along the path of gradual illumination, in a subtle, subliminal sense, through these very high frequency vibrations of sound. Thus far they've been successful in at least somewhat soothing savage humans, who need soothing more than the so-called "savage beasts." This form of enlightenment began during the Dark Ages, thanks to the sacred music of the Catholic Church, and increased during the lifetimes of men like Mozart, Albinoni, Bach, Brahms, Mendelssohn, Tchaikovsky, Puccini, Sibelius and a long list of others. The evolvement of Earthlings through the "music of the masters" was aided by the "art of the masters," as the Higher Powers used the artistic genius of painters like Rubens, Michelangelo, Rembrandt and Leonardo da Vinci to channel the harmonies of color and form into the human mind, along with the harmonies of sound, through music. Chording into the symphony of enlightenment came the poets, beginning with Shakespeare, and even earlier with Greek and Roman drama, who have been similarly channeled to shine the Light of the harmony of the rhythm and rhyming of words into the darkness on Earth.

Without these harmonic impressions on the ethers manifesting into the forms and patterns of music, art and poetry, the scientific and technological "advances" made by man would have long ago destroyed all life on this planet, as they currently threaten to do. But a threat is only a threat. The evidence that it won't result in annihilation is given in Chapter 5, "Numerology." Already, in 1987, a new Russian leader, Gorbachev, has emerged, giving every indication of a sincere attempt to reach across old misunderstandings — if only a genuine communion, based on a full recognition of the past mistakes of both sides can be realized before certain madmen's pet project of Star Wars is launched. Then maybe this latest nuclear insanity can be tossed back into a *Star Trek** script, where it belongs — an opinion shared by astrology's enemy, the nevertheless brilliant Scorpio astronomer, Carl Sagan, who may yet be illuminated to the message of *true* astrology, the mother (as he well knows) of astronomy.

Eagle Scorpio Sagan is aware that all the great so-called astronomers of the past, such as Johannes Kepler, Galileo, Copernicus, Newton and Tycho Brahe, builder of the first observatory in the western world — were astrologers, who had never even heard of the term

---

* Be patient, Trekkies. Count to ten. Wait.

"astronomy" in their lifetimes. True, Carl ? Maybe we can share a cup of peppermint tea and discuss it someday. I've ordained your conversion, so you haven't a chance ! Astrology needs minds like yours, and I congratulate you for going to jail for speaking out against nuclear testing.

Meanwhile, don't forget that it was Johannes Kepler, an indisputable genius, as you've recognized yourself, who wrote in his research notes that: "In me, Saturn and the Sun work together in their sextile aspect . . . to toil up mountains, to stumble over fields and rocky slopes . . . these things delight me. My destiny is similar; where others despair, money and fame come to me, though in modest measure . . . and I meet opposition . . . true astrology is a holy testimony to God's glorious works, and I, for one, do not wish to dishonor it." I suppose you've noticed that he qualified his assertion with the words "true astrology," Carl. That's the kind I just mentioned to you.

Regarding my suggestion of tossing the Star Wars concept back into a *Star Trek* script where it belongs, I hasten to assure my Trekkie readers that I adore *Star Trek* as much as you do, except for the violent wars that sometimes explode in space. I'm sure Captain Kirk agrees with me, not to mention Spock, who certainly has his odd-shaped head screwed on straight, and who needs those enormous ears so he can hear the sounds of silence in the cosmos, which vibrate to the pulsing colors and chords of Pax et Bonum on the higher frequency light waves to which Spock is so finely tuned. Eventually, he'll even pick up the even higher frequency of the emotion of love. Actually, he already has; he's just pretending not to hear. He's waiting for his Twin Self. Like I said, Spock's odd-shaped head is screwed on straight, and his heart, as large as his ears, is likewise properly aligned with the rest of him. He communicates with dolphins. He even writes poetry, and everyone knows one can't become a poet without vibrating to the harmonics of love.

It's just that Spock isn't turned on by all those mini-skirted space women batting their long, sweeping lashes on the *Enterprise*. I happen to know whereof I speak, since one of my personal Gurus (also the long-time Guru of *Star Trek* producer and writer, Gene Rodden-berry), Dr. Charles Arthur Musès, was the behind-the-scenes editor of some of those early *Star Treks* — and the seeder of important concepts dramatized in the series, such as the benign aliens in "Assignment Earth," a top favorite with true Trekkies.

Here's another fascinating example of the synchronicity and the harmonics of the Universe, covering all of the senses, including the sixth sense, color and sound, as well as just about every other known vibratory frequency. As far as I know, it's an experiment which has not yet been attempted or researched, but certainly one deserving of serious attention and study by New Age scientists.

Everything on Earth of a material nature has its origin in the planets. (This wasn't always so; it only commenced at a certain Time, but again, that's a subject for later books following this one. Each planet and each Luminary (Sun and Moon) vibrates to a particular corresponding number . . . the number to a color . . . the color to a mineral and a metal . . . to a flower . . . to a musical note or tone (same word in Lexigrams !) . . . and so forth. Each planet and each Lumi-nary possesses its own individual frequency pattern, even as you and I, the New York Public Library and every television or radio channel — even as your morning grapefruit — the refrigerator where it's kept cold for your breakfast — and all the glasses in your china closet. The dishes too.

The single frequency, increased tenfold, involved in the experi-ment initiates with one of the Luminaries (Sun-Moon) or planets, and since Mars is the one with which I'm most familiar, it being my own Sun Sign ruler, I'll use it to illustrate my example of this intriguing multiple vibration of a single frequency.

It works in a similar, but individual pattern involving color, mu-sical tone or note, gem, metal, herb, flower and so on, with the Sun, the Moon and other planets or stars. The word *planet* is an old Greek word meaning "wandering star" (planets wander, Fixed Stars do not) — so either term is correct, although modern popular usage is planet. I like star. Especially "wandering star."

Before I describe the experiment, I must regretfully (and somewhat uncomfortably) apologize to you for an error in my last two books, *Sun Signs* and *Love Signs,* in which I named the diamond as the gem vibrating to Mars-Aries — and the ruby (along with the onyx) as vibrating to Saturn-Capricorn. To admit an error is painful to Rams, but at least we're honest enough to do so directly, with no sneaking around. I relied on an ancient astrological work, which has proven to be reliable over the years in every way, except regarding this particular gem assignment, and my attention was called to the error not long ago by one of my Avatar-Adepts of impeccable authority, Dr. Charles Musès — so I have no choice but to blush, say I'm sincerely sorry, and correct the mistake here and now.

The truth is — the metaphysical fact is — that the diamond vibrates to Saturn-Capricorn, and the ruby vibrates to Mars-Aries.

Any Aries Ram can see why I accepted the mistake in that ancient tome, stating that the gem vibrating to the Mars frequency is the diamond. Because, you see, the diamond is "the hardest substance known to man," and we Rams do enjoy believing we're tough.

However, even a Ram has to admit that ice-cold, stoney-faced Old Man Saturn, ruler of Capricorn, is . . . well . . . tougher. But only in a material sense of substance ! A rock is a rock, after all. So, I submit, like a meek little white wooly lamb, to the superior esoteric wisdom of my Adept-Guru, and hereby surrender "my" diamond to stuffy grandpa Saturn.

The true gem of Mars is the ruby. The color is certainly logical. Oh, well, rubies are prettier than diamonds. Diamonds are too icy cold, with all that arctic glitter, right ? Rubies are warmer . . . even hotter !

But guess what, fellow Aries creatures ! Our Mars ruby is used in the laser, which is the *only* power capable of penetrating the "hardest substance known to man" — Old Man Saturn's diamond. Warrior Mars can break Saturn's icy resistance, shatter that Saturnine strictness and discipline with typical Martian aggressive penetration. So there ! Saturn didn't really win, after all. It's a draw.

Unfortunately, though, Saturn-Capricorn, with those blasted Goat's horns, still wins the final victory. It annoys me to confess that, speaking numerologically, Saturn vibrates to the number 8, while Mars vibrates to the life force number 9. And . . . when you add Saturn's double serpent circle 8 to the 9 of Mars, you get 17. Having already read the numerology chapter, you know what that means. We end up by adding the 1 and the 7 to get Saturn's 8 again. Curses ! Oh, well, he who is last shall be first, you know. Mars will win yet, you'll see.

At any rate, you can still use the onyx for Saturn, because it is definitely Saturn's secondary gem, after the . . . diamond. Finally, then, here is the Mars single frequency multiple vibration — (now that my former goof is, I trust, fully atoned for with my readers) — and I'll change the reference in my first two books at the earliest opportunity, I promise.

Mars vibrates to the number 9 — which vibrates to the frequency of the color crimson red — which vibrates to iron — which vibrates to the *powerful* (!) ruby — which vibrates to garlic and onion — which vibrates to the daisy — which vibrates to the day of the week, Tuesday — which vibrates to the month of April — which vibrates to the musical note or tone of C Major.

Now, supposedly and theoretically, if one gathered together nine Aries people, who were each born on a Tuesday, April 9 — and placed them in a room on a Tuesday, April 9 — all wearing solid crimson red clothing — with the walls and ceilings painted crimson red — red color filters on the lights in the room (red bulbs) — lots of daisies — plenty of garlic and onions (yuk !) — with a large bowl of . . . uh, rubies — (and security guards, I guess, outside the door of the room !) — and everyone also wearing . . . uh . . . rubies — with plenty of iron furniture in the room — and then, should the note of C Major be played on a musical instrument, such as a violin, and sustained for 27 seconds (adding to 9) — everyone in the room would instantly and simultaneously levitate. Right up to the ceiling !

The reason for such a theory of levitation is based on the great increase in intensity of that particular, individual, multiple-layered vibrational frequency. Harmonics again. It would be an interesting experiment, undeniably. Naturally, it would take some preliminary research, and some cooperation from Harry Winston or Tiffany's for the diamonds. Excuse me, I mean the rubies.

There are infinite demonstrations of the beautiful synchronicity of the Universe, flowing from the harmonics of color and sound and the pulsing rhythms thus set into motion, in every imaginable facet of life. There are discordant patterns, too, but fortunately, the sour notes in the symphony are minor, and more than balanced by the harmonious chords.

Even written words fall into individual harmonic patterns, sans the conscious awareness of the writer. Here's a computer statistic you may find worth a thought or two. (Computers are proving many harmonies and synchronicities of the world around us. Until humans realize that their brains are superior computers, the mechanical ones will continue to enlighten us.) Researchers have learned by computer count of the strange patterns of written words. One example is that the splendid and awesome vocabulary of Shakespeare extended to 29,060 words in his entire works. Yet just forty of them comprise fully forty percent of the text of all his plays. Imagine it ! Forty poor overworked words performing nearly fifty percent of a task that employs 29,060 workers. Doesn't that arouse your sympathy for those forty wretched words ? Or maybe they should be thought of as blessed, not cursed. "Many are called but few are chosen." With all this harmonic evidence, you'd almost believe that words are entities with minds of their own. After reading the following Lexigram chapter, I trust you'll more than "almost" believe it.

Here's another surprising symmetry discovered by computers, which are proving the truth of universal harmony until the human brain learns how to tackle it alone. A brilliant Harvard Professor with the curious name of George Kingsley Zipf (1902–1950) decided to turn to the computer to check the census population patterns of the fifty largest cities in the United States. He began with the year 1930, when the largest city was New York, as it still is, of course. The *second* largest city had *half* the population of New York. The *third* largest had *one-third* the population of New York . . . and so on, all the way down to the fiftieth largest city, which was, incredibly, *exactly* one-fiftieth the population of New York. A series like that: one half — one third — one fourth — one fifth — and so on, is called "harmonics" (appropriately).

From out of this and extensive further such research, was born what many computer researchers and experimenters call Zipf's Law. Zipf's Law has given evidence that any allocation of resources — whether it be human population, words in books, typewriters in stores, kindergarten teachers, video tapes or tools in a tool box — *will eventually settle down into a harmonic arrangement.*

That should certainly knock the stuffing out of anyone who still ridicules the law of harmony or disbelieves in the synchronicity of the Universe (theorized and written about by Dr. Carl Jung) and give the doubting Thomases a healthy respect for these invisible rhythms continually pulsing around us.

Meditating on all these wonders is excellent exercise for the Third Eye (the pineal gland) and helps to connect it to the pituitary gland, a union which then produces remarkable insight. Meditate on these magics as you fall asleep at night. Also, you'll find that, if you concentrate intensely on something — anything — at that floating moment between wakefulness and sleep (between the physical, material world and the astral realms) — when you awaken in the morning, the answer or the perfect solution to what you were wondering about or were concerned about as you fell asleep will flash into your mind, as clear as can be. Try it. It works.

All your Higher Self needs is an order from you to perform all manner of magic "tricks," in the same way as imaging mentally the exact time you want to awaken in the morning as you fall asleep (because you don't have an alarm clock) will code into your Higher Self (who can read time as clearly as you can with physical vision) — and cause Him or Her to waken you at precisely that time. I do that a lot. Haven't you ever tried it ? The effective technique is to image vividly the face of the clock, with the hands set at the time you want to be awakened. Your Higher Self, who sees even more clearly than you do with your physical eyes, will *see* when the clock hands point to that time, and gently, softly and surely awaken you.

Primary
Cell Perception

Another term for — another way of expressing the harmonics or the synchronicity of the Universe — is *The Oneness of the Universe*.

The Oneness of the Universe is what is being studied and observed by my friend and "big brother," Cleve Backster, of San Diego, California, formerly of New York. For a long time, orthodox science scoffed at Cleve's inspired experiments, because they involved matters (and non-matter) scientists couldn't see or hear or touch with their five senses. It's a rare scientist who has activated the sixth sense of sensitive intuition, leading to truth, although in Cleve, who is quite Spock-like, that sense has been finely tuned from the day he was born as a curious Pisces Fish. Finally, even the impeccably respectable, ultra-conservative American Association for the Advancement of Science (AAAS) has been forced to recognize his pioneer work in the field of cellular research, and has accurately, albeit somewhat reluctantly, called him "The Father of Primary Cell Perception."

When he was invited to address this august group in New York some years ago Cleve, with his subtle Neptune sense of humor (part of the sixth sense) told his audience of scientists, after being duly introduced as the Father of Primary Cell Perception, that "the way you people have been receiving my research, I feel more like its unwed mother."

First of all, since it's nothing to be ashamed of, but more likely something to be grateful for, it should be known at the outset that Cleve does not possess a degree, a Masters or a Doctorate in any of the scientific "disciplines." Although he studied civil engineering, agriculture and psychology at Texas University, Texas A&M and Vermont's Middlebury College, he lacks about one semester's credits for a Bachelors degree. However, he does possess a very high "degree" of sensitive perception, logic and common sense (which, of course, is not all that common).

When one's Third Eye is opened as widely and functioning as effectively as Backster's, orthodox higher education can be more of a hindrance than a help, in blocking clear thinking by restricting the imagination. In the same way that Abraham Lincoln became a lawyer, Cleve is mainly self-taught. Even without pursuing a Ph.D., one needs to master bushels of reading and study, but more true knowledge is gained when one studies what one is intensely interested in than from being forced to take courses of study for "credits" prescribed by others simply because this was the custom during the past decades in what was, quite literally, a completely different world. The Aquarian Age has changed all rules.

The majority of those who have discovered or invented concepts that speeded up the evolution of Earth didn't possess the sheepskin many people today consider a necessary insurance policy for career success. But being deprived of that big degree can turn out to be a big plus. Let's make that a Big Plus.

If he had not been "deprived" of a master's degree in whatever scientific "discipline," Cleve Backster, the father of primary cell perception, might never have sired this miracle "child" destined to change the basic thought process of cynical modern science — and that he is surely doing ! Then the scientists all over the world, not to mention you and me, would never have known that you can't cut your finger without it being felt and registered by the celery and brussels sprouts in your refrigerator, or more poetically . . . that "you can't touch a flower without trembling a star."

There's always a compensation for every apparent "curse," ready to turn it into a blessing. Like the old faerie tale. How could the handsome Prince have known the Princess truly loved him for himself, if a wicked spell hadn't transformed him into an ugly, warty toad, and she kissed him anyway, not even knowing that it was a temporary affliction ? Another "curse," which was, in reality, a blessing in disguise. Do I sound like Pollyanna ? Nothing wrong with that. Pollyanna had some very neat concepts of happy. I happen to consider this "degree or not degree" of importance to high-school graduates today, who, for financial reasons, have been unable to enroll in college. You "deprived" ones must remember that Alexander the Great had conquered the world by the time he was eighteen, and had never taken a single course in "conquering" !

Cleve Backster, who is now world recognized for challenging the scepticism of science regarding primary cell perception, began his research campaign in the early morning hours of February 2, 1966, Groundhog's Day (!), most appropriate for the elfin-eared Vulcanite who may be Spock in disguise, for all I know. (I accuse him of this periodically.)

Sitting in the New York lab of his Backster Research Foundation (now located in San Diego), Cleve was lost in one of his Neptunian reveries when he happened to glance at the large green plant in the corner of the lab, which was possibly carrying on a friendly conversation with him on whatever astral level he was mentally jogging around in at the moment. To be precise, the plant's true botanical name is *Dracaena massangeana*. Since it looked a little droopy to our sympathetic Fish, he decided to water it. On the way to do so, he suddenly wondered how long it would take the water to travel from the roots to the leaves, since it looked so desperately thirsty, so after he watered it he connected a pair of polygraph electrodes to one of the leaves, no doubt feeling foolish (an action one trained in scientific "disciplines" would never have been caught taking) — and waited to see if possibly the moisture might slowly and gradually change the plant's resistance level enough to register on the graph paper.

Bingo ! He was shocked (to the degree a Piscean can be shocked; it's hard to surprise them) to see an immediate reaction pattern from the now perkier plant that closely resembled the response of a human under emotional stimulation. Next he wondered, with mounting excitement and curiosity, if the plant would also produce on the graph paper a "human" response to a threat to its well-being and safety, and decided to try burning one of its leaves.

What happened then was most fortunate, because I frankly doubt if the tender-hearted Fish would have been able to carry through such a hurtful attack on his pet Dracaena to its conclusion. He didn't have to, because, before he could even locate a match — (he didn't have a lighter since he's a non-smoker, but a most tolerant one, not one of those paranoid, hysterical, non-smoking dictators) — before he could find a match — well, let's allow Cleve to tell it in his own words. "At the split second I had the image of fire in my mind, the recording pen went wild, and bounced right off the chart. It really shook me up."

It was clear that the plant had, in some manner, through a primary cell communication, perceived the threat to its safety. Since that historic Groundhog's Day, Cleve has carefully conducted hundreds of observations, as he calls them, in an intense and concerted effort to find more evidence of primary cell perception in, not only plant life, but fruits and vegetables, fresh eggs, mold cultures, yogurt, human blood cells, tissue samples and even spermatozoa.

Backster has demonstrated that house plants register visible apprehension when a dog passes by (perhaps at some time having been used as a fire hydrant by a careless canine ??) — and also receive signals from the dying cells in the drying blood of an accidentally cut finger. In fact, of equally vital significance regarding proof of the Synchronicity and Oneness of the Universe, they respond to distress signals issued in response to life threats against the cells of *any member of the living community*. Cleve has further discovered that the plants are able to receive signals from human thought communication over considerable distances. They have registered "pleasure" over Cleve's intent to return and water them when he was fifteen miles away at the time the thought image projected in his mind.

Images and feelings experienced individually by the plants and received by them from others don't consist of spoken words, of course. Naturally, they haven't taken a Berlitz language course, and don't comprehend words that say "one of your leaves is about to be burned" or "hang in there, I know you're thirsty, but water is on the way . . . P.S. I love you" — but when such actions are imaged in the mind by the one speaking the words, the translation into threat, comfort or love is swift and direct.

The reason Backster calls the phenomenon "primary" is that this perception applies to all the cells he has monitored, without regard to their individual assigned biological functions. He's discovered similar responses in the amoeba, the paramecium and all the other single-cell organisms he's tested. He's tried unsuccessfully to block the signals being exchanged by using a Faraday screen, screen cages and lead-lined containers. Still, the communication continues to flow without interruption — just as similar attempts to "block" the invisible communication between humans in esp experiments fail to have the slightest effect on the these "astral wave lengths." The conclusion reached by Cleve, with Spock-like understatement, is that "staggering as it may be to contemplate, there seems to be a life force signal connecting all of creation."

What is staggering today is "ho-hum" stuff tomorrow. Humans become inured to miracles so quickly. The once staggering discoveries of electricity, radio, telephones and television are about as exciting to humans today as playing a game of tic-tac-toe. You don't see anyone falling to his knees in ecstatic wonder when answering the phone, turning on the radio or switching on the TV and seeing the image appear "like magic" on the screen. People become bored with magic almost immediately after it manifests. But maybe that's what drives the human Spirit onward and upward . . . looking for new magic, questing for new miracles.

Some of Cleve's discoveries are amusing, but nonetheless of serious significance, such as the vegetable caper. Electrodes are attached to three different kinds of fresh vegetables. Then "someone" (not Cleve, he's too sympathetic to his new friends) — so someone else chooses one of the three vegetables to be dropped into boiling water, as restaurants do with those poor live lobsters. The one selected "faints" before it's even touched, the instant it's selected in the mind of the chooser — that is, it registers on the graph paper a sudden upward sweep, followed abruptly by a straight line indicating "unconsciousness." The other veggies continue their chart squiggles uninterrupted — until the unfortunate veggie is "boiled": then they respond with sympathetic agitation. Eggs also "faint" when it's been mentally decided to pick them up and break them — and they also register a "nervous" response when another egg is actually broken nearby.

This is certainly a comforting discovery to me, since I hate to put carrots in a juicer, slice a tomato, and so forth. Now I know they'll go into a sort of anesthetic coma as soon as they "realize" what's going to happen, and won't "feel" anything. Cleve believes one should notify the food in advance that it's about to become part of the food chain, so it can put itself into a protective and painless faint or coma, which is what the ancient Tibetan monks used to do: apologize aloud to the food before they prepared it or ate it. I hope those poor lobsters have time to faint before they're boiled alive.

While we're on the subject of "fainting," one afternoon Cleve was visited in the New York laboratory of his Backster Research Foundation, where he conducts all of his research, by a lady from a Canadian university, who was involved with "plant work" and botany. She was curious, and wanted to observe one of the plant demonstrations. Although Cleve dislikes this sort of thing, because he never knows what negativity and scepticism may be in the mind of the observer, capable of short-circuiting the demonstration, he courteously obliged, with some reservations.

At the appointed time the woman knocked on the door, Cleve invited her in and led her directly to the plants, where she sat down to watch. He then hooked up several of the plants to electrodes and waited. And waited. And waited. None of the plants was making even a "faint" tracing. The needles simply would not move on the graph paper. Feeling a combination of embarrassment, annoyance and puzzlement (he had never before seen a complete non-response like this), Cleve tinkered with the electrodes for a while, then finally gave up. The plants weren't "talking." They had cut off all communication, period. And that was that. If they had "fainted," he speculated to himself, it had to have happened before they were hooked up, probably at the instant the woman had knocked on the door . . . . and errant thoughts were floating through her mind. But . . . what kind of errant thoughts ? We shall soon see.

After a few minutes of polite shop talk Cleve asked his lady visitor exactly what type of work she did in her field at the university. "Mostly," she replied cheerfully, "I gather plants, then I take them to the lab, put them in the oven and bake them to get their dry weight." Mystery solved. The frightened plants had picked up, through the strange Morse Code of plant perception, that the "Wicked Witch of the North" had entered the lab, and might be planning to bake them into Brownies. So they "passed out" in a trembling combination of fear and self-defense. Immediately after the woman left the lab a concerned Cleve hurried back to his traumatized plants, and there they were, once again making their normal "tranquility" pattern on the graph paper, no longer taking a botanical Fifth Amendment ! Naturally, this is amusing, but it's also of serious importance. Plants can, indeed, absorb all manner of things in the emotional aura of humans who approach them.

As mentioned in the Preface, and also earlier in this chapter, the word **SIMULTANEOUS** contains the words **NO TIME** . . . and the energy force of communication behind cell perception obviously travels faster than the speed of light, since the plant responses are invariably "simultaneous" with the thought in the mind of the human or the trauma suffered by any living thing.

Backster has conducted so many hundreds of tests, demonstrations and observations, each one more exciting than the last, it's not possible to include a detailed description of all of them in this chapter. But here are a few more, explained briefly.

An unfertilized egg can respond with pulsations that coincide with *the heartbeat of a chick embryo,* regardless of the fact that the egg is unfertilized and that (as a double check of this) even under microscopic examination, the content of the egg shows no evidence of the beginnings of a physically evident cell division to account for the pulsations. More evidence that the male impregnation does not rule life, but that life itself is ruled by the feminine principle or essence, which possesses the subtle seed of future life, even before the male principle enters the picture. Also more evidence that material objects, things or people exist as an impression in the ethers before materialization into physical matter occurs through the use of higher energies. A rooster mating with a hen is only one of those energies . . . but the future event is already present in the feminine aura.

In his original published experiment, Cleve set up an automated device in a separate room near his laboratory that dumps cups of tiny brine shrimp into boiling water at random intervals. The plants attached to electrodes in his lab react with intense agitation on the graph paper at the very instant the tiny shrimp hit the boiling water.

Before giving you a final example of Backster's monitored observations, I'd like you to image his San Diego laboratory. It's full of creatures, from fish to electric eels, plants everywhere, television monitoring equipment, microscopes and glass aquariums, with a stuffed ET, the well-known extraterrestrial, overlooking the operations — a gift from me on a particular Groundhog's Day. One must tread carefully when walking around the lab to examine all the plant and other alchemy taking place there, because if one is not cautious, one might step on the large tortoise who crawls around lazily wherever and whenever it suits his fancy . . . sometimes playing peek-a-boo from his shell with his companion and playmate, Sam, Cleve's super-intelligent, rather arrogant Siamese cat. Every time I go there, those Lewis Carroll lines pop into my mind: "Would you walk a little faster ? said the whiting to the snail. There's a porpoise right behind me, and he's treading on my tail" . . . changing porpoise to tortoise, since Sam is continually teasing that poor creature with his tail, in various, inventive ways . . . and one of these days, tortoise is going to, perhaps not tread on it, but yank it into his shell. *Meow !*

Here's another Backster experiment, one of which Cleve isn't fond, and doesn't like to watch, but of great significance to the Oneness of the Universe.

Police officers and students from several states have observed this one: Six of the officers draw lots to determine who will be the "killer." The officer thus randomly selected then uproots one of two plants which have been "empathizing" next to one another for several weeks or months in the lab. The "killer" rips the leaves of the uprooted plant to shreds, and in other ways violently murders the poor green victim. A few hours later, five of the officers enter the room, one at a time, where the "witness plant" sits, attached to an electrode. The plant continues to trace its normal, individual pattern on the chart, showing no response. But when the officer who murdered the plant's friend enters the room the witness plant immediately reacts with a strong "agitation" response.

A police officer observing one of these demonstrations in the Backster lab scratched his head when it was over, and murmured, "Holy Moses ! Do you suppose that someday in the near future a man can be found guilty of murder in a court of law because of the testimony of a petunia ?" I'm afraid so, officer. This is the Aquarian Age. The witness plant would give the same response to a human being murdered before its "eyes," but naturally Cleve has no desire to conduct a test to prove it. However, homicide detectives, while they're gathering fingerprints from the scene of a crime, might consider glancing around to see if there are any plants in the room, then taking it or them to Backster's lab to be tested in the presence of any suspects, in a sort of "plant lineup." The results, although presently of no legal status, would at the very least be . . . interesting. The same thing would occur with a loved house plant witnessing child abuse or wife abuse. The possibilities are endless.

These are only a few examples of the observations of Backster's research, which range from shrimp and eggs to human blood cells and spermatozoa cells, all of which "recognize" their donors. If you'd like to know more about Cleve's work, it has been partially described in the fascinating book *The Secret Life of Plants* by Peter Tompkins and Christopher Bird, but will be more fully documented in depth, involving the interesting human sidelights, as well as the technical aspects of the research, in a book currently projected for publication in the near future.

Meanwhile, if you have a technician's mind and enjoy assimilating those long words of scientific terminology, you may obtain a copy of "Biocommunications Capability: Human Donors and In Vitro Leukocytes," material written by Backster and Stephen White, and presented by Cleve during several lectures from the Backster Research Foundation, Inc. — 861 Sixth Avenue — San Diego, California, 92101 — USA.

Action at a distance has been in the past attributed to gravitational forces originating with the Luminaries and the planets, and has been so ascribed correctly. However, Backster's primary cell perception research reveals that it is also a feature of a *non-material* field in which the gravitational field is localized by plant growth. The significance of the Backster Foundation research, which, despite its great strides, is in its infant stages, with thrilling worlds of discovery still ahead, is that it has established as a fact that plants are sentient, that they possess what can only be called "feelings."

Plants are creatures without nerves, and are therefore dependent on the auxins they manufacture to achieve growth, phototropism and wilting and such. Yet they have been shown by Cleve's testing to exhibit definite and sympathetic responses to the beneficent or malevolent events occurring to living cells, animals, humans and other plants in their vicinity — and at a distance.

Because plants lack "sense" organs, their responses to feelings cannot be defined as "sensory impressions." They must be defined as evidence of a life force field as yet unsuspected and unrecognized by orthodox scientists, but known for eons to metaphysicians. What, exactly, is this life force ? A chord of music, still unheard . . . a spectrum of color, still invisible . . . awaiting human discovery, but operating in perfect harmony until such discovery is made by Earthlings of good will.

Yale plant physiologist Dr. Arthur Galston has for years been an outspoken critic, not only of Cleve Backster's primary cell perception discoveries, but of the oneness of the Universe in all of its various facets, and has been quoted as calling these harmonies of communication "pernicious nonsense." The colorful, if somewhat vitriolic two word phrase somehow had the ring of a non sequitur to my inner ear when I first came across it. So I decided to turn to good old elf-father Webster again.

pernicious: causing great injury, destruction and ruin; deadly and fatal.
nonsense: absurd; a triviality possessing no relative importance or value.

— Webster, Noah

Dr. Galston, sir, with all due respect, how can something trivial, of no importance or value, kill, cause great injury, destruction and ruin, not to mention be deadly and fatal ? Poor man, we shouldn't be too harsh with him just because he hasn't mastered the proper use of the language. We all make mistakes. His excuse may be that he's just not well read. He's been too busy tinkering around with the organs of plants, and flying to conventions and seminars to squirt his sour grapes on the miraculous research of the Aquarian Age to take the time to browse through libraries of scientific journals with enough care.

If the good doctor had read my first book, *Sun Signs* (which is highly improbable), he would have learned about a number of fascinating discoveries that would have prepared him for the kind of revelations of Backster's research — such as the following.

For example, since Dr. Galston frequently ridicules astrology, in

1953 Dr. Frank A. Brown, Jr., of Northwestern University, made a startling discovery while he was experimenting with the "physiology" of some oysters. Orthodox science had always assumed (through Dr. Galston's "careful" methodology) that oysters open and close with the cycle of the tides of their birthplace. But when Dr. Brown's oysters were taken from the waters of Long Island Sound and placed in a tank of water in his Evanston, Illinois, laboratory, a strange pattern emerged.

Their new home was kept at an even temperature, and the room was illuminated with a steady, dim light. For two weeks, the displaced oysters opened and closed their shells to the same rhythm as the tides of Long Island Sound, one thousand miles away. Then they suddenly snapped shut, and remained that way for several hours.

Just as Dr. Brown and his research team were about to consider the case of the homesick oysters closed, an odd thing happened to Cleve Backster on that Groundhog's Day of 1966. The shells unexpectedly opened wide again, to Dr. Brown's shocked amazement and surprise (just like Backster's). Exactly four hours after the high tide at Long Island Sound — *at the precise moment when there would have been a high tide at Evanston, Illinois, if it were on the sea coast* — a new cycle began.

The oysters were adapting their rhythm to the new geographical latitude and longitude. By what force ? By the magnetic force of the Moon, of course. Dr. Brown finally had to conclude that "the oysters' energy cycles are ruled by the mysterious lunar signal that controls the tides."

Further, the late Harold Saxton Burr, emeritus Professor of Anatomy at Yale's Medical School, Dr. Galston's own alma mater, stated that "a complex magnetic field not only establishes the patterns of the human brain at birth [astrology, Dr. Galston] — but continues to regulate and control it through life." Dr. Burr stated that "the human central nervous system is a superb receptor of electromagnetic energies, the finest in Nature."

We may walk to a fancier step, but we hear the same drummer as the oysters . . . and the plants. Skipping from astrology to plants (a very short distance), your Dr. Burr not only recognized that the 42 billion cells in our brains form a myriad of possible circuits through which electricity can channel, he also, among his many research projects undertaken with an open mind and a most active Third Eye, made a ten-year continuous chart recording of the electrical potential activity exhibited by a *tree*, Dr. Galston — with amazing results, which were neither pernicious nor nonsense.

Then, too, there was the Indian scientist, Sir Jagadis Chandra Bose, who adhered meticulously to Galston's sacred scientific methodology, and used extremely sophisticated instrumentation in his experiments with plant life. He did everything strictly by Galston's rule book, and his results were essentially the same as Backster's, causing Sir Bose to state with absolute certainty that "plants definitely do experience an equivalent of emotions" — the pernicious little rascals.

North - South
Power Points

★ ★ ★ ★ ★ ★

One of the facets of universal synchronicity, a striking evidence of the harmony of the Universe, is the North-South mystery. I initially learned about it on a spring morning on West Fifty-Seventh Street, when I met my first Adept in 1963, who was at the time disguised as a meek and mild employee of the *New York Times*. (Remember, in Chapter 3 I told you that all Gurus have a "cover" that helps to keep private their true identity.) I tried the experiments he suggested, and was never disappointed.

After several months of pondering the awe of it, I located a book published in India at the turn of the century that explained the basis of the North-South mystery — and a couple of years later, Joe Goodavage published his marvelous book, *Astrology, the Space Age Science,* and I was pleased to note that he, too, was aware of this magical harmony of polarity.

Although what I was first taught about the North-South mystery was later supported by the Hatha Yoga book published in India, Goodavage's occult classic and a number of other metaphysical tomes I've since come across, I'll always remember best the excitement I felt on that enchanted morning when my beloved "first Guru" revealed his secrets to me.

Most of you, I imagine, already know that water runs down the drain in a clockwise direction in the Northern Hemisphere — and in a counter-clockwise direction in the Southern Hemisphere. *Conversely,* hurricanes and tornados in the Northern Hemisphere swirl in a counter-clockwise motion, while in the Southern Hemisphere, they swirl in a clockwise motion — exactly the opposite of the Northern-Southern Hemisphere directions water takes when flowing down the drain.

Astrologers chart the course of the planets correctly in a counterclockwise direction on the astrological wheel or circle, while they recognize (as do astronomers) that the "Ages" (Age of Pisces, Age of Aquarius and so forth) move in a clockwise direction. What did someone write in the Christian Bible about "wheels within wheels"?

This is all part of the harmony of a functioning Universe, and nothing can interrupt it or interfere with it — except one thing, as we'll soon learn. How does this inflexible law affect mundane events on Earth, and in what way does it affect you, as an individual? Magnetically. And more importantly than any other than a few Initiates suspect.

Universal Law states that, in the Northern Hemisphere, the North always has been and always shall be dominant over the South. When an opposition or a conflict occurs between them, the North will always win — or there will be a draw or a tie, so that *no one wins.* But in any event, the South cannot dominate or be victorious over the North.

In the Southern Hemisphere, the law is polarized — that is, opposite in its effect. In the Southern Hemisphere, the South always has and always shall be dominant over the North. When an opposition or a conflict occurs between them, the South will always win — or there will be a draw or a tie, so that *no one wins.* But in any event, the North cannot dominate or be victorious over the South — in the Southern Hemisphere.

In the final analysis, however, the North is superior, in a universal sense, because when an opposition or conflict occurs *between the Northern Hemisphere and the Southern Hemisphere, the North will carry the dominant vibration and be victorious — or the outcome will be "a draw" and neither Hemisphere will win.*

As evidence of the latter portion of this North-South polarity law, no civilization has ever originated in the Southern Hemisphere; they have all originated in the Northern Hemisphere. Every modern nation existing today south of the equator was originally founded by people from the Northern Hemisphere. This dominance of the North (in the Northern Hemisphere) and the South (in the Southern Hemisphere) — and the final dominance of the North over the South *between* the two Hemispheres — is manifested in every macroscopic and microscopic way among cities, states, nations and individual humans, in relation to opposition or conflict — from wars to personal arguments and debates.

Let's examine more evidence of this inflexible Universal Law of harmony. The Civil War. America's War Between the States. Although there may be a few die-hard rebels who secretly still sing "Save Your Confederate Money, Boys, the South Will Rise Again" (written by my friend, "Hank" Fort, a southern woman) — it can't happen. The South lost, the North won, and the outcome was decided before the war even broke out.

The religious or occult "Gurus" of the Oriental countries are well aware of this polarity law. Our present-day American leaders' ignorance of the Law is why, when there was no genuine difference between the politics of north and south Korea or Viet Nam, the United States of America was maneuvered and manipulated into fighting on the side of *South* Korea and *South* Viet Nam — and thus the "mightiest nation in the world" was humiliated by being unable to be victorious over North Korea or North Viet Nam — our defeat decided, as with the fate of the rebels in the Civil War, before the conflict ever arose. If our current political leaders would open their Third Eyes and become initiated to esoteric truth, as were our founding fathers, and stop ridiculing everything metaphysical as "pernicious nonsense," like our soon-to-be-converted Dr. Arthur Galston, these defeats need not occur. Better yet, conflict would cease, replaced by Peace, should they become fully illuminated.

As Goodavage has pointed out, spiritual enlightenment moves eastward, and civilization moves westward on the terrestrial sphere. As for dominance, if the borders of two nations occupy the same general latitudes, then the polarity law of whichever hemisphere applies to the *capital city* of the nations or countries thus geographically located.

In the Northern Hemisphere, China maintains dominance over India, and unsuccessfully continues her rivalry with Russia, Peking being *north* of New Delhi, India — and *south* of Moscow; likewise south of Washington, D.C., as India is *south* of Peking, Moscow and Washington. However, since Moscow and Peking are both *north* of Washington, D.C., the United States will never achieve dominance (either political or spiritual) over China and Russia, until our capital is moved to Alaska, *north* of the capitals of these two countries.

France and Germany's great armies were strong and favored when they invaded Russia, and their defeat was attributed to adverse weather conditions. Rather, they were defeated by the North-South Universal Law of polarity, Russia being *north* of both nations. As for the mighty Russia, with millions of men to fight the few defenders of tiny Finland, the Soviet Union was unable to claim a victory over this small country *north* of her. The "great" Russian army could not defeat the Finns.

Meditate on these north-south polarities, and form your own conclusions. Nicaragua is *south* of Israel in the Northern Hemisphere, also south of the United States. However, the Contras are "all over the place," so the resolution of the conflict *within* this country is a rare, Free Will choice, assuming that other countries to the north mind their own business.

Still in the Northern Hemisphere, it should be important to world leaders that Tehran, the capital of Iran, is *north* of Baghdad, the capital of Iraq. Poor Cuba is south of all major powers in the Northern Hemisphere, and must, of necessity, align with either the United States or Russia. Fidel Castro tried the former alliance, with the result that our CIA, with their Organized Crime partners, tried to murder him in various ways, on several occasions. Even his enemies should be able to see the necessity and the logic in his then turning to the latter.

Castro possesses his fair share of faults and flaws (don't we all ?

Including some of our Presidents) — but on his last visit to the USA, he insisted on being taken to the Lincoln Memorial in Washington before being driven to his hotel, remaining there for nearly an hour, openly weeping. I can't fault the man for admiring and respecting Lincoln. Was it a publicity stunt? Perhaps. I have no way of knowing. Castro is certainly no "Honest Abe," but neither is he the devil incarnate, and his office walls are covered with photographs of Abraham Lincoln —not past Cuban leaders.

Speaking of Lincoln and publicity stunts, the annual Lincoln Day dinner in Lincoln's hometown of Springfield, Illinois, might very well fit that description. In reality, it's nothing more than a political platform for the media's sniffing out potential Presidential candidates. I was present at the 1986 Lincoln Day dinner. There were five hundred guests listening to the costumed Civil War band playing "Glory Alleluja" and applauding the passionate speeches about Lincoln's freeing of the slaves. Yet, in that huge hall, there were only two black faces visible in an ocean of white faces, seated up front near the stage, where the TV cameras could pan them. *Only two.*

But what can one expect from such "guardians and protectors" of the image of Abraham Lincoln as the city fathers and museum curators of Springfield, who have recently sanctioned the installation of *neon lighting* in Lincoln's home on Eighth Street? When I visited there, anticipating the experience of a trembling nostalgia, I wasn't sure whether I was in Abe and Mary's home or the Red Apple Supermarket.

If world leaders were more metaphysically oriented, they would find it meaningful and prophetic that the nation of Israel is *north* of Saudi Arabia — and that Tel Aviv is likewise *north* of Cairo, Egypt. Yet Tel Aviv is *south* of Beirut, capital of Lebanon — while Beirut is *north* of Cairo, Egypt. With these complex and intertwined examples of the North-South Universal Law of polarity, it's no wonder the fighting in the Middle East seems to be fated to go on forever . . . . until all of these nations realize that it's a no-win situation, and build a bridge of peace between one another, in a spirit of compromise and respect for the religious faiths of each.

In the Southern Hemisphere, under the reverse or opposite North-South polarity law (with the South superior or possessing dominance over the North), consider these geographical possibilities: while *south* of all *Northern* Hemisphere major powers, which it can therefore never defeat, South Africa is also *North* of New Zealand, and parts of Australia and Argentina, which, under the *reverse* Southern Hemisphere law of polarity, makes these countries also dominant over South Africa. Although the European nation of South Africa will never be conquered by any other African nation, it doesn't have a chance of winning a conflict with the major powers in the Northern Hemisphere, surely meaningful relative to current Northern Hemisphere world disapproval of Apartheid.

The United States has traditionally dominated Mexico, while Mexico in turn dominates its neighbors to the south, except those in the Southern Hemisphere, where the situation is reversed.

And what about Mexico's War of Independence with Spain, in which Mexico won its independence ? A Universal Law is never one-dimensional — there are several levels of intricate interpretation of "dominance" on rare occasions. Regarding this one — true, Spain is north of Mexico in the Northern Hemisphere, and should have been victorious, you might think. You would be mistaken.

First of all, wars of independence, as conflicts go, have a shade of different meaning. In the instance of this one, even though Spain was north of Mexico in the Northern Hemisphere, and therefore possessed (and still possesses) dominance over the country of Mexico, south of it - why was Mexico able to win independence ? The answer is that, although Mexico won her independence in this type of conflict, different from the conflict of other wars, where two *separate* nations (or people) are fighting — Mexico did not escape the *influence* of Spain.

Before the conflict of independence, Mexico was composed of several tribes of Mexican Indians, and an equal number of Mexican Indian dialects were spoken there. Since winning independence, Mexico has remained under the influence of Spain, in both a cultural and a political sense. And what language is spoken in Mexico today ? The language of Spain — Spanish. Now that Mexico is a separate country, should the kind of conflict of war between two *separate nations* ever break out, Spain would not fail to win — or there would be a draw or a tie, where neither nation would win. The North-South rule is only emphasized by this example.

Canada may well be the country of the future in the Northern Hemisphere. It hasn't yet fully developed its potential. Located north of the United States in the Northern Hemisphere, Canada has always come out ahead in various dealings with the United States, even though the latter is a more powerful and industrially more developed nation.

No, I haven't forgotten the midnight ride of Paul Revere, King George of England and that other George who froze his toes crossing the Delaware. Later.

How does the polarity law affect the average man and woman ? Strongly. So strongly that I, in fact, hesitated to expose this secret in print, for fear my readers would pick up on it, solve its riddle and carry through on the knowledge in all sorts of effective but bizarre ways. Does the law work, for instance, in courts of law ? Yes, it does. And so I had images of the attorneys for the Prosecution and Defense fighting over which of their legal teams got to sit in the *north* of the courtroom (guaranteeing either victory over the other side — or a tie or draw (a mis-trial ?) — and which of their legal teams had to be seated in the *south* of the courtroom, condemning them to losing their cases. Then there are the various nuances of whether the jury is seated to the north of the accused — or to the south of him, perhaps causing the defense attorneys to insist on moving the juror bench to the other side of the room. And where is the Judge himself seated, in relation to the person on trial ? Naturally, in this hemisphere, the prosecution would prefer the Judge to sit north of the accused — but if wishes were horses, beggars would ride, and the Judge will sit wherever he sits, period. Can you just imagine a Judge's response if he or she were to be requested by the Prosecution or Defense to move his bench to the other side of the courtroom ? Horrors ! A scene straight out of Gilbert and Sullivan.

The part of the foregoing related to the north-south seating position in the courtroom of the Prosecution and Defense is no joke, and would exercise an absolute influence over the outcome of a trial. But I finally stopped worrying about causing such confusion by realizing that because so few attorneys are even near the state of mind to open their Third Eyes, most lawyers being light years away from illumination, there wouldn't be enough of a problem created to be concerned about.

The same rule applies to corporate Boards of Directors. They don't realize the importance of their seating position. And Congress. The House of Representatives. Private and personal meetings between our American Presidents and the Heads of other World Powers. If only they comprehended how vital the north-south seating position is in whichever hemisphere peace conferences take place — it would make a whole universe of difference to the outcome.

Further, our American Presidents might consider that, of all the world leaders with whom they meet, those from China and Russia might well have selected their seating positions beforehand during past conferences. China, because the Orientals are well aware of the polarity law, whether they wish to acknowledge it openly or not — and Russia, because the Soviet Union has long been conducting extensive research into metaphysical and esoteric matters, and is considerably ahead of the United States in such experimentation, because its leaders realize that technology can be made impotent by a Higher Law put into practice. In conclusion, our Presidents should be wary of where they sit down, when it comes to meetings important to world peace and world survival. The First Lady might want to tuck a compass in the President's overnight bag when he next flies to one of those conferences. It's far more important than a few clean shirts and socks.

The law works with equal strength in your own living room, an office or a friend's house — any place at all. Believe me, I've tried it hundreds of times, with both strangers and those very close to me. When I've had either a mild or serious difference of opinion with any of them, I try to sit North of him — or her — and when I've been able to accomplish this, I've always won the dispute, or else it's left at a draw, and the other person eventually comes around to my point of view. However, those times when I've been unable to manipulate my position, and have been forced to debate from a position south of the person who is giving me "a hard time" over some matter, I always lose — or at least, I never win. Once again I'll emphasize that, although this may sound amusing, it's nevertheless very serious and very real.

I can imagine, when this book is published, all the married couples fighting for the north chair or couch position — not to mention which one sleeps on the north or south side of the bed at night, relative to the position of the spouse or lover. I may seem to be discussing all this in a humorous way, but it's as serious as anything can be, and don't forget that. If you take all this as only humor, you'll regret it!

Now let's analyze the Revolutionary War with England, our "mother country." Both the United States and England are, of course, in the Northern Hemisphere. London is north of, not only our capital, Washington, D.C., but also Boston, Philadelphia and Plymouth Rock. So what happened here ? We won our independence from England, and we also won the infamous War of 1812 with Great Britain. Are we immune to this powerful and inflexible Universal Law of North-South dominance ? Yes, we are. Does that surprise you ?

To begin with, the real America was owned by our American Indian brothers and sisters. Following the North-South polarity law, they unfortunately but naturally lost the country to a handful of English people and a few Frenchmen who came over here and literally stole America from its rightful owners, accomplished through several brutal and violent wars with the red men — because London is *north* of America. The outcome could have been no different. In this case — of the American Indians losing their proud country to the English — the law was humming harmoniously, even though it may have sounded like sour notes and discordant chords to the unfortunate Indians.

Present-day descendants of those brave Indians may wonder why the shameful way they were robbed of their country was permitted by any kind of universal law or harmony, if the word "harmony" is synonymous with the word "peace." It's understandable that they should question the justice of such a law.

Could it be that the Higher Selves of both the American Indians and the Higher Selves of those English-born soldiers who fought them had a larger law in mind — that these Higher Selves of both sides knew the future of America, and knew that it was in the hands of a few Adepts and Avatars with the most glorious dream since the original dream in Eden ?

America's future was certainly in the hands of such as these. George Washington, Thomas Jefferson, Benjamin Franklin, John Adams and other framers of our Constitution were (are you listening, Carl Sagan and Arthur Galston ?) — *astrologers*. They were Rosicrucians and Masons of high degree — all of them, including Lafayette. They chose the birthday of the United States of America by astrology, and were guided by profound occult mysteries in the designing of her Great Seal.

The shimmering dream of these founding fathers of America, these framers of the Constitution and the Declaration of Independence . . . . was not a fragile one. Their dream possessed unlimited and infinite strength — the great power to *shatter for the first time* the inflexible North-South Universal Law, a permission given by our

Creators once an eon or so, for the greater goal of Love and Peace on Earth. Did not Moses "break the law" (of physics) by parting the Red Sea ?

No other nation, no other country since the very Beginning of Time on this Earth has possessed the power to so completely break the Universal Law of North-South polarity. Only America, in her separation from England and her subsequent war with Britain, fought in 1812 — winning — victorious both times, regardless of being geographically located in the Northern Hemisphere's "loser's position," south of the conflict.

America possessed such power because no other nation, no other country since the Beginning of Time on this Earth has been founded on such principles as the United States of America.

Abraham Lincoln, America's visionary and ultrasensitive leader, believed by metaphysicians to have been one of the fourteen soul pieces of Osiris, knew this esoteric secret. Lincoln's voice trembled when he spoke, in Gettysburg, those ringing words: "Fourscore and seven years ago our fathers brought forth on this continent a new nation, conceived in liberty and dedicated to the proposition that *all men are created equal*. Now we are engaged in a great civil war, testing whether that nation or *any nation so conceived and so dedicated* can long endure."

Yes. Lincoln knew the cosmic importance of not allowing this nation "of the people, by the people, for the people" to perish from the Earth.

Our Constitution, with its guarantee of freedom of speech and freedom of religion, is unlike any Constitution of any other nation ever founded on the Earth. Even more importantly, it's the only completely un-ethnic country in the world.

There's no such thing as an American, in the way that there are Frenchmen, Italians, Germans, Russians, Japanese and so on. Other countries, other nations *accept* immigrants, but immigrants *are* America. There are no other kinds of Americans.

Americans are Indians (both kinds, from India and our red brothers and sisters). Americans are French, Irish, Scottish, Welsh, Russian, English, Italian, German, Cuban, Mexican, Spanish, Chinese, Japanese, Swiss, Australian, Finnish, Polish, Yugoslavian, Eskimo . . . and every other ethnic group on the Earth.

Never before has there been a country founded on the dream of being home *to every man and woman, every single Earthling,* regardless of nationality, race, faith, creed or color. The dream of our founding fathers was to establish a nation to test the great ideal of brotherhood and sisterhood of *all races,* working together *as one.* Our Creators smiled upon this courageous dream of all-embracing good will and individual freedom, and protected it from subjugation to the universal Law of North-South polarity.

The United States is still being divinely protected because of this original dream. Never mind the Teapot Dome scandal, Watergate and Irangate. So-called saints and saints of nations are continually being soul-tested. We are still the only country in the entire world where both clear-thinking men and women and misguided thinkers can speak their minds and say whatever they wish — either for or against our government — as can the media spokesmen and spokeswomen. America will continue to be divinely protected, *as long as our First Amendment, guaranteeing Freedom of Speech* remains intact. To keep it so is worth putting up with all manner of printed and spoken ugliness to protect that First Amendment. And it's worth remembering Voltaire's ringing declaration, "I may disapprove of what you say but I will defend to the death your right to say it."

Playing Musical Eagles

★ ★ ★ ★ ★ ★

As we've learned from the singular exception to the North-South law, America is a mystical nation, which was the intention of our founding fathers, the colonial Freemasons, Rosicrucians and astrologers, who perceived the harmonies of the Universe around them, and based their dream for America on esoteric codes, patterned on the harmony of astrology and numerology.

The birth chart of the United States was carefully chosen to give this newborn nation the Cancerian Sun Sign of its chosen birth date of July 4, 1776, for the purpose of instilling the cultural and historic traditions inherent in the Moon-ruled sign of Cancer. The birth date chosen by these "wise men" was one with the ruler of its Cancer Sun Sign, the Moon, in the astrological sign of Aquarius, blessing America with Aquarian ideals of tolerance, brotherhood and sisterhood, a strain of genius and the progressive, intuitive qualities of Aquarius. The Moon rules the emotions. In this way did our forefathers plan that the emotions of America's people would mature in time to match the powerful vibrations of the approaching Aquarian Age they knew, as astrologers, would be the next Age on Earth — so that America might lead the world in Truth and Light during the new Golden Age.

They selected a birth chart having that Aquarian Moon harmoniously training the nation's Ascendent — Gemini. The Gemini Ascendent (or rising sign) was astrologically selected to give America versatility, intelligence, adaptability to change and eloquence of speech. However, because a country possesses the same Free Will as individuals, we have unfortunately chosen in the past to use our Gemini Ascendent in its negative vibration of deception, with typical Gemini, Mercury-ruled glibness, talking "out of two sides of our mouth at once," by preaching equality, while denying first women and then our black citizens the right to vote.

The sign of Aquarius on the ninth house of religion graced America with a Uranus-seeded tolerance toward the many different faiths of her people. The sign of Pisces ruling America's tenth house has caused us to be led by "fathers" or Presidents who have been alternately compassionate, spiritual — and deceptive. We've had a couple of the latter type recently. Yet we've also had our spiritual Presidents. Since our first, George Washington, was a Piscean, this synchronized with our country's nativity in the beginning. "Cancer Cares" is a common and ancient astrological adage, referring to the "Jewish mother" essence of the sign Cancer. Cancerian America started the "Care Packages," and we continue to symbolically feed the world chicken soup. Our money system reflects our Cancerian love for financial security, but that Gemini Ascendent and Aquarian Moon caused America to go into debt. Like any Cancerian, America's image to the world is moody, changing from depression to humor . . . always hinting at the keeping of secrets . . . then the Gemini Ascendent starts talking . . . and it all hangs out.

The mystical philosophers who founded America, those illuminated forefathers of our country also designed the Great Seal of the United States on the same metaphysical principles, and it hides certain mysteries of America's spiritual heritage. Its designers believed that, by the time of the Aquarian Age, all Americans would have become evolved to the point of comprehending its secrets and, indeed, we are currently seeing an upsurge of matters mystical. (The Great Seal is reproduced on the American one-dollar bill.)

There are several books available which tell of various facets of the mystical meanings of our Great Seal, including the Goodavage book — but not all of these works agree on every small detail. Another source for information is a reprint from the Spring 1952 issue of a magazine called *Egypt,* available from the United States Treasury Department.

Have you ever wondered why the Great Seal of the United States features an Egyptian Pyramid, topped by a mysterious Eye ? Before you can understand this secret code, you should know that there are three kinds of Karma. In a layered sense, each Earthling lives within

these three karmic influences: (a) Individual, personal Karma, (b) National Karma and (c) Ethnic or Racial Karma.

Translating the codes of the Great Seal, the Pyramid and the symbolic Eye represent that America is living the Karma of ancient Atlantis, buried on the floor of the Pacific Ocean, awaiting discovery. It was Isis who, long after the murder of Osiris, passed on his principles of ideal government to the founders of Atlantis. America is the reincarnated Atlantis, which itself was the reincarnated Egypt of many eons ago, when it was ruled over by Isis and Osiris.

What has been called by some the "mystical eye" at the top of the Pyramid on the reverse side of the Seal, represents the *Eye of Horus,* usually drawn as ... but it was decided by our forefathers, who designed it, that this rendition would be too occult for the general, as yet unilluminated public, and so it was rendered as "an ordinary eye," which only made it more of an enigma, since an ordinary eye has no historical precedent with any genuine mystical relevance.

Horus was the son of Isis and Osiris, whose tragic tale I will be relating with other "twelfth night secrets" in a later work. According to the "Elder Brothers" of wisdom presently on Earth, the High Priests and High Priestesses of Atlantis, who failed to warn the people in time to prevent the natural cataclysms that caused the Great Flood, have reincarnated in the Aquarian Age, so that they might have a second chance to warn the people — to teach them the precepts necessary to avoid an encore of the Atlantis tragedy — the star sign codes of ancient wisdom holding the keys to illumination.

The Pyramid and Eye of Horus is on the reverse side of the Seal. On the front side is the familiar American Eagle, adopted as a symbol of America by an Act of Congress in June of 1782. The Eagle is another echo or reflection of Horus, who is pictured in a number of Egyptian hieroglyphics as having the head of a Falcon, belonging to the Raptor or Eagle family.

It is also the symbol of Scorpio, the higher essence of Scorpio — the lower levels being the Grey Lizard and the stinging Scorpion. (This entire triune of Scorpio is symbolized by the Serpent of Wisdom, eating its own tail.) The Horus Scorpio Eagle further represents the Egyptian Phoenix, the mystical bird with the power of rising from its own ashes, the esoteric code for both reincarnation and immortality, another reminder that America is living the Karma of Atlantis.

The name **HORUS**, when you re-*verse* two letters (writing a new verse or poem), becomes **HOURS**, which is why Horus, in the secret teachings, is the Master of Eternity, the ruler of the Eternal Now or Higher Dimension of Time, this occult mystery sometimes written for us in initialed code as $\mathcal{MOE}\mathcal{A}$ capped by the Pyramid.

The numerological value of Horus is 23. Study its meaning on page 259. Osiris is a 17 — and Isis is the single number 8, the double serpent symbol of the snake eating its own tail, representing Eternity and Immortality. The 17 of Osiris also reduces to the single number 8. As we learned in Chapter 5, the number 8 is the number of Saturn — and reincarnation is ruled by Saturn and Pluto, the latter being the ruling planet of Scorpio. The numbers of Isis and Osiris together equal 16 ("fall from a high place"), which reduces to 7, the spiritual number (Chapter 5).

The next planet to be discovered will eventually be called Vulcan, the lame *goddess* of thunder, as Vulcan is a feminine planet, the true ruler of Virgo. Following this, the planet Pan-Horus, true ruler of Taurus, which will herald the Earth's understanding of the Eternal Now, placing all Earthlings in a Higher Dimension of Time, including gravitation — and the control of it.

There are two schools of prognostication regarding these two planets or "wandering stars." The other school claims and predicts that the discoveries will be made in reverse order, with Pan-Horus discovered first, then Vulcan. Since neither sighting has occurred, and being a strong advocate of Free Will choice to be mistaken or correct, I firmly cast my personal vote for Vulcan first, and *then* Pan-Horus. Any Taureans want to wager with me ? I promise to be a gracious loser — *or* a generous and humble winner.

The Eagle (representing America in the Great Seal) supports the shield, this code intended to convey that our forefathers intended America to be strong in defending herself, yet always ready to defend and support less fortunate nations and peoples.

The *E Pluribus Unum* legend written across the ribbon in the Eagle's beak — *Out of Many, One* — does not refer only to the single nation formed of thirteen colonies, as many people believe. The esoteric code of this phrase is that the original dream of America was that those concepts upon which she was founded would eventually spread to include all nations — and thus unify them into One.

The arrows of defense against attack clutched in the Eagle's left talon have too often over the past decades been distorted to mean war when war was not necessary, a prostitution of their original symbolism; and they are also prophetic of the necessity of the Civil War to hold the center together — a necessity successfully accomplished, but also profoundly regretted by Lincoln.

It's most important to note that the American Eagle's head is facing toward the Eagle's right, toward the right talon holding the olive branch of Peace.

The shining cloud above the Eagle's head, emblazoned with thirteen stars representing the original thirteen States, was meant to symbolize several things, but none so meaningful as its coded message of being what our forefathers saw as "The Crown of Countless Ages," the reincarnation of an eternal ideal, one possessing the power to break the Universal Law of North-South polarity . . . the same ideal (although with even more layers of truth and love) held in the beginning by the founders of the Lost Continent of Atlantis, before the Free Will choice of that once fair land and its people led to its tragic inundation.

If you've carefully studied the sections concerning numerology in

Chapter 5 you may be able to guess the reason for and the importance of the repetition of the Compound Number 13 on both the front and reverse sides of the Great Seal. Notice how many repeats there are of 13.

There are thirteen stars in the circular glow of the life-giving Sun above the Eagle's head. The total number of stripes on the Eagle's shield is thirteen, representing, again, the original thirteen colonies. The olive branch of Peace clutched in the Eagle's right talon contains thirteen branches and thirteen berries. There are thirteen arrows clutched in the Eagle's left talon — and thirteen letters in the legend *E Pluribus Unum*. All of these repetitions of the number 13 are seen on the front side of the seal.

On the reverse side there are thirteen layers of stone in the *un-finished* Pyramid. Can you guess why it was left unfinished in this image designed by the mystics who founded America ? The legend *Annuit Coeptis* contains thirteen letters. The correct interpretation of these two words is *The Divine Hath Smiled Upon Our Undertaking*.

The printed words across the ribbon banner beneath the Pyramid, *Novus Ordo Seclorum*, mean *The New Order of the Ages*. Leaving the number 13 for just a moment, the numerological value of Novo Ordo Seclorum is 17 (you may read its meaning on page 255) — the *same* Compound Number possessed by Osiris, whose ideals and teaching of perfect government comprise, in reality, what our founders meant by *The New Order of the Ages*.

Back to the number 13. First, read the meaning of this myste-rious number on page 251. Next, read in that same Chapter 5 the section concerning the Compound Number 12, which also explains further the number 13, beginning on page 251.

Another layered meaning of the intent to repeat thirteen so often in our Great Seal is that our founding fathers traced the American dream and birthright, as astrologer Nora Forrest knew, back to — not the well-known twelve tribes of Israel — but to the lesser-known thirteenth tribe of Israel, of which Mannaseh was the leader. Also, General George Washington and twelve of his generals were Freemasons, and therefore numbered thirteen. "To those who understand the number thirteen are given great power and dominion."

The final power of 13 was manifested when America's Declaration of Independence was signed at the hour when the Sun was deposited at exactly thirteen degrees of Cancer.

Another secret code in addition to "adaptability to change" is behind the selection of a Gemini Ascendent for America's birth chart. Gemini is a dual or double sign, meant to symbolize the day when Americans shall have spiraled into the illumination of realizing that matter and energy are inseparable polarities of the same reality. (Two are one.) When we approach this great truth scientifically as well as spiritually, as Cleve Backster's work is gently teaching us, we shall be well on the way to becoming immortals. (See Chapter 9.)

The dark forces on Earth are not lazy; they're always hard at work, under the adage that "light attracts the darkness." Twice, in 1792 and 1884, Congress tried to pass a law to omit the reverse, Pyramid side of the Great Seal, because it was an enigma to the unenlightened. By 1884, America's leaders didn't have a clue as to why our forefathers had designed an image with such metaphysical and Egyptian undertones. After all, what relationship could there possibly be between Egypt and the United States? To some of them, it was downright embarrassing. Especially when they couldn't explain it or decode its message. But Divine protection prevailed, and for reasons now forgotten, such a law was never fulfilled, and today America has the only two-sided official Seal in existence.

The Great Seal of the United States of America, the "new Atlantis," contains all the heraldry, drama and esoteric mystery of the American dream conceived by Masters of astrology and numerology, bearing a profound occult significance, which has left a deep impression on our national character, even without either our present leaders or the American people being consciously aware of it.

Purple Plates
for
Purple Leprechauns

We've already learned that each material object and each human being vibrates to an individual frequency of angstrom units (light waves) per second. This is the life force energy responsible for universal harmony and synchronicity . . . the forgotten rainbows and forgotten melodies creating the Oneness of the Universe established by Cleve Backster's Primary Cell Perception discoveries. In India this life force energy is called Prana, but whatever it's called you could not live without it, and at present you're using only a fraction of its power.

Your third dimensional mind can use it to tune into the fourth dimensional cosmic consciousness (your Higher Self) . . . allowing you to "see the Light" . . . to become in tune with the harmony of the Universe, for within these colors and chords all magic is conceived, all miracles are born. There are many ways to tune in. Not just one or two. Many.

One of them is an Aquarian Age, Tesla-inspired discovery I call "the purple plates," for want of a better term. These plates have been channeled to Earth from the higher realms, through the mind and brain of a man who knew Nikola Tesla, and has studied his discoveries in depth, but who prefers to remain anonymous, as do many Cancerians of profound insight.

These anodized aluminum plates are created in two sizes, one measuring approximately three inches by five inches and the other measuring approximately eleven inches by eleven inches. Just one of the smaller plates will create mountains of magic, but I find it useful to have both sizes, for various purposes. The plates have been anodized with the color Violet, which is the healing ray of the rainbow spectrum. Their atomic structure has been altered, so that they are in resonance with a high-frequency vibration of the life energy force, in a complex way, connected with the known energy of negative ions. The "purple energy plates" (my own personal name for them) possess a field of energy capable of penetrating any living thing — plant, animal or human.

The life force energy, or Prana, can be measured in several ways.

One of them is through radionic equipment. Using this measurement, the energy level of an individual man or woman not yet fully illuminated might register, say, 20 on the scale. When this person is handed a purple plate the reading will instantly increase to 90 or 95. It won't remain at that level, but continual use of the plate will gradually bring the person's energy to 100 permanently. Enlightenment. And higher than 100, since the life force energy cannot be completely measured by any device presently known. And so, the use of this New Age "magic" will eventually raise your frequency rate of angstrom units per second, which is of obvious benefit to your spiritual evolvement, as well as your path toward cell regeneration (see Chapter 9).

Precisely how the plates work should not be of as much concern to you as what they can do for you. There are so many mini-miracles the plates accomplish (some of which you'll discover for yourself) it's difficult to detail all of them. Here are just a few.

First and foremost, the plates will slowly but very surely raise the vibratory frequency of those who use them, and that's of prime importance. They will reduce the negative vibrations in food, water, other liquids and tobacco. Many people who own them place their food on the larger size plates, while it's still in the shopping bag from the market, for about fifteen minutes. Travelers often find that the water in a foreign country makes them ill, but it won't if the water is energized on a purple plate for two or three minutes. Cigarettes become milder after being placed on the plate for fifteen minutes or so, and pineapple, for instance, will lose its sour taste and become sweet-tasting.

The magic I personally find to be the most helpful involves pain. (Aries Rams have a low pain threshold !) When a purple plate is placed on a burn or a cut . . . or tied with a ribbon or cord on an ache or a pain anywhere in the body, healing is noticeably accelerated, and the pain either greatly lessens or disappears entirely with amazing swiftness, usually within five to ten minutes, seldom longer than twenty minutes. This is accomplished by the plate's energy in returning the injured cells or tissue to a normal vibrational rate; thus the healing and disappearance of pain is due to the afflicted area being returned to the proper balance.

One of the construction workers employed by the contractor in the remodeling of my house in Colorado came to work one day with a "splitting migraine headache," and was about to take the day off, until I tied a "magic purple plate" (the small size) on his head with a sash from a bathrobe (making him look like Spock when Spock and Kirk prepared to visit the twentieth century in the film *Star Trek IV*). I asked him to leave it on his head for fifteen minutes. He felt rather foolish, but agreed, and less than five minutes later, when I asked him about his headache, he was up on a ladder, pounding nails. He looked down at me, grinned, and said, "It's gone. Completely gone."

"All right, then give me back my purple plate," I said, smiling back at him, pleased as always to observe the never failing magic. He replied quite seriously, "No way are you going to get this back ! I'm leaving it on all day — and I'm taking it home with me." He was only half serious, of course, but I graciously gave him the plate as a gift, and he was as delighted as if I had given him a magic wand — which, in a way, it is. Anyone who treats a friend with a purple energy plate is going to receive a lot of pressure to allow the friend to keep it, so it's wise to have several on hand for emergencies. The incident I just related is but one of more than a hundred headaches I've observed cured instantly by the purple plate over the years.

Another time (one of literally thousands of examples) a friend was chopping wood for me, and "threw out his arm." His upper arm was causing him severe pain, and he was on the verge of deciding to have someone drive him into Woodland Park to a doctor. I made him sit down on the couch, fixed him a cup of hot tea and tied a purple plate on his arm. By the time he had finished the tea (and a slice of cake) the pain had completely disappeared, and five minutes later he was out in the back yard chopping wood again. New Age medicine !

One of the magics I've depended on numerous times is the energy plate's ability to remove the sensation of nausea almost instantly. Any time I feel severe nausea, for whatever reason, I rush to get a purple plate, lie down on the bed on my back and place the plate on my solar plexus. The large size plate usually works more quickly in this instance, but a small one also does the job, taking only a few minutes longer. Using the plate in this way causes all sensations of nausea to disappear within no longer than five minutes, usually within one to two minutes . . . and sometimes in thirty seconds. I don't know what I would do without that reliable pain and nausea reliever being always available when I need it in a hurry. My women friends with "morning sickness" from pregnancy treat their purple plates as if they were precious jewels.

Some of my friends sleep with the plate tucked into the pillow case (on the bottom side, not the head side) all night. The energy goes through anything and everything except metal. They awake in the morning with more energy, and feel as if they've had a full eight hours' sleep, whether they have or not. A few people are unable to raise their vibratory rate in this manner because they're so sensitive to the energy, they stay awake all night! In any case, this use of the plates should be limited to one or two nights a week, and when it's important to wake up early the next morning with extra energy for the reason of an important meeting or appointment the next day.

As for raising your vibratory frequency with the plates, some people will feel increased physical energy and less fatigue by tucking one in the pocket of a shirt or blouse for thirty minutes to an hour, twice a day. Every individual is different, and experimenting with the plates will quickly tell each person the most effective way to use them relative to his or her own personal response.

In addition to removing nearly all kinds of pain almost instantly, and all the other minor miracles manifested, there is one particular use of the purple energy plates I've found to be truly amazing, nearly unbelievable, yet observably and infallibly true. There's no way to completely convince you of the validity of this, I suppose, unless you try it yourself.

We've already learned that each person vibrates to an individual frequency of light waves, a metaphysical truth or fact that is the foundation of a vast amount of unguessed and unsuspected "magic." Natives in civilized jungles often refuse to allow missionaries and other visitors to take their pictures with a camera, for reasons founded in such "uncivilized" (uncluttered by civilization's mental smog) minds, and seeded by the more active sixth sense and Third Eye possessed by these Earthlings. They claim that the one who photographs them, in some mysterious way, is "robbing them of a piece of their souls."

This isn't true. However, the photographer is "stealing" their frequency rate, and it's not mysterious to anyone who understands the individual vibratory frequency we've discussed. Somehow, through the process of photography, the individual frequency of the person who is photographed is impressed upon both the positive and negative print. Therefore, this particular purple plate magic only works when the "negative" of the positive print used has not been destroyed, and is known to exist somewhere, whether in the home, or even in the files of the photographer who took the original picture — or when using a Polaroid print, containing both the positive and negative on the picture itself, back to back.

Let's say a child, a mate, or loved one or a friend (perhaps an employer or neighbor or co-worker) is behaving in a most negative and exasperating manner, as we all do, from time to time, human nature being what it is. You can literally turn that person around, changing his or her attitude from negative to positive — not permanently, but until the next time — by using your purple energy plate in the following way. (But don't tell the person what you're doing.)

Place either a Polaroid photo or a positive print of a photo, the negative of which you know to be in existence and not destroyed — on a small-size purple plate, face down. Leave it there for *no longer than an hour*. Usually within approximately fifteen to twenty minutes that person's attitude will undergo a startling change, will be completely transformed from "nasty," stubborn, selfish, angry, annoyed or unsympathetic — to apologetic, cheerful, unselfish, sympathetic and pleasant. You really need to experience it to comprehend the sheer wonder of it. Within minutes, the person will contact you by phone or in person, depending on where and how the "disagreement" took place — (or you may initiate the contact yourself) — and will demonstrate a complete change of attitude, often apologizing for the former negative behavior or speech. The first few times it happens you'll be truly stunned . . . almost awed by this kind of energy power. Or you may choose to manifest this magic *before* you communicate with a certain person to ensure that the phone call or meeting is harmonious. Remember never to tell the person what you're doing. The person's mind is then capable of blocking or negating the positive energy infusion.

This kind of energizing with the purple plate should never be attempted for a trivial reason — only when it's genuinely important to change the vibrations between yourself and the other person. And it must not be thought of as some sort of "black magic" to force people to change their own free will decisions, because it will not do that. It's white magic, capable only of temporarily, for a period of time, changing a person's vibratory rate from negative to positive. In other words, if someone has refused to do what you want them to do, this magic *may* cause a change of heart or mind, *only if the individual person wishes to change his or her heart or mind, and is consciously unaware of such a desire*. Otherwise, this process will *not* cause a change of heart or mind, but it *will* have the happy result of creating a new level of understanding between you, a sort of truce or peace, causing both of you to be able to handle your conflicting desires, and work out your misunderstandings in a friendly manner, without rancor or ill will.

Here is only one of many examples from my personal experience. A friend of mine who lives in Colorado Springs visited me one day in Cripple Creek, in tears. Her husband, whom she loved deeply, had become an alcoholic. She'd tried everything, but nothing would convince him to stop drinking, although he was, basically, a "religious man," with a kind heart, who admitted that he wanted to stop drinking but just couldn't. I asked my friend if she would lend me a picture of him for a few days.

She looked surprised, but gave me a Polaroid she carried with her in her pocketbook. Then she asked me, with understandable curiosity, what I intended to do with her husband's picture. Knowing that she wasn't yet at a stage of enlightenment to comprehend the powerful harmony frequencies of the Universe, and feeling that her disbelief might short-circuit what I planned, my response was cryptic. I just smiled, and said, "Oh, I'm just going to try some 'white witch' magic."

She left, and that evening I placed her husband's picture on one of my small-size purple plates, leaving it there for the full hour. Never having used the photograph process in this way before, I wasn't sure what might — or might not — happen.

The next morning my friend telephoned me from the restaurant where she worked, in a combined state of happiness and bewilderment. "You can't guess what just happened about an hour ago !" she exclaimed. "Jim (not his real name) stopped in on his lunch hour, and told me he's decided to stop drinking, 'cold turkey,' and he's going to start going to church every Sunday ! I could tell he really meant it. He's never been that serious about it before. What did you do to make that happen ?"

I told her I was very happy to hear the news, but not to be concerned about the "why" of it — just wait and see how serious he was. Two months later, she visited me again in Cripple Creek. "Jim" had been making her go to church with him every Sunday, and he hadn't had a drop to drink. A year later, he was still sober. At this point, I let her believe I had "prayed," using his picture, and gave her back the photograph. Two years after his period of being sober he began drinking again. Then I told my friend the purple plate story, and was rewarded by hearing her express absolute faith in the magic, with no scepticism.

Although her husband had by then left to go to another state, and they were legally separated, she asked me for a purple plate, and I gave her one, warning her that no prediction could be made, as with "ordinary" use of it, when it came to something like alcoholism, regarding the length of time it would take for the magic to manifest. Instead of the usual 15 to 20 minutes or so, it could take much longer treatment, once a day or several times a week. She understood. That was last year. A week ago she called me in California to tell me that "Jim" had come back home, and was now permanently cured. He had entered a cure center in another state, and hadn't wanted to return until he knew he was free of the desire to drink. They're as happy as two bugs in a rug, as my Irish elf-mother used to say. Naturally, I can't promise that the purple plate will always cure alcoholism, but it certainly can't hurt . . . and who knows ? That's what experimentation is for.

The reason for not leaving a photo on the plate for longer than one hour at a time (and preferably no more often than once or twice a week) is because some people are extremely sensitive to its energy, and too much "exposure" can cause the person being so "treated" to exhibit nervousness or hypertension. If anyone uses the photo experiment for such an evil purpose *deliberately,* it will *not* cause such a reaction, because the law of the Universe regarding the life force energy will absolutely block such a result, boomeranging the tenseness back upon the user. This is an unbreakable law of magic when one tries to use such a sacred life force for evil. The only time to be concerned about overexposure is when the motive has been to be of benefit to someone, and then the tension will be felt briefly, because the overexposure was not intentional. Otherwise, the user will be mighty sorry for having attempted to cause harm to another. The sensitivity of some people to these energies has been demonstrated by what occurs when the plates are brought into the vicinity of mentally disturbed patients in institutions. They react in various ways, but always *intensely;* therefore, it's advisable to use the photos of any severely mentally disturbed people you'd like to help for no longer than a half hour each time.

While you're pondering what I realize you may believe to be the bizarre nature of the energy of the purple plates, especially as used with photographs, you might keep in mind that scientists have been for several years successfully experimenting with eradicating insects by irradiating a *photograph* of the diseased fields. Orthodox scientists, that is. (I knew that would make some of you feel better!) By the way, it doesn't matter whether the photograph you expose to these life force energies is one taken recently — yesterday — or when the photographed subject was a child or an infant. The individual vibratory frequency doesn't change.

The only pain or discomfort the purple energy force field has not relieved, in my personal observation for more than ten years, is the pain caused by a twisted muscle, a slipped disc, or misplaced vertebra. All other pain is swiftly either greatly relieved or completely banished. I almost forgot a special message to plant lovers. Water your plants with water treated on a plate, and notice the difference in their growth. Also, place a purple plate under fresh flowers from a florist, and they'll last nearly twice as long before wilting. Regarding plants, there's another bit of magic that's been developed by the same Nikola Tesla–inspired researcher, along with several other energy innovations. You can obtain the purple plates and these other life force energy "magics" by writing to Energy Innovation Products — P.O. Box 5011, Scottsdale, Arizona 85261 — USA.

Under normal circumstances I don't believe it's proper to include this sort of information in a book of this kind, but since I believe it's important to plant the seeds of such Tesla-inspired high frequency harmonics of the golden Age of Aquarius, I know my readers would be cross with me for sharing these esoteric secrets and ancient mysteries without also sharing the knowledge of how they can obtain them for personal experimentation.

No medical healing claims are made for the purple plate energies. They're not intended in any sense to replace the proper treatment of serious health problems by a professional holistic medical doctor, and I'm sure my readers have the common sense to realize, for example, that complaints such as chest pains need immediate medical attention. But as for the other magics I've described here, you'll discover for yourself how effective the purple plates can be, and you'll never be without one after you've seen what they will do . . . . far more, I promise you, than the over-the-counter medications that receive such high-profile advertising in all media, to which the medical profession doesn't object.

One final incident of the purple plate life force energies (you'll discover lots of uses on your own): A teacher friend of mine in Colorado has found the perfect remedy when one of her grade-school students is being naughty and disrupting the class. In her schoolroom is a chair with a pillow on the seat. No one is allowed to touch the pillow or go near the chair. It's called The Magic Good Pillow. Any student who is behaving badly is told to " sit on the Good Pillow" for fifteen minutes. When the child returns to its seat he (or she) has turned (at least temporarily !) into a perfect little angel. Of course one of the large plates is beneath the pillow. My teacher friend has discovered her own personal way of creating purple magic.

The plates have been in use by many people for more than fifteen years — I've had my own for more than ten years — and they still function as effectively after that length of time. Once the structure of the atoms of the aluminum have been altered, they will remain in that condition . . . probably indefinitely. The plates are not "charged"; they are simply altered to vibrate with life force energy of the Universe — what Nikola Tesla called "free energy."

Translating my personal choice of "purple" plates to describe these energies (possibly because my favorite faerie tale as a child was about a "purple elf named Leser") . . . into the true color of the plates, which is the rainbow spectrum musical "tone" of violet, it represents the seventh ray and the "violet flame" of the Avatar-Adept, the Comte de St. Germain. In metaphysics, violet is the healing ray of the spectrum.

To lead us "harmonically" into the next chapter, on the study of Lexigrams, here's an introductory Lexigram for you. The word VIOLET contains the words LOVE and LIVE . . . also LET. And so, VIOLET whispers softly to us the perfect healing prescription for all illness. Do you want to heal others . . . or yourself ? Well, then . . . . .

First LOVE . . . then LET LIVE !

★ ★ ★ ★ ★ ★

If you're a male reader of this book, and you should happen to come home from work some evening to find the woman you love waiting for you with a purple plate tied around her head — and then discover she's moved your favorite, cozy armchair to the south side of the fireplace for no rational reason, don't panic and think the space people have landed and zapped her into such weird behavior.

Because there's so much controversy flying around among astronomers and astrologers these days about the actual, scientific date of the Age of Aquarius — and his book seems to be so involved with the Aquarian Age — I believe I'll end this chapter with some lines from *Gooberz* in an attempt to close the gap between the pros and cons of the actual date marking the beginning of the new, golden Age.

★ ★ ★ ★ ★ ★

do not listen
to those smug prophets and Cassandras
    who argue endlessly and monotonously
that the Aquarian Age is, technically, not yet here

    and who babble and quarrel among themselves
    about the stern astronomical Precession of the Equinoxes
    ignoring the Uranian Procession of Children
    walking through the loneliness with lighted candles
                              chanting *Peace*
    all we ask . . . is give Peace a chance

we are well within an astrological
        orb of influence
of those unpredictable Aquarian vibrations

    as a matter of fact . . .
    a matter of both astronomical and astrological fact
    we are as close to them now as the Earth was
    to the trembling vibrations of the Piscean Age

    when the symbolic Fish of Christianity
    first swam into the muddy streams of ignorance
        on this dark and dreary planet
    at the time of Mary and Joseph's weary ride into Bethlehem
    to the teeming Inn, where there was

                        no room
    with the same over population problem

no room

        for the hungry and the homeless
                or for the despairing oppressed
      in our selfish, seeking hearts

      no room for those who wear the robes of a different
skin
      or who hear the call of a distant drummer

no room for those who follow a different star
whether it be the Star of David
or the Hopi Indian star of harvest faith

so . . . is it any wonder . . . that we're having a sexual revolution
that we shake under the Uranian thunder
of individuality of hairstyles, music, clothing, politics
and religious convictions ?

with women clamoring to be Ministers and Priests
and riots on campus, introducing the Seventies, taking
their toll

didn't you see it all coming, Mr. Gallup and Mr. Poll ?
didn't you feel Kent State coming ?
or do you scoff at the stars — and ignore the planets too
as blind astronomers and other scientists are wont to
do ?

I see them all squatting
in their Kindergarten of Knowledge

the professors and the shrinks
the scientists and the astronomers
the sociologists and poll takers
and an occasional politician

playing with Truth
as children play with colored blocks
lettered A B C
for Apathy — Blindness — and Cop Out

then, when their blocks topple over
from too much emphasis on Equatorial Equinoxes
and such
they rage in childish petulance
and bang each other over the head
with the offending chunks of wooden facts

do not bang *me* over the head with your A B C
blocks

colored with half-truths
you disciples of Thomas, the Doubter

you will not break the Ram's tough horns !

The Aquarian Age is here !

and its pulsating, powerful, contradictory orb
mixing with the Sun rays of the roaring Lion
. . . Leo, the sign opposite Aquarius . . .

is ominous, if not heeded

locking the New Age in your scientific closets
with boring, tiresome technicalities
will not cause it to disappear

yes, the vibration of Aquarius is here
and much too close for comfort . . .

it burns my soul
and sears my mind
with unanswered questions

★ ★ ★ ★ ★ ★

8

LEXIGRAMS
. . . AND THE WORD DRUIDS

the use of words to penetrate the meanings of
ancient codes . . .
the profound mysteries of the English language . . .
and how to lexigram the secrets of words,
names, titles, and phrases

words divine, words sublime . . . holy, holy words !
  a picture is worth ten thousand words
so the Oriental sages say . . . and therefore is the higher
    nay, nay . . . for shame !
for it takes words to tell . . . even of that ancient claim

   the hidden glory of every story
     shines forth in words, words, words !
   the miracle of the Easter gladness
     overcoming death's morbid sadness
   is told in words, words, words !

words have wings, like birds
to fly through the sky of the mind

. . . be ye aS wiSe aS a Serpent
  yet aS harmleSS aS a dove . . .

  words . . . those mysterious scribbles on a page
  holding the wisdom of every age
   the experience and teaching of every sage

  oh! the beautiful rhyming of the proper timing
       of words !

  powerful words, that ring with truth
   words that sing, forsooth !
  yes, words that ring and words that sing
  words of spring and every good thing . . . like kitties

★ ★ ★ ★ ★ ★

HAT ARE Lexigrams ? Lexigrams can be used in several ways to solve riddles and penetrate mysteries. First we'll need to learn more about what they are . . . then the rules of how to calculate them . . . and finally, the reason behind the mighty power of words.

And so, this chapter will be patterned as follows:

> What Are Lexigrams ?
>
> How Do They Work ?
>
> The Rules for Calculating Them
>
> Some Examples
>
> The Mystery of Their Origin
>
> More Examples
>
> Perhaps . . . a Final Secret

★★★★★★

You may lexigram a word, a name, a title or a phrase. We'll begin with words. Each word possesses its own immutable meaning, which is, even when not immediately apparent, the genotype of the word — its gene. In fact, **GENE** is a Lexigram of **GENOTYPE**, thereby containing the basis of this word's meaning. Sometimes the origin and formation of words is consciously deliberate, as with "genotype" and "gene," but more often it's not.

It's simple to deduce why, for example, the noun "failure" contains within it the verb "fail" — why the word "consequence" contains the word "sequence" (first you act, then, in sequence, comes the consequence of your action). It's not simple, and not nearly so obvious to penetrate why "consequence" should contain the word "queen!" Could the word have been conceived in antiquity, when royalty was born in a matriarchal society, and it was the Queen who ordered the punishment or consequence of an action ? Yes. It not only could have been, it was. Neither is it quite so simple or obvious to comprehend why the word OCEAN should contain the word EON. After you've become accustomed to the thought process developed in mastering Lexigrams, you'll know why.

As we've just seen, a certain percentage of all words in the English dictionary were formed consciously and deliberately by human wordsmiths or from common usage, with logical patterns and obvious progressions. However, a much larger percentage were conceived and born from the mass collective *subconscious* womb of whispering memory . . . and these are the words holding the greatest riddles, hiding the deepest mysteries.

As with other such occult secrets, the Lexigram star sign code has chosen to hide itself, in this instance behind the bland mask of anagrams, a word game played for intellectual exercise and amusement. Lexigrams are *not* for amusement or intellectual exercise. They probe behind anagrams to uncover higher knowledge and wisdom, hiding-in-plain-sight, where many esoteric mysteries hide, unsuspected and therefore undiscovered. Most satisfying of all to those who master them, Lexigrams can verify what intuition has only hinted at, concerning history, science and people.

Naturally, not every single word in your dictionary will lend itself to valid or revealing lexigramming — please remember that — nevertheless, many an English word is, in itself and of itself, a kind of concentrated poem or verse, masking symbolic images and concepts. Taking the time to examine each word having a bearing on your thoughts at the moment opens up a whole new uni-verse of perception, so you can harmonize and "sing along" with the one true verse of the life force energies we studied in the "Forgotten Melodies" chapter.

Sometimes lexigramming will bring the polarities of the material and spiritual realms into communion in your mind. It's as exhilarating as an electrical storm when you experience an instant lightning flash of realization, accompanied by the thunderous recognition of a long forgotten truth . . . suddenly recalled.

The mystic from Lebanon, Kahlil Gibran, wrote that "thoughts are like birds, which, when imprisoned in a cage of words, can indeed spread their wings, but cannot fly." However, when words are lexigrammed, the resulting thoughts are released, and *can* fly . . . not only "over the rainbow" . . . but measureless miles beyond.

Anyone can surely fly into the sunrise of a richly rewarding astral trip, for example, simply by concentrating (as mentioned in Chapter 1) on why the word IDEA, belonging to the material realm, should become an IDEAL by adding the letter L for Love, belonging to the spiritual realm.

Also mentioned in an earlier chapter (and it bears repeating), the word UNTIED, meaning "separation," becomes the word UNITED, simply by reversing 2 letters. Re-*versing* them. Write a new verse ! This realization leads you swiftly into the thought that, if two people (or two nations) become separated, all they need do is re-verse their viewpoints to become once more united. Or as the American Indians counseled, if each would walk a mile in the other's moccasins.

Not only by reading books, but also through the quiet contemplation of Lexigrams, you can receive insights occasionally even leading you into a penetration of both the truth and falsehood of myth and legend. There's much buried treasure in that area — also in matters omitted from history as chronicled by those ignorant of certain past events, as well as by those motivated in preventing future generations from learning them.

As for probing history, the Church of England was formed when King Henry VIII divorced his wife, Catherine of Aragon, who had borne him no sons, so he could marry Anne Bolyen. Henry's divorce so outraged the Pope in Rome, he sent word from the Vatican that Henry was forthwith to be ex-communicated from the Catholic Church. Unruffled and arrogant, Henry founded his own church, the

Church of England, and made himself the head of it, dropping his allegiance to the Pope. When the Church of England formed its American branch it was called the Episcopal Church. The word **EPISCOPAL** contains the letters of the words **LOSE A POPE**, which they did, undeniably. It also contains the word **ELOPE**, which is religiously what Henry did with Anne. Why it should contain **LIES** needs to be studied and pondered more deeply. Here's a hint. I shall someday soon be writing a book about the long-kept secret that history has "lied" in saying that Anne suffered a miscarriage in prison, where she was placed by Henry to await her execution.

Instead, shortly before she was beheaded, she gave birth to a premature, redheaded male infant, by the locksmith–jail keeper, Moner Hughes, who smuggled the infant out of prison, and named him William Moner, to hide the truth from Henry. The child grew up to father a son he named Moner Hughes, the ancestor of Howard Hughes. The word **LIES**, therefore, belongs in the word **EPISCOPAL** for more than one reason.

Because every ancient secret is revealed at its allotted time (when the student Earthlings are thought to be ready) — and never prematurely, before its time — it follows that the Aquarian Age has rung the bells of this particular secret, allowing it to be channeled to the world as the ancient star sign code I've christened Lexigrams.

The word *Lexigrams* equals the Compound Number 27 in numerology, an appropriate identification number, as discovered through its sister art and science. Lexigrams, astrology and numerology are sibling codes. I have a still secret reason for giving only the first one a capital letter.

All three codes are of invaluable help to anyone who wants to learn how to analyze people, events and entities. You already know what "entities" are from reading the definition in the earlier chapter about numerology. The same definition applies to lexigrammed "entities."

More basic knowledge of life can be comprehended through lexigramming than by reading only the surface of words in all books ever written (including this one), because Lexigrams help you revive your sleeping sixth sense, which will, in turn, gently coax open your Third Eye, allowing you to then uncover layer after layer of the mysteries swirling around you — the enigmas of Heaven and hell and everything in between, including the intricacies and complexities of human relationships. When you become an expert in calculating Lexigrams it's possible to learn as much as the wisest Guru could teach you. Because it possesses such a startling code key to truth, let's take the word *Guru* itself, as an example of one of the multiple facets of lexigramming that is slightly different from the calculation of *basic* Lexigrams.

Pronounce each of the four letters comprising the word **GURU** as G-U-R-U, separately, aloud. Do this three times. When these four letters are pronounced separately aloud they form a speech "sound" in the ethers, making it seem as if the word Guru is saying: Gee ! You are . . . **you** ! Which happens to be precisely the mission of any Guru — to bring you to the realization that you, too, are an Avatar. You, too, are a Guru. You, too, are a Messiah.

As with all forms of lexigramming, the apparently innocent and simple meditation of this *one single word* spirals our thoughts into higher truth. You don't believe that you are a Messiah ? You are. And the "second coming" was not intended to be the appearance of a man from Galilee, with a beard and white robe, floating down from the skies. He may — or may not — be on Earth now, in a physical body, but only a few Initiates will know his identity, to protect the truth he taught and will teach again — from a new distortion caused by the defeating doctrine of "Divinity."

Yes, Jesus was "the son of God." But so are you the son — or the daughter — of God. So far, still the "prodigal son" or "prodigal daughter" — but, nevertheless the child of your Creators, your Mother and Father "Who art in Heaven" whether they be called God or

Jehovah or the Almighty. Divinity implies that "the imitation of Christ" is a hopeless quest, doomed to failure, for how can "lowly you," only a human, ever attain anything near the goodness, the "power and the glory" of one who was "the son of God"? Jesus was born to remind all people of their original birthright of divinity, to speak to the slumbering "angels" within them — their Higher Selves.

The Nazarene tried so hard to make it clear each time he said "Be it done to you according to your faith" . . . in other words, "I did not heal you because I am special or above you. Your own *faith* that I *could* is what healed you." But spiritually lazy humans kept responding with "Master, heal me," because the doctrine of Divinity didn't require the discipline necessary for self-healing. It was much easier to just let him do it. Jesus also repeatedly said "*All things that I have done, you can do also.* Go, thou, and do likewise — *and more.*" Now, how could any words be more clear than these ? Yet the masses continued to beg, "Master, heal me."

Jesus was "only" human, only a man, although a very enlightened one, whose mission on Earth was to teach each soul that he or she could perform the same magic as he, if they were willing to listen to the slumbering angel within, and to practice the same disciplines as he: giving, caring, compassion, forgiveness, selflessness and above all . . . love.

Jesus was human, but Jesus "the Christ" was a different person (albeit the same flesh body) — one who had achieved the power of immortality (see Chaper 9) through mastery over the physical body and harmonious communication with his Spirit or Higher Self — as you may do and become also.

The "second coming" is not what is now expected, just as the true mission of the babe born in Bethlehem was not what the Jews expected it to be two thousand years ago. The "second coming" will be in the heart of every man and every woman on Earth of good and pure, unselfish intent: "Behold," said the Angel, "I bring tidings of great joy . . . to *men of good will.*" This, too, is the awesome revelation of Easter, which will be recognized when all people realize that they are also "messiahs" — gods and goddesses (no one above or below anyone else), possessing great powers they have too long forgotten.

Let's try to find evidence of this eternal truth of the wondrous birthright possessed by all "fallen angels" on Earth, through Lexigrams. Can each man and each woman become a "messiah" if they live as he lived ?

The word **MESSIAH** contains the following ringing words, as a message to those whose Third Eyes are open to truth:

HE IS HIM . . . HE IS SAME AS HIM . . . HE IS SHE . . . SHE IS HIM . . . HE IS SAME AS ME . . . I AM SAME AS HIM . . . SHE IS SAME AS HIM . . .

Hiding also behind **MESSIAH** is the celebration of the Catholic **MASS**. This Lexigram is as logical and clear as any message could be to those who use their intelligence and intuition. Those who do have, perhaps, already tuned in to those 3 vowels and 6 *separate* letters in the word *Messiah.* Remember the 3-6-9 mystery in numeroloy ? Here it is again. Three vowels: the holy trinity of the you-of-you. Six *separate* letters: 6 is Venus — Love. Together, 3 and 6 add to 9. The Alpha and the Omega — the Beginning and the End. The *total* number of letters in *Messiah* is seven. Seven . . . the spiritual number, in its higher dimensional vibration.

This is one example of the way Lexigrams can cause your thoughts to spiral into a major or minor revelation you may not otherwise have had cause to ponder. I call this process one-word-spiraling, although it can also be done, using the same kind of spiral thinking, with a name, a title or a phrase containing more than one word. By spiral thinking I mean that the process sends your thoughts spiraling upward with the power to penetrate the place where all mysteries are born. Like a mental screwdriver . . . and that's a near perfect analogy.

The rules of working Lexigrams are both different from and sim-

ilar to the game of anagrams. But you must never think that Lexigrams are synonomous with anagrams. The latter is merely a game
for light intellectual amusement; the former is a serious spiritual process of decoding.

When you're decoding secrets through Lexigrams you first make
a list of all the words contained within the single word — the name —
or the multiple word phrase you want to penetrate. Remember that
you don't need to use *all* the words in your final Lexigram — *only as*
many of them as you need to make the meaning you're seeking clear.

After you've made your list of words you tune into your Higher
Self, through intuition, using your sixth sense, as you place the words
together, on a separate sheet of paper, to form short phrases or sentences. Your own instinct will then overshadow you, filling your
mind with inspiration, as you place the words on the page in patterns
that reveal such astonishing insights, you'll sometimes gasp aloud in
the sheer delight of discovery.

It takes a little practice, then all of a sudden you find that you can
do it, and you'll feel as though someone had switched on a bright light
in a dark room. After that it's like eating potato chips or Goobers
Peanuts. You can't stop. You quite nearly are tempted to scribble on
walls and such, which is why it's a good idea, if you're going to become enlightened by lexigramming, to carry a small notebook and pen
or pencil with you at all times. I blush to confess that I once came
close to writing on a friend's lampshade, but caught myself before any
damage was done. And, more times than I like to count, I'm afraid
I've scribbled a hasty Lexigram on my wrist or the flesh of my palm,
when I was stunned by a sudden concept and there wasn't a scrap of
paper to be found in the vicinity at the time. Thus my counsel, born
from experience, to have a proper pad and pencil on your person, at
the ready.

Lexigrams do churn up the adrenaline irresistibly, and it's difficult to pull in the reins, once the race to solve the riddles of yourself

and the mysteries of the Universe has exploded through the starting gate of the Mind.

Remember the Zebra Rule in the numerology chapter ? Lexigrams also have a Zebra Rule to follow.

Let's say you lexigram a person's name, and it contains the word *liar* or the phrase *he lies* or *she lies*. Or any other such negative word, such as *thief* or *steal*. Any word indicating negative action or an extremely negative trait.

When a negative word appears in a name Lexigram, and the letters N and O or N and O and T (which can be used to cancel the negative, forming, for example — "he is *not* a liar" — or "she does *not* lie") do not appear in the Lexigram, then that person has a problem, and needs to change his or her name to cancel the negative word or phrase, also changing to a more favorable numerological vibration — and also needs to be aware of the necessity of bringing this personal character flaw under control.

This is especially true if the foregoing "cancel" letters and words do not appear in the Lexigram — and in *addition,* the letters forming YES appear, which would cause the negative words to read: "Is he a liar ?" *Yes.* Or: "Does she lie ?" *Yes.*

However, when a negative word appears, and the letters N and O — or N and O and T also appear, as the words "no" or "not" to cancel the negative — while the letters forming YES do *not* appear — it means that the person (or word) being lexigrammed will have been *accused* of whatever the negative word implies, but is not guilty. The person (or word) is guilty only when the word YES appears in the Lexigram *without* the cancel power of the words NO or NOT. I realize that this sounds complicated, but if you read it over several times, you'll understand it, because it's inherently logical. The Zebra Rule is necessary in lexigramming so that you won't accuse a person (or word or title) of something he or she or it is not guilty of doing or being.

Here are the remaining rules for calculating Lexigrams. If they aren't observed, you won't learn anything of consequence or dependability.

1. Each letter of each word in your Lexigram must be contained within the original word, name or phrase you are lexigramming. You can use each letter in the original more than once in forming each separate word of your Lexigram, but *not* in the *same* word. For example, you can't produce the word "wishes" as a Lexigram if your original word, name or phrase contains only *one* letter "s." But if the original contains two of the same letter, you may. Example: the word "moonlight" contains two *o*'s; therefore so may any single word in your Lexigram.

2. The word, name or phrase you are lexigramming *may not* contain more than four of the five vowels (a-e-i-o-u). It's *best* if the original contains only three or fewer vowels. Remember that four vowels are not ideal, but they are permissible. All five vowels are not. If the original word, name or phrase contains five vowels, it does not want to be lexigrammed, and is too complex to allow you to learn anything from it.

3. The original word, name or phrase *may not* contain more than fifteen different and separate letters of the alphabet, although it's permissible for the original to contain a particular letter two or more times, such as "moonlight sonata," and, in such a phrase, the extra *o*'s don't count, under the rule of "no more than fifteen separate and different letters of the alphabet." Example: The original single word *moonlight* contains two vowels and only eight letters. It actually contains nine letters, but that second *o* doesn't count. *Only* the first one.

4. The reason for Rules 2 and 3 is that, if an original word, name or phrase contains five vowels and more than fifteen separate and different letters of the alphabet, you could form just about every word in the dictionary, and your Lexigram won't reveal anything personal or reliable.

5. Make all the words you can from the original word, name or phrase. Then study them. Look at them. Use your intuition and instinct to then form the words into short sentences. Complete your final Lexigram in ALL CAPITAL LETTERS, as demonstated in the examples later on in this chapter. If necessary, you may add *in lower case,* an *a* or a *the* or a *but* — in parenthesis — to bring more meaning to a sentence, but this should be done sparingly, and only if necessary to comprehend the full meaning of a sentence in the Lexigram. As you study both the single word and multiple word examples in this chapter, it will be clear to you how to calculate your own Lexigrams.

Here are a few samples of brief Lexigrams, which, even when they're only amusing or slightly humorous (depending on which side of any particular fence you're on) also bear more than a grain of truth. Later, we'll study some "heavier" ones.

Original	*Lexigram*
Diplomacy	Mad policy
Moonlight	Thin gloom
Weird nightmares	Withering dreams
HMS Pinafore	A name of a ship
The South Sea Islands	A thousand islets shine
Republican	Incurable clan (if you're a Democrat)
Democratic	Rated comic (if you're a Republican)
South	So hot
North	Not hot
Armageddon	Mad god near
Postage	Paste to pages
Violent	No love
Murder	Red drum

Test your sensitivity, esoteric ability, your sixth sense and your talent for word-spiraling on the last word on the list. Do you see *why,* in a sixth or an esoteric sense, this is valid? Murder: Red drum.

Many words convey a more subtle and meaningful message than was consciously intended when they first "appeared" in the English language. The truth is that *people* do not, in reality, originate words. Words are conceived and born of their own S-elves, with definite minds of their own, and you'll soon see why. Words are *alive*. They live ! Shortly, we'll examine the evidence of this.

Lexigrams can be silly, trite, serious or sacred. The examples just given were partially silly or trite, partially serious. Yet even the silly ones are shaded with subtle implications. Evidence that people don't consciously create words with surprising Lexigrams is the word Democratic. Would Democrats have consciously created a word describing their political behavior as "comic" ? Would Republicans have consciously created a name to describe their party that reveals their conservative policies seem to be "incurable" ? And it must be admitted that "comic" and "incurable" are apt definitions of the behavior of both political parties on occasion.

The fact that the name of opera singer **BEVERLY SILLS** contains **SILVERY BELLS** is an example of one of the perhaps trite but nevertheless fascinating aspects of Lexigrams. By thus naming her, Beverly's parents unknowingly reflected the singular quality of her voice, which would be the foundation of her career. Maybe not so trite a Lexigram after all !

Not sacred but certainly not silly or trite, is the Lexigram of feminine rights leader, **MS. GLORIA STEINEM**, which tells us that **GLORIA SMITES MEN**. Random thought: They need a bit of smiting, Gloria, until they get it together.

One of the strongest evidences of the undeniable validity of Lexigrams is that the Lexigram of one person's name cannot be transferred or used to describe another person. There's no reason for Gloria Steinem's name to contain "silvery bells," so it doesn't — just as there's no reason for the name Beverly Sills to contain "she smites men," so it doesn't. "Silvery bells" belongs to Beverly Sills, and "she smites men" belongs to Gloria Steinem. *Lexigrams are not interchangeable* because they are born from the alphabetical letters of the person they describe. There's no arguing with such an obvious fact, and we'll see more irrefutable proof of it in a number of examples of lexigramming the names of well-known public figures later on in this chapter.

I'll also be demonstrating many more single word Lexigrams later, but before continuing with additional examples, so that you can fully appreciate them, you'll need to understand the startling reason *why* the words of the English language possess such power . . . and such uncanny intelligence. We learned the great importance of sound in the "Forgotten Melodies" chapter concerning the harmony and synchronicity of the Universe, and it should have prepared you to next comprehend the mighty power of words themselves. But . . . *why* should words vibrate with such power ? Why do they hold such unguessed secrets ? Why are they able to solve so many riddles and mysteries, at the same time being capable of inflicting so much pain and creating such confusion ? From whence did they come, these entities called words, belonging to the "race" of the English language ?

You've heard the phrase "a dead language," and you've heard the phrase "a living language." The former is a language no longer used, of real value only to scholars. The latter is believed to mean " a language still written and spoken." But the phrase "a living language" when employed to describe English hides more layers of meaning than are apparent on the surface of it.

The English language, formed from the Anglo-Saxon alphabet, is — literally — alive. All other languages, whether based on the Anglo-Saxon or different alphabets, only exist, and aren't truly alive in the sense I mean, and this is not to be construed as prejudice from an English-speaking person. *Lexigrams do not work; they are not valid in any language other than English.* This is something for you to seriously ponder, because the reason behind it is perhaps the most profound of all mysteries. We'll discuss it after we first learn to comprehend that words are not just marks on a page but living entities, capable of many unsuspected magics. As you will shortly see, there was a time when they became so, and a reason for their becoming so.

Like any living thing, the English language keeps growing and evolving, *even leaving the fossils of "dead" words behind.* ★ ★ ★ ★ ★ That sentence may possibly become important at the end of this chapter, which is why I marked it with stars.

Now, will you open your mind a few inches while we consider why I've said that words are "living entities"?

Some words are mutants of original words, and so words undergo mutation. They meet, "fuse" or fall in love, so to speak — and they mate. They can and do produce "children." Hybrid words and varieties of compound words are the progeny or offspring of "parent" words, who (not which) earlier "fused" (fell in love) — and mated.

Yes, mated. After they tamed each other. You see, **MATE** and **TAME** are synonomous words in the art and science of Lexigrams. Because mate is tame, and tame is mate, when you switch the letters around. Of course. To mate is to tame — or should be. Remember how the fox taught St. Exupéry's "Little Prince" to tame him, by moving a few inches closer each day, with great patience, to gain his love and trust? It is not necessary to mate because you have tamed, but it is most desirable to tame before you mate.

Most important, each entity word, even those words which "look alike" (like human twins, astral twins and doubles), such as tame-mate and mate-tame, are nevertheless distinct individuals, regardless of an "inherited" relationship to any other word or words. Just like people. Each word's individuality is hidden within its "soul" or "spirit," waiting to be discovered.

Although the following rightfully belongs in a later book, this particular "twelfth night secret" must be mentioned here in general, not in detail, as a foundation for the mighty power of words. I won't make any attempt to defend it in these pages, nor to offer the source of the revelation. Therefore, many of you may at first tend to disagree. But whatever your initial response, try to accept the premise that English — yes, English — was the first language spoken upon this Earth — and on all other Earths, in all solar systems and Universes.

Humans tend to insist that anything of vast antiquity must be strange, complex and "foreign." On those rare occasions when Earthlings think at all about the language spoken "in the beginning," when Eve *allegedly* said to Adam, "Have a bite of this delicious apple, darling," it's usually imaged (by Americans) as some long-forgotten form of ancient Hebrew, Eskimo or gobbledygook — anything, as long as it's weird and not familiar.

Linking antiquity and the familiar is taboo, one of those rules accepted as having been engraved in stone, like the Ten Commandments, one of those rules that are merely wisps of custom, having no relationship to reality. Yet each such unfounded *rule* continues to *lure* humans into accepting it as "gospel truth." That's to be expected, I suppose, since the word **RULE** hides the word **LURE**. Rule is lure, and lure is rule. *Quite* ! as Guru Nahtan would say, in his wonted *quiet* way. Naturally, since **QUITE** is also **QUIET**, through a quick switch of letters.

The reason it's such a shock to people to conceive that English was the original language spoken in the Eden-Heaven now called Earth is that it's difficult for them to recall any memories of Eden and Eve in a time so many eons before the Tower of Babel, although they should be able to evoke memories of Eve in the garden, since **EVOKE** contains **EVE**.

The symbolic building of the Tower of Babel describes the wanton destruction of primordial English, which originally vibrated so purely to the Music of the Spheres that it fell as gently on the ethers and human ears as singing . . . or chanting. To speak in those original tones and rhythms was truly to sing ! Well, what do you know ! **ENGLISH** contains **SING**. *Quite*. English, however, lost its musical, harmonious purity after Adam began to tell **HIS LIES**, two words also hiding in **ENGLISH**. Note that it does not contain *her* lies, for a reason related in a forthcoming work. It's interesting that to **RELATE** something means to tell what is **REAL** — **LATER**, after it has occurred. **RELATE** tells you all this. *It defines itself.* It's easy to get lost in thought and revelation when you're tuned into Lexigrams. Where was I ?

As that future book will relate, many lies were seeded by Adam, after he became **MAD**, the word being prophetically hidden within his name, **ADAM** — and that's the truth, even if it offends and hurts the mistaken images promoted by the patriarch-minded. All truth hurts to some degree, since it digs out falsehoods by the roots, sometimes as painful an experience as a trip to the dentist for root canal work, as truth itself warns, since **HURT** is found there, hiding-in-plain-sight in **TRUTH**. Adam's lies, and the reason for his madness will explain why Earthlings can never become fully **EVOLVED** concerning the matter of their origin until they learn to **LOVE EVE**, and stop believing that she initiated the original temptation, as the word **EVOLVE** has been telling us, in Lexigram, for such a long, weary time. This is not some manufactured promotion for Women's Liberation, but a long buried truth even **ERA** supporters have thus far not listed to with the inner **EAR**.

After the Fall, English remained, but in a much less pure form of pattern and tone, and was no longer "sung" or chanted (remember incantations ?) in its original rhythms and vibrating notes, until the symbolic building of the Tower of Babel, at which time it disappeared entirely into the mass subconscious, remaining dormant until, by Divine Will, it was slowly and gradually resurrected in the Celtic region of Earth. It's part of the great mystery of English that **NOTE** is **TONE**, and vice versa, because **MUSIC** was once the **SUM** total of *all that was*. *The word* **MUSIC** itself tells you that, does it not ?

The Master of Music and the English language, the Master of the **MUSES**, who knew of its dormancy and eventual destined resurrection was one whose Egyptian identity was Hermes Thoth. He was also the

Master of Mathematics and, indeed, the word SUM hides within the word MUSES, as harmoniously revealing as other Lexigram secret codes. And, of course, since Hermes THOTH was sometimes called "the god of Thought," it's only natural that the word THOUGHT should contain his name.

A brief and deliberate musical digression back into the sister of Lexigrams, numerology. Since we're speaking of music, a piano has 88 keys; 88 adds to 16. The meaning of the Compound Number 16, given on Page 254, accurately describes the tragic fall of the Music of the Spheres, as once channeled through the pure tones and rhythms of primordial English. 16 reduces to 7, and 7 is the number of Neptune, the planet ruling music in astrology. 7 is also the spiritual number of higher enlightenment, as explained in the chapter about numerology. There are seven notes in the musical scale. And . . . "Music hath charms to soothe a savage breast." Have I said that before ? Quite probably I have. Important truths always bear considerable repetition before they take root and flower into illumination.

I find I'm spiraling higher mentally, and can't quite stop yet. NEPTUNE, astrology's ruling planet of music, contains TUNE. There are 44 black keys and 44 white keys on a piano — 44 black (or negative) keys and 44 white (or positive) keys needed to create the notes and chords of perfect harmony (likewise true of the perfect blending of all positive-negative polarities in elecricity, man and woman, etc., and these 44 black and 44 white keys add to that total of 88 I just mentioned. Keys — *think*. Why call them that ? Because they are *keys* to the codes of wisdom. Are KEYS codes ? YES ! The Lexigram answers the question.

Yes, 44 negative and 44 positive "keys" add to 88. Just look at all those 4s and 8s ! Remember what was said about these fated numbers in the numerology chapter. But they finally reduce to the spiritual 7. (44 plus 44 equal 88 . . . and 88 adds to 16 . . . which reduces to 7.) On the way to the enlightenment of the spiritual number 7 is the danger threatened by the Compound Number 16 (read again its meaning on Page 254), the warning of "a fall from a high place." It can be avoided if the **LOGICAL MAGIC OF NUMEROLOGICAL** counsel is heeded. Back then, it was not. Lexigrams tell us that anything **NUMEROLOGICAL** contains **MAGIC** and is **LOGICAL**, because the word Lexigrams the revelation of its own mystery.

By the way, the three words *Tower of Babel* possess a numero *logical* value of 18, which is surely "logical" when you read the analysis of the number 18. Of course, 18 reduces to the powerful single number 9, and we know that 9 represents both the beginning and the end. So, if the beginning holds the end within it, then the end holds the beginning within it. "I am Alpha and Omega," spoke the Nazarene, offering a great truth in the form of a riddle to those of his time. And to us.

All right, now we'll return from our musical saga, our spiraled hegira initiated by the explosion of a few simple Lexigrams, and continue the story of the demise of this once fair language — English.

I mentioned in an earlier chapter that the Socratic method of teaching consists of asking questions, since no one can teach you anything; they can only help you remember what your Third Eye *already knows*. So let's get Socratic for a moment. First, before continuing our Tower of Babel story, I'd like you to "remember" something. Because the word **MEMORY** contains the words **MORE ME** you'll regain more of the you-of-you as you remind yourself — **RE-MIND** yourself (change the thought forms in your mind) to remember an important truth. Think about it while you re-mind yourself in quiet, calm contemplation, and realize that **CONTEMPLATION** whispers to you of its reward — spiritual **ELATION**. See it hiding there, like a secret promise to you ?

What I'm requesting you to remember is that when English was the pure and musical language spoken (sung) on this planet in the beginning, there was **NO TIME** on Earth. You should have channeled that from your **CONTEMPLATION**, since the word itself tells you clearly by its own Lexigram that there was **NO TIME** when *someone* decided to **TEMPT** *someone* with that delectable, delicious apple. The reason there was no Time is explained in the next chapter. Do you see the words "no time" and "tempt" winking their star sign codes at you from "contemplation" ? Or twinkling. No difference. **TWINKLING** contains **WINKING**.

Aside from the enigma of illusionary Time explained in Chapter 9, what you need to k-now now (omitting the *k* temporarily) is that the original English language, bruised and battered as it already was after the Fall, was further split, fragmented, cut and sliced into a myriad of alphabets, symbols and speech patterns during the period of the Tower of Babel — and humans have been "babbling" to each other ever since, — with a lot of "sound and fury, signifying nothing," as poet Will Shakespeare wisely observed. Even wiser was his counsel of "The first thing we do, let's kill all the lawyers." I'm sliding away from my subject again. Sorry, but you see, the word **LAWYERS** contains **YEARS**, and it does sometimes seem as though they've been "babbling" in courtrooms, waging **WARS** between prosecution and defense, under-helping and over-charging us for years — yes ? Even the word **LAWYERS** chimes in agreeing with our **YES**. I hasten to add, however, that three lawyers I know, Arthur Klebanoff and Jerome Perles, of New York, and Garry Appel, of Denver, Colorado, are exempt from my frustrated legal lexigramming of the current jest called justice. The word **JUSTICE** itself confesses that it's too often, in today's society, a **JEST**. It's hard for a word to disguise its flaws under the revealing light of lexigramming.

I apologize for the legal digression, but you'd best become accustomed to it, because it's a sample of what you'll experience yourself when you "tune" into this star sign code. You'll see. Just wait.

Before continuing the explanation of why words are "living entities," you may need some sort of a shock absorber, some foundation of both the laws of physics and metaphysics. I believe the most effective way to accomplish this is for you to give me your word, druid honor, that you will meditate for several minutes on the following sentences you've already read in the beginning pages of the previous "Forgotten Melodies" chapter, before you proceed to read any further. Promise ? Read them again, and really *think* about them.

I refer to these sentences.

Just as there are *tones* of *colors* in the Rainbow Spectrum which can't be seen with physical vision, such as ultraviolet and infrared, there are *colors* of *tones* in the Music of the Spheres which can't be heard with physical hearing. "In the Beginning," certain sounds produced differing sets of vibrational frequencies in the ethers. Some of these were of such low frequency that they formed particles of what we call "matter," or physical substance.

There would be no Light, as we know it, without minute specks of matter in the ethers to reflect it.

There is an intimate connection between color and sound and all other expressions of life. Sound is on a lower level of the scale, and comes just above the *form and substance of matter*. Consequently, *sound* is the intermediary between the higher level of abstract ideas in the Mind — and *concrete form*.

Sound is capable of molding the ethers into *shapes,* and through these shapes, the corresponding power of the Mind (especially the Minds of our Creators) is able *to make an impression on the ethers which can manifest into physical matter*.

Have you read the foregoing several times, and memorized it ? Good, then we may continue.

Following the Tower of Babel language cataclysm (which very nearly contains "asylum," except for the *u,* so perhaps it should be spelled "catuclysm" — we still have to watch for distortion of spelling) — following this *murder of the music of English,* a major cosmic event of vast importance to Earth and Earthlings transpired.

Because the destruction of the rhyme, rhythms and musical tones of primordial English inflicted such severe damage to universal synchronicity, short circuiting as it did the former harmonious communication between Earthlings, our Creators divinely manifested the wee nature spirits, called druids by the Celtic people, with a lower-case *d*, who were and still are *quite real* entities — also shy and quiet.

Remember . . . in the Beginning, our Creators spoke certain sounds which produced differing sets of vibrational frequencies in the ethers. *Some of these were of such low frequency that they formed particles of what we call matter or physical substance.*

In this manner were the tiny word druids created.

Many Indian tribes called their "god" by the name Manitou. But the Algonquian Indians were the first to employ the name Manitou. Manitous were conceived by them as *nature spirits, of both good and evil influence.* This will take on a most important meaning in a few pages. Remember it. And so, the tiny word druids may also be called elves, sprites or manitous. (They never like capitals, always lower case, since they don't want to call attention to themselves.) But the word is spelled wrong in the dictionary. For numerological (magical and logical, remember ?) reasons, both Manitou and manitou must be spelled with two *n*'s . . . as in Mannitou . . . mannitou and mannitous. This gives mannitou (and Mannitou, the "god" of some tribes) a vibration of 33 — and gives the plural mannitous a vibration of 36. Both Compound Numbers are supremely appropriate, as you will recognize by referring to the definition of these particular double numbers in Chapter 5.

The nature spirit druids were charged with the sacred mission of hiding and protecting the Anglo-Saxon alphabet until the preordained time for it to be resurrected and gradually re-seeded into the mass collective subconscious, of humans. When this occurred the Anglo-Saxon alphabet began to take a wrong fork in the road, as it were, twisting itself into several new languages, such as Latin, Greek, German, French, Italian and so forth. It took a while for the basic essence of English speech to return to human consciousness, first incarnating itself into a form called "Olde English."

It was at this point of a pretzel twist in the English language that the druids, who possessed (and still do) magic powers bestowed upon them by their — and our — Creators, multiplied or "cloned" themselves in a kind of desperate spiritual and mystical attempt to keep matters under control. To accomplish this, they *mattered* themselves, superimposing themselves on each word, to protect each word from oblivion, while simultaneously causing it to gradually assume its former shape and *sound*.

The druids took over their mission of "mattering" themselves, cloning themselves and superimposing themselves over individual words in the Celtic regions where "Olde English" began to *reappear*: England, Ireland, Scotland and Wales. After a short time the little nature spirit words became so hypnotized by and enmeshed within this mission (much as did our own Spirits when they created flesh bodies: See Chapter 9) that it became somewhat of a fun game to them. Losing their perspective, from time to time, like mischievous small children, they began to spring little unexpected mini-pranks on humans who "used" them — spoke them. When the druids were spoken (as words) they proceeded to create an action, to materialize, so to speak, the meaning of the "word spoken," as Earthlings tossed the little nature spirits into the ethers *as sounds*. Perhaps, who knows, they may have felt that this was an added benefit to humans, helping them to learn the *power* of the words they spoke, thus gently leading them back into recalling the primordial purity of the English language.

Now do you understand why it is that the people of England, Wales, Scotland and Ireland all have their legends and stories of — their firm belief in — the wee folk, druids, elves, faeries, leprechauns and the like? Some of them lead humans to pots of gold, some trick humans by leading them on to an illusionary end of the rainbow — others sour the cow's milk, cause humans to trip, hit their elbows and knees sharply. The good wee folk, superimposed upon harmonious words, bring bundles of good luck. The unfortunate, sacrificing wee folk who volunteered to "matter" and superimpose themselves upon disharmonious and ugly words carry out their mission in a polarized version, bringing nasty little annoyances to the humans who toss them out into the air without thinking as unpleasant sounds, likely landing, as often as not, on their tiny heads, which would naturally cause them to be occasionally cranky.

You still don't believe these nature spirit druid words possess magical powers ? You think I'm jesting, trying to be amusing, telling you faerie stories ? Remember the scientific evidence of the Eidophone in Chapter 7, "Forgotten Melodies" ? Read it again. Now. Then read it a third time. *Think.*

Truly, I am not jesting, trying to be amusing — or telling you faerie stories — although these true stories are, admittedly, about faeries, nature spirits or sprites and wee folk. I'm perfectly serious. As serious as James Barrie and Lewis Carroll were in writing *Peter Pan, Alice in Wonderland* and *Through the Looking Glass.*

You didn't know these books are serious, as well as charming and imaginative ? Oh, they are, they are ! It just takes a long time for adults to learn to read between the lines of such works and discover the real messages here. When Peter and Wendy and Michael and John were flying around the room they were levitating, you see. When Alice grew taller, then shorter, she was visiting various astral levels. When Peter spoke of always remaining a child, and never growing up, he was expressing the principles explained in the following chapter, "Physical Immortality." And so on . . . and on . . . and on. If you read these books again, with your Third Eye open and your sixth sense singing, you'll see them in a completely new light.

What I'm relating to you here is as serious and as real as anything else I've ever written, whether it's that Aries is impulsive, Cancer is moody or Libra is indecisive, etc. — all of which I presume you've found to be true and reliable. Trust me. Mostly, trust yourself. Ask your own Higher S-elf. To repeat my own s-elf and the Galilean for perhaps the one hundredth time in this book, "Let those who have eyes, see — let those who have ears, hear." (And let all others soon become enlightened.)

Speaking of yourS-elf and myS-elf, you've probably wondered while reading this book why I frequently spell these identification words in such an odd way. The druids very much like it. It makes their small hearts happy. You see, they have come to think of themselves as nearly human, these druid words, and they refer to each other as we do. They think of "themselves" as myself, himself, herself, yourself and ourselves, too, just like us. But unlike humans, the word druids are only too painfully aware of the need for separation within these words — and the reason for the need.

The reason is the Serpent Mystery. "Be ye therefore wise as serpents, and harmless as doves." "Your eyes shall be opened, and ye shall be as gods." (Third Eyes.) The thing is, there are two "good" serpents and one "bad" serpent, a total of three, and it all goes back to the much distorted and twisted story of Genesis. The distinction between and the identification of the three serpents is related in a later book. All you need to understand about it now is that it's the "bad" serpent who has tried to keep hidden the truth within these oft-used pronouns: ourselves, himself, yourself, herself and myself. Not to mention your Higher Self.

Let's first lexigram the word "sprite," since it's just another term for the wee folk or nature spirits (druids). SPRITE is very close to the word SPIRIT, is it not ? SPRITE, then, TIES itself tightly to the word SPIRIT. Sprite and spirit are also closely tied and related in a meaningful way in numerology, the sister discipline of Lexigrams, SPRITE being represented by the Compound Number 23, and SPIRIT being represented by the Compound Number 19, in their vibration to Higher Power. Consequently, to borrow a phrase from Abraham Lincoln, it is altogether fitting and proper for a sprite to be a spirit. Let's continue spiraling. We'll soon enough get back to that serpent, coiled there and waiting for us to expoSe his attempted deception over the past eonS. Note the pronoun — *his*.

Now, since a sprite is an elf — and a sprite is also a spirit (sometimes called *nature* spirits, without the *e*) — and since humans possess a Spirit (which is the Higher Self or Overself), then it logically follows that, just as the tiny sprite-druid words are elves — the Spirits of humans *may also be called elves*. Let's image, then, and quite truly so, that each tiny druid word has a spirit of its own — and to differentiate it from a human Spirit, the spirits of the druids are spelled "sprites," with a lower case *s*. Therefore, *you* possess a Spirit, and the little word druids possess a "sprite." And both Spirits and sprites are elves.

Both kinds of elves — *nature* spirits and *human* Spirits — possess magical powers, do they not ? Yes, they do.

Webster: elf or sprite; nature spirit, druid: *exercising magical powers*.

And so, the you-of-you, the Higher Angel of your-s-elf is, in reality, a most powerful **ELF**. Here is one of those "coincidences" which is not really a "coincidence" but a typical tongue-in-cheek little code-trick of the words druids.

Your brain, as I've already pointed out in a previous chapter, is actually an electrical device containing more than 40 billion electric cells, each with a faint electromagnetic field, continually sending out weak signals in the radio part of the sound spectrum, carrying a frequency of between 1 and 30 hertz. The signals from your heart likewise lie in this faint electromagnetic field.

Remember these words — once again: "In the Beginning, certain sounds produced differing sets of vibrational frequencies in the ethers — and some of these were of *such low frequency* that they were capable of forming particles of *matter* or *physical substance*. (The way elves were created!)

The low frequency field can possibly be used for *external control of the mind* and plausibly also perhaps be used to plant perceptions in the brain (seeding by Gurus ?). Since the Earth Herself generates a faint electromagnetic signal in the very low 1 to 30 hertz range, certain natural conditions may trigger responses in humans . . . . and most certainly "creates" or produces the "physical matter" of plants, trees and flowers.

Now for the "coincidence," which is not a coincidence, but one of the little "jokes" of the word druids. Do you know what science calls this *Extra Low Frequency* field when scientists refer to it among themselves ? They've named it after its initials — **ELF** !! Most appropriate, don't you agree ? I just heard Nahtan whispering into my inner ear *"Quite* !"

By the way, since we're speaking of the Higher Angel of the S-elf, the word **ANGEL**, when you switch the letters around, is **ANGLE** and, as Einstein's Higher S-elf knew, in channeling through Albert by way of the extra low frequency of **ELF** the wonderland of mathematical relativity, *all reality* depends *entirely* upon the relative **ANGLE** from which it's viewed in the cosmos . . . in its relative relationship — or **ANGLE**— to space and that great imposter, Time. Time and space. Relativity. **RELATIVITY** contains **REAL**, so what is **REAL** is relative to its **ANGLE**. No wonder **ANGLE** is **ANGEL** ! Angels can help us judge what is real in any given time or space, past, present or future.

Mentioning the Wonderland of Einsteinic Relativity spiraled me into Lewis Carroll's magical tales, which spiraled me into the heroine of them, the little girl who inspired Lewis Carroll's *Alice in Wonderland, Through the Looking Glass* and all his other books — an actual little girl of whom he was very fond, named Alice. Without Alice, we would never have known about the Mad Hatter, the Red Queen or the White Queen, and we would never have heard about the time when "'twas brillig, and the slithy toves did gyre and gimble in the wabe." Since Alice was the author's muse, it was quite logical, then, for **LEWIS CARROLL** to hold within both his heart and his name . . . **ALICE**.

Before we leave her, there's one more thing. The word druids have asked me to send all of you a special secret code message — personally from them to you, using Lewis Carroll's words:

> *In spring, when woods are getting green*
> *We'll try and tell you what we mean*
> *In summer, when the days are long*
> *Perhaps you'll understand the song . . . .*

What does Alice have to do with the serpent we were about to expose ? Absolutely nothing. But I keep telling you that's what happens over and over with Lexigrams. When you start to get lost a dozen times a sentence, a hundred times a page, a thousand times a day when you're writing or speaking, on lexigramming detours of your own, you'll forgive me. When you experience it yourself. Ah, yes, yourS-elf . . . back to that sneaky snake.

Good grief ! **SNEAK** is **SNAKE** and **SNAKE** is **SNEAK** ! How very marvelously appropriate. While the "good serpents" (remember, there are both kinds) have been coiling into words like wiSdom, bleSS, Serene and so forth, what he (oh, yes, definitely *he*) has been doing for so many centuries, sneaking and snaking around throughout the English language, is driving the tiny word druids bonkers, by in-SiSting on planting the letter *S*, representing him (as it also does in "good" words, the good serpents) anywhere he can; in particular, sneaking into the middle of all those *identity* words, such as: ourselves, yourselves, himself, herself, yourself, myself and even your Higher Self or Overself.

Until the exposure on these pages, he's gotten away with it. Surely you can now see clearly what those words have always in-tended to convey to you. SanS that Sneaky Serpent *S*, those words are **NOT** (give it caps) *single* words. They are *double* words. Removing the *S*, they become our elves . . . your elves . . . her elf . . . your elf . . . my elf . . . and your Higher Elf or Over Elf.

Now let me demonstrate how our teeny-tiny friends, the word

druids or druid words, whichever, reveal some surprises about current grammar. Obviously, the word "herself" (herS-elf) actually refers to *her elf*. Right ? Right. Stay with me. But it is poor *actual* grammar to say *himself*, since it can't be *him elf*. That's ridiculous. Although, as we've seen, it's correct to say *herself*, because it means her elf. Don't leave me yet. I'm just warming up to a revelation. All right, so we've correctly and properly tossed the grammatically incorrect *masculine* "himself" (him elf) out of the druid dictionary for excellent cause — leaving in the druid dictionary the *feminine* "herself" (her elf) for equally excellent cause.

By the same rules, we can't use the feminine "sheself" (she elf), but that doesn't matter because we still have one feminine identification we *can* use: *herself* and her elf. However, what about the men, what about the masculine elves ? We can't use *himself* (him elf), as we already know. And clearly it would be dreadful to use *hisself* (hisS-elf). Our human wordsmiths will not permit such a gross usage. Therefore, the masculine sex has been exiled from elfdom by both the word druids and the human wordsmiths.

Because we know that these small nature-spirit-sprites are much smarter than our dictionary compiler human wordsmiths, that they are just and wise druids who were given a sacred mission by our Creators, they must have good cause for having banished the masculine sex from the language paradise of Elfdom, a reason lost in antiquity, and for-eons-forgotten. It will be remembered in a later book, and the shattering truth will finally win a victory over our so long entrenched patriarchal society, not making women superior, but harmoniously equal. The **PATRIARCH** system is a **TRAP**, as the word admits.

However, the feminine sex hasn't entirely escaped "the mark of the beast," the negative serpent "S." It's *not* there in "he" but it *is* there in "She." And it's there in *both* "hers" and "his." Also note that the serpent "S" coils around "maSculine," not around "feminine." And that the maSculine "himself" and "hisself" are not valid elf words.

Remaining with the "druid log book" or the druid dictionary of Elfdom for a moment longer, notice that the word "themselves" is also incorrect elf grammar. One can't very well remove the serpent "S" from themS-elves, and be left with "them elves." There's a good reason for that, and if you meditate on it for a while, you'll see it.

Since the Fall and the later symbolic Tower of Babel language cataclysm, English has not yet returned to its original musical purity, although it has progressed to a fair measure of its former power, unrealized by **EARTHLINGS**, who still possess the power to **SING** the language in their very name, but are presently too filled with **HATE** to **HEAR** the Music of the Spheres. There are lots of **STAR SIGN** codes to make a wish on sparkling from the word **EARTHLINGS**, in addition to these five.

Yet two of these five present a happy bit of knowledge, telling us that each **EARTHLING** is an individual **STAR SIGN** himself or herself ! Do you see **STAR SIGN** hiding-in-plain-sight within **EARTHLINGS** ? Yes, hiding in plain **SIGHT** !

Men and women have thus far not heeded even the fraction of former power still available to them in the continually evolving English language. Further, they fail to notice the negative side of that power, as they speak thoughtlessly. Too many people today use **WORDS** as a **SWORD** to wound each other, by switching the last letter to the first, and the first to the last. They will continue to do so, in some degree, until they fully recognize that the words of the English language were meant to fly through the mind on **WINGS** (another word hiding the secret that words can **SING**) until they realize that English (which also contains **SING**, as we've already noticed) is the only one of all **LANGUAGES** which can be **SUNG** in the harmonious chords of the Music of the Spheres.

Did our Creators actually charge the nature spirit druids with such a **MISSION** as we've discussed ? Any mission must be carried out by those who commit **NO SIN** (at least no serious sin . . . mini--

pranks don't count) as the word itself reveals. So, did our Creators give such a mission to the druids ? Yes, they **DID**, for the very word **DRUID** contains the message that they **DID** — to **RID** the world of the babble of confusion. **WORLD** contains **LORD**, plus the inverted double pyramid letter *W,* which has a vital meaning of its own, as an inverted double pyramid.

Earthlings in the Aquarian Age must learn (and one must **EARN** learning — do you see why ?) — they must learn to stop using **WORDS** as a **SWORD**, and begin to realize that each single **WORD** they speak is, in reality, a magic wand, as powerful as the **ROD** of Moses, when they discover how to use them properly. Remove the mystical secret of the inverted double pyramid "*W*" from **WORD**, and you are left with a wand or a **ROD** as potent as Aaron's rod, the one he lent his brother, Moses, to convince the Pharaoh to "let his people go."

Even the plural form of **WORDS** loses its power to become a **SWORD** and hurt when humans cease to re-verse it into a word that doesn't rhyme with happiness and compassion, but with pain and misery. Each single word is a verse that must be molded to rhyme with the harmony of the Uni**VERSE**, the one true verse, so that the lost chords of the Music of the Spheres may once more, like the voice of the turtle, be heard throughout the land.

Let's remain with **UNIVERSE** a spiral longer. The word contains such a clear definition of what constitutes it. First, the most apparent. Universe or Uni-verse means one verse, since Uni is one. One verse signifies the Music of the Spheres, with everyone and everything singing in perfect harmony. **UNIVERSE** also contains, in addition to that one (or Uni) **VERSE**, these words: **SUN . . . VENUS . . . NURSE . . . SEER** and **US.**

In astrology, the **SUN** represents the life force, while **VENUS** represents Love, the most important word in the entire English language. What more does one need, other than Life and Love ? The word **SUN** in **UNIVERSE** has another layered, more deeply hidden meaning, referring mysteriously to our lost Sun. (You'll read about what happened to it in Chapter 9.) The word NURSE gently chides the patriarchs, reminding them that She (our Mother Who art in Heaven) still lovingly and protectively NURSES US, as she does all humans in all UNIVERSES. The word SEER means that She also sees into a future when Her children will "come home" to Her, remembering when they were nursed and nurtured by Her infinite Love. UNIVERSE also contains EVEN, or perfect balance and harmony. Likewise, EVE, another reminder to open the Third Eye to the truth of that sneaky serpent and the apple.

The word VERSE alone gives us SEE ("let those who have eyes" — Third Eyes — see) . . . and, again, SEER. Yes, our poets, those who write verses channeled by their Spirits, are our true prophets. We need them now far more than we need our scientists. Those who write VERSES are our SEERS, who will gradually, with the help of the word druids, mold the English language back into its pure and primordial shape and form . . . and music. For what are verses without music to sing of them — and what is music without its melodies emphasized by verse ?

"In the beginning was the Word . . ." "And God spoke the word . . ." "The Word was made flesh, and dwelt among us." (The latter quote delves into very deep waters, and can't be interpreted in this present work.) The word, the word, the word! In the beginning, there was a Word . . . a Sound . . . a chord of Music . . . capable of creating and manifesting matter out of the ethers. *The Word of Creation.* The lost chord. Obviously, an awesomely powerful word-elf . . . (Extra Low Frequency sound — ELF, remember ?)

As the tiny druid nature spirits were assigned the task, by our and their Creators, to guard and protect the English language down through countless eons of Time, they were also given the most sacred and holy of missions . . . to guard the Word of Creation Itself from Earthlings as yet unenlightened, who might use it for unthinkable destruction. They have performed their mission, these tiny word druids, and kept this word hidden from even the most illuminated Avatars and Adepts. While gently and gradually seeding into humans the English language . . . they have done the opposite with the Word . . . keeping it buried . . . revealing to humans all words but this . . . one at a time . . . over the centuries.

Where have the druids protected the Word ? The answer is perhaps a most profound mystery, and as I sit here typing this page, I tell you truly, druid honor, that I have not yet channeled whether or not to reveal it in this book. I promise I shall, either way, when I approach the end of this chapter. Of course, the geographical location of it is only the initial step of a long and secret alchemy formula required to decode the Word, which may be revealed only to two once "lost angels" who have once more become immortal. (See Chapter 9.)

Lexigram spiraling can result in a brief, lightning flash mentalastral trip, or a long journey back into the truth buried within your sleeping subconscious. The ones we've been using as examples so far have taken us on relatively short trips. Shall we take a much longer one by spiraling a particular nine-letter word ? Yes, let's. Because the word I have in mind is one which is currently causing a vast amount of tragic controversy all over the world, in both a religious and a medical sense. Abortions.

We'll Lexigram the plural of the word, not the singular, since we're going to try to discover if the word will lead us into illumination, by giving us a reliable cosmic answer to the pros and cons of the issue — and that issue isn't relevant to one single abortion (for which there may be various justifications), but to abortions, plural, as they are presently being attacked by the Right to Lifers and defended by those who champion women's rights over their own bodies.

Are abortions morally defensible — or a sin against defenseless human life? Are abortions *murders* ? As always, the word itself posesses the answer, as it defines its own true meaning, hidden within the alphabetical letters comprising it. The word "abortions" offers us a coded solution to the raging abortion issue, seeded by the recent emancipation of women. Some of you will be greatly comforted by the answer given so clearly in the word's Lexigram; others of you will be resentful of that answer. Speaking to the latter group, please keep in mind that the answer has no relation whatsoever to my own personal feelings, prejudice or lack of prejudice. The answer comes directly from the wisdom of the word druids. If, by now, you still refuse to acknowledge the evidence of their power, you'd best skip the next several pages, whichever side of the abortion controversy you're on. Conversely, if you have, by now, learned to respect the word druids and their sacred mission involving the English language, you'll find "abortions" to be new evidence of it.

One more request. If you're a Right to Lifer, and become offended at any particular point along the way of our spiraling, stay with us. You hate being called prejudiced, don't you ? The only way you can prove you don't deserve such an insulting label is to *first* pay close attention, with an open mind, to the counsel offered by the word druids, and immediately following it, by astrology — and *then* make your decision, based on all the information available, not just part of it. This request is meant for Catholic readers too.

The Lexigram of **ABORTIONS** does not quibble about the answer to this issue. Its revelation is quite emphatic, leaving no room for doubt or dispute.

ABORTIONS

It lexigrams into the following words:

**IT IS TORN. IT IS NOT BORN. IT IS A ROBOT.
A ROBOT IS NOT BORN - NO SIN
IS ABORTION A SIN ? NO. IT IS NOT A SIN.**

The Zebra Rule applies.

Read the Zebra Rule again. When a negative word appears and

the letters N and O — or N and O and T also appear, as negating words, while the letters Y and E and S do *not* appear — it means that the person (or word) will have been *accused* of whatever the negative word implies, but is not guilty.

Catholics and Right to Lifers, stay with us, please. We're going to spiral higher to discover just why this Lexigram says what it does. That's the real value in Lexigrams, to use them to rise to a higher consciousness through further thought spiraling, based on the initial Lexigram revelation. That's where lexigramming becomes an art.

First let's spiral into the pages of good old Noah Webster's rule book, which usually does not contradict the druid dictionary (it just doesn't reveal as *much* as the latter). *Webster* has the following comments to help us define further what our Abortions Lexigram called the entity which is aborted: a Robot.

Robot: a machine that *looks* like a human being, and performs various *acts* of a human being, but is *without human emotions*. A mechanism guided by *automatic controls*.
Webster [Italics mine]

The word druids do not err; they had some reason for hiding the term robot within the word abortions to describe the entity being aborted. The words infant, baby, child and even fetus were missing when the word *abortions* appeared in the language.

Does the *Webster* definition of "robot" relate to the fetus in the womb ? Yes, it does. The fetus *looks* like a human, and performs various *acts* of a human while immersed in fluid in the uterus, but is yet *without human emotions*, and is guided, most definitely, by *automatic controls*, those controls being in the hands of a particular Spirit or Higher S-elf, who has decided to build this house, this flesh temple (the body is the Temple of the soul — and Spirit — and Mind), and to take up residence when it's completed. The Spirit, therefore, is the Landlord-Owner of the house or flesh temple being constructed, and the parents are the architects, yet always using the blueprint of the Spirit who ordered the building of this Temple of Flesh.

Now let's spiral further, to penetrate higher truth, which leads us into both mystical or spiritual truth founded in the Christian Holy Works . . . and astrology, the mother of astronomy (not the other way around), religion, mathematics and all science.

The "miracle of birth." What is it, precisely, this miracle ? It is the trembling awe felt by the mother and onlookers at that sacred instant when the infant draws its *first breath of life,* that magical moment when what has been, in effect, a "water-breathing creature," is miraculously transformed and transmuted into an air-breathing human — and a *new life is born.* Life renewing itS-elf again.

As medical science recognizes, tremendous biological, chemical and physiological changes occur in the organism called the infant at that instant of its drawing *the first breath of life.* Turning to the Scriptures, do they not refer to God saying "And I shall breathe the breath of Life into them . . . ?"

Spiraling into astrology, it is at this moment that the more than 40 billion electromagnetic cells in the brain are programmed, like a computer (of which the human brain is the ultimate prototype), by the invisible, yet powerful cosmic frequencies — or light waves — emanating from the Sun, the Moon and the planets — in a pattern commensurate with their position in space, and their mathematically and astronomically measured aspects to one another at that magnetically charged instant of Time — so that the human thus born will feel a powerful electromagnetic "tug" (which can be accepted or rejected through the holy gift of Free Will) each time in the future when the Sun, Moon and planets either conflict or harmonize with their brain-computer-programmed positions in "the sky" at birth.

Spiraling next into metaphysics, it is likewise at this magical instant that the Spirit and its individual Mind and Soul, from which it is never separated (and which always remain outside the body) connect with or lock-in to the body temple of the now human infant this Holy Trinity ordained to be constructed approximately nine months earlier.

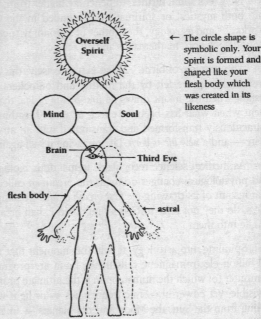

← The circle shape is symbolic only. Your Spirit is formed and shaped like your flesh body which was created in its likeness

The three symbolic circles comprising the *upper pyramid* are never separated, either during the life of the flesh body "puppet" or after its death.

And so, you see, the entity called "the fetus" by medical science and "a robot" by Lexigrams, is not human — is not alive — until this instant of the first breath when the brain is programmed, when the first "breath of life" occurs. This is, by the way, why your horoscope or nativity is not correctly calculated without the astrologer's tedious work of rectifying the exact time of birth, the instant of the first breath, which is seldom the same time given on the birth certificate or by "mother's memory." Since astrologers who have mastered the art and science of rectification are so very rare . . . it creates a problem. Personally, I will neither calculate nor interpret a nativity I have not been able to rectify to this exact instant of *actual life*. Even though I am one who has mastered rectification, it takes sometimes only a few hours if I'm lucky, up to several days or weeks or longer with some nativities to accomplish rectification reliably. Each chart is an individual challenge.

The abortion controversy is like so many things on this planet. It concentrates with such intensity upon the flesh that it ignores the Spirit. So much ado is there about the mirror-reversed prologues of birth and unnecessary death (see Chapter 9), and so little attention given to the great drama in between.

True, it's very sad to lovingly build a temple that a Spirit, Mind and Soul intend to possess, a sanctuary woven of tender, gentle dreams, and then, for any one of a variety of reasons, see that dream of a body temple disappear. But it isn't the end of the world. It's agonizing, but it isn't the *end* — of anything.

There are few experiences more emotionally devastating than the accidental miscarriage of the flesh "house" a deeply desired infant is intended to occupy. It's one of the most painful trials a man and woman who love must occasionally endure. But it would be so much less hurtful if they could realize that, when the grief of disappointment has healed, another flesh body temple may be designed and built, a new "house," constructed with the same blueprint — to be the residence of the *very same* and equally disappointed trinity of the Spirit, Mind and Soul who, when fused with the new body temple at its first breath, will create the very same human infant wrongly believed to have been lost. If only such bereaved parents realized this, they would be deeply comforted by the comprehension that there is no real cause for grief — except the waiting period of another nine months, surely a short span as Earth time goes.

I won't invade the parents' privacy by giving their names, but I know a couple in Ohio who were ecstatic when their first child was conceived. They looked forward to the birth of their baby with such joy and happiness. Then, a few weeks before the delivery date, the mother was told by her doctors that the "baby" had died — that she was carrying a dead infant — *robot,* remember. There are no druid words in the English language to describe the agony and courage of both parents, especially the mother. Who can find words to describe what she felt during her first long and painful labor, knowing that, at the end of the pain, there would be no joy . . . no life. ?

This brave mother bore her heartache and physical pain, suffering her great soul test alone. Not even her equally heartbroken husband could conceive of what it was really like for her. I told her that their baby, a female "robot," was not dead; that because of their love and courage, she would become a miracle baby very soon . . . that she (her Spirit) had changed her mind, and wanted a different birth date, for complex astrological reasons . . . that she would return to them if their desire (electromagnetic energy) remained strong enough. She believed me. She quickly learned to *know* this, not just "hope" it.

A year later, on the *same day* as the earlier delivery, she gave birth to a beautiful, healthy baby girl. Their miracle baby returned. The very *same* baby (Spirit, Mind and Soul) they had thought was lost, with the same generally designed body temple (horoscope), with only a couple of minor architectural (planetary) improvements, and the same colored glass windows (the eyes are the windows of the soul). All the little girl had done (her Spirit) was to decide to arrive a little later, that's all.

This sort of miracle has manifested hundreds of thousands of times, all over the world, and it would manifest an even greater number of times if the parents of a "miscarried" or otherwise thought to be lost flesh body temple . . . recognized the truth.

To plan for a visit from someone very dear, and then to learn that the visit must be postponed indefinitely, is certainly cause for deep disappointment, but . . . *no one died*. And the more intensely one images the postponed visit occurring, the sooner the happy event will manifest. How long ? When ?

When is the least important part of the knowing that a baby — or anyone else — who has temporarily disappeared from your life will return. If people who are separated could only comprehend this truth, the time of their coming together again would arrive so much sooner. The delays of reunion are caused by failing to recognize the in-significance of *when*.

That's another facet of Lexigrams. "Insignificant," in the druid dictionary, does not possess the same meaning as *not* significant. **IN-SIGNIFICANT** should give you a Lexigram **SIGN** that something is significant *within*. When you've mastered the word alchemy of the *in*-significance of when, you can simply *ordain* the "when" of the event. Clocks and calendars aren't in control of it. *You* are. That may be the greatest thing you'll ever learn. Next to Love, which comes first . . . always.

It takes a while to get the hang of it, of learning how to read the druid dictionary correctly, but once you do the Force will be with you . . . forever. Once mastered, it's like swimming or riding a bicycle. You never forget how.

I said that there are few things sadder (for the yet unenlightened) as the involuntary loss of a deeply desired infant's partially con-structed body temple (house), before the new human life has had a chance to occupy it. However, there are many things sadder and more devastating to life itself than the deliberate abortion of an un-wanted "house" which prevents a robot from becoming alive and hu-man at the first breath — such as the hideous nightmare of child abuse unwanted children suffer, to name but one of them.

Destroying body temples is not a good thing. It's obviously

wasteful, as senseless as building a new home, then tearing it down before anyone has had a chance to live in it. (The death of adults is an equally wasteful and senseless destruction of "houses" or body temples. See Chapter 9.) Such abortive destruction of a robot, of a temple-under-construction, may perhaps correctly carry the stigma of vandalism, but it is not murder.

The robot or flesh temple thus destroyed was only *intended* to be the residence of a human at the time of fusing with a particular Spirit, Mind and Soul, who would have been spending all their time outside the house (body temple) in any case. When the intended residence becomes unavailable by being torn down (aborted) these three inseparables simply ordain the building of a new one, sometimes in the same location, using the same parental architects — at other times in a different neighborhood, city, state or country, using other architects — entirely depending on the degree of desire (electromagnetic energy) of the parents.

Most people aren't aware that when a man and woman mate a powerful auric light is sent out into the ethers, visible to millions of trinities of Spirits, Minds and Souls awaiting a birth channel. If the mating occurs for no reason but lust, the auric colors of the spectrum are muddy and indistinct, a rust-red color, and attract, as a birth channel, a Spirit who is not highly evolved but a spirit who, *nevertheless*, deserves his or her spin on the Karmic wheel of life.

When a man and woman mate in love and tenderness the brilliant auric light projected by such a trembling, ecstatic union attracts a much higher evolved Spirit, who chooses this mating as a birth channel, which is what is meant by a "love child," and does not necessarily require a piece of paper called a marriage license. Neither Spirits nor our Creators pay any attention to pieces of paper — since many of those who possess such a piece of paper mate in lust only. Parental channels are thus *chosen* by Spirits awaiting incarnation.

Interesting that **LUST** is **SLUT**. It's difficult to determine whether these two words were deliberately formulated by human wordsmiths or word druids. Lust describes mating experienced for one partner's selfish sexual pleasure only.

Sexual union experienced by those who have **TAMED** each other before they **MATED**, as we've already discussed, is blessed, and need not be experienced only for the purpose of conceiving. The ecstatic reward of love is a holy experience, whether or not it results in a voluntary or involuntary conception. To create new life is a blessing, but so is the creation of mutual peace and fulfillment.

As for abortions, humans ought to be more concerned with the Spirit, and less concerned with the flesh temple or body. In the long run, it would be greatly beneficial to everyone involved, including future body temples, which, like all houses, would be considerably improved if designed by enlightened architects, working in harmony with the Owner-Landlord. It's both sad and ironic that the misguided Right to Lifers destroy and burn down abortion clinics in retaliation against those who destroy flesh houses of their own volition, creating heavy Karma for themselves by this sort of "revenge." Perhaps the balanced Karma of their own miscarriage of a new life they so wrongly, cruelly and angrily tried to defend ? That's how the law of Karma works, in this Incarnation or the next.

Returning from that very long trip initiated by a mere one-word Lexigram, when the word "abortions" seeded itself — its elf — into the language as a word druid, it already contained the answer to the abortion controversy, even before it became an issue.

Remember the Lexigram code of "in-significant" ? Here's another secret. Some of the word druids are disgruntled and disgusted because human wordsmiths have tacked a "dis" to them, and it sticks like glue, refusing to be dis-engaged. They seem quite pleased when I refer to feelings I have of a very joyous and happy nature by saying I'm both gusted and gruntled — which means I'm extremely pleased. That's the meaning of gusted and gruntled, is it not ? Or it should be, to any thinking human who has studied the druid dictionary. If pleased is the opposite of displeased, integrated is the opposite of disintegrated, order is the opposite of disorder and satisfied is the opposite of dissatisfied, then gusted is the opposite of disgusted and gruntled is the opposite of disgruntled — to any logical Earthling. The word druids who were in charge of "gusted" and "gruntled" have had nothing to do for so long, they're really quite bored, and would appreciate it if they could become useful again by these words returning to common usage, through your use of them. So, do start describing your happy feelings and satisfied feelings as gusted and gruntled, won't you ?

Shall we spiral into a few more Lexigram mental-astral trips ? Then we'll lexigram some names together.

Personally, I've found the word "lie" to be the most meaningful exposure of truth I've discovered in Lexigrams, and I know that sounds like a contradiction, the ultimate non sequitur. What you must understand, however, is that the word *lie* possesses multi-layered meanings. Some lies are born from (the children of) deliberate deceptions. Others are born from (the children of) kindness and consideration. These are sometimes called "little white lies" to save someone's feelings from being hurt. Like telling a friend you loved the cookies she baked for you and brought to the hospital, when in reality they tasted like cardboard, sprinkled with bird seed. Still other "lies" are born from (the children of) faith and knowing.

For instance, anything you can't see with physical vision — or can't prove with visible evidence — is considered by some people to be a lie, if you insist to them it's there and they can't see it. After whatever it might be finally manifests into matter or beingness, whether it's a missing child or any other miracle, the "lie" the believer was accused of suddenly . . . Abracadabra ! . . . becomes the truth. The "liar" becomes a prophet.

If you say to a friend "Look at that beautiful rose bush in the front yard" (you planted the day before) — and no rose bush has yet manifested into "matter" visible to physical eyesight, the friend is likely to say, or secretly believe, that you're lying. The rose bush might very well be cheerfully growing there, in an etheric sense, waiting to be ordained to manifest itself into dense matter, but as long as it's not visible to the physical vision, pointing to it and insisting that it's really there is defined by everyone as telling a lie. Just as children, when they tell their parents about their "imaginary" playmates . . . sometimes tiny faeries and nature spirits who converse and play with them . . . are told to "stop lying."

There are more interesting insights about what constitutes a lie or does not, but as you begin to master Lexigrams, you'll discover them for yourself.

Here's a small Lexigram of two words, as an initial step to your comprehension of "lying."

Lexigrams often start rusty wheels turning in your brain. Some of them may be frustrating when you first calculate them, because they don't seem to make a bit of sense. But don't stop. Keep spiraling, and you'll find the answer is always logical, even though it may be hidden at first until you penetrate the meaning. For example, why should such a positive word as "believe" contain the word "lie" ? It's a real stumper when you're first learning about Lexigrams. But if you continue to ponder it, you'll be rewarded for your calm **CONTEMPLATION** with, as I pointed out earlier, a kind of spiritual **ELATION**.

BELIEVE contains **LIVE** a **LIE**. That doesn't seem logical, at first. The word **MIRACLE** contains the word **LIE** also. More confusion. Why ?

Keeping in mind the definitions of "lie" we just considered, realize that **MIRACLE** also contains the word **CLAIM** — and so, if you continue to **LIVE A LIE**, eventually you'll be able to **CLAIM A LIE**.

If you **BELIEVE**, you will eventually manifest a **MIRACLE**.

Believing (living a lie) is a process that will gradually manifest invisible etheric concepts, dreams, ideas and ideals — and *convictions* — into visible, dense matter. First comes hope, faint and weak. Then comes belief, much stronger. Next comes faith, and you're almost there ! At last comes *knowing,* the real power that makes it happen. The word KNOW hides the words NOW and WON. So, when you're able to really KNOW a thing it places you in the Eternal NOW, and you've WON. (More about the Eternal Now at the end of this chapter.)

As for BELIEVE lexigramming the word LIVE, some of you may be wondering why the word LIVE itself is EVIL, spelled backward. Lots of people have noticed that. Fewer have noticed also that EVIL is VILE. It's nothing to be concerned about; in fact, it's something to be ELATED about, when it's been carefully CONTEMPLATED — perhaps the most important truth revealed by Lexigrams. Because . . . there's another word in LIVE besides EVIL and VILE . . . and that word is, again, as we just saw, LIE. This is a perfect example of how you must train your mind to work with Lexigrams. What does it really mean, when you penetrate the word *live* and find the words "evil" and "vile" and "lie" within it ?

It means that humans, hypnotized by false religious doctrines and dogmas, believe that to live one must know the vile experiences of evil; that evil is an absolute necessity to the process of living. But there sits that three-letter word, telling you that this is a LIE. To live need *not* involve evil. Humans only *believe* that it does. (When one believes a falsehood, *"believe"* is not such a positive word, is it ? Another reason the word druids seeded the word "lie" into it.)

The *truth* is, as we discussed earlier, that this WORLD, containing LORD, is but a distorted mirror reflection of the real world, of the level of awareness called Heaven, where your Spirit, the you-of-you, dwells. And where your body could also dwell, if you understood how to live with "one foot in Heaven, and one foot on Earth" (as explained in the next chapter). When Earthlings finally penetrate the true meaning of the fourth and fifth lines of the Lord's Prayer (pene-trated in Chapter 9) . . . "Thy Kingdom Come, Thy will be done . . . on Earth, as it is in Heaven" . . . then to **LIVE** may not any longer be called **EVIL**, and to claim that it is will be exposed as a **LIE**, as it's a lie even now, when it's still not fully comprehended.

Through the absolute imaging, ordaining and knowing of the Mind, you have the power to manifest any kind of miracle — Ordain, Image, Believe, have Faith and Know — in other words, impress your image upon the ethers with such intensity that the image will be trans-muted into physical, dense *matter*. One way to impress it on your mind and to always remember the alchemy of it is through yet another facet of Lexigrams — meditating on two simple sentences. At least, that's how I re-mind my own S-elf of the alchemy of it. I find it irresistibly amusing, like a private joke with my Higher Elf, so that when I happen to speak the sentences aloud, musing to myS-elf in the presence of others who don't have a clue as to what I'm up to, I can't suppress a giggle — which doesn't do much for my desired image of dignity, I must say. These are the two alchemy-reminder sentences:

If you *mind*, it *matters*. If you don't *mind*, it doesn't *matter*.

When you read or speak the word *mind* in these two sentences image it mentally as a verb, synonymous with using your Mind to ordain a thing. Understand ? A verb. And when you read or speak the word *matter* in these two sentences, image it as synonomous with the verbs "materialize" or "manifest." See ? In other "words," you need to firmly "mind" (verb) a thing to materialize it into visibility, to "matter" it — manifest it into dense matter.

And so, if you mind something, it certainly does matter.

But if you *don't* mind, it certainly *won't* matter.

You'd be surprised how often I have to chuckle and appear to be a little pixilated during a day's normal conversations, keeping "in mind" the foregoing alchemy secret of Lexigrams. Like, someone in a theatre lobby will rudely press ahead of me in the popcorn line, re-marking sarcastically, "Excuse me, do you *mind* ?" — and I answer, with a silly elf grin on my face, "Well, usually I do, but not this time, so I guess it won't really matter."

Or when a friend asks, "Are you sure this doesn't matter ?" And I reply, grinning again, "That depends on whether or not I mind it." The confused stares I get only make my Higher Elf and my own S-elf giggle louder. I think most of my acquaintances have just written me off as a little eccentric, you know ? You'll find out. When they ask you to explain what you mean it just becomes more and more amus-ing, until you're finally overcome with an uncontrollable fit of laugh-ter. Like . . . remember when you were in Sunday School or grade school and someone said something funny to make you laugh, and you couldn't stop until you were sent from the room in disgrace ? It's like that.

Now, you may want to ask yourself what the human wordsmiths believe they really mean by those two words ? Are they verbs or nouns ? How are they defined ? By this time you may have guessed that these are two of the many jokes played on humans by the word druids, who roll over in the ethers, clutching their tiny tummies, laughing every time they hear them used . . . and mis-used.

If you could use a good laugh yourS-elf (or if your elf could use one) while you're reading this, check *Webster's*. Their confused at-tempts to define the word *mind* are amusing, as they valiantly struggle on and on, taking up more than half an entire page with this one word. Somewhere in the middle of all this verbal stuttering, the hu-man wordsmiths come up (or down) with: "never *mind* — don't be concerned; it doesn't *matter*" (!).

Then one is tempted to look up the word *matter* a few pages back from "mind," and discovers that the dictionary takes up roughly the same amount of space, using about the same number of contradictory words as were used in attempting to define "mind." They should be able to leave it with "a substance of which all material things are made," but they dare not stop there. As they go on for more than half a page with the enigma of "matter," one feels a sharp pang of sympathy for those of foreign birth who are trying to learn the English language as it exists presently.

Under the *Webster* definition of "matter" is, however, a sentence that shines forth from the page like a beacon of light, one which should impress upon the most sceptical brain computer the great power of the Mind. *Webster* states, quite truly, that matter is "what all material things are made of" . . . and that "matter and energy are regarded as equivalents, mutually convertible, according to Einstein's formula. $E = MC^2$ (energy equals mass multiplied by the square of the velocity of light). Remember those angstrom units, which are actually light waves, we discussed in the "Gurus, Ghosts, and Avatars" chapter ? *Webster* further re-minds us that, in dualistic thinking, "matter" is regarded as the *opposite* of Mind and Spirit, but neglects to tell us that the former is *created* by the latter. That's an important omission. It's disturbing to metaphysicians. Does it bother you ? You don't mind it being omitted ? Well, then, I guess it won't matter.

Sometimes the word druids play audio jests with words, such as: I *threw* the ball *through* the window . . . I am *through* with you . . . and it's *through* the light wave energy of the Mind that matter is created. Or the words *edition* and *addition*. They sound alike, and really are sibling words, since each "edition" of anything is an "addition" of the former number of "editions." We could remain with this facet of Lexigrams for an entire book, but we'll move on now to more Lexigrams of the basic sort.

I must warn you of a particular experience you're certain to have as you begin to master Lexigrams. (And they must be *mastered*, or they'll try to take control, in their mischievous ways.) You'll seldom complete a Lexigram of a word (or a name) the first time you calculate it. That is, you'll think you have, you'll firmly believe you have — especially if it's a word of only four or five letters — how could a word escape you dealing with such few letters ? But as I keep telling you, Lexigrams, the dictionary of the word druids, have definite minds of their own.

Sometimes Lexigrams will hold back their most startling secret for days, even months or years. Then one day you'll look at your Lexigram again, and there it is, peeking out at you ! The answer you'd been blinded to when you first tried to solve the mystery of the word or short name you needed so to penetrate. You'll be annoyed, and be unable to understand how you, as an intelligent, careful person, could possibly have missed that one revealing word, after having spent so much time concentrating on a simple Lexigram. Timing is everything in Lexigrams, and the word druids prove *themselves* (Oh, them-elves !) to be alive when they simply will not allow you to learn anything prematurely that they decide you're not yet ready to know. That's just part of what I meant by saying they have a mind of their own. Or minds of their own. It's one of their most exasperating habits. I've never taught a single person Lexigrams who hasn't had this frustrating experience with them.

It was my own elf mother who first tuned me in to words, teaching me bushels of fey and in-significant secrets (she was Irish). Actually, she was "me grandmother," as the Irish say, but I've always called her my elf mother, a term I believe everyone should adopt. After all, by the time your babies have babies, you should have become quite druid or elflike in your wisdom. The same with elf fathers. It's ever so much truer a description than the old label and its stuffy image, don't you think ? Anyway, it's a rather Hobbity idea I like.

After she first seeded me with the fascination for words along came A.G. and C.A.M., two of my wisest Gurus, who verified it all, and introduced me to their word druid friends, telling them I was not the enemy, but was working toward the same ideals as they were. After consulting with them privately A.G. brought me the message, several years ago, that they were now ready to come out of hiding, if people were ready to accept them, and not ridicule them. They felt, he said, that letting humans know of their existence might speed things up a mite before the catuclysms (that's the way *they* spell the word). C.A.M. then informed me that the word druids told him they would be watching me carefully as I write my books, especially this one, which "stars" them in feature roles, one might say — and that their constant kibbitzing of me at the typewriter is the reason I always, without fail, type the American word *theater* as the English spell *theatre*, and become quite annoyed when an editor at a publishing house tries to change it to "theater." It's their way of re-minding me of the geographical location of their protection of the language. Also where the sect known as the Essenes originated. Did you notice the word *mite* in the middle of this paragraph ? " . . . Might speed things up a mite . . ." Did you also notice that **MITE** is **TIME** — and **TIME** is **MITE** ? What does that tell you ?

Another strange thing about Lexigrams that seems most odd, but is nevertheless true, is that Lexigrams often expose the secrets of the one who is working on them. They frequently reveal as much about the one doing the lexigramming as the Lexigrams reveal to the one trying to penetrate them. You might say it's a kind of mutual mystery . . . simultaneously unfolded . . . which is why I say that Lexigrams are a bridge to your own Higher Elf, allowing you to gradually learn how to possess all the power He or She possesses, and has been patiently waiting to channel into you.

Therefore, you'll sometimes notice that someone else will pick up something entirely different from what you discovered by lexigramming the same word. Even lexigramming itself is individual, just as you and the word druids are individuals.

The Lexigram I've found to be the most puzzling and disturbing personally, and for the longest time was unable to spiral into a satisfactory answer concerns the word **EARTH**.

I had no problem with the discovery that **EARTH** hid within it the words **EAT** and **HATE**. It was obvious, as it would be to any vegetarian, that to EAT meat means that one HATES our animal brothers and sisters, and I already knew that EARTH was once an Eden Heaven (again, see Chapter 9) — that one of the reasons (only one of them) for the Fall was the EATing of meat, which is a sure way to spread and demonstrate HATE. Then I found the words EAR and HEAR, and this discovery was also logical. It's related, of course, to that counsel from the Nazarene I repeat so often in this book, "Let those who have eyes, see — let those who have ears, hear." I realized that humans on EARTH are being given a message to use the inner EAR to HEAR once more the Music of the Spheres, a message intensified in the word EARTHLINGS, hiding SING, which we discovered earlier in this chapter.

But then . . . then I realized that EARTH is HEART and HEART is EARTH, by taking the last letter of Earth and making it the first letter of Heart — and vice versa. The two words must vibrate to the same musical language chord, because each is the other, with a simple switch of one letter of the alphabet — H. This was a deep enigma to me. First of all, *why* should Earth and Heart be word druid identical twins ? What is happening here ? I wondered. What are these identical twin word druids named EARTH AND HEART trying to tell us ? Clearly, something of deep in-significance. Even CLEARLY also contains EARLY, we know that what we are supposed to hear that will make everything clear was known in an EARLY age . . . in the beginning. All very well, but it still didn't solve the basic mystery of those druid twins, HEART and EARTH. I told myself I needed to spiral higher, and so I did.

As I continued, with Aries determination and persistence, to ponder and puzzle and try to spiral higher and higher to penetrate the message from a higher level of awareness, I felt a little like a "temporary angel," who flew up into the sky, then saw her wings drop off as she drifted back down to Earth again, still not fully enlightened.

On my mental-astral spiraling flight, I came up with a few codes and clues, but not the final answer. Suddenly, as I sat in the quiet and calm contemplation necessary for a full penetration of Lexigrams, I saw before me the shape of a human **EAR**. Quickly, I drew it on my sheet of Lexigram paper. Then I added an opposite **EAR**. Next, I drew the two ears joined together, and realized that they looked like a **HEART**. Draw two opposite ears, joined together, and you'll see what I mean. But that was only another clue, not the answer to the enigma of these twin druids, superimposed over the words **EARTH** and **HEART** — although it's worth remembering that two **EARS** equal a **HEART**.

Still spiraling and flying through the sky of my Mind on the wings of thought, I printed, in capital letters, the following related words (meaning that all these word druids belong to the same "family":

AURAL   related to what the dictionary calls the *"ear-sense* of hearing"

AURICLE   the external part of an *ear* — *and* an atrium of the *heart*

AURUM   the geologist's Latin-based word for *gold*

AURA   the human aura

AURA   the same word, also a medical term for "a warning sensation that precedes a seizure, such as a *heart* attack." Strange

AURIC   derived from gold — *gold* again

What have we here, enigmatic word druids ? Clearly, there is some musical chord linking the Earth, the human Heart, the human Ear . . . and *Gold*. The **EARTH-HEART** Lexigram code is a tough one to decode because it's been so intricately encoded by those little word druids. My thoughts next spiraled into the word **GOLD** itself, and a discussion about it I had with the turbaned one. (See Preface.)

He told me, this lovable Avatar-Adept-Guru, that **GOLD** was a most important word in the fallen but still living English language, as is the metal it defines. Gold is the only metal that cannot be destroyed or changed into something else. It remains gold. It's the only hard metal soft enough to be malleable, allowing itself to be pounded or pressed into various shapes, *without breaking*. Gold is "immortal"; it never dies, and cannot be "killed." Again, it remains itself, and whatever you do to it, it never breaks.

It seems to be, in some mysterious way, seeded into the mass collective subconscious that gold is linked to the human **HEART** and human emotions, because gold is what is given always as a sign of high esteem (gold watches to valued employees who retire, and so on) . . . and what lover doesn't prefer to give the beloved gold over any other precious metal or stone, even a diamond? Gold says something complex to the hearts of humans. It's found in the **EARTH**. "Gold," Nahtan told me, "possesses unsuspected healing power, as the ancient Egyptians knew, which is why they used so much gold in their tombs and healing rites; why they always wore it against the skin. But," he continued, staring deeply into my eyes, "what *is* gold, in reality ?"

I pondered his question for a moment . . . I thought that, when you remove the **L** for Love, the word **GOLD** then becomes **GOD**.

"Is **GOLD**," I asked him, "the gentle-powerful vibration or musical chord for Love ? Is **GOLD** . . . . Love . . . *solidified* into a precious metal ?"

As usual, Nahtan turned Socratic on me. He smiled, then asked me several questions. "Can Love be destroyed ?" he asked. "Can Love be pounded and pressed into various shapes, without breaking ? And last, but not least . . . can Love heal ?"

The answer to each question, of course, was obvious. Then he smiled again, saying, "Well, then, it does seem that Gold and Love have much in common." He hesitated, then said, "Even in a monetary sense. Gold is sold . . . and so, unfortunately, is Love sold . . . and both financial transactions are regrettable."

"But . . . what about Earth and Heart and Gold . . . and the Ear and Hear . . . and Eat and Hate . . . I still can't penetrate the **EARTH-HEART** Lexigram."

Nahtan replied simply, "You will," and as was his wont, indicated that the subject was closed for the present.

Over the years I found another word hiding in **EARTH** and **HEART**, as tears of pure frustration stung my eyes each time I tried to complete the **EARTH** Lexigram. Of course. I'd missed it before. **TEAR**.

No matter how I tried, the Lexigram remained locked. But I did make an interesting discovery about **GOLD**. That it contains **GOD** is obvious, and we've already covered that. But it also hides the words **OLD** and **LOG**. The Bristlecone Pine is the oldest tree known to this continent — an "old log." In America, the gold strikes and gold rushes have occurred in California, Nevada and Colorado. These are the three states where the Bristlecone Pine grows most profusely. I haven't checked South Africa, but then, we're penetrating gold in America.

One spring morning in Cripple Creek, during a thunderstorm, I had one of those dreams you wake up in the middle of, you know ? As I sat up in bed, I remembered my dream so clearly it awed me. My dream had solved the Lexigram puzzle of **EARTH** and **HEART** and **GOLD**. Even the **EAR** and **HEAR** and **EAT** and **HATE** part of it. I was elated and overjoyed, and wanted to tell Nahtan immediately. But, as usual, I had to be content with sending him an astral telegram over our "Eastern" Union. It worked, and he phoned me a few days later. I must say he was quite happy that I had solved the Lexigram all by myself. But when I told him enthusiastically that I planned to reveal it in the Lexigram chapter of *Star Signs* his voice took on a rare stern tone, and he cautioned me that I must not do this. "Some Lexigrams," he said, "must be solved by the Higher S-elf of each individual, and this is such a one. You do not help people by doing all of their spiraling for them. No one becomes illuminated in this manner. They will see, and they will know, at the allotted time for each individual."

I'm sure this annoys and frustrates you. I can well understand it, because your annoyance matches my own. Nevertheless, as I'm sure you will understand, one simply does not deliberately and Free Willfully disobey a Guru on a level as high as Nahtan. And so, I risk your displeasure and annoyance with me by telling you only this much — enough to start you on your own journey to penetrate this Lexigram . . . and may the Force be with you !

★ ★ ★ ★ ★ ★

As I wrote earlier, Lexigrams of words, names or phrases can be silly, serious, sacred or sublime. The silly ones can be thought of as masks the word druids wear on Halloween.

To demonstrate a silly one, here are a couple of lines from a verse in one of my poetry books: "What freaky creatures we are . . . to speak a language in which rats spelled backwards is star."

To demonstrate a serious and sacred one, I'll share with you how a Lexigram spiraled me into solving only a small portion of my puzzlement with the fourth dimension of Time: the Eternal Now.

Ever since I can remember I've tried to penetrate the fourth dimension of Time, which is an Eternal Now, where Past, Present and Future are all one, not separate slices of "Time." Einstein, Abstract Al, came closer to it than anyone else, but even his theory of Relativity leaves a few veils still concealing the whole truth of it . . . or, at least a clear comprehension of it.

Clock time just creates more tangles in the cobweb. I suppose that's why I seldom listen to the radio. Every few minutes the announcer or disc jockey interrupts to say "The correct time is now . . ." And who cares ? Not I.

It's also why I keep all of the clocks in my Tesla-haunted, slipping-off-the-time-track house in Cripple Creek, including the old grandfather clock in the corner, each set at a different — and incorrect — hour. When the latter chimes, then, it doesn't send me into a state of panic to realize how little "time" I have left to do something I haven't yet done, you know ? When I become nervous over time I've found I'm even later than usual for appointments and such, just because I'm *aware* of it. I count on friends to "get me to the church on time" — to the airport or wherever.

My friend and make-believe big brother, Cleve Backster, the Spocky researcher you read about in the previous chapter, has a simply dreadful time hang-up. When he visits me he absolutely insists on arriving at the airport for his return trip at least two hours before his plane is scheduled to take off, creating the necessity of hanging out in those dreary airport coffee shops forever-and-a-day. I've reached the point where I refuse to accompany him to the airport. I say good-bye at my front door and send him off in a cab, or in a car with a friend — and let him idle the hours away in the terminal however he chooses.

Howard Hughes used to continually tell his close friends (he only had — that is *has* — one or two of them) that "time is on *our* side." Well, time may be on Howard's side, even now — (yes, another riddle) — but it's definitely not on *my* side. Never was. Never shall be. Time and I are not allies. We're cautious enemies, engaged in a never-ending cold war, behind a dark curtain of nameless fear.

All right, here's a Lexigram of the phrase *Eternal Now*. Let's see what it might have to tell us.

I also lexigrammed *The Great Pyramid*, because I know it's also closely related in some manner to the fourth dimension.

I didn't include every single word of either Lexigram. You may want to do a little lexigramming exploration yourself. But these Lexigrams contained enough words to spiral me into reveling in some revelations — and further fantasizing about that tempting and elusive relativity of space.

★ ★ ★ ★ ★ ★

ETERNAL NOW

RENEW WATER . . . RELATE A TONE TO RA . . . A TONE NEAR EAR
AN EON TO ATONE

NOW NEAR TO LATER . . . . . EON and ERA RELATE TO NOW

NOW and LATER ARE ONE

is NOW *NEAR* TO LATER ? NO ! NOW and LATER ARE ONE !

THE GREAT PYRAMID

THE EARTH GRID IS HERE

RA HATED TIME . . . because . . . TIME HARMED THE EARTH

TEAR TIME APART . . . RAH MADE TIME DIE IN THE PYRAMID

(Nothing decays in the Great Pyramid)

THEY (Isis and Osiris) PRAYED IN THE PYRAMID
RAHRAM (esoteric name for our Creators)
RAHRAM HEARD HIM . . . RAHRAM HEARD HER . . . THAT DAY

THE GAME IS TIME
I DARE TIME !

The final three words of the Pyramid Lexigram are personal to me. You may find some that are personal to you.

Unlike any other Lexigrams you'll ever calculate, these two — The *Eternal Now* and *The Great Pyramid* — are, in a certain sense, interchangeable. *Others* are *not.* They fit only the word, the person, phrase or entity they describe. These are closely related concerning the mysteries they hide, and that makes a difference, you see.

I'll give you only a couple of examples of the thought spiraling these two created for me. It's best for you to spiral some of them yourself.

To realize that Past, Present and Future are all One, it's first necessary to realize that none of the three of them actually exist, in reality . . . as well as in relativity. Shall we try to prove that ?

All right, now answer only with either "yes" or "no" the following questions. No fair to answer in more detail. Just a simple "yes" or "no."

Consider the Present. Will you admit that the Present is nothing but a *moving stream of the Future becoming the Past* ? **GORILLA !** That word was in the Future before you read it, but instantly it was in the Past *as* you read it. *Nothing* remains, not even the ticking of the clock. *Everything* keeps moving, *constantly.* Therefore, once again, do you admit that the Present can only be defined as a *constantly moving stream of the-Future-becoming-the-Past,* never stopping, even for a split second ?

We can, therefore, ignore the Present, since it doesn't exist. Right ?

Now, let's move along in that constantly moving stream to consider the Past and the Future.

Will you admit that what you now call the Past — was what you once called the Future ? Think. Was the Past once the Future ?

Next question. Will you admit that what you now call the Future is something you will someday *surely* call the Past ?

Then, will you further admit that, therefore, following pure logic, the Past is *equally* as much the Future as it is itself ? Will you admit that, following the same pure logic, the Future is *equally* as much the Past as it is itself ? That these two imposters are *interchangeable* and totally equal ?

Then they do not exist as separate entities, right ? They cancel one another out — except for that instant called the Present, when one is becoming the other — which we just proved doesn't exist ! Right ? So we just tossed all three of them into nothingness.

A second bite of mystical food for thought you may want to munch on and ponder.

Sit down somewhere so that a wall is *behind* you, and a clock is in *front* of you. The wall is behind you, and the clock is ahead of you, in front of you.

Now, let's make the phrase "behind you" synonymous with the Past. Let's make the phrase "ahead of you" or "in front of you" synonymous with the Future. Is that clear ?

Now someone walks up to you, where you're seated, and asks you: "*Where* is the wall ?" You will answer, of course, "The wall is *behind* me." (Behind being synonymous with the Past, remember.)

Then that person asks you, "Where is the clock ?" Staring straight ahead at the clock on the table, you will answer, of course, "The clock is in *front* of me." (In front being synonymous with the Future, remember.)

Now pretend (pretend intensely) that you have a pair of eyes at the back of your head, performing exactly the same function as the pair of eyes on your face. Do you have the picture set in your mind firmly ?

If so, you'll know that the eyes on your face and the eyes at the back of your head are *both* flashing simultaneous images into your brain, your front eyes projecting the image of the clock — your "rear" eyes projecting an image of the wall behind you. For the purpose of this illustration, let's say two simultaneous images, one superimposed upon the other.

Now someone walks up to you, where you're seated, and asks you: "Where is the wall ? Is it in front of you or behind you ?"

Your answer would have to be, "I don't understand what you mean. The wall *is*."

Then that person asks you "Where is the clock ? Is it behind you or in front of you ?" Your answer would have to be the same. "I don't understand what you mean. The clock *is*."

The reason you wouldn't understand the questions, or be able to answer them, would be that you've never comprehended behind you — or in front of you. You've experienced only those simultaneous images. Therefore, you'd have no way of interpreting "behind" and "in front." The only experience you would have is in *selectively tuning out one image in favor of the other, whenever you chose to do so — or blanking out (erasing) both together when you chose.*

When you read the last four paragraphs substitute the words *Past* and *Future* for "behind you" and "in front of you," and read them aloud. It won't make you totally *comprehend*, but it will bring you a few feet closer to doing so. It seldom works, though, unless you substitute the words, as I told you — then read the paragraphs *aloud*.

After pondering these two mental jogging exercises you'll eventually tone the muscles of your Soul, symbolically, and begin to spiral higher and higher answers to the Eternal Now with more ease.

By the way, did you notice, on your own, in the clock-wall example, that whether you place either of them behind you (Past) or in front of you (Future) *depends entirely on which direction you're facing ?*

In other words, someone in the room who is seated so that he or she is facing the opposite direction would find what you called "in front" (Future) to be "behind" (Past) — and would find what you called "behind" (Past) to be "in front or ahead" (Future). Therefore, the Past and the Future *are the same*, to two people facing opposite directions. It's all relative. Back to Abstract Al again . . . and the Lexigram of **ANGEL** and **ANGLE**.

✫ ✫ ✫ ✫ ✫ ✫

Speaking of clocks, Time and relative angle-angels, remember I told you in Chapter 3, "Gurus, Ghosts, and Avatars," that I was eventually enlightened with the solution to the "twenty till and twenty after" phenonemon Finbar O'Malley and I discussed the morning he drove me to Cripple Creek ? I promised to share it with you (there's an extremely thought-provoking Lexigram linked to it) — and so, if you haven't discovered the solution through your own mental spiraling, here is what I learned during my mountain retreat.

In the midst of a brief contact with one of my "teachers" there, we fell into a discussion about this old Gaelic "superstition." (Please read about it again at this point. It begins on Page 122 in Chapter 3.)

Why does this strange *silence* periodically occur within a group of people, and what does it mean ? "It occurs when reincarnated Atlanteans are talking together," I was told. "The mystery of the memories contained in what has been called 'the mass collective subconscious' or 'racial memory' has never been fully explained or penetrated. In this case, what occurs is a sudden, deeply buried group memory, triggered by whatever 'force' allows you to awaken at a certain time in the morning that you ordained the night before, when the clock hands point to that time — a subconscious group 'race memory' of the tragedy of the terrible inundation of Atlantis.

"Legend truly claims that this Atlantean inundation began, as measured by Earth time or 'clock time,' at twenty minutes before eight o'clock (O ! Clock !) and that by twenty minutes after eight, this once fair continent of Atlantis was submerged beneath what is now the *Atlantic* Ocean (so named for just that reason), the entire cataclysm beginning and ending in what seemed to be the 'twinkling of an eye' — taking only forty minutes in all. One might say that the 'silence' phenomenon could be interpreted as a *subconscious* gesture of 'respect' or 'remembrance of tragedy,' like unto those similar, but *conscious* moments Earthlings observe collectively in church or on a national observance of some major catastrophe."

Having been thus seeded by the Avatar, I inquired about the "scientific" cause of this swift inundation of an entire continent, remarking that I had heard legends claiming that Atlantean scientists (whose technology-existing-without-equal-spiritual-enlightenment our present-day scientists are now dangerously close to matching) caused the cataclysm in this way: They are said to have designed and created a very large crystal by a carefully calculated mathematical formula, but their calculations were in error for some reason — and instead of producing the great power (for various purposes) they had expected, the crystal in some manner shattered the Earth's crust, causing it to slip upon its axis and initiate the Ice Age.

"This is correct," I was told emphatically. "As for the nature of the earthquaking error committed by the Atlantean sciences, continue to spiral your thoughts in meditation, keeping the aspect of *Time*, as indicated by the 'twenty till and twenty after' phenomenon in mind as you do so. Then we shall meet again and discuss what you discover in this manner. Remember that the Atlantean cataclysm concerned took place at twenty minutes till and twenty minutes after eight, but the group phenomenon you have observed can occur at twenty minutes *before* — or twenty minutes *after* — *any hour*," as an astral code to conjure the *position* of the clock hands at the time of the tragic event.

I did as instructed. I meditated. For a while I was not inspired. Then one day, while I was staring at the face of the old grandfather clock in my "haunted house" in Cripple Creek, perhaps assisted by the "ghost" of Nikola Tesla in the corner of the parlor (see Chapter 3), I began to draw the face of a clock on paper — a large clock face. Next, I marked the position of a clock's hands at twenty till and twenty after eight (A.M. or P.M.), which is the same position indicating twenty till and twenty after noon or midnight. I then saw that, when the clock face was turned upside down or re-versed, the markings indicated *ten* minutes till and *ten* minutes after ten the 3 tens equaling 12, reducing to 3. Just as 20 till and 20 after 8 equals 12, reducing to 3.

I also observed that these four markings, when connected, created a double pyramid shape, with one "layered" over the other, as in the following sketches.

The triangle or (tri-angle . . . three angels ?) re-minded me simultaneously of the Great Pyramid of Giza, designed and engineered by Osiris *after* the fall of Atlantis. I remembered that I had been taught that *beneath* the Giza Pyramid is another pyramid, built to precisely the same exact measurements of the one on top of the ground, the two being joined, *base-to-base*, an engineering feat not yet suspected by our present scientists. I recalled that I had also been taught the reason for these two identical pyramids having been thus designed and constructed, base-to-base. It was "to keep the Pole Star centered," to "prevent any further axial excursions of the North and South Poles."

I had also learned (been taught . . . or remembered) about the "hidden generators present in the bottom, unseen and unguessed pyramid, sending out mighty forces," used to guide the "spacecraft" of the time. Another reason for the base-to-base construction was to neutralize the awesome power and energy which would otherwise "escape" through the top or tip of each pyramid, causing this awesome power and energy to *centralize* itself at a point near the base-to-base joining, so neutralized and centered through the law of *magnetism* and *the magnetic field*. This centering of the energies of the "tops" of both pyramids made it possible for Master Avatars from other Earths in other solar systems to heal the people in the "Queen's Chamber," under the guise of the priests of the day.

The source of this immeasurable power and energy may be attributed to the unique *measurements* of the Giza pyramid (or pyramids), the shape itself in some manner "bending the light waves," so that anything in the center of this *controlled* energy would *not decay*. I hastily scribbled another drawing, and saw that this pyramidic magic was *not a Hexagram*, such as my first clock-face sketches, but *diamond shaped*.

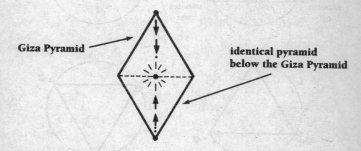

Giza Pyramid

identical pyramid below the Giza Pyramid

Swiftly, I spiraled another thought image, and drew it on the paper. A light flashed in my brain, but only for an instant. Then darkness again. But while the light flashed, I realized that my diamond-shaped drawing created the figure 4.

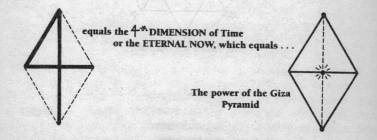

equals the 4-th DIMENSION of Time or the ETERNAL NOW, which equals . . .

The power of the Giza Pyramid

Suddenly, I glanced once more at the **LEXIGRAMS** of **ETERNAL NOW** and **THE GREAT PYRAMID** . . . and they had new meaning. I

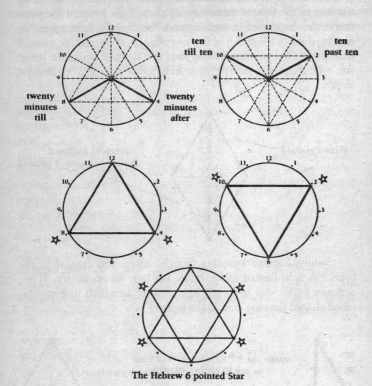

ten
till ten

ten
past ten

twenty
minutes
till

twenty
minutes
after

The Hebrew 6 pointed Star

couldn't wait to discuss my discoveries with my teacher. We met the following day. When I excitedly told what I had spiraled through the meditation-elation I had been counseled to try "Guru" responded by saying:

"You have channeled truth. Not in its entire mathematical complexity, but nevertheless, truth. Knowing of the awesome power and energy created at the top of a pyramidic shape of the precise measurements of the Giza Pyramid (although the latter had not yet been engineered), the Atlantean scientists constructed an enormous *crystal pyramid* to these same measurements — then overlaid upon it, as in your drawing, a second and identical crystal pyramid — realizing that this created a six-pointed star, with four *additional* power points. However, since their technology was *not equaled by their spiritual enlightenment* (even as today) — they failed to realize the spiritual reason behind the necessity of *controlling* such power and energies in exactly the same way as you illustrated in your final sketch.

"Consequently, when this Atlantean crystal was activated the resulting unchecked energy force exploded, cracking the Earth's surface and creating an axial excursion upon your planet. In this manner was Atlantis inundated and destroyed. It must not be allowed to occur again in the Aquarian Age."

"But . . . how can there be an encore of the Atlantean cataclysm, since the pyramid secret is known to most scientists today, and no one would re-create such a destructive crystal ?"

"It need not happen in the same manner," he replied sadly. "At this level of time, the destruction will be nuclear . . . if not prevented. And the Giza Pyramid can no longer repair the damage, due to certain changes made to its structure by various pharaohs over the centuries. You see, after the fall of Atlantis Osiris designed and engineered the Giza Pyramid to prevent *the same kind of cataclysm* from repeating itself. It was not, however, designed to prevent the kind of destruction caused by nuclear power."

For weeks following this discussion with my teacher, I spiraled thought images continually. I couldn't seem to ignore the term HEXAGRAM. When I created a Lexigram for Hexagram I saw that it contained REX . . . RA and RAM . . . HER RAGE . . . and then I pondered the puzzle of the number 6 this spiraling had produced. As we learned in the numerology chaper, 6 represents Venus. It's the number of love and peace. Then why should a six-sided Hexagram have caused such a tragedy ? Unbidden, I recalled what I had earlier been taught — that the esoteric code name for our male-female Creators is RAHRAM, also present in this Lexigram.

When I expressed my confusion to my teacher he answered, "You are right to be puzzled. It is a great mystery, indeed. The solution is that, in the Atlantean instance, the number 6 was inverted and mirror-reversed into the 9 and all of the negative vibrations of 9." He noticed the question in my eyes, and anticipated my next query. "No, I do not choose to answer your question of *how* — in what manner — this 6-9 reversal took place. You must channel the answer yourself. It is so written in the Akashic Records."

"Do you mean the Lexigram of G-U-R-U (Gee ! *you* are *you* !) ?" I asked.

"Yes," he replied. "By the time you have spiraled the answer to this particular 6 . . . 9 question, you will have realized the identity of the teacher from whom you have learned the *most* during your mountain retreat."

"I know who that is," I replied. "My own Higher Self, right ?"

He looked at me sternly. "As long as you have to end any statement with a question, as you just did, you have learned nothing." And he left.

For the longest time I pondered a second part of this particular 6-9 mystery. I thought it odd indeed that, with a Hexagram being a six-sided figure, and six (6) representing Venus . . . Love . . . Peace, that somehow — and as always, *not coincidentally* — the word HEX crept into the English language, with such usage as "I'll place a HEX upon you !" a most negative "curse." I finally figured it out. Please write and let me know when you, too, have decoded this mystery and solved it.

Later, my friend, Philip di Franco, channeled another facet of this shining diamond-shaped and Hexagram mystery. He noted that all pictures of watches and clocks in advertisements display the watch or clock face with the *hands set on either twenty after eight . . . or* pointing to *ten after ten*. The reason given by jewelers is that this is "a more balanced and attractive setting of the watch or clock hands, in a visual sense." But . . . is this the *real* reason ? Or is the true reason buried in the subconscious "race memory" of the jewelers ?

Now, before we leave the Lexigram-Hexigram mystery and go on with some incredibly revealing name "Lexies," are you ready for two additional mysteries concerning Atlantis and the later Giza Pyramid ? All right, open your mind, open your heart and open your Third Eye to prove to yourself the truth of the foregoing paragraphs.

First, before the Hexagram comes the Hexagon. From the Hexagon, by extending it, the Hexagram is produced. Meditate on the Atlantean crystal double pyramid again. Then lexigram the word HEXAGON. It contains these words: EON GONE. A clear code that, when the Atlantean scientists, with their technology, first started with the Hexagon crystal, the whispering warning was there within the very word that the next step of extending it to a double pyramid Hexagram would be *the end of an eon,* would signal an EON GONE too soon, with its possibilities of future glory destroyed by technology not founded on spiritual law.

The second magic requires you to send away for two small and relatively inexpensive objects, from which you will learn secrets of immeasurably more value than the reasonable cost. Xanthium Crystal . . . Suite 40 . . . 712 Wilshire Blvd. . . . Santa Monica, CA . . . Zip: 90401. (213) 394-7333

One is a two-inch, pure Austrian crystal *Hexagon* holder for a tiny crystal ball. The other is a two-and-a-half-inch pure Austrian crystal Pyramid. The crystals sparkle and glow with flashing light and every color of the rainbow spectrum. And, since they are pure crystal, they are solid; a pleasure to hold in your hand.

Take the glittering crystal ball holder, lift it to the light, and stare into the flat bottom of the object. You will immediately see clearly the *Hexagon* shape (see figure below), then notice that it extends into the 6 pointed Hebrew Star of David (the *Hexagram* — see figure below) . . . whispering to your Third Eye the many mysteries contained within this lovely crystal.

Hexagon

Hexagon with sides extended is a Hexagram

Then take the glittering Pyramid crystal, which has four sides. Hold it to the light, with *one of the edges* directly in front of your eyes, and look through it. You will see, magically and miraculously, a second pyramid hiding within it. Meditating with these two crystals will, I promise you, be an enormous "booster" to your spiraling of ancient codes and mysteries. There are some I've not told here so you may discover them yourself.

★★★★★★

ATLANTIS

serpent

Here are some Lexigrams of well-known names (and titles) for you to consider. As you study them, remember this positive evidence of the credibility of Lexigrams. We've already discussed it in relation to opera singer Beverly Sills and feminist Gloria Steinem. Still, it bears repeating, as all "golden rules" do. Name Lexigrams are absolutely not interchangeable. Nor are they born from coincidence. You cannot take the message or description gleaned from one person's name and apply it to another person, because each one is clearly sui generis. The Name Lexigram describes individually the person from whose name the words were born, and no other. This is only one of the several ways you can be sure that Lexigrams are a valid art and science, not just a game.

Before presenting the examples of name lexigramming, I should remind you again of the Lexigram rules for a word, a phrase or a name — that it is not valid if more than four of the five vowels appear (three is better) — or if more than fifteen *different* letters of the alphabet appear. And don't forget that Zebra Rule ! (On Page 220.)

One more thing to remember regarding Name Lexigrams: Some names contain very few letters; consequently the Lexigrams of such names are brief, consisting of only a few words.

Some names contain the full allowance of vowels and alphabetical letters; therefore the Lexigrams of these names are longer, more detailed and more revealing.

However, in both cases Name Lexigrams, like all Lexigrams, have a mind of their own. In the instance of a Name Lexigram with only a *very few* words, this can mean either that (a) the person whose name it is will be found to be an extremely private person, keeping many personal secrets — or (b) the person whose name it is happens to be a simple and uncomplicated human, lacking any complexity in the personality, who leads a rather ordinary life.

In the instance of a Name Lexigram with *many* words, this can either mean that (a) the person is a complex personality, with intricate facets of character, who has a busy, multi-layered life-style — or (b) this human is likewise a very private person, but in this case the privacy is achieved by the subconscious "burying" of secrets in a flurry of words. In the latter case, it doesn't do any good — the revelations discovered in your Lexigram will, in the final analysis, tell you what you need to know, if you're patient, and use the power of your sixth sense . . . your intuition . . . with your Third Eye wide open !

Blending Name Lexigrams — the astrological Sun Sign — and the numerological value of a person's name and date of birth — will give you a surprisingly comprehensive summary of anyone — or any *thing*. (Yes, you may apply numerology to words, too — also to initials.) And so, astrology, numerology and Lexigrams together can turn out to be your own personal crystal ball. These three star signs of ancient wisdom are exciting codes you may use in a variety of ways to quest for truth and knowledge.

★★★★★★

ADOLF HITLER

**HITLER HAD OLD FOE (Jews) HE LEFT FOE TO ROT (Jews)
ROLE OF HITLER; FOE OF LIFE (and) LORD OF HATE**

OR

FOE OF HATE and LORD OF LIFE

Hitler had the above choice. To see why he did, read *Spear of Destiny*, listed in the "Pilgrim's Progress" section in the back of this book. It should be required reading in all schools. Hitler was an avid student of the occult, superbly trained in all esoteric arts and sciences, including mass hypnosis of crowds. He could have used his amazing knowledge as white magic, to advance humankind. He had a choice. He chose instead to use his metaphyiscal training for black magic, to spread hatred in the world. His Lexigram makes this clear. It also contains the following prophetic words about the German dictator:

HE TORE AT HAIR . . . HE HID AT FORT

RAID AT FORT

FATE OF HITLER; FATED TO DIE AT FORT (in) FIT OF HATE

HE TRIED TO HIDE FEAR . . . HE LEFT OLD FOE (Jews) TO DIE OF FIRE

FATE OF HITLER: TO DIE OF LEAD TO HEAD (shot)

TO DIE OF HOT FIRE (cremated at Fort)

THE DEATH OF HITLER FATED

★ ★ ★ ★ ★ ★

ABRAHAM LINCOLN

When we Lexigram only the ten separate letters comprising Abraham Lincoln we discover three of perhaps the most important facts about the man. Plus a word for further meditation and mind spiraling. **RAIL.** He was known, of course, in his political campaigns, as the rail splitter. Then we discover:

BORN IN A CABIN . . . A CALM MAN . . . COMA IN BRAIN
(referring to the assassination)

When we study the short name a bit longer, we find: **HAM** (Abe was accused of being a bit of a "ham," who enjoyed making his audiences at political rallies laugh at his jokes). **COIN:** Every school child knows the incident of Lincoln walking several miles to return to a storekeeper a penny he owed him. This is an excellent example of what I told you about one-word-spiraling. One word alone in a Lexigram, when you open your mind and use your sixth sense, will pour out a stream of thoughts, progressively leading you on and on . . . and on . . . until a light flashes suddenly in your brain, and a computer card pops out to enlighten you about some secret you were trying to learn about the person or entity you were lexigramming. Next let's see how much more we can learn about Lincoln by using, as permissable in Lexigrams, assuming the other rules are observed, his name plus his title, President Abraham Lincoln, the vibration of which has been sent into the ethers equally as often as the name Abraham Lincoln alone, to learn more about the man.

★ ★ ★ ★ ★ ★

PRESIDENT ABRAHAM LINCOLN

This Lexigram gives a more complete picture of the man who kept the center together, so that this nation of the people, by the people and for the people did not perish from the Earth. First, **HE SPLIT RAILS.**

HE HEALED A TORN NATION . . . OTHERS HATED HIM . . . HE HATED NONE

A SAD MAN, ALONE IN A MOB . . . HE TOLD NO LIES — OTHERS LIED TO HIM

HE LED THE NORTH, AND CALMED THE REBELS

THE NATION REMAINED UNITED

HE HAD NO PRIDE . . . HE HAD A CALM MIND AND A CLEAR HEAD

HIS DEATH CAME FROM A SHOT IN THE HEAD

THE LORD SENT ABRAHAM LINCOLN TO LEAD AMERICA HOME

HIS STAR IS ETERNAL

HONEST ABE

This Lexigram contains **LINCOLN IS NOT THE SAME AS HITLER.** There is no "Adolf" in the Lincoln lexigram.

SAINT FRANCIS OF ASSISI

Francis was not married; therefore he produced no son. Although he conquered his fear of leprosy by embracing a leper, and spent his life helping to heal these outcasts of the day, he was never able to conquer his strange fear and dislike of ants. His Lexigram, formed from three vowels and nine letters, contains:

NO SON FOR FRANCIS . . . FRANCIS SAT ON ANTS . . . FRANCIS FRANTIC !

IN FRANCIS IS NO SIN . . . NOT A STAIN OF SIN IN FRANCIS

FRANCIS TRAINS FOR A FAST IN A SOFT RAIN . . . FRANCIS IS FAIR
(He often fasted)   (He was a Libra)

FRANCIS FAINTS IN FRONT OF CROSS

Francesco had a vision before a crucifix at San Damiano where he went into a trancelike state, and heard, through clairaudience, the voice of Jesus saying, "Francis, rebuild my Temple."

FRANCIS RISES TO STARS ! He was often seen levitating by his monks.

Do you recall, at the end of the Numerology chapter, the legend beginning on Page 283, which tells that metaphysicians have always claimed that Francesco Bernadone, Francis of Assisi, was one of the reincarnated "14 pieces of Osiris" ? Again, Lexigrams answer such soul-probing wonders. The above words comprising "Saint Francis of

Assisi," the name which is still most commonly and frequently used when referring to him, and therefore carries the strongest vibration, lexigrams into:

OSIRIS ARISES IN FRANCIS

FRANCIS IS OSIRIS !

★ ★ ★ ★ ★

HOWARD ROBARD HUGHES

HEAD OF (TWA) BOARD . . . HUGHES GOOD, but SAD HE HAS A HARD HEAD

HUGHES, SR., HAD HUGE GUSHERS . . . WAGES GREW . . . HE HOARDED DOUGH

Hughes, Sr., made his fortune in the oil fields, and was not known to be overly generous with his money.

USA SUED HUGHES . . . OR . . . HUGHES SUED USA ?

A good question, on several occasions in the past.

HUGHES HAS A BAD EAR

Hughes has been nearly deaf in his left ear for most of his life. Notice that, under Lexigram rules, I could have used the past tense "had" in this Lexigram, but I chose to use the present tense "has" instead. That's a riddle, one that may be solved sooner than you expect.

HUGHES SHREWD True. And the word applies to his identical twin and fraternal twin half brothers too. Another riddle, soon to be solved.

BAD GUARDS USED HUGHES Right on. But justice will triumph.

HUGHES SOS WAS HEARD As the world will soon know.

HUGHES HAD SAD DOGS . . . HUGHES DREW DOGS Howard has owned several loved dogs as pets over the years. Once, when driving to dinner at a country club with a film star I know well, they passed a dog lying on the side of the road. Howard ordered the driver to stop for the dog, and drive straight to an animal hospital. He sat there until the dog was pronounced out of danger, hours after the country club had closed. When he lived, for nearly a year, in the home of a friend of mine, he often liked to "doodle" while seated at the dining room table, and some of his occasional doodles were of dogs.

GOD HEARD HUGHES . . . GOD REWARDS HUGHES . . . HUGHES SOARS !

This Lexigram is an enigmatic prophecy, a promise for tomorrow.

JESUS OF NAZARETH

SEE THE ROSES . . . HEAR THE NOTE . . . HEAR THE TONE

JESUS NEAR TO ZEUS AT SUNSET
(Zeus was the Greek "Father god")

THE HEART OF JESUS (was) **TRUE TO HER** . . . (and) **TRUE TO US**

THE STAR OF JESUS SHONE ON EARTH

HE AROSE ON EASTER
This Lexigram contains the deep Earth-Heart mystery.

★★★★★★★★★★★★★★★★★★★★★★★★★★★★★★★★★

| MARY MAGDALENE |

MARY A RAM . . . MARY RAGED . . .
MARY ANGERED . . . MARY DREAMED

MARY HAD A MAD DREAM ON A GREY DAY

MARY HAD MANY MEN . . . MANY MEN DAMNED MARY

MARY LEANED ON A GREAT MAN
"though your sins be as scarlet
they shall be as white as snow"

MARY MADE AN ANGEL

Nor are the Lexigrams of these two names . . . interchangeable.
Like all Name Lexigrams, they are distinctly, individually descriptive.

★★★★★★

| CENTRAL INTELLIGENCE AGENCY |

CIA CAN TRAIN AN INTELLIGENT AGENT IN A LYING GAME IN A
YEAR

RENT . . . TEAR

A CIA AGENT CAN CREATE ANGER and RAGE

CIA CAN LIE . . . A GENTLE GIRL CAN CRY LATER

CIA CAN GET REAGAN . . . . CAN GET NANCY ILL

CIA EAGLE not REAL EAGLE . . . CIA EAGLE A LIE

Obviously, neither Harry Truman nor anyone else involved in
naming this government agency and approving its seal had the slightest notion that the USA symbolic Eagle would appear in the name of

the agency — and naturally had no idea that Ronald Reagan and wife Nancy would be in the White House thirty-seven years later. There's a subtle message here for President Reagan and the First Lady, in view of Irangate and perhaps subsequent events.

THE SALVATION ARMY

A NATION MAY LIVE IN LOVE . . . AS SAINT MARY

NO LIES . . . ONLY LOVE

It's unfortunate that the Salvation Army Lexigram can't apply to the Central Intelligence Agency Lexigram. It would be a better world. But a Lexigram can never live the Karma of any other Lexigram — only its own — another evidence that the words forming them are living entities and totally individual, even as you and I are totally individual.

There's an effective way to prevent any harm resulting from your sending the sounds of spoken negative words into the ethers — and I trust that by now you understand how much harm really can be caused by this, because of the invisible, yet powerful frequencies of sound. There are many negative words and phrases and, naturally, they can't all be listed here. You know which ones they are. Phrases like: Drop dead. This job makes me sick. He (or she) makes me sick. Let's kill two birds with one stone. If it's the very last thing I ever do, I'm going to . . . . . Wouldn't you just *know* that would happen ? (something negative, of course). He probably won't call. I'll never be able to get this straight. I'll tell her, but she's never going to understand. We'll never make it to the airport in time. We're sure to get there after the movie has started. I'm not going to get enough sleep, so I'll be half dead tomorrow. Look at that pimple ! I'm going to look terrible for the party tomorrow night. I'll see him dead first, before I'll let him . . . (whatever) And . . . it always sends cold chills through me, but I've actually heard mothers say, jokingly, innocently, never realizing what they're doing — a new popular "jest" — to their children, when they're misbehaving, "Oh, go play in the traffic !"

After you've realized the reality of the power of words and sounds, but haven't been able to change your bad habits completely, you'll catch yourself uttering something negative without thinking, and feel concerned. (But don't say, "Darn it ! I could bite my tongue for saying that" — or you just might, and you know how painful that can be !) Instead, after unthinkingly speaking a negative word or phrase, just say aloud the word *cancel*. And say one *cancel* for each negative word in the phrase or sentence you spoke, imaging the words being zapped down with a laser beam with every *cancel*. The word *cancel* has the power to do just that. You may feel a little quirky at first, but after a while you'll realize it's worth it, and besides, your friends won't laugh at you. They'll just think you're being mysterious; that you know something they don't know and, of course, you do.

When you've learned how to read between-the-lines of the Compound Number definitions in the numerology chapter (since each analysis possesses multi-layered meanings) you'll understand why the word *cancel,* which has a numerological value of 20, has the ability to erase a negative sound, and "clean the slate," so to speak, for a new birth of positive frequencies.

Two exercises you can learn to do fairly quickly, which may have the strongest effect on your comprehension of the powers you possess when you tune into your Higher S-elf, are the ones I used my own s-elf in the beginning — and I'm just as awed and overwhelmed by them each new time they prove their magic as I was the very first time. The wonder never becomes stale to me. I marvel at it every time it happens, which is every time I call on it, without a single exception.

The first one is a magic for remembering something you've forgotten, and it happens to all of us. It can be a telephone number, someone's name, a particular date, an address — or a word or phrase you know very well, but simply can't recall, if you're a writer, sitting at the typewriter, and need that word or phrase quickly.

The second one is a magic for finding something you've lost in the house. (It also works for lost objects at a distance, but that's more complicated.) I mean those times when you misplace something — or when you've put it away so it *won't* get lost, then forget where you put it — or those occasional times when a paper, a check or some other item was there moments ago in front of your eyes, and seems to have simply de-materialized; it's just nowhere to be found. Where could it have gone ? It obviously can't have grown feet and walked away !

Before I tell you the two magic mantras, you must be absolutely certain that you understand this rule. You can't tune in to your Higher S-elf until you firmly *believe* you can, without the faintest shadow of a doubt. You must also understand that the *first time* a "magic sound mantra" works, that's it. It will never fail to work after that. Do you see why ? Because once you've observed the power of it is real, every last tiny seed of negative doubt will have disappeared from your conscious mind. You'll then be as confident of it as you are when you flip on a light switch, *knowing* so surely that the light will go on, you don't even think about it — and you certainly don't pray "Oh, please, *please* let the light go on !" It's more or less like that.

It's so simple. You say whichever of the following two sentences apply — *aloud*. Then put the problem completely out of your mind, and do something else — anything else. Within no longer than two or three minutes, and usually within thirty to sixty seconds, the magic will manifest. The word or name or whatever you haven't been able to recall will pop up in your mind like an electric light bulb flashing — or like a computer card read-out. Bang ! There it is ! Or . . . the object you've lost or misplaced will magnetize you toward it. You'll turn around, or take a few steps, after you've said your mantra and dismissed it from your mind . . . and BAM ! there it is before you — often in a spot where you've already looked and simply didn't see it. Sometimes it will fall through the air, blown by a breeze from an open window, or fall on the floor as you brush by it. That's when it can seem very spooky.

1 Divine Spirit of my Higher Self, instantly — now — seed my mind and my brain with that which I have forgotten. I *ordain* this, under grace.
Thank you !

2 Divine Spirit of my Higher Self, instantly — now — lead me directly to that which I have misplaced. I *ordain* this, under grace.
Thank you ! (With this mantra, also *image the item as you speak.*)

I've given up trying to find a way to fully express the wonder, excitement and gratitude you'll feel when these two relatively minor magics become a permanent part of your daily life.

I've found that I have two kinds of friends and acquaintances. Those who laugh in embarrassment when I tell them about this magic wand of words; that spoken words truly are a wand — and the other ones who believe me, and with all the excitement, faith and innocence of a child immediately try it, find that it works and won't stop talking about it. They call me several times a week to shout over the telephone "I did it again ! I did it again !" I'm very happy for the latter ones, of course, but sometimes I do wish they would become accustomed to the magic a little sooner — never take it for granted, of course, but give me some peace !

Which kind are you ? If you're the latter kind, isn't it perfectly marvelous never to have to worry about losing anything or forgetting anything — ever again ?

Best of all, once you've mastered these two first steps toward communication with your own Spirit, you can advance forward, creating your own mantras for *whatever* minor or major miracle you need in your life for your happiness, as long as it doesn't bring unhappiness to anyone else. "For whatsoever thing you desire, pray as if you had *already received it,* and you shall surely have it." That kind of praying is the kind with power. It's called *ordaining.* "Ask, and it shall be given you." "Knock, and it shall be opened." All three of these counsels of the Nazarene referred explicitly to what you can infallibly expect when you tune in to your Higher Self with absolute confidence. The major miracles take a little more time, but will manifest just as surely. Time is not important. Only the certainty of the eventual result.

★ ★ ★ ★ ★ ★

You will need to achieve a certain state of mind if you want to receive the full benefits of lexigramming. Otherwise, you'll just be playing anagrams. You must allow your Higher Self to take over your thoughts until you reach a dreamlike state, difficult to describe. It begins when a Lexigram stimulates your imagination to produce ideas and images which seem to flow on their own, bringing a steady stream of associated images. This sort of channeling occurs when you fall into a half-conscious, half-dreamlike state of mind.

Mozart once explained that music came to him while he was strolling through the mountain woodlands early in the morning. Melodies would rush into his head in complete, finished compositions; then he would dash home to set the notes down on paper.

Keats recalled that the inspiration for his description of Apollo in the third book of Hyperion came to him in a manner he called "by chance or magic . . . as if it were something given."

The poet Shelley described this state of "creative seizure" by writing . . .

> Sudden the shadow fell on me
> I shrieked and clasped my hands in ecstasy

Shelley also observed that "When my brain gets heated with thought, it soon boils and throws off images and words faster than I can skim them off." This is the state of mind that will allow you to penetrate mysteries through Lexigrams. It's somewhat like the familiar question, "How will I know if I'm in love ?" . . . and the answer,

"When you are, you won't need to ask." The same may be said of the state of mind allowing you to solve the mysteries hiding in Lexigrams. You will know when you achieve it. No one can teach you but yourself.

Don't forget that your Lexigram will be as individual as you are. Remember I told you that Lexigrams often reveal as much about the person calculating them as about themselves, in a sort of mutual enlightenment.

Since this is a chapter about words, it shouldn't end without an attempt to penetrate the second most powerful word — the Word of Creation — the Word with the power to manifest physical matter. Yes, it comes second — after the word *Love,* which will always reign supreme.

In the beginning was the **WORD** . . .

I wasn't certain when I began to write this chapter, but now I've decided to share with you my own thought process involving a Lexigram concerning the sacred word of creation and its protection by the word druids, down through the ages.

A legend, its origin lost in antiquity, claims that the Word shall be rediscovered when Earthlings are sufficiently enlightened to ensure it will not be misused as before . . . . . discovered by Isis and Osiris, his fourteen separated soul pieces joined in one man . . . "with all his scattered pieces whole" . . . accompanied by the purified reincarnation of their son, Horus . . . and that this rediscovery shall take place during the Aquarian Age. That gives us roughly two thousand years to manifest a universal thought transformation. Legend gives us little more information than this, except that the Word will be sung or chanted by these two, and their son, Horus, at a cosmic moment, calculated astrologically. ". . . and the stars shall lead them."

Knowing that the druids are the protectors of all words, I meditated upon this for a very long time, wondering where this great resurrection of former glory would take place, in a geographical sense.

Remember the lines near the beginning of this chapter marked with ★ ★ ★ ★ ★, I said might become important near its end ? It was when we were considering why words are living entities . . . that they fused or mated, produced children (hybrid words) . . . and so on.

These are the starred words:

Like any living thing, the English language keeps growing and evolving, *even leaving the fossils of "dead" words behind.* ★ ★ ★ ★ ★

As I wrote that sentence in the diary I kept in Colorado, where I had been sent by Nahtan to be taught some of the secret codes of the Universe, I stopped suddenly. The sentence seemed to stand out on the page in red letters. Especially the word *fossils.*

My mind spiraled instantly from the word *fossils* to rocks and stones. Then came a memory fragment of a line from the stage play and film *Superstar* . . . "the very rocks shall start to sing" . . . a lyric sung by Jesus on Palm Sunday, as he rode on a donkey.

Druids. Rocks. Stones. Fossils. I remembered how carefully I had been taught by one of my Avatars that the nature spirit druids first appeared in the Celtic area . . . that they were *not* the cruel druidic priests who falsely used the term *druidic* for their ancient, evil rites in England . . . at . . . Stonehenge.

Druids. Rocks. Stones. Fossils. England. English. Celtic. Stonehenge. Stonehenge, the true home of the word druids. Once again I glanced at the sentence I had just written: . . . . *even leaving the fossils of "dead" words behind.* An image of Stonehenge flashed into my mind, and I could see the shapes of those huge stones as clearly as if I had been standing there, under a New Moon. They seemed to form the letters of a word . . . . similar to a Hebrew word. Then I thought that, if they moved slightly, they would take on a different shape and form. Swiftly came the thought of Osiris, levitating the huge stones into position to form the Great Pyramid . . . by chanting . . . singing . . . producing sounds with the high frequency energy to levitate these large chunks of "matter."

And I wondered . . . could it be that a certain sound, chanted at a particular time . . . by chosen ones . . . possesses the power to move the stones of Stonehenge to form . . . the sacred Word of creation ? Has the Word been hiding there all these eons, waiting for the enlightenment of Earthlings to be once more spoken ?

This is what I mean by spiraling . . . .

The next thought was formed from a logical progression of these musings. What would happen if I lexigrammed three words: Druids of Stonehenge ? I decided to omit the word *the,* as in The Druids of Stonehenge, because I wanted to be sure the revelation of the Lexigram was clear, and the fewer words the better. Anyway, the letters of *the, t — h —* and *e,* are already contained within the word Stonehenge itself.

Would the Lexigram verify the legend . . . and my own illumination ? It could have said so many things.

First, I tried to lexigram The Great Pyramid, and you've already seen its message. The Great Pyramid obviously is not the place where the prophecy will be fulfilled. But . . . is Stonehenge the place ?

Here is my Lexigram. No other sacred location on Earth I've lexigrammed in my quest contains these singing messages. The word druids allowed me to discover their secret. And now I share it with you.

Some of you won't even be interested in it. Others will find it amusing, but not of any serious import. But there may be a few of you who will tune into the musical chords of the vibratory frequency of the *Druids of Stonehenge* Lexigram's deeper mystery.

DRUIDS OF STONEHENGE

THE ONE NOTE IS NOT GONE

THE DRUIDS HID IT HERE IN THE RUINS EONS AGO

AS THE SUN ROSE

IT IS HIDDEN IN THE HUGE STONES . . . SEE THE STONES ?

OSIR (i) IS (i) S GUIDED HERE (by) DRUIDS

TO SING THE TRUE NOTE FOR US (at) SUNRISE

THEIR SON HORUS GUIDED HERE TOO . . . TO SING

THE TRUE TONE

A SONG SUNG AT SUNRISE

THE GREAT GODS (HE-SHE) ORDAINED THIS

THIS IS RIGHT (and) THIS IS TRUE

A SONG OF GOODNESS SUNG (at) SUNRISE

THESE THREE (shall be) LED THERE by THE DRUIDS

HORUS IS HIS SON (Osiris) . . . HORUS IS HER SON (Isis)

STONEHENGE SINGS TO US !

SEE HIS TEARS ?   SEE HER ROSES ?

HEAR THE STONES   OH ! HEAR THEIR SONG !

SOON

★★★★★★★★★★★★★★★★★★★★★★★★★★★★★★★

A LEXIGRAM POSTSCRIPT

a mystery

for your contemplation . . . and elation

★★★★★★★★★★★★★★

A second Lexigram of Jesus of Nazareth

with secrets the word druids hid from us

in the first one

JESUS OF NAZARETH

JESUS NEAR TO NATURE . . . AND TO THE SEA

JESUS (is) THE SON OF THE SUN

HE HEARS THE ONE TRUE NOTE OF THE STONES

AT STONEHEN(G)E

!

JESUS (and) OS(I)R(I)S ARE ONE

HEAR THE STONES

HEAR THE STONES

HEAR THE STONES

SEE HER ROSES ?   **SEE HER TEARS ?**

Claire Faverone, Francesco's "Lady Poverty," had a rose garden at San Damiano, the church rebuilt by Francis in Assisi. Her roses were her greatest pleasure. Legend says that she and Mary, the Mother, Mary Magdalene and Isis are pieces of the same soul — the Twin Self of Jesus, Francis and Osiris.

HEAR THOSE NOTES . . . SEE THOSE HEARTS

THOSE TONES, THOSE HEARTS AROSE . . . (and) ARE ONE

Artist: Rob Schouten
Visionary Publishing, Inc.
Isis Unlimited Beverly Hills, Ca.

Stonehenge, England

9
PHYSICAL IMMORTALITY

a thought transformation,
leading to the achievement of
cell regeneration

This chapter is dedicated to:

Annette and Robert Kemery . . . and Pauline Goodman

the three most magical Earthlings I know

with much love

and a promise for tomorrow

"I am weary
of religious and spiritual abracadabra
        the churches have failed
can't you see that *the churches have all failed?*

and the biggest ghost story of them all
the biggest ghost-hoax of all Christian churches
is the Easter resurrection conception
                which is nothing but a cruel deception

        a cruel deception !

            a joke played on the broken-hearted and bereaved
                    a joke of such poor taste
        and I tell you . . . I *swear* that I will not be so deceived !"

            my voice, then, shattered into bitter splinters
                of remembered cold and lonely winters
                and I could not continue

        he slowly shook his head
        and his voice was low and
        gentle
        when he spoke . . .

        "no, the resurrection of Jesus
                    is not a joke
        it is quite literal
        more tangible and real than
        anything you feel
        at this moment . . .

                                Easter is Truth !

★ ★ ★ ★ ★ ★

HEN AN ancient building, built on a strong foundation, has outlived its time and must be destroyed so
that a new building may be constructed on its site,
there is only one way to accomplish such a transformation of matter. Dynamite. An explosion.

Likewise, when an ancient falsehood, built on a strong foundation of lies seeded into the mass collective subconscious for thousands
upon thousands of years, has outlived its time and must be destroyed
so that a new realization may replace it, there is only one way to
accomplish such a transformation of thought. Dynamite. An
explosion.

The words in this chapter may very well be perceived by your
falsely programmed brain as an unexpected blast of dynamite. An
overload, to use a common computer term, since the brain is, after all,
the ultimate computer. Close your mind against the initial shock if
you must, but keep your soul open. Later, your mind may join it in a
new realization, and you could experience a thought transformation.

At the outset, let's face the prime objection most people give as
their reason for believing that physical immortality is impossible because of being impractical. You may ask yourself, "Even if I should
want to live eternally in my present body, without the repeated coma
of death and rebirth, such a thing could never be possible for every
human on Earth. Already we're facing worldwide famine, just around
the corner — so, with new babies being conceived and born every
hour, if everyone achieved eternal life and never died — the Earth
would become so overpopulated as to be unthinkable."

Your argument is understandable, and appears to be reasonable.
However, there is a beautifully harmonious, sensible and even logical
solution to this apparent flaw in physical immortality for everyone —
and it does not include a mandate that men and women who become
immortals not mate or reproduce. Babies will still be born. Yet, there
will be no overpopulation.

I realize this seems to be a contradiction, a non sequitur, but it is not. The explanation, while surprisingly simple, nevertheless requires a foundation of layered esoteric knowledge to be properly understood, and once again I must apologize for the necessity of telling you that my own teachers have counseled me to offer the answer in the long-delayed but forthcoming *Gooberz*, giving as a reason that revealing it now would be premature. The situation echoes once more the ancient adage quoted, of necessity, so often in this book: *When the student is ready, the teacher will appear.*

Meanwhile, you can move forward to begin now to achieve eternal life, if that should be your desire. By the time you've chosen to do so, and have begun to practice it, the answer to the overpopulation question will be available — and you may even be able to answer it for yourself before then.

Until the dawning of the golden Age of Aquarius, only a rare few dreamed of physical immortality — eternal life in the same, but continually improved and transfigured flesh body. Others have believed in it only as a possibility for a few initiated Masters, the founders of the world's religions (some of them). Today, however, those who ponder such a possibility for themselves are increasing in number. More people are beginning to realize that physical immortality is actually the foundation of genuine religion.

Yes, physical immortality — eternal life in the material sense — was the original cornerstone of all religions, worn away by the ravages of illusionary time, and replaced by false deathist dogma and doctrines. The Christian Bible says accurately that "God hath put eternity into the heart of man." And into the heart of woman too.

Yet today's religions, and even the new occult movements, continue to sell the "glory of death" concept.

During recent years there have been various attempts to break the stern and dreary deathist philosophy by portraying the experience of death as almost a fun thing, floating around like a balloon in the ethers, and gazing down on the discarded cocoon of the flesh body — or flying dreamily in and out and around the Moon or Pluto on a glittering silver cord, in what is intimated to be a kind of practice session for death.

The "silver cord" is actually seen by the Third Eye as sparkling silver, possessing an unlimited stretch capacity, and is not only a visible cord — but also an audible (to the inner ear) musical *chord* of extremely high frequency. In one of the incidents dramatized in the television mini-series *Out on a Limb,* actress Shirley MacLaine remarked that her own astral trip on her silver cord ended the instant she imaged "limitation," when she wondered if her silver cord would stretch far enough for her to actually touch the Moon she saw herself approaching. True. A thought of any kind of limitation instantly blows the fuse in all attempted magic, including the magical reality of physical immortality.

All these attempts to erase the dread of death are admirably motivated. They're saying, in effect, "Don't be afraid. Dying is a marvelous trip. You'll love it !" But such images are impotent to defeat and permanently destroy death. They succeed only in making it a shade more palatable, and they certainly don't do anything to comfort the bereaved, those grief-stricken loved ones left behind when the dead go flying off into the cosmos on their silver cords.

These silver-cord-astral-trips may occur during sleep, or in trance, under the proper conditions, but they are not "mini-deaths," and are not "dress rehearsals" for an inevitable and final "crossing over."

By the way, it's interesting and meaningful to contemplate the similarity between the silver cord attached to the body while astral traveling (or dying) . . . the umbilical cord of the newborn infant, attached to its mother . . . and the cord attached between the mother ship (space capsule) and an astronaut landing on the Moon. The three experiences are closely related.

Today's religious leaders on the stages of church, synagogue and television who are so cheerfully selling death as pie-in-the-sky, somewhere out there in the-great-by-and-by, have failed dismally to manifest the third and fourth lines of the Lord's Prayer: *Thy Kingdom come, Thy will be done . . . on Earth, as it is in Heaven.* They have not been successful in creating Heaven on Earth, and they never will be, the way they've been going about it. Religions rely upon the goodness of their various founding Immortals to bring about such a miracle.

But it's not the Immortals who seeded their spiritual doctrines who cause the wars, sicknesses, disasters, personal misery and "man's inhumanity to man" (and animals) on Earth. These evils are caused by mortals, playing carelessly with their Free Will Tinker Toys. And the only way to end this hell on Earth (which, in case you haven't yet noticed, has always been its geographical location) is to turn all of Earth's mortals into immortals, because the process will not only "wipe away all tears from their eyes," as John prognosticated in Revelations, but will also remove all desire to be evil from their hearts and minds. "And there shall be no more death."

The truth is that all mortals were once immortals. Even you. You only need to both *remember* and realize this for the battle to be won, the victory to be yours. Victory is the thought transformation resulting from comprehending that physical immortality — perpetual longevity, sans illness and aging — eternal, healthy, youthful life in your living flesh is not a fantasy, but a practical and attainable possibility.

The Hindu Hatha Yoga Masters in India who have already achieved it (and there are more of them than you've ever dreamed) claim that at least half if not more of the people alive in the 1980s may learn how to live forever in continually increasing health and youthfulness, by simply the *knowing* of this truth, which will, in turn, bestow mastery over the physical body. Naturally, there are certain disciplines to follow, but the first step is a releasing of your religion-seeded loyalty to death. That takes immense effort, admittedly, but it's certainly worth a try, isn't it ? You have nothing to lose and a lot to gain. And believe it or not, dying takes much more effort.

Why ? Because physical immortality is natural — and death is unnatural. Therefore, people need to exert so much (subconscious) effort to die that it causes illness and pain. Ask yourself if you choose to remain among the masses of humanity who have subjected themselves as slaves to a deathist theology that condemns them into finally sacrificing their bodies to dust — or to the extinguishing fire of cremation. To worship the grave, if you'll pardon the pun about such a serious issue, is a grave offense against both truth and happiness.

The High Priests of deathist philosophy are the Life Insurance companies, who keep telling you that "the life span is . . ." and everyone accepts this illusionary number as gospel. In the time of Francis of Assisi, the imaginary "life span" was not much past forty, which is why they married at twelve and thirteen. In the time of Moses, it was around six hundred years, during the Civil War about fifty-five or sixty. Now they dictate that the arbitrary "life span," based, one presumes, on the age of people who have died each decade, is eighty. Obediently, then, in submissive follow-the-leader fashion, men and women check that illusionary double number on the calendar, and when they're getting close, make out their wills and wait to die.

Someone once said that thoughts are angels, and some thoughts are, like this one: You are alive now, and so obviously your current and true life urges are stronger than your programmed death urges. As long as you continue to strengthen your life urges, and ignore your programmed death urges, you'll go on living. Read this thought over and over until you completely comprehend what it's saying.

You die because you *believe you must,* and you believe it because your computer brain has been falsely programmed that it's a necessity. Not only has your brain been programmed, your mind and soul have both been subjected to mass hypnosis from parents, relatives, friends, radio, television, newspapers and magazines. You die because you're reacting and predictably responding to post-hypnotic suggestion. Your mind and soul have submitted to it (the soul more reluctantly) — but your Spirit (Overself, Higher Angel of your S-elf, the you-of-you) knows better. Ask the wise Guru of your own S-elf, and He or She will level with you about the myth of dying.

Just the belief in death is enough to kill you, even without accident or disease. This is what medical people call "dying of nothing specific except old age."

All deaths are suicides, do you realize that ? Every single one. The only distinction is that, with some people, suicide is a subconscious choice — and with others it's a conscious choice. Otherwise, those who commit suicide and those who succumb to accident, illness or "old age," die for exactly the same reason: belief in the inevitability of death. In America, suicide is against the law — a punishable crime. In a way that's amusing, since it can only apply to unsuccessful suicide attempts. The successful ones are obviously beyond the reach of the law. Actually, all deaths are against the law — the law of eternal life — but it's too late after the "guilty ones" have escaped what religion and even the new occult movements call "the prison of the flesh," and traveled to a different dimension.

Now, there is the real culprit — the concept of "the prison of the flesh." No wonder everyone longs to escape, even though they're nervous and apprehensive about what happens after the "prison breakout." Who wants to remain in prison ? But . . . is the flesh body, called the Temple of the soul — a prison ? It is only when you fail to understand what is meant by "keeping one foot on Earth and one foot in Heaven."

Before continuing, let's understand that the following terms are synonymous: Higher Self . . . the Angel of the Higher Self . . . the Overself . . . the Supraconscious . . . and the Spirit. All of them are terms for the real you-of-you. They are interchangeable. For clarity and brevity, now that this has been explained, I'm going to choose to use the term *Spirit* when I'm referring to the you-of-you. But remember that your Spirit is not a synonym for, not the same as — your soul. The "Spirit" and the "soul" are two different terms describing two separate parts of the "holy trinity" of you. (See drawing on Page 116, Chapter 3.)

You were once, countless forgotten eons ago, a Spirit. You still are, essentially, but now you are a Spirit —*plus* a Mind and a Soul — a flesh body and an astral body. One might say you have more or less cloned your S-elf.(Your S-elf is another synonym to add to the foregoing synonyms for your Spirit.)

I employed the word *clone* because it describes what I'm trying to explain. But don't ever forget that modern man's attempt to clone the flesh body is against Universal Law. Cloning may be successfully accomplished only when it has been chosen for complex reasons by the Spirit of an Adept, Avatar, Guru, Master or Immortal (these terms also being synonymous to each other). Cloning attempted by the unenlightened — and modern science is, to date, about as synonymous with the word *unenlightened* as you can get — is doomed to failure, fated to collapse from its own weight of negativity — and will be halted by our Creators before it causes irreversible harm.

Returning to those countless forgotten eons ago, you were once a pure Spirit. A Spirit who (not *which,* but *who*) existed in a higher dimension, now called "Heaven," where there was (is) no illness, no aging, no death, no murder, no theft, no envy, no violence or anything else of a negative and unhappy "nature" — and no Time — with a body in every way identical to physical bodies, except composed of a finer substance. In every way but . . . certain differences related to particular organs of the body, which need not concern you quite yet. In appearance, identical. That's the thing to know.

One fine day your own Creators divinely decided to create infinite zillions — many times over the number of grains of sand on this planet — infinite zillions of dense physical dimensions of matter called Eden Heavens (each with its own solar system) — Eden Heavens called Earths only after the "fall" of each, brought about when certain immutable laws of each planet's Mother Nature were disobeyed. Before such transgression, there was no Time here, as there was no Time in the higher astral dimension of "Heaven." There were two Suns; consequently no darkness on the face of the planet. Without darkness, Time cannot be measured. And the Earth did not spin, so there was no gravity. I know all this opens up a Pandora's box of questions, and some of them will be answered later on in this chapter. Some must wait for later books.

Through your precious gift of Free Will choice, you decided, as did other Spirits, to exist *partly* on this planet, this mirror-reflection of the higher Heaven dimension, and partly in the higher dimension itself (the real world), keeping, in a manner of speaking, one foot in Heaven, and one foot in the Eden Heaven now called Earth. Other Spirits did not so choose, and remain, even now . . . Angels.

To accomplish such a dual existence, you created a flesh or physical, material body, in your own (your Spirit's) image, with an astral body superimposed — as the vehicle for those round trips between dimensions. Again, see the drawing on Page 116, Chapter 3.

This original physical body was, unfortunately, due to "free-willful" disobedience of Universal Law, later to multiply itself through many thousands (in some cases, many millions) of successive flesh incarnations.

Your Spirit cloned itself, gave birth to or created this original material, physical body in imitation of your Creators' act of giving birth to (creating) this Eden Heaven, in this solar system (and an infinite number of others) — later called Earth. And since it was a physical, material world of matter, this mirror-reflection of "Heaven" (the higher dimension), your Spirit needed a material, physical, flesh body, in order to experience its delights, which are presently called the five senses: taste, touch, sight, smell and sound.

Actually, in the beginning, there were six, not five senses necessary to keep "one foot on Earth, and one foot in Heaven." Have you ever heard anyone remark that "he must have a sixth sense?" Before defining the elusive sixth sense, let's try a Lexigram code. As we discussed earlier, Jesus spent part of his eighteen "lost years," which were removed from the Christian Scriptures — with the Essenes. The word ESSENES contains within it the letters of the word SENSES. The spiral thought thus initiated by Lexigrams may seed a question in your mind. Did the Essenes possess all six senses, and was one of the magics they taught the carpenter from Nazareth how to regain, strengthen and use the *sixth* sense?

You might think of your sixth sense as having the "good sense" to remember, therefore realize that you can travel back and forth between the two dimensions of Heaven and Earth as often as you choose, whenever you like, using sometimes your flesh body, sometimes your astral body, and sometimes both at once, depending on the requirements for any particular trip. And don't forget your numerology lesson about the number 6 (as in sixth sense) which is the number of Venus . . . and Love.

The brilliant crystal of the sixth sense is reflected in many prisms, such as: human auras and Third Eye vision (your contact with the Higher Realms) telepathy, teleportation, psychometry, esp, clairaudience, clairvoyance, sensitivity, intuition and so on. But, in general, the sixth sense has been dulled by an eons-old amnesia of the mind and soul, which has short-circuited or cut off their communication with your Spirit.

The Spirits who chose to create and occupy (part-time) flesh bodies, so that they might experience the pleasures of the senses, by losing the *sixth* sense, also lost touch with their minds and souls, and consequently lost control of both the physical and astral "puppet bodies" they once divinely manipulated with the wisdom of Love and Light — breaking the line of communication between the world in which the Spirit dwells and the world of matter where the physical body dwells, with its superimposed astral body "spacecraft."

When the mind and the soul once more communicate with the Spirit, acting as intermediaries, then the Spirit may once more guide the physical and astral bodies in manifesting the magic and miracles of the beginning "faerie tale" world on Earth, of which the faerie tales of old are a transparent image, a faint echo.

Each mind and soul at last became so emeshed in the vicarious pleasures of the five physical senses experienced through the material body, they no longer remembered that the astral body possessed a *sixth sense,* giving them a round-trip ticket between "Heaven" and "Earth," with no cancellation date.

The real and actual presence of the Spirit was likewise forgotten; the vital communication with Him or Her cut off. Another revealing Lexigram to spiral your thoughts: the word **COMMUNICATION** contains the word **COMMUNION** — and both words contain **UNION**. Instead of the original intent to keep "one foot in Heaven, and one foot on Earth," both "feet" (symbolically) became firmly planted on Earth. The only traveling between here and other levels the majority of Earthlings do presently is through the dangerously deceptive hegiras of hallucinatory drugs — in trance — or during sleep. None of these trips are satisfactory because they're followed by spiritual amnesia, as the astral experiences called dreams are distorted through the "scrambling device" in the brain, much like the one on the President's telephone. Just as it wouldn't be much fun to visit Europe and remember nothing when you return. You can't even bring back postcards or photographs as souvenirs of your astral travels. Perhaps an occasional nightmare, but that's hardly ideal.

Yet, without sleep the physical body would die. It's literally kept alive, refueled and refreshed by these hazy astral trips to your "Heaven home." Not all trips are to the higher dimension of your Spirit. Some are to different levels of awareness. You might call it time traveling, as your astral body is transported, on its silver cord, to the experiences of

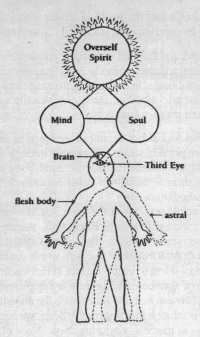

The "circle" is symbolic only. Your Overself of Higher Self is, in appearence, exactly like your physical body, which was created in its image, except for one difference, which need not yet concern you.

Past, Present and Future incarnations, which exist simultaneously in the relativity of time and space. Such trips are the source of the flashes everyone periodically feels that "this has happened before." You may have visited next Friday during your sleep last Thursday.

Unfortunately, each return to this world takes a heavy toll on the dense body, because of a lack of communication with your Higher Self (the puppeteer). Consequently, your physical body needs a re-charge of its battery every twenty-four hours or so. But even these periodic sleep charges can't halt its gradual deterioration due to gravity. Physical gravity and mental gravity. Take charge of the latter, and you can control the former. More about the "gravity" of the subject of gravity a little later. Understanding it is an urgent necessity for those who choose to live, and not to die. We'll return to it.

Ultimately, the human body is an energy system. Anyone can learn to de-materialize and re-materialize the human form by mastering the nature of the body as light. Even though, in your present state of forgetfulness of your divine powers, you use only your astral body on these trips to the higher dimension — and other levels of past, present and future, it's possible to travel there and back, taking along *both* your astral and physical body, once you get the hang of it. Metaphysician Analee Skarin has written that "death is the dreary back door into other worlds, but there is a great front door for those who overcome" — (who overcome gravity). The door between the higher dimension of "Heaven" and Earth can swing both ways for immortals who realize their potential of eternal life. On a microcosm level, wouldn't it be dreadfully dreary and a bit of a bother if, every time a friend or loved one went to visit Disneyland or Aunt Ethel, they never returned ? It's ever so much nicer all the way round for everyone when all such visiting consists of round trips, whether astral or physical, don't you agree ?

We'll discuss the how-to-do-it aspect of eternal life and physical immortality shortly, but now we need to further discuss the concept in general, at least those readers who are still in shock from the very idea of it need further discussion, so they can apply some logic to measure its truth. There is logic to it, yes, there is, as you'll soon see, enough I trust, to satisfy even a biologist or a physicist. First, however, you must be convinced that it's attainable, that you already possess immortal life. You've only forgotten that you do. I'll try my best to accomplish this. But I'm only a channel for a message from a higher level of awareness, and all I can do is plant the seeds. Your own Free Will controls whether or not they blossom and bear fruit.

Physical death is unnatural. Neither is it a free trip to Heaven, as most religions would have you believe, because its consequence is repeated rebirth into flesh bodies, until you're enlightened to truth. "Seek the truth, and it shall set you free." This counsel from the Avatar-Adept, Jesus, cannot be repeated too frequently. The people of his time could not and would not have comprehended the whole truth at their stage of evolvement, so it was necessary to impart wisdom to them in parable form, many of which seem like mystical riddles, which is, more or less, what they are.

Eternal life is natural, a truth which always was, is now and ever shall be. You are now and always have been in harmony with it, but you've been programmed to believe you're not, and this false belief causes you to gradually destroy your body, a body intended to survive as long as the Earth survives.

The difference between one person and another — between, for instance, a mortal and an immortal — is what they think about. Whatever thoughts and ideas are in the mind have the power to produce direct results in the body. The body is totally obedient to the ideas and thoughts in the mind. Therefore, what you think about habitually will become dominant, and possess the greatest power to control your body.

What most people think about habitually, after a certain illusionary chronological number called "age," is death. And so, the body obeys, becomes ill and dies.

Those of you who have taken these remarks about physical immortality seriously may be wondering, "How does this affect the law of Karma?" An excellent question.

Whether you decide to allow your present physical body to live or die, you cannot escape the law of Karma — but don't forget that you experience karmic rewards, as well as karmic retribution. Also remember that there are ways to dilute or even negate the latter. (See Chapter 4, "Déjà Vu.")

To choose eternal life in your present flesh body does not remove your Karma. But you would be paying (and receiving) it anyway, so nothing will change there, except that the very act of choosing *not* to die, the very realization that death is not a necessity, will negate a great deal of the unpleasant Karma of past incarnations.

The supreme demonstration of this is the incident of the two criminals who were crucified with the Nazarene. Translating that incident into modern idiom, one of the criminals began to sarcastically taunt Jesus as he hung on the cross in agony, reminding him that he was supposed to be "the son of God," therefore why didn't he call on his omnipotent Father to miraculously rescue all three of them? The other criminal quickly spoke up in defense of Jesus, saying, in so many words, "Leave him alone. We deserve to be here, because we have committed great sins. He is innocent, and should not be questioned." Whereupon the Nazarene turned to the second man who spoke, and said, "Verily, verily, this day thou shalt be with me in Heaven."

I'm aware that most translations use the word *Paradise* instead of "Heaven," but I happen to believe Jesus used the latter term. I've always mistrusted the word **PARADISE**, since it contains the words **RAPE** and **DIE** (albeit also **ARISE**), whereas **HEAVEN** Lexigrams into **HAVEN** and **EVE** (there's a reason for that, but it doesn't belong in this book) — also **EVEN** — and Heaven is where everything is balanced evenly (harmoniously).

The word *Heaven,* a.k.a. paradise, is synonymous with enlightenment. (Even though lower-case paradise is suspect.) Metaphysicians translate this crucifixion incident as allegorical to the "spontaneous remission" of Karma. In other words, the *very act of faith* demonstrated by the second criminal — complete faith in a man who was despised by all, deserted by his few friends, apparently possessing no power, and who appeared to be impotent to save others or himself — was an act of faith so powerful, so pulsating with conviction and innocence in the face of all contrary evidence, that it balanced the man's karmic scales, allowing that particular physical body to die totally free of the chains of Karma (until and unless in a future incarnation he created new Karma for himself).

It's certainly fair to assume that anyone who dares to face friends, relatives and the world today with an outspoken, unashamed and confident belief in physical immortality, despite all the vast programming otherwise, is demonstrating an act of faith of equal weight in the karmic scales as that of the man crucified with Jesus.

The danger of creating new negative Karma (becoming a fallen angel) is always there for the man or woman who chooses (again) immortality, as it was when your Spirit originally chose to spend *part-time* in a physical, flesh body. Nothing has changed there either, except that choosing eternal life gives one a new slate and a new opportunity to also choose not to create new negative Karma.

Ask yourself this: Is not a person more likely to create new negative Karma when he or she is still suffering from spiritual amnesia of past incarnations — cannot recall what transgression brought on present "bad luck" — and can't become too interested in a hazy, dim, uncertain future incarnation when present negative acts must be atoned for and balanced ? Isn't that person's attitude likely to be "who cares" ?

Conversely, however, when a person has demonstrated the great act of faith of totally believing and practicing physical immortality, knowing, therefore, that he or she is now under the law of "instant" Karma — and that the karmic scales will be balanced, not in some misty future life, but in this very present and continuing life, with total recall, the karmic retribution occurring to this present identify and flesh body — would that person not be far *less* likely to create new negative Karma, and be far *more* likely to earnestly attempt to create new *positive* Karma ? Too many books on Karma neglect to teach that there is both positive and negative karmic cause and effect.

Therefore, when physical immortality has been chosen and achieved by more and more Earthlings the negative behavior causing

Earth's unhappiness will gradually and finally cease. The pollution of the planet will stop when those responsible for it become immortal, and realize that it's themselves, not "future generations," who will inherit the wasteland caused by nuclear madness and other forms of destruction of the water and air in our environment.

We fear acid rain and the holes being torn in the Earth's ozone layer, endangered species and a multitude of acts of violence and cruelty to Mother Earth and her creatures. Yet, the belief that death is inevitable — that death is beyond an individual's control — is still the biggest killer of all. The belief that "God" is out there somewhere, but not on Earth, and not within the flesh body. Fortunately, this belief is gradually being replaced by the dawning awareness that each man and each woman is God to his or her own body. Immortals clearly have the greatest motivation for ecology — for sanity in politics — for technology that helps, but doesn't kill — for universal prosperity.

Immortal humans also have all the Earth time they need to master body purification techniques, including the mastery of eating habits and sleep with conscious recall of astral experience. What I mean by the mastery of eating habits is explained in Chapter 4. Improper eating and lack of control over sleep are barriers to total awareness.

Many people have no desire to conquer death and live forever because they image themselves living in ill and aged bodies, but this is in direct contradiction to the real meaning of physical immortality.

Your body was gloriously designed by your Spirit, as your Spirit's body was gloriously designed by your Creators, to be eternal. Your flesh body is a self-sustaining electromagnetic battery, forever capable of being recharged with energy, continually improved and transmuted into perfection through the process of cell regeneration. And it all begins in your mind.

Through the process of cell regeneration you can accomplish either (a) age prevention — or (b) age reversal, if necessary — and free your material body of all disease and imperfection. Don't look to the medical profession. Look to yourself. "Physician, heal thyself." The choice is yours and yours alone, whether you're eighteen or eighty by illusionary chronological measurement. If you're eighteen, you must learn how to *prevent* aging, in order to conquer disease and death. If you're eighty, you must learn how to *reverse* aging, in order to conquer disease and death. These are simply polarities of the same magic.

The eternal and suppressed, long-buried truth is that you may exist within your present body, and continually improve it, for as many centuries or eons as you desire — all the way to eternity or forever — healthy, youthful and fully functioning, projecting and actually *being* whatever chronological "age" you wish, based on the human concept of these impotent "numbers." Some Master Avatars and Adepti who have become physically immortal deliberately choose to project and *be,* for however long or brief a period as they may prefer — the present "image" of the illusionary chronological age of forty, fifty or sixty, in order to be believed by those still mortal to be worthy of respect, so that they may successfully teach. (It's difficult to possess several doctorates and master's degrees and *appear* to be twenty or thirty.) However, in the final analysis, each newly immortal man or woman may choose to project and *be* any chronological "age" seen individually as ideal, switching the numbers around at his or her option, from "time" to "time." Rather like pressing the control switches on your washer from hot to cold to warm, whichever suits your current needs.

Whether you choose to believe it or not (I believe it, because I have impeccable cause to do so) — there are many among you who are already immortals. And before they became so, they were no different from you . . . or me. One of the problems of achieving eternal life in the same physical body while so many millions of mortals have not been thus enlightened, they tell me . . . is the problem of the programming of chronological age.

These Avatars and Adepti are forced, therefore, to pretend to "die" at whatever chronological age any current time period "requires" based on the "life span" then expected of them. He or she simply disappears, and is presumed dead, with the body never found, or never actually identified. Then the Avatar turns up in a different part of the world, with a new identity, a new birth date and a few friends (other Avatars) to substantiate the false birth date, when necessary. It's really quite a bother, they claim, and one can see why. It will be much easier when immortality catches on.

Just imagine what happens when a true Adept (immortal) announces to someone who asks his or her age, "I'm six hundred years old, going on seven hundred, as calculated by your erroneous Earth Time." (Or two thousand, going on three thousand, as the case may be.) What happens depends on the period of history. During one time period, such a person would have been labeled a witch or a warlock, and burned at the stake. During a later time period, such an answer would have condemned the Avatar to an insane asylum. Today, in the Aquarian Age ? Well, we're gaining ground. Such an answer to an age inquiry presently wouldn't result in being burned at the stake or committed to the funny house. But it probably would result in the loss of a certain degree of credibility, eliciting such whispers as: "George is obviously a most brilliant person, quite intellectual really, but a little . . . well, you know . . . *weird*. I don't think he's playing with a full deck." Or words to that effect.

Since credibility is needed for teaching truth and for other missions of immortals, that's not the ideal type of response an Avatar desires, even though it's an undeniable improvement over yesterday's witch burnings and asylums. Whether one is immortal or mortal, it takes courage to face a loss of respect and credibility.

By the way, did you know that, among the many "crimes" women (and a few men) were accused and found guilty of during the shameful witch burnings in Salem and other places, mostly by the Catholic Church, a large percentage included the "crime" of agelessness ? Many witches went up in flames because their neighbors swore under oath as to their birth dates, yet they looked and behaved many decades younger than their dates of birth indicated. A most interesting bit of history, strongly suggesting that many of these "witches" were immortals.

No wonder that the secret knowledge of age reversal and physical immortality was buried even deeper around that time period. Most enlightened ones, not possessing the financial means to pop up in Europe or somewhere with a new identity, chose the unpleasant path of aging and death to being tied up to a stake and having their bodies set afire. That's one of the most painful deaths imaginable. Poor Joan of Arc was turned into a human torch simply because she honestly revealed her powers of clairaudience. Even today, "hearing voices" can get you a sanity hearing if you're careless about the people in whom you confide. Shhh! Silence is, indeed, under certain circumstances — golden.

I'll interject here a personal incident, based on a commitment test of spiritual honesty I've been taught is necessary to the complete achievement of immortality. Two or three Earth years ago, I was interviewed by a Capricorn reporter from a Denver newspaper. The article about me closed with these words: "Goodman was asked her age, but refused to answer, based on her explanation that any discussion of chronological age is against her spiritual beliefs. However, when pressed, she finally admitted to being four hundred."

I'm still trying to figure out if the reporter wrote that with a straight face or with his tongue in his cheek. Since he was a Capricorn (the astrological sign of reverse aging), it may have been the former. I doubt if I would have been so courageous in Salem. As an Aries all through the past four hundred years, I have a very low pain threshold, and I'm a shameful coward about burns. Not only would a flaming torch have intimidated me into projecting four hundred years of wrinkles, an asylum would have been an even more frightening alternative, with everyone claiming he or she was Napoleon or Josephine. I must digress for a moment, because I'm reminded of an old joke with a hidden meaning related to these matters.

A man in an asylum was always strutting around with one hand thrust in his nightshirt, wearing a hat with a feather, and shouting to everyone within earshot, "I am Napoleon Bonaparte ! I am Napoleon ! And I won the battle of Waterloo ! The history books lie !" One day, as he was thus proclaiming his message, an elderly man sitting on the floor in the corner rose up and asked, "Who told you that you are Napoleon ?" "God told me !" came the offended "Napoleon's" reply. Then, from another corner of the room, a man with a white beard stood up, and, with great dignity, announced in a ringing voice, "I did *not* !"

The Denver newspaper interview incident has a moral. This is one of the steps in the how-to-do-it process of achieving eternal life. To question the necessity of the deathist theology, whether seriously or with a sense of humor, is a blow against death. Some of you braver ones — even if you're still a high-school or college student — when casually asked your age, might reply, "Two hundred next May" — or "seven hundred last February." Then give the questioner a steady, laser-beam, mysterious, Scorpio-like gaze. You'll be surprised at the variety of responses. It's fascinating. Try it. As for myself, I confess that I lied to the reporter. I won't be four hundred for another one hundred and thirty-two Earth years yet.

Still, even sans witch burning and psychiatric commitment, Avatars today must continue to "die" and start all over with a new name and identity somewhere else after a "reasonable period" in the same body and its original identity, in a deception oddly similar to that practiced by those in the Government Witness Relocation program.

You might find this information I've been given helpful someday. You can't judge a female Avatar or Guru (immortal) by her motherhood. It's both natural and possible to conceive and bear a child even when one is several hundred years old, by Earth time. The Karma of menstruation has nothing to do with pregnancy, even in this imperfectly (at present) formed physical body. Someday medicine will discover this truth — well, actually, they already have discovered it. They just don't believe it yet, and aren't quite ready yet to announce the discovery. Female children of nine, ten and eleven years of chronologically measured age have, within the past decade, become pregnant and delivered infants, before ever having their first lunar period. And this is not a rumor from sensationalist magazines. It's a medically witnessed fact. Remember the law of polarity. If one may conceive and bear a child before the menstrual periods begin, one may do the same after they have ceased. Sarah did. Abraham didn't want to believe it either, but he finally had to, when he saw it with his own eyes. There are many such miracles waiting around the corner, like shooting stars, to amaze you in the Aquarian Age.

And so . . . just because that woman down the street gave birth to twins last month, don't be too certain that she's not an immortal. Not even if she shows you her birth certificate.

A postscript to the foregoing paragraph: When astro-biology birth control catches on, medical science will be forced to take a second look at the "old wives' tale" of the connection between female lunar periods and conception, since Dr. Jonas, of Czechoslovakia, has already proven, through careful research with thousands of women, that some women can conceive only *during* their menstrual periods. As for giving birth after the menstrual cycle has ceased (after ancient Karma has been balanced), it's far more common than most people realize — women giving birth (over the past century, in fact) at ages ranging from fifty to sixty. Records are available. When it happens today the confused medical profession calls them "menopausal babies." Here's a friendly, not ominous warning regarding all this.

A number of conscientious objectors in the sixties chose to adopt the name, identity, birth certificate, school records and so forth, of an actual person, a mortal who had submitted to death, using the dead person's identity. Secret agents in the CIA and the KGB are known to do likewise, from time to time. The same procedure is occasionally chosen by some Avatars and Gurus who need, for reasons already explained, a new identity. So . . . how well do you really know that wise friend who's been enlightening you regarding various New Age ideas and ideals ? Remember the biblical warning that one may "entertain angels unawares."

You'll recall what was written in the chapter "Gurus, Ghosts, and Avatars," concerning the Adept known as St. Germain (or the Comte de St. Germain) who was, according to metaphysicians of high credibility, also Shakespeare, Francis Bacon and Isaac Newton. You may have wondered how that could be, since all three men lived during the same "life span" period of history. Remember what I said a few pages back on the subject of cloning? I said that scientific and involuntary cloning by mortals is an extremely negative research, but that the Spirit of an enlightened Avatar may — just as was done "in the beginning" — clone himself or herself for various cosmic causes of spiritual intent. Consequently, an Adept who has become a completely illuminated immortal may "overshadow" more than one flesh body (or physical identity) simultaneously, with the Adept's Spirit watching over and controlling several material bodies at the same time. This can be accomplished by the takeover of a body born in the usual Earth manner — or by actually creating from the ethers a physical body. A Spirit, mind and soul may not be created in this manner, but a flesh body, complete with brain and all the necessary physical parts may be so created, under the guidance of an Overself — the "puppeteer," who in this manner manipulates the strings of several "puppets" at once. See once again the drawing on Page 116.

Let's return to the problem of programmed chronological age images confronting both immortals and would-be immortals. Note that the words *mature* and *maturing* are not synonyms for *age* and *aging*. The former is necessary and desirable for a human body, the latter is neither necessary nor desirable.

What causes the process we call aging ? You've been falsely programmed to believe that it's caused by a chronological count of how many "years old" you are — your "birthday count." Not true.

This GIGO (garbage in — garbage out) programming of the computer brain insinuates that the man-made and inaccurate calendar — and the illusion of Time — are the stern "gods" that cause the human body to age. Again, we're referring to the negative phenomenon of aging, not maturing. It takes eighteen to twenty-one years for a body to mature.

Using this time-calendar yardstick is the same as saying a person ages because of how many sunrises and sunsets that person has observed or "lived through." How can something so obviously untrue be accepted ? Why ask the question ? I know the answer. Post-hypnotic suggestion and centuries of false programming. What happens when you "live through" or watch two or three sunsets or sunrises . . . or several thousand of them ? Nothing. Not a thing. They haven't the slightest effect on your body. To be precise, it's not sunrise and sunset anyway. It's earthrise and earthset. But science has so many things upside down and backward, I suppose it's to be expected that their terminology for the Earth's trips around the Sun would be the same. You can toss holier-than-thou astronomers into the bucket too.

Time is an illusion. It allows humans to measure it because of the stark comparison between light and dark. That's the only "beginning and end" there is to measure. But when there was no darkness on Earth — before the "fall," and before this planet's second Sun exploded, causing the Earth to spin around the remaining Sun like a billiard ball hit sharply with a cue stick — there was no Time. Does it really deserve a capital letter ? Yes, I suppose it does, since it makes such an impression on everyone.

A question to ask the wise elf of your S-elf: If the light outside were to remain exactly as it is now —assuming you're reading this in the daytime — and never changed in the least — how would you measure or refer to Time ? You couldn't refer to "last night" or "yesterday morning" or "last week" or "next month," because there would be no calendars, no clocks. When would you begin to set the clocks ?JUThere would be no *when*. Only the present. Only *now*. An

Eternal Now. Really think deeply about it. Neither plants nor people would need to "begin or end" (die). They would simply just *be*.

How would you measure Time if you were locked in a room with continual artificial light — or continual darkness ? With a clock ?JU(In the latter case, with a visible-in-the-dark face ?) Well, yes. But those clocks would have been set — started — in a world of dark and light, the only measurement of Time there is. The dark and light periods of the presence and the absence of the Sun also created the season of the illusionary calendar year.

And so, Time is the Great Deceiver. The Great Imposter. Therefore, to accuse what is not even real of being the enemy that causes the process of aging is foolishly illogical.

However, the aging process, regrettably, does exist. There's no denying it. You see it everywhere — in the reincarnations of trees and flowers, after they "age and die." You see it in your "older" relatives and friends. And, after the illusionary chronological calendar "age" of thirty or so illusionary "years" of 365 sunrises and sunsets each, you may begin to believe you see it in your mirror. If you believe you see it, you will. Swiftly. Your face and body will meekly acquiesce and obey the image of your Creator Mind.

Yes, the aging process does exist, an end product of the deathist programming. But the enemy that causes aging is not make-believe birthdays. It's *gravity*. Italics may not be sufficient. Let's give it capitals and bold face, so you won't forget the true identity of the enemy that causes the aging process. **GRAVITY**. You'll see shortly why you mustn't forget what I mentioned earlier: that there are two kinds of gravity — the gravity of the physical, material world — and mental gravity.

Physical gravity began when the Earth started that billiard ball spin around the remaining Sun, after being sharply struck on one side, while it was *not* spinning, by the exploding other Sun (creating animal, plant and human mutation — dinosaurs and the like). And so,

Time and Gravity began simultaneously. (I'll be writing about more of these "twelfth night secrets" later, at the allotted time).

While we're on the subject of the exploding Sun is a good "time" to meditate on the purpose of the Moon. Our Moon is what remains of our eons-ago second Sun. Francis of Assisi often referred to Brother Sun and Sister Moon. His sexual definition was right, but these Luminaries are more correctly defined as Father Sun and Mother Moon. (The Moon rules the astrological sign of Cancer, which represents the eternal essence of maternity.) What a lovely "angel of a thought," to conceive of the infinite compassion of our Mother Who art in Heaven, when her "child," this Eden Heaven now called Earth, suffered such indescribable horror. Mystics have channeled that She charged the pock-marked, dusty, burned-out Sun with Her gentler light (He is Love — She is Light), and divinely ordained its appearance as the Moon, above the now-in-darkness Earth, to light the night sky each time the remaining Sun disappears from sight . . . as Her promise for tomorrow.

How sad that the patriarchal theology has even entered the realm of Father Sun and Mother Moon by seeding repeated references to "the Man in the Moon," when it is not His face, but a faint echo of Her tender, maternal and nurturing image on the surface of the Moon, as gazed upon from Earth, which is seen mystically by the Third Eye — and even with physical vision, when one meditates and tries.

This is all symbolism, of course, but with an eternal message for the "fallen angels" of Heaven, here on Earth. Everyone to whom I've pointed it out succeeds in seeing it clearly after trying several times, most of them on the first try. If you'd like to try it yourself, when the Moon is full — or near full — when it is round in shape, not crescent — here is what to look for. The supremely feminine, cameolike face is seen in profile, facing toward the left, in appearance the features very much like those you've seen in a cameo ring or brooch, with the hair piled high on the head, in what might be called, for the purpose of recognition, a sort of Gibson girl style. Once the image springs into clarity for you, it's unmistakably the facing-toward-the-left profile of a woman of "unearthly" beauty and sadness. Do write and tell me when you've discovered it, won't you ? It's a moving experience, and once you've seen it clearly, you will always see it clearly, each night when you look up into the sky.

To some Cancerians I know, and to others also, when Her image suddenly manifests into vision, the sight brings tears, from a fragment of soul memory of the profound sadness any mother so very long forgotten by the children she deeply loves . . . must feel in her heart.

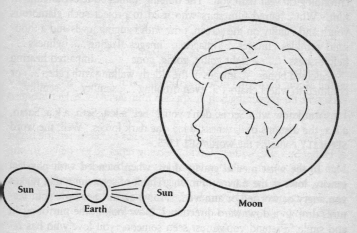

Back to gravity . . .

Remember when you were a small child in school, and the teacher held up an orange or an apple, representing the Earth, and you wondered, in your innocence, why the people on the bottom of the orange didn't fall off into space ? When you raised your hand, troubled, to ask, the teacher replied with one word: "Gravity." Tons of it keep your feet (both of them, unfortunately) planted firmly on the ground.

Gravity presses down on your mind, your face, your body and all of its organs with a "heavy hand." After enough of such pressure your mind submits even more meekly to the deathist theology. The skin on your face begins to sag, your body organs press downward and become tired. That's what *physical* gravity does. *Mental* gravity finishes off the process with images. Images all around you, from when you were a tiny tot, multiplying themselves every illusionary year of your life — Images of the elderly — the sick and the old. Within your own family. Friends and neighbors born in an earlier illusionary chronological year than you. The nursing homes on television and in film. White-haired film stars who used to project such glamorous youth and vitality on the screen, now with hanging jowls and a thousand wrinkles. Images . . . images . . . images of aging . . . ugliness . . . helplessness . . . eyesight going, going, gone . . . . . impaired hearing . . . calcified bones . . . images of the elderly walking with canes . . . or confined to wheel chairs . . . even drooling . . . senility . . . senility.

You know who Set is, don't you ? Set, a.k.a. Seth, a.k.a. Satan, a.k.a. the demons of darkness, a.k.a. the dark forces. Well, the word **SENILITY** contains the words **SET LIES**.

To see what mental gravity does, when blended with physical gravity, look in the mirror. Frown. Think of something that makes you angry or worried or annoyed. Frown again. See how your features drop in a downward direction ? Now look in the mirror again and smile. Pretend you've just seen someone you love who has returned after a long time. *Think* about it vividly, then smile and call out, "Well, **HI** there !" See how all your features form themselves in *upward* curves ? Including the lines around your mouth, your eyebrows, your whole face.

Fully aware of what physical gravity does to the face, body and all the body's organs, some Yogis choose to spend an hour or more each day standing on their heads — *to reverse gravity*. Physical gravity, that is. It's really dreadfully hard work, makes you dizzy besides — and it doesn't do all that much reversing. It barely makes a dent in the rest of the ninety-nine percent of the "time" the Yogis are walking around upright, submitting to those tons of physical gravity. That's not how you "reverse gravity." There's a much easier and far more effective way.

The more than 42 billion electric cells in your brain have a power immeasurably stronger than gravity, when they are controlled and guided by your Mind. You just proved it by looking in the mirror — if you did as I suggested. Did you ? If not, please do it now. All right, are you back ? Then think about this: Mental Gravity (let's give it caps; it deserves them) — Mental Gravity, *in both directions,* is what you were using to manifest those instant results in the mirror.

Could mere physical gravity do that — *instantly ?* Of course not. No way could it do that. So, you see, physical gravity is a light-weight, compared to the power of Mental Gravity. This isn't merely a mystical, esoteric statement. It's the absolute, measurable truth. Another truth even a physics professor can't deny is that physical gravity *cannot reverse itself,* never mind how many tons of pressure it contains. This alone should expose it for the weakling it is. But Mental Gravity can do so, as we shall see. (We're going to cap those two words from now on.)

The way to reverse physical gravity, the silent, sneaky enemy that causes aging, is to seriously and consciously guide and control those more than 42 billion electric cells in your brain with the infinitely greater power of your Mind. Mental Gravity. Up until now, it's been working in a misguided partnership with physical gravity, thanks to the age programming that began when you were a child. Break off that relationship. When you do you will eventually, and most certainly, be able to use Mental Gravity to *reverse* physical gravity, without head stands yet ! — for the very simple reason that the former is literally stronger and more powerful than the latter when you allow it to be, and don't hold it back. It can't be accomplished overnight. All those GIGO weeds must be pulled out by the roots and your computer brain re-programmed. It takes lots of practice, but doesn't everything ? It even takes lots of practice to become a liar, addicted to drugs or alcohol, forgetful, suspicious and fearful. Everything takes practice, from racial prejudice and male chauvinism to mistrust between nations. Right ? Right.

The pull of gravity, like everything else, without exception, is polarized. It works up and down, vertically. You've heard that "what goes up must come down," correct ? Do you know what that endlessly repeated saying means ? It's paying homage to the power of physical gravity. But have you ever heard that "what comes down can go up" ? No, you haven't. Because that saying applies to the well-kept secret that Mental Gravity can control physical gravity.

What is the phenomenon of levitation but the *reversal of gravity* ? And who levitates ? Saints do. Spiritually enlightened men and women do. Francis of Assisi, among a number of other holy ones, was seen frequently levitating several feet above the ground while saying his prayers, by witnesses of impeccable credibility and integrity. A couple of Yogis from India toured America in 1986 (and may still be here as you read this) — demonstrating levitation before crowds of hundreds. One of America's most popular magazines ran a feature story on these two men, including photographs taken of them sitting in the lotus position, arms crossed, several feet in the air. The article stated that they could remain there for a half a minute to a minute, and that they were practicing to be able to achieve an hour or more in the air.

In direct polarity are those possessed by "Satan" (dark forces of negativity), who also levitate, as in William Peter Blatty's book *The Exorcist,* and the film of the same name, based on many such true incidents of possessed people levitating, witnessed by both reputable priests of the Roman Church and medical doctors. Yes, observed levitating. *Reversing gravity.* Remember that all magic works both ways. The great power of the Mind may be used as curse or blessing, just as fire can be a faithful friend or a cruel master.

Currently it requires about one hundred years of illusionary

Earth Time for physical gravity to cause the features and body organs to fall and objectify "old age." It would take even longer, if it were not helped by the booster of Mental Gravity, which can work in both directions. Mental Gravity is capable not only of hastening the down direction of physical gravity, but also of reversing the downward direction to upward, either instantly or gradually, whichever speed is chosen by your Mind — another proof of its superiority over the physical gravity that "keeps people from falling off the bottom of the orange," and simultaneously causes aging. We know for certain, from scientific evidence, that Mental Gravity can cause physical levitation of the body. Possessing the awesome power of gravity reversal, and not using it, is like owning a car, and keeping it in the garage — or like owning a magic wand, and keeping it in a trunk in the attic. Such a waste.

The reason physical gravity has been able to get away with it for so many hundreds of thousands of years is that, as already pointed out, Mental Gravity has been its willing co-worker. Once more, break off that relationship ! You don't need to stand on your head like the Yogis. All you have to do is *use* your head for something besides getting headaches and a garden for your hair to grow in — on ? Whatever.

At some time during the sixties and the seventies, medical science discovered an odd and fascinating, yet very sad (they think) phenomenon. A disease called Progeria — premature aging. In a bizarre heralding of the Aquarian Age, popping up here and there, like some strange Uranian flowers from another galaxy, were young children, from six to twelve years old, or thereabouts, who aged with breathtaking speed, right before the eyes of their shocked doctors. Like watching a plant grow with speed photography, a process requiring weeks or months, happening before your eyes in seconds. You've seen such camera work on various Nature programs and specials on television.

These children, within a few swift years, age all the way from six or twelve to eighty or a hundred years old. They suffer all the known geriatric diseases of senility, everything from arthritis and rheumatism to calcified bones, loss of hair, teeth, sight and hearing. They resemble little old men and women, septuagenarians, octogenarians . . . and older. Some appear to be past one hundred. Toothless, horribly wrinkled, nearly deaf and blind. Pathetic youngsters.

Pathetic ? Don't be so certain. One of the strangest things about these Aquarian Age medical marvels is their dispositions. Doctors and nurses who care for them are amazed and at a loss for words to describe the lack of any negative response to this premature aging the children are suffering. Their dispositions remain cheerful, they are completely uncomplaining, they're unusually bright and alert, and they smile a lot. The medical people just can't figure it out. They behave almost like . . . well, almost like . . . miniature saints.

That's understandable. Indeed. Because . . . these children are illuminated Spirits, who have chosen to manifest these particular flesh bodies to demonstrate the Great Truth of the golden Age of Aquarius to the medical profession — and to men and women everywhere. They have a mission . . . but thus far it is failing, and can use your help.

They are here to teach a glorious lesson, the first magical step toward the realization of the miracle of physical immortality. They are objectifying in their flesh bodies the mighty Law of Polarity, the law Earth scientists and physicists know well and respectfully genuflect to, but too often fail to recognize.

These gentle children are here to bring an Easter message to Christians, Buddhists, Jews and those of all other Earth religions. They are saying silently and eloquently, through their poor, afflicted flesh bodies: "Look at us ! *Look* at us, please ! Don't you see ? We are living, visible proof, undeniable evidence of the polarity law of physical gravity. Look ! See ? *Think*. Hear us with your inner ears.

See us with your Third Eyes, as well as with your physical hearing and sight."

They are saying, with such love and sacrifice: "See me ? If I am nine years old, by your illusionary chronological Earth age measurement standards — yet I look and feel and project your image of ninety years old — then, by your own polarity law of physics, it is equally possible for one who is ninety years old by your false calendar to look and feel and literally project your image of nine years old — or any other illusionary double number. If nine can be ninety, then ninety can be nine. If seven can be sixty, then sixty can be seventeen, in the higher dimension mathematics. See us ? We are living, tangible proof of this ! What other proof could you possibly need than this evidence you see before you with your own eyes ? Perhaps if you opened your Third Eyes . . . . ."

But does medical science really look and listen ? No. They concentrate on trying to *treat* this new Aquarian Age "disease" of premature aging — on trying to analyze what flesh body functions went wrong to *cause* it — ignoring the irrefutable truth it is proving undeniably, without equivocation: that physical gravity is reversible, and contains polarity, as does everything in this world, hot and cold, dark and light, up and down, backward and forward . . . and on . . . and on . . . and on into infinity. All of you, look and listen.

I have a suggestion to make to clergymen and religious leaders everywhere, "for the love of Jesus," "the love of Moses," "the love of Buddha, Mohammed, Krishna and all the rest. Take all of those wide-eyed, trusting millions in your auditoriums, television audiences, churches and synagogues, and lead them to the new Lourdes. Tell them to kneel before the Easter altar of these children of the New Age, thanking them and gratefully blessing them for the shining message of truth, simplicity, love, innocence and eternity, the message of Pax et

Bonum they are trying to communicate to all Earthlings through their patient and cheerful suffering. Nurses and physicians, realize that you may be "entertaining Angels unawares."

Amen . . . Awomen

How many of you have noticed the paranoid, near-pathological and fanatic fixation on illusionary chronological "age" of certain magazines ?

I won't list them by name, but you know which ones they are.

The publishers, editors and staff writers of these magazines seem absolutely incapable of presenting any story at all, about anyone at all, without dropping "numbers" every paragraph or so. Their hypnotic fixation on this is very much like a hypnotized person who has been told to hold his arm in the air, that it is made of cement, and can't be lowered. That arm stays there, exactly as though it were actually made of cement, until "permission" is given by the hypnotist to lower it.

For example: Actress Jane Marshall, 32, and her husband, stockbroker Peter Thomas, 31, were seen yesterday at a White House luncheon with the President, 77, and the First Lady, 69. They took along their children, Toby, 17, Helen, 12 — and their adorable twins, 16 and 16 and 5 minutes. Or . . . Prime Minister Osgood, 72, met today with Premier Zhivago, 75, and his wife, Elsa, 68. They enjoyed a lavish banquet, along with other notable guests, such as film star Robert Hemmingway, 47, industrialist Anthony Perles, 51 and Olympic champion, Heidi Armstrong, 23, who came with Broadway producer, Hymie Castor, 64.

Now, I ask you, is this urgent information you're seeking as readers about all these people ? I certainly hope not. Otherwise, you're in trouble. I mean, who *cares,* for God's sake ?

Are they, perhaps, attempting to help their readers image the person they're writing about, believing that these numbers will best help in imaging them ? Then wouldn't the images be more clarified by writing: "Actress Jane Marshall, 5′ 2″, 118 lbs., and her husband, stockbroker Peter Thomas, blue eyes, black hair, were seen yesterday at a White House luncheon with President Ronald Reagan, of Irish ethnic stock, with dark-brown-hair- reporters-have-repeatedly-failed -to-prove-is-dyed-by-stealing-samples-of-it-from-the-floor-of-the- barber-shop-where-he-gets-his-hair-cut (now *that* is an interesting and informative piece of news, which happens to be true) — and his wife, Nancy, a blue-eyed Cancerian. Marshall and Thomas took along their children, Capricorn Toby, a law student, Helen, in nurse's train- ing — and their adorable Gemini twins, 5′ 3″ and 5′ 3″, one with brown eyes and one with green eyes.

When two public figures fall in love, especially actors and ac- tresses who have ignored the numbers lottery, these magazines have a real field day. Susan Astor, 32, plans a New Year's Day wedding to Oscar winner Charles Murphy, seven years her senior, and . . . **WAIT ! HOLD THE PRESSES !** The magazine editors forgot that, according to the months they were born, on New Year's Day Murphy will, for three months into the new year, actually be **EIGHT** years her senior, not seven. Wow ! Good thing we caught *that* goof in time ! Our readers would never have forgiven us. Or . . . Academy Award nominee Jerry Cranshaw, 21, has announced in a press conference that he's been living in Paris with his leading lady in *Here Come the Clowns,* Pamela Richards, who, at 23 is two years older than Cranshaw. Laurie Adams, 19, has confessed that she and Andrew Nottingham, 44, were secretly married in London last year . . .

The writers of these magazines are compelled and driven to re- mark upon the numbers imbalance between lovers and mates, whether the disparity in numbers between them amounts to thirty years, twenty years, ten years, five years — or only one or two years, which is about as silly as you can get. Even thirty years' difference is meaningless when you realize the illusion of the calendar abacus. But one or two years ? Good grief. Charlie Brown, do you realize that Lucy (I believe) came along a year or so before your appearance in the comics. Holy Moses ! That means she's a year or two older than you. And how old are *you*, Charlie ? Certainly old enough to stop talking to your Aquarian dog, Snoopy, as if he were a real person. For shame, Charlie. Act your age. Does someone, perchance, know where an illustrated book might be obtained, detailing, with posed models, exactly how one should "act" in order to "act" one's age at 17, 33, 20, 23, 56, 42, 87, 35, 64, 19 . . . etc. . . etc. ?

Language is a reliable reflection of brain programming. Think about this. Don't just flip it through your mind, but *think* about it. When a child displays or demonstrates a thought process or behavior usually attributed to maturity, everyone pats him on the head approvingly. It's considered very good form for a child to behave like an adult. Good little boy. Good little girl. Mama and Papa are proud of you.

But when an adult behaves like a child, everyone frowns, and says "Act your age." Meditate on the verb used. "Act." Think about it a little longer. The common usage of the verb "act" in this manner is most revealing. "*Act* your age," says quite clearly that the person society observes behaving in a carefree, childlike manner should become an actor or actress, and ACT (a make-believe profession, right?) . . . and act out whatever particular image the Director (Society) has of any double number. But *you* are the Producer of this drama of your life, and you can fire the lower case director whenever you choose, without severance pay. *You're* Cecil B. DeMille. Sack the cowardly custard !

Can't a person simply *be* his (or her) age — just *be* whatever it really means ? Yes. Must a person actually *act* in order to project what society dictates as the image ? No. You know what ? It proves that the subconscious minds of those who say "act your age" are basically and wisely "with it." The subconscious mind *knows* that what is being requested in such a command needs to be pretended or acted out to be successful. What if one has no acting talent ? Then how would such a one "act" his or her age ? They don't give out Academy Awards for it, do they ? Even if they did, is an "Oscar" really worth it ? And so, if there ever is such a book, with illustrations explaining how to "act one's age," it would have to be published in Hollywood.

Now, look, let's get serious. What does all this pathological chronological behavior mean ? It means that these magazine people believe that everyone holds a sharp, clear and precise image of each double number in the numerical system. Dare I say it's a myth ? Yes, I shall dare, because, to give but one of hundreds of examples, one day last month I was having lunch with two unenlightened, follow-the-leader-type business people. One of them asked me the age of my attorney. "How old is he ?" I replied that I thought he was thirty-four, in violation of my usual refusal to discuss illusionary numbers, since the question took me by surprise.

"*Thirty-four* ?? !!" one of them exclaimed, apparently nearly in a state of shock. "I could have *sworn* he was at *least* thirty-seven, if not thirty-eight." This was just too much for me. I asked the waiter for a sheet of paper and a pen, which I then offered to my two luncheon companions, asking them, "Would you mind drawing three faces for me, please — one of them age thirty-four — one age thirty-seven — and one age thirty-eight ? I'm genuinely curious and interested in learning your system." For a few moments they doodled with the pen on the paper, by turns, then stared at me, as one of them asked, "What system ?"

"Your system of differentiating between thirty-four, thirty-seven and thirty-eight," I replied. "I mean, seriously, is there an extra wrinkle or wart or something, somewhere, that people can spot if they look hard ? It would be a big help to, say, for instance, private investigators, when they don't have fingerprints or anything like that, but they do have the birth data, to help them decide if the guy in the red Volvo is the criminal they're looking for, or just an innocent citizen."

They weren't sure if I was being serious or funny, but I was being very serious. I really would like to know. People don't have rings to count, like trees, do they ? If so, I must have been asleep in high-school biology class. I've asked literally more than a hundred people this sort of question, and not a single one of them has been able to answer — or to draw their number images.

Obviously, anyone can come close to winning the chronological Wheel of Fortune when they're choosing between a twelve-year-old and an eighty-year-old — or even between a twenty-year-old and a seventy-year-old (assuming they aren't dealing with an enlightened mortal, on the way to becoming immortal, who has mastered the first courses in cell regeneration). But . . . today's "sheep" believe they can tell the difference between twenty-three and twenty-six — forty and forty-three — sixty and sixty-seven. They actually believe that. It boggles the mind. What is amusing is that each one of the guessers has a totally individual and differing image of each of those numbers — yet are helpless to either draw or describe them. I guess that's because their images were programmed into their computer brains without a Code Key.

This chapter is about destroying the deathist illusion with the enlightenment of physical immortality, through cell regeneration.

What exactly is cell regeneration ? Just that. The regeneration of the cells of the rechargable battery of your physical body, which has been called "the temple of the soul," but which is also the material, flesh temple of other equally invisible and vital parts of the you-of-you. It will be easier to picture in your mind if you realize that the process is related to the spiral mystery.

The spiral is the basic principle of Nature's laws, and can be observed anywhere you look. The spiral of the conch shell. Spiral tendrils of ivy and other plants wind around porch railings and fences. Flowers form themselves in a spiral, leaves are coiled in spiral form before they miraculously unfold. Plants, grass and flowers shoot in spiral growth to literally screw their way through the hard surface of the ground, when spring calls to them. There is spiral movement in the Yin-Yang forces of the Hexagrams of the I-Ching.

Linus Pauling, Nobel Prize-winning discoverer of the magic of Vitamin C, also discovered what scientists have labeled polarized molecules. Pauling observed that the strings forming the structure of the molecule have a spiral motif, with the joining units linked to form a helix in the shape of a loosely coiled spring, much like a spiral staircase with each step made from a different grained wood. These molecular units of matter are unsymmetrical, like a pair of gloves or sandals possessing two forms which are mirror images of each other. All spirals of living matter twine around in the same direction — *although everything would work equally well the other way around.* This is important to cell regeneration, as we shall soon see.

"We are all built of right-handed corkscrews," stated another Nobel Prize-winner, Sir Laurence Bragg.

The spiral mysteriously seems to possess some subtle quality of its own. Wind a piece of copper wire into a spiral and it magically acquires properties it did not previously possess. The spiral used mechanically makes it possible to penetrate wood and iron. In the science of electronics, John Nelson, of RCA Laboratories, told me when I worked for NBC that the spiral is used to convert radio waves into electrical impulses.

Your doctor can tell you that the spiral is discerned in many organs of the human body, and many of the body's functions operate through spiral movement. It is of more than passing significance that all of Earth's "creatures," beginning with the tiny amoeba, all the way to men and women, when they move without any means of stimulation, will be invisibly urged to take a spiral path. The horns of a Ram, all horns — are spiral. The umbilical cord is a spiral. Thumb prints are spiral. So is your humerus, the pelvis and likewise your sweat glands. The spiral appears in cell division — and even in astrology's mathematics a logarithmic spiral occurs. Of course, astronomers and mathematicians use logarithms too. But they may not be as sensitive to the meaning as esoteric astrologers with a mystical leaning and a respect for the illumination of intuition.

Lakhovsky, in his book *The Secrets of Life* drew an analogy between the spiral formation found in all living cells — and the coil in an electric current. Nikola Tesla, of course, with his alternating current discovery, knew this, even as a child. Lakhovsky further suggested that, just as in an electrical oscillating circuit, radiations are emitted through the functioning of a spiral of wire, increasing its capacity — *"in the living cell, radiations are emitted in a like manner."*

Now, let's travel back, in a spiral trip, to an important statement a few paragraphs ago. All spirals of living matter twine around in the same direction — *although everything would work equally well the other way around.*

I clearly remember John Nelson, in the NBC cafeteria, telling me that "because the spiral is used to convert radio waves into electrical impulses, it is evident that the capacity exists to move from one level to another — or from one vibration to another."

Here is a rather clumsy drawing to help you comprehend the spiral mystery, and how it relates to cell regeneration.

Do you see the tiny star ? It marks the beginning of your flesh life, therefore the beginning of the life of each cell in your body, as it spirals in a right-handed direction toward the programmed brain's expectation of aging and death, brought on in a material sense by physical gravity, assisted by Mental Gravity.

Now, do you see the black dot ? It represents where your cells are on their spiral trip at this moment, while you're reading these words. Never mind if you are nineteen or ninety or more. (The higher your illusionary chronological number, the more spirals, of course.)

Look at the black dot; picture that you are looking at the black dot of every cell in your body. Then intensely, vividly, use your Mental Gravity to image the spiral turning in the *opposite* direction. Draw it — all the way back, not to the initial tiny star (after all, you don't want to return to your crib or the hospital delivery room) — but to whatever point along the way represents whatever present image you may have of whatever illusionary chronological year, and *will it* to stop right there — until and unless you give each cell a new command. Don't just think about it. *Do it.*

You will have begun the process of cell regeneration.

Repeat these three statements aloud, until you have memorized them.

"All spirals of living matter twine around in the same direction — although everything would work equally well the other way around."
LINUS PAULING

"We are all built of right-handed corkscrews."
SIR LAURENCE BRAGG

"Because the spiral is used to convert radio waves into electrical impulses, it is evident that the capacity exists to move from one level to another — or from one vibration to another." JOHN NELSON

Keep imaging, keep repeating these sentences aloud, and finally your sleepy, drugged, falsely programmed brain will register it, and re-program itself. It truly will.

Despite all those blind spots we've discussed in earlier chapters, medical science still manages to make some marvelous discoveries from time to time. One of them is the discovery that every cell in the human body replaces itself over a period of seven years. Except for the human brain cells, a most important exception for you to remember. (Alcohol burns out brain cells, and even though you have over 42 billion of them, becoming magic requires as many as you can keep healthy.)

Meanwhile, think about this seven-year cycle. There's not a cell in your body (other than in the brain) — not a hair on your head or on your body, not a fingernail or toenail you possess right now that was there seven years ago. You are, therefore, in a cellular sense, a brand-new person every seven years, commencing with your birth. If a body organ has a defect, the defect will remain (until you cure or heal it yourself), but the cells making up the organ will be new.

Moreover, many humans have been found in Russia and elsewhere who possess the roots for a third and even a fourth set of teeth. (You've already gone through two sets — your baby teeth and your "second" teeth.) Unfortunately, these extra roots don't get to grow into teeth because the death urge chokes the body's battery and kills it before they get a chance to manifest. More waste. Obviously, your body can produce the roots for as many sets of teeth as you need, in perpetuity, which will certainly save a lot of dental bills when you become immortal.

Why does your body do all this? It's your life urge again, desperately trying to keep you alive, giving you new opportunities every seven years to begin your immortality. The life urge is so strong, so insistent in man and woman, you'd think it would win an easy victory. It would, except for the ever increasing physical gravity and mental gravity combining to defeat its repeated attempts to make you immortal.

What is the difference between "old cells" which have run their right-handed screwdriver spiral to an end — and new cells — regarding the process of cell reversal we just discussed? Not much. As you gradually reverse the spiral of each cell in your body, stopping at whatever point (chronological "age" image) you've chosen between the black dot and the tiny star in the previous drawing, *no new cell will be needed to replace the cell thus freshly regenerated*. The only reason for the replacement is that your double gravity pull wears out the cells. Eventually, you won't need more of them, because you'll be keeping those you have in perfect condition.

Does this spiral your mind into a revelation ? It should, because it means that all cells spiral because of the illusion of Time. Your cells did not so spiral when your body was on Earth with two Suns, and was not spinning (causing gravity). Neither did plants and flowers spiral. They simply *were*. The reason they screw themselves through the ground now in a spiral is a demonstration of their own life urge, imitating your body's life urge. When you have recognized Time for the imposter it is the cells of your body will no longer spiral and need to be reversed — although their general shape will still be spiral, symbolic of the "serpent circle of eternity."

Until the cell regeneration cycle is completed, while it's still in progress, when you image a new cell image it stopping its right-handed spiral *at the same point* in the drawing you've imaged your old cells to stop, when they're spiraling in a reverse direction. You needn't keep count of all your old and new cells with a Chinese abacus to do this. Just give the dual order applying to both kinds of cells, and your body will take care of the details. Ordain your powerful Mind to program your computer brain with this command, then trust your body's wisdom to comply.

Now . . . isn't it fortunate that your brain cells don't need to be replaced every seven years, and don't die (unless you kill them) ? And now do you see why you have so many, and why you haven't yet begun to use ninety percent of them ? They're going to be needed when cell regeneration becomes the rule, until immortality is achieved. There is good cause for these extra "chips" in the computer brain, waiting to be activated for the big task of eternal life.

Here are the first eleven steps along the path toward physical immortality. When you've mastered them your cell regeneration will have commenced, and you'll be able to walk the rest of the way yourself, guided by your own Higher Elf.

1. Know the truth. Don't hope it's true. Don't have faith that it's true. Don't believe that it's true. **KNOW** it. Your ability to

achieve physical immortality is real. You already possess it. This is the most difficult of all the steps along the way to master, yet the most necessary. Without it, the others mean nothing, and will accomplish nothing.

KNOW IT NOW
Then you will have **WON**

2. Image the spirals of your cells turning in the opposite direction, and repeat aloud: *I am immortal, and I now ordain my body to demonstrate this,* each morning and each night of your eternal life. Boost and assist your cell regeneration by taking 1,000 mgms of PABA (para-amino-benzoic acid), 5,000 mgms of Vitamin C and 2,000 mgms of d'alpha tocopheral Vitamin E every day, and use moisturizers all over your body, not just on your face. Get lots of fresh air, especially while you sleep. Instead of cars, buses and cabs, *walk* as much as you possibly can. Drink at least two full 8-ounce glasses of unsweetened grape juice every day of your immortal life. (Red grape juice tastes better, and the plumpies need it also, but blue grape juice is an equally potent cell stimulator.) Eating grapes is fine, but you still need the grape juice. You'll see the difference in the skin on your face within one week, or sooner. Four glasses a day are not too many, but at least two. Step 2 contains all the cosmetology you need. Vitamins B-12 and B-Complex are not priorities, but will help.

3. Don't be ashamed of your new enlightenment. Talk about it to every person you meet. Friends, relatives and business associates. Ignore their ridicule. Out of every ten people who ridicule you, there will be one or two who will believe you. Then, when you're 500 or 600 years young, you'll have a few people you know to pal around and hang out with you.

4. If you're a woman, when you become pregnant for the first time, or the next time, try to have your infant delivered under water to avoid the birth trauma that results in a continuing pattern of im-

proper breathing. There are more people around who can do this than you may realize. Search for them. If you're a man, support your wife in this maternal wisdom.

5. Stop drinking. A little wine, *very* occasionally, nothing else. No drugs, quite naturally. And, alas ! Stop smoking as soon as you feel you can without serious emotional trauma. Substitute something for smoking. Like . . . sexual union with the person you really love . . . smelling flowers . . . Ferris wheel rides . . . listening to symphonies . . . making a few baby miracles for someone who needs some magic . . . swimming . . . singing . . . taking a shower . . . running with your dog or dogs . . .

6. No sexual promiscuity. It short-circuits your soul. No unnatural sexual union — and don't pretend you don't know why. Any behavior in opposition to Nature's laws is the enemy of the *natural* process of physical immortality. No pornography. It sets up images that block the discovery of your own Twin Self, through the law of magnetic attraction. And you cannot become a *full* immortal until you have achieved union with the missing half of your Spirit, of the you-of-you. Just the decision to become immortal in itself guarantees that you'll find each other, at some point along the path. Isn't that what you've been secretly searching for and aching for all of your life anyway ? Face that truth. However many sexual partners you may have had — or are having now — you're still empty, still lonely, and you always will be until that miracle manifests. If you've practiced negative sexual behavior in the past, forgive *yourself* completely, then forget it. The true "confessional" is within.

7. Likewise, forgive your enemies. "Do good to all those who harm you and say all manner of evil against you." Being kind to those who are kind to you doesn't cause your cells to spiral in a reverse direction. Being kind to those who hurt you through word or action does. Give away half your money to friends and strangers equally. Read the "Déjà Vu" chapter and the "Labors of Love and

the Money Mystique" chapter, until you've memorized what they say — then **do** what they say. The counsel given within them is not from me, but from those who are many cosmic light years beyond me in illumination. Stop clinging to material possessions. Let go. Be generous with, give freely of your time and money.

8. Firmly and permanently reject all fear about every aspect of your life: fear of flying, fear of accident, fear of poverty, fear of loneliness — *all fear*. Including fear for friends and loved ones who are ill. Stop expecting them to die.

9. Become a vegetarian in the way outlined in the "Apple a Day" chapter. Do not kill any living creature for any reason. Hunters and fishermen cannot achieve eternal life, are not candidates for physical immortality. I'm truly sorry about that, because some of the dearest and most enlightened people I know are fishermen or fisherwomen, with only this one blind spot keeping them back. To repeat, do not kill for any reason. Learn karate and other Oriental self-defense arts if you must, but *do not kill*. You must not remove any person's or creature's Free Will choice to live or to die.

Not killing is so basic, it shouldn't even need to be mentioned. If you have formerly killed "in the line of duty," with the mistaken notion of "patriotism," forgive yourself and cleanse yourself. There's never a real reason for killing anything or anybody. There is always a way to solve a "dangerous," existential situation where your murder or another person's murder is threatened, without killing the aggressor. There is always a way to prevent the death of one person without killing another. Wounding an arm, hand, foot or leg is not desirable, but is better than killing.

10. Fast one day a week, every week in the year, drinking only fruit juice, and when you can handle it, only fresh spring water — no

fruit juice. Work up to fasting in this manner one week out of every month. It purifies both your mind and your body. Jesus fasted, and look at all the miracles he manifested. So did Francis of Assisi, and he was able to converse with birds and wolves and other creatures in their own language.

11. The number 11 is a Master Number in numerology, as you've already learned in Chapter 5. Therefore, it's appropriate that the eleventh step in becoming an immortal (synonymous with becoming a Master) is numbered in this way, not by my own design, but by the harmonics and synchronicity of the Universe. It doesn't matter whether you are fourteen or forty when you read this step — or eighty or ninety illusionary chronological years. *Memorize it,* even if you're a teenager, *memorize it* — because it's of urgent importance to anyone seriously intending to achieve cell regeneration and either the prevention of aging or the reversal of it — and to conquer death.

By now, do you realize that the most basic step in achieving immortality is to know that, *in reality,* there is no time ? Do you understand that it's your false belief in the power of time that blocks your cell regeneration ? Do you know now that time is your enemy — that if you allow it even the smallest acceptance in your mind, you cannot become immortal and your cells will not regenerate ? Good. Now consider the word **RETIREMENT**. It lexigrams into **RE-TIME**. Webster thus defines the word **RE**: "to appear over again . . . to renew." And that's just what happens when you retire, either because your employer has silly rules about a forced retirement age, or because you believe yourself that it's necessary and desirable at a certain illusionary chronological age. In other words, when you accept **RETIREMENT**, Time "reappears over again anew" — *it returns to master you again.* Retirement is the most powerful of all the influences causing unnecessary aging, and even death.

Retirement is a huge mistake. Take a year or two to goof off when you want to relax or travel, but no more than a year or two at a time. *Permanent* retirement is an unsuspected, deadly killer. It will kill you as surely as a shot from a rifle — it just takes a little bit longer to die. It destroys completely your life urges.

Retirement is comprised of two pure ingredients: pure laziness and pure fear. It's a false dream of lazy days, with nothing to do but sleep and play — a false fear that you're "too old" to be of any value — that you only have "a few years left" and you have to desperately do nothing to enjoy them, to make the most of them.

Retirement doesn't make "the most" of anything. It makes "the worst" of everything.

What keeps the juices of your life urges flowing, what keeps your mind recharging your body, is your career, profession, job or work. *Being needed* by whomever for whatever. Giving out to the world what only you have to offer it. And the world *still needs you — more than ever now.*

If you haven't yet retired — don't. Take a couple of years leave of absence, get all that playtime and travel time out of you, then return to your work, which you're becoming more superbly capable of executing every year of your immortal life. If you're in a profession where you are your own boss, working for yourself, the decision is yours. Be grateful for that. If you work for an employer who insists that you retire, do it if you must. Then get another job. You say that's nearly impossible "at your age" ? It won't be as easy as when you were a chronologically illusionary twenty-one, but if you try, you'll be surprised.

If you genuinely, sincerely and seriously try, and can't find orthodox employment, then *create* a new career or profession for yourself. There are so many *thousands* of ideas and concepts along this line, I have no intention of listing any of them here. Use your own imagination. That's what it's for.

Be a consultant to someone. Your wisdom is needed. In a few

years you'll be able to plunge into the job market again, because immortality will have begun to be dimly realized by many more people than before this book was published. You'll see. Besides, if you forget that fear-based "Big Brother" Social Security number, and *righteously* "lie" (tell the real truth) about your age, the way you're going to *look* soon, no one will know the difference.

You don't need a birth certificate to get a *good* job, and certainly not to begin a new career. Avoid retirement playgrounds like poison, because that's exactly what they are.

I've tried for years to convince a retired person very close to me, whom I love dearly, that his retirement to one of these places was a subconscious death wish that would bring about just that — his death.

He wouldn't listen. I offered him a number of responsibilities I knew he could handle better than anyone else I'd ever met, better than people half his illusionary chronological age. He kept responding with, "I'm too old. I can't handle it. Why, *do you realize how old I am ?*"

Men and women of a certain "age" love asking that question. They revel in it. They brag about it, as if it were a badge of honor. It's not. It's a badge of disgrace, of surrender to the programmed deathist lies. Yet it contains a trace of wistfulness, implying "isn't it wonderful that I've made it to this number, and I'm still here ?" It would be more wonderful if you made it to that number and thousands of years beyond it.

The person I referred to just now will read this book, and I pray that he gets the message. It's a last resort. Both he and a woman I also love dearly look and behave and think about thirty years "younger" than the age they keep bragging about. I **HAVE ORDAINED** that they wake up, look in the mirror — and *get moving*. Likewise with another woman I dearly love, who only needs part of this message, because she's always secretly believed what this chapter is saying, but was afraid everyone would think she was crackers if she dared to express it. She's a Pisces. My message to her is: Come on, express it. It's time. No one will laugh at you. The mission of this book is to prepare people for the miracle you've known about inside yourself all along — and it will accomplish its mission. Nothing can prevent its seeds from sprouting because it's been ordained by our Creators. You don't need to be afraid anymore. Go for it ! I have a job for you to do, beginning in a few months, so get ready to start to work. Also, you'll be moving to another state within the year— like those other two people. That's a white witch prediction for the future, and three promises for tomorrow.

These are the 11 steps for achieving gradual physical immortality through cell regeneration. Step 4 is not an absolute necessity, but it will help the "flesh of your flesh, bone of your bone" to begin becoming an immortal at birth.

If you can change, for instance, your programmed belief in poverty, you can also change your belief in aging and death. If you can control the physical effect of gravity in only one small area of your life, you can do it in all other areas. I know a man who has requested that I not make his name public. His bones, in particular, those in his back, had calcified, and he was told by doctors that he would never walk again. He firmly committed himself to immortality, and began to practice all the steps of cell regeneration. It took five and a half years, but his bones gradually began to soften, to de-calcify. It may be ten years or so longer until they have returned to the perfect condition they were in his youth, but what is ten years to an immortal ? He is now walking without pain.

If you have a physical handicap, overcoming it to any degree at all will give you the evidence you need to conquer aging and death. Developing an athletic ability often helps greatly. Learning to help and heal others will help enormously. Each negative attitude and habit you overcome, however small, will strengthen your belief in your personal spiritual, mental and physical powers, and allow you to establish effective communication with your own Spirit, who possesses all power for all purposes.

Bob Wieland, a Viet Nam vet, lost both of his legs when he stepped on a land mine. As he says, "My legs went one way — and my life went another." In 1982, Wheeler decided to "walk" from California to Washington, D.C., wheeling himself along highways and roads with a "scooter," the stumps of his legs protected by thick bandages. It took him three years, eight months and six days to complete the 2,764-mile "walk." But he made it to his destination, the Viet Nam War Memorial in Washington, bearing the name of his buddy, a soldier who was killed beside him when a mortar went off. Bob Wieland is clearly a candidate for physical immortality, even though he doesn't realize it yet. He's also a candidate for the miracle of growing both legs back, good as new.

Notice that Wieland's courageous "walk" across the country, in taking 3 years, 8 months and 6 days, adds to 17 — and the 2,764 miles he covered add to 19, making the Compound Numbers of his trip 17 and 19. Look up their meanings in the numerology chapter.

There are a multitude of ways you can tell that cell regeneration has started in your body. The skin becomes clear, the breath becomes sweet, the odors of elimination begin of diminish. Your tongue will gradually become pink and soft, sans rough bumps. Your eyes will sparkle and your voice will take on a subtle but detectable musical tone. Your emotions will grow ever more easy to control. You will begin to recall your "dreams" (astral travels) clearly. You'll require less sleep. If you have lines in your face, they will slowly but surely become invisible.

According to Gurus, and I have no reason to doubt it, there's a strange chemical reaction in the body when the cells begin to reverse their spirals, perhaps five to seven calendar years after the process has begun, occurring at uncertain intervals. It varies. An odor. It's been compared to the unpleasant but not unbearable odor of an athlete's tennis shoes, after extreme exercise. Pungent, somewhat sour, and quite strong. Distinctive. It's also been compared to the musty odor detected when an air conditioner in, say, a large 747 type plane, is turned on, after having been shut off for several hours. Perhaps it's related to oxygen, since cells do contain oxygen, which may be changed in some way, as the spiral reverses. It's unmistakable, and it's said that there's a reliable way to identify it. If you sniff your skin or any part of your body to locate the source, it becomes apparent that the strange odor is not coming from there. No one else can even detect it. Others will swear there is no odor, should you ask them, as they gingerly smell your hair and skin. They'll think you're joking, but you'll be serious. Finally it will dawn on you that the odor you smell so strongly is coming from *within* your body, not from without, and that you're aware of it through the olfactory or cranial nerves, transmitting the odor to the forebrain and mucous membranes in the upper part of the nose. This is why no one else can detect the slightest hint of it from being close to you. Only you can smell it. Perhaps some biologist, chemist or physicist whose mind is open to cell regeneration could define its origin. You shouldn't be overly concerned with it, because it's a sure sign that your cells are reversing their spirals. And "even this shall pass away."

★ ★ ★ ★ ★ ★

I have a memory. A deep, deep memory, and recurrent. From my childhood. I trust that people of the Hebrew and other religions can relate to it, even though it's founded in the Christian celebration of Easter. When I was small I used to look at "elderly people," now called "senior citizens," and think about growing up to look and behave and feel like them myself someday. Did you ? That day seemed far away in a misty future time, but it still troubled me. Did it trouble you too ?

Then, when I became a little older, I made a private decision, a secret pact with myself. That could never, never happen to me. And that was that. Period. Did you make a secret pact like that with yourself too ?

And . . . Easter Sunday. I was so . . . ambivalent about it. On the one hand, it filled me with bursting balloons of happy. On the other hand (I sound like an afflicted Libra) — it puzzled my twelve-year-old mind. On the happiness side, there was the delicate scent of the lilies around the altar . . . and the heavy, rich scent of all the other Easter flowers everyone wore pinned to their dresses or suits. The spanking-clean and brand-new white gloves, white anklets and shiny new, black patent Mary Jane shoes, the rustling silk of a pink (one year, daffodil yellow) dress, the creamy straw bonnet, trailing rosy velvet ribbons. And the Easter bunny basket, stuffed with jelly beans and chocolate goodies, colored eggs, and maybe a surprise, like a charm bracelet to wear with my new clothes to church. The angel music of the choir . . . and the pounding, echoing chords of the organ . . . blended with the dizzying, heavenly scent of spring outside, the warm breezes and budding green leaves on the trees . . . the tulips lining the walk to the church door.

It all made me certain that I could actually fly, if I'd only make the effort, and my heart swelled with a thrilling joy impossible to fully describe, when the choir and everyone else, including me, sang those magical lyrics, punctuated by Alleluias . . . Christ, the Lord, is risen today . . . sons of men and angels say . . . born like him, like him we rise ! Join the triumph of the skies ! . . . Where, O death is now thy sting ? . . . Alleluia ! Alleluia ! Alleluia ! . . . with the rolling waves of the organ music blending with the flickering candles, the holy scents and flower fragrances all around . . . I felt an overwhelming, over-powering joy tingling from head to toe !

But . . . on the puzzlement side, I kept wondering . . . if Jesus was the Son of God, then why wasn't there a Daughter of God ? And I wondered why everyone was so happy about Easter, if it only meant that just one man could experience such sky-rocket magic, and none of the rest of us would ever have a chance to know such a miracle. Especially me.

But my puzzlement faded away as soon as I returned home from church and buried my nose in the hyacinths my mother filled the house with every Easter. There is no way to express this. You'll just have to press your own nose deeply into a hyacinth's blossoms . . . and inhale. Or have you already noticed yourself that something about this particular spring flower's fragrance makes your heart soar up to join your Spirit ? It makes you *know* that Easter is truth for *everyone*, as your entire being is flooded with the mystery of this knowing. Not even logical, metaphysical, intellectual and personally tangible evidence of cell regeneration brings such certainty.

The "sense of smell" is surely the strongest of the other five. It leads you so swiftly into at least momentarily possessing the sixth sense. Rain on the grass . . . lilacs drenched with dew . . . the scent of spring in the air . . . the cold, clean smell of falling snow . . . damp earth . . . can float your astral into a higher dimension for fleeting moments. So, when your new commitment to physical immortality wavers briefly, go out and smell a hyacinth . . . or walk in the rain. Re-spiral yourself !

There are three kinds of immortals. Those who became so hundreds or thousands of years ago, and communicate it to a chosen few apostles in a subtle manner. Those who became so equally long ago, but who choose to pretend they are still pilgrims, so that they may empathize with others newly initiated to truth. And those who have just learned the secret, and are delighted with the evidence they can share with others. It's not always easy to make the distinction.

Nadine Star, an "elderly" resident of Louisville, Kentucky, wrote these words: "If I had my life to live over, I would like to make more mistakes." (She means behavior society labels as mistakes.) "Next time, I'd relax. I'd start barefoot earlier in the spring, and stay that way later in the fall. I would ride more merry-go-rounds. I would pick more daisies."

Nadine is clearly a candidate for cell regeneration, and doesn't quite realize it yet. Perhaps she will soon. Then she won't need to "live her life over." She can just go right on living it, improving it in all those ways she wrote about, and amazing everyone by growing magically younger . . . and younger . . . and younger . . . until people say, "Who is that lovely young girl out there running through the daisy fields ? It looks like Nadine Star, but it can't be. Maybe it's her granddaughter. She sure takes after Nadine, doesn't she ?"

Those who teach immortality do not deny or reject reincarnation as a choice each person has a divine right to make. One of them said to me, "I can't understand why anyone would not prefer staying alive and helping to change the world to the traditional and popular practice of using up bodies and disposing of them as trash. They are going to survive flesh death anyway, and continue to reincarnate until they become illuminated and initiated, so why not just stay around in the same body, maintaining the same appearance — or improving it ?" I had to agree with his logic.

Physical death will always be available, but it is and always has been a matter of personal choice. Your body is an energy system, capable of infinite improvement and perfection. It may be difficult to conceive of your own self as the source of all healing, but to believe anything else is to accuse the Creators of your Spirit of doing a poor job. Just as your Spirit created your first incarnated physical body in His or Her own image, so did your Creators manifest your Spirit's in Their own image. This chapter is not an attempt to deprive you of the right to die, only an attempt to cause you to wonder about the sense of it — by using your sixth sense.

Look at it this way. Your flesh body does not have the power to destroy itself. It is only Mental Gravity, used in its reverse direction, that has the power — and you control your Mental Gravity with your

Mind. Your Mind survives the death of your body, whether you want to believe it or not. Not believing in Universal Law hasn't yet stopped it from working. When you think about it you have to be innately immortal in order to kill yourself.

When you decide to allow your body to outlive your programmed death urge you'll see many a miracle. The deathist theology can last only as long as you cling to it. The moment you let go of it — all the way — you'll be startled to see yourself manifesting love, wisdom, giving, forgiveness, confidence, joy, peace and physical health. You'll be able to actually feel these qualities expanding within you, with little or no effort.

Julian Davis, the former Cripple Creek gold-miner to whom I dedicated my verse about the town in the beginning of this book, was in his seventies when we met. All of his life until then he was a hunter, and drank everyone in the local bars under the table, night after night. He was a brilliant student of miracles; all he needed was to be told, and after we'd talked for a time, he vowed he would never again hunt deer or take a drink of whisky. He never did. Unexpectedly, then, he discovered he was a poet, and wrote a delightful book of poems, which was published and sold all through Colorado. He was designed to be an immortal, and would have made it if he had learned about it just a few years earlier. When he returns in his next flesh body he'll breeze right through it, becoming an immortal before he even reaches his teens. Cell regeneration and reversing gravity isn't difficult, but it's always a mite easier to prevent it than to turn it around later. You chronologically "young" readers had best remember that. You chronologically "older" readers, don't be concerned. The process of regenerating your cells and reversing their spirals carries its own kind of excitement and magic. It doesn't matter when you conquer the myth of aging, before or after, as long as you conquer it.

I remember one morning when Julian stopped by my little, slipping-off-the-time-track, haunted house on Carr Avenue, to have some tea and a slice of blueberry pie. He'd just returned from the funeral of an old friend and was depressed, a rare state of mind for him. Shaking his head sadly, as he sipped his Red Zinger tea, his favorite brand, Julian said, "He was only eighty-nine, can you believe that, girl ? They sure are takin' 'em young these days." Right, Julian. They sure are.

Another Cripple Creeker, my neighbor, schoolteacher Ruth Cook, is a Pisces. (So, by the way, was Julian.) I taught Ruth how to "image" a parking spot in the Springs at the Mall on crowded days, by ordaining it of her Higher Self (you must always add the words, "under grace, with no inconvenience to anyone"). She quite probably could have managed it herself, without my instruction, since she was born with esoteric magic in her very pores, as most Pisces Fish are.

One winter night, sitting by the Ben Franklin and talking over a cup of coffee, I was slightly wavering in my own magic, and asked Ruth if she believed in the certainty of someone's eventual return to Colorado, a return representing a personal miracle to me. I will always remember her answer. "Well, I should certainly hope so," she said. "With the power of all that faith you've been demonstrating for so many years, if it didn't happen, I'd never be able to get my 'park' at the Mall on a weekend."

What Ruth was expressing was an eternal truth, humorously, but very wisely. Should you believe in physical immortality ? All such wonders are irrevocably linked, and cannot be separated. If physical immortality isn't real, Ruth could never get her "park" at the Mall, for goodness' sake ! (And it never fails to manifest for her, smack on the spot, every time.)

One bitter cold winter morning in the mountains, when everyone was weary of snow and ice, snow and ice, snow and ice, including me — I entered the Cripple Creek Market, stomping the snow from my boots, blowing on my frozen fingers . . . and saw a familiar leprechaun. Pokey, they called him. He worked in the small grocery store, commuting each day from the magical "twilight zone" of neighboring Victor. Walking up to him as he was sweeping the floor, I said in an exasperated tone, "Pokey, it seems like it's been winter forever. It's already the end of April. Will spring ever come ?"

Pokey went right on sweeping, glanced up at me, flashed his elf grin, and spoke just two words. "Always does."

They reached deep inside me, those two simple words. Yes, I thought. Spring always comes. With all the broken promises in the world, it's good to know that spring is an eternally unbroken promise. Like the Moon's nightly promise of sunrise . . . rainbows after a storm . . . and the Easter hyacinths of physical immortality.

★ ★ ★ ★ ★ ★

Children and grown-ups. Polarities. Adults have lost their awareness of their divinity, and are afraid to admit the truth, which is that children are more divine and wiser than they are. All children could become immortals in a twinkling, if it weren't for the adults around them with their deathist mentality, who can't unravel the parental disapproval syndrome, causing the children's Third Eyes to solidify into stone. Now the children of the world are being physically and sexually abused, their innocence murdered.

Facing the opposite polarity, the tragedy of nursing homes is that the "senior citizens" are forced to die right in the middle of their youthing process of cell regeneration, from the gloom and doom surrounding them. Meditate on the term "second childhood" Really *think* about what it means. A second chance to be a child. A second chance to begin cell regeneration and eternal life. What society calls "second childhood" is a natural form of primal therapy. It's the Mind and body's final attempt to allow the life urge to conquer the programmed death urge — a trembling and miraculous process of rediscovering the child within. If "senior citizens" in their "second childhood" could be left alone, away from deathist environments and people, encouraged instead of ridiculed and rejected, they would swiftly begin to master their bodies, experience cell regeneration and return to their youth. That's the next step. But they're stopped before they can take the next step. The Spirit is calling them with this one last chance to recognize the truth of eternal life. Society drowns out the voice, and the elderly surrender.

Some continue to fight the death urges around them by moving into retirement "playgrounds" instead of nursing homes. For a while they hop about merrily, dancing, biking, jogging, swimming, taking great strides toward regeneration and mastery of the body — reversal of gravity. Then, gradually, as they watch ambulances and morticians' wagons cart away the dead and dying all around them, they give up. They would rather die than continue to suppress the child within them, demanding to be heard. Suppressing natural immortality is so very un-natural, so painful — and takes so much effort.

It's time to start loving and respecting the "senior citizens," to make it socially acceptable for them to heal themselves — and to demonstrate their miraculous return to a second childhood, allowing it to progress, as intended, to cell regeneration in the body. There are three kind of humans presently on this Earth. Children, the wise ones. Adults, the confused and blind ones. And the elderly, cruelly stifled in their expression of gravity reversal and cell regeneration called "second childhood" — blocked right in the middle of the Spirit's rebuilding program to give them mastery of the body and a return to youth by the death urges all around them. By their own death urges, too, just as they were about to be replaced by a new and powerful life urge. What a tragic waste.

When society permits its "elderly senior citizens" to act like children their cell regeneration process will begin, gravity will be reversed, and they will gradually begin "youthing" themselves back to the appearance and physical health they originally enjoyed. Then the magic of "the fountain of youth" will become ordinary. Ponce de Leon was looking in the wrong place. The fountain of youth was gushing within him all during his search. He was looking in Florida, wasn't he ? Odd, isn't it, that so many "senior citizens," secretly feeling these strange new Life Urges are magnetized to Florida, perhaps subconsciously following Ponce. Unless they recognize the truth of their own immortality, their own ability to achieve mastery over the body, they'll be as disappointed in their quest as he was. The fountain of youth is not in Florida or Palm Springs. The fountain of youth is within. Remember this. The easiest times to conquer death, to become an immortal are in childhood — and in "old age."

Our Creators' love for the world will allow the Earth to survive, even though present world leaders seem determined to annihilate it. The world doesn't need to be saved. The question is whether or not humans are finally willing to open their Third Eyes, use their sixth sense — and save *themselves*. After all, this is the Aquarian Age and, in astrology, the sign of Aquarius rules and represents "second childhood." That's encouraging and, hopefully, prophetic.

I have two friends, a married couple living in Santa Barbara, California, who realize that they are immortals, and who have been experimenting with the often amusing false images of chronological age. Most people believe this husband and wife are around twenty-one to twenty-three years old, and invite them to frequent college affairs. Then they meet the couple's twenty-five-year-old son, their thirty-year-old daughter, and her new baby, and they go into a state of shock. These two people won't discuss their chronological age with anyone (not even me) because they don't want to submit themselves to the myth that aging is necessary, knowing full well that unenlightened mortals have individual images of all the double numbers, and are capable of powerfully projecting those images when they hear or see a "number," which can have a temporary but most damaging effect on the person they "see" as whatever chronological age. It can cause the cells to spiral back in a different direction for a brief time, and actually cause physical "aging" to manifest once more. It's not worth it. Consequently my friends let everyone guess away, as much as they like.

The wife — we'll call her Melanie — is always amused when she takes her baby elf daughter (granddaughter, but that term has such false images graven into it) — when she takes her elf child for a walk. People never fail to stop to admire the infant, and ask my friend, "Is this your first baby?" However, when she goes to a movie in town with her daughter, and the latter happens to call her "Mom" while they're buying tickets, my friend is inevitably asked, "Do you want a senior citizen ticket?"

One weekend when Melanie and her husband were in Los Angeles they went to a theatre in Westwood and were asked, when they bought their tickets, if they had their UCLA "student passes."

The power of a self-hypnotized human mind is an awesome thing when it's investigated in this way. People really do actually see what they believe they see.

Another friend, who lives in Boulder, Colorado — another immortal — has been experimenting with the aging myth. When he was thirty-two he decided to reverse the spirals of his cells, regenerate them, and become twenty-four again — physically. His identification was so intense and powerful, he told me, that he even got "keyed in," as he expressed it, to some of the emotional and financial hang-ups he had when he was that "age." It took some practice and some effort to toss them away. But he succeeded. He wrote to me last month to share with me an amusing but troubling experience.

He went to a finance company for a loan to buy a house. Without thinking, he filled out the credit application with his *real* age of twenty-four. The credit manager looked at him suspiciously, and challenged his age. "You don't look twenty-four," he told my friend. "You probably aren't even twenty-one yet, are you?" Having no proof of his age with him, my friend didn't know how to respond. Then the credit manager noticed that the loan applicant had a college degree and seven years' work experience. (It's hard to remember all the details when you're youthing yourself.) At this point, the man behind the desk became genuinely angry, told my friend that he was lying, and flatly refused the loan. In his letter, my Colorado immortal friend said, "I guess he thought I was a bad risk, being such a "liar." I thought the whole situation was rather humorous, but it sure reminded me once again of three things: how incredibly people's minds can be programmed regarding the myth of age — how swiftly cell regeneration works, making it necessary to stop before it goes too far (!) — and the problems being an immortal creates in a practical and financial situation."

Physical immortality is a truth whose time has come in the Aquarian Age. Those who seek it need not concern themselves with the overpopulation problem it only seems to create, because, as I mentioned earlier, by the time they have achieved the beginning mastery of their bodies, they'll understand what must be done next. It will be revealed to them "when the student is ready." And they will smile when they discover the very simplicity of the answer.

If you accept that this is the Golden Age when death will be conquered — if you'd like to make a dent in the power of death in the history of the world, there are several things you can do.

You can spread the truth courageously. The more swiftly erroneous mass thinking about death is changed, the sooner eternal life will become commonplace. Every person who questions the inevitability of death — whether seriously or even humorously (a sense of humor is part of the sixth sense) — weakens its power. Spreading the truth of physical immortality through thought transformation and the resulting cell regeneration will save your own life and the lives of those you love, while you'll also be helping to save the environment and to prevent the "natural" disasters predicted for the Earth. It's the most effective method you can use to stop war and violence. The mass subconscious, falsely programmed death urge is the primordial cause of earthquakes, flood, drought, nuclear mistrust — and even the shattering of personal relationships, the destruction of human love.

If there are, for instance, enough immortal-minded men and women practicing truth, simplicity and love — in time — California will stay above the water. Each person who clings to the death urge, who is dedicated to the necessity of death, is voting for disaster. The purpose of prophecies of doom is to warn us, so that we may then have a chance to use our wisdom to prevent disaster.

You can do other things also. You can begin your own physical immortality simply by changing each negative and fearful belief into a positive one — *one thought at a time.* Use the always successful ordaining or affirmation technique (communication with your Overself Spirit). Instead of fearing and believing you might die of a disease or be killed in an accident at any moment, simply affirm and ordain aloud: "I am completely in control of the fate of my physical body. Nothing can harm me without my consent, and I do not choose to give my consent. I choose to live."

When you begin to genuinely question death the death urge programmed into you starts to crumble. Realize how difficult it actually is to destroy your body. When you pay attention to your suppressed life urge it warns you again and again of imminent danger before a fatal accident. There's a tremendous margin of safety in the Universe, and you can tap into it through your sixth sense, which connects you to your Spirit —your Higher Self.

Even so-called "fatal" illnesses take a long time to kill, giving you plenty of warning to *change and transform your thoughts* — to lose your death urge. Over ninety percent of all suicide attempts are unsuccessful. Your suppressed life urge is trying to make you immortal right now, if you would only listen to it. Pay attention to the messages flashed into your Mind by your Overself — and the messages from your own body, as every cell composing it struggles to live. Honor and act on these messages. All pain is firmly anchored in fear and negative thoughts, and if you throw them firmly out of your consciousness, you can live forever. Try it. If you prefer your old death urges, you can always change your mind.

"There are many roads to Rome." That oft-repeated saying has multiple meanings. Using oversimplification, it's the same as saying that everyone begins the journey in New York, and everyone will reach the final destination of Los Angeles, regardless of the mode of travel or the speed of travel chosen. Or the other way around, from Los Angeles to New York, if you prefer. It's only allegorical. The point is that different people achieve the same goal by using a myriad of road maps and esoteric pathways through the woods.

Everyone even slightly interested in pursuing the goal of immortality — and, in particular, those of you who are sufficiently evolved to be aware of the higher occult mysteries — will want to read *The Lion Path*: "A Manual of the Short Path to Regeneration in Our Times," written by the brilliant metaphysician, Musaios, containing ancient astrological and astronomical disciplines and regimens for achieving immortality swiftly. A short path it may be, but a complicated one despite the fact that its author presents the formulas with unwonted crystal clarity, relative to such profound mysteries.

I warn you that *The Lion Path* is fathoms deep, although it will be easily comprehended by the already illuminated, especially those who are educated in the studies of astronomy, astrology and mythology. To them, it will be a sheer delight, as they discover its never-before revealed Egyptian secrets of regeneration and immortality. This is book urgently needed in our Time. It's an incomparably valuable guide for Initiates desirous of mastering the ancient disciplines for the purpose of quickly joining the ranks of the Masters now upon the Earth in their mission to save the planet from a premature and unnecessary Götterdämmerung. Metaphysical beginners, however, may have some difficulty in comprehending this fine work, prepared by one of the world's true Masters and Meta-Magicians.

If you're among these, you needn't trouble yourself with such strict disciplines as the book details. They're not necessary to become immortal. You would be wise to add *The Lion Path* to your library now for that day when "the student is ready," but you needn't immediately involve yourself with its prismatic pathways until that time comes — and when it does, you'll know it.

Meanwhile, you may successfully follow the slower, easier and simpler path of the eleven steps outlined in this chapter. They will give you the needed and necessary mastery over your body to begin cell regeneration, and will make you an immortal as surely as the more complex path. To repeat: There are many roads to Rome.

Not everyone is destined or designed to be a leader at History's Twilight Hour. The "ordinary" happiness and love you'll experience and project as you become an immortal in the ways described in this chapter are of equal value to the rescue of Earth during these troubled times, which will begin in 1988. The Higher Masters are aware of this — even Musaios himself. Still, *The Lion Path* should be in your library, since one never knows when one might "entertain angels unawares." The book is published by the Golden Sceptre Publishing Company, and you may learn how to order a copy in the "Pilgrim's Progress" section on Page 601.

How do you begin preparing yourself for taking the steps toward cell regeneration outlined here ?

Spend as much time with children as you can. They are the wise ones. Talk with them, not down to them. You'll learn much more than you guess, if you really listen to them. The truth of this is summarized in the following brief excerpt from the Prologue to *Gooberz*. (The text of *Gooberz* is in story form, unlike the Prologue, with plot progression, dialogue and such. The Prologue is intended only to seed the mind before the narrative begins.)

SSshhhh ! Listen to the children. They know.

all children's hearts contain the Serpent wisdom
of coiled and spiral secrets
never dreamed of nor suspected
by those who do believe the wells of childish minds are shallow
and thus careless, then may overlook some ancient mystery
lying   silent,
fallow

sleeping there unseen, invisible . . . beyond the ken of all those
unaware
that children meditate and dwell on things O ! never told
when their thoughts are brushed with fleeting gold
by passing angels, rustling silken wings, and murmuring low
above these softer forms of clay
too recently exiled from Heaven to pass judgement . . . and so
who harken with still open souls
as yet not sealed by the ponderous gravity of Earth experience

only later, after trials of torment and temptation
are the doors to Truth slammed shut, and firmly locked
by the flesh inheritance of fixed opinion, engraved while in the
womb
then do such shining Spirits become the self-imprisoned, final
minions
of the Body Temple's narrow, echoing tomb
crumbled from a promised alabaster . . .. into a common dust

******

I saved my favorite Lexigram for this final chapter. Of all the
mysteries contained in the lexigramming of English words, using the
Anglo-Saxon, druid-protected alphabet, this one is, to me, the most
profound. The only word that doesn't rhyme with any other. The
fruit my grade-school teacher used to demonstrate gravity. Orange

ORANGE contains: NO ANGER — NO RAGE — NO AGE

One of my personal and dearest Gurus told me that immortals have a secret greeting among themselves. When an Avatar recognizes another Adept they exchange two simple gifts, bearing a silent, coded message. They give one another, he said . . . a hyacinth . . . and an orange.

I'll share with you his parting words to me, before he "disappeared" the most recent time (although I know he'll manifest again soon, in his usual sneaky way). "Regarding physical immortality," he said, "before miraculous revelation may be received, there must first be a confident and unswerving *knowing*. Then comes initiation. There is no way, in Heaven or on Earth, that this divine order may be reversed." He paused. Then he smiled, and as I closed my eyes, he placed his hand gently on my head, and repeated these words, first uttered 2,000 years ago. "O thou of little faith, wherefore didst thou doubt ?"

I believe it was he who spoke those words (in English or Hebrew ?). Or . . . is it possible that I experienced a trembling moment of clairaudience ? I must remember to ask him when he returns.

The Los Angeles affiliate of the ABC television network is KABC. After every news broadcast the station flashes on the screen a 13-word, inspired message. Please look up the meaning of 13 in the numerology chapter. As I sit here typing the last page of this book, perhaps through the pulsing synchronicity of the Universe, I can see, to my left, the television screen, with the picture on, but the sound off, a habit of mine while I'm working and feeling an author's loneliness. The KABC message is twinkling at me, silently, a star sign code.

> We bring you the world as it is
> Imagine what it could be

★★★★★★

AFTERWORD

remarks from the author
to her readers
on the subjects of astrobiology and *Gooberz*
for all of you who have written, including
those who have been so patiently waiting
for *Gooberz*

Because I chose to quote from my forthcoming book about reincarnation, *Gooberz,* within the pages of my last book, *Love Signs,* I have received over the past seven years more than a thousand letters from you, from all over the world, telling me you've been unable to locate *Gooberz* through my publishers or the bookstores, and asking me how you can obtain a copy. Your confusion is justified, since a footnote at the bottom of each *Love Signs* page quoting from *Gooberz* informs you that this book "will soon be published by Harper & Row."

According to a friend of mine who works for a firm handling mass surveys for politicians and major market products, such letters are estimated to represent less than one percent of the number of people who feel the same way, but who don't take the time to write about it.

Based on these statistics (and the postmarks), there must be well over a million of you everywhere from America to India to Europe, who have been trying to find *Gooberz*. So I'm taking this way to thank each of you who have written to inquire about it — as well as those of you who have written to me about many other matters over the years, among them inquiries about my missing daughter, Sally — and the astro-biology birth control method I mentioned in the section of *Love Signs* called "A Time to Embrace."

First I'd like to respond to your concern about Sally, then to your questions about astro-biology — and finally — explain why you haven't yet been able to locate *Gooberz*.

Concerning your many hundreds of sympathetic and much appreciated inquiries about *Sally, a book about her disappearance is currently being planned, to be called either *Spider Line* or *Forget Me Not*, to be written by David Sikes, one of the government agents who conducted the investigation, and a co-author. Sally is still missing, and I've been told by concerned friends in the Justice Department and other government agencies that the publication of a book about her disappearance is what will lead to her recovery. I'm absolutely certain that we'll find her.

To all of you who have written that you're praying for her return, I send my heartfelt thanks. I keep all of your letters in two large baskets in the small chapel in my Cripple Creek home, near the altar. Sally's pictures are on the altar, and six candles, burning constantly for her. Each time I receive a new letter from one of you, I place the latest letter on the altar near one of her photographs, until the next one arrives, then I place it in the basket with the others. And so, your letters are read and re-read, treasured and kept, and *every single one* spends time performing its magic on the little altar. Some of them are tear-stained. They've all moved me deeply.

I am so grateful for your letters and your prayers. The magnetic

---

*As with *Gooberz*, Linda's readers have written about Sally because of her "Open Letter to Sally," printed in her last book, *Love Signs*. R. A. Brewer, consulting editor.

energy of the power of the love they contain will soon manifest the miracle of Sally's return. Please know this. And please continue to keep the faith with me, as you've been doing from all over the world (even Iceland and Poland) for so many long and weary years of waiting. It has meant . . . and will mean . . . much more than you may realize.

★ ★ ★ ★ ★ ★

As for your inquiries about the astro-biology birth control described in *Love Signs*, the anticipated author of that book, "R.C.," has decided not to write it after all. Instead, I am planning to bring out a small, hand-held astrological computer-calculator, tentatively to be called RAHRAM, accompanied by a small book, which will allow you to calculate your own individual ovulation periods yourself. Meanwhile, a word of caution: If you try to obtain your astro-biology dates from an astrologer, should the astrologer not give you a full ten-day period of celibacy each month, within which is your *exact* and *individual* ovulation period, you will not get the one hundred percent reliability I promised you. It relates to the life of the spermatozoa and other factors, and is not something to be taken lightly. Make sure that any astrologer whose help you may seek knows what he or she is doing.

I've kept all your letters, and I will soon use them to convince a particular computer company to underwrite RAHRAM, so send me — and this urgent project — the blessing of lots of white light and energy. I've ordained it to be available within perhaps twenty-four months subsequent to the publication of this book, but I need your help. Your letters are a powerful persuasion for those who control the financial funding for such projects.

★ ★ ★ ★ ★ ★

And now, regarding *Gooberz*, since you've all told me that you've received no response to your written inquiries from either my publishers or the bookstores, leaving you puzzled and frustrated, I feel it's my responsibility to explain. Seven years is a long time to wait. You deserve the truth, so, as complicated as it is, I'll share it with you. It's more than a touch unusual, but I guess you're accustomed to the unusual from me by now. I wish I led a nice, normal life, but does anyone, really, these days ?

I assume you've already read the Preface to this book; otherwise you won't understand what I'm about to relate.

The turbaned one was correct in all of his prognostications. As you learned in the Preface, I went on my learning retreat "to the mountains," as he foretold, kept a diary of my experiences, and have used it as a basis for this book.

At the end of the year of my retreat to the mountains of Colorado, I returned to California, also as he foretold, and on December 7, 1970, Pearl Harbor Day, in Pickwick Bookstore, on Hollywood Boulevard (now called B. Dalton Bookstore), I met the man he predicted I would meet, right on schedule.

Approximately a year later, I sat down and wrote a book about that experience, including the experiences of other men and women I know, and called it *Gooberz*. When it was completed I put it away as too intimate to share with the public and book reviewers. It was channeled, manifested through what has been called "automatic writing," which I once believed had to be accomplished with pen or pencil and paper. I now realize that the same process can occur while using a typewriter. Channeled, automatic writing is a most disturbing experience, I can assure you — something like suffering daily amnesia.

I wasn't quite sure, when it was completed, just what kind of a "literary brain child" this strange book was. *Gooberz* eluded description, and came out of the typewriter in a completely unconventional style. Regardless of my decision to never publish it, I was persuaded to allow a number of people to read the manuscript. Some of them were married couples, many were college students reaching out for something they could use as a guide to help them measure love and analyze their relationships in a deeper sense. There were some who requested to read the manuscript because it's very much about the experience of death and bereavement, as much so as about love and sex — men and women who had just experienced the agony of losing someone close to them, and didn't feel like continuing to live themselves. Others read it to quench their thirst about mystical mysteries, from reincarnation to . . . well a variety of occult secrets. They were not disappointed.

I was genuinely and unexpectedly amazed by the responses of everyone who read the manuscript version of *Gooberz*. It seemed to possess a life of its own, completely separate from me or my control. In the strangest way, it appeared to contain some power, to vibrate to some indefinable energy. Several couples who read it after they had separated or divorced, were reunited, three couples married — and two couples actually re-married. Those who had suffered agonizing bereavements, who had been crushed and shattered by death, found, not only consolation, but a certain miracle that transformed their grief into unexpected joy and excited anticipation. (I can't explain here why, but when you read the book, you'll understand.)

At some point in time, observing what kept happening in the lives of people who had read the manuscript, I was forced to realize that *Gooberz* didn't belong to me. It belonged to Higher Forces over which I had little or no control. One male college student who read it described it in an odd way. He called it "everyone's personal biography," an unusual description coming from a man, since the book is obviously written from a woman's viewpoint and experience.

That's one of the inexplicable facets of *Gooberz*. It has this diffi-cult-to-analyze chameleon quality, so that, whoever is reading it, at some early point along the way, kind of "locks in" to the plot, as one person said, and from that point on, whether the reader is male or female, the story becomes, not the author's, but the very personal history of his or her intimate relationship with someone. I've even had some readers of the manuscript ask, "Were you looking in our bedroom window? Did you tape record our conversations and phone calls? How could you possibly know the exact words we said to each other when we met . . . when we fought . . . when we parted . . . and so on ?"

Well, of course, I didn't know. How could I ! Yet, in that strange chameleon way, the experiences in *Gooberz*, whether related to childhood, maturity, death, a love affair or marriage — seem to allow the people reading it to translate them into their own experiences. I can't explain it. So I guess I should stop trying. I only know that's the way it is — that's what happens. I suppose it's somehow connected with the *way* it was written, in the sense of it having been channeled by Higher Forces, who evidently know the alchemy of causing words on a page to change their meaning for each individual who reads them. I've been told that the book is "multi-layered," that what one reader sees between-the-lines, another misses, yet sees a different message the first one misses . . . in each instance what is seen applying to a particular individual.

Despite my growing awareness that I had no control over the book I had more or less involuntarily channeled, I continued to try to exercise control over it anyway. I placed it firmly on a closet shelf, returned to the haunted suite at the Hollywood Roosevelt Hotel, and commenced work on *Love Signs*, a book I had already contracted to write. (*Gooberz* was "put away forever" and this book, *Star Signs*, was still in the form of my Colorado diary — see Preface.)

Unexpectedly, when *Love Signs* was nearly completed, I felt a sudden urge to quote from *Gooberz* in this astrological compatibility book, when I felt some of its passages were appropriate. You certainly had every right, then, when *Gooberz* failed to appear in the bookstores several years later, to write and inquire what happened to it.

This, essentially, is what happened. One of the messages the turbaned Guru you read about in my Preface to this book had given on that New Year's Day of 1970, at some eternal point during our fast-forward-speed discussion of cabbages and kings and other odd, assorted esoteric things — was a message I found to be distinctly uncomfortable, so I erased it from my mind at the time. Shortly after *Love Signs* was completed and published (although the events actually began a few years earlier), his words came back to me . . . only too clearly.

"On the level of your Higher Self," he had said, "you have chosen in this incarnation what is called by the Masters *the thunderbolt path of accelerated Karma,* often chosen by those about to be initiated, at the time of approaching Earth cataclysm."

He then explained that this was for the purpose of paying off karmic debts swiftly, more or less in bunches, so that one may move along with one's mission on Earth, sans the burden of the chains of Karma for too many lifetimes postponed. I recall thinking it would be something like cramming for a test in college, when you've goofed off for several semesters and now it's nitty gritty time. I've explained this in more detail in Chapter 4, "Déjà Vu."

If ever truth was spoken, that prognostication was surely it. There have been numerous and repeated occasions to remember his words over these past eons . . . has it really been sixteen years ? Seems like sixty. *The thunderbolt path of accelerated Karma* indeed — with, I might add, several bolts of lightning thrown in for good measure to punctuate the earthquaking events in every sphere of my life, from emotional to health, to financial to professional . . . and spiritual . . . perhaps especially the latter, since my faith was severely shaken. I realized, dimly, that I was experiencing what many of you have also suffered, judging from your letters: a great soul test of worthiness. By the way, I read all your letters carefully, and wish so very much I could answer them personally, but it's simply impossible. Instead, I try to answer all but the most personal and specific questions through the books I write, and I trust this necessary alternative has been — and is —helpful to you.

Even though I was, as I said, dimly aware of the reason for what I was experiencing, such awareness, as I'm sure you've also discovered, doesn't make it any easier to bear, never mind what you're told by religious zealots who aren't always capable of practicing what they preach. What *did* make it bearable was trying, as I did constantly, to hang on tightly to my childhood faith in magic and miracles — no matter how great the mistakes, how muddled the tangle, how hopeless the outlook.

I don't know what my grades were at the end of my personal soul test, since one isn't given a report card for these things, but I assume that I passed, because I'm still here. I may not have made A plus every single time, but I tried, and as my Irish elf mother used to say of trying . . . "the angels can do no more."

Early in 1980, after *Love Signs* had been published with its quotes from *Gooberz* announcing that it would be available to you soon — right in the middle of the upside-down world I was living in, while I was thunderbolting down the path of some of that very heavy "accelerated Karma," out of the blue I received a phone call from the turbaned one. The stranger.

This time he offered me his name. It was Nathaniel, he said, but he preferred to be called Nahtan. Somehow, he had located me and learned my unlisted telephone number. I let it pass. Who questions Avatars ? One must "save face" for them at all times, and not press too many questions. They'll just avoid answering anyway, so it's a waste of energy to probe, as I've discovered with more than one of them.

Nahtan told me he had enjoyed reading *Love Signs*, gave me a much welcomed and needed little pat on the head for living up to my spiritual responsibility by writing it — then said he was disturbed by the indication in it that *Gooberz* would be my next published book.

He reminded me of the counsel he had given me on that New Year's Day in 1970 regarding the order of publication of *Gooberz* and the book about my experiences in the mountains, saying . . .

"The book *Gooberz* has a mind of its own, and I'm sure you've already discovered that. It will be published when it wants to be — not when either you or a publisher want it to be — neither before nor beyond its allotted time." His tone was quite emphatic, even stern. "This book will select its own timing synchronized to the harmonics of the Universe. As I advised you nine years ago, you must first write and publish the book based on the diary you kept in Colorado, and I believe you should call it *Star Signs* . . ." (he was even dictating the title, and I bristled, but remained silent) ". . . the book about what you learned during your mountain retreat, before you met the man about whom *Gooberz* was written, which, by the way, I assume you did, at the time ordained."

"Yes, I met him," I replied, "just as you predicted I would. Everything happened right on schedule. But I wrote this book about it, called *Gooberz,* as you know from reading *Love Signs,* and I really feel that, because it's been promised to my readers in the book which is out now, I should certainly keep . . . ."

He interrupted me quickly. "No. Your thinking about this is in error."

"But . . . what will my readers think of me, when I promised them that it would . . ."

"They will understand. They will wait. It's now time for you to share with them what you learned in Colorado in 1970 for those who are searching for the many magics of understanding themselves and others you discovered while you were there. Then, after *Star Signs* is published, it will be time to share *Gooberz* with your readers, because they will be better prepared to comprehend its message."

I still remember my shock at hearing his compelling voice over the wires. I suppose I'd imagined that one so . . . ethereal . . . would not use ordinary mechanical devices like telephones. When I mentioned this to him, he laughed heartily (even his laughter had a British accent) and said, "Actually, you and I do not need a telephone to communicate. But since you are not yet aware of this, that is, you don't *believe* it yet, which is the same thing, I reached you today through your present level of understanding such things. Try to remember, however, in the future, that you may always contact me without the instrument, any time you wish, simply by using the electromagnetic energy of intense desire. I will hear and answer you as surely as I have today."

After this unexpected and bossy message from the stranger I began to feel like a puppet or a marionette, with my strings being pulled first in one direction, then another, by very dictatorial Higher Forces. Aries Rams do not accept gracefully such manipulation, even from Divine Will. Nevertheless, I obediently agreed to first write and release *Star Signs,* to be published before *Gooberz.*

Soon after the conversation with Nahtan, your letters started to pour in from all over the world, asking, "Where is *Gooberz* ?" — even some telegrams, stating just those three words ! This is the first chance I've had to answer each of you.

Druid Honor, the foregoing is essentially the entire truth concerning why you have been unable to find *Gooberz.* You've no idea what a relief it is to finally share this literary trauma with you at last. Again, I apologize to you for the long delay, and once more thank you for your letters, your patience and your faith.

Now you know the book's past, what about its future ?

Since I've obeyed Nahtan, completed *Star Signs,* and released it for publication, I can turn my full attention to *Gooberz.* I'm confident that it will be winging into the bookstores before 1988 ends.

Keep those cards and letters coming, but this time mail them directly to me. Linda Goodman — c/o the Postmaster — Cripple Creek, Colorado — Zip: 80813. If we remain united, we shall overcome !

As for those of you who have written that you've been recently unable to locate a hardcover copy of *Love Signs* please be patient a short while longer. *Love Signs* will be available in a new hardcover edition soon.

Returning to *Gooberz* in closing, the "allotted time" of its "birth" foretold by the turbaned one will be the manifestation of *your* miracle, through your letters of inquiry and concern. That's the way the Universal Law of Image-Ordain-Manifest works.

All that electromagnetic energy projected by so many of your minds has already made a powerful impression on the ethers, which will materialize *Gooberz* and "matter it" into the bookstores soon.

I assume you've already read and mastered the "Mind-Matter" lesson in Chapter 8. The perfectly marvelous thing is that you were creating the magic of materializing *Gooberz* (in a large sense, your own personal biography of your quest for love) even before you read this book or that chapter — before you consciously realized that you knew the formula for such magic !

Do you see the wonderful thing this proves ? It proves that you are already magical, and have been since you were born . . . that everything in this present book you were subconsciously aware of, before you even turned the first page ! Because, as I've told you, you are all gods and goddesses, possessing great powers you have too long forgotten.

Concerning *Gooberz*, you "minded" very much, and so it shall soon "matter" !

Now that you know the code, what are you waiting for ? There must be many other miracles you've been dreaming about. Stop dreaming and go right ahead . . . *manifest* them !

Abracadabra !

Linda Goodman

★★★★★★

For The
Pilgrim's Progress

A RECOMMENDED READING LIST OF BOOKS ON METAPHYSICAL
AND OCCULT STUDIES . . . BOTH FICTION AND NONFICTION

VER THE years, I've received such a blizzard of letters asking me to recommend books for the fledgling astrologer and the occult beginner, I'm offering here some suggestions for further study — these all being either my past and current personal astrological "bibles" — or books that have expanded my own awareness in the myriad metaphysical fields, at various times.

There are many hundreds of astrology textbooks published, most of them repetitious, some of them of no help whatsoever — and only a very few of them of any real value to the serious, esoteric professional. One can waste a good deal of money, since astrology books are so expensive, using the slow process of trial and error. I don't claim that these are the only valid textbooks. There are a number of other fine ones. But these, in my own opinion, constitute a *required* library for the sincere student of astrology. They are basic. After these books have been acquired, others may be added according to personal preference.

Also, in answer to those many who have written to ask, I use the

Equal House system of the ancients in calculating a horoscope myself, having tested and found the modern Placidian system not nearly so dependable or revealing. In my own experience, the Placidian "intercepted houses," which claim to give more depth to astrological interpretation of the nativity, only serve to cloud the issues and to create ambivalence. Human nature is strange. People always tend to lean toward the more "complicated" methods in any field, rejecting the simplistic — when the fact is that "truth" invariably is hidden within simplicity. To each his own, of course. And to each *her* own. The catholic-minded student should learn all the common systems, and then decide for himself or herself. I merely state here my personal faith in the decided superiority of the Equal House system of the ancients for those who have inquired, and who have expressed an interest in my private preference. For me, the Placidian system results in many inaccuracies of interpretation. But if it works for you, by all means use it. The very finest technical explanation of why the Equal House system is the more accurate and reliable is contained in the front section of Sydney Omarr's excellent book, *My World of Astrology*.

The following astrology textbooks are listed in order of importance to the novice in the beginning stages of learning to calculate a nativity (natal chart or horoscope). If possible, it's desirable to purchase at the start all the books listed. If you can afford only a few at a time, my recommendation is that they be purchased in the order in which they're given here.

In answer to the many requests for recommended reading in the entire occult or esoteric-spiritual field (supplementary to astrology itself) I've also listed here the books I've personally found the most inspiring and enlightening for the beginner. This is by no means a complete list. There are many others. But these are the ones that bestow a more comprehensive "awakening," and which I therefore believe should be read *first*. This second list of recommended books is not given in any particular order of importance. If I were pressed to advise which of the books among these should constitute the *initial* introduction to these matters, I would say *There Is a River,* by Thomas

Sugrue, because this book is a sound general preparation for the wisdom to be found in all the others and holds the reader's interest completely, whether a believer or a disbeliever. It is a good place to begin.

Not all but some titles are annotated for the reader's greater convenience.

TO LEARN TO CALCULATE AND INTERPRET A HOROSCOPE

Ephemeriden 1890-1950 (Zurich), calculated for noon GMT (Greenwich Mean Time)

or

The Complete Planetary Ephemeris, calculated for midnight GMT for 1950 to 2,000 A.D.

If the Zurich ephemeris is used, the student will also need *Die Deutsche Ephemeride* (calculated for midnight GMT) for any ten-year period after 1950, such as the current one for the years 1980 through 1990, inclusive.

The Rosicrucian Tables of Houses

This contains, in addition to the necessary information for locating the Ascendent and MidHeaven of a nativity, a surprisingly comprehensive listing of the latitudes and longitudes of both American and foreign cities. (When such a list contains Cripple Creek, Colorado — *that's* comprehensive!)

Time in the U.S.A. Compiled by Doris Chase Doan.

This is a "must" for accurate calculation and for birth hour rectification. It contains the very necessary Daylight Saving Time information, which cannot be found in any other book. This is the best book of its kind — and since a chart is not accurate if you don't know the facts about DST in various places at various times, it is vital. For many decades in the U.S.A., each state and town and city has had an individual rule about DST, rather like the Mad Hatter's Tea Party. The only time the entire nation was on DST simultaneously was during the years of World War II, when it was called War Time — and it lasted consecutively all year long, every year, during the period of the war. *Time in the U.S.A.* explains War Time, gives the period when it was in effect — and also gives the DST of other years for different hamlets, cities and towns within the States, for which there is considerable variation.

My World of Astrology, by Sydney Omarr. New York: Fleet Publishing Company, 1965.

No published astrological textbook so clearly and definitively demonstrates the CORRECT WAY to cast a chart. All other books written on the subject are to some degree confusing and misleading. Sydney's book is the only one that explains (or at least the only one that makes it CLEAR to a beginner) the urgent importance of the position of the SUN in a horoscope. The Sun must fall at the right "Time" in the chart. Otherwise, you can be sure that you've either made a mistake in your math calculations — or that no baby could have been born on that particular day, month and year — at that particular time, in that particular longitude-latitude.

This constitutes the greatest proof of the validity of astrology. It's also an enormous help in the rectification of the true birth time. (Mother's memory and the Nurse's accuracy are both less than ideal.)

The World-Breath has definite and periodic pulsations — a systole and diastole action — whereby birth is controlled. Nature's infinite periodicity may not be altered nor disputed. Births may take place in respect to any single locality and date *only* at intervals that are in accordance with certain Lunar motion. Only particular conditions involving the World-Breath permit birth to occur in a given location, at a specific moment in Time. Repeatedly, I and others have challenged sceptical astronomers and scientists to allow us to prove this profound proof of the holiness of astrology — to no avail. Omarr's book also contains fascinating accounts of the author's several successful debates with various "erudite" critics of astrology — and a wealth of other assorted natal and esoteric information.

The Manual of Astrology, by Sepharial. London: W. Foulsham and Company, Ltd., 1962.

Perhaps the one book I would place at the very top of the list of absolutely indispensable interpretive textbooks. This book alone can make anyone who has a natural aptitude for such work a competent astrologer of natal science.

The Complete Method of Prediction, by Robert de Luce. New York: ASI Publishers, Inc. 127 Madison Ave., New York, N.Y. 10016, 1978.

An exceptional and extraordinary interpretive guide on a level with the Sepharial textbook. In particular, this is a fine book regarding transits and progressions in *predictive* work; whereas the Sepharial book is more helpful concerning the interpretation of the natal horoscope (character and potential, etc.).

Heaven Knows What, by Grant Lewi. St. Paul, MN: Llewellyn Publications, P.O. Box 3383, St. Paul, MN. 55165, 1962.

A classic, and deservedly so. This book can bring a quick comprehension of astrology to even the amateur, and is written in Gemini Lewi's wonderfully readable and witty style, without his sacrifice of a single thread of the scientific foundation of astrology. Lewi was a mathematical genius, as well as a fine creative writer, a rare combination. This book is concerned mainly with character analysis and potential, on the basis of the Luminary (Sun-Moon) positions and other planetary aspects in the birth chart — and the reader doesn't have to know how to calculate a horoscope to find it useful and amazingly reliable as a measurement of character and personality on the basis of more than the Sun Sign alone. Charts in the back allow the reader to look up the natal aspects of any birthday. But caution should be used in relation to the Moon Sign. It's best to have this particular position calculated *exactly*.

Astrology for the Millions, by Grant Lewi. St. Paul, MN.: Llewellyn Publications, P.O. Box 3383, Saint Paul, MN. 55165, 1975.

The same kind of classic as the above book, except that this one deals mostly with the predictive facet of astrology for the amateur and professional alike. Both books contain a wealth of additional reading material regarding the entire field of astrology, easily understood by those who know nothing about this art and science whatsoever — and are useful as well for the serious student of astrology.

Astrology and the Human Sex Life, by Vivian Robson. London: W. Foulsham and Company, Ltd., 1963.
    An excellent book for the purpose of comparing two horoscopes in detailed compatibility work.

How to Handle Your Human Relations, by Lois Haines Sargent. Washington, D.C.: American Federation of Astrologers, 1958.
    A most reliable guide concerning compatibility aspects between horoscopes, on the same level as the above book but not quite so in-depth regarding this particular branch of astrology.

Aspects, by Charles Carter. London: L. N. Fowler & Co. Ltd.

Any book at all by Alan Leo.

Any book at all by Manly P. Hall.

The Dictionary of Astrology, by James Wilson. New York: Samuel Weiser Publications, 1974.
    This is an indispensable book for the student who intends to make a serious study of astrology — or to become a professional astrologer. A really urgent guide for all manner of astrological terminologies and methods.

Horary Astrology, by Robert de Luce.

Horary Astrology, by Geraldine Davis. N. Hollywood, CA.: Symbols and Signs, P.O. Box 4536 N. Hollywood, CA. 91607.

Linda Goodman's Sun Signs. New York: Taplinger, 1968.

Linda Goodman's Love Signs. New York: Harper & Row, 1978.

Linda Goodman's Star Signs. New York: St. Martin's Press, 1987.

Any good Pluto ephemeris.

Showing the "movements" or the sign positions of the planet Pluto over the years — and giving an interpretation of Pluto's natal aspects in the birth horoscope (potential) as well as the meaning of Pluto's transiting and progressed aspects in predictive work. The German books concerning Pluto are the most definitive and reliable.

The Technique of Prediction, by Ronald Carlyle Davison. London: L. N. Fowler & Co., Ltd., 1971.

One of the finest textbooks available concerning the interpretation of transiting planets and progressions.

Lectures on Medical Astrology, by Davidson, M.D.

You'll be extremely fortunate to locate and possess this series of lectures by Dr. Davison on Medical Astrology. It is not easily available. At one time it was printed by astrologer Charles Jayne, of New York. This is, without question, the most accurate, perceptive and comprehensive study of medical astrology thus far published, to my knowledge.

Any book by Margaret Hone.

Any book by or about Evangeline Adams.

The Astrology Annual Reference Book. N. Hollywood, CA.: Symbols and Signs P.O. Box 4536, N. Hollywood, CA. 91607.

This reference guide has been compiled with loving care and rare integrity as a quick and easy, reliable source for a multitude of purposes, and is republished and re-created every year — with many new astrological concepts for study, which the editors neither endorse not condemn but offer for consideration and research.

FOR READING INVOLVING THE GENERAL OCCULT FIELD

Reincarnation in World Thought, edited by S. L. Cranston and Joseph Head. New York: Julian Press, Crown Publishers, Inc.

This is an excellent and incredibly detailed book concerning the vast subject of reincarnation, even giving the private experiences of many famous people regarding déjà vu. It is scholarly and utterly fascinating, and would prove for the most sceptical the sound common sense of this basic truth of all Life — the original foundation of all religion.

Reincarnation. The Phoenix Fire Mystery (same authors) is also very illuminating, although I personally prefer the earlier published book. New York: Crown Publishers, Inc., 1978. Obtain both if possible.

The Search for the Girl with the Blue Eyes, by Jess Stern. New York: Doubleday & Co. (Reincarnation) (Used bookstores.)

The Game of Life, by Florence Shinn. Marina Del Rey, CA.: De Vorss & Co.

You Forever, by Lobsang Rampa. London: Corgi Books, 1965.
Other Rampa books are fascinating, but not nearly so helpful as this one, in my personal opinion.

There Is a River, by Thomas Sugrue. New York: Henry Holt & Co., 1942.
Or, The Association for Research and Enlightenment, Virginia Beach, VA.

Any book about Edgar Cayce.
Any book published by the A.R.E. (Association for Research and Enlightenment) Virginia Beach, Va.

The Sexuality of Jesus, by the Reverend William Phipps. New York: Harper & Row, 1979.

Any book by the Reverend William Phipps.

The Aquarian Gospel, by Levi. Marina Del Ray, CA.: De Vorss & Co., 1964.
A truly necessary classic.

The Essene Gospel of Peace.

Available only through Academy Books, 3085 Reynard Way, San Diego, CA. Any book at all published by Academy Books, above address, is excellent reading for enlightenment. They will send you a complete list of titles and content.

Do You Really Need Eyeglasses? by Marilyn B. Rosanes. Berrett, New York: Popular Library, 1978.

Your eyes are the window of your soul. You owe them the gift of reading this very fine and unusual book to bring about that "clear day" when you can "see forever."

Astrology, the Space Age Science, by Joseph F. Goodavage. New York: New American Library, W. W. Norton & Co., Inc. 1967.

This book should be required reading for all schools.

Before going any further, I'd like to say that Goodavage's book should be one of the "bibles" of all New Age thinkers. It's packed with colorful confetti of esoteric knowledge, and chorded with ancient wisdom, backed up by scientific data for the sceptical. If this splendid book were to be made required reading in schools, the education system would be powerfully transformed, as would the students exposed to it.

Our Threatened Planet, Goodavage. New York: Simon & Schuster, 1978.

Storm on the Sun, Goodavage. New York: New American Library, 1979.

The Secret Life of Plants, by Peter Tompkins and Christopher Bird. New York: Harper & Row, 1973.

The Secrets of the Great Pyramid, by Peter Tompkins. New York: Harper & Row, 1971.

The Mysteries of the Mexican Pyramids, by Peter Tompkins. New York: Harper & Row, 1976.

Cheiro's Book of Numbers, by Cheiro. New York: Arc Books, 1964.

The Kabala of Numbers, New York: Samuel Weiser Publications, 1913.
    One of the finest, if not the finest book in the field of spiritual numerology, closely aligned with astrology. Extremely enlightening and awakening.

Psychic Discoveries Behind the Iron Curtain, by Sheila Ostrander and Lynn Schroeder. New York: Bantam Books, 1971; Englewood Cliffs, N.J.: Prentice-Hall, Inc., 1970.
    A superlative basic book regarding the entire occult field of worldwide scientific investigation of the metaphysical.

Health and Light, by John N. Ott. New York: Pocket Books, 1976.

The Life Everlasting, by Marie Corelli. Alhambra, CA.: Borden Publishing Co., 1855 West Main St., Alhambra, CA. 91801.

Ardath and *Romance of Two Worlds,* by Marie Corelli. Try used bookstores.
    The above books are classics concerning Twin Souls and mystical awareness. Other Corelli books not so helpful, but always interesting. Corelli writing is inspired and will be extremely enlightening for those curious to learn more about "Twin Souls." Her spiritual revelations are reliable and follow all the higher precepts of metaphysics, with the single exception that the author, at the time she wrote these books, had not yet been illuminated regarding the falsehood of the "Divinity" of Jesus — that he was an exceptional and extraordinary human, but only a man and not Divine. Other than this one misleading factor, the Corelli books are flawless regarding all occult matters.

A Dweller on Two Planets, by Phylos. Alhambra, CA.: Borden Publishing Co., 1855 West Main St., Alhambra, CA. 91801.

For the advanced student of the occult.

Any book by Dion Fortune. St. Paul, Minn.: Llewellyn Publications (or secondhand bookstores).

Dion Fortune books are only for the *very* advanced initiate.

Consciousness and Reality, by Dr. Charles Musès.

The Lion Path, by Musaios. Sceptre Publishing, 1442-A Walnut St., Berkeley, CA. 94709.

The Essene Christ, by Upton C. Ewing. The Edenite Society, Inc. P.O. Box 115, Imlayston, N.J. 08526.

The Prophet of the Dead Sea Scrolls, by Upton C. Ewing. The Edenite Society.

These two Ewing books should also be required reading in schools, for the awakening of all the children of the Aquarian Age.

A Time For Astrology, by Jess Stearn. New York: New American Library, W. W. Norton & Co., Inc., 1972. East Rutherford, NJ.; Coward, McCann & Geoghegan, Inc., 1971.

Design for Destiny, by Edward W. Russell. New York: Ballantine Books, Inc., Division of Random House, Inc., 1973.

A most important book, containing serious answers to those who are sceptical of all spiritual phenomena.

The Last Days of the Late Great State of California, by Kurt Gentry. New York:
G. P. Putnam's Sons, 1968 (probably available only through secondhand bookstores).

A Wrinkle in Time, by Madeleine L 'Engle. New York: Dell Publishing Co., Inc.

Any book by George Hunt Williamson.

Any book by Michael D'Obrenovich.

The Little Prince, by Antoine de Saint-Exupéry. New York: Harcourt Brace Jovanovich, 1943.

The Spear of Destiny, by Trevor Ravenscroft. New York: G. P. Putnam's Sons, 1973.

The Gospel of St. John, by Rudolph Steiner. Spring Valley, NY.: The Anthroposophic Press, Inc., 1940.

From a cycle of twelve lectures given by Steiner in Hamburg, Germany, in May 1908.

Any book by Rudolph Steiner.

For a list of all books by Steiner, check with the Goethe Society, New York. Rudolph Steiner was a metaphysician unequaled before or since his time regarding all spiritual writings.

Four Arguments for the Elimination of Television, by Jerry Mander. New York: William Morrow & Co., Inc., 1978.

The subject matter concerns far more than television itself. It concerns your literal survival, and is one of the most important books of the dawning Aquarian Age. It should be required reading in schools, but probably won't be because it offends those who make large fortunes from activities that harm us all.

A Tree Grows in Brooklyn, by Betty Smith. New York: Harper & Row, 1947.

A book about metaphysical truth, and all forms of love, disguised as everyday living. My personal favorite of all books written during this century. It will carry an open mind wherever it wishes to go, especially inside itself. Reading it for the first time is like finding an old friend you thought you'd lost a long time ago, even if you're not from Brooklyn! You're as much in need of its wisdom and promise for tomorrow as was the generation of the forties, when it first appeared. Maybe more.

Any book by Vera Stanley Alder.

Any book by Dr. Paul Brunton.

Beauty: A Retelling of the Story of Beauty and the Beast, by Robin McKinley. New York: Harper & Row, 1978.

One Bowl: A Simple Concept for Controlling Weight, by Don Gerrard. New York: Random House, 1974.
    A powerfully beneficial but as yet unrealized concept that explains the unsuspected hindrance of physical health and spiritual enlightenment in "social dining," i.e., the blending of conversation with the partaking of food and drink.

Evil and World Order, by William Irwin Thompson. New York: Harper & Row, 1976.

The Last Blue Whale, by Vincent Smith. New York: Harper & Row, 1979.

A few of these books may only be obtained as indicated. If your local occult bookstore doesn't carry any of the others, most of them may be obtained by writing to:
    The Bodhi Tree, 8585 Melrose Ave., L.A., CA 90069
    B. Dalton (Pickwick Books), 6743 Hollywood Blvd., L.A., CA. 90028
    Gilbert's Bookshop, 6278 Hollywood Blvd., L.A., CA 90028
    Samuel Weiser Bookshop, 132 East 24th St., New York, N.Y. 10010
    Zoltan Mason Bookstore, 789 Lexington Ave., New York, N.Y. 10021
    Chinook Bookstore, 210 North Tejon, Colorado Springs, CO. 80903.
    (They will order any of these books for you.)

If any of these fine books, which should be always available to the public, happen to be "out of print," I suggest that you write to the publisher and strongly urge republication. Publishers have no right to withhold from you books which could so benefit your lives, which perhaps did not sell as quickly as their publishers would like — for the good reason that they were not properly promoted and advertised.

About the Author

Linda Goodman was born during a spring thunderstorm on an April day. She has four children: a Goat, an Archer, a Water Bearer and a Scorpio Eagle, who are currently pursuing their assorted dreams, and with whom she celebrates Groundhog's Day and other important holidays frequently. Linda lives in the Colorado mountains with her dogs, Benjamin and Bear, Cancer and Gemini respectively. Ben and Bear are vegetarians. One is twelve years old and one is nine years old, so they are still puppies. A lion who was born free sometimes visits Linda's home, but it is quite tame and friendly, despite an occasional grumpy growl. The author's favorite songs are "When You Wish Upon a Star" and "On a Clear Day," of which there are an abundance in her home town of Cripple Creek (stars and clear days). Her favorite perfume is vanilla extract and sweet peas in the rain. Her favorite book is *A Wrinkle in Time*. She is 5′ 4″ or 5′ 5″ depending on whether she is wearing shoes or barefoot, so most of the time she is 5′ 4″. So much for vital statistics and biographical background.

AGENT UNDER SIEGE

LENA DIAZ

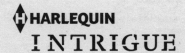

My prayers and condolences to all who have lost loved ones and
friends during the horrendous, unimaginable pandemic that
gripped our world in 2020. I hope that this story gives you a few
hours of escape and that it puts a smile on your face. God bless.

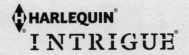

ISBN-13: 978-1-335-40148-9

Agent Under Siege

Copyright © 2020 by Lena Diaz

Recycling programs
for this product may
not exist in your area.

This edition published by arrangement with Harlequin Books S.A.

For questions and comments about the quality of this book,
please contact us at CustomerService@Harlequin.com.

Harlequin Enterprises ULC
22 Adelaide St. West, 40th Floor
Toronto, Ontario M5H 4E3, Canada
www.Harlequin.com

Printed in U.S.A.

Lena Diaz was born in Kentucky and has also lived in California, Louisiana and Florida, where she now resides with her husband and two children. Before becoming a romantic suspense author, she was a computer programmer. A Romance Writers of America Golden Heart® Award finalist, she has also won the prestigious Daphne du Maurier Award for Excellence in Mystery/Suspense. To get the latest news about Lena, please visit her website, lenadiaz.com.

Books by Lena Diaz

Harlequin Intrigue

The Justice Seekers

Cowboy Under Fire
Agent Under Siege

The Mighty McKenzies

Smoky Mountains Ranger
Smokies Special Agent
Conflicting Evidence
Undercover Rebel

Tennessee SWAT

Mountain Witness
Secret Stalker
Stranded with the Detective
SWAT Standoff

Marshland Justice

Missing in the Glades
Arresting Developments
Deep Cover Detective
Hostage Negotiation

Visit the Author Profile page at Harlequin.com.

CAST OF CHARACTERS

Bryson Anton—This former FBI profiler's redemption hinges on him saving the young woman who believes her attacker is the killer Bryson failed to capture years ago.

Teagan Ray—This criminal justice student puts her life on hold to convince Bryson to help her catch the man who attacked her. But her decision sends them both down a path that could cost them their lives.

Mason Ford—After his life is nearly destroyed by a corrupt small-town government, this former chief of police uses his lawsuit winnings to form the Justice Seekers. He offers former law enforcement officers a second chance to redeem themselves and obtain justice for others.

Avarice Lowe—He was once suspected to be a serial killer but managed to disappear when the police turned to another suspect. Now more people are dying with the same signature used in the original murders.

Leviathan Finney—Imprisoned as the Kentucky Ripper, is he really the serial killer who once terrorized his state? Or, as Teagan believes, did the real killer get away?

Gage Bishop—One of the Justice Seekers, he helps Bryson and Teagan when they need it most. But will his help come too late?

Chapter One

Long before the shadow fell across the end of the dock and hovered over Bryson Anton's wheelchair, he knew the man was there. Motion sensors and security cameras had made Bryson's watch buzz against his wrist when the man parked his car in the driveway. More messages warned when the man crossed the back patio. And again, when he'd descended the gently sloping lawn that ended at the creek. Bryson didn't care who was now standing behind him, as long as he didn't have to engage in conversation.

"Nice place," the man's voice rang out. "Probably one of the highest views in the Tennessee side of the Smoky Mountains. I'll bet at night you can see nearly every light in downtown Gatlinburg from here."

Bryson sighed but didn't turn around. "My former boss took pity on me after I got myself hurt on the job. He gave me a boatload of money, and I was selfish enough to take it and buy this property. But that doesn't mean he can drop by any time he wants."

"I'm still your boss. I haven't accepted your resignation."

"That's not how it works, Mason. I resigned, whether you accept it or not. I'll never be a Justice Seeker again. I'm not going back to Camelot. You and your knights of the round table are better off without a washed-up former profiler jacking up your investigations."

"Is that why you're sitting out here drinking like a fish, because you think you jacked up everything?"

"Something like that." Bryson grabbed a can of beer from the cooler beside his wheelchair and popped the top. He took a deep long swallow, more to irritate his unwelcome visitor than because he wanted it.

Mason retrieved a beer and eyed the label, then tossed it back unopened. "Fish biting?"

"Do you see a fishing pole around here somewhere?" Bryson emptied his can in the water and dropped it on his lap before wheeling around. "Enjoy the view as long as you want. You paid for it." He rolled his chair up the flagstone walkway toward the house.

"Dalton and Hayley missed you at their wedding last week." Mason fell into step beside him.

"Yeah, well. I didn't have time to learn the latest dance steps." He stopped at the sliding glass doors and tossed the empty beer can in the recycle bin. When he reached for the door handle, Mason leaned past him and held it closed.

Bryson swore. "What do you want from me?"

"I want you to do your job. A new client came to Camelot yesterday. She specifically wants to hire *you*."

He scoffed. "You expect me to believe she asked for a washed-up former FBI agent to screw up her case so someone else will die? If she did, send her on over. I can accomplish that without lifting a finger."

Mason leaned back against the door. "That's a heck of a guilty conscience you're nursing. Or are you just feeling sorry for yourself?" He waved toward the wheelchair. "If you'd actually go to your physical therapy appointments instead of being a no-show half the time, you'd be out of that thing by now. Don't look so surprised. I pay your insurance premiums. I see what's billed. And there've been a surprising lack of medical invoices lately. You've given up, Bryson. The question is why?"

"Why?" he gritted out. "Let me remind you that when I was the FBI's golden boy, everyone treated my profiles like biblical text. So when I presented them with a profile for the Kentucky Ripper, they focused all their efforts on Avarice Lowe, the suspect at the top of my list. Meanwhile, Leviathan Finney—the real Ripper— was no longer under surveillance. To celebrate, he kidnapped and *gutted* another woman. Because of me, he was able to kill again."

"*Because of you*, the police were able to significantly narrow their list of suspects much faster than they could have otherwise. The choices they made after that weren't your fault. Hell, Bryson. If it wasn't for the work you did, it would have taken far longer to catch the Ripper and put him in prison."

"Tell that to the family of the last woman he killed."

Mason shook his head. "I hear someone anonymously sends money to the last victim's family every month. While I admire the generosity and kindness of the gesture, that person is making payments on a debt he doesn't owe. The only person responsible for that woman's death is the man who killed her—Leviathan Finney."

Bryson fisted his hands on the arms of the wheelchair. "Are we about done here? It's getting late."

"Big plans tonight?"

"I have to wash my hair."

Mason let out a deep sigh. "Just explain one thing, then I'll go. Why now? You left the FBI over three years ago and started working for me as one of the Justice Seekers. Why is the Ripper case bothering you again after all this time?"

Bryson stared at him incredulously. "Bothering me *again*? It never *stopped* bothering me. But I tried to make something good from the bad, atone for my sins by working investigations for you. And what did I do? I nearly got Hayley killed, got myself shot and here I sit with shrapnel they can't dig out of my hip without risking the loss of my leg. Do I sit here feeling sorry for myself? No. I don't deserve anyone's sympathy, least of all my own. The people who deserve sympathy are the ones I've hurt, those who nearly died because of me, and the one who *did*. Accept my resignation and leave me alone. I'm not going to risk hurting anyone else. I'm done."

Mason's jaw worked as he stared past him toward the creek. A full minute passed in silence before he finally met Bryson's gaze again. "Sounds like you've made up your mind."

Bryson arched a brow. "Sounds like you're finally listening."

"Oh, I've been listening. I just don't like what I'm hearing." He pulled a thick neon green folder covered with pink polka dots out from beneath his suit jacket and dropped it onto Bryson's lap. "Guess you won't be needing this."

He eyed the folder like he'd eye a coiled rattlesnake. "What is that hideous thing?"

"I was asked to give it to you. It's from the client I told you about, the one who requested that you work on her case. She put her pursuit of a master's degree in criminal justice on hold to perform research on an alleged serial killer. She believes that you're the only person who can convince the police that her conclusions are reasonable and help her catch him. She provided a summary of her research in that folder."

Bryson snorted and shook his head. "If she's convinced that a failed criminal profiler is the key to her theory, then she needs to go back to school. Her deductive reasoning is skewed."

"Personally, I found her work intriguing, her theories compelling. And I've already got my master's in criminal justice, not to mention a decade of experience as a chief of police and another seven years after that running The Justice Seekers." Mason straightened and tugged his suit jacket into place. "But I can see that I'm not going to change your mind. The funny thing is, I never took you for a quitter. Even after the FBI."

"Yeah, well. I never thought I'd be responsible for

another innocent person almost being killed either. Guess we were both wrong."

Mason stared at him a long moment, then looked past him again toward the dock. "That really is a gorgeous view. Let me know when you decide to go fishing. I can bring a pole, throw out a line." He gave him a hard look. "*All* of your brothers and sisters at Camelot would love to toss you a line, including Hayley. You just have to ask." He shoved his hands in his pants pockets and strode away without waiting for a reply.

Bryson dropped his gaze to the ridiculous-looking pink-and-green folder in his lap. He stared at it long after he could no longer hear the sound of Mason's car driving away. Long after the sun began to set and the mosquitos started buzzing around his ears. Long after the twinkling lights of Gatlinburg reflected in the sliding glass door, studding the night sky like glitter on a black velvet canvas.

Then he tossed the folder in the trash.

Chapter Two

Teagan whistled as she stepped out of her car onto the brick-paved driveway. It was as if she was standing on top of the world, with the entire Smoky Mountains range spreading out around her in 360-degree views. There wasn't another house in sight, just the rambling one-story stone-and-brick mansion set so far back from the main road that she hadn't seen it until she'd almost passed it.

She wasn't sure what she'd expected of the home of a former FBI special agent, but it wasn't this. Either the FBI was paying way better than most people realized, or Bryson Anton's post-FBI career paid *extremely* well. He'd spent three years so far with The Justice Seekers, an agency of former law enforcement officers and ex-military whose professed goal was to obtain justice for people who couldn't get it via the traditional route. Having seen their quirky, state-of-the-art headquarters that they'd dubbed Camelot, she figured it was a safe assumption that's where Bryson had made his money.

When she reached the front porch, she was surprised that in addition to the broad front steps there was a ramp concealed behind the landscaping. No rocking chairs dotted the wide expanse. No flowers decorated the empty cedar window boxes, even though it was the middle of spring. If she had to describe the expensive, sprawling home in one word, it would be...*lonely.*

She was about to knock on the frosted glass double door when the left side jerked open. She blinked in slack-jawed admiration at the incredible work of art that greeted her wearing nothing but a frown and a white towel draped around his hips. His dark, shoulder-length hair was damp. Beads of water clung to the hair on his golden, sculpted chest. It almost killed her not to reach out and trace the trail of one very happy bead that ran toward his six-pack abs and disappeared below the top of his towel. On a scale of one to ten, she rated him sexy-as-hell.

"Hi." Of all the compelling, intelligent, well-formulated introductions that her summa cum laude education could have provided her, she came up with that one-word bit of brilliance. She cleared her throat so she could properly introduce herself.

"It's about time you got here," he practically growled. "I've been trying to work the cramps out of my hip all morning. If the muscles aren't loosened up soon, I'll end up in the wheelchair the rest of the day abusing an exquisite bottle of scotch."

Leaning heavily on the cane in his right hand that she only just noticed, he limped across the expensive-looking shiny white floor before stopping beside one of the biggest black leather couches she'd ever seen. Except for the other couch in the room, which was just

as big. The two of them formed an L with their backs
to the bump-out of windows near the garage.

"Where do you want me?" he asked.

Was that a trick question? On a bed, on the kitchen
counter, *anywhere*. Since he appeared to be waiting for
an answer to his ridiculous query, she had to rewind
the brief conversation in her head and remember what
he'd said when he'd opened the door. Her previously
absent brain clicked into gear, and she realized he was
likely expecting either a massage therapist or a personal trainer. For his left hip, the one he was favoring
as he leaned toward the cane on his right side. Apparently he wanted her to tell him where he should sit, or
lie down, or whatever was required so that she could
work out his muscle cramps.

Her ovaries screamed at her to say yes to anything
he wanted. But it wouldn't be ethical to let this go on
any longer when it was obviously a case of mistaken
identity. All she had to do was tell him who she was
and why she was there.

Now if she could just stop drooling long enough to
remember her name.

He frowned. "What's wrong?" He glanced down at
his towel. "I've got boxers on if you're worried that I'm
naked under here."

"Oh, no, trust me. That wouldn't bother me *at all*."
Drop the towel. And the boxers. *Please*. She cleared
her throat. "What I meant to say is that—"

The doorbell rang, followed by a knock on the glass.

He swore. "Ever since my old boss came by yesterday, you'd think this was a Walmart on Black Friday. This makes the third person to come by in two days."

"Three visitors in two days. A veritable siege."

He gave her an odd look.

She smiled. It was either that or give in to the barbaric urge to grab his towel and toss it away. She curled her fingernails against her palms, trying her best to keep him safe.

His face was a study in pain as he limped to the door. She wondered at the source of that pain. His employer hadn't mentioned anything about an injury. Mason had only stated that Bryson was on temporary leave, but that he'd be more than happy to return to take her case. She had a feeling that Mason might have stretched the truth. A lot.

He opened the door with a bit of wariness this time, keeping his lower half hidden behind it.

Unable to make out what was being said, Teagan imagined it was far more clever than her conversation since they spoke longer than it took to say, "Hi." When he stepped back, a rather impressive woman entered. Bright, attention-getting red hair floated above baby-blue scrubs. She marched across the room with the authority of someone who had a legitimate reason to be there. Teagan was quite certain that the woman's muscular arms would have made a linebacker blush with envy. After snapping a white linen in the air and tucking it around the couch cushions, she ordered Bryson to lose the towel and lie down.

Teagan debated what to do. Should she go or should she stay?

"You." Bryson pointed at her. "Sit over there until I can stand again without wanting to drown myself in a bottle of tequila. Then we'll find out who you are and what you're doing here."

He dropped his towel and lay down on the couch, his left leg facing out toward the room. His thighs were just as muscular and beautiful as the rest of him. *Wowzah*.

The woman that Teagan mentally dubbed "Helga" placed a pad on the floor by the couch and propped her knees on top of it. Strong, man-size hands were stuffed into latex gloves. Then she shoved the side of Bryson's boxers up his leg and proceeded to squeeze and pummel his hip.

Personally, Teagan wouldn't have bothered with the gloves.

She tossed her purse onto the other couch and plopped down to enjoy the show. It was over far too soon. She almost groaned in disappointment when Bryson pushed to his feet, then pronounced his cramps gone and thanked the therapist. A few minutes later, Helga had left and Bryson returned from his bedroom in a pair of jeans and a black T-shirt.

Since the jeans caressed his muscular thighs and tight rear end and the T-shirt did nothing to hide the perfection of his pecs, Teagan decided that she didn't mind that he'd put on some clothes. It was a pleasure seeing the perfect male specimen in varying stages of undress. She just wished she could see him *completely* undressed for a fair comparison.

He limped to her couch, looking just as adorably grumpy as he had when he'd jerked open the front door and complained about her taking so long to get there. Well, complained that *Helga* had taken so long.

"Spill it," he said. "Mason sent you, didn't he?"

"I wouldn't put it that way."

"How would you put it?"

"I'd say that I went to Mr. Ford and asked if I could hire you. He said he was certain that you'd be interested, but that I'd have to ask you personally. He graciously provided your address and here I am. Technically, I sent myself." She remained seated on the ultra-plush couch and offered her hand. "Teagan Ray. Nice to meet you."

He didn't bother with a handshake. "Bryson Anton. I don't work for Mason Ford anymore. Get out of my house."

Chapter Three

"No."

Bryson stared at the defiant young woman sitting cross-legged on his couch. There was nothing about her sensible flat shoes, her conservative navy blue dress pants and short-sleeved white blouse that buttoned all the way to her neck to indicate that she was a radical militant bent on destroying the rest of his miserable morning. Even her black hair, which appeared to be curly based on the little wisps that framed her face, was mostly tamed in a tight braid that hung down the middle of her back. So why wasn't she cowed by his sour disposition and gruff commands? And why was she still sitting on his couch?

"Perhaps you didn't hear me correctly, Ms. Ray."

"Call me Teagan. I'll call you Bryson." She flashed a bright white smile that probably cost her parents a second mortgage.

"Ms. Ray, you may call me Mr. Anton, or the jerk who's throwing you out of his house. Because that's exactly what I'm doing. Tossing you out. I didn't invite you here so—"

"Actually, you did."

"Excuse me?"

She tapped her temple as if that would explain everything. "I have a photographic memory. I basically see words—"

"I know what a photographic memory is," he bit out.

"Excellent. It's good to use terminology we're both familiar with for the absolute best understanding, with no confusion. A common frame of reference will help us communicate better. Don't you think?"

"You lost me at *no confusion*."

She grinned. She seemed to do that a lot. "Let's go back to the part where you invited me here."

"I didn't invite you."

"When Mr. Ford told you about me, you told him, 'You expect me to believe she asked for a washed-up former FBI agent to screw up her case so someone else will die? If she did, send her on over.'" She spread her hands out beside her. "Here I am. Plus you invited me in at the front door. It's kind of like with vampires, once you let them in, that's it. You can't just throw them out."

"Watch me." He tossed his cane on the other couch, then scooped her up in his arms.

Her dark brown eyes got so wide he could see the beautiful little golden flecks around the irises.

He whirled around, then stumbled and had to steady his shin against the coffee table to keep from tipping over.

She boldly looped her tawny-brown arms around his neck and stared up at him with a look of concern. "I'm not sure you should be holding me like this without your cane. I don't want you to hurt yourself. Plus, even as gorgeous—with a capital *G*—as you are, I still think we should get to know each other better before we jump into each other's arms. Don't you?" She fluttered her impossibly long, thick eyelashes.

Actually *fluttered* them.

"Has anyone ever accused you of insanity?" he asked.

"All the time. It's one of my best qualities—the ability to act crazy while I outmaneuver and outsmart everyone around me."

He scowled down at her.

She tightened her arms around his neck. "I could literally do this all day. We fit together perfectly. My soft curves, your hard muscles. Very comfy."

"Are you flirting with me, Ms. Ray?"

"I believe I am, Mr. Anton."

"Because you're trying to confuse and outmaneuver me so I'll let you stay?"

"Mostly. Is it working?"

"The jury's still out on that. But my hip's starting to hurt like the devil again, so I'm either going to drop you or set you down. I'm leaning toward dropping."

"I prefer setting."

"No sense of adventure." He let her legs slide down until she was standing. Then he gingerly let her go, trying not to move too fast and lose his precarious balance.

She grabbed his cane and handed it to him. "Is this one of those cool FBI things? Like if you twist the head it opens and becomes a rifle? Or maybe the tip has poison in it? You jab the bad guy and he dies a horrible death a few minutes later. Am I right?"

"It's a gun, of course. Poison is so beneath an FBI agent."

Her grin widened. "James Bond has nothing on you guys."

He rolled his eyes. It was all he could manage with the pain slicing through his muscles. When he thought he could shuffle across the room without falling to the floor in an embarrassing heap, he headed toward the kitchen. He eyed her morosely as she used her two perfectly healthy hips to hop onto one of the bar stools at the marble-topped island.

"Don't get too comfortable," he warned. "You haven't achieved victory. Once I liquor up enough to be able to haul you to the front door, I'll be throwing you out as promised."

"I consider myself forewarned." She motioned toward him. "Mind if I ask what's wrong with the leg? I noticed the ramp outside, and a wheelchair in the corner of the family room."

"You can *ask* all you want. And I can choose not to answer." Bypassing the scotch that he preferred for late-night drinking—alone—he grabbed a bottle of tequila along with a shot glass.

She motioned toward the cabinet. "Can you at least pretend that you have some manners and act like a host for a few minutes?"

"Are you even old enough to drink?"

She rolled her eyes. "I'm sure I don't look *that* young."

He sighed and reached for a second glass. After pouring two generous helpings, he set the bottle between them. "Ms. Ray. You seem like an intelligent young woman—"

She grimaced. "You say young as if you think I'm a child. I can't imagine that I'm more than ten, maybe eleven years younger than you."

He arched a brow. "Meaning that while you were in elementary school, I was losing my virginity to the homecoming queen at my high school."

She hesitated with a shot glass halfway to her mouth. "Can't top that. But I did have my first kiss quite early. Third grade. Behind the jungle gym. Ricky Southernton." She tossed her shot back with one gulp.

"On the lips?"

"On the cheek."

"Doesn't count. I was in *second* grade when I kissed Becky Louis. She bit my tongue."

"Maybe you shouldn't have shoved it down her throat."

He reluctantly smiled. "Maybe not." He tossed his own shot back and reveled at the smooth burn as it went down. A few more shots and he might be able to avoid the wheelchair until at least the dinner hour.

"Have you thought about getting prescription painkillers instead of drowning the pain with alcohol?"

He shot her a look that should have frozen her to the bar stool.

She held up her hands in a placating gesture. "Sorry. The filter between my brain and my mouth is defective. I shouldn't have asked."

The completely unrepentant look on her face, in direct opposition to her words, forced a laugh out of him. How long had it been since he'd laughed, or even smiled? He had no idea. But the novelty of both had him starting to relax, if only a little. "I was on pretty strong pain pills in the beginning, but it was like living in a brain-fog all the time. Had to wean myself off them. Drinking works better for me, and it's a heck of a lot more fun." He refilled his glass, then paused in question with the bottle poised over hers.

"Yes, please."

He topped off her shot, then drained his while watching her. If he hadn't been paying close attention, he wouldn't have noticed the tiny, involuntary shudder when she tossed it back.

"That's a waste of some pretty great tequila for someone who doesn't even like it."

She shoved the glass across the island for more. "What makes you think I don't like it?"

He poured more for himself, but not for her. "When you have ten or eleven more years of experience behind you, maybe you'll figure it out. Go home, Teagan. There's nothing for you here. I can't help you."

"You mean you *won't* help me?"

"The intent doesn't matter. The result is the same."

"Then I guess we're back to drinking. Shots with a hot guy before noon. I can think of worse ways to spend my morning." She grabbed the bottle.

He tugged it away from her. "If you're trying to win me over with the hot guy talk, you can stop right now. Like I said, I'm not going to help with your case. And

I'm not buying this over-the-top happy, flirty personality you're presenting. Nobody's that cute. You're trying too hard."

"You think I'm cute?" She grinned and fluttered her long lashes again.

"I think you're nervous and overcompensating. It's time to drop the act."

Her smile dimmed and she seemed genuinely confused. "What do you mean?"

He rested his forearms on the island. "Profiler, remember? At least, I used to be one. It took me a few minutes to realize what was happening. Probably because I'm out of practice and I do my best to avoid people these days. But you don't have to keep pretending, trying to be something you're not. Maybe it's the tequila that I drank, maybe it's that I admire your spunk and the effort you've put into this. Whatever it is, you've earned a slight reprieve. I'll listen to your spiel so you can get it out of your system. *Then* I'll throw you out."

She stared at him, wide-eyed, then grabbed his full shot glass and tossed it back before he could stop her.

He silently cursed himself for not being more careful. Given her small stature and the strength of the tequila, her ability to safely drive herself home was now seriously in question.

"Better?" he asked dryly.

"Better. Although I'll admit that scotch I saw in your cabinet is more to my taste."

"Don't even think about it."

She grinned.

"This is where I warn you that I haven't read the information that Mason left me."

"I kind of figured, since the folder I gave him is hanging half-out of your garbage can on your back patio." She motioned toward the glass doors on the far side of the kitchen.

"Observant, I'll give you that. Then again, it's hard to miss a neon green folder with hideous pink polka dots."

"Not a polka-dot fan?"

"Not in the least."

"Pity."

He shifted his weight to help ease the tightness in his hip. "Maybe you can brief me on what's in the folder. Mason mentioned you think you're on the trail of a serial killer."

She nodded and ran her hands up and down her arms, looking slightly less eager now that the discussion was at hand. She reached for the tequila.

He swore and placed the bottle on the counter behind him. "Trust me. You're already going to have a heck of a hangover. No more alcohol. Now, for a common reference, so there's *no confusion*, what name are you dubbing your alleged killer?"

She drew a deep breath, then straightened her shoulders as if she was about to head into battle. "The Kentucky Ripper."

Chapter Four

Bryson froze, then slowly straightened. "That's not funny."

Teagan's eyes widened. "I'm not making a joke. I'm serious. The Ripper is the killer I've been researching."

"At least now I know why you asked Mason for me, specifically. Well, forget it. Rehashing past failures isn't my idea of fun."

She held up her hands. The overhead lights winked off several gold rings. "Just hear me out. I've been researching this for a long time. I'm not here to cast blame. I'm here for your insight. And I'm here to ask a very important question." She squeezed her hands together. "What if the guy they thought was the Ripper is actually a copycat and the real serial killer is still at large?"

He winced, then eyed his empty glass with longing. "If that's true, then I screwed up even worse than I thought."

"Not at all. *You* didn't make the mistakes during the Ripper investigation. The *police* did."

He tore his gaze from the shot glass. "Maybe I drank

too much tequila too because that one went right over my head. I'm lost, in spite of our *common frame of reference*."

"Then I'll be happy to explain. First, profiles are tools, not biblical text."

He stared at her as his own words were thrown back at him. "Did Mason say that to you?"

She frowned. "No. Why?"

He shrugged. "Just wondering. Go on."

She crossed her arms on top of the island. "When your profile indicated that one of the two top suspects was the most likely killer, the police went after him with everything they had. Meanwhile, their other prime suspect was no longer under surveillance. He took advantage of their mistake to abduct and murder a woman. Instead of thinking of your profile as a divining rod, they should have stayed the course, kept their surveillance on both suspects until some evidence tipped the scales." She motioned in the air as if waving away her words. "Regardless, my point is that, based on my research, I think your profile was spot-on. The first guy *was* the real Ripper. The guy they put in prison is a copycat. The police got sidetracked by the last murder and pursued that killer to the exclusion of everyone else. So, while there's plenty of blame to go around for how everything turned out, none of it should have ever blown back on you."

He was going to filet Mason for giving this misguided, albeit beautiful woman his address. Her theories were bogus. Unfortunately, he could tell how vested she was in them and he didn't want to destroy her confidence before her law enforcement career was even off the ground.

Using his nonjudgmental teaching voice, the one he'd adopted while presenting guest lectures at Quantico, he explained, "For that theory to hold water, the first requirement would be that the Ripper is still active. But no other women have been tortured and brutalized per his specific signature since he was put away. Explain how your theory addresses that."

"No other women *that you know of.*"

"Fair enough. That I know of. But if new cases had popped up, I can't imagine the media not making a connection even if the police didn't. The Ripper case was bread and butter to them. It made for great ratings. If something that sensational happened again, they'd be all over it."

"The media in Kentucky, yes, absolutely. Other places, not necessarily. They don't know about the original cases and wouldn't realize there was a serial killer operating in the area."

"Maybe."

"Definitely," she countered.

He admired her confidence, even if she was dead wrong. "Why would the killer change locations?"

"Because he's smart. He knew he'd been given a tremendous opportunity, that a mentally disturbed fall guy had taken credit for his crimes and turned attention away from him. He knew that if he killed again in the same area, the police would know right away that they'd caught a crazy guy bent on enjoying the spotlight and confessing to crimes he didn't do. They'd be back on the trail of the real Ripper, reassemble the task force. But stopping, not killing anymore, isn't an option either. Our psychopath is driven by an urge to kill that he can't control. So in addition to changing locations, he also changes his MO, his modus operandi, the way he kills."

He could see why Mason had found her compelling. She spoke with authority, like someone who'd had real-life experience with this sort of thing rather than just book knowledge. He decided to press her some more, see whether she'd backtrack and second-guess herself, or hold firm and defend her theory. "Don't serial killers always keep the same MO?"

She gave him a wounded look that almost had him feeling guilty. "You're treating me like a student, testing me, aren't you? Pushing to see if I know what I'm talking about."

"Do you? Know what you're talking about?"

Her gaze dropped to the island. "Yes," she whispered. "I do."

Her ragged tone put him on alert, had him studying her body language. The best indicator of honesty and genuine emotion as opposed to lies and bravado was how a person moved, how they spoke, not the words they used. Her body language told him that something else was at play here, something she wasn't yet ready to say out loud, something that had dread curling in his chest. "You were talking about modus operandi."

She cleared her throat. "What I was saying is that serial killers don't always maintain the same MO, their method, *how* they kill. Modus operandi is a conscious choice. They can change it if necessary. Like if a killer starts out tying his victims with shoelaces. If one of them manages to break a shoelace and escapes, the next time he abducts someone he'll use handcuffs. Different MO, same killer."

"That's a good way to explain it," he allowed. "But I'd add that MO is more about what's necessary, or what the killer *feels* is necessary, in order to carry out his crime. Outside of forensics, with no fingerprints or even DNA, what would convince you that some murders were done by the same killer if the MO had changed?" Again, he watched her closely, trying to decipher the subtext, the meaning beneath her words.

"Signature. A serial killer, a true psychopath, is driven to kill. He can change parts of what he does, but the signature is an intrinsic part of his killing ritual. It's the part of his crimes that he *can't* change. Signature is a subconscious action, something he doesn't choose to do or not to do. It's something he's compelled to do." She clasped her hands on top of the island. "Like the Ripper carving an *X* across the abdomen of each of his victims after he abducts them. That's his way of branding them, of letting them know that he… he *owns* them."

She wasn't meeting his gaze anymore. Instead, she slowly traced the veining in the marble top of the island. Her stark words had his throat tightening as he carefully watched her, weighing every move, even the tone of her voice.

"Signature is often a reliable means for linking crimes," she continued. "But the police often confuse

MO with signature, or assume something is the signature when it's just another thing the killer does each
time, but isn't *compelled* to do. And even though it's
been documented many times that serial killers can
and sometimes do change their victimology, go outside
their comfort zone and choose a victim that doesn't fit
with their history, the police automatically think that
means it's a different killer. It's not their fault. Most
will never come across a serial killer case their entire
career. They're not equipped to evaluate the complexities, dive deeper, weigh a killer's thirst to kill versus
his desire not to get caught. They don't understand his
willingness or ability to adapt."

"You've circled back to the Kentucky Ripper again."
He kept his voice gentle, encouraging her to finish
what she came here to say, what she so obviously
needed to say. And all the while he cursed Mason for
sending her, for *using* her to get to him. "His original
victimology included Caucasian women in their mid-
to late thirties, married, with children. They all lived
within the same fifty-square-mile geographical region
in Eastern Kentucky. None of them worked outside
the home."

She nodded. "Yes, but I'm saying he could have
changed all of that. He could have moved to another
state, gone after someone who was younger, single,
without children. Someone who worked outside the
home, even if only to take temporary odd jobs to make
ends meet. Even if the signature was the same, most
people in law enforcement would think it was another copycat, a one-off, since the alleged real guy is

in prison. They wouldn't realize what they're dealing with, or even that they have a serial killer operating in their midst."

What he'd started to suspect just moments ago had solidified into a cold hard knot of dread that had him clenching his teeth so hard they ached.

Holding on to the edge of the countertop to maintain his balance, he limped around the island until he was standing beside her. Then, keeping his voice as gentle as possible, he asked, "How old are you? Don't give me a flippant answer either. I'm serious."

His question didn't seem to surprise her. "Just turned twenty-six. My birthday was last month."

Younger than he'd thought. Her guesstimate of their age difference was off by several years. "You're not Caucasian."

Her perfectly shaped brows rose. "Gee, what gave that away?" Her sarcasm did little to hide the underlying pain in her tone.

"Mason didn't mention where you're from. I'm guessing it's not Kentucky."

"Never even been to Kentucky. My home is in northeast Florida, Jacksonville." Her bottom lip trembled.

He tightened his grip on the island. "Single?"

She nodded, her eyes over-bright, as if she was fighting back tears.

"No kids?"

She squeezed her eyes shut, then shook her head. "No kids."

"You take odd jobs to make ends meet while doing your investigation?"

She slowly nodded.

"Show me," he whispered, still praying that he was wrong, but just as certain that he wasn't.

Without hesitation, she gripped the hem of her blouse, then pulled it up to her chin.

Angry puckered welts marred her skin, forming a five-by-five-inch X on her abdomen. His hands shook as he gently pulled her blouse back down. "When?"

"Two years ago." Pain leached from every word. "I was halfway through my master's degree program. But I had to put it on hold until...until I recovered. But after that, I couldn't focus, couldn't even think about going back. The police had no leads, no suspects. They still don't." She shook her head. "That's when I put my education to the test, began my own investigation. That folder I gave you is a year and a half of my life. My conclusion is that the man in prison known as the Kentucky Ripper killed *one* person, even though he claimed responsibility for many more. The real Ripper changed locales and victimology."

She finally looked up, her tortured gaze meeting his. "I believe that I'm a victim from his second spree. There are probably others as well, cases no one has connected, including me. And more women will suffer and die if I don't stop him. I'm also worried that I'm a loose end for him, that he'll come back to finish what he started." Her gaze searched his, as if looking for answers. "Please, Bryson. Help me find him and send him to prison. I don't want to die." The tears she'd been holding back spilled over and streamed down her cheeks.

He swore and lifted her into his arms. Daring his hip to interfere, he cradled her against his chest and strode from the kitchen.

Chapter Five

Teagan rubbed her bleary eyes and rolled her head on the pillow. She was in Bryson Anton's bedroom. In his bed. But he wasn't there, and his side of the bed hadn't been disturbed. She didn't know whether to applaud his old-fashioned gentlemanly conduct or curse him for it. She sighed and threw the covers off her before shuffling to the open bedroom door.

Bryson glanced up from the couch behind the coffee table, a stack of papers in his hand and more spread out across the wooden surface.

She stretched her arms above her head as she padded across the family room in her dress socks. She had no idea where her shoes and purse were. "Not to bruise your ego, but after you took me to bed, I don't remember anything. Maybe we should have a redo so you can refresh my memory."

He gave her the side-eye. "Trust me. If I took you to bed, you'd remember."

She grinned. "I have a feeling you're right."

He rolled his eyes. "You passed out in my arms, and

I generously allowed you to use my bedroom to sleep it off. You're a lightweight when it comes to alcohol."

"Won't argue that." She yawned and gestured toward the cup on the table beside him. "I don't suppose that's coffee?"

In reply, he held the cup out to her.

She took a huge gulp before handing it back to him. "I think I'm half in love with you."

"That's the tequila talking. You're still drunk."

"Can't be. Had to have slept it off by now. How long was I out?"

He glanced at his watch. "Seventeen minutes."

"Oh. Then I'm definitely still drunk. More please."

He handed her the mug without looking up.

She shifted around to see what he was doing, then sat beside him, her thigh pressed to his.

"Boundaries, Teagan." He glanced pointedly at their legs, plastered together.

She sighed and moved over, just enough so they weren't touching. "You're either married, have a girlfriend, or we play for the same team, because nothing I'm trying is working."

"Never married. My girlfriend dumped me months ago because hanging with a guy with a limp cramped her style. And, trust me, you and I are definitely *not* playing for the same team."

"What is it then? I haven't struck out this many times since high school softball."

"Maybe you're not my type."

"Pfft. Have you *seen* me? These legs go all the way up."

He arched a brow. "We need to work on this low self-esteem of yours."

She laughed and shuffled through some of the papers he'd spread out in front of him. When she realized what he was looking at, hope flared in her chest. "You're reading my file?"

He shrugged. "I was bored. I had seventeen minutes to kill."

"Does this mean you're going to help me?"

"My history of helping people isn't exactly stellar. I'm only committing to looking through your research to offer suggestions that you can take or leave. Maybe I can put a different spin on it so you can think in new directions. I wouldn't get excited, if I were you. Like I said, I don't have a great track record. This ruined hip is because I messed up a pit maneuver a rookie could have performed in his sleep. I managed to knock the killer's vehicle into a ditch, but knocked myself silly in the process. Before I could even scramble for my gun, I'd been shot, shoved out the door, and the killer was taking off in my car with a hostage. The only reason the hostage survived is because one of my coworkers was able to rescue her after I nearly got her killed."

"I have a feeling there's way more to it than that." She started to pat his leg, then jerked her hand back at his reproachful look. "Have I mentioned that I'm a touchy-feely sort of person? I'll try to behave." She bit her lip. "You're still going to help me, right?"

He blew out a breath. "I thought you were *acting* earlier, that you were overcompensating."

"Sorry to disappoint. This is the real me."

"I didn't say I was disappointed."

She stared at him, hoping he'd explain *that* comment. But instead, he turned back to the papers in front of him. After a few minutes, she said, "If you change your mind about you and me, and I miss a signal, just let me know, okay?"

He let out a deep sigh and pinned her with an exasperated look. "Teagan?"

"Yes, Bryson?"

"Shut up."

She grinned and scooted back on the couch to sit cross-legged while he reviewed her research. It was taking him far longer than she'd expected. The folder wasn't *that* thick. She'd brought the summary, not the detailed reports. But he kept thumbing through the pages, comparing things, rereading. She was dying to know what he thought. She was also dying for an entirely different reason.

She climbed off the couch. "Where's the nearest toilet in this monstrosity? I'm about to pee my pants." She hopped back and forth from one foot to the other. "Never mind, I'll figure it out." She ran into his master bedroom and chose door number one. "Found it!" she called back, before slamming it closed.

BRYSON STARED AT his bedroom doorway where Teagan the Tornado had just disappeared. He'd expected a different woman when she woke, figuring her earlier actions were a type of bravado, a coping mechanism because of what had happened to her. Then again, she hadn't slept long enough to sober up.

He took his cell phone from one of the piles of paper on the coffee table, idly rubbing his aching hip as he reluctantly pressed a programmed number that he should have deleted months ago. When the line clicked he said, "You're trying to kill me."

"Delightful, isn't she?" Mason chuckled.

"You mean she's always like this? There isn't a cure?"

"I'm not taking her back. If that's what you want, I'm hanging up."

He turned his head, looking through the glass doors at the back of the kitchen. The creek was too low to see from here unless he stood. But the pilings holding the dock in place reached like spindly fingers toward the bright blue sky overhead, a reminder of his last conversation with Mason. Had it been only yesterday?

"Bryson? You still there?"

"I'm here. You mentioned when I was ready, that you'd throw me a line. Looks like I'm going to at least dip my toes in, whether I want to or not."

"She's a hard person to say no to."

"Yes. She is."

"Whatever you need, it's yours. Just name it." Mason's tone was all business now.

"My files, all those boxes I foolishly—and against FBI policy—saved from the Ripper case with the Bureau. I asked you to store them along with other case files you archived for The Justice Seekers. Is it possible to get them sent here, when you have time?"

"You'll have them within the hour."

Teagan appeared in his bedroom doorway, looking slightly green and more than a little woozy as she gripped the doorframe. She really didn't know how to hold her liquor, which for some reason he found adorable. "Thanks, Mason."

"For the files?"

He tightened his hand on the phone. "We'll start with that, for now." He hung up. Then he grabbed his cane and laboriously climbed to his feet.

Teagan trudged toward him and stopped a few feet away, her hand clutching her stomach. Bryson had a feeling he was about to finally meet the real Teagan.

She looked up at him, misery drawing tight lines at the corners of her eyes. "Did I really tell you I had to pee?"

He smiled. Maybe he'd already met the real Teagan after all. "Come on. I'll make you some fresh coffee and my special hangover blaster."

Chapter Six

When Bryson had mentioned a hangover blaster, the name alone should have warned Teagan to just say no. But she had to admit, even sitting on his master bathroom floor with her head hanging over a toilet, that awful concoction had done the trick. Too bad that meant throwing up everything she'd eaten or drank for the past *week*.

She shuddered and sat back. At least she could be grateful that the man was a neat freak. Either that or he hired really great cleaning people. His bathroom floor was spotless. She winced. Or it had been, until she'd come along. With her tummy finally settling, she pushed herself to her feet and then wobbled to the sink.

After rinsing her mouth out with some mouthwash that she'd found in a cabinet and brushing her teeth with her finger and a dab of toothpaste, she felt almost human again. She washed her face, made sure her stubborn hair hadn't escaped its braid, then did a quick refresh of the bathroom. The sound of voices engaged in conversation had her hurrying through the master bedroom and opening the door.

The front double door was wide open. Bryson was in his wheelchair directing a man with a hand truck full of bankers boxes toward a hallway that ran across the back of the house. Careful not to get in the way, she plopped down cross-legged on a leather padded bench just outside the bedroom and waited.

By the time the man was finished and Bryson locked the door behind him, she'd counted over a dozen boxes.

He wheeled his chair up to her. "Feeling better?"

"Much. Although I'm not sure whether the cure is worse than the hangover." She motioned toward his chair. "I see you ran out of tequila and traded in the cane."

"My liver cried uncle for the day."

"If you strip, I'd be happy to play Helga and massage your hip for you." She rubbed her hands together in anticipation.

"Helga?"

"The masseuse from this morning. What I lack in professional training I'd more than make up for with enthusiasm."

He coughed as if to cover a laugh. "Yes, well. I appreciate the offer but another massage isn't going to do the trick at this point. The hip gives out once the muscles get overworked and won't support me anymore."

"Are you doing physical therapy?"

"Let me guess. You can help me with that too?"

"If I'd known I'd meet you one day, I would have changed majors in college so I could say yes."

This time he laughed out loud. "Let me worry about the therapy, or lack thereof." He waved toward the back hallway. "Go on. Ask me about the boxes. I can tell that your curiosity is eating you alive."

She frowned. "Your earlier theory about your girl-friend dumping you because of your limp probably isn't right. I think she left you because you're always profiling people and reading their minds. Okay, yes, the curiosity is driving me batty. What's in the boxes?"

"I don't read minds. Profiling, or more accurately, Criminal Investigative Analysis, is science, not art. Although some might argue it's both. And the answer to your question is that the boxes contain my research on the Kentucky Ripper. I was fresh out of polka-dot folders."

"All you had to do was ask. I could have let you borrow some of mine." She waved toward the cased opening where he'd directed the man with the hand truck. "Did the FBI send over copies of their research on the case?"

"The FBI doesn't allow former agents access to their case files. Those are copies I made of everything that passed my desk back when I worked on the investigation. Well, more accurately, when I worked on the profile. Technically, I wasn't an investigator. But the case consumed me and left me with more questions than answers, even after the killer was convicted. I religiously copied as much as I could and snuck it home every chance I got. From start to finish, the case took two years. Those copies added up."

She put her hands on her hips. "I knew it. You don't think the right guy was put away or you wouldn't have risked your career taking that stuff home. Admit it. My theory holds water."

"I admit nothing. But I'm willing to take a fresh look, which is why I had this stuff brought out of storage." He motioned toward the doorway at the end of the room. "Come on. Might as well give you a tour of this *monstrosity* and show you where those boxes went."

"That monstrosity comment I made earlier was under duress. I didn't mean it."

"Yes, you did. And I don't take offense. It *is* a rather large house, too big for one person. But it met my requirements when I was house shopping."

"Let me guess. Requirement number one, no carpet, for easier mobility with the cane and wheelchair?"

"Anyone could have guessed that."

"Requirement number two," she said. "It's only one story. You're not ready to tackle stairs just yet."

"Again, too easy. What about the third requirement?"

She shook her head. "Stumped on that one."

"The isolated location so people wouldn't bother me." He arched a brow at her.

She winced. "Ah, well. Two out of three isn't bad. That's sixty-six percent, still a passing grade, in high school at least."

"Somehow I can't imagine you ever being satisfied with anything less than an A. You were valedictorian, weren't you?"

"Takes one to know one?"

He smiled. "Come on. You've already seen the kitchen, family room, and made yourself completely at home in my master bedroom and bathroom." He waved toward two more doors on the far right wall. "Closet and half bath."

"I was so close earlier. Didn't realize there was a half bath over there."

"At least you made it to a bathroom. Can't complain about that." He wheeled his chair toward the back of the room.

She fell in step beside him. "What is this floor made out of? I can't figure it out."

He leaned over the side of the chair as if noticing the floor for the first time. "Beats me. Came with the house. Come on, right turn, obviously, since the hall starts here."

Along the way, he pointed out the various rooms but didn't stop until they reached the far end.

"He motioned toward the door in front of them. This leads—"

"Let me guess. Man cave?"

"Home office."

"Oh. Kind of anticlimactic after walking all this way."

"It wasn't *that* far."

She gave him a droll look. "Says the man who *rolled* all the way here. I've already gotten my ten thousand steps for the day. And that's just since I walked out of your bedroom."

"Do you want to see the coolest part of the house or not?"

"Coolest? Robert Downey Jr. in *Iron Man* cool or Keanu Reeves in *John Wick* kind of cool?"

"More like Bruce Willis in *anything* kind of cool."

She grinned and they fist-bumped. "Then my answer is most definitely yes."

He shoved the door open. Then he moved back and motioned her forward. "After you."

The excitement on his face had her expecting something amazing when she stepped inside the room.

She wasn't disappointed.

Chapter Seven

Bryson rolled into his office behind Teagan and did something he rarely did these days. He simply enjoyed the moment. He didn't worry about his aching hip or rehash the would haves, could haves, should haves of his life. Instead, he basked in the sheer joy on her face as she turned in slow circles, taking it all in.

There was a lot to take in.

The expansive room was a microcosm of the house itself, fully contained with a kitchenette in one corner, a bathroom, a bedroom intended for those all-nighters if he needed a quick nap before heading back into the main room to continue his work.

On the left side was the library. Floor-to-ceiling cherrywood bookshelves were filled with all kinds of law enforcement textbooks on topics like forensics, crime scene analysis, and profiling. Past the library, nearly every inch of wall space was adorned with matching cherrywood cabinets, drawers and open shelving. Storage would never be a problem here. The boxes that Mason had sent over were neatly stacked beside some of those storage cabinets. Something for him to tackle later, after everything was scanned electronically. That was the real beauty of this room—the technology.

A large round stone table in the middle of the room was control central for the massive daisy-chained monitors that took up most of the opposite wall. From that table, he could bring up reports or photographs or even the internet and display the information on any individual monitor, or slide it across all of them to form one picture. It was a profiler's dream, to be able to have everything at his fingertips at one time so he could make comparisons and see the entire case at a glance.

Too bad he'd never actually used the darn thing on a case.

Teagan had made a full circuit of the room, opening doors and checking behind them, looking into the storage cabinets. But she surprised him by returning to the library, rather than the round table. She traced her hands almost reverently across the books, like a beautiful butterfly, flitting from tome to tome. When she finally turned around, she motioned toward the two leather wing chairs and circular rug that completed the library effect.

"This is amazing. You have books I've only dreamed of reading, rare ones that my college couldn't even get their hands on when I tried borrowing them through our library system. Two of the books have your name on them. I didn't know you'd authored any texts."

"Neither do most people," he said dryly. "My publisher lost a fortune on those."

"Then they don't deserve to be your publisher. They

obviously don't know how to market your work or it would have sold a gazillion books."

"Are you one of the six people who bought a copy? Is that how you know they're amazing?"

She rolled her eyes. "I'm sure you're exaggerating."

"Not by much, unfortunately."

"Well, based on your reputation in the field, I'd love to become reader number seven, if you'll let me borrow them."

"You can *have* them. I've got plenty more. What about the rest of the room? You don't seem as impressed as I'd hoped. My ego's a bit deflated. I thought you'd run straight to the table and start salivating."

"I would have, if it wasn't for your library. I'm a book lover, through and through. But the entire room is incredible." She strode to the table and ran her fingers across it. "You must have enjoyed being a Justice Seeker more than you've let on. This is fit for the *knights of the round table*, just like the one that Mason told me that you all have in some super-secret hidden room at The Justice Seekers' home base."

"Almost. It's not quite as large as his since I don't have twelve Seekers, or so-called *knights*, to fill it up. But I admit I enjoyed his flair for the medieval and the fun of the whole Camelot concept, so I stole some of that for myself. I converted an existing study and two bedrooms into this office with the intention of using it to work from home while recuperating from being shot. But the recovery has been slower than I'd expected, and I ended up with way too much time to think about my failures. Resigning seemed like the reasonable thing to do."

"Wait. Are you saying that you've never used this office, or *great hall*, if you call it that like Mason does? Once it was finished, it just sat here unused?"

"I don't call it a great hall. It's got the stone floors, walls and table, but nothing else that resembles a castle like Mason's does. And, yes, you're absolutely right. I can't remember the last time I've traipsed across the house to this room. If it wasn't for the cleaning company that comes in once a week, there'd be cobwebs and dust all over the place."

"Wow. If I'd known that, I'd have snuck in through a back window and claimed squatters' rights long ago. I could happily live here for weeks and not come up for air." She lowered herself into one of the cushy leather chairs at the round table. "Ahhh. World class. You have great taste." She waved toward the monitors. "Feel free to feed your ego by giving me a demonstration. How big are those screens anyway? Six or seven feet tall?"

He rolled one of the other leather chairs out of the way and positioned his wheelchair beside her. "Each one is six feet by three feet. I wanted twelve, to keep with the Camelot theme. But it seemed like overkill and would have restricted the space too much, so I settled on nine. They work together as one monitor if I want, or I can load something different on each one. That's the real benefit, being able to put up information about different crimes on each screen and compare them. I can use a computer tablet at the table to select which screen I want and use a light pen to draw circles around different items or highlight them, edit them, whatever."

"Definitely cool. Can I drive?" She held out her hand. "Give me the reins. Let's do this."

Instead of popping up one of the computer tablets from a hidden compartment in the table, he adjusted his chair to face her and took her hands in his.

Her eyes widened and a slow grin spread across her face.

"Don't," he said. "Whatever sexy, funny, or smart-ass comment you're about to make about me holding your hands, just wait. I need to have a serious conversation with you. Can you focus for a few minutes without any wisecracks?"

A look of wariness crossed her face. "Why do I feel like I'm about to be sent to the principal's office?"

He sighed and let her go.

"Okay, okay." She grabbed his hands with both of hers. "No jokes, no tangents. I'm listening."

He arched a brow, not sure whether or not to believe her.

"Really," she said. "I can be serious when I need to. Go on. What is it?"

"I just want you to be sure that you know what you're getting into before we go any further. You've been like a whirlwind, blowing into my life. I met you, what, a few hours ago? And somehow you've managed to make me excited about working again. That's why I brought you to this room, to show you the tools we've got at our disposal so we can work together, if that's truly what you want to do."

"Are you kidding? It's all I've wanted since I first came across the Ripper case and saw your contributions to the investigation. I want to work with you to catch the Ripper before—"

"We're not going to work on the Ripper case."

She blinked. "My turn to be confused."

He gently entwined their fingers, trying to convey that he was there for her if she needed his support. "I'm going to hire a temp to scan in and catalog the data in those boxes. That will take several days, maybe even a week. In the meantime, the only case that I've had a chance to scan is yours. While you were recovering from your tequila binge, I used the scanner in my study to process your folder. That's what I want to bring up on these screens. But there's a world of difference between looking at something on an eight-by-ten sheet of paper, and seeing it on a six-foot-tall screen. A lot of this stuff is deeply personal. Are you sure you can handle it?"

"I don't understand your concerns. I put that folder together. I know what's in it. I want you to see it, to review it with me."

"Your descriptions of the most recent attack that you allege was made by the Ripper didn't mention you by name. That's quite telling. And there's far more detail to what happened to you than what you had in that folder. A lot more. We have to review all of the information, not just some of it, if we have a chance at solving this thing."

"Well of course there's more, all the detailed reports that support the summaries I wrote. I didn't bring those with me."

"That's not what I mean. There are other details, things you didn't reference even at a high level in your summaries."

"Like what?"

He squeezed her hands before letting go. Then he pushed down on top of the table in front of him and the section flipped over to reveal a computer tablet. He typed some commands into the control program, then pressed enter. Teagan looked up at the screens. Her eyes widened and she put a hand over her mouth before turning away.

"Where did you get those?" she whispered.

He tapped the tablet and the screens went dark. "I still have a few contacts in law enforcement."

She crossed her arms over her middle. "Well, they shouldn't have shared my hospital photos with you. They're—"

"Too personal? None of my business?"

She flinched and dropped her gaze.

He rolled back from the table. "Come on. It's okay. Forget all this. You're not ready."

"Wait. Just…give me a minute to catch my breath, okay? I can handle it. Really."

"Teagan. There's no reason for you to have to catch your breath, to handle it. You lived through the abduction, the torture, once already. You shouldn't have to do that again, reopen old wounds. Leave the investigation to me. Maybe because I admire your spunk, or maybe just because I'm ready to jump back in the game and didn't realize it until now. Regardless of the reason, I want to do this. But the only way I can is by going through every piece of data surrounding your abduction, everything that happened to you. *Everything*. It's the only way to make sure nothing was missed, that every possible clue has been considered. Meanwhile, you can go back to Florida, get on with your life. When I have something to report, I'll contact you." He wheeled to the door and held it open for her. "Come on. We're done here."

Chapter Eight

When Teagan crossed her arms and gave him a mutinous stare, Bryson sighed and let the office door close. She'd made no move toward the doorway. She wasn't backing down without a fight. But neither was he. "Teagan, we should—"

"You caught me off guard. That's all. I didn't expect to see…those pictures, okay? You should have warned me."

"If I'd warned you, I might not have received an honest reaction. You would have covered up your true emotions, or at least tried, with false bravado. Now I know the truth. This is all still too raw for you to be involved in the investigation. And there's nothing wrong with that. Victims don't typically work on their own cases, for good reason."

"I'm not a victim," she snapped. "I'm a survivor."

"Fair enough. That doesn't change anything that I said."

She waved toward the stacks of boxes. "Why can't we start with these? I already know the man who attacked me is the real Kentucky Ripper, not Leviathan

Finney, the guy in prison. There's no reason to review every nitty-gritty detail about what happened to me. We're past that. We know who did it, that first guy you profiled back in Kentucky, the one the police let get away, Avarice Lowe."

"Did you tell the detectives on your case that you believed Lowe was the one who'd abducted you?"

"Yes. I did."

"And? Let me guess. They did a cursory look at him and either couldn't locate him at all or said he had an alibi. And they went no further than that."

"They couldn't find him. But they didn't try very hard."

"Why do you suppose that is?"

She threw her hands in the air. "I don't know. Probably because they're lazy and wanted to work on easier cases."

He wheeled over in front of her. "Can you think of another reason? Come on. Set aside emotion and use that valedictorian mind of yours."

She gave him another mutinous look. "They don't believe Lowe is the Ripper and had no evidence to tie him to my case. But that's because they refused to listen."

"Detectives, good ones at least, follow the evidence. The only reason you feel that the Ripper is the one who abducted you is because the man who hurt you carved that X on your abdomen. Everything else about your case is different, including the fact that you survived."

"Then let's go through your case files and find more similarities. That's why you brought them here."

He shook his head. "I brought them here to review *after* I review your case, and then, only if we decide the two cases are connected, or highly likely connected. What happens if we do it your way, spend all our time on the Ripper case, and discover that you're wrong? We've wasted weeks, or longer by that time going through all of the Ripper's cases. We'd be starting over at ground zero without having made any progress figuring out who attacked you. If you truly want my help in finding out who hurt you, I'm all in. But I have to do it my way. I follow the evidence. And that means, starting at the beginning, with what happened to you."

She stared at the stacks of boxes for a long moment. When she finally met his gaze, naked pain radiated back at him. "I spent over a year and a half on this to find the man who hurt me. I don't want to start over. I can't."

Disappointment shot through him, but he forced a smile. "Then don't. Keep doing what you're doing. Follow the leads where you believe they'll take you."

"Without you."

He nodded. "Without me."

"Bryson's way or the highway, is that it?"

He hated the hurt in her voice. He especially hated that he was at least partly the cause. But it would be far worse if he gave in, if he went against everything he'd learned as a Justice Seeker in how to run investigations as well as his profiling experience with the FBI. She'd managed to awaken a hunger in him for justice again, a desire to right the wrongs of his past and prove he was better than the mistakes he'd made.

Starting out by making another mistake wasn't how he'd atone for his sins.

Steeling himself against the censure and sense of betrayal in her beautiful brown eyes, he responded to her accusation. "Bryson's way was to enjoy his hermit-like existence and never talk to another human being again. I was perfectly happy here all by myself until you showed up. So don't act like I'm suddenly pushing you to do something that I want you to do. You came here for my help. I was willing to help you the only way I know how, by using my training and experience and following the right steps from beginning to end to build a profile. I would have gathered as much evidence along the way as I could. Then, I would have worked with the police to get them moving on it. None of that is sexy or flashy. It's a heck of a lot of work. But that's the way it's done. Period. And you said you can't do that, which means *we're* done. Follow your own path and I'll follow mine. There's a creek full of fish in my backyard. Maybe I'll get a pole and cast a line. There are worse ways to spend my time. Go home. I mean it. I wish you the best, I truly do. But when I come back inside, I want you gone."

He wheeled out of the room and a few minutes later he was on the dock, nursing a can of beer as if the twenty-four hours since Mason's visit had never happened. But as he listened to the creek splashing over the rocks and watched the cars far below that seemed like toys from this distance, he realized that everything had changed. There *was* no going back. Mason had started a quiet rumble inside him. Teagan had built that rumble into an earthquake that had rocked him from his complacency. She'd reminded him of the thrill of the chase, the satisfaction of solving a puzzle, and the reason he'd gone into his line of work to begin with—to help people. But just as he hadn't helped Hayley when he'd gotten shot, he hadn't helped Teagan.

He swore and crumpled the now-empty can in his hand. He'd been far too rough on her. Every word he'd said had been true, his truth at least. But she obviously wasn't ready for that kind of honesty. She wasn't one of his peers, a hardened or jaded agent who he could talk to without guarding his words. She was a victim, a survivor. She deserved nothing but respect and kindness as she struggled to come to terms with what had happened to her. If going after the Ripper was her way of coping, then who was he to stand in her way? He should have encouraged her. Instead, he'd lectured her on the "right" way to conduct an investigation.

The distant sound of her car starting up in his driveway had his shoulders slumping in disappointment. Not with her. With himself. She'd probably head back to her hotel room, or wherever she was staying, and continue her research like a hamster on a wheel never getting where they truly wanted to go. She needed guidance from someone willing to pursue the angle she wanted to pursue, not the angle that Bryson had insisted was the right place to start. So how could he help her?

It all boiled down to contacts.

He'd joked earlier that he still had a *few* contacts in law enforcement. In reality, he had far more than a few. After all, he'd only gone on hiatus as a Justice Seeker six months ago. Before that, with his combined years as a Seeker and an FBI special agent, he'd worked with hundreds, maybe thousands of peers in his field. Many of them had become close friends that he still had to this day. Maybe, just maybe, he could give Teagan what she wanted—someone to talk to who'd worked on the Ripper cases.

He pulled out his cell phone and placed a call to Special Agent Pierce Buchanan. There was the usual small talk, asking about Pierce, his wife, Madison, and their toddler, Nicole. That was followed by some groveling and apologizing for Bryson having refused the couple's many requests to let them visit him after the shooting. But they worked out an agreement. In exchange for Pierce contacting Teagan and offering her an insider's view of the Ripper murders, Bryson would fly to Pierce's home in Savannah for a long weekend later this summer. Bryson wasn't sure if he was the winner or loser in that negotiation. Three of Pierce's four brothers and his father were in law enforcement. They'd likely show up and grill him about every detail of the shooting and its aftermath.

After ending that call, he made one more.

To the airport.

Chapter Nine

Death and its close cousin, extreme violence, had walked this meandering path before. They'd held hands in the dark shadows beneath these towering live oaks. They'd carefully avoided the bulging tree roots that lifted and cracked the concrete, quietly stalking their prey. Here, in the near-darkness where thick branches and leaves blotted out the hot Florida sun overhead, they'd crouched in this ten-foot-wide space lined on both sides by six-foot-tall wooden fences. The fences were supposed to ensure the privacy of the homeowners whose properties backed onto the nature trail in The Woods subdivision while joggers and walkers enjoyed these paths. But two years ago, these same fences had protected and concealed evil.

This was where Teagan Ray had been attacked, brutalized and then abducted.

There were theories that extreme violence, whether or not it ended in death, left an indelible mark on a place. It tainted the soil, the trees, even the air with its negative energy and could be felt for years afterward. Standing here now with a sense of dread and oppressiveness weighing down on him, Bryson was more inclined to believe those theories than to dispel them. Because it wasn't the GPS coordinates that had made him stop when he'd reached this spot. It was an overwhelming feeling of doom.

He shook his head at those thoughts. It was more scientific than that. He'd stopped here because he'd tried to mentally place himself in the role of a man stalking prey. This is where he'd have lain in wait for a potential victim. It was a particularly dark spot, with thick overgrown bushes providing the perfect cover. And over two years ago, unfortunately, Teagan was the one who'd happened through here at just the wrong time. And she'd paid for that dearly.

After the initial attack, the belief was that she'd been drugged. Still able to walk with assistance, but not coherent enough to fight back or even understand what was happening to her, she was led by her abductor to wherever he'd parked his vehicle. Or, at least, that was the theory. There weren't any witnesses to fill in those details.

Her first lucid memories, after the attack on the path, were that she was blindfolded and tied up in the shack where he'd taken her. Two weeks later, when he'd left on one of his so-called supply trips that he took every few days, she'd miraculously escaped. But she'd gotten lost in the wilds of the Florida backcountry for days. By the time a hiker had found her, she was dehydrated and sunburned and half out of her mind. Once she'd recovered enough in the hospital to explain that she'd escaped a kidnapper, over two days had passed.

The police used scent dogs to backtrack to the shack where she'd been held. Turns out she'd been about an hour and a half from her hometown of Jacksonville, deep in the woods outside of Live Oak, near the Suwannee River. But the abductor wasn't there, and he never came back after that.

The owner of the shack was cleared. Not because Teagan couldn't pick him out of a lineup. She couldn't pick *anyone* out of a lineup. She'd been drugged, blindfolded, deprived of water and food. Her abductor had kept the shack mostly dark, with room-darkening drapes and few sources of light. He'd told her from the beginning that he planned to kill her. But until then, he was super careful, obviously in case she somehow escaped, which she did.

Because of his extreme care to conceal his identity, she'd told the police she could probably pass him on the street and would never know it. That was likely one of the reasons she had put her education and the rest of her life on hold to try to find the man who'd attacked her. Knowing he was in prison and could never hurt her again would no doubt be the only way she could ever live without the fear of him finding her again, and finishing what he'd started.

Too bad her abductor hadn't been the owner of the shack. That would have made everything neat and tidy and it would all be over by now. But the owner lived in Canada, where he went to work every day and had plenty of people to vouch for that. The shack was where he stayed two or three times a year when he came down to work at clearing the land around it in preparation for building the retirement cabin he dreamed about.

Bryson made some notes on the police report, marking things on the map of the trail that he'd noticed today. Then he tucked the report into his jacket pocket and took one last look around. He intended to walk all of the paths in this community today if his hip could handle it, or use his wheelchair if he had to, which seemed likely by how badly his hip was already throbbing. He wanted to see whether there were other good ambush spots on other trails. If so, then maybe someone with homes backing up on those paths might have spotted a man walking the trails back then, choosing his ultimate hiding place. There could be some witnesses who didn't even realize they'd seen something important.

There were 4.1 miles of nature walks and trails in this community, according to its website. Other statistics that he'd gleaned about The Woods were that it had 811 homes and 18 man-made ponds. It boasted a so-called natural setting, thus the name. From his perspective, that meant there were a heck of a lot of trees and overgrown bushes, providing great hiding places for would-be attackers. But because the community was gated, the residents had been lulled into thinking they were safe.

Maybe that explained why Teagan had thought nothing of walking through this overgrown, dark, far less traveled section of the trails as the sun was going down. Her parents lived just a few streets away, and she'd been home from college on a visit. Having grown up here without any major crime incidents in an upper-middle-class area that was generally considered safe, she had felt there was nothing to worry about. In a perfect world, there shouldn't have been. But unfortunately, there were some very bad people sharing the same air as the rest of them, and Teagan had the misfortune of coming across one. Wrong place, wrong time.

Or did that really explain it? Could the attacker have been after her specifically?

That was one of the questions Bryson needed to answer. The assumption all along in the police reports, and by Teagan and her parents as well, had been that she was a randomly chosen victim. There wasn't any evidence to the contrary. But Bryson wasn't the type to assume anything.

A low growl had him turning around, leaning on his cane with one hand as he flipped back his jacket with the other to grab the pistol holstered on his hip. But he didn't pull his weapon. Instead, he let his jacket fall back into place and rested both of his hands on the cane to steady himself as he glanced from the impressive, still-growling German shepherd to the gorgeous young woman holding its leash.

Teagan.

The accusation that she might have somehow gotten Pierce to tell her where he was and then followed him to Jacksonville died on his lips unspoken. She hadn't expected to see him here. It was evident by her wide eyes and the way her left hand was pressed against her throat.

"What are you doing here?" he demanded. "I thought you'd be in Savannah by now." His accusatory tone did exactly what he'd intended. It gave her something to focus on instead of the fright from seeing a man standing in the shadows where she'd once been attacked.

She dropped her hand and gave the dog a command that had him sitting on his haunches. His tongue lolled out as if he hadn't been poised to rip out Bryson's throat seconds earlier.

"Why would I be in Savannah?" She sounded genuinely confused.

It was his turn to be surprised. "Didn't you get a call? From FBI special agent Pierce Buchanan?"

She shook her head. "No. But I haven't checked my messages since leaving your place yesterday. My phone number listed in the folder I gave you is a landline at my apartment. It's not one that I share with many people. And it's not registered under my name."

The truth sent a wave of anger and sympathy straight through him. "You carry a burner phone, don't you? You're worried that your attacker might trace you."

Her gaze was her answer, darting toward the fences on either side of the path and the thick trees and bushes blocking the view of anyone behind them. He wondered why the homeowners association hadn't voted to clear out these dangerous hiding places, especially after what had happened to Teagan. But mostly, he wondered why she was here.

He took a step forward, hesitating when her dog emitted another threatening growl.

"Zeus, stop." She shook the leash and the dog quieted, but his dark eyes followed Bryson's every move. "Why would an FBI agent be looking for me?" Her eyes widened again. "Have they found something? In Savannah? Oh no. Someone else wasn't attacked, were they?"

Ignoring the new round of growls from her dog, he limped toward her, stopping just out of lunging distance. "No. I'm not aware of any more attacks linked to the man who hurt you. Pierce is a good friend of mine who lives in Savannah. Because of his experience with serial killer cases, he ended up assisting on the task force in Kentucky. We worked the Ripper case together. After you left yesterday—"

"After you threw me out, you mean," she accused. "I thought you Justice Seekers were supposed to be honorable and help people in need."

He smiled, pleased to see a return of the sassy confident woman he'd met in Gatlinburg. "Yes, well. I was on hiatus from the Seekers at the time. So you weren't officially my client. But I did want to help you. So after I threw you out, I called Pierce and asked him to give you an insider's reading of the Ripper cases and to answer any questions that you had."

Her brows crinkled in confusion. "Why would you do that? You told me that looking into the Ripper case was the wrong approach."

He started to move closer, but Zeus stood up, his ears flattening. Shooting her dog to defend himself was the last thing he wanted to do, so he took a step back.

"I'm glad you have Zeus with you, for protection," he told her. "That's smart."

She winced and looked away.

Understanding had him filled with regret. "I wasn't trying to say that you shouldn't have been out here without him that first time." When she didn't answer, he leaned to the side, trying to get her to look at him. "Teagan?"

She sighed and met his gaze. "What?"

"It wasn't your fault." He waved his hands along the path. "None of this is your fault. A woman should be able to dance naked through the streets without worrying about some Neanderthal attacking her. It's *never* the victim's fault. The only person to blame is the monster who hurt you."

A reluctant smile tugged at the corners of her mouth. "You sound like my parents."

Now it was his turn to wince. "Ouch."

She laughed, then winked, looking more like her old self again. "Don't worry. There's exactly zero chance of me confusing Hot Guy with my parents."

"Good to know. I think. Assuming I'm Hot Guy?"

She grinned. "Definitely." Her smile dimmed, and some of her earlier uneasiness had her glancing around again. "I'm staying with my parents for a few days. And like I do every time I see them, I walk this trail. Not because I want to go...where it happened...some survivor's weird hang-up or something. But because it's the same routine I had before the attack. I've walked these trails almost daily since I was a little girl. And I refuse to change that because of...because of what happened. He took so much from me. It might seem silly, but letting him take away my joy of nature and long walks would be letting him win." She patted the dog beside her. "My only concession now is to bring my mom's dog Zeus and Annie along."

The dog seemed to be licking his lips in anticipation of sinking its teeth into his hide—if dogs had lips.

"Wait. Annie? Who's Annie?"

She slid her hand into the pocket of her jeans and pulled out a compact .22-caliber pistol. "Meet Annie."

"Let me guess. After Annie Oakley?"

Her gorgeous smile made another appearance. "Very good, Sherlock. Maybe you should be an FBI agent." She shoved it back into her pocket.

"Been there, done that." He gestured toward her pocket. "Should I ask for your concealed carry permit?"

"That depends. Did you become a police officer since the last time we met?"

"Touché. Don't worry. Your secret's safe with me. I won't call any of my JSO contacts to tell them about Annie."

"Is that how you got past the gates? Someone from the Jacksonville Sherriff's Office told the guard to let you through?"

"Actually, I got in the old-fashioned way."

"The old-fashioned way?"

"Ben Franklin. A bribe."

He'd expected a laugh. Instead, her face turned ashen.

"Teagan? Are you okay?" Risking the wrath of Zeus, he leaned toward her.

Predictably, the dog barked and pulled against the leash trying to reach him.

She frowned and yanked him back. "Zeus, enough. Friend. He's a friend." She motioned toward Bryson. "Hold your hand out for him to sniff, palm down."

"You're kidding, right?"

"No. I'm serious. Let him smell you." She slipped her hand under the back of the dog's collar. "Friend, Zeus. Friend."

Telling himself he was an idiot, he did as she'd asked, holding his hand out.

Zeus snuffled his hand for a good ten seconds, then his tongue lolled out and he gave it a long sloppy lick before sitting back on his haunches.

Bryson made a face at the saliva on his hand, then looked up in time to see Teagan trying to hide a grin. He narrowed his eyes suspiciously. "You did that on purpose."

"Yeah, well. It's kind of funny, seeing you dressed up in a business suit with dog slobber all over your hand."

After a quick glance at Zeus, who seemed far more interested in a butterfly flitting around a nearby bush now that he'd supposedly accepted Bryson as a non-threat, he reached out and wiped his hand on Teagan's shirt.

She gasped in dismay at the wet stain on her formerly white blouse. "I can't believe you did that."

"We're even now. Don't go planning your revenge."

"Hmm. We'll see about that." She glanced around again. "You said you bribed the guard at the gate to let you in? You didn't show him some kind of old FBI credentials or anything like that?"

Now he understood why she'd paled earlier. "You're surprised at how easy it was for someone who doesn't live here to get in. Is that it?"

She nodded. "Not that I should be surprised. After all, the police ruled out the suspect as living in the community. They supposedly researched every single resident. We knew he had to have come from outside somehow. I just didn't think it would be that easy to drive on in."

"Yeah, well. It's not like you have to be a former cop to be a security guard. Pretty much anyone can be one. And they aren't paid enough to make them above reproach, some of them anyway. I'm sure most are great people and genuinely try to do a good job."

She snorted. "Now you're pandering, trying to make me feel better. I preferred it when you were being brutally honest."

"Brutal? Ouch again."

"If the truth fits." She shrugged, then winked as if to soften her criticisms.

"This isn't going at all the way I'd planned when I flew down here late last night."

"You thought I was in Georgia. You didn't plan on running into me."

"No. I didn't. But now that I have, I'm wondering why I did. After being so intent on finding information on the Ripper, why would you come back to Jacksonville? Are you taking a break from the investigation? Returning to school to finish your master's?"

She straightened her shoulders. "No break. I'm digging

in harder than before. And I'm taking your advice. I'm starting at the beginning. And this—" she waved her hand toward the trees and bushes around them "—is where it all began."

Chapter Ten

The look on Bryson's face had Teagan stiffening. "Why are you so surprised? I went to you for help and advice because I respected your experience and expertise. Did you think I'd completely ignore your suggestions?"

He nodded, surprising her with his honesty. "I assumed anyone stubborn enough to work past my annoyance over the mistaken identity thing and then pretend they liked tequila enough to make themselves sick would be far too one-track minded to give up over a year of research to essentially start over."

"Yeah, well. Maybe you shouldn't judge people so fast when you meet them."

His mouth quirked up in that sexy half-smile that had her practically drooling again just like the first time she'd seen him. Good grief he was dangerous, the kind of danger that had her wishing she'd worn shorts instead of jeans. She was actually sweating now, and it couldn't be more than eighty degrees. A mild spring day around here.

"Looks like my profiling skills are even dustier than I'd realized," he said. "My apologies for making assumptions." He shifted on his feet, and she didn't miss the telltale wince as he rested both hands on the top of his cane.

"Your hip is bothering you."

"Are you playing Watson to my Sherlock now?"

"Oh heck no. I'll never be the sidekick. If anything, I'm Wonder Woman and you're Steve Trevor."

"Doesn't he die in the end?"

"Everyone dies in the end."

His grin faded. "I didn't mean to bring up bad memories again."

She shook her head. "Trust me. You didn't. They're always there, in the back of my mind. That's why I'm doing this investigation. When I escaped that day, I got out of the shack. But I didn't escape him. He's still out there. Until he's put away for good, I'll never be able to move on. Not really."

He sighed heavily. "I was worried that might be a big part of this for you. What happens if you never find him?"

Zeus whined beside her and she realized she was unconsciously tugging his leash, transmitting her agitation to him. She forced her hand to relax and rubbed his head. "That's a problem for future Teagan to worry about. Right now, I'm on the case, determined to do everything I can to bring this guy to justice. The real question is, now that we're both committed to this endeavor, do we work on it together or go our separate ways again?"

He subtly shifted, resting his back against one of the live oaks lining the path. This was the longest that she'd seen him standing without giving in to his wheelchair, and he'd been out here before she'd arrived. He had to be about ready to collapse.

"How about we discuss it over dinner?" he asked.

She blinked. "Dinner? Did I miss a signal somewhere?"

He laughed. "It's just dinner. I'm hungry, and to be honest my hip is going to give out soon if I don't sit. Rather than fall down in an embarrassing heap on the concrete, I'm inclined to head to my car then off somewhere to eat before my next appointment which isn't for—" he glanced at his watch "—another two hours. What do you say? Want me to drive you home so you can put up Zeus and then go eat with me?"

"What appointment?"

"It was too much to hope you'd let that pass." He pushed away from the tree and leaned on the cane. "I'm interviewing the Brodericks tonight, a couple who used to own one of the homes that backs up to this spot on the path. They moved shortly after everything happened, to one of the homes in the back of the subdivision, on Beautyberry Circle. Tomorrow I'm interviewing some other people who live along this path to see if they've remembered anything in the years since your attack. But also to get more of a lay of the land, try to get more of a sense of what your abductor may have been thinking back then."

She stepped toward him, not stopping until she had to crane her head back to look him in the eyes. "Don't tease me, Bryson. You're mentioning these interviews because you're offering to let me participate. Is that right? You wouldn't be cruel enough to bring them up otherwise, would you?"

He smiled sadly and feathered a hand across her cheek. The touch was so unexpected, so soft and gentle that she'd swear her heart skipped a beat. Even more of a surprise, he leaned down and pressed an equally soft kiss against her forehead before straightening. But he didn't drop his hand. Instead, he left it there, cupping her cheek, his thumb gently stroking her skin as if he didn't want to break the connection between them.

"I'm not teasing," he said, his voice a strained whisper. "And I would never deliberately be cruel to you. I shouldn't have been so harsh, so short with you in Gatlinburg. I thought I was being noble, protecting you. But I had no idea that instead of influencing you to go off in an innocuous direction where you'd be safe, you'd come back here to start over on your own. If the man who hurt you is still around here, and he realizes you're back in town trying to find him, then you're putting yourself in danger."

She frowned, ready to argue. "But I can—"

"Let me finish. While I'm not trying to send any signals…" He dropped his hand, his face reddening slightly as if he just realized that he was still touching her. He cleared his throat. "I'll admit that there's something about you, something special, that has me thinking about you far more than I should in ways I really shouldn't be thinking, not when I'm working a case. It's hell on my focus."

She blinked up at him. "You think I'm special?"

His gaze dropped to her lips. "No question." He

shuddered as if waging some kind of internal war with himself. Then he moved back a step. "The point I'm trying to make, and not doing very well, is that it would be really hard to work this case with you and to also stay objective the whole time and not get…sidetracked. But it would be even more impossible to work the case alone, knowing you were somewhere out there potentially putting yourself in danger with no one to watch your back. I'd worry about you the whole time and wouldn't get anything done. So, I guess you've won this particular battle. To be crystal clear, no misunderstandings, I'm inviting you to work with me on your case, starting with the homeowner interview this evening. But only if we agree to keep our relationship professional." His gaze dropped to her lips again. "At least until the case is over."

Her stomach jumped at his last statement. She couldn't stop smiling. But not just because she now realized he was as interested in her as she was in him. Far more important was that he was going to help her find and put away the monster who haunted her dreams at night, who cast a pall of fear over her every waking hour no matter how hard she tried to pretend that he didn't. Bryson was the answer to her prayers. And she was going to enjoy every single minute that they were together, because the man was hopelessly fun to tease. Keep their relationship strictly professional? Pfft. Not a chance. But, of course, she wasn't going to admit to that. He'd figure it out eventually and by then he'd be so hooked on her that he'd be helpless to do anything about it.

That was her hope at least.

"I'll be crystal clear in my response." She hooked her right arm around his left one as if to flirt, when really she could tell he was struggling to remain upright and was probably too proud to ask for help. "I would love to work with you, starting with dinner, and then conducting the interview tonight. But first, as you mentioned earlier, we need to drop Zeus off. Like I said, he's my mom's. I just borrow him when I visit."

They started down the path together, him leaning heavily on the cane, her holding on to his left arm to keep him from falling over, and Zeus happily sniffing and following along at the end of his leash.

When they reached his rental car, she was surprised and a little disappointed to see that he'd chosen a luxury BMW sedan. Its dark blue color and the four doors gave it a decidedly mature, boring appearance even though it was definitely a nice car. Bryson Anton was still a young guy, in spite of his teasing her for being several years younger. And he really was hot. He'd look much better sitting in a red, sporty convertible with the top down than a glorified grocery-getter. Or maybe even a jacked-up four-wheel-drive truck with a gun rack in the back, although that seemed a little too country for him. He was refined, but not upper-crust. Definitely the convertible sports-car type.

But after he insisted on holding the door open for her, then slid into the driver's seat, his deep sigh and the look of relief on his face explained why he'd chosen this car. He needed the plush seats and comfort of a vehicle that would smooth out a bumpy road because of his bad hip.

"Have you thought of getting a second opinion on your hip?" she asked. "I mean, there has to be a way to fix it so it doesn't hurt so much all the time."

"I've had second, third and fourth opinions. The bullet is lodged close to my spine and presses on a nerve that makes the hip ache. Surgery isn't an option. I'm told there's a fifty-fifty chance that it will loosen on its own one day and then be removable and I'll be good as new, or it will loosen on its own one day and nick my spinal cord, putting me permanently in a wheelchair."

She pressed a hand to her mouth. "Oh my gosh. I'm so sorry."

He shrugged. "I'm learning to live with it. Partly thanks to you. I admit to wallowing a bit in self-pity before you came along. Now, if the bullet shifts and I can't walk anymore, at least it will happen while I'm trying to do something good rather than sitting around my house all day drinking tequila." He put the car in drive but kept his foot on the brake. "Enough about me. Where to, Ms. Ray?"

"Do a U-turn, Mr. Anton."

With Zeus taking up the tiny space behind the seats and lolling half-across the console that separated them, Bryson followed her directions to her parents' home, at the end of a long pond on Birch Bark Court, and pulled into the driveway. Beautiful mature crape myrtles dotted the sides of the yard, their hot pink flowers waving in the warm spring breezes. And standing out front on the walkway between the garage and entry were both of her parents, currently in the process of planting a batch of white and pink periwinkles in one of the flower beds.

"Give me a minute to get your door," he said as he popped open the driver's door. "Please don't embarrass me by getting out first. My mother would never forgive my poor manners if you do."

She grinned and gave him a thumbs-up. Of course she didn't need him to get her door. But she didn't mind the show of chivalry and old-fashioned manners, especially since he thought that she was special and made it hard for him to focus. She couldn't help chuckling at that declaration as he leaned on his cane, obviously struggling not to limp very much as he rounded the car to her side. Behind him, her dad and mom were staring with unabashed curiosity at the gorgeous white guy who'd brought her home, no doubt wondering what was going on.

After she and Zeus got out and he closed the door behind her, she gathered the dog's leash to keep him from taking off and looped her arm around Bryson's left one again.

He arched a brow in question. "That's probably not a good idea. You might give your parents the wrong impression about our relationship." He kept his voice low even as he nodded in answer to her father's wave.

Instead of letting go, she tightened her hold. "Did I ever mention that my dad has a bad heart?"

His eyes widened as they started up the driveway toward her parents. "I'm sorry. I had no idea."

"Oh, it's under good control. But it would probably

make his heart go into palpitations if he realized that I'm investigating the killer again."

He stopped beside her. "They don't know?"

"Nope. And I aim to keep it that way. To protect Daddy." She tugged his arm to get him going again.

"Then what are you going to tell them about why I'm here?" he whispered harshly before passing his cane to his left hand so he could do the expected handshake with her father. Her mother hung a few feet back, glancing curiously between the two of them.

"I'm Nick Ray, Teagan's father. That's her mom, Sylvie."

"Nice to meet you both. I'm—"

"Bryson Anton, from Gatlinburg." Teagan flashed her best smile at her parents before dropping a bombshell. "My boyfriend."

Chapter Eleven

"Your boyfriend?" Bryson hissed almost two hours later as he was finally driving Teagan away from her parents' house. "And after telling that zinger you left me at the mercy of your very curious mom and dad while you disappeared to take a shower. I haven't had to dance that loose with the truth or change the subject so many times to avoid being pushed into a corner in, well, ever."

"But you did it. You managed to get through the inquisition and dinner while spinning the truth like a practiced politician—minus the lies. I especially liked it when my dad asked how long it had been since we'd first met and you said it felt like only yesterday." She flashed her magazine-cover smile at him.

He swore beneath his breath. "Why did you do it, Teagan? Lying by omission, or by not correcting what someone else said, is still a lie. And why trap me there for dinner when we were supposed to be there just long enough to drop off Zeus?"

Her smile faded and she looked out the window as he wove through the maze of streets toward the back of the development where the newer houses were built, where the Brodericks now lived.

They didn't want to be reminded of what had happened any more than Teagan did. It had taken quite a bit of cajoling to get them to agree to talk to him tonight. Thankfully, when he'd stepped outside of the Rays' home to make a call to ask them whether it was okay to bring Teagan, they'd said it was. He didn't want to surprise them by showing up with her. And he hadn't wanted to disappoint her either, since she was so set on going.

"Teagan?" he pressed, when she didn't answer.

She finally sighed and turned in her seat to face him. "I'm not going to apologize for doing it. Because I'd do it again if given the choice. But I do regret that I didn't warn you, and that it was so difficult for you. Honestly, I was selfishly focused on myself. I love my parents and assumed you'd enjoy their company. And my mom is a terrific cook. I hoped you would love her zucchini lasagna as much as I do and have a fun couple of hours before we—" she waved her hand toward the road as he made the last turn "—dove back into…this. I needed that break, that moment with my parents to prepare for the interview."

The sound of dejection in her voice had him feeling like a jerk. He pulled to the curb a few houses short of their destination, but left the air conditioner running to beat back the heat. He didn't know how people lived here in the summer. The humidity in March made it feel like he was stepping into a sauna every time he went outside.

"I liked your parents very much. Or, I would have, if I wasn't working so hard not to tell a bunch of lies that I'd have to apologize for later. And your mom is a fabulous cook. We couldn't have bought something at any restaurant around here and had better. But that's not the point. I'm already getting over my anger. But I deserve the truth. Why tell them I'm your boyfriend when I could have just been a friend or a friend of a friend? Now, when they ask you about me later and you tell them we broke up—or whatever your cover is going to be when I don't come back around—it will be that much harder. And it will probably make me look like a heel, thank you very much."

She clutched her hands together in her lap, and he suddenly felt like the heel he'd just described. After everything she'd been through, and the upcoming interviews about her ordeal, here he was dumping on her. Regardless of the little drama that had just played out, it was nothing compared to what she'd endured.

He placed his hand over the top of hers. She glanced at him in surprise.

"I'm sorry, Teagan. I'm making it out to be far more important than it was. Let's just drop it and—"

She shook her head. "No. I owe you an explanation. And it was far more important than you realize. Yesterday, at your house, you mentioned that your girlfriend left after your injury. Well you're not the only one. Except it was my longtime high school sweetheart. It wasn't official yet, but we'd always assumed we'd get married after we both graduated from college and got our careers going. He couldn't…he couldn't handle knowing what happened to me. Or how messed up I was for so long afterward."

He took her hand in his and entwined their fingers together. "You don't have to do this. It's okay. I understand—"

"No. You don't. Look, I'm over him. Way over him. Anyone who can't stick around through the bad isn't the one you want with you during the good. It was a blessing that I found that out before vowing to spend the rest of my life with him. The breakup was just a few months after the attack. I barely even think about him anymore. But I've never...since then I haven't... well, it's been hard to—"

"You haven't dated since?"

She squeezed her eyes shut, then nodded.

He waited in silence until she looked at him again. He tugged one hand free and gently smoothed back a recalcitrant curl that had escaped the long braid down her back. "Since someone as gorgeous and bubbly as you could have a date any time she wants, that's obviously a personal decision. But your parents don't understand your choice, do they? They worry about you because you haven't, in their eyes at least, moved on."

She blinked as if in surprise. "How did you figure all that out so fast?"

He glanced down at his shirt and frowned. "Where's my I'm a Profiler badge? I could have sworn I was wearing that today right along with my Eagle Scout badge."

She managed a weak laugh and it warmed him inside to see her smile again. "You, Bryson Anton, were never a Boy Scout."

He pressed his free hand against his chest. "You wound me to think I couldn't be a scout." He winked. "What gave me away?"

She shook her head, her smile more carefree. "You'd have been bored to tears doing all the things they make you do to earn a badge. Instead, you'd rather be out there in the thick of things, getting lost in the woods just to see if you could find your own way out. Or setting a fire to see if you could put it out. Not exactly good scouts material."

"Looks like I'm not the only profiler around here." He squeezed her hand before letting it go. "If using me helps to make your parents worry less about you because they think you have a boyfriend, then I suppose the subterfuge is okay. Just give me some warning before you throw me in a fire next time, okay?"

He barely had time to blink before she was straddling the console, one thigh plastered against him, her generous breasts flattened against his chest. All his logical, well-thought-out arguments about not getting involved with her, especially while working the case, were incinerated the second her lips touched his.

So much for warning him before throwing him into another fire.

His whole body was being scorched from the outside in, her tongue doing amazing things with his, her long nails raising goose bumps of pleasure across the back of his neck. But he wanted more, so much more. He groaned deep in his throat and wrapped his arms around her sensuous body. Then he half turned, pulling her the rest of the way onto his lap. He kissed her the way he'd wanted to since the moment she'd stood in his doorway looking so adorable as she breathed the word "Hi." If the pain from his hip hadn't stopped him that day, he'd probably have done something juvenile, like drool. Instead, he'd focused on the pain to keep from acting like a letch.

Teagan was unlike any woman he'd ever met. He never knew what to expect from her. Half of him was annoyed that he couldn't predict her reactions even with his years of training as a profiler. The other half of him was sliding his hands around to the front of her shorts, grasping her zipper. Realizing what he was about to do, he drew on deep reserves of strength and forced his hands to release her zipper. Instead, he gently grasped her shoulders and eased her back to straddling the console instead of him. His lungs labored in his chest as they blinked at each other from only a foot apart. And he couldn't help but be pleased that she seemed to be struggling for air just as much as him.

"Holy smokes," she whispered, her voice breaking. She cleared her throat, her hands shaking as she reached up to check her hair. "Lennie what's-his-face was junior high compared to you. Heck, elementary school. That was *amazing*. I can't even remember what he looks like anymore. And we were an item for over eight years."

He grinned, his ego ridiculously inflated by her compliment. "Wait. Lennie? Your old boyfriend's name was *Lennie*?"

"No judging. People don't choose their own names." Her tongue flicked out to wet her lips, making him groan. "Kiss me again, Bryson. Before I start remembering what what's-his-face looked like."

He grabbed her upper arms and gently but firmly pushed her back. "Hell, no. We need to talk about this… thing going on between us before it goes any further. Besides, another kiss like that and I won't be able to walk for a week." He grimaced and shifted in his seat. "As it is, I won't be able to walk for a few minutes, at least."

Her gaze flew to his lap and her eyes widened. "Oh, mercy. Lennie *really* had nothing on you."

He laughed and pushed her farther away. "I'm starting to feel sorry for this Lennie guy."

Her lips firmed. "Don't. Trust me. He doesn't deserve your sympathy." She settled back down on her side of the car and drew a ragged breath.

Seeing her mood change so quickly, as if swimming through a layer of dark memories, had an ice water effect on his traitorous body—which was a good thing right now. But it also had him wanting to punch her ex-boyfriend for the hurt he'd obviously caused her.

"I've got a few friends at the Jacksonville Sheriff's Office," he said. "Where's Lennie live? I bet I could rack him up enough speeding tickets so he'd be riding the bus to work for the next six months."

Her mouth quirked in a reluctant smile. "Mercedes-Lennie on the city bus. Now that might be fun to watch."

"Just say the word."

She laughed, then pointed to the digital clock on his dash. "Didn't you say the interview was supposed to start about now?"

He noted the time and grimaced. "Hopefully a couple of minutes won't make them change their minds. You sure you want to do this? You can drop me off and pick me up when I call."

"I've never wanted something this hard in my life. I've been in limbo for years. If you can help me end that, put this monster in prison once and for all, it will make all the difference. I can handle it. I promise."

He wasn't nearly as optimistic as she seemed to be. But he wasn't going to argue with her. If she wanted to be a part of this, as far as he was concerned, she had every right to be. Because it was her life and all about making her feel safe again.

"It's that gray-blue stucco over there, two houses down. Close enough to walk but with my hip, I'm going to be lazy and drive the last fifty yards." Once they were parked in the driveway, he grabbed his briefcase from the floorboard behind her seat.

Unlike at her parents' home, she didn't wait for him to open the door. He silently cursed his hip for slowing him down. But there was no way he could go even one more step without his cane. He hefted it from the back seat and limped after her, pain his constant companion.

He'd pushed himself harder today than any day since he'd been shot. And it showed. His hip was so stiff and ached so much that he was running more on willpower than physical strength. And after that little stunt that he and Teagan had just pulled in his car, he was practically a cripple. But he'd grit his teeth and keep going, somehow. At least until this interview was over. And the moment he reached his hotel room he was going to collapse on his bed, down some painkillers and not move until morning.

At the door, he rang the doorbell then started when Teagan clutched his right arm.

"Teagan—"

"Don't fuss at me. I'm not flirting, Bryson. Just give me a second."

He noted the stress lines around her eyes, the ashen gray tint to her brown skin. He wanted to take her hand in his, offer his strength. But he didn't have any to spare. If he let go of his cane he was afraid he'd fall down. All those times he'd blown off a rehab appointment were really coming back to bite him.

"It's okay, you've got this." He offered a reassuring smile. "*We've* got this. We're a team, together. I'm here for you, all right? Trust me."

She blew out a shaky breath and nodded just as the door opened.

A woman stood there, looking even more stressed than Teagan, her face so pale it was shockingly white in the dimly lit foyer.

Bryson lamely nodded rather than hold out his right hand since it was currently clutching his cane so he could remain upright. "Mrs. Broderick, it's nice to meet you in person. I'm Bryson Anton. This is Teagan Ray. Is this still a good time to speak with you and your husband about Teagan's abduction two years ago?"

"Of course." Her gaze darted from one to the other, then behind them before she stepped back. "We've been expecting you. Please, come in." Without waiting, she turned and strode through the long, dimly lit foyer away from them.

Bryson hesitated. "It seems as if this impending interview is far more upsetting to Mrs. Broderick than I'd expected. Maybe you should wait in the car."

"No way. I don't want to blow my chance. If I can't handle the emotions of this first interview, you won't let me go to the ones tomorrow. I'll be okay. You'll make sure of it. We're a team. That's what you said. Right?"

He regretted agreeing to take her with him for so many reasons. But they couldn't stand here waiting and make the Brodericks think they'd changed their minds. He motioned for her to step inside. She gave him a tight smile, and they started down the foyer together.

Mr. Broderick's deep voice sounded from the family room that was just visible through the arched opening a few feet away.

Teagan gasped and stopped.

He turned to see what was wrong. Her eyes were opened wide, a hand pressed to her mouth. She looked absolutely terrified.

"Teagan? What's wrong?"

"That v-voice," she croaked, obviously struggling to push any sounds out. "*His* voice."

Bryson swore as understanding dawned. He dropped his cane and clawed for the pistol holstered at his waist as he struggled to turn around without falling. White, hot pain exploded in his head and his hip crumpled beneath him. Teagan's scream was the last thing he heard as everything went dark.

Chapter Twelve

Teagan stood frozen, the horror of what was happening—again—seeping into her bones like leaden concrete, anchoring her in place. Her pulse hammered in her ears, blocking out the sounds around her. It was as if her mind had separated from her body and all of this was happening to someone else.

Bryson. Sweet, wonderful Bryson lay dead at her feet, his dark hair matted with blood. She'd only caught a glimpse of his battered body before jerking her gaze up toward the man who'd hit him, fully expecting the next blow from the baseball bat to land on her. Even so, she couldn't raise her arms to defend herself. She. Couldn't. Move.

Instead of hitting her, he'd taken Bryson's pistol out of his holster, then shoved his hand in her pocket and yanked out her gun too, all before she could even blink. How had he known she had the gun when even she, in her moment of need, had forgotten it?

He'd been just inches from her but after taking the guns, he'd walked away. She watched helplessly, uselessly still as a statue, as the man—oh God, *that voice*—crossed the family room to the woman cowering in the corner. What was her name? Broderick. Mrs. Broderick. A trap. She'd led Bryson and Teagan into a trap. Why? Why would she do that?

The woman's lips moved. She was looking up at the man, hovering over her with the bloody baseball bat in his right hand. She was saying something, pleading? The words were lost in Teagan's fractured mind, unable to penetrate the sound of her own heartbeat rushing in her ears. *Thump. Thump. Thump.* Her heart pounded against her rib cage, white noise that masked everything around her. The tableau played out like a silent movie before her, a nightmare. Because surely none of this was real. It couldn't be.

Not again. Not again. She couldn't survive this again.

The man lifted the bat.

No. Teagan tried to yell, to get her legs to move. She had to help the lady. But her throat was so tight she couldn't make a sound. Her legs were shaking so hard she couldn't take a step.

He brought the bat down in a deadly arc.

Bam! Bam! Bam!

Oh dear God, please, no! The bat. The woman. Bile rose in Teagan's throat. A low-keening moan filled her ears, and the man jerked around to look at her. She realized that she was the one making that awful sound.

The room around her darkened, like a tunnel, narrowing down to one point where all she could see was the man across the room, watching her. Everything centered on what she'd never seen until this very moment.

His face. She'd known that voice, the devil's voice. To this day, it haunted her dreams. But that face. How could such evil hide behind such an average, kind-looking face?

There was nothing remarkable about it. He was white, clean-shaven, his light brown hair streaked with blond that had no doubt cost a fortune at some expensive salon. Which meant this man had money, a job, likely a home, a car. A family? He was just like anyone else she'd pass on the street.

Except that he wasn't.

The eyes. The eyes gave him away. They were dark, almost black, completely devoid of warmth. An abyss of emptiness, a deep well of evil with no soul to warm them. They were the eyes of the monster who'd hurt her two years ago. The same monster who'd just brutally killed Mrs. Broderick. And the wonderful man lying at Teagan's feet.

She couldn't look down. Couldn't stomach seeing the damage the bat must have done. She didn't want that image burned into her retinas. Bryson. Smart, gorgeous, sweet Bryson Anton, who wouldn't even be here if it wasn't for her.

Forgive me, Bryson.

Evil stared back at her from twenty feet away. Blood dripped from the bat in his hand. She shuddered as a wave of nausea gripped her.

He smiled, as if pleased at her distress. Then he started toward her, still holding that awful bat. Slowly. Like a lion stalking the weakest member of the herd, separating it out, readying for the kill.

Her mind screamed at her. *Move. Run. Do something.*

But she couldn't. Why not? She'd run before. Two years ago, when her attacker injected drugs to put her to sleep, but missed the vein, she'd taken advantage of his mistake. She'd pretended to be asleep. And then, after hearing the sound of his car driving away, she'd forced one foot in front of the other. She'd gotten away.

There were neighbors close by. Some of them had to be home. Most of them had to be home. The work-day was over for the nine-to-fivers. All she had to do was turn around and...no.

She couldn't leave Bryson.

She didn't deserve to survive yet again when he lay at her feet in his own blood. It was her fault. This, then, would be her penance. Face the monster. Pay the price for bringing Bryson here, for destroying a wonderful man.

Shoes echoed against the floor. Hardwood. Like her parents' house. He was coming closer. Relentlessly. Slowly. Savoring her fear.

She whimpered, and hated herself for it. She was about to die. She wanted to face him with dignity in her last moments. But the wounds of the past were too much to overcome. Her body wasn't her own anymore to command. She couldn't stop shaking. Maybe she was already dead.

Evil stopped three feet away.

She forced herself to meet his gaze, to memorize every line, every bump, every angle of his ridiculously ordinary face, refusing to look away as fate raised the bat once more. If she couldn't run, at least she could

stand here and pretend courage she didn't possess.
There would be no defensive wounds for her. But as
she stared at him, a strange sense of déjà vu swept
through her. She'd seen him before. Not at the shack.
He'd always concealed his identity back then. So she
had to have seen him somewhere else. But where? Who
was he?

He raised the bat higher, watching her, as if waiting
to see what she would do. As she remained motionless,
his smile faded. She wasn't giving him the satisfaction
of cowering. She was ruining his fun.

Hooray for her. Finally she'd beaten him. If only in
a very small way. This time it was her turn to smile.

Hate glittered in his eyes as he slowly lowered the
bat. He tossed it onto a nearby chair and reached behind
him. Metal glittered in the overhead lights. A gun? No.
Silver circles. A short chain connecting them. Handcuffs. He'd bound her last time, tied her with strips of
cloth. But never handcuffs. She'd cut through the strips
with her teeth after the drug had failed to knock her
unconscious. Perhaps he'd changed his routine since
then. He'd learned from his mistakes.

He moved with a swiftness that was terrifying. Too
late, she tried to twist away. But the sound of one of the
cuffs ratcheting onto her left wrist echoed in the foyer.
He yanked her wrist down toward the floor. She fell
to her knees, sliding in the sticky wet blood. Bryson's
blood.

Dear, sweet Bryson. Lying on the floor, his face
turned toward her. Eyes closed forever.

His murderer slapped the other handcuff onto

Bryson's right wrist and ratcheted it closed, anchoring her to his body. She looked up in question. He'd retrieved the bat, but instead of slamming it down on her, ending this, he turned away. His shoes clomped across the floor as he headed down the hall to the left. Dress pants. He was wearing gray dress pants and a white shirt. A formerly white shirt. Had he just left work? What kind of person did this—entered someone's house and beat them to death after getting off work, like it was a normal part of their day?

A hysterical laugh bubbled up in her throat, but died before reaching her lips. The monster had opened a door and headed inside. A muffled sound echoed from the room. Was someone else there? The sickening unmistakable crunch of wood on bone had her gasping in horror. The other half of the couple who lived here, Mr. Broderick. He must have been in the room, probably tied up. A bribe so that his wife would do what the monster told her to do.

Bile rose again in her throat. She turned away from Bryson's body just in time to empty the contents of her stomach against the foyer wall. She shuddered and wiped her mouth.

"Dear Lord," she prayed, the whisper finally passing through her tight throat. "Please let me die quickly. And don't let me grovel or beg for my life. Give me strength. Please, God. Help me."

Something fluttered against her shoe.

She gasped and whirled around. The fingers of Bryson's right hand moved against her, tapped her toe.

She shot him a look of shock, and met his pain-filled startling blue gaze.

"Bryson," she whispered. "You're alive. Oh my God. Bryson." She lifted her shaking right hand to his face and gently cupped it. "I'm so sorry. Please forgive me."

His eyes seemed unfocused. He coughed and blood dribbled out of his mouth to the floor.

"Shhh," she whispered. "Don't try to talk." She jerked her head up, realizing there weren't any sounds in the other room anymore. He'd be coming out soon. Coming for her and Bryson. "Close your eyes," she whispered. "Play dead. He thinks you're dead. Just, no matter what happens to me, just lay there. Don't move. Do you hear me? Play dead. It's your only chance."

His fingers tapped her again and his lips moved.

She glanced down the hall, then leaned down, trying to hear what he was saying.

"Run. Get. Away." His whisper was so low she could barely make it out. "Go."

Tears splashed onto his face and she realized she was crying. "Oh, Bryson. I'm sorry. I thought you were… I thought it was too late. And I couldn't make myself leave you. And now, I can't." She lifted her left hand, showing him the handcuffs that bound them together. "It's okay, though," she whispered, looking down the hall again. What was taking the monster so long? What was he doing in there? "It's okay," she repeated. "There's nothing I can do to save myself. I accept that. But he thinks you're already dead. Lie very still. No matter what. You'll make it. Just play dead."

His lips moved again, his eyes pleading with her to listen. "Cane. Get. Cane."

"You think you can stand?" A rush of hope flooded through her. "Here. I'll help you."

"Cane," his hoarse whisper was louder now. "Get the cane."

She stretched out their linked hands and scrambled over, reaching out her right hand as far as she could. It took some contorting, but she was finally able to grab it. "Got it."

"I'll take that." The monster jerked it out of her hand and backed up several feet. "Getting feisty, Teagan? Planning on trying to beat me over the head with this like I did your friend?" He chuckled and motioned toward Bryson. "Give me his cell phone. And yours. Hurry."

"Mine is in my purse." She motioned toward her purse where it had fallen to the foyer floor earlier.

"Prove it. Turn your shorts pockets inside out."

She did as he asked.

"Now his. Get his cell phone and toss it to me so I can verify that you don't do something stupid, like try to press 911 before you give it to me. If you do that, you're both dead. Understood?"

She drew a ragged breath and nodded, then dug in Bryson's suit jacket pockets until she found his phone. For the briefest second, she hesitated, desperately wanting to press the three precious keys that would call for help. But the monster was watching. And he'd shifted the aim of his gun toward Bryson's head as if in warning. She hurriedly stood as best she could with her arm cuffed to Bryson and tossed him the phone.

After checking the screen, he threw the phone on the couch, then motioned toward Bryson again. "Take that watch thing off his wrist and get rid of it. I don't know what it can do, whether you can make calls with it. I'm not taking chances."

She quickly took it off and tossed it down the foyer.

"Help him up. We'll bring him with us. I need to know how much he knows before I kill him."

She hesitated. "He's already dead. Just uncuff me and I'll go with you."

He made a clucking, disapproving sound with his mouth. "Now, Teagan. Don't lie to me. I doubt I hit him hard enough to kill him. But if you'd rather I take care of things right now, to make it easier for you so you don't have to help him walk, I can get the bat—"

"No!" She shook her head. "Please. Don't. Just… give me the cane. I'll help him. But I need the cane to get him on his feet, to help him walk."

He tossed the cane down beside her. "I'd help but I don't want to get his blood on my nice clean shirt."

She blinked and realized he was wearing a different shirt now, a light blue one tucked into navy blue dress pants. Even his shoes, which had been black earlier had been exchanged for gunmetal gray ones. He must have washed himself off and changed into some of Mr. Broderick's clothes. Right after killing the poor man.

Swallowing hard, she looked down. Bryson's eyes were open again. He was staring at her.

I'm so sorry, she mouthed, regret heavy in her heart

that she'd wasted her chance to get help for him. Had she suspected he was still alive, she would have forced herself to turn around, to run to the nearest neighbor and call 911. Instead, she'd been frozen by fear and the belief that he'd been killed. She'd given up. And because of her cowardly actions, now he was still in horrible danger, when she might have been able to save him.

"Get him on his feet. Now. If you take too long, I'll shoot you both and be done with it."

She wanted to demand that he be done with it right now. But that was no longer an option. It wasn't just her life on the line now. She had to be brave, strong, and somehow figure out how to get Bryson out of this mess. She awkwardly straightened his legs, apologizing profusely every time she jostled him because of their hands being handcuffed together.

Finally she got him into a sitting position with his back pressed against the opposite wall of the foyer from where she'd been sick. White lines around his mouth clearly mirrored his pain. His hip had to be excruciating right now, on top of the awful bump on his head. She reached up to test it and he winced, ducking away from her hand.

"You're not bleeding anymore," she whispered. "That's a good sign."

"Hurry up," the monster ordered. "The daughter will be home soon."

Teagan and Bryson exchanged a look of horror. The idea of a daughter coming home to find her parents slaughtered by this man was beyond awful. But still being here when she got home would ensure that she too would be killed. As if coming to the same realization, Bryson began pushing against the wall, struggling to get to his feet.

She faced him, their hands clasped together as she helped him up the rest of the way. As soon as she was sure he wasn't about to fall, she got the cane and put it in his left hand. He normally held it in his right, to compensate for his bad left hip when he raised his right leg. But with his right hand cuffed to hers, that wasn't an option. It would be rough going. She hoped she had the strength to keep him from falling.

"Come on. Out the back." The monster was holding a gun now. Bryson's gun. He motioned with it and stepped out of reach of the cane or a well-aimed kick, not that they could manage either one shackled together with Bryson hurt.

More from willpower than physical strength, the two of them managed to hobble out the open French door, across the patio, all while being directed by the gunman. He closed the door behind them, probably to throw off anyone trying to find the perpetrator who'd murdered the Brodericks. But where was he going? He stopped at the six-foot-tall wooden privacy fence that encircled the large backyard.

He motioned them forward with the gun. When they stopped a few feet away, he lifted one of the sections of fence back from the post it should have been nailed to. Perhaps this was the way he'd gotten into the Brodericks' home? He'd come from behind them, loosening the section of fence to act much like a gate.

Just the way he'd abducted Teagan years earlier?

Until this very moment, she'd never remembered how he'd managed to get her off the path without anyone seeing her. It had always been a confusing image in her mind—a creaking sound that she'd attributed to the breezes in the branches overhead, but that she now realized must have been him opening a pre-loosened section of fence; her turning around just as the bite of a needle plunged into her neck and a hand clamped over her mouth. Darkness descending around the edges of her vision as he'd tossed her over his shoulder. That creaking sound again. He'd closed the fence behind them. That must have been what happened.

"Teagan?" Bryson whispered, between lips white with pain. "We have to move."

The gunman was pointing the pistol at her. He must have told her to get going and was threatening to shoot her. She squeezed Bryson's hand, then struggled forward with him leaning heavily against her, their cuffed hands clutched tightly together.

The gunman waved them toward the back of the house whose yard they were now in while he secured the section of fence behind them. As they reached the screened-in porch, the cut screen on the door told the story that she had feared. She exchanged a look of misery with Bryson before helping him through the door that the killer had obviously gone through earlier.

But how had he known that she would be at the Brodericks'?

That question was eating at her. And she had no answers. She wanted to ask Bryson, but doubted he could think much beyond the pain that was clearly radiating through his whole body. It was taking everything he had to remain upright, as evidenced by how hard he was leaning on her and how often he stumbled. It didn't help that the house was carpeted. It was much harder for him to keep his balance, and he fell against the wall more than once.

"To the garage, that door over there." The gunman motioned ahead to the right, then ducked through an archway to their left into the kitchen.

"Where are we?" Bryson whispered as they hobbled toward the garage.

"Bentwater Place," she whispered back. "The subdivision directly behind The Woods. The entrance to this subdivision is about a mile, maybe more, from the Hodges Boulevard entrance to The Woods."

He nodded as they reached the door that led from the house into the garage. It was standing wide open, revealing a small package delivery truck inside. Any hope that Teagan had that he hadn't hurt the driver died when she saw the piles of packages taking up most of the space on the other side of the garage. No driver would have willingly allowed someone to dump the contents of his truck. How many people had to be hurt or die because of whatever sick fantasies this guy had?

"Find the button that opens the garage door," Bryson urged. "If someone's outside, we can try to get their attention."

"Do it and I'll shoot both of you," the killer said from behind them.

Teagan stiffened and looked over her shoulder. His

dark, empty eyes bored into hers. The maw of the pistol was pointed directly at the back of Bryson's head.

"What do you want us to do now?" She steadied Bryson's shaking body against the garage wall beside the doorway. He was so pale she was afraid he was about to pass out.

"Get in the back of the truck." The sound of sirens filled the air, coming from somewhere behind them. The killer froze, cocking his head to listen. The sirens got louder. There could be no mistake. They were racing toward the Broderick's' house. The daughter must have gotten home and called 911. And the police had to have been close by to be responding this quickly. Any minute now, they'd be standing in the home that was separated from this one by about fifty feet of grass and a privacy fence.

If she screamed, would they hear her?

As if reading the intention in her expression, the killer shoved the gun's muzzle against the back of Bryson's head. "In the truck. Now. If you scream, if you do anything to alert the police, I'll shoot both of you, him first. Then I'll find another family a few houses down to kill and drive away in their car as the police try to figure out where the shots came from. You'll be dead, another family will be dead, but I'll be just fine. Is that what you want? Me to kill your boyfriend and another innocent family, all because you refuse to follow instructions?"

"We're going." She forced the words out between clenched teeth.

Bryson looked like he wanted to argue. But he was

in no physical condition to do so. They hobbled to the end of the truck. The gunman twisted the handles and yanked open both of the doors. Just as expected, it was empty. No windows. No pass-through to the cab. Just a metal box, with no way out but the back doors. Which required getting past their armed escort.

It took some grunting and contorting because of how their hands were cuffed together to get both of them into the back. As soon as their feet cleared the doors, one of them slammed shut.

The gunman paused in the opening of the other door. "I'll take that cane for now. Don't want you trying to poke me with it when I open the door again." He yanked the cane away from Bryson and sealed them inside.

Chapter Thirteen

"He didn't blindfold us," Teagan said.

Bryson hated the fear in her tone. He knew exactly what she was afraid of, that because the man who'd abducted them hadn't blindfolded them, it meant he intended to kill them. He wasn't worried about witnesses, or that they could identify him later. But reassuring her right now was beyond Bryson's abilities. He was struggling just to stay conscious. That blow to his head had really done a number on him.

The darkness in the back of the truck was absolute, which was disorienting enough. But his aching hip and throbbing head were each trying to outdo the other in the pain department, which made his efforts to wrangle his scattered thoughts next to impossible.

"Bryson?" She moved her left hand against his right one and interlaced their fingers. "How bad does it hurt? Your head?"

He gently squeezed her fingers. "Don't worry about me. I'm fine."

"Maybe if you said that without pain making your voice so raspy I'd believe you." She clasped her right hand over their joined hands. "I'm so sorry. None of this would have happened if it wasn't for me involving you. I never should have gone to Gatlinburg and interfered with your life. That was beyond selfish. And now, we're both going to die—"

"Hey, hey. Stop that. You didn't do anything wrong. I'm the professional. I should have been on guard against this type of possibility. But what matters right now is that you don't give up. You hear me, Teagan Ray? Don't you dare give up." He waited, but when she didn't respond he said, "If you're nodding or shaking that beautiful head of yours, or making some kind of rude gesture, your effort's wasted. I completely forgot to pack my night-vision goggles this trip."

A brief laugh reassured him like nothing else could have. He needed her present, engaged, not frozen and helpless the way he'd seen her in the foyer after he'd finally managed to swim through the darkness that had threatened to drag him under. He wasn't sure how long he'd lain there after that awful slam of the bat against his head. He hadn't even seen the bat until later, when they were leaving, lying on one of the chairs. It had shocked him that he was still alive with the amount of blood covering the bat.

Then he'd seen Mrs. Broderick.

She'd been curled in a lifeless heap on the other side of the room. He knew then that not all of the blood on the bat was his. The poor woman had been brutally attacked. Even though it didn't feel like it, he was lucky to be alive. For now.

"Aren't you going to say I told you so?" she asked, interrupting his thoughts.

He had to draw several deep breaths to push back the hazy fog that kept trying to drag him into unconsciousness. What had she said? Something about I told you so. "What are you talking about?"

"Avarice Lowe. I'd pegged him all along as the man who'd abducted me. But I was wrong. It's this man. Whoever's driving this stupid truck. The thing is, Lowe never seemed to fit the image of the monster in my head. I know it sounds wonky. But I always thought I'd know my abductor if I ever saw him, by the way he was built, his profile, something. Nothing ever clicked for me when I saw Lowe's pictures. And, to be honest, nothing clicked when I saw this guy today. Not really. I mean, his voice, yes. Definitely. And yet, even though he seems familiar, he doesn't seem…right. It's still not clicking." He could feel her shoulders move against him as she shrugged. "Listen to me. I'm not even making sense."

"Always…trust your instincts." He swallowed hard against the bile rising in his throat. Obviously he had a concussion. All he wanted to do was lie down and sleep. Or throw up. Or both. He cleared his throat and tried again to follow the conversation. "Instincts. They're telling you something. What did you mean when you said he seemed familiar?"

"His face."

"His face?"

"It just seemed…familiar. He's the kind of guy you could pass on the street a bazillion times and you might think, okay, he's kind of good-looking. Clean-cut. But nothing amazing. Just a typical, white-collar kind of man, you know? And yet, I would swear that I've seen him before. Not just once. Several times."

He rubbed his left temple, desperately trying to beat back the throbbing pain and focus on what she was saying. There was something important here, more important than her thinking she'd seen him before. But he couldn't seem to grasp what was bothering him about what she'd just said. Finally he dropped his hand to his side, giving up for now. Whatever was bothering him would come to him, eventually.

"Maybe he lives in The Woods," he offered. "You've passed him on the street, on the sidewalk. Or saw him at that amenity center. Do you ever use the tennis courts, the pool?"

"The pool sometimes. But I haven't in a long time. Not since, well, I never was a fan of a one-piece bathing suit. Too grandma for me. But I don't think wearing a bikini is exactly a good idea now."

He wanted to reassure her, tell her that no one would notice the X that had been cut into her skin. But people could be cruel. Some probably would stare. Others might ask a question, innocently thinking she'd had that X carved there on purpose, like a tattoo. They might wonder at the symbolism and significance, without realizing they were bringing up a horrific memory that she'd rather forget.

He'd just started to doze off again when she asked, "What are we going to do?" Her voice was a low whisper, as if to keep the driver from hearing them. "Please tell me you have a plan."

He didn't have a clue. He tightened his hold on her hand. "We'll figure it out. Together. Two against one. We've got this."

The truck hit a bump in the road, knocking them against each other. He scooted back against the wall, trying to keep from slamming into her. But she had no such compulsion. She moved closer, her body plastered against his side. But unlike earlier, there was nothing suggestive about her actions. He could feel the slight shaking of her shoulders and realized she was silently crying. Carefully, so he wouldn't hit her face, he maneuvered their handcuffed hands so that he could put his arm around her, pulling their linked hands tight against her belly. She cradled her head against his neck.

He tried to pay attention to the changes in road noise, traffic sounds, the turns the truck made. But everything was so muffled that he had no clue where they might be. Had it been an hour? Two? He had no idea. With his watch gone, and his mind a fog, time as he knew it didn't exist anymore. His every moment was measured by stabs of pain that shot through his body with every beat of his heart. His hip had long ago gone numb. But, if anything, the pain in his head was worse than before. He felt every shift of the truck's wheels on the pavement, every pothole, every slide of gravel.

Wait. Gravel?

"We're slowing down," she whispered.

He nodded, then remembered she couldn't see him. "Yes. We are. And we've turned onto a gravel road.

Wherever he's taking us, we're close." He carefully pulled their linked arms over her head so they were side by side again, instead of nestled against each other.

The brakes squealed as the truck lurched to a halt.

Her fingers clenched his. "Now would be a good time to share your plan."

Right. If only he had one. His thoughts were so jumbled. "Stay alert. Be observant. As soon as that door opens, evaluate your options and react. If he's stupid enough to stand in striking distance, we tackle him. But I don't expect he'll do that."

"So we have no plan."

He sighed. "Pretty much. But that doesn't mean there's no hope. All it takes is one mistake on his part, one moment when his guard is down. Then we'll get the upper hand."

"Do you really believe that?"

"I have to. We both have to. I'm not operating on all pistons right now, and my vision was blurry at the Brodericks' house so I'm not expecting much better when he lets us out of here. I need you to fill in the gaps. Pay attention when he opens that door. Get a three-sixty view. We need to know what's around us. Where to run if we get a chance."

"Okay. I'll… I'll do my best."

The driver's door creaked open.

"Come on," he urged. "Let's scoot to the end in case we can surprise him, take him down."

Getting to his knees was beyond his capabilities at the moment. Instead, he had to scoot across the metal floor of the truck. Thankfully, it wasn't that large and they were soon positioned beside each other at the doors.

The sound of shoes crunching on gravel came from outside. He was heading toward the back.

Bryson could feel her shivering against him. He silently cursed the man with all the power right now, the man who'd hurt her more than most people endured in their entire lifetime.

He gritted his teeth and braced himself, hoping she was ready to dive with him to tackle the man. There was no other option since they were still handcuffed together.

The left door flew back. Bryson hadn't planned on near total darkness and hesitated for a moment. But Teagan was already hopping out of the truck. He hurriedly followed and together they rushed forward, hoping to wrap arms around their attacker. They both met empty air and stumbled against each other before falling back against the closed right door. It was the only reason Bryson managed to remain upright.

Laughter sounded off to the left. A powerful flashlight switched on, forcing them to squint and shield their eyes against the brightness.

"Good try." The man chuckled again. "But I assumed you'd pull a stunt like that so I stayed behind the door, out of reach." He lowered the light to point at the ground, directly in front of them. Dirt and gravel mixed with pine needles and other debris. Since the only sounds were insects buzzing close by, it was a safe bet that they were somewhere outside of town, an hour, two, maybe more from Jacksonville if his judgment on how much time had passed was accurate. But he couldn't be sure. Their captor may have driven in circles to disorient them and then drove to some rural part of town. Jacksonville was the largest city in the country by landmass, so they could easily still be in Duval County but nowhere near any homes or businesses.

Teagan's fingers curled around his. Perhaps she was beginning to realize how isolated they were, and wondering the same thing that he was—what happens next?

Without the flashlight in his eyes, he was able to make out more details now. The moon and stars provided enough light to see that they were surrounded by trees and Florida scrub, mostly small thin bushes and sharp palmettos ready to skewer anyone foolish enough to go for a walk in the woods.

The gunman stood about twenty feet away, out of reach, a dark silhouette with his arm extended, pistol gleaming in his grip. "Get moving." He motioned with the flashlight to their right, aiming it at what was apparently their destination, a tiny cabin.

"I need my cane," Bryson called out.

The flashlight swept back toward their captor. He aimed it up toward his own face, a slow smile spreading across his cheeks as he pulled something out of his pocket. "Let me guess. Because you wanted these?" He shook the two tiny keys on the end of a chain, making them click against each other. "Handcuff keys hidden in the cane's handle. I knew you were awfully insistent on wanting that stupid thing. Took me half the trip fiddling with it to figure it out."

He threw the keys into the trees, then leaned down and grabbed the cane, which had been lying at his feet. "Afraid you'll have to do without it. I'm not risking another trick in that thing that I haven't figured out yet." He tossed the cane into the woods behind him. "Now go on." He swept the flashlight in an arc toward the cabin again. "Teagan, stop standing there like a statue and help your boyfriend before he falls down." He chuckled.

Bryson looked at her. She hadn't moved since they'd tried tackling the gunman without success. Her fingers holding his were cold, stiff. Her body shook as she stared wide-eyed at the little house in the clearing. And then it dawned on him why. He'd seen it before, in crime scene photos.

The killer had brought them back in time, two years to be exact. He'd brought them to the infamous shack where he'd once held Teagan captive.

Chapter Fourteen

The world had disappeared for Teagan. Everything had faded away the moment she'd jumped out of the truck and the flashlight revealed what she should have expected, but hadn't allowed herself to believe. He'd taken her back to the dilapidated shack where she'd spent two weeks in a drug-induced stupor, drifting in a haze of pain from the torture that her captor had put her through.

She pressed a hand to her belly, remembering that first night, when he'd slowly carved the X in her flesh. The pain had been excruciating. With her arms and legs tied and him straddling her, there was nothing she could do to escape the slow awful burn of the blade. She'd screamed so loudly that something in her throat burst and she'd almost drowned in her own blood.

After escaping this hellhole, she'd charted a new path for her life. She'd focused her energies on becoming stronger, both physically and mentally. When the police seemed to be getting nowhere with the investigation, she'd taken it over herself, doing everything she could to try to discover the identity of the man who'd reduced her to the broken woman she'd become for those fourteen days. And she'd thought she had. She'd been so sure that Avarice Lowe was the real Ripper, the man who'd branded her like a steer. The fact that no one else believed her didn't dissuade her. Instead, it made her angry, and even more determined to find someone who'd help her put Lowe away. She'd thought Bryson was that someone, the one person who would read her file and finally tell her that she was right.

But she wasn't right. Bryson was right, had been all along.

It was as if everything she'd done for the past twenty-four months and nineteen days was a sham, a waste, a farce. Here she was again, where it had all started. And she'd managed to condemn Bryson to share this hell with her. This time, both of them would die.

"Sweetheart, look at me," Bryson's whispered words seemed to come to her from the end of a long tunnel. "Come back to me. Don't give up. Don't let him win."

She couldn't see him, couldn't see anyone, or anything. Not the dark shapes of the trees, or the twinkling lights of the stars, or the moon, or even the gravel rocks at her feet. The devil himself, the one who'd brought them here, had faded too. All she saw was the little shack.

Hovel was more accurate.

Four walls covered in weathered gray wood that was splintered and warped. No electricity, which meant no air-conditioning, unless that had been changed. The inside consisted of a small bedroom and bathroom on the back left corner, a tiny main room and a kitchen up front. Although calling the cooking area a kitchen was being generous. It consisted of a handful of homemade-looking cabinets and drawers, a tiny refrigerator like those in hotel rooms and a compact gas stove fed by a propane tank outside. The bathroom, as she remembered it, was so filthy she'd had to close her eyes when he'd shoved her inside and stood guard at the open door, watching. Always watching. Or touching, hurting her in unspeakable ways.

Dear Lord, please, let me die. Strike me with lightning, something, just don't let him...touch me...not again. Please.

"Teagan, look at me. Open your eyes." Bryson's gentle but firm voice cut through her terror, snapped her out of her semi-stupor.

She openly stared up at him. The moon's light wasn't enough to see the blue of his eyes, but she remembered their beautiful color, and the kindness in them. She remembered how ruggedly handsome he was. He was so sweet and smart and...*and he was going to die.*

A low keening moan slipped out between her clenched teeth. Her hands shook as she started to lift them. But her left hand pulled up short because of the cuffs. He bent his arm to allow her more movement, frowning, apparently wondering what she was doing, but helping her. Always helping her. She lifted her arms again and this time she was able to cup his face.

"We have to kill him," she whispered. "Before he makes us go into that horrible shack. He won't shoot me, not right away. That would spoil his fun. We'll refuse to go inside and he'll have to come close. As long as you duck down in front of me, I can shield you—"

"The hell with that." His clipped tone brooked no argument. "I'm not using you as a human shield." He grabbed her left hand and pulled it down with his, their handcuffs rattling against each other. "I don't have a plan yet but putting you in the line of fire isn't at the top of my list. It's not even *on* the list. Forget it."

"Hey, you two. Get moving." *Bam!*

The warning shot kicked up dirt near their feet. Teagan threw herself against Bryson's chest, desperately trying to shield his body with hers.

He swore and shoved her as far from him as the cuffs would allow. His glare told her exactly what he thought of her attempt to protect him. But without her to lean on, he stumbled. She rushed forward and jammed her left shoulder beneath his right, bracing him again. The pained look on his face told her he hated that he needed her help. But he didn't push her away again.

"Next one goes in your head, FBI guy. Or Justice Seeker. Is that what you go by? Seems I heard that somewhere. You need to do what I say, when I say it. Or you can seek your justice six feet under."

Justice Seeker? Bryson probably mentioned that he was a former FBI profiler when he spoke to the Brodericks to lend him credibility so they'd agree to speak to him. But would he say anything about being a Justice Seeker? Not likely. It had taken her months of digging to track Bryson to the Seekers. How did this animal know about them?

"I need my cane." Bryson's voice was hoarse, a testament to the amount of pain he was in after their little dance in the dirt. "I can't walk without it. Unlock these handcuffs and send Teagan to retrieve it for me."

"So she can take off and escape? I don't think so. Good try though. But I'm tired of waiting." He aimed the gun at Bryson's leg.

Teagan rushed in front of him to his left side to better help him, their cuffed hands pulled awkwardly across his waist. He was really struggling, his left leg shaking as if it was about to collapse.

His look of regret confirmed that he realized the same thing. He gave her a curt nod of thanks, then lurched forward.

The thirty or so feet to the shack felt more like a mile trudging through wet cement. But finally they were at the two steps that led up to the tilted, rotting front porch. There was no railing, nothing for Bryson to cling to except her. But they made the climb together, pausing just outside the front door.

Instead of the dry-rotting wood she remembered, this door was shiny and new, its glass front encased in a black wrought-iron frame with a network of vertical bars just like she'd expect to see on a jail cell. And both of the small front windows, to the left and right of the door, were covered in the same black bars. He'd converted the shack into a jail.

There'd be no escape this time.

She pulled the door open and glanced up at Bryson. His eyes were glazing over, unfocused. He tried to say something, but couldn't seem to get the words out.

She practically dragged him inside as he teetered

back and forth. Thankfully the couch was right where it had been the last time, four or five feet from the door. If turned sideways, it would probably scrape both walls, if it would even fit.

He fell from her grip onto the cushions, pulling her down with him. She managed to push off the back cushion so she didn't fall on top of him. Instead, she slid to the floor, her left arm raised to not jerk his right arm. Not that he would have felt it. His eyes were already closed. He'd passed out.

The sound of metal grating against metal had her jerking her head around to see what the gunman was doing. To her relief, he hadn't followed them inside. But to her horror, he'd just locked the door. He grinned as he pulled his key out of the round lock that required a key on both sides—not the kind where you could flip it from the inside.

He aimed the flashlight up, casting an eerie, sinister look across his face. "I'll give you two lovebirds some alone time," he teased, adding a wink that had her wanting to throw up again. "Make sure he's ready to answer my questions when I get back. I want to know what the cops know. If he can't talk, he's of no use to me."

She'd wondered why he'd gone to the trouble of taking both her and Bryson instead of killing him at the Brodericks'. Now she knew it was because he wanted to interrogate him.

"Today caught me off guard, I gotta admit," he continued. "I'm not really prepared. Don't have my... supplies handy. But don't you worry. I remember everything you like. I'll make sure I come back with just the right stuff." He leaned closer, pressing his face against the glass. "How's my mark on your belly looking?"

She automatically pressed her hand against her stomach, her entire body shaking as she stared at him. Hot tears coursed down her cheeks in spite of her efforts to hold them back.

His grin widened, his bright white teeth sparkling in the light. "Don't worry. I'll freshen it up a bit, make sure it hasn't…faded, since our last meeting." He chuckled and hopped off the porch, the flashlight's beam bouncing across the gravel as he headed toward the truck.

Chapter Fifteen

Bryson blinked in the near darkness, a fog of confusion roiling through his mind. Where was he? How did he get here? And why was he lying on a couch that, judging by the lumps and musty smell, clearly wasn't his?

He braced his hands on the cushions to push himself up but the tug of a cold chain against his right wrist had him stopping to look down. A small form lay curled up on the floor, her left arm propped against the couch. As his eyes adjusted to the dark and he was able to make out more details, he noticed the gleaming silver circle around both their wrists. They were handcuffed together. Still confused, he leaned down for a better look. Teagan. She was on the floor, without even a pillow for her head.

What was going on?

Her eyes were closed and she was asleep, albeit a fitful one, her elegant brows drawn into a frown. Having never seen her hair anything but perfect, he was surprised to see curls forming a halo around her face, escaping the tight braid that hung down her back. Even worse, there were dark splotches on her blouse. The color was lost to him in the darkness, but there was no mistaking the metallic smell.

Blood.

Memories slammed into him. Awful glimpses of the reality that had happened, and where those dark splotches had come from. He softly touched one to make sure it wasn't wet, then pulled his hand back in relief. It wasn't her blood. It was his. Thank goodness she hadn't been hurt. But that would change the moment their captor returned.

Careful not to jostle their joined wrists, he managed to push himself to a sitting position so he could take stock of their situation. It didn't look good. The front iron-barred door was closed, no doubt locked, but the glass provided a moonlit view of the gravel road and clearing out front. They were empty, the delivery truck nowhere in sight.

He studied all four walls in the main room as best he could in the limited light. Both of the front windows were covered in bars. He imagined the one other window that he'd seen in police photos, the one in the tiny bedroom down a short hall, was also barred. The adjacent bathroom didn't have a window, unless that had been changed over the past two years.

The place was too small to be called a hunting cabin, which was what the owner had called it in the police reports. Had he been the one to install the bars and new door after what had happened here? Or had he sold the cabin, unknowingly, to the very killer who'd been using it all along as his own? Maybe the original owner was the killer, and the police had mistakenly cleared him.

Those were only some of the questions going through his mind. Along with the one that had been niggling him since the tragedy that had happened at the Brodericks': How had the killer known that Teagan would be there?

"Bryson, are you feeling better?" Her voice sounded groggy.

She was shoving to her knees, already reaching up to check on him. He grabbed her hands in his and kissed them before letting go.

"I hate that I slept at all. But I needed it. I'm thinking more clearly."

"What about the pain? Your head? Your hip? I could massage—"

He stopped her wandering hands and teased. "Boundaries, Teagan."

She smiled, somewhat reluctantly. "I sure never thought our first time sleeping together we'd actually be, well, sleeping."

"Maybe next time it will be different."

Her eyes widened like an owl's in the darkness. "If you really mean that, I'll bust out one of these walls to get us out of here. And I'll hold you to your word."

He laughed, amazed that he *could* in a situation like this. "Now there's the sassy, sexy, smart woman I remember. I think that sleep did both of us some good. But we can't sit around any longer. We have to get out of here before he comes back."

She moved her arm, frowning when the short chain between their wrists stopped her movement. "You had handcuff keys in your cane. Why didn't you tell me?"

"I wasn't even sure they were still there. It was a gag gift from Bishop, one of the Justice Seekers, after the shooting. He gave me a set of handcuffs and put the keys in the head of the cane, teasing that I could use them to keep my girlfriend at my side through my convalescence. That was after the nurses complained about how bad a patient I was in the hospital."

The corners of her mouth turned up in a small smile. "I can imagine that. I've seen how grumpy you are when your hip hurts."

"I never thought about those handcuff keys again until I was lying on the floor in the Brodericks' foyer and realized we were cuffed together. That's the main reason I kept asking for the cane. But he kept us under such close scrutiny that I never got the chance to get them out. You have to twist open the top and tilt the cane up in the air. Not something you can do on the sly. Once he put us in the back of the truck and kept the cane, I figured I'd lost my opportunity so there was no point in bringing it up."

"I don't suppose there was a gun in there too," she said. "I asked you in Gatlinburg if there was a gun hidden inside and you said there was."

"I was joking. Being a jerk, really."

"No. Never a jerk." She squeezed their joined hands.

"We need to get these handcuffs off. It's the only way we'll have a fighting chance if he comes back before we get out of this shack."

"You really think we have a chance?"

Her left hand clutched his right one so hard that his

fingers started going numb. She was trying to put on a brave front. But inside, she was obviously terrified.

He leaned down and tilted her chin up, their eyes meeting with understanding, before he pressed a soft kiss against her lips. He'd only meant to distract her for a few seconds, to make sure she knew that he was here for her and would do whatever he could to protect her. But with both their emotions running high, touching her was like putting a match to gasoline.

Suddenly she was straddling him like she'd done in his rental car. And the temperature went up a thousand degrees as they tangled against each other like two horny college kids on spring break. It was only when she moaned into his mouth that he realized he'd slid his hands up her belly and was working on the front clasp of her bra. The logical part of his brain was yelling at him to stop this madness, that they were wasting valuable time. The rest of him, which seemed to be winning, was arguing that maybe this was exactly what he should be doing in case these were his last moments on earth. What better way to go out of this world than making love to the most amazing, interesting, adorably sassy woman he'd ever met?

"The back," she whispered against his mouth. "The clasp is in the back."

What few brain cells he had left registered what she'd said, that to take off her bra he had to slide his hands around to her back. But if that was the case, what was the hard part in the front of her bra he'd just felt?

Underwire.

He broke the kiss and stared down at her. Somewhere along the line, either she or he had discarded her shirt as best they could. It was hanging over his forearm caught in the handcuff chain. And in the dim light filtering in through the windows and front door, two perfect breasts sat in all their glory, exposed, freed from the cups of her bra that was still fastened beneath them. More than almost anything, he wanted to pull each nipple into his mouth, treasure those soft, warm, incredible curves. But, as impossible as it seemed, there was something else he wanted more.

Her underwire.

He slid his hands around her back and fumbled with the clasp. She sighed with pleasure as he pulled her bra off, but her eyes flew open in surprise when he sat back.

He held the bra up, felt where the underwire ended, then tore at the delicate fabric with his teeth.

She stared at him in confusion. "What…what are you doing? If you want to put your mouth on something, trust me, there are better places to put it." She motioned toward her breasts.

He grinned even with the fabric in his mouth. She was definitely the type of woman who knew what she wanted. If he could go back in time and keep her at his house instead of turning her away, he'd probably still be in bed with her days later.

"Bryson?" She was frowning now, obviously getting annoyed.

He made one last tear and the wire hit his teeth. He sat back, working at it with his fingers now, pulling it out of the fabric.

She gasped in dismay. "That bra cost over a hundred dollars."

He hesitated. "You're kidding. You wear hundred-dollar bras?"

"It's my only hundred-dollar bra. I was saving it for a special occasion." She arched a brow. "Why do you think I took a shower at my parents' house? Who do you think I put that bra on for?" She waved her hand toward her shorts. "I have matching panties too."

Boy oh boy did he want to see those matching panties. But more than that, he wanted her to *live*. He glanced toward the door, and the blessedly empty gravel road out front. "I'll buy you another hundred-dollar bra, a dozen. And matching underwear. But right now, I need this." He finally yanked the wire free and held it up. "Handcuff key."

Her eyes widened in surprise.

"Hold up your wrist. I'll try your side first."

She did as he'd asked, and he ran his fingers along the flat side of the metal circle until he found the little slot for the key, just where the metal was locked into the hole. He slid the end of the underwire inside, then carefully worked it back and forth. The cuff backed out one slot with a loud click, giving her a little more wiggle room.

"It's working!" Her voice was full of awe.

"Long way to go. Give me a minute. I have to be careful or the wire will break." He ratcheted the metal back one slow click at a time.

"I'm guessing our captor took Annie from you at

the Brodericks'," he said as he twisted the wire in the cuffs. "Otherwise you'd have shot him full of holes."

"Annie? Oh, my gun?" At his nod, she shook her head. "I don't understand it. I had so many opportunities to get away, to get help. But I just...froze. In that foyer. He took your gun and mine before I even thought about trying to use them. Or run out the front door to a neighbor's. I can't believe I just...stood there."

The handcuff loosened another click. "It's the trauma from before. If he'd been anyone else, I imagine that wouldn't have happened. But your brain shut down the moment you realized who he was. That's not your fault. It's not something you could control."

"Nice of you to say, but I'm not so sure that—"

Click. He pulled the handcuff off her.

She rubbed her wrist and grinned. "I'm free!"

"Not quite. That was step one. Step two is getting out of this shack. Step three is disappearing into the woods long before he gets back." He slipped her end of the handcuffs over his still-cuffed wrist and clicked them loosely into place.

"What are you doing!" she exclaimed. "Why did you do that?"

"To save time. I can do whatever I need to do with both cuffs on the same wrist. I'll worry about getting them off later." He waved toward her shirt, which had fallen to the floor. "I'm having enough trouble focusing with this concussion without your gorgeous breasts distracting me. Mind putting your shirt back on?"

Her smile beamed at him, full wattage. "You think my breasts are gorgeous? What a sweet thing to say."

She winked and grabbed her shirt. "Let's get out of here, Bryson. I want you to buy me those matching underwear sets so you can take them right back off again."

He laughed and tried to shove himself to his feet, but his hip gave out and he collapsed against the cushions. His face heated with embarrassment as he cleared his throat. "Looks like I'll need a little help standing. I should be able to walk but getting up off this couch is beyond my current abilities. I always get stiff after lying down for a while."

"I sure hope you do."

He glanced at her in confusion, then realized what she meant when she winked.

He shook his head, grinning. "You've got a one-track mind. Help me up." He held his hand out to stop whatever she was about to say. "Without another sexual innuendo. We're running out of time."

Her smile faded and fear took its place. He regretted being so blunt, but even though her natural tendency to block out her fears and worries by flirting and teasing was adorable in most circumstances, they were a liability in this one. Especially since the blow to his head had him thinking far less clearly than usual.

She helped him up, and thankfully he was able to limp unaided to the door.

"What do we do now?" She settled her shirt into place. "Try to pull out the hinge pins?"

He was already sticking the underwire into the door lock when her innocent question had him glancing up in surprise. The hinges were on the inside. Because doors like these were intended to keep people out, not in.

Their abductor might have finally made a mistake.

Chapter Sixteen

"You, Teagan Ray, are brilliant," Bryson told her. "I'll try the lock first, but I was worried this metal will be too soft for this. The hinge pins will likely be our ticket out of here. But we have to find something to use to pop them out." He motioned toward the stove, which was only about three feet from the door, and beyond that to the handful of cabinets that formed the tiny kitch-enette. "Look through this kitchen, in the bedroom, under the couch. We'll need something we can either wedge under the end of the pin to pull it or something to stick in the hinge on the bottom to push it."

"I'm on it."

She moved past him and started slamming open cabinets and drawers. He could follow her progress through the tiny shack by the sound of her cursing and the sounds of her either kicking or hitting walls.

He blocked all that out and focused on trying to pick the lock using the underwire.

After half a dozen attempts, he realized it wasn't going to happen. The metal was just too soft and kept bending. He tossed it aside as she ran to him holding up a long metal rod and a foot-long piece of wood.

"Will this work?" She was breathing heavily from exertion. "I figure you can stick the metal up the bottom of the hinge and use the wood like a hammer to push out the pin."

"Do I even want to know where you got the steel rod? And why it's wet?"

"Probably not."

"Were you in the bathroom?"

"Like I said. You don't want to know."

He grimaced. The rod looked like one of those old-fashioned toilet-tank float rods that controlled how the toilet flushed. As to the wood, it was either a piece of baseboard or a piece of the floor itself. Judging by the dilapidated shape of the building, neither would surprise him.

The steel rod was the perfect size and slid in place beneath the middle hinge pin with ease. Hope flared in his chest as he slammed the wood against it. He slammed it over and over and over, but the pin wasn't moving. He finally stopped and leaned in close, trying to see if there was something keeping it in place. Then he took a closer look at the hinges in the door frame and cursed.

"What is it?" she asked.

"Locking hinge pins."

"Never heard of them. But I don't like how that sounds."

He tossed the wood and rod on the floor and wiped his hands on his dress pants. "I thought our captor made a mistake with the hinges on the inside. But he didn't. There's an extra screw that prevents the pin from being backed out. We'd need an Allen wrench and a screwdriver to get it out. No homemade tools are going to back out that screw. It's drilled into the wrought-iron frame."

Her shoulders slumped. "That's why he didn't try to drug us, or tie us up. He knew there was no way to escape."

"Don't give up on me now. I haven't thrown in the towel just yet."

She nodded. But he could tell she was rapidly losing hope.

"Talk to me," he said. "Tell me how you escaped the last time while I see what else is in here."

"There's nothing. Just the couch and a few aluminum pots and pans. The utensils in the drawer are plastic or rubber. There's nothing we could use to stab or hit him."

"He's got a gun. Nothing much trumps that. We need to get out before he returns. We have to think outside the box." He limped past the front door and the stove, then yanked open one of the cabinet drawers in the kitchenette. "Tell me about the shack, and how you got out."

"It's basically the same. Well, the bars are new. And the iron front door. There isn't a back door. He tied me up when he left, with cloth. He didn't use handcuffs. Mostly he used drugs to keep me docile. He'd knock me out for hours, and I wouldn't wake up until he was back. I was in detox for weeks after I got away."

He pulled the hardware, tested the corners of the drawer boxes. "Go on. What else."

She sighed heavily. "I was blindfolded whenever it was light outside. And he wore a hooded mask most of the time. That always gave me hope, thinking he'd eventually let me go because he was keeping his identity secret. But I don't know that he ever would have. He was just extra cautious, in case something happened and I got away. He's not worried about us identifying him. He's going to kill us."

He'd just started into the bathroom but turned around when she said that. "Not if I kill him first. Do *not* give up on me."

Her eyes widened, but he didn't stand around talking. The sense of time passing was making him feel edgy and nervous. He couldn't imagine that whatever their captor was doing would keep him gone much longer.

The bathroom was a total bust. It was pitch dark, for one thing, but tiny without even a cabinet under the sink to hide anything. No bleach or cleaners that he could toss in the gunman's face. He didn't know how Teagan had managed to think about the toilet rod or even how she'd gotten it out of the back of the tank in the darkness. He had to give her a lot of credit for ingenuity.

The bedroom was much the same as the rest. Bars on the lone small window. An empty closet. No bed, just a mattress lying on the floor. It looked new, thankfully. Not the one that had been here two years ago.

He paused in the tiny hallway outside the bedroom.

As run-down as the place was, maybe they could push through a wall like Teagan had teased about earlier. He doubted it, but he sent her off to look for weaknesses in the walls while he returned to the kitchen corner of the main room. With her distracted, he leaned down to study the two-burner gas stove.

It had caught his attention earlier as he'd considered what he could do given the lit pilot light and the fact that the gas line ran through the wall to a propane tank on the outside. Filling the cabin with gas and causing an explosion would likely burn the dry-rotted cabin like kindling. And the fire could be seen for miles around. It would get first responders out here for sure. But being blown apart in the explosion or burning alive were both wholly unappealing.

"What are you looking at?" she asked.

"Nothing helpful. I'm going to check the bedroom again. Did you find any weaknesses in the walls?"

She followed him as he limped into the bedroom.

"No. But I'm no expert at building construction. And it's still so dark in here that I might have missed something. Unless you want more baseboards."

He straightened from his study of the wood beneath the window where he'd been hoping moisture might have rotted out the frame. "Baseboards. That's what you handed me to use as a hammer. Where did you find it?"

She pointed toward the closet. "In there. The board was broken already so I was able to kick out that piece I gave you." She rubbed her hands up and down her arms. "He'll be back soon, won't he?"

The wobble in her voice had him longing to hold her, to try to comfort her. Instead, he dropped to his knees to study the baseboards, grimacing at the jolt of pain that sizzled through his hip.

"You didn't finish telling me how you got away." He felt along the bottom of the closet as she talked behind him, telling him how her captor had missed the vein the last time when he'd tried to drug her.

"He was going on one of his supply trips," she said. "The injection made me groggy but didn't knock me out like usual. I pretended to be unconscious. After he left I shoved the blindfold up and used my teeth to loosen my bindings and got myself untied. The old front door was mostly rotten so I kicked it until it split away from the frame. Then I took off. Nothing amazing. I just ran until I couldn't. Then I walked. Then I crawled. A hiker found me several days later. Not that any of that matters. Our situation is different. We're good and stuck here."

He tugged on the board he'd been testing, pulling as hard as he could. It broke in half with a loud crack.

She jumped beside him. "What was that?"

He glanced over his shoulder. "The walls might be solid. But the floor isn't. Those baseboards came out easily for you because the whole floor in this section has been eaten up with termites." He waved toward a foot-long, four-inch-wide hole he'd made in the floor. "That's dirt down there. The crawl space under the cabin. This is how we're going to get out."

She was shaking her head before he finished. "No,

Bryson. That's not the sound I heard. There was something else, out front."

He lurched to his feet, then limped as fast as he could into the main room. She ran after him and they both stumbled to a halt when they saw the headlights bouncing crazily across the trees. A vehicle was coming up the gravel road toward the shack.

They were out of time.

Chapter Seventeen

Teagan watched the lights bouncing across the trees. The road faced those trees but ran perpendicular to the front of the shack. They wouldn't be able to see the truck until it made the last turn and pulled up. But there was no reason for anyone else to come down this road. The killer was back. And when he came inside and saw they were out of their handcuffs, he'd cuff them again. Then he'd make a circuit of the shack and find the small hole that Bryson had started. He'd decide Bryson was too big a liability to keep around. He'd kill him for sure.

And then he'd come for her.

"Kill me, Bryson." She grabbed his arm. "Please. I can't do this again. Choke me. Hit me over the head. Something. It will be a mercy killing. Please."

He shook her hand off his arm. "This isn't over. You hear me? Don't you dare give up." He pointed to the couch. "We have to block the door. As small as this room is, we should be able to jam one end against the wall and the other against the door. He won't be able to get inside."

She looked from the lights outside to the couch

and back again. "We'd just be delaying the inevitable. What's the point? I have a better idea. I'll make him so angry he has to shoot me. Then at least I won't have to bear his touch again."

He yanked her around to face him as the sound of gravel crunching beneath tires echoed outside. "All we have to do is break three or four more boards in that closet and we're out of here. But we have to buy some time. Help me get this couch into place." He grabbed her arm and tugged her away from the door as the headlights turned toward the shack.

"Grab that other end," he yelled. "We'll have to slide it past the hallway to turn it. Hurry."

She ran to the other end and together they slid the couch across the floor.

"It's clear," he said. "Now, turn it, turn it. This end toward the door."

They slid the couch sideways, one end facing the door, the other the hallway.

"He's here! He's here," she yelled. The truck had parked in front of the cabin.

"Slide it back. We have to wedge it between the wall and the door. Hurry!"

She pushed her end but couldn't get it against the wall. "It's too long. It won't fit. He'll be able to push the door and the couch will slide down the hall."

The engine cut off outside. A loud creak sounded. The truck door opening?

She started to shake. "Oh, God. He's here."

Bryson leaped over the back of the couch, stumbling and nearly falling before catching himself. Then he limped to her end. He bent down and somehow lifted the couch in spite of his bad hip, his face turning red as he shoved the couch up in the air. Then he dropped it against the wall just past the hallway opening. It fell down, but stuck with another foot to go. She didn't see how it would hold. When the killer pushed the door, if he pushed hard enough, the couch would slide up the wall and he'd still be able to get inside.

Bryson must have thought the same thing because he climbed onto the end of the couch that was against the wall and hopped up and down, one-legged, favoring his hip. He jumped again, and again. The couch springs squeaked in protest. Then it dropped down into place, wedged tight.

Keys rattled outside. "Hey, what are you doing in there?"

Bryson grabbed her arm and tugged her toward the hallway. "Go, go, go."

"Open the door!" The gunman pounded against it, his voice thick with rage.

Once they were inside the bedroom, Bryson released her and limped into the closet. Jamming his bad hip against the wall to keep his balance, he slammed his right heel down on the boards beside the hole, over and over. Wood crunched beneath his boot, dropping below. But the hole wasn't large enough for them to get through. Not even close.

Bam! Bam! Bam!

Teagan jerked around as bullets burst through the wall from the front of the shack and plowed through the opposite wall, throwing splinters up in front of her face.

"Down, get down!" Bryson tackled her to the mattress on the floor behind her.

More shots exploded through the wall, right where
she'd been standing. She buried her head against his
neck as he covered her with his body.

The front door rattled, followed by furious cursing and shouting. Then, nothing. Silence fell over the
shack like a heavy blanket, except for the sound of their
breathing and the blood rushing in her ears.

"What's he doing now," she whispered. "Where is
he?"

He lifted off her and held a finger against his lips,
telling her to be quiet.

She nodded to let him know she understood.

A thump sounded outside. Bryson grabbed her,
stumbling and limping as he pulled her into the corner away from the window. Moments later, a flashlight shone through the glass. They both scrunched up
against the wall, watching the light as it moved around
the room. Then it stopped, shining directly on the hole
in the closet floor. The light flicked off.

"Oh, no," she whispered.

He swore softly. Then he pressed his fingers to his
lips again, and edged to the window to peer out.

A thump sounded from somewhere beneath them.

She covered her mouth to keep from screaming.

He grabbed her, pushing her in front of him toward
the door, motioning for her to be as quiet as possible.
He was obviously struggling to keep up, his unbal-
anced gait evidence of just how badly his hip must be

hurting. But they made it to the hall, then hurried into the main room.

He limped to the door and tugged the handle. It moved just enough to prove it wasn't locked. But there was no way to open it with the couch against it. He motioned for her to put her hand on the knob, then bent down next to her ear. "When I lift the couch, run like hell. Get out of here. Run to the woods and don't stop for anything."

"What about you? You can't run."

"Don't worry about me."

"Bryson, I can't leave you—"

The sound of wood splintering in the other room was followed by a guttural yell. "You're dead, you hear me? I'm going to kill both of you!"

Shots rang out. Glass shattered. He must have shot out the window.

"He'll be through that floor soon. I need you to run. I need to know you're safe. Then I'll run a different way and hide. Our best chance is to split up. Promise me you'll run and won't look back. Promise!"

More wood splintered in the other room.

"Promise me." He lightly shook her.

"Okay, okay. Promise."

Bracing his left side against the door, he grabbed the bottom of the couch and pulled and tugged, wrestling to get it to move after being wedged in so tight.

A shot rang out.

She ducked, then looked at Bryson, who'd frozen in place. "Are you okay?"

His mouth tight, he nodded. "Get ready. Remember what I said. Run as fast as you can. Don't stop for anything."

She nodded and tightened her hand on the doorknob.

He heaved again. The couch finally jerked free and seemed to practically fly upward and over on its side, out of the way. As soon as it cleared the door, she tugged it open and ran. She ran as if the hounds of hell were on her heels, because that's exactly what it felt like. She didn't stop until she reached the far end of the clearing. Even though she'd promised not to stop, she did. She had to make sure he was okay. Ducking behind a pine tree, she peered around it at the shack. The front door was hanging open and the headlights didn't reveal anyone inside. He'd made it. He'd gotten out.

She turned and ran.

As soon as Teagan took off running, Bryson dropped to his knees, grimacing as he scooted himself back against the wall, tucked between the door and the stove. He hadn't lied to her, not at first anyway. He'd thought he could run, or at least limp really fast. With a head start, he would have had a chance. But then things had changed. He slid his hand inside his suit jacket. It came away sticky and wet. That last bullet had hit its mark. He wiped the blood on his pant leg and closed his eyes.

Another shout of rage sounded from the bedroom. The man sure had an anger problem. Bryson wondered what he did for a living, because it would be really hard to hide that type of a temper in a nine-to-five office job. Something or someone would be bound to set him off. Whatever he did, it would be a solo kind of job. He'd have the freedom to set his own hours so he wouldn't be missed for weeks at a time when he was on a sociopathic spree. He'd have made an interesting profile.

A series of loud thumps and cursing echoed from the back room. The gunman was finally breaking through the floor.

Bryson coughed and blood sprayed out of his mouth. Not a good sign. Darkness was closing in on the edges of his vision again. He shook his head to stay awake. He still had one more thing that he had to do. Step one had been to get out of the handcuffs. Step two was to get Teagan out of the shack to safety. Step three was still to come. He had to ensure that first responders came out here to help her so she wouldn't die in those woods. And at this point, there was only one way he knew to do that.

He slid his hand behind the stove beside him, then yanked hard on the gas line. Like most things in this shack, it was old and brittle and much easier to pull loose than he'd expected. Finally something was going his way.

"I'm coming for you now!" the killer yelled from the other room. Shoes stomped on the hardwood floor and a hulking dark shape appeared in the hallway. Dawn was finally breaking on the little glade in the woods. And the first rays of sunlight shone through the door, glinting on the pistol in the other man's hand.

He narrowed his eyes at Bryson, his face red with anger and exertion. He looked left and right, not that he needed to in such a small space. One glance could clearly show that they were alone.

"Where is she?" He lifted his gun, aiming it at Bryson. "Tell me right now or I'll shoot."

Bryson smiled and held up the gas line, which was hissing and spewing out foul-smelling propane. "She's gone. Go ahead and shoot me. The flare from the muzzle will take us both out. And Teagan will never have to be afraid of you ever again, you scum-sucking, piece of human excrement. You're not even fit to lick the bottom of her shoes, pervert."

The other man's gun started shaking. His face was so bright red it looked like he would have a stroke at any moment.

As gas continued to fill the room, Bryson piled on more insults, trying to prod the killer's temper so he'd shoot. He wanted him to shoot. Because Teagan would be safe. She could finally live the life she deserved, without fear. And the explosion would bring the help she'd need to make it back to civilization.

"You stupid cop."

"Is that the worst you can think to say? Really?" Bryson clucked his tongue. "You're dumber than I gave you credit."

He roared with rage, then strode across the room toward Bryson and shoved the gun against his temple. But when he glanced at the gas line, he swore. He tossed a few more curses Bryson's way, then yanked open the door and headed outside.

Bryson swore a few choice curses himself. He hadn't defeated the devil after all. But he'd get the help Teagan needed. Of that he was sure. As soon as the gunman was far enough from the cabin to feel safe, he'd shoot that propane tank. He was too mad not to. The explosion would be spectacular. Half the firefighters and cops in the county would be here in minutes.

"Bryson, what are you doing?"

His eyes flew open. Teagan was running toward him from the hallway. "What the hell? The place is full of gas and he's going to—"

"Shoot the propane tank, I'm guessing? Was that your stupid plan?" She put her hands beneath his shoulders and hauled upward. "Help me. Hurry."

He swore a blue streak and drew on reserves of strength he never knew he had to push to his feet.

"Go, go, go," she yelled, repeating his earlier words to her.

They hobbled into the bedroom and she hopped down into the hole. He winced as he tried to lower himself, then gave up and went headfirst. She was reaching back to help him, but he shoved her toward the patch of sunlight just a few feet away. She hurried forward and he half-scrambled, half-crawled after her.

Out front, the truck engine started up. Tires crunched and the engine roared as he drove away from the cabin.

They cleared the structure, him leaning heavily on her once again as they stumbled toward the tree line. Just past the first stand of trees, palmettos viciously scraped their flesh.

"Down," he yelled. "Over here!" He yanked her behind a fallen tree log and rolled on top of her.

A shot sounded. The shack exploded, turning the clearing into a fiery inferno.

Chapter Eighteen

Teagan restlessly paced the hospital conference room. From the exasperated looks on the faces of most of the men sitting at the table, she knew they were getting tired of her jumping out of her chair. But she was too nervous, too freaking scared about what was going on with Bryson that she couldn't sit still for more than a few minutes.

"Ms. Ray," one of the Jacksonville Sheriff's Office detectives called out to her.

Which one was he? Burns, Rodriquez, Bunting? The names of the other two sitting at the long table had been forgotten right after they'd introduced themselves. How many detectives did it take to question one lone abduction victim? How many did it take to change a stupid light bulb?

"Ms. Ray," he called out again.

Burns. That was his name.

He motioned toward the other side of the table. "Will you please sit and answer some more questions?"

Five against one. JSO on one side, her on the other. Not that they were enemies, exactly. But their lack of interest, or ability, to solve her abduction and torture two years ago didn't make her much of a fan now. The only reason she was talking to them was because Bryson was in surgery after being life-flighted from Live Oak to the trauma unit at UF Health Shands Hospital here in Jacksonville.

It had nearly killed her watching the helicopter disappear in the sky with him on board. And she'd hated being stuck with a Florida Highway Patrolman as her assigned bodyguard, wasting time making her get checked out at a local Live Oak emergency room. When the doctors there confirmed what she'd said all along—that she was fine—the patrolman had finally taken off down Interstate 10 to drive her to Jacksonville. They'd arrived two hours ago, and she still didn't have an update on Bryson's condition other than that he was in surgery.

"Ms. Ray—"

"Tell you what, Detective Burns." She flattened her palms against the table but didn't sit. "How about you get me a real update this time on Mr. Anton's condition. Something more detailed than a simple acknowledgment that he's still in surgery, and then, maybe I'll answer more of your endless questions."

He sighed heavily, then left the room, presumably to get the information that she'd requested.

Another detective motioned toward her seat. "There are three murders attributable to your abductor—Mr. and Mrs. Broderick and the driver of the delivery truck that he hijacked. We need to catch this guy before he hurts someone else."

"Don't you think I know that?" She shook her head at his seeming callousness. Her heart ached over the senseless, brutal murders her kidnapper had carried out while trying to get to her. She wanted him caught just as badly as anyone else, probably more so. Because even though she wasn't the one who'd hurt those people, she'd always wonder whether she could have done something differently to prevent their deaths.

"Ms. Ray," he began again. "I know this is nerve-racking, especially when you're worried about your fiancé. But we really need your help."

A twinge of guilt shot through her over the fiancé lie. But she'd wanted to make sure that the hospital would share information with her on Bryson's condition. Not that it had served her well so far. She'd been stuck in this room, answering dozens, maybe hundreds of questions during this inquisition. There just wasn't anything else she could tell them. Maybe if they'd actually work on the investigation, using the information that she'd already given them, they'd figure out the killer's identity and arrest him.

She plopped down in her chair. "I honestly don't know what else you think I can tell you. We've been over the timeline again and again. I told you the guy looked familiar but I couldn't figure out why, still can't. I sat with your sketch artist and you've got his likeness now. Why don't you put an APB out based on that and try to find the guy?"

"They don't use the term APB anymore, Ms. Ray," a familiar voice spoke from the doorway. "It's called a BOLO—be on the lookout."

Relief had her slumping in her chair at the sight of Bryson's boss from The Justice Seekers, Mason Ford. "Mr. Ford, thank you so much for coming."

He stepped inside the room. "I'm just glad that I was already in the state working a case when you called."

"Who the heck are you?" one of the detectives demanded. Rodriquez, she believed.

"A friend of the family. If you don't mind, I need to speak to Ms. Ray." He opened the door wider when they didn't move. "Privately."

The detectives shot sour looks at both of them but finally got up. As they headed out the door, Rodriquez turned back to Teagan and slid a business card across the table. "When you're ready to cooperate, give me a call. We need to jump on this case fast. Please don't take too long." With that he headed out the door.

She threw her hands in the air. "When I'm ready to cooperate? I've done nothing but cooperate. They keep asking me the same questions over and over."

Ford shut the door behind him and gave her an apologetic look. "And I'm about to ask you to repeat everything you just told them. Sorry about that. But you did call. I'm here, and the full force of my company is at yours and Bryson's disposal. I'm pulling everyone off noncritical cases effective immediately. We'll do everything we can to catch this guy."

Some of the tension that had taken hold of her for the past twenty-four hours began to melt away at his words. "Thank you, Mr. Ford. I can't tell you how good it is to hear someone say that. Those detectives treated me as if I was a suspect, the jerks."

His mouth tilted up in what she assumed passed for a smile for him. Back at The Justice Seekers headquarters he'd never cracked even a shadow of a smile. But he'd been nothing but courteous and had jumped at the chance to help once she'd called him on the way from Live Oak to Jacksonville to tell him that Bryson was hurt.

He set a leather portfolio on the table and sat across from her. "First, please call me Mason. After all, you being Bryson's fiancée makes you family, more or less."

She felt her cheeks heat. "I'm sure you realize we aren't really engaged. I made that up so the hospital would share updates about his condition. Not that they've bothered."

"Since you only met a few days ago, I kind of figured that was a ruse. The offer to call me Mason still stands."

"A few days ago? It feels like I've known him forever."

"Not surprising, given the trauma and emotional turmoil you've weathered together. As to those detectives being jerks, I'm sorry it feels that way. They're under a lot of pressure to solve this thing and probably don't even realize how they come across. Not that it excuses poor manners. As for Bryson's condition, I can update you on that."

She straightened in her chair. "The hospital gave you information?"

"Let's just say that I got the information from the hospital and leave it at that. Sometimes the end justifies the means. Don't you think?"

She grinned. "I like how you work, Mason. Please tell me how he's doing. Is he…is he going to—"

"He's going to be fine."

She dropped her face in her hands, unexpected tears flowing down her cheeks.

He waited silently until she regained control of her emotions. A few minutes later, she drew a ragged breath and sat back. "That's very good to hear. Thank you."

"Of course. He's actually in recovery now and should be awake soon." He placed his cell phone on the table. "The second he's lucid, that's going to vibrate. I'll take you right to him."

"Thank you," she whispered, fighting to hold back more tears.

"The bullet nicked his spleen but no other organs," he continued. "It went through and through. He lost a lot of blood. That on top of the concussion pretty much shut him down. That's why he was unconscious after the blast. Luckily you were both behind a log when the tank exploded, which shielded you from the shock wave. Otherwise, your insides would have liquefied."

She winced.

He smiled apologetically. "Sorry. That was graphic. Bottom line, he's going to be okay, eventually. He was lucky. You both were. If the explosion and resulting fire hadn't alerted authorities so that help arrived quickly, he'd have bled out."

She wrapped her arms around her waist. "Once again, he saved me, in spite of how badly he was hurt. He saved both of us. He's an incredible man."

"Yes. Yes, he is. And I want to do everything I can to protect both of you. We need to catch this guy and get enough evidence to ensure he'll either be executed or locked up so he can't hurt anyone else ever again. I know you're weary of answering questions. But I'm coming in late on this. So I'd very much appreciate it if you'd start from the top, right after you left my office in Gatlinburg." He pulled a computer tablet from his portfolio and set it on top of the table. Then he took out a small electronic device and set it a foot away from her. "To save time briefing my team, and to make sure I don't miss anything, I'm going to record this as well as take notes. If you're okay with it?"

"Absolutely." Covering the same ground yet again didn't bother her since it was Mason who was asking the questions. She believed that he'd actually do something with the information. None of the detectives she'd spoken to earlier had inspired that kind of confidence. "Did the police give you a copy of the likeness their sketch artist came up with?"

"Not yet." He picked up his phone. His fingers practically flew across the screen as he typed out a text. He waited a few seconds, then the phone buzzed. He checked the screen, then set it down. "My team will have the sketch within minutes." He poised his hands over the virtual keyboard on the tablet. "You were going to tell me the timeline. Don't leave anything out."

Half an hour later, a knock sounded on the door. Mason was out of his chair, gun in hand but hidden behind him before the door opened.

The detective who'd gone for a status update stood

in the opening, a look of surprise on his face when he saw Mason. He took a quick glance into the room. "Where is everyone?"

"Not here. What can I do for you?"

"I, ah, wanted to let Ms. Ray know that Mr. Anton is out of surgery."

"Thank you." Mason closed the door before the detective could say anything else. He holstered his gun, then sat down. "You were saying?"

She clenched her hands together beneath the table. "You drew your gun. You think he'll show up here? At the hospital?"

"It's possible. Don't worry. I had a guard stationed outside the surgery room. He'll stay with Bryson in recovery as well."

She blinked. "How do the police feel about that?"

"I'm always as accommodating as possible with law enforcement. But I'm not about to leave the security of an injured member of my team to their care. The hospital administrator was more than okay with it after I offered a substantial donation in Bryson's name." He winked. "Now, if you don't mind. Please continue."

"Yes, of course. I, um, I guess I was up to the point of where I ran like a coward for the trees."

"No. I think you were telling me that you did exactly what Bryson asked you to do, so you wouldn't put him in more danger by making him worry about having to protect you rather than make his own escape. But I'm puzzled. If you ran into the woods at the front of the clearing, how did you end up behind the shack when it exploded?"

Her face heated. "I didn't exactly follow Bryson's instructions. I know he wanted me to keep going, to run as far away as I could. But I hadn't seen him leave the shack, and I was worried that he might have been pretending to feel better than he did, just to get me out of danger. All throughout our ordeal, he kept telling me to have faith, that it was two against one, that we could beat the bad guy together. And there I was running away. I just couldn't do it."

He crossed his arms on top of the table. "So what did you do?"

She wrapped her arms around her middle, remembering. "I circled through the woods to the back of the shack."

"Where was the gunman?"

"I wasn't sure. The truck was still parked out front. I didn't see him anywhere."

He stared at her, waiting.

"I got down on my belly and tried to see beneath the shack, through the crawl space. When I didn't see anyone moving around under there, I was terrified that the gunman was inside with Bryson. So I ran to the shack and crawled up into the closet through the hole in the floor."

He still didn't say anything. But his eyes widened slightly.

"I heard the gunman shouting in the other room. And I smelled gas. It was filling up the cabin. A moment later, the front door creaked. I peeked around the corner and saw the gunman running for his truck." She swallowed hard. "And Bryson, he was just sitting there, his back to the wall, holding the gas line in his hand."

She swiped at the tears in her eyes. "For a split second, I thought he was dead. But then I saw his chest rise and realized he was still alive. I yelled at him to get out. We dropped through the hole in the closet floor and made it to the woods just before the explosion." She wiped her tears again. "Like you said earlier, if it wasn't for Bryson getting both of us behind that log when he did, we'd both be dead. He deserves a medal of honor. Not a bullet in the back."

He cleared his throat. "That's quite a story. I gather you sat with him until help arrived?"

"Of course. I know CPR. But that's about the limits of my nursing abilities. He was breathing, and his heart was beating. But he wouldn't open his eyes. I didn't know what to do. All I could think of was to apply pressure to the wounds, even though they didn't seem to be bleeding all that much. I had no idea he was bleeding internally."

She squeezed her eyes shut for a moment and let out a shuddering breath. "Thank goodness the fire department and police arrived so quickly. I heard the sirens and ran to the clearing. They were amazing, ran with me around back, no questions asked. They immediately started an IV and got him on a gurney. I think they flew him out in a helicopter within a couple of minutes. They saved his life."

He slowly shook his head. "No, Ms. Ray. I think that distinction belongs to you. If you hadn't been stubborn enough and brave enough to go back into that shack to check on him, he'd be dead right now." His voice sounded oddly hoarse, and he cleared his throat before continuing. "Thank you. On behalf of all the Justice Seekers, thank you for saving our dear friend and coworker."

She was about to argue that he wouldn't have even been in danger in the first place if it wasn't for her, but his phone vibrated against the table.

He picked it up, then stood.

She shoved out of her chair. "Bryson's awake?"

He shook his head. "Not yet. But I'll go check on him right now. Meanwhile, you have visitors."

"Visitors?" She frowned. "The police are back?"

He hesitated at the door. "When you called me to help Bryson, I took the liberty of calling someone to help you. But I asked them to give me time to interview you first. They've been very accommodating. But they're out in the hall now, demanding to see you." He smiled his first real smile. "You're an incredibly brave and smart young woman. Thank you again for everything you did." Without waiting for her reply, he left the room.

A moment later, two people rounded the corner and paused in the doorway.

She let out a shriek and ran around the table, tears flowing again.

Her mother and father gathered her to them in a bone-crushing hug.

Chapter Nineteen

Teagan sighed deeply and shifted positions in the plastic chair a few feet from Bryson's hospital bed as he slept the morning away. Three days. It had been three days since she'd cried all over him in the recovery room after he woke up from surgery, only to have him gruffly tell her that he needed his sleep. Since then, he'd hardly spoken a word to her. He was acting just like the surly bear she'd encountered the first time they'd met. But they'd moved beyond that. Far beyond it. So why was he acting like they were strangers and he was the grouchy hermit again?

She'd asked him that very thing.

His answers were many. He had a headache. He was feeling fuzzy from the concussion. The pain from his surgery had him feeling bad and he just needed to sleep. All of that was probably true. But he was a strong man, and had overcome far worse to save both their lives. And he'd been at his kindest in the past when he was in tremendous pain, because he'd risen above it to save them. So none of his actions now made sense.

Thankfully, his boss—Mason Ford—didn't seem

worried about Bryson's less than friendly attitude that seemed to extend to anyone unfortunate enough to be in his vicinity. He simply ignored Bryson's gruff responses and went about his business. And he kept Teagan up to date on everything going on with the investigation.

Which, unfortunately, wasn't much.

Even with half the Justice Seekers working the case here in Jacksonville, none of them seemed to be making any more headway than JSO. No one had discovered the identity yet of the man who'd abducted them and killed three innocent people. But Mason assured her they were doing everything they could and weren't giving up. And he did something else—he gave her a company credit card to use for all of her and Bryson's needs. He told her the card had no limit and to use it for anything at all, no questions asked.

He'd also ordered Bryson to let her make all the arrangements to get him set up at a local hotel after being discharged so he could get strong enough for the trip back to Gatlinburg. Teagan decided that she liked Mason Ford very much, especially since he made no secret that he was rooting for her to win this little cold war between her and Bryson.

She crossed her arms and waited another half hour before the doctor's morning rounds finally brought him to Bryson's room to perform a final evaluation before giving him discharge papers. Miraculously, he woke up just as the doctor stepped into the room. Teagan snorted and looked out the window, pretending indifference, when she was fuming inside.

The hurt had long ago faded. Or, at least, it was buried down deep. No more crying in front of him. She had her pride after all. And no crying on her mama's shoulder either, given that her mother now thought—along with the hospital staff—that she and Bryson were engaged. That was going to be a huge disappointment for her parents once he went back to Gatlinburg and she told them the "engagement" was off. They'd half fallen in love with him when he'd had dinner at their home. They fell the rest of the way after hearing everything he'd done to protect their only child.

But they wouldn't be the only ones nursing a broken heart.

She kept her face averted, pretending interest in something out the window while she wiped the wetness from her eyes. How could she still have all these inconvenient feelings for a man who didn't return them? She took a few deep breaths and reached down for her anger again, wrapping it around her other emotions like a shield, to keep her safe.

"All in all, you're an incredibly lucky man," the doctor said behind her as he apparently finished his exam. "Any one of your injuries—the blow to the head, the gunshot, the half-dozen pieces of wood that the explosion drove into your back—could have killed you. You might not feel lucky right now, but once the pain fades and you're back on your feet, I think you'll begin to realize just how fortunate you are. Someone was looking out for you."

She turned around, but steadfastly looked at the floor while he thanked the doctor and discussed the discharge instructions. Her anger had evaporated beneath the shock of what she'd just heard. She hadn't known about the wood driven into his back. On top of everything else that he'd endured, he'd basically been stabbed, *six times*, as the remnants of the shack rained down on them. But not one of those pieces of lethally sharp wood had hit her— because he'd protected her. Again. She had no right to be angry with him. And he had every right to be angry with her. He'd be sitting on his dock enjoying a cold beer right now, listening to the rippling water of the stream behind his house if it wasn't for her. Healthy, content, his only worry the ache in his hip when the tequila and scotch weren't enough to dull the pain.

What a selfish immature idiot she'd been, thinking only of herself.

The squeak of metal had her glancing up to see him struggling to lower the railing. The doctor must have left while she was consumed with her own thoughts.

She rushed over to him. "Here, let me." She gently pushed his hands away and lowered the railing. "Just, please, don't try to get out of bed on your own. I know you don't want my help, so I'll get the nurse to help you get dressed."

"Teagan, I—"

"It's okay. I understand. I'll have the car brought up and will meet you and the nurse out front."

He frowned. "What do you think you understand?"

Without answering, she hurried from the room.

BRYSON EASED BACK against the pillows that Teagan had just stuffed behind him so he could sit up in the hotel bed. "Thank you." He motioned toward the impressive fifteen-hundred-square-feet, two-bedroom suite that she'd reserved for them at the Omni hotel. The accommodations were luxurious, but more important, it was close enough to the hospital that he hadn't had to endure the agony of a long car ride. And since she'd insisted on him taking more pain pills after reaching the hotel, he was feeling pretty good right now. Physically at least. "Thank you for everything, Teagan."

She seemed surprised by his words, acknowledging them with a quick nod. Then she turned to finish putting away his clothes that she'd had brought from the other hotel he'd originally been staying in, closer to The Woods subdivision. Her surprise that he'd actually thank her had him feeling like even more of a jerk than he had since the moment he'd woken up in the recovery room.

All the memories of what had happened had slammed into him, stealing his breath. He'd made so many mistakes that could have cost her life. The very first one was in agreeing to take her with him to that ill-fated interview at the Brodericks'. Everything had gone downhill from there.

The worst part was knowing what had driven him to include her, to give in to her request even though he was the one experienced in law enforcement and knew better, knew the dangers. What had driven him was pure selfishness, his ridiculous fixation on her and desire, no—*need*—to be around her as much as possible. His obsession had clouded his reason. And just as soon as he was able to manage on his own, he'd set her free, break this tenuous bond that had developed between them. He'd ensure that none of his bad decisions could ever risk her life again. Obviously he hadn't learned the lessons of his past—from his sloppy handling of the Kentucky Ripper case to his failure to save Hayley from the person who'd ended up shooting him in the hip all those months ago. He had no business thinking he could really protect Teagan.

She was much better off without him.

Finally she stopped running around the suite putting things away, and stood by his bed. "I guess it's good that you already had a wheelchair and had it at your other hotel," she said. "Saved me from having to rent one while you're here. Goodness knows you'll need it for a while until you're back on your feet." She motioned beside the bed where she'd stored it within easy reach. "There's a cane too, for when you're feeling good enough to try to walk. It's nothing fancy. I got it at the hospital gift shop. Your other one, unfortunately, is locked up in evidence. It practically took an act of Congress just to get my purse released after the police took it from the Brodericks' home. They wouldn't even discuss the cane, for some reason. Anyway, in case you've forgotten your discharge instructions, they're in writing in the top drawer of your bedside table. But part of it is that the doctor wants you to try to stand and take at least a few steps several times a day. If you're in bed the whole time you could get blood clots and—"

"Teagan."

"Do you need something? A glass of water? Soda? There's a bar over there but you really shouldn't have any alcohol with the pain meds you're—"

"No. Thank you. I don't need anything. I—"

"Okay, then. I'm going to explore my room, catch up on some sleep. I haven't slept well at the hospital and—"

"Teagan."

"—if you need something, just text me on your phone. I left it on the nightstand. The police have both our phones in evidence so that's a new one. I had Mason program your team's numbers in there, so that should help. My new number's in there too, obviously, so you can text me. I'll check on you in a couple of hours."

"I need to talk to you."

"No, right now you need to sleep. We both do."

"Wait, please. Just give me a minute to—"

She hurried into the other bedroom, shutting the door hard behind her. But she hadn't turned fast enough to hide the tears in her eyes.

He swore and punched a fist into the mattress beside him.

Chapter Twenty

After spending five grueling days and nights in a tension-filled hotel suite with Bryson, Teagan was more than ready to see the last of the place, no matter how amazingly luxurious it was. She could have had a home health-care nurse take care of him while he recuperated. But since part of the reason that Mason had suggested they stay there together was to ensure that both of them were out of sight in case the killer came looking for them, it just made sense for her to take care of him herself.

But it hadn't been easy.

They'd hardly said two words to each other after their arrival. And since it wasn't looking promising that the killer would be found any time soon, it was time for both of them to try to get on with their lives. Well, as much as possible anyway. The police would have someone watching her parents' home while she was here, not that anyone expected the killer to be brazen enough to try to hurt her again. He was long gone, on the run.

Now, as the rented limo pulled up at her parents'

home to drop her off so Bryson could fly in Mason's private jet back to Gatlinburg, she was so antsy to get away from him that she was pulling open the door before the driver had even come to a complete stop on the street out front.

"Wait," Bryson called out. "Let me walk you to the door."

"I've got it. No need." She grabbed her one piece of luggage from the seat beside her and hopped out, not even giving the driver a chance to open the door. "Take care, Bryson."

She heard him swearing as she slammed the door shut. Tears were already running down her cheeks by the time she sprinted across the front lawn and threw open the front door. "Mom, Dad, I'm home. Don't get up," she yelled, hurrying toward her old bedroom on the right side of the house. "I'll put away my stuff and freshen up. Talk to you in a few."

"Teagan? Are you okay?" her mom called out from the kitchen where insanely amazing smells were coming from. She must be cooking dinner.

"I'm great. Need to use the restroom, that's all," she lied, hurrying to toss her bag on the bedroom floor then running into the bathroom before her mother could stop her.

She shut the door, then turned around and slid to the floor, finally letting the tears fall that had threatened all morning. She hated crying, especially since she'd probably cried more lately than most people cried an entire lifetime. But it seemed to be the only outlet for her tumultuous emotions. Admitting to her mom that she was more upset over the way the relationship between her and Bryson had ended than the fact that a killer was still out there wasn't something she was keen about. Especially since the so-called relationship had never really begun in the first place. It wasn't real, none of this. It couldn't be. They hadn't even dated. So how could she possibly be in love with him? It wasn't love. It was lust, and shared trauma. In a few weeks, or months, this ache deep in her soul would be gone and she'd forget all about Bryson Anton.

Now if only she could convince her heart of that brazen lie, she'd be just fine.

After crying for a ridiculously long time, she actually felt better. She blew out a shuddering breath, then climbed to her feet. The mirror above the sink was not her friend. Her eyes were puffy and red. Her hair was escaping her customary braid. And her makeup was a disaster.

Thankfully, her mom and dad wouldn't care about her makeup. But they would care if they realized she'd been sitting in here crying for the past ten minutes. She grabbed a washcloth from the cabinet under the sink and washed her face, scrubbing off all of the makeup she'd painstakingly applied in the hotel bathroom. Not that Bryson had noticed. Her throat tightened. *Good grief. Stop it, Teagan. He's not worth it.* She lifted her gaze to the mirror and shook her head. Maybe if she kept lying to herself, she'd eventually believe the lies.

Straightening her shoulders, she drew a bracing breath and headed off to find her parents. Her mom smiled at her from the archway into the kitchen.

"Teagan, baby. Finally you're home." Her mom tossed a dishcloth onto the countertop and wrapped her arms around her.

"It's so good to be here. I missed you and Daddy so much." After a good long hug, she let her mom go and glanced around the kitchen. "It smells amazing in here. Did you cook all my favorites?" She crossed to the stove and bent down to smell the tantalizing aroma rising from the huge pot. "Jambalaya. You're the best, Mom."

"There's apple pie baking in the oven. It'll be ready by the time we finish supper."

She turned around to hug her mom again, then froze. Bryson was leaning against the wall beside the table at the other end of the kitchen, looking like a model out of a magazine in his charcoal gray tailored suit.

He straightened away from the wall and smiled. "Hello, Teagan."

"What...what are you doing here?" she demanded. "You're supposed to be on your way to the airport."

"I wanted to pay my respects to your parents and they invited me to dinner. You don't mind, do you?"

"Well, of course I mind." She put her hands on her hips. "You need to leave."

"Teagan Ray," her mother chided her. "That's not how we treat our guests, especially your fiancé."

"He's not—"

"Teagan!" Her father had just stepped inside from the backyard, holding a pitcher of sun tea that her mom must have had steeping on the porch table. Behind him, Zeus lay on the grass, sunning himself. Her father's mouth widened in a broad smile. "Your mom said you were finally home. Come over here and give dear old dad a hug." He nodded at Bryson, apparently unsurprised to see him, and set the jug on the table.

She reluctantly stepped into his embrace, glaring at Bryson over her father's shoulder. This farce had to end now. No way was she going to sit through dinner pretending everything was okay. When he let her go, she moved back beside her mother.

"Mom, Dad, there's something I need to tell you."

"You can relax," Bryson said. "I already told them."

Her jaw dropped open. "You told them?" She glanced from her mom to her dad. "Neither of you look furious with me. What exactly did he tell you?"

Her mom pressed a kiss against her cheek. "The truth. That you were never engaged, that you weren't even boyfriend and girlfriend. He explained how you told the hospital you were his fiancée so you could be in on his care plan, which I think is really sweet. I was just teasing you a minute ago about being engaged. I shouldn't have done that."

She blinked at her mom, then shot Bryson a confused look. "What did he tell you about why I said that he was my boyfriend?"

"*He* is standing right here and can speak for himself," Bryson teased, sounding lighthearted, which had her even more confused after everything that had happened. "I explained that you didn't want them to worry about you because of the bad breakup with your ex. You wanted to protect them, to keep them from thinking you hadn't moved on in your life."

"You said that?" she whispered, her throat tight.

"It's the truth, isn't it?"

She slowly nodded. "I still don't understand why you're here. You should be on the plane."

He stepped toward her, his limp barely noticeable. Then, to her complete and utter shock, he took both her hands in his.

"I couldn't leave with things the way they are between us," he said. "I need to explain why I've been a complete and utter jerk since waking up in recovery."

Her chin wobbled, and to her horror she realized she still had tears left to shed. She furiously blinked them back and glanced at her parents, who were both avidly watching without making any pretense at not trying to listen. She leaned forward, lowering her voice, even though she was certain they could still hear. "You don't owe me any explanations."

"Yes. I do. We can talk now, in front of your parents. Or somewhere private. But I'm not leaving until I apologize and give you an honest explanation."

"Why are you being so nice all of a sudden?" She leaned in so close she was almost touching him and whispered, "You don't owe me anything, Bryson."

He slowly shook his head. "I owe you my life."

"Damn it," she muttered, stepping back. "You're making me cry again."

"Teagan—" her mother began.

"I know, I know. Language. Sorry, Mom." She wondered if her mother would still treat her like a kid when she hit thirty. She swiped at her wet eyes. "We'll talk in the backyard, Bryson. Then you can go."

"After dinner," her mother said. "Whatever you two have to say can be settled later. Now go wash up. Henry, show Bryson to the other bathroom so he can wash up too."

Teagan's face heated with embarrassment at being ordered around in front of Bryson. But since he was currently following her father to the master suite to the second bathroom, at least she wasn't the only one being bossed around like a child.

"You can thank me later," her mother whispered. "Now go fix your face before that handsome man comes back."

She gasped in dismay, remembering that she'd washed off her makeup, and ran for the bathroom.

"YOU DIDN'T NEED to put on any makeup, you know," Bryson said after dinner as they both rested their arms on the top of the picket fence and stared out over the backyard pond.

Her face heated yet again. "I'm amazed you even noticed."

He sighed heavily. "I owe you a tremendous apology. I've been an absolute beast since waking up after the explosion."

She hesitated, his words surprising her. "I didn't think of it that way, that when you woke up in recovery it was your first time being awake since the explosion. You must have been really confused. In your place, I think I would have been terrified. Not knowing what had happened."

He turned to face her, his left hand braced on top of the fence. "I was beyond terrified, about you."

"About me? But… I was right there in the recovery room. You saw that I was okay."

"By the grace of God, yes. Teagan, what were you thinking coming back inside that shack? Just a few seconds earlier and that madman would have still been there to kill you or take you with him. A few seconds later and you'd have been killed in the explosion. You shouldn't have risked your life like that, especially after promising me you'd run as fast as you could and wouldn't stop."

"Sort of like you promised me that you'd run out of the shack too? If you'd told me you'd been shot, I would have helped you instead of running off and leaving you. If you'd been killed, how do you think that would have made me feel? How could I live with that kind of guilt on my conscience? If you think I'm the kind of woman who thinks it's romantic for a guy to die for her, then you don't know me at all. I don't want you to die for me. I want you to live."

His jaw tightened, and he turned to face the pond again.

She did the same, counting silently until she could speak again without her voice shaking. "So that's it then?" she finally said. "You've been mad at me ever since then because I couldn't bear for you to die if there was anything I could do to prevent it? Is this your apology? Because as apologies go, it totally sucks."

He suddenly turned and grasped her forearms, pulling her close. "Don't you get it, Teagan? When you walked in my door in Gatlinburg, you changed everything for me, everything. You made me care when I didn't want to. You made me want...you. And instead of shutting myself away to protect someone else from being hurt by another one of my lousy decisions, I decided to give it another try. I thought maybe, just maybe, I could help you and not be a bringer of doom. But look at how that worked out? I'm a jinx. Bad luck. Whatever you want to call it. If it hadn't been for me, you wouldn't have been at the Brodericks'."

She shook her head. "What you're saying doesn't even make sense. Mason told me what happened with Hayley, when you were shot in the hip. You were the only person for miles around who saw her with the kidnapper. You rammed her truck with your car to try to save her, and paid for it by getting shot." He started to interrupt, but she pushed his hands away to stop him. "The only one who thinks you were a failure in that incident is you. From what Mason said, the delay you caused before the abductor took off with Hayley again was enough of a delay to save her life. It gave other Seekers the time they needed to catch up to them. She's alive because of you. Period."

His jaw tightened. "Are you done yet?"

"No. I'm not. I won't bother getting into the details about the Ripper case. I already told you my own investigation proved to me that you were the only one who had that right. And, hey, look at me, I was the one who was dead wrong on who abducted me. It certainly wasn't Lowe. But as far as me going with you to interview the Brodericks, give me a break. You know me well enough by now to realize that if you hadn't agreed to work with me after running into Zeus and me on that path, I would have continued my investigation on my own. So what do you think would have happened when I took the steps you did, set up an interview with the Brodericks, and others. Eventually I'd have stumbled onto the killer, like you and I both did. But I'd have done it alone. How do you think that would have turned out? Without you to save me, I'd have never figured out how to get out of handcuffs, or thought to make a hole in the floor to escape the shack. Without you, I'd be dead right now. Don't you see that?"

His gaze searched hers. "After everything that's happened, how can you have such faith in me?"

"You've never let me down, not once. Why wouldn't I believe in you?"

He lifted her hands and gently pressed a kiss on the back of each of them. "I've been angry at myself, angry at you, because I care so much about you. I don't want anything bad to happen to you."

She tugged her hands free and cupped his cheeks. "Then maybe instead of pushing me away, you should be pulling me close. Because there's no one I'd ever trust more than you to keep me safe."

He groaned before taking her in his arms and kissing her. The kiss was so sweet, so tender, that she was crying when it was over.

He frowned and gently wiped away her tears. "I'm sorry, sweetheart. What is it? What did I do?"

She laughed through her tears. "You did everything exactly right. These are happy tears, for once."

He pulled her against his chest. "I don't know that I deserve your trust. Or that I deserve you at all. But you make me want to." He pressed a kiss against the top of her head.

She reveled in the feel of him in her arms, finally. The sweetness of his hug, and the kiss they'd just shared, melted away the hurt of the past week. Finally, she was exactly where she wanted to be. And it felt far better than she'd ever imagined it would.

"I'm so glad I took Zeus for a walk that day," she said. "And that you were with me when the killer found me. You're an amazing man."

He grew still, then gently pushed her back. "That's it. The missing puzzle piece. The path where you were abducted the first time, and where we met while you were walking Zeus. That has to be it."

She stared up at him in confusion. "What are you talking about?"

He pulled out his cell phone. "It's always bothered me that the killer knew you'd be at the Brodericks'. And that he had enough lead time to have carjacked the delivery guy and hidden the truck in that garage. He also had time to loosen a section of fence, all in anticipation of us coming over. Who knew you'd be with me that night?"

She shook her head. "No one. No one but you and me. I didn't even tell my parents where we were going."

"Exactly. You and I didn't talk to anyone about our plans. And there's no reason to assume the Brodericks would have told anyone either, or that they'd just happen to mention it when the killer was nearby."

"Okay, then the killer would have had to hear you and me discussing it. Is that what you're saying?"

"Bingo." He pressed a speed-dial number on his phone. "Mason, yeah, it's Bryson at my new number. Listen, are any of the Seekers in The Woods subdivision right now, maybe interviewing witnesses?" He shook his head for her benefit. "Okay, right. That's fine. I can—" He listened for a few moments, nodding. "JSO. Of course. I forgot they were conducting extra patrols out here. I'll call them now. I'll catch you up later. It's just a hunch."

"Bryson, what's going on?"

"Just a minute, sweetheart. One more call." He pressed another speed-dial number. "Detective Burns? Bryson Anton. Yes. I have a favor to ask." He idly turned away, slowly walking down the length of the fence as he explained whatever hunch he had to the detective.

She leaned against a post, smiling as she noted how well he was walking, without using his cane. His limp was barely noticeable. The last several days of rest had done wonders. And thankfully his surgery had been laparoscopic, making the recovery much easier. Still, he hadn't had a miracle cure. If he pushed too hard he'd end up having to use the new cane she'd gotten him to replace the old one. Or, worse, end up in his wheelchair for the rest of the day. What he really needed was to go home, to get on that flight to Gatlinburg, and give his body more time to fully recover.

As he turned back toward her, still talking on the phone, she wondered what was going to happen next.

Not with the case. She was content to let others handle it at this point. What she wanted to know was what would happen with them. After all, he'd kissed her, in full view of her parents who were no doubt watching them through the back sliding glass doors this very minute. And he'd called her sweetheart. Twice in as many minutes. That had to mean something serious, didn't it?

He stopped a few yards away and leaned against the fence looking out at the water, phone still to his ear. But he wasn't talking. He seemed to be waiting for something. He suddenly straightened and looked at her, a slow smile spreading across his face. He said something else to the detective, then shoved his phone in his pocket and closed the distance between them.

"What is it?" she asked. "Did they...did they catch him?"

"Not yet. But we've got a great lead. I asked JSO to look for some kind of camera tucked up in the trees that overlook the path, at the spot where we were that day I met you with Zeus."

"And where I was abducted."

"Yes. It dawned on me that the only reasonable way the killer could have known about you going to the Brodericks' was if he heard us talking about it. And the only place we spoke about it was—"

"On the path."

"Exactly. The camera was about twenty feet up in an oak tree, tucked into a juncture with two other branches, with a fake bird's nest concealing all but a small hole for the lens. And it has audio capabilities as well as visual. He was watching and listening. There may be other cameras along the path too. Now that JSO knows what to look for, they'll be able to find them, if they exist. More importantly, they'll be able to get an expert on this, figure out the camera's range and triangulate the area where someone would have to be in order to receive the transmission."

"Wouldn't he have to be close by?"

"Probably. Which means it's likely he lives or works in this subdivision, and I'm guessing he did two years ago, as well. I doubt he targeted you specifically, not the first time. You just happened along the trail and met whatever criteria he has for his preferred victims."

She pressed a hand to her throat. "I'm still stuck on the first part, about him living or working here. JSO cleared everyone back then, everyone in the whole development."

He cocked his head. "They didn't clear everyone in the one next door."

She gasped. "Bentwater Place. The house where he took us and put us in the truck. He might live there?"

He shrugged. "JSO's looking into it. I would have thought if he did, they'd have figured that out already as part of the Broderick murder investigation. But it's possible he lives in one of the homes next door and would have known the house was empty the night we were doing the interview. Then again, he may live here in your subdivision and the police cleared someone they shouldn't have when your case was being actively looked into. Like you, I'm a bit skeptical since they missed that camera and it's remained there all this time.

But from what the officer said who found it, he never would have seen it if I hadn't specifically told him to look for one."

"Wait. Are you saying it's been there for *years*? Not that it was put there recently?"

He clasped her hands in his. "Based on the condition of the outside casing, it was probably there back when you were abducted. My guess is when the police didn't find it, the killer didn't risk going back to get it. And when months passed without it being discovered, he kept it active and checked in on the video every now and then."

"Which is how he knew I was here in Jacksonville, and where we were going that night."

He squeezed her hands. "I believe so, yes."

She stared up at him. "I was bound and determined to walk that path all week for my planned visit with my parents. I naively assumed I'd be okay with Zeus and my gun. But the way I froze back at the shack, and at the Brodericks' house, we both know I wouldn't have drawn my gun in time to protect myself. And knowing what I do now, I don't think Zeus could have stopped him either. Thank God you were there that day."

He leaned down and pressed a quick kiss against her lips. "That camera will hopefully lead them to the killer. And the BOLO they have with the police artist's sketch will ensure he doesn't get very far. But I'm not taking any chances. Pack a bag, Teagan. You're going with me to Tennessee."

Chapter Twenty-One

If any other man had *informed* Teagan that she was going to do something, or go somewhere, without asking her, she'd have ripped right into him. But this was Bryson. She knew his authoritarian dictate wasn't his typical way of operating, that he wanted to keep her safe, which was incredibly sweet. Besides, flying on a private jet to his home for who knew how many days or weeks of seclusion with him wasn't exactly a hardship. Especially since they'd worked through the tensions and self-recriminations of this past week. She was looking forward to this time alone with him.

But as she watched him snoozing in the limo seat across from her on the last leg of the trip to his house, she couldn't help feeling a twinge of disappointment. Between the toll that his injuries had taken on him and the effects of the pain pills and antibiotics, he'd slept most of the way here. He needed the rest to get better. But she was so hungry for time with him, quality time. She wanted that *get to know you* phase of the relationship that they'd skipped during their life and death struggles. She was greedy to learn the little things.

Like his favorite color.

His favorite food.

Was he partial to country music as so many people around here were?

Would it shock him to know that she hated country music but loved classical?

Since he hadn't mentioned his family before, and none of them had called or visited him in the hospital, was that because he didn't have any family? Or was he just trying to keep them from worrying? Did his boss know that he wouldn't have wanted them told about what had happened?

She couldn't help feeling jealous if he had siblings. She'd always wanted brothers and sisters. Well, mostly sisters. Brothers could be so mean, at least from what her dad said about her uncles. But growing up an only child, she'd always longed for more. She wanted a house full of her own children one day. Did he want children too? Would he love and cherish them and protect them from a world that could be hateful and mean when people didn't fit into those neat little racial categories?

"Want to talk about it?"

She met his questioning gaze. "You're awake."

"I am."

"How's your pain level? Need some pills?"

"I need to know what's bothering you." He grimaced as he straightened in his seat, but shook his head when she reached for the bottle of pills in her purse. "Don't. A little twinge here and there is better than sleeping my life away. Those things knock me out." He glanced out the window. "Almost home. But we still have time for you to tell me what has you frowning as if you want to kill someone. Hopefully it's not me," he teased.

When she didn't answer, his smile faded. "Seriously. What's wrong?"

"Nothing. Random thoughts. Silly things."

"You can be outrageous and deliciously sassy. But you're never silly. What are these random thoughts? If you have questions about the investigation—"

"What's your favorite color?" she blurted out, even though it was the least important question rolling around in her mind right now.

"Ah. Now I understand the frown. You're contemplating some of life's most vexing problems."

"How do you feel about interracial marriages, and children?"

His eyes widened. "Well, Okay. That was unexpected. The answer is gray, by the way."

"Gray?"

"My favorite color."

"Gray can't be your favorite color. Gray isn't a color. It's a…shade."

He shrugged, unconcerned with her assessment. "As to interracial marriages and children, I'm against children getting married regardless of their race."

She stared at him deadpan. "When did you develop a sense of humor?"

"Apparently never. You're not laughing."

She looked out the window. "How much farther to your home?"

In answer, he tapped on the glass partition. It lowered and the driver met his gaze in the rearview mirror. "Yes, Mr. Anton?"

"Take the long way to my house."

"But, sir. We're already—"

"Up and down the mountain, then. We have a few things to settle before we arrive."

"Of course sir. Just let me know when you're ready to get there."

The glass went back up, sealing them in privacy again. He moved from his seat to settle beside her, then took her right hand in his left. "I'm assuming this is a hypothetical question. Or is there something else you want to add, so that it's more specific?"

Her face grew warm. "Forget I asked. It was a ridiculous question and completely inappropriate."

"It's a serious question, a deep question, and it deserves a serious, respectful and honest answer. As to being inappropriate, I can't imagine how it could be, unless maybe it's not hypothetical after all and you're talking about you and me—and you're worried about how I would take it?"

It didn't seem possible for her face to get hotter, but it did. "Like I said, forget I asked. It was inappropriate, because it assumes all kinds of things, like that whatever this is between us could ever grow into something to where the answer to that question would matter."

"You're talking marriage, between you and me."

She crossed her arms. "You don't have to sound so stunned. It's a logical progression in relationships. Not that I'm saying we're in a relationship, exactly, or that it would become a logical step for us. I mean, if we ever even, you know, dated. Which we haven't, really—"

He covered her mouth with his and gave her a slow, lazy and incredibly thorough kiss. When he pulled back, all she could do was sigh, and melt against the buttery leather seats.

"Wow," she finally managed to say. "If I could bottle you up and sell you, I'd make a fortune."

He laughed, then grew serious. "I'm not going to pretend that I can see into the future and tell where you and I might end up. We've had a rocky couple of weeks, and that's the biggest understatement ever. But I can say with absolute certainty that we are definitely in a relationship."

She swallowed, and managed a shaky smile. "Good to know."

"As to your other questions, the first one is easy. In case you haven't figured it out, I think you're one of the smartest, funniest and hottest women I've ever met."

She blinked up at him. "You think I'm hot?"

"Oh. Yeah. And that's not *in spite* of your brown skin or any other feature that makes you different from me. It's *because* of those features, because of all the things that make you uniquely you. You're an amazing, sexy, wonderful woman, Teagan Ray. Whoever you end up marrying, if you decide to marry, that man would be incredibly lucky and should feel honored that you chose him. And if he doesn't feel that way, then he doesn't deserve you."

She settled against him, resting her head in the crook

of his shoulder as he put his arm around her. "You're an amazing man, Bryson Anton."

"You're not so bad yourself. And, Teagan?"

"Yes, Bryson?"

He kissed her neck just below her ear, making her shiver. "I couldn't begin to understand the ugliness the world may have shown you, the prejudice you've likely faced in your life, or the fears you live with every day about things I would never encounter, simply because we were born looking different from each other. But I can tell you this. Hypothetically, if you and I, for example, were to marry and were fortunate enough to have children, I would do everything in my power to protect them in every way. Above all, I would love them, and make sure they knew they were loved, always, unconditionally. And that I've got their backs, no matter what." He kissed the top of her head. "Does that answer all your questions?"

She shook her head. "Not even close. I have dozens more."

"Dozens?"

"Scores, actually."

He laughed. "Then I guess we'll be riding around this mountain for a good long time." He settled back more comfortably, pulling her with him. "Go ahead. Ask your questions. But be prepared. I might have a few of my own."

Chapter Twenty-Two

Teagan had learned so much about Bryson during that conversation in the limo two days ago. It had been fun learning about his family, his rather *large* family of three younger brothers and two older sisters who were both married and had six kids between them.

His family was spread out across the country from coast to coast. While his parents split their time between Canada and traveling all over the US, fully enjoying their retirement, they popped in throughout the year to visit their children and grandchildren.

Bryson had explained that after seeing how difficult it was for his family when he'd been shot during his last Justice Keepers assignment, he'd made Mason promise not to tell them if he got hurt again. That was why they hadn't been at the hospital. While she couldn't fathom not keeping her family informed about something like that, she respected his decision.

But in spite of the many new details that she'd learned about him, she realized she'd already known everything that really mattered. He was smart, loyal, considerate, and a million other wonderful things rolled up in an incredibly mouthwatering package that she wanted to devour.

Except that she couldn't. Not yet.

It was torture not being able to move their relationship forward the way she wanted to. But he couldn't stand the way the pain pills made it hard to focus and concentrate on the investigation, so he'd all but stopped taking them. And that meant he was hobbling around on an aching hip again in the mornings, stuck using the wheelchair most afternoons. Her heart ached for him as she watched him limping across the family room right now with the aid of his cane, smiling at her and pretending he wasn't in pain. But the small white lines around his mouth weren't something he could hide.

"Ready?" He paused by the front door where she'd been waiting for him.

"Ready." She took his cane so he could grab his suit jacket from the hall tree and shrug into it.

She picked up her purse and let him open the door. It seemed to matter to him to open doors for her, so she'd stopped trying to run ahead or open them herself. As they crossed the front porch, she asked, "You really think a brainstorming session with the Justice Seekers is going to crack the case open?"

"We have to try something new to shake things loose. Plus Bishop texted me that he's back from interviewing Leviathan Finney and wants to talk about what he found. He'll meet us at Camelot."

"First of all, I forget, who's Bishop? Second, he interviewed the Kentucky Ripper in prison?"

He stopped on the walkway at the end of the porch.

"Gage Bishop. He's one of the Justice Seekers, the first one Mason hired when he created the company. Everything I know about him would fill about a third of a sheet of paper. He keeps to himself, doesn't socialize with the others outside of work. Mason's the only one who knows whatever traumatic event ended his law enforcement career before he started over as a Justice Seeker."

He limped down the path again, toward the driveway.

"I'm confused. Traumatic event? I thought you didn't know anything about him."

He stopped again, leaning heavily on his cane. "I assumed if Mason was impressed enough to give you carte blanche with a company credit card after I was discharged from the hospital that he would have confided in you. I thought you knew."

"Knew what? I'm lost."

"The Justice Seekers. The whole reason the company was formed was to give a second chance to people who'd had their law enforcement careers destroyed through no fault of their own. It's a second chance for all of us."

"I had no idea. But I guess it makes sense. You felt you'd failed as a special agent—"

"I did."

"No. You didn't. But I understand now why you became a Justice Seeker. After you quit the FBI, you felt you had something to prove. And Mason gave you that chance."

"Not that I've done much with that second chance. He probably regrets hiring me."

They'd started down the path again, but she moved in front of him, blocking his way. "Don't you dare talk like that. I'd have been killed half a dozen times by now if it wasn't for you. I'm not going to listen to any more self-recriminations. You're an amazing guy with fantastic instincts. It's time you gave yourself some credit."

His jaw tightened, telling her he didn't agree. But to his credit, he didn't argue.

She stepped aside and followed him toward the driveway where she'd backed his metallic-blue Ford pickup out of the garage in preparation for the drive into town. It was decked out, with all the options. It wasn't the red convertible she'd pictured him driving. But Hot Guy in a pickup revved her engines even more than she'd thought possible.

A luxury car, like the rental he'd had in Jacksonville, would have been much easier on his hip. But the car that he'd owned, a classic older car he'd planned on restoring, had been totaled that day he'd been shot trying to save Hayley from a kidnapper. So it was either take his truck or hire another rental. She wished he'd opt for the rental because she knew it would be easier for him to climb in and out, and the bumps in the road wouldn't hurt so much in a car. But she also knew he was a proud man and didn't want to look weak in front of the team. To him, renting a car to drive when he had a perfectly good truck in his garage would be a neon sign that he wasn't okay.

At least he was letting her drive. That was the one

concession he'd made. She was pretty sure he was relieved when she'd asked, even though he pretended to debate her question. Her insistence that she loved trucks and wanted to drive this one, which was certainly true, wasn't completely accurate since her main reason to drive was to help him save face. It was obviously much more comfortable to be a passenger than to pump his foot on the pedals.

Twenty minutes later they were at The Justice Seekers' headquarters, an enormous two-story modern-day castle that fully lived up to its nickname of Camelot. Even though she'd been here once before when she'd met with Mason Ford about hiring Bryson, she was still in awe. Especially when Bryson took her into a secret passage to a room few clients ever got to see, a truly medieval looking meeting room with an enormous round table in the middle. It had been dubbed the Great Hall. It was a much bigger version of Bryson's so-called office at his house. And judging by the enormous monitors forming a semicircle a short distance from the table, this Great Hall had all the technological gadgets that Bryson's did, maybe more.

"Welcome to Camelot," he whispered in her ear as they stood off to one side, just past the secret passage they'd walked through. "What do you think of Mason's pride and joy?"

"Stunning. A bit overwhelming, really. But super-cool." She waved toward the round table, where three other people were seated. "Are those Justice Seekers?" At his nod, she said, "I thought they were in Jacksonville."

"Five of them are. The rest were working cases here

and couldn't leave right away. There's one more Seeker we're waiting on before we start. When fully staffed, there are twelve of us, plus Mason, our fearless leader."

"Fully staffed?"

"One of our Seekers was killed last year. Mason's just now looking for a replacement. But let's not dwell on that. Like I said, there are basically twelve of us, plus the boss."

"The knights of the round table. And King Arthur?"

He smiled. "Yes. But if you call Mason King Arthur he'll never forgive you. That's the one part of his little game he hasn't adopted. He thinks it's pretentious." He motioned toward the right side of the table where a man just as broad-shouldered and tall as Bryson was pulling up a chair. "That's Bishop over there. When we sit down, you'll see that everyone has an assigned seat with their name and their moniker engraved on the stone table in front of them."

"Moniker? Like, what, Hot Guy?"

He laughed. "Don't say that too loudly or I'll never hear the end of it. The monikers are based on their former occupations. Bishop is The Bodyguard."

"I thought you didn't know what he did before he became a Justice Seeker?"

"We know he protected people, but we don't know who he worked for. A good guess is one of the alphabet agencies—FBI, CIA, NCIS. But only Mason knows for sure. That extremely extroverted lady on the left who's waving at you is The Cop, Brielle Walker. She used to be a Gatlinburg police officer."

She smiled and returned Brielle's wave. "And the guy beside her?"

"Han Li, The Special Agent."

"You both have the same moniker? Special Agent?"

"No. He was a special agent with Homeland Security. And he started here first, so he got to choose The Special Agent for his title."

"Then what are you?"

His mouth tightened. "The Profiler. Not my choosing. Mason stuck me with that title."

She splayed her fingers against his chest. "You're an amazing profiler, Bryson. If I have to tell you that a hundred times until you believe it, I will."

He arched a brow. "A hundred times, huh? That implies you're planning on sticking around for a while."

"If you want me to stay, I'm sure I'd enjoy you trying to convince me." She gave him an outrageous wink.

He was about to say something but the door to the hidden passageway opened and another man, wearing a Stetson, stepped into the room. Bryson's grin faded and his answering nod in response to the other man's friendly "hello" was decidedly cool.

"Who's that?" she kept her voice low.

"The Cowboy, Dalton Lynch."

"Why don't you like him?"

He gave her a surprised look. "What makes you think I don't like him?"

"Oh, I don't know. Maybe because it felt like a polar vortex descended on the room when you barely returned his greeting."

His jaw tightened. "I have no problem with Dalton.

But I don't go out of my way to inflict my presence on him. His wife is Hayley, the woman who almost died because of me."

She blinked in surprise. At the table, Dalton's expression as he eyed Bryson seemed to be more of regret, maybe even frustration. But there was absolutely no animosity or reproach. When he caught her looking at him, he nodded, then turned toward the others.

"Bryson, I don't think he blames you for what happened to his wife any more than you should blame yourself."

He put his hand on her back. "You're sweet to worry about me. But the only thing that matters right now is figuring out the identity of the man who almost killed you. And putting him away for a very long time. Come on, they're waiting."

He introduced her to the others. Then they all got really serious, really fast. She sat in the chair beside him, in the seat for Zack Foster, The Tracker. He'd whispered that Zack was the one who'd died, which had her feeling like an interloper. But he insisted no one minded her sitting there and it seemed to be true. They were all very respectful and nice to her.

Each of them had a computer tablet in front of them, and what they brought up was displayed on one of the huge screens at the front of the room so they could see everything at the same time. As efficiency went, it was amazing. They shared reports, pictures, investigative notes, all at the touch of a button or the swipe of a finger across their tablets that were each-hardwired into the computer for security.

She was a bit overwhelmed hearing what they'd been doing. Every one of them was working her case now. It was humbling that they were all so vested in helping her. But then again, they were doing it for Bryson too. He was their brother-in-arms. The man they were after had almost killed him. And it was obvious that none of them were going to let a stone go unturned in their quest to bring the killer to justice and avenge their friend and fellow Seeker.

The hours ticked by, with short breaks here and there so everyone could use the restroom or make phone calls.

Lunch was brought in by some efficient person who suddenly appeared from the secret passageway and quietly set the food and drinks down on a table against one wall, then quietly disappeared.

They seemed to have exhausted just about every lead and angle possible by midafternoon. But there was one person who hadn't presented his findings yet—Bishop. The others sat back and the room went quiet as his notes from the prison interview with Finney, the Kentucky Ripper, filled the screen.

Chapter Twenty-Three

"A few days ago," Bishop began, "Bryson requested that I look into Leviathan Finney in relation to this case. The reason is obvious. Ms. Ray was abducted two years ago by a man who carved an X on her stomach, just like the Kentucky Ripper did to his victims. But since that same man abducted her again, and Finney is in prison for the Ripper's crimes, the question is whether Finney is the real Ripper or a copycat. The reason that matters is that if he's a copycat, then it's possible that the man who abducted her is the Ripper. Knowing that provides a lot more data to use to find this man. But we don't want to send ourselves, or the police, down the wrong investigative path. So it was important to figure out whether we could rule in her abductor as the Ripper, or rule him out."

He typed a few buttons on his tablet, then a table of dates, names and comments appeared on the screen.

"Those are the Ripper's victims," Teagan said.

"They are," Bishop agreed. "Along with the dates of their abductions and murders. I created this table to keep track of what Finney was supposedly doing at the time of each abduction or murder. It's his alibi list, basically. Or it was supposed to be. When I checked through court transcripts, the alibi information was rather thin. His lawyer didn't present much of a defense. Regardless, I dug as deep as I could in the time that I had. And then I went to the psychiatric hospital where Finney was being held before being deemed fit enough to be placed in the general prison population. I spoke to his doctors and was able to convince them to share information to help with my victim/alibi matrix."

Teagan blinked and shot Bryson a look, but he didn't seem fazed by Bishop's last statement. As far as she knew, doctors, especially a psychiatrist, would never disclose that kind of information about a living patient without a warrant. She wondered what Bishop had done to "convince" them to talk.

"After that," Bishop continued, "I spoke to Finney, for hours." He highlighted a handful of rows in the table on the screen. "After piecing together witness statements from the investigations, court transcripts, what his doctor said, and then interviewing people to corroborate what Finney told me, these four rows are the only ones where I couldn't positively alibi him out. But even these I'm fifty-fifty on." He sat back and glanced around the table, apparently finished speaking.

Teagan looked at the others. Brielle was furiously typing on her laptop. Han was swiping through screen after screen on his, as if searching for something. And the guy in the Stetson, Dalton, had jumped up from the table and was standing off in a corner on, of all things, a wall phone. She hadn't seen one of those in years.

At her questioning look, Bryson asked, "The phone? Most of Camelot is a giant Faraday cage."

"Fair a what?"

"Faraday. Electronic signals can't get in or out. We have to use dedicated landlines. It's for security. Even the computer tablets are hard-wired through the table to the main computer."

She thought that seemed like total overkill, but didn't really care at the moment. What mattered was that she was completely lost. "Why does everyone else seem to understand whatever Bishop just said about Finney? I'm confused."

Bishop remained silent, apparently content to let someone else explain.

Bryson took her hand in his. "To sum it up, he was able to prove, maybe not court of law proof, but proof to us, that Finney couldn't have killed most of the victims that he's accused of killing. He had solid alibis that either weren't presented at trial or weren't known at trial. There are only a few that Bishop couldn't speak to. Which goes to say that you were right all along. Leviathan Finney very likely isn't the Ripper. But he's not a copycat either. He was set up. Framed."

"By the police?"

"Doubtful. Most likely the real killer, to take the heat off."

"An innocent man is in prison. That sucks."

"We'll contact one of the Innocence Project groups to look into his case."

"Already did," Bishop chimed in.

"Great," she said. "I guess. But what does all this

mean as far as finding the guy who abducted us? Are you saying he's the real Ripper?"

"It's a definite possibility, highly likely actually. The police never linked your case with the others in spite of the signature X because the Ripper was already in prison. But now that we know the Ripper was never caught, all of the murders attributed to him have to be reexamined in relation to your abduction. This is a huge break. There's an FBI field office in Jacksonville. Once our team brings them up to speed on this development, they'll be back in the game, looking into your case and reopening the Ripper investigation. Obviously there are formalities, like convincing JSO to call them in to help. But Mason will get that done. Just a matter of time. The number of people working this case is about to quadruple, easily. With some of the brightest law enforcement minds around. They'll catch this guy in no time."

Dalton returned to his seat. The others turned their attention toward Bryson.

"What about you?" Dalton asked. "Any theories about who this guy might be?"

"A few," Bryson said. "It's been bothering me that he was able to abduct Teagan two years ago without anyone seeing him. She was apparently drugged. She thinks she remembers him injecting her right after he accosted her on the path. After that, her memory is blank until she woke up at the shack. But that path through her neighborhood is well-traveled. And the entrance to the path on both ends is in even busier sections of the neighborhood. It seems far-fetched that he could have led or carried a drugged woman from the path without anyone seeing her. Which is why I called Mason early this morning and asked him to have our Seekers in Jacksonville re-interview everyone who lives close to that part of the trail and ask very specific questions."

"Like what?" Dalton asked.

"Like whether he could have loosened a section of fence like he did behind the Brodericks' house and taken her through the opening to someone's backyard. From there, if he did the same trick he pulled with us, he could have gone through someone's home while they weren't home and into their garage where he had a car waiting. Then, all he had to do was drive out of the subdivision. There's a guard shack at each of the two entrances. But the cameras only record people coming in, not going out. If he came in via the subdivision behind The Woods, like he did recently, he wouldn't be on any of the guard gate's cameras."

Teagan raised her hand.

Bryson smiled. "You don't have to ask permission to speak."

She felt her face heat and lowered her hand. "You said earlier that you thought he might live in one of the houses in Bentwater Place, near the one we went through to that delivery truck. Did anything ever come of that?"

"The police ruled that out. He definitely isn't one of the homeowners on that street or the neighboring streets. But one of those homes was vacant because it's for sale. He could have seen that for sale sign and broke in to conduct quick surveillance on the house next door. Once he was sure the owners weren't home, he used that house as part of his plan to abduct you."

Dalton tapped on the table as if in deep thought. "How close is that path to the Bentwater subdivision?"

Bryson looked at Teagan in question. "What do you think? Half a mile? The Woods is huge. That path is in the center of the subdivision."

She nodded. "Maybe even a mile, or more really if you consider all the twists and turns you'd have to take because of all the streets in between."

"He didn't walk from Bentwater to the path," Bryson concluded. "It's too far. There would have been multiple reports in the interviews that the police conducted after your abduction, reports of different people seeing a man walking toward that trail. There weren't any reports. None."

"Then how did he get in?" she asked.

He sat back, considering the question. "Getting back to basics, we have two choices. He walked or drove. Since no mysterious strangers were seen on the cameras at the guard shack, driving is out. But since he wasn't seen walking through the subdivision by anyone interviewed after your abduction, walking is out too. Which leads to one conclusion. The time frame that the police covered when canvassing the neighborhood was inadequate."

A few chairs over from him, Dalton nodded. "That's the only explanation. He was already in place. He went into the subdivision before the time range that the police checked." He turned toward the former police officer. "Brielle, I think you had that report on the video from the guard shack. How far back did they check?"

She was already typing. Then she punched a button and a report popped up on one of the big screens. "One week. Our killer had to be in place prior to that." She turned her focus on Teagan. "I haven't been in that development. But from what I've read, there aren't any actual woods where someone could hide out that long and not be found, are there?"

Teagan shook her head. "No. I mean, there are plenty of areas with lots of trees and bushes. But it's all personal property, or it backs up behind a strip mall on one side. The community areas are too heavily traveled, like those walking paths, to allow someone to camp out and not be seen."

"I agree," Bryson said. "And it goes back to the sheer volume of witnesses in that area. Even if he camped out, someone would have seen him at some point and reported it. Nothing like that happened. Which means he was in one of the houses. We already know he's not one of the owners, based on the extensive reports the police did on every homeowner. If he was visiting someone who lives there, again, they would have mentioned it to the police. That leaves one last possibility. He was using someone's house when they were out of town. We need a list of everyone who was out of town over a week before the attack."

"On it." Brielle started typing on her computer again. "I've got all of those types of records already from our earlier canvassing but didn't put it together the way you just did. I just need to cross-reference a couple of spreadsheets and I'll have it."

A few minutes later, the dejection on her face told the story even before she spoke. "Sorry, guys and gals. As impossible as it seems in a place with that many houses, no one was on vacation in that time span. At least, no one who didn't have a house sitter or friend at their place while they were gone."

Bryson sat forward in his chair. "Then the house was empty. Whoever owned it didn't live there anymore. How many homes were vacant, either for rent or for sale during that time frame?"

The tension was palpable in the room as they waited for Brielle once again.

She popped up the latest search results. "Three. All for sale, all vacant."

"Bentwater Place, the house that was empty and for sale that the police thought our killer might have used as his home base with the Broderick murders," Bryson said. "Does anyone have any additional information on that house?"

"Like what?" Dalton asked.

"The realty company. Better yet, the Realtor who listed it."

Dalton smiled. "Of course. On it."

"I'm on it too, for the ones in The Woods," Brielle said.

A few moments later, Dalton sat back. "Pine Acres Realty."

"Dang, I almost beat you," Brielle said. "I'm calling it a tie. Two of mine are with Happy Meadows Properties." She rolled her eyes at the name. "My last one, which happens to back up directly onto the path where Ms. Ray was attacked, is Pine Acres Realty."

Teagan blinked in shock. "He's a Realtor?"

"It appears likely," Bryson said. "And he probably works for Pine Acres Realty. We need pictures."

Bishop, who'd been quietly working on his own computer all along, punched a button. The screens filled with pictures of the smiling men and women who worked for that realty company.

Bryson arched a brow. "Thanks, Bishop."

Bishop nodded.

"Bottom row." Teagan's voice was hoarse. "If the screen wasn't so huge, I wouldn't have even noticed. And now I know why no one in the neighborhood recognized the police sketch."

"Why?" Dalton asked.

Bryson reached for Teagan's hand beneath the table and she gratefully clung to it. "Because he looks completely different in that picture. Hair color, hair style, glasses. There's only one thing that's the same."

"What's that?" Dalton pressed.

"His eyes." Teagan's hand tightened on Bryson's. "Pure evil, dead inside. That's him. It's definitely him. I've probably seen him on real estate flyers in the neighborhood. But I never connected the dots. His name?" She paused to draw a choppy breath. "I need to hear his name."

"Chris Larsen," Brielle announced.

She shook her head. "So average. So…normal."

Brielle started typing again. "I'll get this information to Mason and the team in Jacksonville right away."

"I'll give him a call," Dalton added. "I'll answer any questions he has about our thought processes and how we arrived at this conclusion." He smiled. "How *Bryson* arrived at it. Good job, Profiler. And it's good to have you back."

Bryson seemed surprised by Dalton's statement, but he nodded his thanks. "Call me with Mason's update on the hunt for this guy?"

"You don't want to hang around? If our team's in on the takedown we might get a live feed."

"I would, but my hip's aching something awful." He pushed to his feet, leaning heavily on his cane, and motioned to Teagan. "I know you'd rather hang around, but I don't think I can drive right now. Do you mind?"

She was struggling to maintain her composure with all of this information crashing down on her. And here he was, pretending that he was the one who needed to leave. She gratefully went along with his ruse. "I can get the updates later. I don't mind."

Once they were in his truck, the stress and worry that had been eating at her seemed to magically fade away. He had that effect on her, made her feel safe, more in control. "I know your hip really does hurt. But I also know you'd never admit that in front of your team. You did that for me, because you saw how I was struggling to hold it together. Thank you."

"It was nothing. But you're welcome anyway. How are you holding up? I can drive if I have to."

"I know, but I'm fine. It was all so…intense back

there, finding out who he was, and realizing he's just a person. You know? Not some mythical monster impossible to stop. Hearing he's a Realtor kind of takes the drama down a notch. Makes it somehow bearable, especially knowing it's only a matter of time now before this is over."

When they pulled into the driveway, his phone buzzed in his pocket. She parked while he spoke to Dalton. When she got out, he frowned, obviously wishing she'd wait so he could open her door. He'd just put his phone in his suit jacket pocket and grabbed his cane when she opened his door and offered her hand.

"There's no one here but us, Bry. You can suck up your pride for a minute and let me help you. It *is* okay for a woman to help a man sometimes, you know."

He avoided her hand and hopped out on his own.

She rolled her eyes and moved to his side. "What did Dalton have to say? Is JSO cooperating? Did they put out a new BOLO on the killer now that we know his identity?"

He smiled and unlocked the front door. As he pushed it open for her he said, "Yes, JSO is *cooperating*, although I'm sure they think it's the other way around. A new BOLO was put out, but they already contacted the realty company to see if they had a lead on his whereabouts. That's why Dalton called, to give us an update about the realty company." He shut and locked the door, before giving her his full attention.

"They got him, Teagan. He's on his way downtown right now in the back of a squad car. It's over."

She burst into tears.

BRYSON TOSSED HIS cane to the floor and lifted Teagan in his arms. He couldn't make it very far, but he managed to stumble to the couch without dropping her. He settled back with his precious burden and held her while she cried out the hurt and the fear and the anxiety she'd been suffering for years.

It was a long time later before he settled Sleeping Beauty in his master bedroom that he'd given up while she was here. She'd readily invited him to stay with her in his bed that first night. But he knew the dangers. It didn't matter how his head hurt, or the wounds on his back, or his hip, or where the bullet went through him, or, good grief, how sore his belly still was from the surgery. He was a mess, physically. But if he got horizontal next to her none of it would matter. There'd be no stopping either of them from taking full advantage of that situation. And then he'd probably end up in the hospital again. But oh how he wished it could be different.

He quietly shut the door. But he didn't head to the guest room where he was staying. He had another destination tonight. And this one was too far for him to make using his cane. He'd used up the last of his stamina carrying Teagan. It was time to admit defeat, for now, and get the wheelchair.

A few minutes later he reached his office. As he opened files on the computer and began moving bits of information onto the various screens, he reflected on what Dalton had said at Camelot. He'd referred to his old moniker, Profiler. That one word, spoken by a fellow Seeker, had started an avalanche of thoughts in his mind.

Even though he'd been trying to work this case as best he could with a lingering concussion and his other injuries, he hadn't tried to approach it as a profiler. He was too used to scorning his previous profession, thinking of his failures instead of focusing on his successes. But he didn't think of it the same way anymore. Teagan had done that for him, made him start to accept that maybe he wasn't the big failure he once thought himself to be. And Dalton, of course, welcoming him back. That had been a surprise. If Dalton didn't blame him for Hayley's near miss, maybe he needed to rethink that whole episode.

But mostly it was Teagan's faith in him that was giving him a new perspective. Like that maybe he should trust himself, listen to the warning bells going off in his head. They were telling him that something wasn't right.

They'd caught the man who'd abducted Teagan. They'd caught the man who'd killed the Brodericks. So why did he feel like there was something left unfinished? The niggling feeling wouldn't leave him alone. So he was going back to the beginning as he'd once told Teagan to do. He was reexamining everything. And once he did that, he'd do what he hadn't done in years, and had never thought he'd do again.

He was going to build a profile.

Chapter Twenty-Four

Teagan finished brushing her teeth just as the morning sun began to peek through the windows. After giving her braid one last adjustment, she left the master bedroom to find Bryson. Much to her frustration, even though he'd ensconced her in the master suite since she'd come here, he was sleeping in a guest room. She understood it was because sleeping together was too tempting. Neither of them would want to *sleep*. Which would just set his recovery back. But she was getting so frustrated wanting him to get better, and just plain *wanting* him.

Everything about him appealed to her. And the more she got to know him, the worse her obsession became. Whether he was in butt-hugging jeans and a T-shirt or one of those sexy tailored suits that showed off his broad shoulders, she wanted to peel off his clothes and explore *every inch*. As if his sexy exterior wasn't enough of a turn on, Hot Guy was also intelligent, with a kind soul and the heart of a steadfast, loyal, intensely protective warrior. It was becoming nearly impossible

not to weep with longing and desire every time he entered a room.

She could definitely fall in love with him. She was
more than halfway there already. But she had no clue
whether he felt the same. Oh, he liked her, a lot. And he
wanted her. There was no denying the hungry look in
his eyes that he tried so hard to hide. Clearly he suffered
from the same affliction that she did. If they ever *really*
got together, they'd probably spontaneously combust.
But did he care about her? *Really* care, as in I could
love you forever kind of care? She just didn't know.

Shaking her head at her fruitless thoughts, she
headed to his room just down the hall. He wasn't there.
The bed didn't even look as if it had been slept in.
Growing concerned, she checked the main rooms in
this part of the house. She even looked out the back
door at the dock, where he could be found most eve-
nings. But he wasn't there. She was just passing the
little alcove to the left of the TV when she realized it
was empty. Each night he stored his wheelchair there
and used the cane the next day until the pain forced him
to use the chair once again. But the wheelchair wasn't
there. Why? Had he suffered a setback to his recovery?

Increasingly anxious, she headed down the back
hall and looked in every door that she passed until
she reached the end, his office. Light shining under
the door had her letting out a relieved breath. He must
have come here last night for some reason, then ended
up sleeping in the attached bedroom rather than head
all the way to the front of the house.

She knocked on the door. No answer. She knocked

again. When he still didn't answer, her overactive imagination conjured up all kinds of awful scenarios, like him lying on the floor in a pool of blood, his wounds ripped open. Just the thought of him in pain, needing her, had her opening the door.

He wasn't on the floor dying.

And he wasn't sleeping in the guest room.

He was in his wheelchair at the round table, oblivious to her entry as he spoke to someone on his cell phone. All nine of the giant monitors were filled with documents. But that wasn't what had her gasping in surprise.

It was the pictures.

He glanced over his shoulder, then punched a button on the control panel, clearing the screens. "Mason, I'll call you back in a few minutes. Send me that list of dates as soon as you have it, all right? Yeah, thanks. Bye." He set the phone on the table. "Sorry. I didn't realize you were there or I wouldn't have had those pictures up."

She fought against the nausea the graphic, violent images had awakened in her as she joined him at the table. So many women. So much...carnage.

"I heard you talking to Mason. Does he have you working on a new case already and you stayed up all night studying crime scene photos?"

He hesitated, clearly uncomfortable with her questions. "I'm not working a new case, not exactly. I'm... reexamining an old one."

"Why would you do that?"

Again, he paused.

She glanced at the blank screens, her mind's eye trying to reconstruct what she'd seen seconds earlier. But she'd been too broadsided by the unexpected tableau to recall many details, even with her photographic memory. "How old is this case you're looking into?"

He looked at his wrist as if to check the time. But he hadn't replaced the fancy computer watch yet that Larsen had taken from him. "Is it morning already? I can whip us up something to eat." He backed his chair away from the table. "How about omelets? I can't remember the last time I—"

She leaned past him and punched the same key that he had earlier. The pictures popped back onto the screens.

He swore and cleared them again, but not before she saw a bloody X carved on one of the women's bellies.

"The Kentucky Ripper," she accused. "You're looking at the Kentucky Ripper cases. Why? The FBI is covering that angle. You said so at Camelot yesterday. And don't try to change the subject by acting like you suddenly love to cook. We both know better. You forget we played twenty questions times ten in the limo on the way home from the airport. I know a lot of things about you now that I didn't before. Like that you hate to cook. So spill. Why have you been here all night looking at murders that happened years ago instead of celebrating that the man who tried to kill both of us is sitting in a Jacksonville jail cell?"

He sighed heavily. "I didn't want to wait for a report from the FBI. I needed some answers now, to quiet some doubts I had, and make sure we'd covered every angle."

"What doubts? What angles?"

"Little details that don't add up. With Finney possibly innocent, the FBI is focusing on Larsen as the real Ripper. And it makes sense, given the signature and other details about the crime scenes, plus things we're starting to learn about Larsen."

She pulled out the chair beside him and sat down. "If it all makes sense, then what's bothering you?"

He hesitated.

"I'm not dropping this. You might as well tell me now or we'll be here all day," she warned.

He grimaced. "All right. What's bothering me is the puzzle pieces that don't fit. It's like with the original Ripper investigation. There are things that never matched Finney. But there was enough so-called evidence that some other evidence was basically ignored. And once he was in prison, the murders stopped. Everyone was content to let it drop, to ignore the inconsistencies."

"Not you," she reminded him. "You kept looking at the case long after it was over. You stored all those copies of the case files. That's what you were going through just now, isn't it? I'm guessing that means you hired that temp you talked about when I first arrived, to key everything into the system."

"I had Brielle work with someone while I was in the hospital," he admitted. "I'd always wanted everything digitized to make examination of the evidence easier. With you having been abducted again, I wanted to have the previous case information handy when I got a chance to review it. The obvious conclusion at the time was that Larsen was likely the Ripper, even before Bishop spoke to Finney. I expected when I eventually got home and went through this stuff, that conclusion would be cemented in my mind."

"But it wasn't."

"No. Far from it."

She shivered and rubbed her hands up and down her arms. "The man who attacked me, who attacked us, is behind bars. It shouldn't matter whether he's the Ripper or not. So why do you look so serious? And why am I starting to feel concerned?"

He took her hands in his. "Whatever I've found, or think I've found, there's no reason for you to worry. You're safe here, with me. There are four fellow Seekers twenty minutes away if we need them, which we don't. And I've got a pistol in the nightstand in my bedroom."

"Then why have you been up all night looking at the case file?"

A flicker of unease crossed his face before his expression cleared. "I like being thorough. And, as I said, I don't like puzzle pieces that don't fit."

"Show me those pieces."

"Teagan—"

"We're in this together. And we'll still be in this together when Larsen is brought to trial and we're both called to testify. Don't shut me out now. Show me."

His reluctance was obvious, but he wheeled back in front of the computer tablet. "I can clear the pictures. There's no reason for you to look at those. I was using

them to double-check details in reports." His fingers
flew across the keyboard as he closed files and moved
things around on the tablet in front of him without sharing them to the big screens. Then he punched one of
the keys, and the various Ripper case files appeared
on the large monitors. True to his word, there weren't
any pictures.

He continued to move things around, mostly closing out various documents until he was left with only
one screen of data. It was essentially a huge list with
different headings with bullets of information beneath
each one.

She read some of the headings out loud. "Race, sex,
age, marital status, victimology, criminal psychopathy,
location, signature…" She shot him a look of surprise.
"A profile. You're working up a profile."

"More or less. I compiled the information from the
Ripper murders along with what we know about Larsen's recent crimes." He scrolled to one of the sections
labeled *Organized vs. Disorganized.* "I'm sure you remember a lot of this from your criminal justice classes.
An organized killer is one who plans his crime ahead of
time, brings his weapons with him. The disorganized
killer grabs a knife out of a victim's kitchen drawer to
stab her. He's more spontaneous, less controlled and
tends to make a lot of mistakes. A disorganized killer
is generally easier to find than the organized one because of those mistakes. Which one would you say
Larsen is?"

"Easy. Organized. He planned everything down to
the last detail, from the camera hidden in the tree over

the path where I went walking to the section of fence he loosened behind the Brodericks' home. He had to have spent months getting that shack set up as his own personal prison, installing the bars on the windows and doors."

"You get an A plus. He's definitely an organized killer, which gives us insight into his mind and how he thinks. Mason confirmed that Larsen purchased that shack over a year ago. I don't know whether he planned to go after you again, or someone else. But he was definitely preparing it well ahead of time for another victim. Knowing he was an organized killer helps predict other things, like that he probably had a steady job."

"He worked for a realty company," she said. "Not exactly nine to five, but he would have had some kind of schedule, checked in now and then, attended meetings." She crossed her arms, remembering what she'd researched on the Kentucky Ripper's crimes. "But that doesn't fit what I know about the Ripper."

"Maybe. Maybe not." He punched a few buttons and a list of names and dates appeared on the screen to the left of the main one they'd been looking at. "You should recognize those."

"The ripper's victims. Six of them."

"What do they have in common?"

"Other than the obvious? The carved X's in their bellies, the fact that they were abducted for days or weeks before being killed? That all of them were stabbed, including the ones you haven't listed. Some were shot too."

"Other than all of that. What type of killer was responsible for the kinds of crime scenes we found in those examples?"

She thought about it, then shrugged. "You're going to say whoever killed them was organized. I remember those crime scenes were pristine. Very little forensic evidence was found. No weapons were left behind. I could go on, but I can't argue that point. Those particular crime scenes were indicative of an organized perpetrator. But there were eight more killings. And those were the opposite of organized. They were...sloppy."

"Yes. They were." He displayed another list of names on the monitor to the right of the main one, the eight victims she'd just mentioned. "All of these were similar because they seemed to be the work of a disorganized killer."

"Right," she agreed. "Given the mix of organized and disorganized crime scenes, the conclusion goes more to a mental disease, like Finney suffered from. He was, is, bipolar. The theory was that he killed some in his manic state—the disorganized killings—and some in his depressive state—the organized ones."

"It's a popular theory, one the police bought into back then." He motioned toward the first list. "Consider these victims again. Although they were brutally killed, the number of stab wounds is low. Only three for the first victim, six on another, and something in between for the rest." He waved toward the second list. "These, however, had anywhere from twelve to thirty-one stab wounds in addition to being beaten in two of the cases. One victim even suffered cigarette burns all over her back."

"I remember." That sick feeling was roiling in her stomach again.

"It's called overkill," he said. "The killer inflicted far more wounds than necessary to kill his victims. Normally, that might suggest that he knew them, had personal feelings of hate toward them. But it can happen with a disorganized killer as well, with or without a mental defect. He kills in the heat of the moment, because of some imagined slight or explosive anger over something seemingly inconsequential to you or me but that is blown all out of proportion in his mind."

Again, he motioned toward the screen on the list, the names of the six victims that he'd grouped together. "Here's another take on these. In each of these cases, there's evidence that the killer spent a lot of time in the victim's home during the stalking phase while the victim wasn't there. What does that indicate?"

"I'm not sure. Maybe I need a refresher course on my college classes."

He smiled. "I'm sure it will all come back to you when you go back to finish your master's degree. Familiarity is the missing link here. We spend time somewhere when we feel comfortable there, because the location isn't foreign or unknown to us."

She stared at him a long moment. "I'm trying to follow, but all that tells me is that the Ripper likely lived in Kentucky, close to the crime scenes. That was part of the original geographical profiling. That's why Finney was such a good fit."

"And Lowe. Don't forget him, the second potential Ripper on the original suspect list. He was from Kentucky too, born and raised in the same general area as Finney."

"Okay. Yes, I remember that. It's part of the reason that I thought Lowe might have been the one who abducted me."

He swiveled his wheelchair to face her. "Think about the other things we know about those crime scenes. In the first list of victims, the bodies were left where they'd be easily found, potentially indicating the killer had some religious background, that he wanted them to get a Christian burial, or whatever religion he followed."

"The bodies weren't hidden in the rest of the killings either. They're the same."

"I'm going to disagree on that," he said. "In the overkill list, the victims were, well, slaughtered for lack of a better description. Discarded. There was no caring emotion behind that action. The bodies were easily found only because the killer couldn't be bothered to try to hide them. Not so with the organized killer list. Those bodies were treated, after death anyway, with a modicum of respect. Left clothed or covered, lying down, almost as if they were sleeping as opposed to being tossed out like garbage. It's subtle, but it's a difference. If you look at every kind of comparison that can be made, those two lists of victims each present evidence of a very different kind of killer. In fact, it's my opinion that it proves there wasn't one Kentucky Ripper. There were two."

She sucked in a breath. But it really shouldn't have been a surprise after everything he'd just shown her.

She glanced from list to list, read the headings on the middle screen, the bullets beneath them. "But, if you're right, then your original profile was wrong."

He surprised her by smiling. "Don't look so worried. You're not dashing my newly found confidence. There's more to the original profile than appeared in any police reports."

"Okay. Now you've lost me."

He shifted in his chair, a quickly hidden grimace telling her how much his night of research had cost him physically. His hip was aching. He needed a hot soak in a tub and a long nap. But she didn't want to embarrass him by pointing out the obvious, so she remained silent.

"When I profiled the murders allegedly attributed to the Kentucky Ripper," he continued, "I presented the police with *two* profiles. Two different killers. When Finney was arrested, it was the profile I gave them that most closely matched his characteristics that they used. The other profile I gave them was ignored. That's why you never saw it in any of the official case files that you researched."

"I still have to wrap my head around this. You've turned the investigation I did upside down."

"No. I haven't. I've proved that your original conclusions were right all along."

She threw her hands up in the air. "Now I'm beyond lost."

"Sorry. I'm not explaining this very well. To try to put it succinctly, if I look at Larsen and everything we now know about him, including that he used to live in Kentucky, he fits that first list of victims to a T."

"Larsen is the Ripper."

He sat forward in his chair. "He's one of them. That's where your research comes into play. Everything about that second victim list—if we consider that Bishop is right and Finney was a mentally ill fall guy who didn't kill anyone—that second list fits the man you believed all along was the Kentucky Ripper."

She pressed a hand to her throat. "Avarice Lowe."

He nodded. "All I'm waiting on for confirmation is a list of dates and alibis for Larsen. Mason's working on that to see if Larsen was on vacation or sick or whatever on the dates when the first set of victims was abducted. I've already cross-referenced everything I had on Lowe."

She glanced up at the dates he'd mentioned, the ones beside the disorganized list. They all had check marks beside them. "Lowe doesn't have alibis for the second set?"

"No. He doesn't."

She sat back. "Two Kentucky Rippers, and a third guy in prison who had nothing to do with the murders."

"It's worse than that," he told her. "There's one more puzzle piece that you haven't seen." He typed on his computer tablet again.

"What could be worse than two killers?" she asked.

He hesitated with his finger poised over one of the function keys. "How about this?"

A picture displayed on the screen. She stared at it a moment, trying to figure out what was supposed to be significant about what she was seeing. There was a small crowd of people standing behind yellow crime scene tape. Behind them were homes and police cars parked up and down the street.

"One of the Ripper's crime scenes? A crowd shot?"

"That's exactly what it is. Standard operating procedure in a case like this. The police photographer hides out of sight and takes pictures of any people watching the activity, just in case the killer ends up being in the crowd."

"Because killers often come back to the scene of the crime," she said. "They get a thrill from watching the police."

"Now observe the cropped, close-up version I made of that same picture." He pressed another key and the screen changed. "What's worse than two different killers?"

She gasped in shock. "A tag team of killers, partnering together." She stared at the close up of Avarice Lowe and Chris Larsen standing in the crowd, side by side, watching with riveted interest as the police worked one of the Kentucky Ripper crime scenes.

"Congratulations, Teagan."

She tore her gaze from the screen. "For what?"

"You were right all along. Lowe was the Kentucky Ripper. But so was Larsen. None of us saw that coming."

"You did," she said. "You created two profiles."

"Yes, well. My mistake was in not following through and pursuing both after the police went after Finney. I assumed I'd messed up. Instead, I should have pushed for more investigating. Maybe then, Finney wouldn't be in prison. Lowe would be in prison, along with Larsen. And then you'd have never been hurt. I'm so sorry." His jaw tightened.

She shook her head. "No. Don't you dare go there. What happened to me was not your fault. It was Larsen's."

He swallowed. "Thank you for that. But it gets even worse. I'm not sure it's just Larsen's fault. It may be Lowe's too. Remember that you said, even after knowing Larsen had abducted you, that he didn't seem like the right man, that he didn't fit your memories except for his voice?"

It took a moment for his words to sink in. When they did, she pressed a shaking hand to her throat. "Oh my God. You think that I was abducted by...both of them?"

He gave her a short, clipped nod. "I don't have any real proof. Just theories. But I think we should tell the police and the FBI to consider that they may have been a tag team on some of the same crimes, including what was done to you." He took her hand in his again. "I'm sorry. I probably shouldn't have even told you that."

"No, no. I don't want any secrets between us. I want to be included in everything." She forced a smile. "Honestly, it's not as huge of a shock as you'd expect. I was wrestling with my own doubts because some things didn't seem to fit with Larsen. Now, well, it kind of all makes sense." She squeezed his hand. "I assume you already told Mason about this?"

He kissed the back of her hand before letting go. "I was discussing it with him when you walked in. He's corroborating some data, but as soon as he saw that picture of Lowe and Larsen together, he was convinced. He's pulling the Seekers onto this right now."

"I guess everything's in good hands, then."

"The best."

She pushed to her feet, still feeling a bit nauseated and shaky after the latest revelations. "I need to push all of this ugliness out of my head for now. I'm going to go call my mom and let her know I'm still alive. She's gotten a bit paranoid after this last...episode. She made me promise to call her every day, but I fell asleep last night and never did. I'm surprised she's not already blowing up my phone this morning." Her face heated. "Sorry about falling asleep with you as my pillow. But thanks for putting me to bed. Next time maybe you can join me." She gave him an outrageous wink, desperately trying to lighten the mood.

He gently cupped her face and pressed a soft kiss against her lips. "One day, very soon, sweet Teagan. I'll do more than just join you in that big bed."

She sighed with longing, already feeling better. He always made her feel better, even in her darkest moments.

He put his phone in his pocket before turning off the equipment. Backing away from the table, he said, "Hop on. I'll give you a ride." He arched his brows in a suggestive manner.

She laughed and eased herself onto his lap so she wouldn't jar his incisions. When they reached the family room, she carefully got up. "I'll call Mom from the bedroom."

"And I'll make breakfast. Toast or an omelet? Those are the only two breakfast meals in my culinary arsenal."

"Omelet. Always."

"Good choice. My toast always comes out burned.

Meat lover, veggie lover, or deluxe?" He wheeled toward the kitchen.

"Deluxe. With sour cream on top, if you have it."

"You got it," he called back.

She smiled and went into the bedroom. But after three tries on her cell phone without the call going through, she gave up and headed to the kitchen.

He'd left his wheelchair sitting by the island and was leaning on his cane as he pulled ingredients for the omelets out of the refrigerator. He glanced up in surprise when she started helping him. "That was a quick call."

"It wouldn't go through. I think there must be a problem with the cell tower or something."

He frowned as he set a carton of eggs on the counter. "Is your battery low?"

"No. But there weren't any bars. No connection. I tried three times. All I got was static."

"Static?"

She nodded.

He pulled out his phone and checked the screen. Then he punched a button and held it to his ear. He swore and tossed his phone on top of the island. "Run back to the office and lock yourself inside." He hobbled to his wheelchair and plopped down.

"Why? What's going on?"

He wheeled around the island. "Someone's jamming the cell signal. And there's only one person I can think of who would have a reason to do that."

The blood rushed from her face, leaving her cold and shaking as she hurried after him into the family room. "Avarice Lowe. You think he's on his way here?"

"No." He glanced up at her as he wheeled past the L formed by the two couches. "I think he's *already* here. Probably lurking outside, gathering his courage." He glanced at his wrist and swore. "I should have replaced my computer-watch the moment I got back. It would have warned me if someone was on the property. Go to the office, Teagan. Hurry. There aren't any windows in there. Lock the main door, then lock the doors that lead into the bathroom and bedroom. Wedge a chair beneath the door to the hallway. *Go*."

Ignoring his dictate, she ran after him into the master bedroom. "I'm not leaving you. Come with me."

He wheeled to the nightstand. "I've got this. I'll take care of Lowe. But I have to know you're safe, out of harm's way. Go on."

He yanked open the top drawer.

"Okay, okay." She headed toward the door. "But I wish you'd let me help you instead of—"

He was suddenly beside her in his wheelchair, shoving her back into the room. She stumbled but caught herself in time to see him shut the door and lock it. His face was drawn and pale as he met her questioning gaze. "My pistol's not in the nightstand. *He's inside the house*."

Chapter Twenty-Five

He's inside the house.

Those horrifying words ran through Teagan's mind over and over as she watched Bryson leaning against the master bathroom counter after ditching the wheelchair because it was in his way. He was using duct tape to secure the thick towels that he'd wrapped around her arms. She didn't ask why. She knew why. The disorganized killer, the one who'd murdered eight of the Kentucky Ripper's victims, was quite the fan of knives. Bryson was using the towels to protect her in case Lowe got past him and came after her next. As to why he had duct tape in his bathroom, that was a discussion for another day. *If they lived another day.*

The psychopath in the main room had already tried to get into the bedroom once. He'd scraped knives underneath the closed door, swiping at Bryson's feet. Then Lowe had used his body like a battering ram, screaming obscenities as he tried to crash through the door. It was only because Bryson had used his own strength against the door that Lowe had given up. But not for long. He was still out there. Planning his next assault. Even now she could hear his shoes thumping and squeaking across the floor as he paced back and forth mumbling incoherent words to himself.

Dear God. Please help us.

Bryson tossed the roll of duct tape onto the counter and reached under the sink. "This is a last resort." He handed her an aerosol can of deodorant. "I don't want you near enough to him to use this. God willing, when you climb out the bedroom window, he'll be so busy with me that he won't get a chance to go after you."

She sucked in a breath, fear for both of them making her flush hot and cold.

"But if he gets past me," he continued, "and he catches up to you, spray his eyes. He won't expect that. It will hurt like hell and he'll be temporarily blinded. Run past him and go for the truck." He dug the keys out of his pocket and shoved them into her jeans pocket. "Drive down the mountain like a bat out of hell. Don't stop. Go straight to the police station. You hear me? Do not stop at some neighbor's house or a little country store. If he ends up following you, he could go after you again. Go straight to the police. It's almost a straight shot once you reach the bottom of the mountain. You remember the directions I told you?"

He lightly shook her when she didn't answer.

"I do. I remember," she said. "But none of this makes sense. Why don't you put towels on your arms too? And climb out the window with me?"

He gave her an exasperated look. "I was up all night. My hip never had a chance to recuperate. I'm not running anywhere. And the towels would make it too hard for me to maneuver in a fight. This is the way it has to be. He's already cracked the doorjamb. The next time he tries to get through the door, he'll be inside the bedroom. While I keep him occupied, you're going to climb out that window and run for the truck."

"I don't want to run away like a coward and leave you. Don't ask me to do that again."

He grabbed a small pair of scissors from one of the drawers and set them on top of the counter. Next he grabbed a folded sheet from beneath the cabinet and tucked it under his arm. "You have to leave me. It's the only way."

She frantically shook her head and set the can back on the counter. "No. It's not. Two against one, remember? You and me against the world. He can't kill both of us. If we attack him together, we'll defeat him."

"No, Teagan. You heard his roar of rage earlier. You saw the knives he was shoving under the door. Probably the only reason he didn't shoot his way through is that he doesn't want to end his fun that quickly. He's a cutter. He wants to enjoy himself first. But if he sees you running for the truck through the front windows, he'll use the gun. You can't outrun a bullet. I have to distract him, try to get the gun to give you a chance."

He shoved the can in her hand, grabbed the pair of scissors and pulled her out of the bathroom.

A shoe squeaked against the polished floor outside the bedroom door.

Bryson scowled and dropped the folded sheet on top of the bed. He limped to the window and quietly eased it up. Rather than risk the noise of loosening the screen's frame and dropping it outside, he used the scissors to cut an opening. He motioned for her to stand in front of the window.

"The truck will detect the key fob in your pocket," he whispered. "All you have to do is press the button under the door handle and it will open. The engine's a push-button start. You remember, right? You've got this." He framed her face with his hands. "All you have to do is run, sweetheart. Everything's going to be okay."

Tears spilled down her cheeks as she looked into his beautiful blue eyes. "Bryson, I—"

Another squeak sounded outside the room. Lowe was getting restless, working up his courage for another assault. Then there was another sound, something scraping across the floor. Something heavy. What was that?

Bryson pressed a quick, hard kiss against her lips. "You can do this," he whispered next to her ear. "Don't let me down."

Her pulse was rushing in her ears so loudly that she almost couldn't hear him. She grasped the windowsill. It was awkward with the ridiculous towels wrapped around her arms. But she managed.

Grabbing the sheet off the bed, he shook it out, quickly rolling and twisting it, holding it in both hands like a length of rope. It shook her to her core when she realized what he was doing: planning to use the sheet to defend himself against the knives. Her heart slammed in her chest so hard she marveled that it didn't crack one of her ribs.

She hated this, hated the thought of abandoning him. And yet, if she stayed, she'd be a distraction that could get him killed. All she could do now was follow his instructions and pray he was able to defeat Lowe.

With a concussion.

A bum hip.

Stitches both inside him and outside. Bruises all over.

With nothing but a sheet to defend himself against a madman with butcher knives and a pistol likely in his pocket.

This was insane.

A thump sounded against the door.

Get ready, he mouthed.

She clutched the stupid can of deodorant and prayed that a better plan would come to her than leaving him here to his likely death. But what could she do? How could she help?

Something heavy crashed against the door. The already cracked frame exploded in a hail of wooden shards as a side table from the family room flew through the ruined opening. Bryson ducked, then lunged forward, arms outstretched with the sheet between them as he grappled with Lowe. Both men moved backward into the family room, a flurry of flashing knives and billowing cloth as Bryson ducked and weaved and wielded his sheet in an effort to avoid being diced into pieces.

"Now, Teagan," he yelled, furiously fighting Lowe's flailing arms. "Go!"

She let out a sob and jumped.

WITH TEAGAN SAFELY away, Bryson focused his undivided attention on the psychopath trying to hack him to death with a knife in each hand. Bryson wrenched his left arm up, using the sheet to deflect yet another blow. This time he twisted the sheet, then wrenched it back. The butcher knife in Lowe's right hand flew across the family room, skittering onto the floor with a metallic twang.

Lowe dropped to the floor. Without his weight as a counterbalance, Bryson's hip gave out. He crashed down on top of Lowe. A sickening scrape sounded and white-hot pain lanced through his side. Lowe's mouth curved in a delighted smile as he grabbed the knife now embedded beneath Bryson's ribs and yanked it out.

Bryson gasped, fighting for air now as he twisted and rolled with Lowe, desperately trying to gain control of the knife. He grabbed Lowe's wrist, muscles burning and shaking as he slowly won the tug of war, turning the man's hand. Bryson swiped the blade across the man's neck. A thin red line immediately formed. But it was only superficial. Lowe didn't even blink. He kept straining against Bryson, trying to turn the knife the other way. Muscles bunched and cramped as Bryson fought back.

The floor turned slippery with sweat and blood. They rolled like two alligators in a death roll, each struggling to get the upper hand. Lowe was strong, and big, but he still wouldn't have been that difficult for a man Bryson's size to defeat. Except that Bryson had begun this match in a much-weakened state. And Lowe's knife had done considerable damage. His life-blood was seeping from his side. A cold numbness spread across his middle, making him shiver. If he didn't end this, soon, it would be lights out. For him.

He threw everything he had left into fighting back. But his muscles ached. Weakness crept relentlessly through his body. It was a struggle just to hold up his arms.

Lowe gave one of his guttural yells, this one of satisfaction and triumph. He was winning. It was almost over. And he knew it.

Taking advantage of Lowe's distraction, Bryson managed to twist and jerk the man's knife hand again. This time he sliced deep into Lowe's biceps on his right arm. But before Bryson could follow up with a killing blow, Lowe twisted and rolled on top of him. Bryson couldn't get traction on the slippery floor. Blood saturated the knife handle. Bryson lost his grip. Lowe plunged the knife deep into Bryson's side again, and twisted.

Bryson arched off the floor, an inferno of lava-like pain scorching him from the inside out. He dropped back down, gasping, struggling to catch his breath. The rest of his strength seemed to drain away, leaving him limp, muscles twitching in agony as he squinted and blinked, trying to focus.

Lowe was a dark blur, climbing to his feet, staggering and clutching himself as he lumbered out of Bryson's sight-line. He rolled his head to the side, trying to follow the other man's progress. Cold. He was so cold. His teeth chattered as he frantically pushed against the floor, like a fiddler crab, trying to slide away. But all he could manage was a few inches.

His nemesis stopped by one of the couches and leaned down. When he turned around, Bryson blinked, trying to see what was in the man's hand. A gun. Probably Bryson's own pistol.

He held it up, no doubt gloating with triumph. Bryson could no longer see well enough to make out the man's expression. Maybe that was a blessing.

"Chris said you'd put up a good fight and you did." He spoke for the first time since their fight had begun, his words choppy as he too struggled to catch his breath. "I was his one call from jail. Imagine that. He called me instead of a lawyer." He shook his head. "What a gift. And I'm here paying him back. This is for what you did to Chris." He held his gun arm out toward Bryson. "After you're dead, I'll enjoy that girlfriend of yours. I'll gut her like a fish."

Bryson swore and tried to push himself up. But it was as if his body was glued to the floor.

The sound of a roaring engine had both of them jerking their heads toward the front windows. Bryson's pickup crashed through the house, tossing one of the couches across the room like kindling, and slamming into Lowe so hard he flew across the room.

Someone hopped out, but all he saw was a blur.

"Bryson! Bryson, I'm coming. Hold on."

Teagan.

She crawled over the destruction she'd wrought on his house. He wanted to yell at her for risking her life yet again for him. But he was so glad to see her, alive, and safe, because she'd killed Lowe. He didn't yell. He was too proud of his little warrior to risk hurting the tender feelings that she tried to hide with her sassy quips. He despised himself that it took dying for him to realize just what she meant to him.

And that he loved her.

Her shoes squeaked and slid across the wet floor as she scrambled toward him. He tried to tell her that he loved her, that he was proud of her. But he wasn't sure if the words came out or not. He was so tired. And cold. At least the awful pain had faded. He barely felt anything anymore. He closed his eyes, at peace, knowing that she was safe. That she would be okay.

TEAGAN GRABBED THE discarded gun she'd spotted on the floor next to a smashed piece of electronics that she could only guess was whatever Lowe had used to jam the cell signals. But Lowe was no longer a threat. He was lying in a lifeless heap about ten feet away.

After a treacherous slippery slide across the blood-streaked floor, she dropped to her knees beside Bryson, gun still clutched in her left hand as she knelt over him. "Can you hear me? Speak to me," she ordered through a cascade of tears.

He blinked, then slowly opened his eyes. "Teagan?" Her name was slurred. He seemed confused as he struggled to focus on her face.

"I'm here, baby. I'm here." She set the pistol down and leaned over him, pressing her hands against the floor on each side of him to keep her balance. Something bumped against her arm. She pulled back in horror to see the handle of a knife sticking out from his left side, embedded all the way to the hilt. Blood pooled beneath him, forming macabre rivulets across the formerly polished white floor. "Oh, no. Oh, no, no, no."

"You...okay?" he whispered, his lips an odd, bluish tinge. "Where's... Lowe? The...gun?"

She motioned toward the body on the other side of the room as she tore at the duct tape holding the towels around her left arm. "I hit the piece of scum with your truck. I drove it right up the front steps. Your gun's right here." She patted the floor beside him. "Don't worry. He can't hurt you again."

He blinked. "Truck?" He rolled his head to the side, obviously trying to make sense of what she was saying.

She finally freed the towel and leaned across him, pressing it around the wound while trying to not move the knife and make it worse.

"Down!" he rasped.

She automatically ducked as the sound of a guttural yell sounded off to the side. Bryson swept the pistol up and fired over and over and over. Then his hand dropped to his side and the pistol skittered across the floor. It was as if he'd gathered all the strength he had left to protect her, once again, and was completely spent.

She looked over her shoulder. Lowe was impossibly close to them, just a few feet away. She'd thought she'd killed him. She must have only knocked him out. Or he'd pretended to be unconscious. Neither of which mattered now. Bryson's aim had been true. He'd shot him in the head.

A sob escaped her. "I can't believe it. After seeing him through the window, holding that pistol, I drove through a wall to save you. But once again, you saved me." She turned back toward him, smiling through her tears.

His eyes were closed.

His jaw was slack.

"Bryson?" She frantically bent over him. "Open your eyes. Bryson?"

"Move. Get out of the way."

She whirled around, shocked to see Gage Bishop kneeling beside her. Behind him, Brielle, Dalton and Han had just stepped in through the ruined wall and were sweeping their pistols back and forth, looking for threats.

"Move." Bishop none too gently shoved her out of the way. He pressed his fingers against the side of Bryson's neck.

"Come on." Brielle was beside her now. "Let's give him room. The police and an ambulance are on their way. Mason told us he'd tried to call Bryson back and couldn't get through. He called us, then 911."

Teagan pressed her fist to her mouth to keep from screaming.

Bishop was performing CPR.

Chapter Twenty-Six

Three months later

Long before the shadow fell across the end of the dock and hovered over Bryson Anton's wheelchair, he knew someone was there. Motion sensors and security cameras had made Bryson's new watch buzz against his wrist when they parked their car in the driveway. More messages warned when they crossed the back patio. And again, when they'd descended the gently sloping lawn that ended at the creek. But he didn't turn around.

Not yet.

"It's been nearly three months since you sent me away yet again, Bryson. One minute I'm at the hospital, thanking God that Bishop was able to keep you alive long enough to even get you there. Then I'm on my knees thanking God that you survived yet another arduous surgery. Only to visit you in recovery to discover you're acting like a grizzly bear, just like last time, proving you're the worst patient ever in the history of the universe. And then, when you're finally in your hospital room and we're alone, I'm ready to pour my heart out to you, and what do you do? You tell me to get out! You order me back to Jacksonville to work on my master's degree. What the heck, Bryson?"

"The summer semester was about to start. I didn't want you to have to wait until fall to start back again."

She said several unsavory things. "No phone calls from you. When I tried calling, you didn't answer. I don't even count the pathetic, generic texts you occasionally sent me. Then I find out that you've been talking to my dad every few days, asking how I was doing. If you were worried, all you had to do was talk to *me*, Bryson. Not my family."

"I was busy."

"Really? What's her name?"

He turned the wheelchair around to face her. She was wearing hunter-green shorts and a lime-green tank top in deference to the warm weather. As always, her rich brown skin was flawless, her full high breasts a reminder of the incredible body beneath those clothes. But his favorite part of her was that gorgeous bright mind of hers. And her beautiful, sassy mouth. He never knew what outrageous thing she was going to say next.

"Helga," he said.

She frowned. "Excuse me?"

"You asked me her name. Her name is Helga. Or, well, I actually don't even know her real name. But that's what you called her when she was here that first day you showed up on my doorstep."

She put her hands on her hips. "Does this mean that you've been doing the rehab the doctor ordered?"

"It does. I have."

She crossed her arms, looking only slightly less aggravated than before. "Well, that's good. But I still don't see why you couldn't text me a real hello, with feeling, every once in a while. Or actually speak to me on the phone. What makes you think you could just text me last night to come back and everything would be fine?"

He smiled. "You're here aren't you?"

She narrowed her eyes, then whirled around.

He caught her arm just before she could get out of reach and yanked her backward.

She let out a little squeak and landed right where he wanted her. In his lap.

"Let me go, Bryson. I'm not kidding."

He gently turned her face so she'd meet his gaze. "Is that really want you want, Teag? You want me to let you go?" The flash of unshed tears in her eyes surprised him. "Sweetheart?"

"You already have. You wouldn't let me stay to help with your recovery. You sent me back home like some child—"

"While I could never mistake you for a child, not even close—" he gently stroked her arm, unable to resist touching her "—there's definitely an age difference between us. Something to think about. You're young, still working on officially starting your career, although I heard the FBI is interested in grooming you as a future candidate."

She smiled. Not full wattage, but enough for him to know that he was right, that the FBI opportunity was important to her.

"There might be a nibble there," she admitted. "They

were impressed with the detailed investigation I conducted, and that I was right about Avarice Lowe being a serial killer. Apparently my notes on him have helped them narrow down facts that blow apart his alibis for some of the killings. He may not be around for a trial. But at least some of his victims' families will have true closure now."

He pressed a kiss against her cheek and settled her more comfortably against him. The fact that she didn't resist being snuggled close was encouraging. "You have the most beautiful mind I've ever had the pleasure of knowing. It's about time the rest of the world figured that out."

She gave him the side-eye before looking away. "I'd say thank you, but it sounds like you're building another excuse to justify why you wanted me to leave you."

"Not leave me. Go back to school. Huge difference."

She shrugged.

"Teag, you're young, energetic, just starting out in life. I'm more toward the middle of mine."

She snorted.

"Okay, maybe not quite the middle just yet. Hopefully."

"Is this going somewhere?"

He motioned toward the wheelchair. "I wouldn't want you to ever regret spending time with a cripple when you could be out with guys your own age doing whatever you want."

She rolled her eyes with a dramatic toss of her head. "I think you're confusing me with the self-centered stuck-up jerk who used to be your girlfriend. I'm a little more creative than her. I can figure out lots of fun things to do with you even if you can't twirl me around a dance floor."

"Does that mean you could be happy if I never walked again?"

Her mouth fell open and she cupped his face in her hands, all signs of teasing and anger gone as she stared into his eyes. "Oh, Bry. Is that what the doctor said? Are you...are you paralyzed?"

He gently pulled her hands down and kissed them before letting go. "No. I'm not paralyzed. I've been very lucky, actually, after being shot twice in my life. Then stabbed. Twice. I just wanted to make sure that if something like that did happen, maybe down the road—considering how dangerous my career can be— that you'd still be okay sticking around."

Her brows arched in confusion. "Love isn't based on how mobile you are or what you can do for someone else. Love is when your happiness revolves around the other person's happiness. Once again, I think you're confusing me with the ex who shall not be named."

He grinned.

She frowned.

"Did you just say that you loved me, Teagan? In that unique sassy way of yours?"

She crossed her arms. "That depends."

"On?"

"On why you're asking me these stupid questions and why you texted me last night that you had first class tickets waiting for me so I could fly up here today. Thanks for the first class, by the way. That was cool."

"You're welcome. Thanks for coming."

She twisted her mouth as if trying to figure something out. "You're acting awfully strange. And my infinite patience is wearing thin. Out with it. What exactly do you want? Are you asking me to be your girlfriend and you're worried I'll dump you because of the chair?"

"Will you?"

"Be your girlfriend? Are you asking me to be your girlfriend?"

"No."

"We're done here. Have a nice life, Bryson." She hopped off his lap and started up the dock.

"I'm not asking you to be my girlfriend," he called after her.

She raised her hand in the air and made a rude gesture without looking back.

He grinned. "I'm asking you to be my fiancée. For real this time."

She stopped so fast that she wobbled and almost fell into the water. Once she regained her balance, she slowly turned around. "What...what did you just say?"

He leaned down and flipped the top back on the cooler beside his chair. Then he pulled out a red velvet box and held it up in front of him. "I love you Teagan Eleanor Ray."

She gasped in outrage. "Did my mother tell you my middle name? I hate it. It makes me sound like an eighty-year-old."

"Well, maybe that will help with the age gap between us." He winked.

She marched back to him and stopped a few feet from his chair, eyeing the velvet box in his hands. "Be honest, Bryson. Exactly how much older than me are you?"

"Old enough to teach you a few things that I know you'll really, really enjoy. And young enough to demonstrate them with an expertise that will make your toes curl."

Her gaze flew to his. She swallowed, then cleared her throat. "Toes curl?"

He nodded.

"All of them?" she squeaked.

"Oh yeah."

She fanned herself, then wiped her hands on her shorts. "Um. Wasn't there a question you asked me, a moment ago, when my back was turned?"

He nodded again.

She put her hands on her hips. "Don't you think you should ask again? Face-to-face?"

"No."

Her eyes widened. She started to turn away.

He stood.

She froze and stared in wonder as he dropped down on one knee on the dock.

"I think I should ask it down here, do this the right way, on bended knee." He opened the box and tilted it so the ring would catch the light.

She pressed a hand to her throat. "You stood on

your own. No cane. And you're on one knee. I don't understand."

"By the grace of God, when Lowe stabbed me, it knocked the bullet loose instead of into my spine. The doctors were able to extract it. And I've been doing everything the therapists ordered me to do. I'm not pain-free yet. But there's a good chance I will be. Eventually."

Her expression turned sad. "Are you in pain right now, Bryson?"

He shook his head. "No. And it's not because of tequila."

"Scotch?"

"Pain pills. Like I said, I'm following doctor's orders this time. No self-medicating with alcohol. No more skipping rehab appointments. And even though I hate how the pills make me feel, I wanted to be able to do this without grimacing. So I'm all doped up and feeling good. Now, about that question I asked—"

"The ring is beautiful," she breathed, stepping closer and eyeing the box again. "But not half as beautiful as you, you frustrating, stubborn man."

He smiled as he pulled the ring out of its bed of velvet. "I wanted something special, something as unique as you."

She moved even closer, then pressed her hand against her chest. "Opals. And diamonds. And rubies. I love opals and rubies. How did you know?"

"All those calls to your mom and dad weren't for nothing."

"Sneaky."

"Necessary. I wanted to surprise you. You just confirmed that you love opals and rubies. Diamonds too I hope?"

She rolled her eyes. "Everyone loves diamonds. Or they should. I couldn't ask for anything more beautiful. Thank you." She held out her left hand.

He poised the ring in front of her finger. But before sliding it on, he looked up, meeting her gaze. "It's selfish of me to even ask you to marry me, because I think you could do a lot better. But I can't imagine my life without you in it. I love you, Teagan Ray. I think I loved you the moment you knocked on my door and the only word you could get out was *hi*." He grinned. "Will you do me the honor of being my wife? Will you marry me?"

"Are you kidding? Put the ring on already."

He laughed and slid the ring onto her finger. Then he stood.

Tears glittered in her eyes as she put her hands on his shoulders. "I can't believe you're standing here like this. I'm so happy for you."

"No happier than me, that you said yes. I wasn't sure how this was going to go."

"That makes two of us. I had no idea why you wanted to see me. I believe you owe me a kiss, future husband." She lifted her lips toward his and waited for him to bend down.

"Hold that thought. I have something else for you." He turned back to the cooler and reached inside.

She groaned. "You're killing me, Bryson. I don't want anything else but you."

"Oh, I don't know. I'm pretty sure you want this. And I did make a promise after all." He handed her a pink bag with little pink ribbons tied all over it, and the name of a very exclusive store on the outside of the bag.

Her eyes widened. "You didn't."

"I did."

She opened the bag and peeked inside, then squealed with delight as she shoved her hand in and pulled out an aqua-colored lace bra and panty set. "They're gorgeous, perfect. And they're my size. Oh my gosh, please don't tell me you asked my mother my sizes." She gasped. "Or my dad!"

"Give me more credit than that. I asked your mother for your best friend's name. Then I asked your best friend."

She laughed with obvious relief and sorted through the contents. "Twelve. You bought me a dozen bras and matching panties. Bryson! This cost a fortune!"

"I can afford it. I'd pay ten times that to see your eyes light up and your glowing smile."

The tears that had been threatening spilled over and down her cheeks. "I'm so happy."

"Because we're going to get married?"

She shook her head. "Because you promised that when you replaced my hundred-dollar bra that you'd buy me more, and then you'd take them off me."

He threw his head back and laughed harder than he had in ages.

"Hurry, Bryson. I'm not waiting one more minute for you to keep your promise. I'll strip right here on your back lawn if I have to."

Still laughing, he scooped her up in his arms and

ran with her to the house. But before going inside, he let her legs slide down him as he'd done so long ago. And this time, he did what he'd wanted to do since the first time he'd seen her. He kissed her. Really kissed her. Kissed her with all his pent-up emotions, love and longing and lust all rolled into one. And when he was done, he pulled back to soak in the haze of passion in her eyes and the love reflected back in them.

His hands were shaking as he cupped her face. "I don't know what I did to make you love me. But I'll thank God every night for the rest of my life that you showed up on my doorstep. You're a treasure, Teagan. A gift to my battered soul. I love you so much."

She shifted the bag of lingerie to her left hand and grabbed his right in hers. "I love you too, Bryson Anton. But you have one more promise to keep. You have to make my toes curl."

"Challenge accepted." He scooped her up in his arms and kissed her again as he strode through the house.

Her toes were curling before they even reached the bedroom.

* * * * *

Look for more books in award-winning author Lena Diaz's miniseries, The Justice Seekers, coming soon!

And if you missed the previous book in the series, look for Cowboy Under Fire, *available now from Harlequin Intrigue!*

#1977 HUNTING A KILLER
Tactical Crime Division: Traverse City • by Nicole Helm
When K-9 handler Serena Lopez discovers her half brother's a fugitive from justice, she must find him—and his dangerous crew. It's a good thing her partner is lead agent Axel Morrow. But as cunning as the duo may be, it's a race against time to catch the criminals before they kill again.

#1978 PURSUIT OF THE TRUTH
West Investigations • by K.D. Richards
Security expert Ryan West's worst fears come to life when hotel CEO Nadia Shelton is nearly killed. Someone will do anything to find the brother Nadia thought was dead, and Ryan will have to stay strictly professional to protect her. But the sparks igniting between them are impossible to ignore.

#1979 HIDEOUT AT WHISKEY GULCH
The Outriders Series • by Elle James
After saving a woman and baby from would-be kidnappers, ex-marine Matt Hennessey must help Aubrey Blanchard search for the baby's abducted sister. Can they bring down a human trafficking cartel in the process?

#1980 THE WITNESS
A Marshal Law Novel • by Nichole Severn
Checking in on his witness in protective custody, marshal Finn Reed finds Camille Goodman fighting an attacker. Finn is determined to keep the strong-willed redhead alive, but soon a serial killer's twisted game is playing out— one that the deputy and his fearless witness may not survive.

#1981 A LOADED QUESTION
STEALTH: Shadow Team • by Danica Winters
When a sniper shoots at STEALTH contractor Troy Spade, he knows he must cooperate with the FBI. As Troy and Agent Kate Scot get closer to the truth, secrets from Kate's family will be revealed. How are they involved...and what are they willing to do to keep themselves safe?

#1982 COLD CASE COLORADO
An Unsolved Mystery Book • by Cassie Miles
Vanessa Whitman moves into her eccentric uncle's remote castle to ghostwrite his memoir, but then Sheriff Ty Coleman discovers a body in a locked room of the Colorado castle, transforming everyone in Vanessa's family into potential killers.

SPECIAL EXCERPT FROM

⊕ HARLEQUIN

INTRIGUE

*When K-9 handler Serena Lopez discovers her half
brother's a fugitive from justice, she must find him—and his
dangerous crew. It's a good thing her partner is lead agent
Axel Morrow. But as cunning as the duo may be, it's a race
against time to catch the criminals before they kill again.*

Read on for a sneak preview of
Hunting a Killer *by Nicole Helm.*

Prologue

The tears leaked out of Kay Duvall's eyes, even as she tried to
focus on what she had to do. *Had* to do to bring Ben home safe.

She fumbled with her ID and punched in the code that
would open the side door, usually only used for a guard taking a
smoke break. It would be easy for the men behind her to escape
from this side of the prison.

It went against everything she was supposed to do.
Everything she considered right and good.

A quiet sob escaped her lips. They had her son. How could
she not help them escape? Nothing mattered beyond her son's
life.

"Would you stop already?" one of the prisoners muttered.
He'd made her give him her gun, which he now jabbed into her
back. "Crying isn't going to change anything. So just shut up."

She didn't care so much about her own life or if she'd be
fired. She didn't care what happened to her as long as they let
her son go. So she swallowed down the sobs and blinked out as
many tears as she could, hoping to stem the tide of them.

She got the door open and slid out first—because the man holding the gun pushed it into her back until she moved forward.

They came through the door behind her, dressed in the clothes she'd stolen from the locker room and Lost and Found. Anything warm she could get her hands on to help them escape into the frigid February night.

Help them escape. Help three dangerous men escape prison. When she was supposed to keep them inside.

It didn't matter anymore. She just wanted them gone. If they were gone, they'd let her baby go. They had to let her baby go.

Kay forced her legs to move, one foot in front of the other, toward the gate she could unlock without setting off any alarms. She unlocked it, steadier this time if only because she kept thinking that once they were gone, she could get in contact with Ben.

She flung open the gate and gestured them out into the parking lot. "Stay out of the safety lights and no one should bug you."

"You better hope not," one of the men growled.

"The minute you sound that alarm, your kid is dead. You got it?" This one was the ringleader. The one who'd been in for murder. Who else would he kill out there in the world?

Guilt pooled in Kay's belly, but she had to ignore it. She had to live with it. Whatever guilt she felt would be survivable. Living without her son wouldn't be. Besides, she had to believe they'd be caught. They'd do something else terrible and be caught.

As long as her son was alive, she didn't care.

Don't miss
Hunting a Killer *by Nicole Helm,*
available February 2021 wherever
Harlequin Intrigue books and ebooks are sold.

Harlequin.com

Love Harlequin romance?

DISCOVER.

Be the first to find out about promotions,
news and exclusive content!

Facebook.com/HarlequinBooks

Twitter.com/HarlequinBooks

Instagram.com/HarlequinBooks

Pinterest.com/HarlequinBooks

ReaderService.com

EXPLORE.

Sign up for the Harlequin e-newsletter and
download a free book from any series at
TryHarlequin.com

CONNECT.

Join our Harlequin community to
share your thoughts and connect
with other romance readers!
Facebook.com/groups/HarlequinConnection

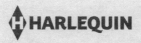